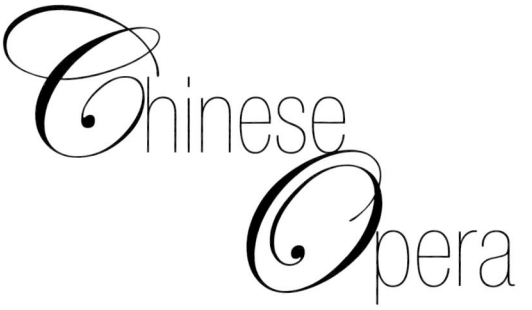

Chinese Opera
The Actor's Craft

表演者的技藝

Siu Wang-Ngai
with Peter Lovrick

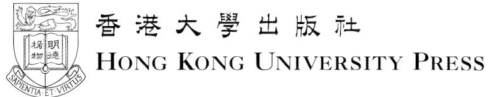
香港大學出版社
Hong Kong University Press

Hong Kong University Press
The University of Hong Kong
Pokfulam Road
Hong Kong
www.hkupress.org

© Hong Kong University Press 2014

ISBN 978-988-8208-26-5 (*Hardback*)

All rights reserved. No portion of this publication may be reproduced or transmitted in any form or by any means, electronic or mechanical, including photocopy, recording, or any information storage or retrieval system, without prior permission in writing from the publisher.

British Library Cataloguing-in-Publication Data
A catalogue record for this book is available from the British Library.

10 9 8 7 6 5 4 3 2 1

Printed and bound by Kings Time Printing Press Ltd. in Hong Kong, China

This book is a labour of love dedicated to all the performers of Chinese opera who have invested their lives in this great performing arts tradition as their own labour of love. It is the hope of the authors that their precious work will not only be preserved, but also flourish for future generations.

Contents

Preface	ix
Chapter 1 How Chinese Theatre Solves Theatrical Problems	1
Chapter 2 Using Stage Movement	5
Mime 5	
Acrobatics 16	
Poses 23	
Special Moves 30	
Playing the Dwarf 34	
Chapter 3 Using Props	39
Horsewhip 39	
Fan 51	
Handkerchief 59	
Ribbon 65	
Table and Chair 69	
Cloud Whisk 75	
Paddle and Boat Pole 80	
Flag 84	
Cloud 89	
Chapter 4 Using Weapons and Skills for Stage Fighting	93
Spear 93	
Mace 101	
Quarterstaff 105	
Polearm 107	
Sword 110	
Sabre 113	
Bow and Arrow 115	
Special Weapons 118	
Preparing for Battle 122	
Chapter 5 Using Costumes	131
Pheasant Tails 131	
Headgear 138	
Hair 141	
Beards 148	
Water Sleeves 154	
Outer Robe 161	
Big Belt 167	
Chapter 6 Using Special Skills	171
Face Changing 171	
Fire Breathing 177	
Opening the Eye of Wisdom 182	
Balancing the Oil Lamp 185	
Ladder Skills 188	
A Final Word—from the Photographer and the Writer	191
Glossary	193
Appendix I: English Guide to the Photographs	195
Appendix II: Chinese Guide to the Photographs	203
References	211
Index	213

Preface

Many years ago, a director of Chinese opera took pains to train me for a part in one of his productions. He had a habit of suddenly stopping to burst out, "Chinese opera is just wonderful!" With all his experience, he kept discovering new facets to admire. Chinese opera is indeed one of the great cultural achievements that China offers to the world. It is also a wonderful window into China itself, combining its music, poetry, history, folk tales and philosophy. Actually, the term "opera" is somewhat misleading for a Westerner. That term conjures up images of Verdi, Puccini or Wagner—dramatic productions entirely set to music from beginning to end. In China, right up until the twentieth century, drama meant musical theatre—a mixture of dialogue, poetry, song and dance. Chinese opera can be traced back through extant scripts as far as the eleventh century and to descriptive accounts dating from centuries before that. The over 360 styles of Chinese opera are differentiated chiefly by their music and the Chinese dialect they use. Much more unites them, however, than separates them.

The Chinese developed an approach to theatre—to solving theatrical problems—that forms a common thread through all opera. Theatrical problems require finding ways to present on stage what the dramatist calls for. How do you bring a horse on stage? How do you bring in two armies to fight a war? How do you climb a mountain or cross a river in a boat? Chinese theatre never opted for realism or naturalism as a solution. It did not call for complex sets, scene changes, accurate period props and costumes, or lighting to solve these problems. Instead, it opted to solve them all through stage conventions immediately understandable to the audience. Those conventions included complex but standardized face painting that essentially writes the personality of the character on the actor's face for all the world to see; stylized costumes to identify rank and status; role types; and codified stage movements with and without props. Many books can be found on face painting, costumes and role types. This book intends to focus on the physical performance art of the actor. Traditionally, Chinese opera has been not a director's art, but an actor's art. This remains largely true despite the practice in modern times of using directors. The actor bears much of the responsibility for defining space, marking time and creating place through a demanding skill set in mime and acrobatics.

This book, like its predecessor, *Chinese Opera: Images and Stories*, owes everything to the magnificent collection of photos taken by Siu Wang-Ngai of many genres of Chinese opera in performance. Siu, a prominent photographer from Hong Kong, has a special love for theatrical photography. His book, *The Hong Kong Ballet*, published by Hong Kong University Press in 2003, is a stunning collection of his photographs taken of that dance company over fifteen years. Siu Wang-Ngai is also an aficionado of Chinese opera. He has taken tens of thousands of photographs of hundreds of operas for over thirty years. The body of Siu Wang-Ngai's work has won him fellowship in the Royal Photographic Society of Great Britain for theatrical and pictorial photography. These photographs, some of which appear in this book, are nothing short of precious. Not only are they splendid examples of photography, but taken together they provide a unique window into the wonderful art of the Chinese performer.

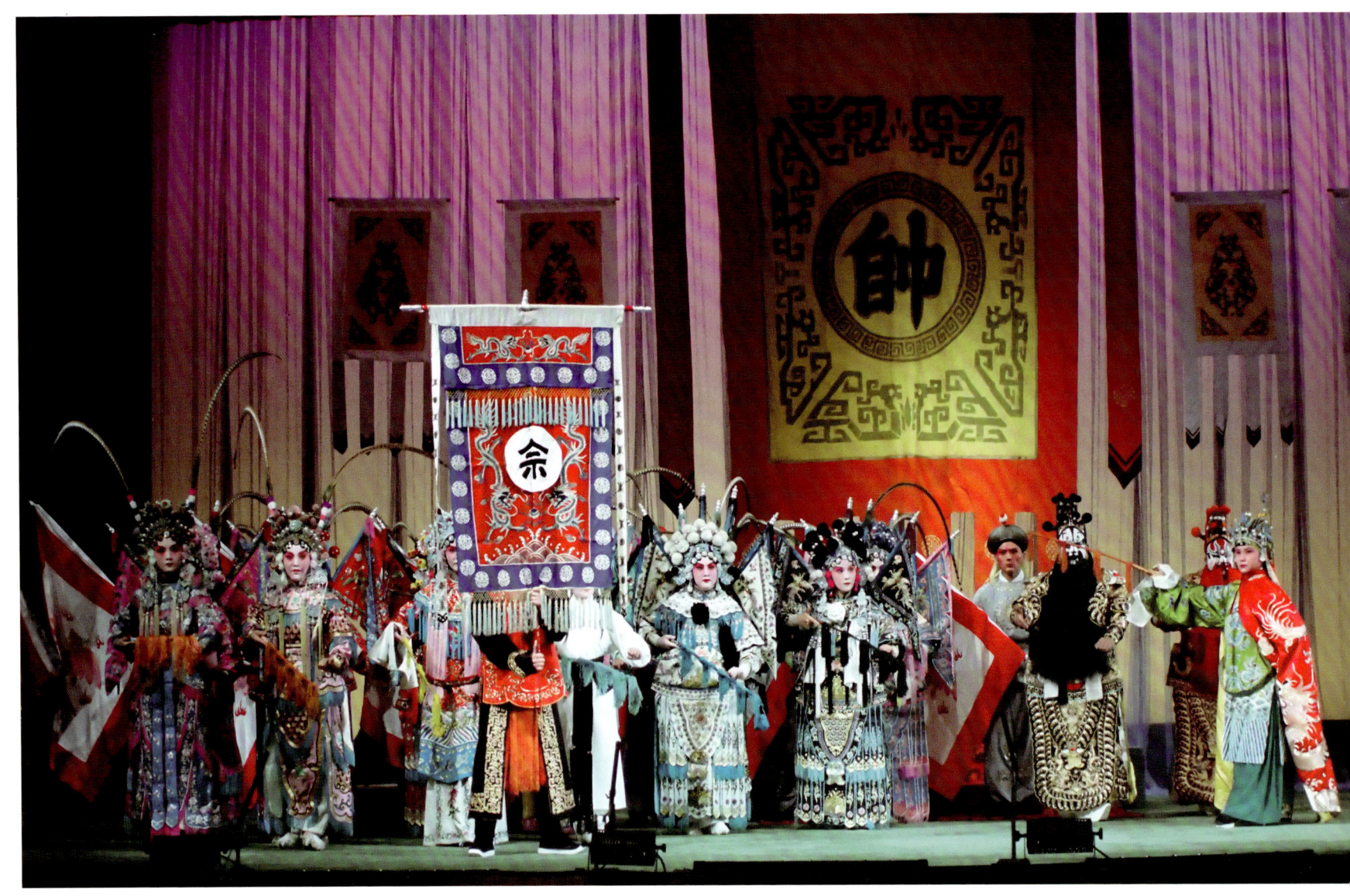

Photo 1.01 *Women Warriors of the Yang Family*, Peking Opera

Chapter 1

How Chinese Theatre Solves Theatrical Problems

A FIRST VISIT to the Chinese opera can be mystifying, if not overwhelming. Audiences used to realistic theatre are lost. Their usual frame of reference is gone. Instead, high-pitched falsettos, clanging gongs, stylized movement, and unrecognizable props thread through the play in an often glorious, but frequently confusing, way. Audiences new to the Chinese opera hearing the explosive cries of approval *"Hao!"* from seasoned opera goers wonder just what they are missing. They realize then that watching a Chinese opera requires more than just knowing the story, which they can easily get from reading a plot synopsis or following subtitles in translation. The difficulty is not simply the language. After all, fans of Western opera are not necessarily fluent in Italian, French or German, but enjoy such operas nonetheless because they are also familiar with the theatrical conventions. There is another language in Chinese opera, the language of the stage. It is a stage technique made up of movement, costumes, face painting, and props, all of which convey meaning. These are not translated into subtitles over the stage or in the programme. New audiences need to learn this language. Familiarity with Chinese stage technique is the key to appreciating Chinese opera.

This stage language is the Chinese opera's response to particular theatrical problems. What does the actor do when the play calls for him to ride a hundred miles on horseback? How can a boat ride down the river be accomplished? And how, in heaven's name, does the cast show two mighty clashing armies? Various theatrical traditions have devised their own solutions to these and other problems. The ancient Greeks and the Japanese Noh theatre use masks to convey personae. Realist and naturalist Western theatres use detailed scenery and curtains to hide scene changes and thus take the spectator from one place to another. The Elizabethan and traditional Chinese theatres use little scenery, depending instead on suggestive props and elaborate costumes.

Over several centuries, Chinese opera has developed a series of stage conventions that has become familiar to regular theatre goers. They know when they see the oily white-faced actor that they have a villain before them. When they see the actor walk in a circle they know that he or she has made a journey. Knowing the conventions of this stage language means the new audience is no longer excluded from the rich theatrical experience of Chinese opera. The centre of all these conventions is the actor. Traditional Chinese opera has focused its attention upon the actor rather than the lighting, scenery, or even the director. The audience already knows the stories well. They come not to see what happens, but rather how highly trained actors present that familiar story in their singing and their mastery of stage technique. In other words, the real pleasure in store for a new audience to the Chinese opera is savouring how the actors unfold the story through their mastery of stagecraft.

Chinese opera is a broad term that needs some defining. The term "opera" is misleading for Westerners to whom opera means full orchestration and characters that sing throughout. In China, opera is more akin to a Western operetta or musical. It is a mixture of singing and speaking, prose and poetry, and even dance and acrobatics. Even with such knowledge, Chinese opera can be hard to pin down because it is a generic term for well over 360 different styles of opera that differ greatly in music styles and dialects. Taiwanese, Cantonese, Sichuan and Peking operas are connected to places. They use the language and musical forms of the localities. So what, then, makes these vastly different performance arts recognizable as Chinese opera? The answer lies in the stage conventions, which are largely, although not completely, shared. These different opera styles have generally approached theatrical problems in similar ways.

This general approach can be traced back well over a millennia. One of the great artistic achievements of the Yuan dynasty (1279–1368) was the Yuan *zaju*. This was the opera that Marco Polo would have seen. These highly polished dramas in four acts moved from prose to singing, and they had clearly established role types like the clown, the villain, the female and the male roles. Yuan *zaju* also depended upon the actor to set the scene rather than on scenery. The scripts continue to be celebrated as masterful pieces of literature exploring themes as varied as social justice and marriage.

Following the short-lived Mongol Yuan dynasty, the Han Chinese Ming dynasty (1368–1644) saw the growth of what has come to be seen as the classical drama of China, *chuanqi*. This highly refined drama included many acts, exquisite poetry, dance and mime. It adopted a southern musical style polished by the sixteenth century musician Wei Liangfu in the city of Kunshan—and thus became known as Kunqu opera. That music with its characteristic flute, unlike the music of the earlier Yuan *zaju*, has survived, and the Kunqu continues to be performed today.

The beauty of Kunqu accounted for both its rise and demise. It became too erudite and subtle to hold much of an appeal for audiences beyond the scholar class. In its place, popular local opera using folk tunes and regional dialects became popular all over China. These operas were shorter and more accessible. They presented a wide range of stories with ghosts, heroes, beauties and emperors. The local flavour of each of these opera styles makes them distinct from each other. They also shared a common heritage of role types, face painting, and mime, among other stage conventions.

All of these threads came together in a marvellous way in China's last dynasty, the Qing (1644–1911). China's longest lived emperor, Qianlong, celebrated his eightieth birthday in 1790. Part of the celebrations included famous opera troupes from different provinces like Anhui and Sichuan coming to Peking to perform. The result of this mix of opera styles was the growth of something new—something that was later to be called the Peking opera. It brought together musical and performance styles from other traditions into an opera that took on a life of its own. In it, one sees the four basic role types of the painted face, the clown, women and men. It traditionally uses a plain stage with only a table and two chairs representing a room in a house. Yet the audience knows that the same chair placed on top of the table can make it a mountain or that the table can become in another scene an altar in a temple.

One of the great Peking opera performers of the twentieth century, Mei Lanfang (1894–1961) was instrumental in introducing the conventions of Chinese opera technique to the West. He was one of the four greatest performers of the female role. His vocal qualities and exquisite movement were a sensation in his tours to Japan, the USSR and the USA in the 1920s and 1930s. The Chinese solution to theatrical problems, and Mei Lanfang's skills in particular, impressed the great German dramatist, Bertolt Brecht (1898–1956), who developed the *verfremdungseffekt* or alienation device of the epic theatre, which became a major force in Western drama. In Peking opera, Brecht saw a stage technique that described a story rather than one that tried to recreate it realistically on the stage. He saw an approach to theatre that broke the imaginary fourth wall of Western theatre and could speak directly to the audience. He saw how small props or gestures were used in that theatre to suggest location or event. He called this *alienation* because the technique both called attention to the fact that the audience was watching a play and evoked what the dramatist wanted it to experience. Constantin Stansislavski, Lee Strasberg, Charlie Chaplin and other great forces in Western performance arts were also enthralled with what they saw on Mei Lanfang's Western tours.

The Chinese opera has not been static in modern times, thus saving it from becoming a museum piece to be admired, but without life or vigour for modern audiences. Mei Lanfang was involved with reformation of Peking opera throughout the 1950s, experimenting with changes in costume, scenery and performance style. New types of Chinese opera, like the all-female Yue opera from Zhejiang Province, developed and came into their own. Opera was updated and applied to propaganda in the Model Revolutionary Opera style of the 1960s in China. The Contemporary Legend Theatre Company of Taiwan has been integrating Peking opera technique with Western theatre practice since the 1980s, adapting Greek dramas, Shakespearean plays, and even theatre of the absurd pieces to the Chinese opera stage. In all of this experimentation, whether it be the revolutionary opera of the 1960s or the experimentation of groups like The Contemporary Legend Theatre, there is a common thread. The approach to theatrical problems has been to solve them in non-realistic ways, relying on a conventional language of performance technique recognizable to the audience. It suggests rather than completely presents. The suggestion is enough to evoke the entire reality.

When an audience new to Chinese opera invests the time to learn some of these conventions, it is rewarded with an ability to appreciate a rare and wonderful theatrical tradition that has developed through the centuries and offers the world a unique approach to drama.

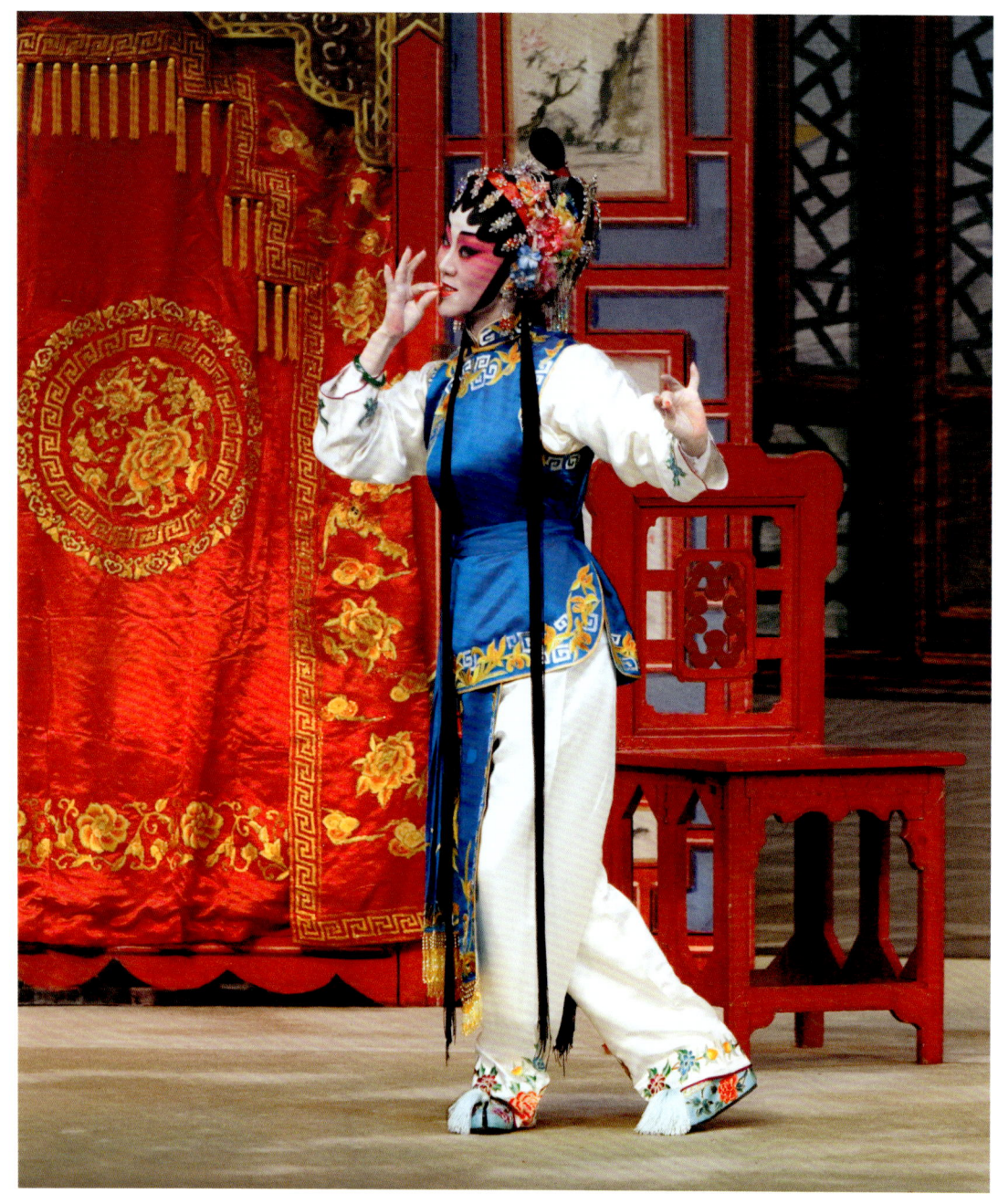

Photo 2.01   *A Comedy of Eight Errors*, Cantonese Opera

Chapter 2

Using Stage Movement

Mime

Relying on mime, or pure stage movement, to indicate physical realities is one of the primary solutions that Chinese opera developed for theatrical problems. The Chinese opera blends mime into performance. It is a tool that actors use along with singing, manipulating costume, and handling props to express a reality rather than recreate it as is the practice in Western naturalist theatre. This approach means that Chinese opera does not need to develop extensive sets or use a wide range of realistic props. In fact, operas can be performed in an empty space with little more than a table and two chairs, and often without even these. Mime creates the buildings and props called for by the story. It can also suggest long journeys without the need to change scenery in order to indicate a new location. Mime in Chinese opera is a stage language with which the seasoned audience becomes familiar. It telegraphs what an audience needs to know to keep the story moving and keeps the focus on the actor.

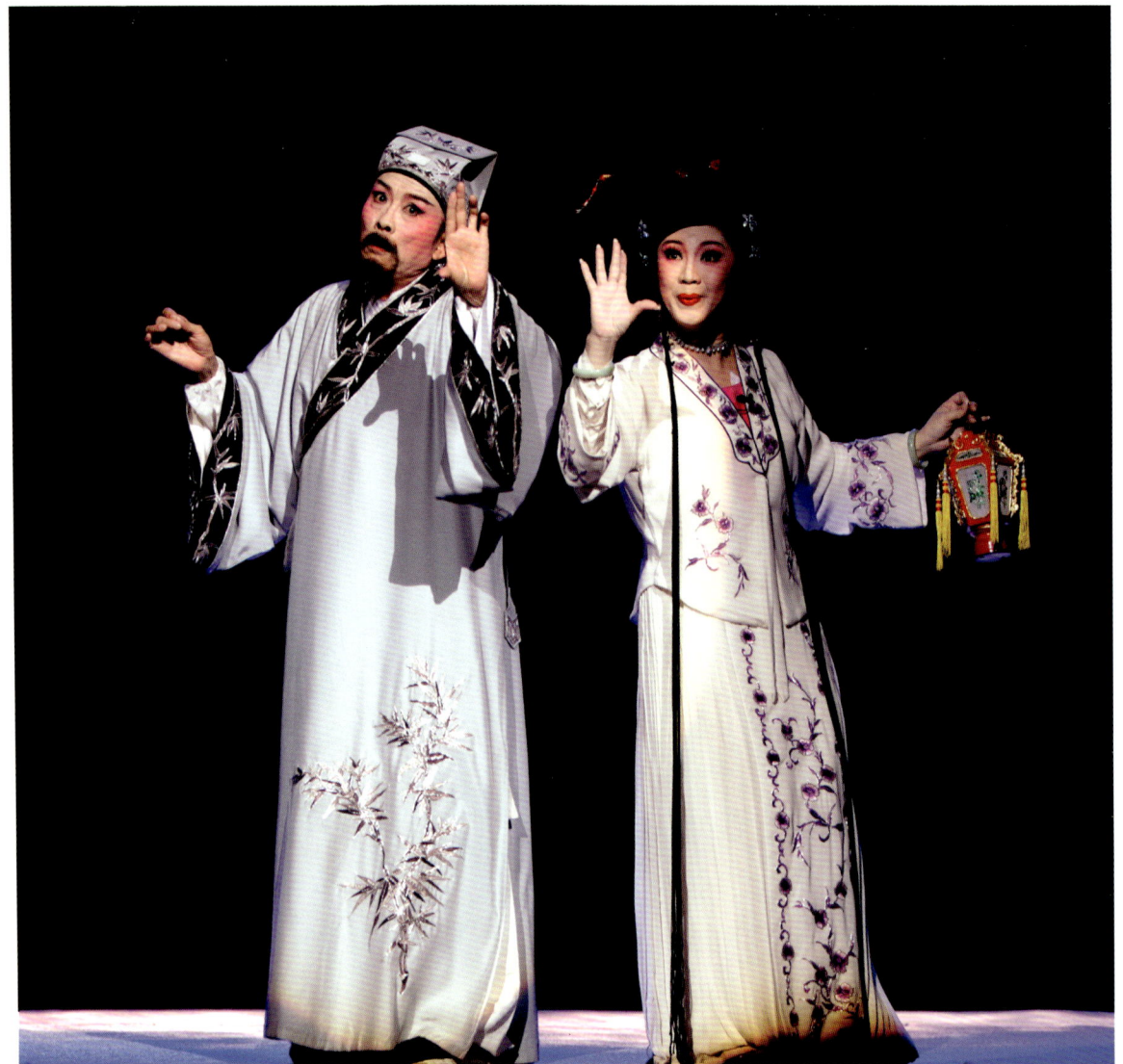

Photo 2.02 *Dong Sheng and Li Shi*, Liyuan Opera

One common use of mime is to open and close doors and windows. In the story of *Dong Sheng and Li Shi*, the couple sings, "Let us bolt the door and close the window shutters," and they proceed to shut up their imaginary house on a completely bare stage (see Photo 2.02). Even without this line, the audience recognizes a standardized movement for closing windows and doors, and pulling a bolt across to lock them.

Mime is used in Chinese opera for a great many other activities drawn from daily life. *Picking Up the Jade Bracelet*, for example, makes extensive use of mime to further the story line. At the beginning of the opera, the young country maiden, Sun Yujiao, chases after the chickens using mime. Then, she feeds them in her front yard. The actress accomplishes this by scooping up her apron to hold the imaginary chicken feed. She mimes scattering the feed, using her body and eye movements to indicate a large flock of chickens in front of her (see Photo 2.03).

Later, the country maiden, alone at home, decides to while away the time by working on her embroidery. She deftly presents the act of embroidering through a series of precise mime movements all

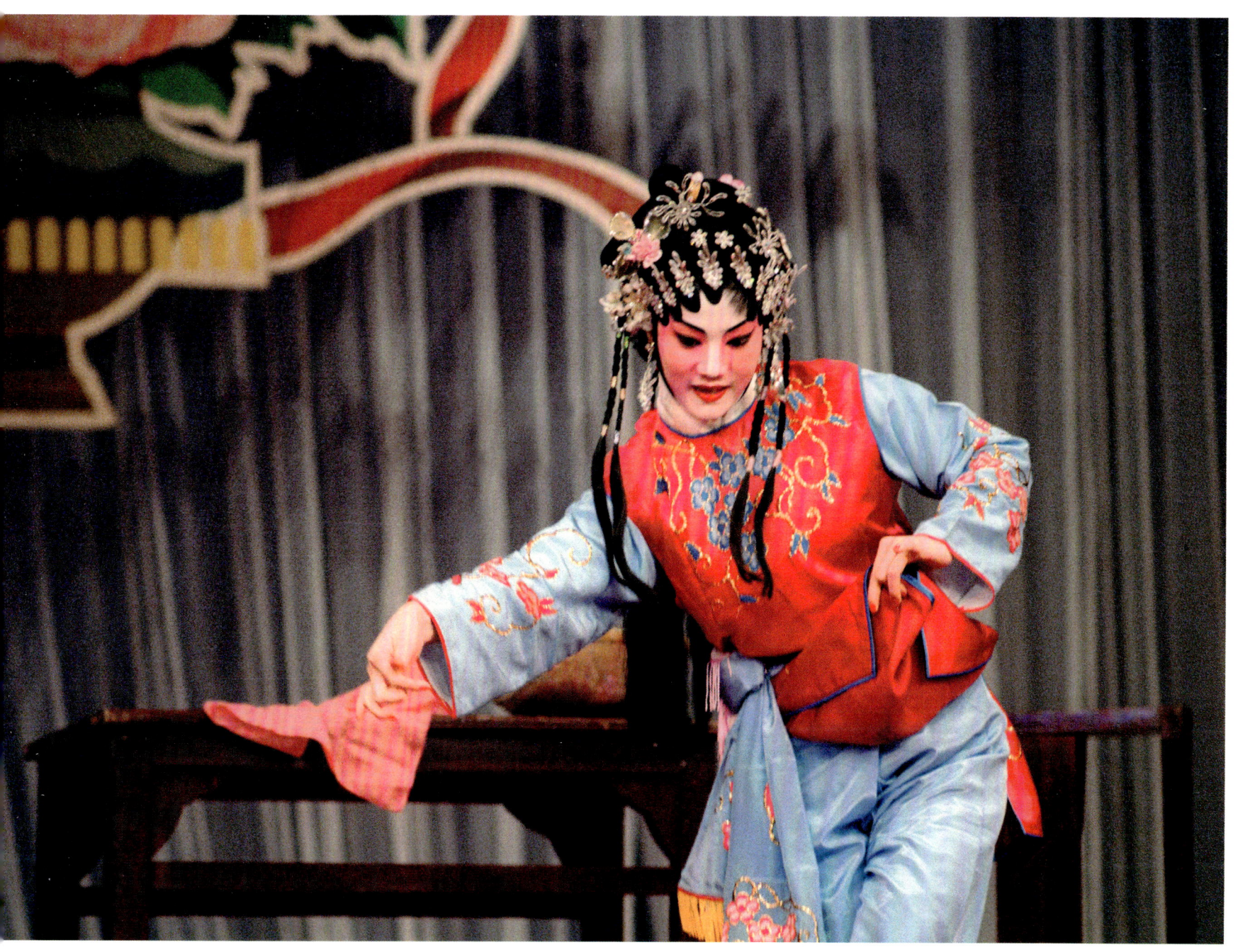

Photo 2.03 *Picking Up the Jade Bracelet*, Cantonese Opera

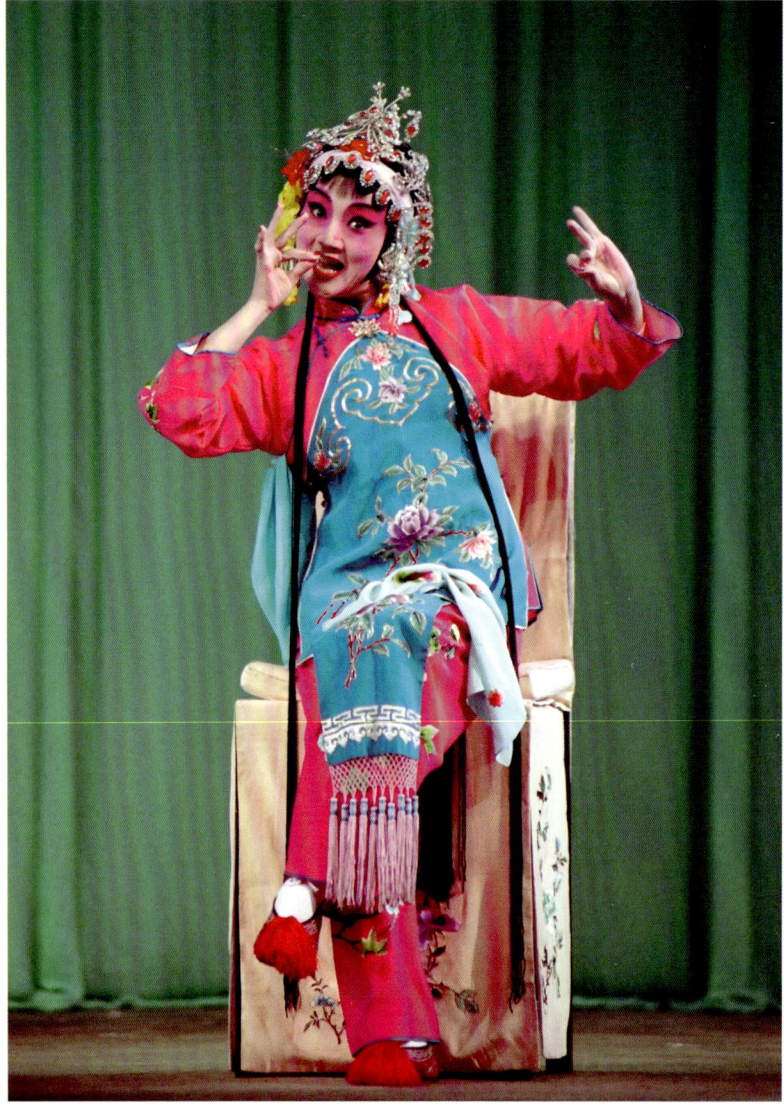

Photo 2.04 *Picking Up the Jade Bracelet*, Ping Opera

instantly recognizable to the audience. Sun Yujiao pulls and twists the thread after choosing the right colour. Then, she bites the thread, attaches it to her needle and begins her task. This series of moves is magical to watch as it invokes the reality of needlework (see Photo 2.04).

Another young woman in a different opera, Pan Jinlian, has eyes for her handsome young brother-in-law, Wu Song, and decides to tempt him by making buns. No props of any kind are used for this marvellous sequence. Wearing her apron, she proceeds to mix the flour and knead the dough (see Photo 2.05).

Aside from daily activities like closing windows, sewing and cooking, mime can also be used to indicate a journey. If a character needs to travel a great distance in the opera, there is no need to close the curtain and change the scenery. One way to express the idea of a journey is a mime move called "circling the stage" (see Photo 2.06). The actor simply moves in a large clockwise or anti-clockwise circle on the stage. When the circle is completed, the audience knows that we are now in a different location. Sometimes, particularly in a long chase, characters will exit the stage to the audience's right and

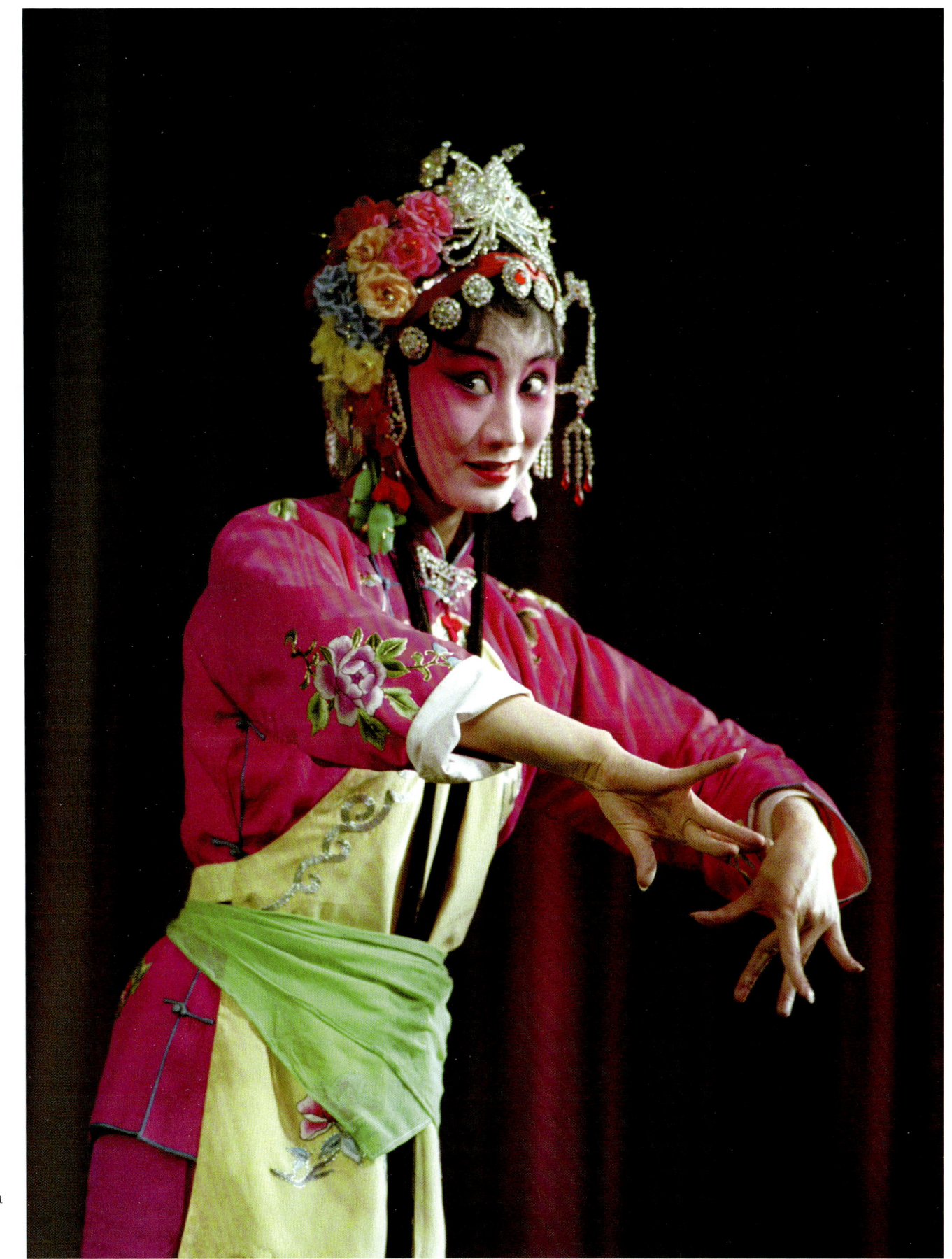

Photo 2.05 *Pan Jinlian Tempts Her Brother-In-Law*, Sichuan Opera

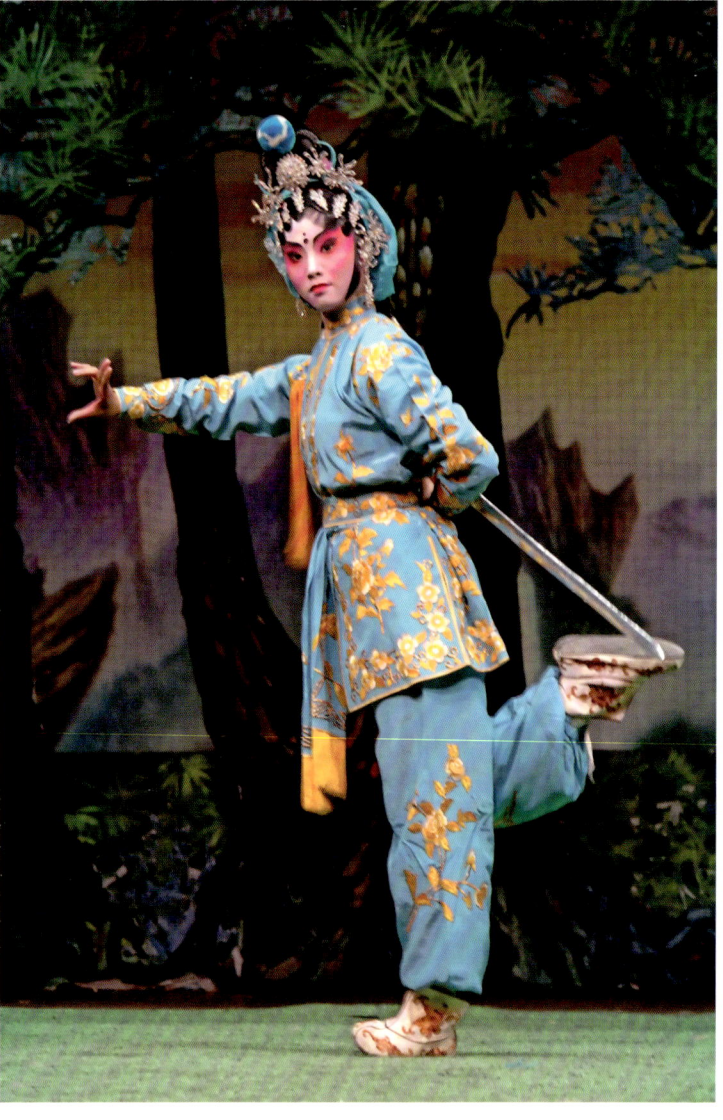

Photo 2.06 *The Magic Lotus Lantern*, Cantonese Opera

re-emerge on the stage at the audience's left indicating that they have crossed a great distance. Characters will also mime travelling by night through careful footwork, and by indicating how alert they are as they take each step. This move is called the "side step".

The female warrior, Mu Guiying, has learned a secret pathway to escape an enemy's ambush in a valley. Following the instructions of an old man who collects herbs in the valley, she makes her way out on the narrow, winding pathway. The performer walks in a counter-clockwise circle to demonstrate her journey (see Photo 2.07).

Mime can also present a journey in a carrying chair. The clever and vivacious maid, Spring Grass, has used her wit to get an official to let her ride in his carrying chair while he walks. Four chair bearers mime holding up the poles and walk in unison with a distinctive swaying gait that denotes porters or chair bearers. Although Spring Grass stands and walks in the middle of the four bearers, the audience understands that she is in fact sitting in the chair supported by them and enjoying the ride (see Photo 2.08).

Photo 2.07 *Women Warriors of the Yang Family,* Cantonese Opera

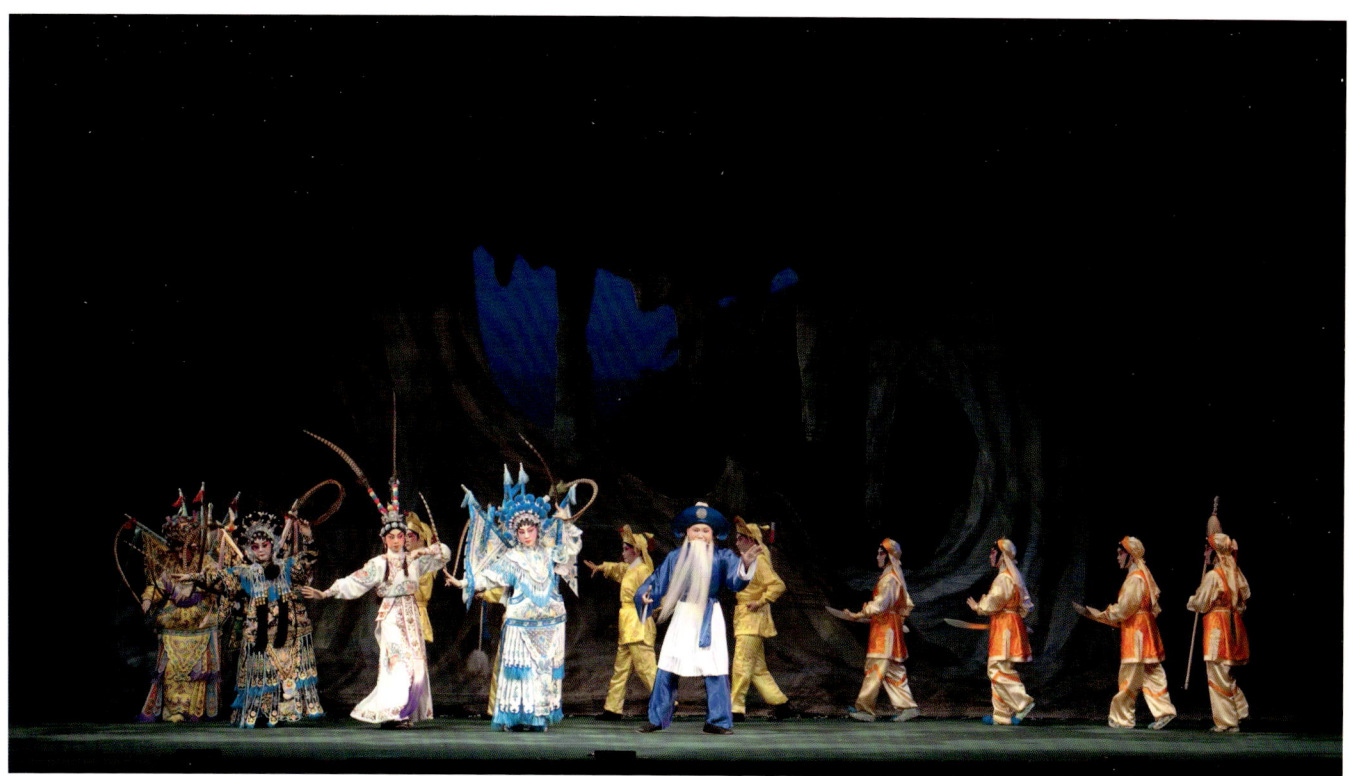

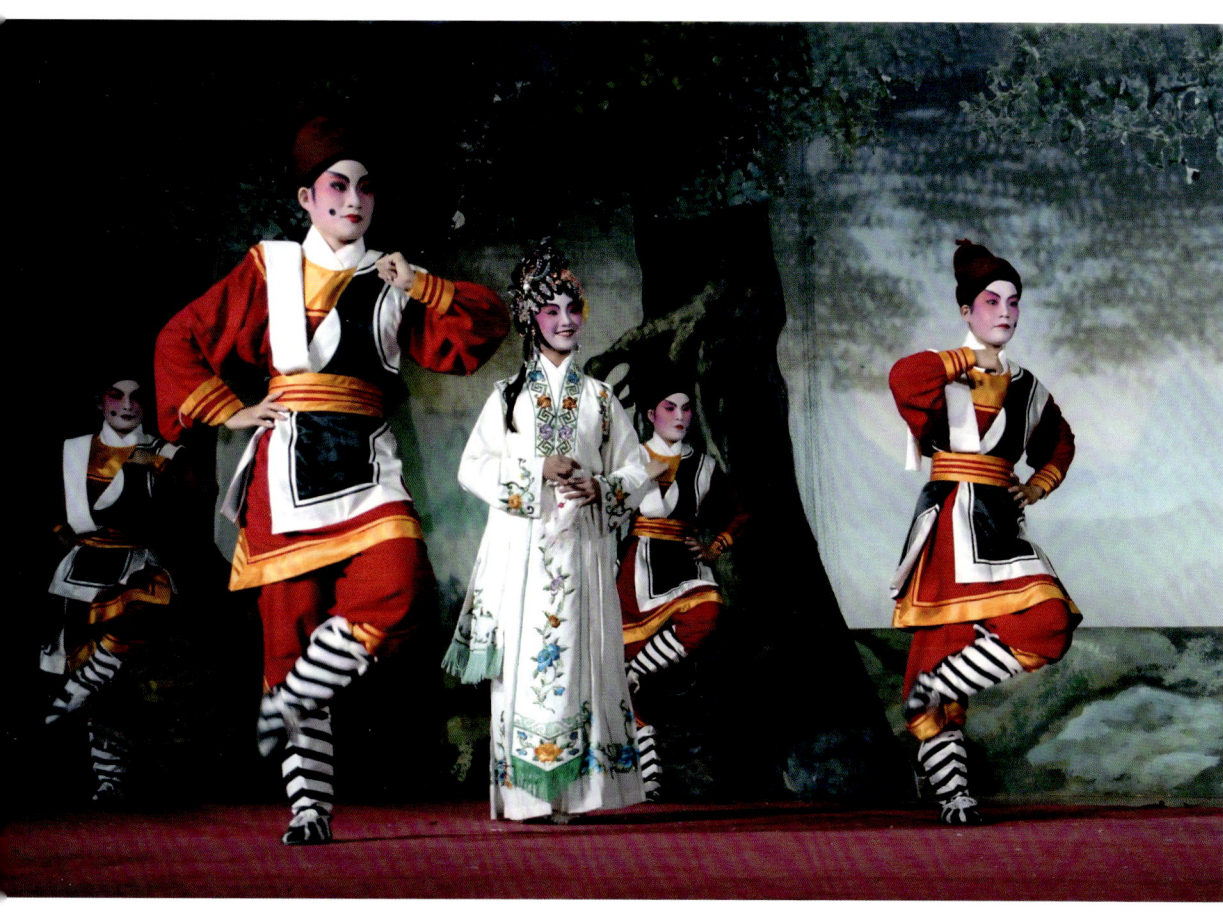

Photo 2.08 *Spring Grass Rushes to Court,* Cantonese Opera

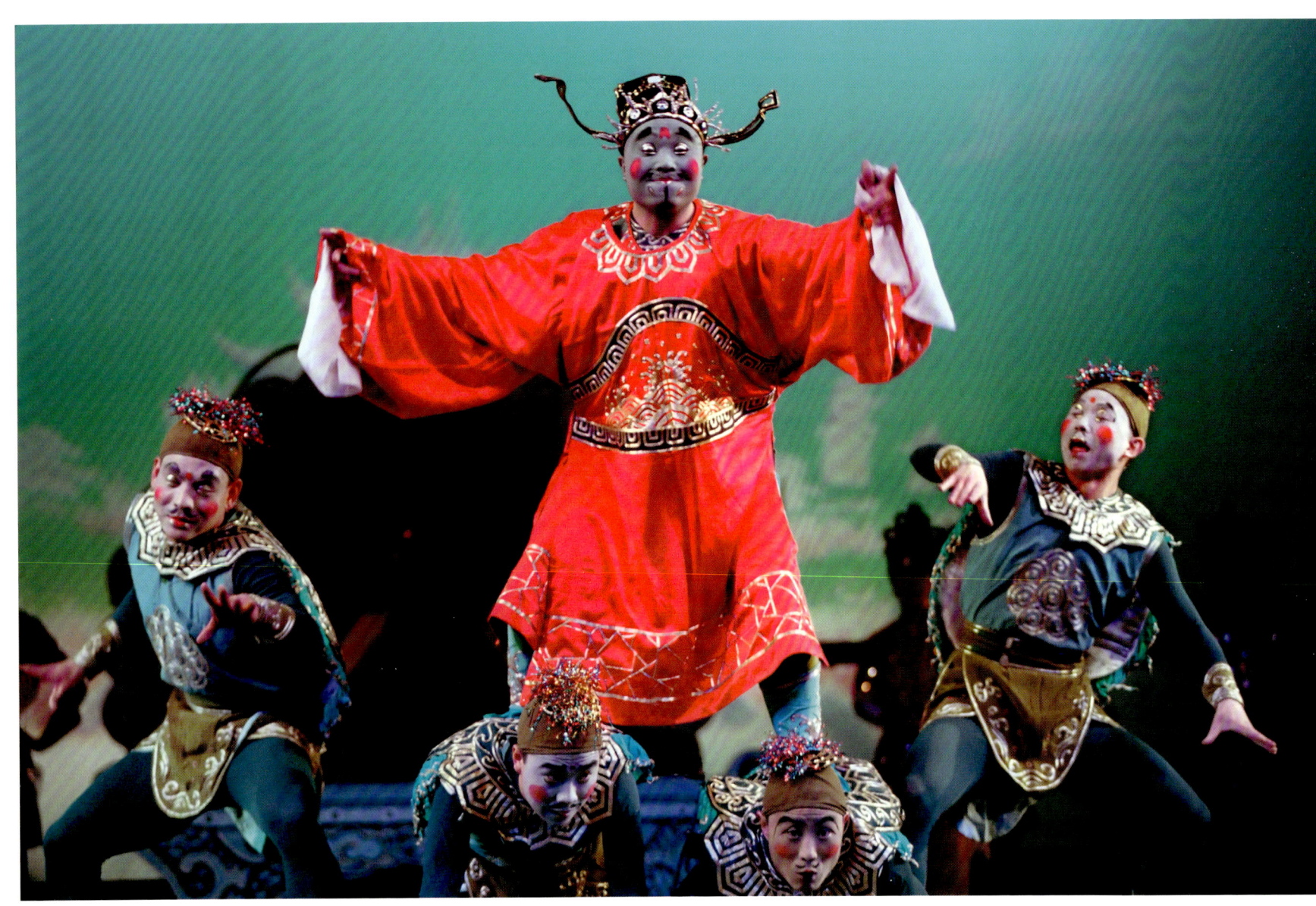

Photo 2.09 *Wreaking Havoc in the Eastern Sea*, Hebei Clapper Opera

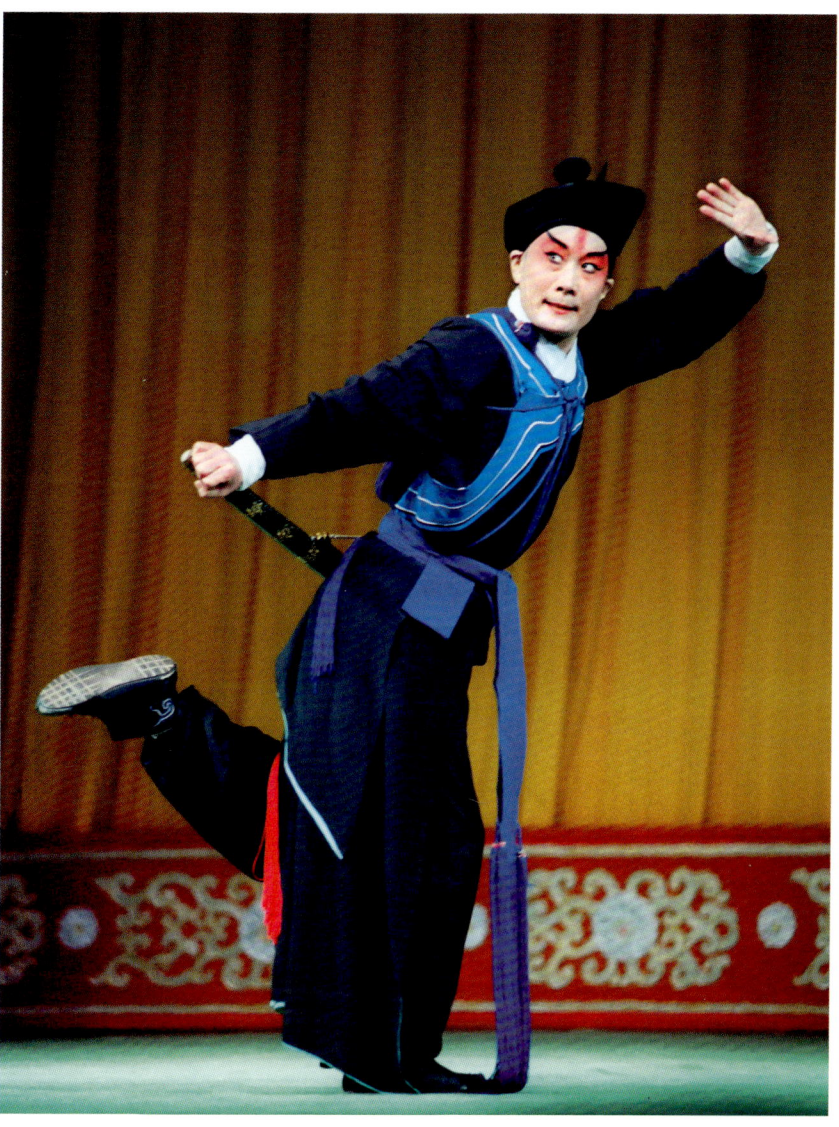

Photo 2.10 *Lin Chong's Night Flight*, Hebei Clapper Opera

Mime can also indicate a fantastic journey as in *Wreaking Havoc in the Eastern Sea*. In this opera, the turtle magistrate swims through the water with his turtle troops. The actors mime swimming under the sea in a turtle fashion (see Photo 2.09).

Another type of mimed travel is the "side walk". Typically used for night journeys or reconnaissance, the "side walk" indicates that the character is in difficult or unknown terrain off the main road. The character is simply dressed, sometimes carries a weapon or other prop, and moves adroitly so as not to be observed. He must depend heavily on careful listening as he moves through the darkness unsure of what dangers lurk around the corners or behind the trees. His eyes convey the sense of constant alertness. The character sometimes sings an aria as he goes, and thus this mime is also called "singing side walk". The "singing side walk" is used in *Lin Chong's Night Flight*. The hero Lin Chong, falsely accused, sentenced, and now in danger of his life, must make his escape at night on Liang Mountain. He mimes his way through the treacherous mountain passes, jumping across a stream while singing an aria (see Photo 2.10).

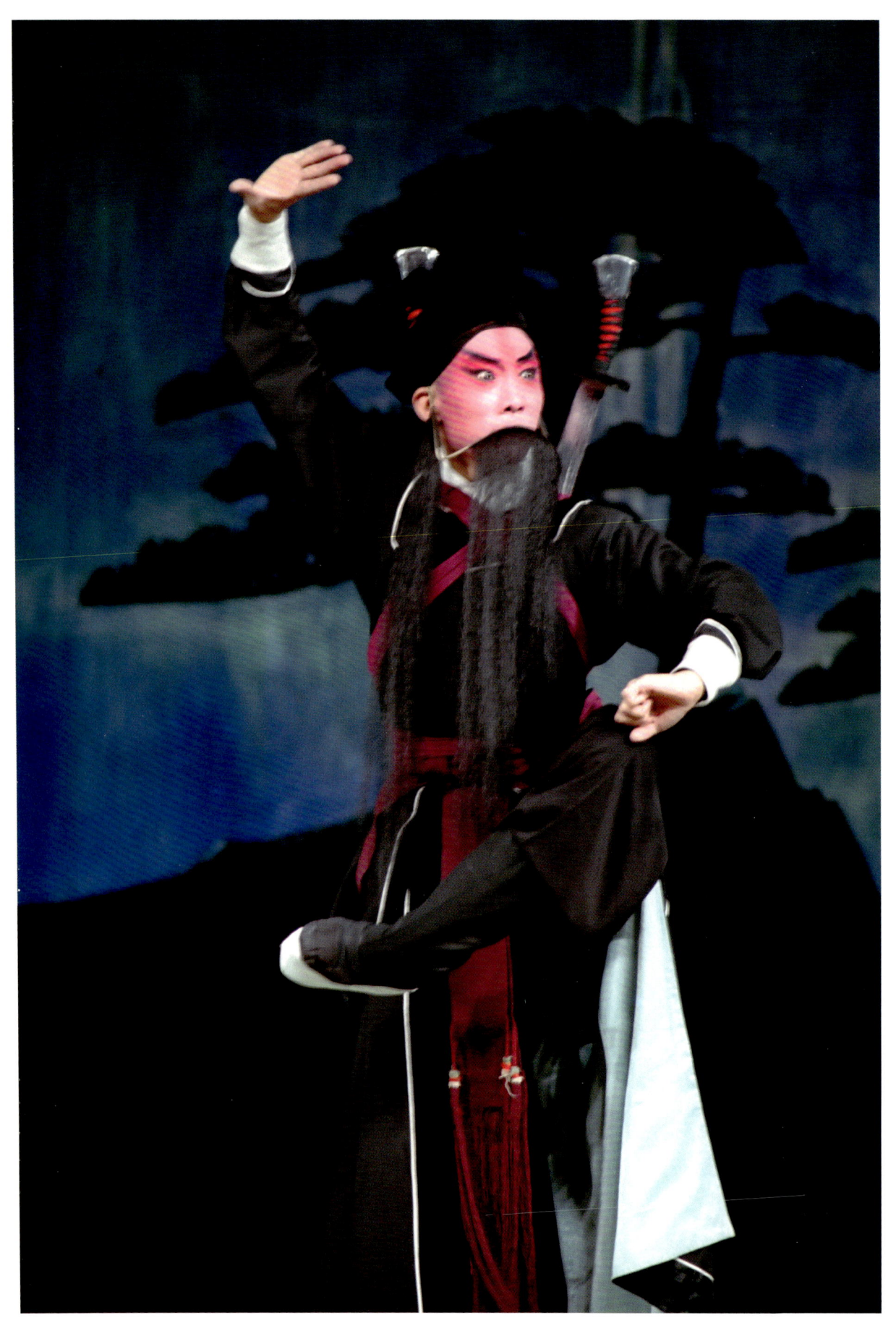

Photo 2.11　*Cleaning Out the Bandit's Lair*, Peking Opera

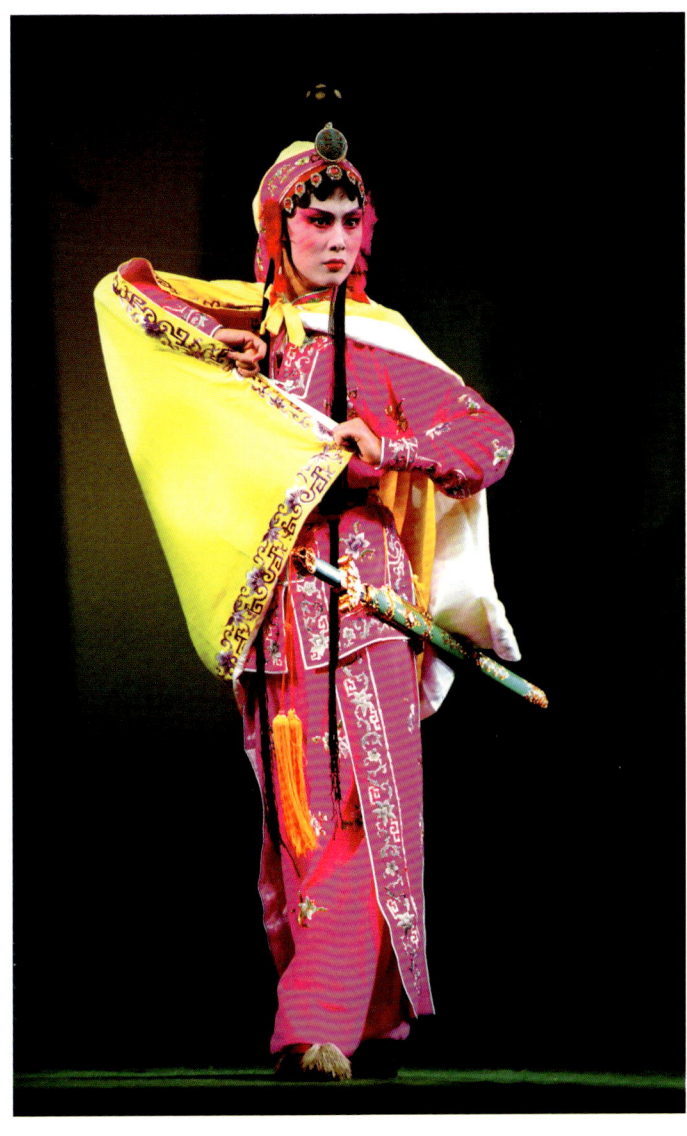

Photo 2.12 *The Prime Minster of Wei*, Shao Opera

The warrior He Tianbao also mimes a journey through dangerous mountain terrain at night in *Cleaning Out the Bandit's Lair*. Having been sent to scout out the mountain base of local outlaws, He Tianbao must make his way in the darkness over difficult terrain. Listening carefully, he demonstrates that he is on alert as he moves deftly through the darkness. His left fist faces the earth like a hammer, while his right hand is opened to the sky. He balances in readiness on one leg. His eyes are fixed, bright and determined (see Photo 2.11).

The young maiden Yue Yan also takes a night journey. She leads her father, the commander of the Wei forces, into the darkness. Falsely accused of treachery, he has been expelled from the camp. She keeps vigilant, leading the way through the wilderness (see photo 2.12).

Mime opens up endless possibilities in Chinese opera. It expands the story line by relying upon the skills of actors executing familiar moves that invoke, rather than recreate, reality.

Acrobatics

FOR MANY WESTERNERS, acrobatics and Chinese opera are synonymous. A trip to Chinese opera carries the expectation of dazzling displays of tumbling and breath-taking flips across the stage. A Western audience can be excused for thinking that Chinese opera is primarily physical because touring companies from China coming to the West often choose to highlight acrobatic operas, or a series of acrobatic scenes. The concern is that the music, singing styles and language of Chinese opera are inaccessible to Westerners. It takes some time after all to familiarize oneself with the conventions of traditional opera. Consequently, troupes will often choose what is easily understood, or at least most appreciated. Chinese acrobatics is universally admired and so seems the right choice for a performance in the West.

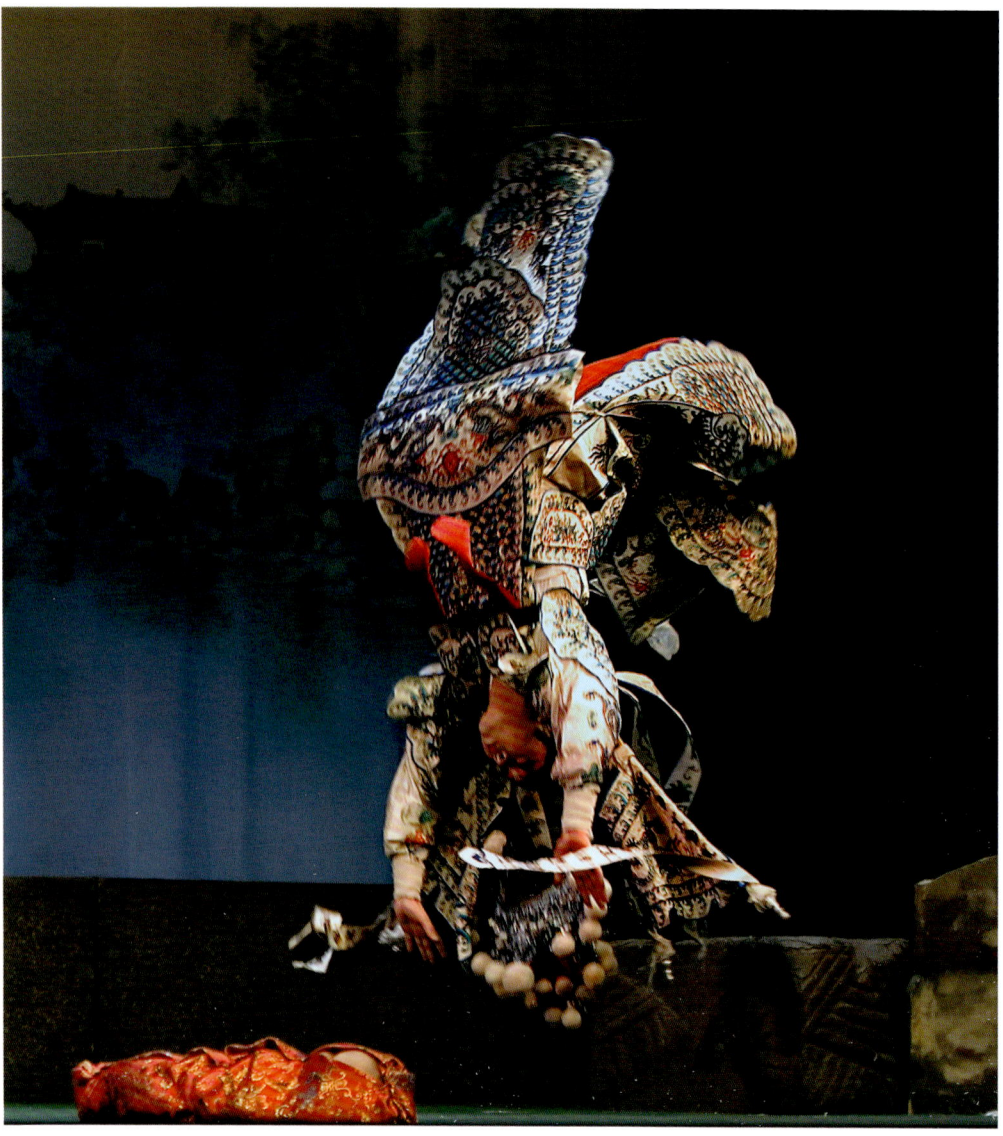

Photo 2.13 *Zhao Yun Hides the Baby Prince*, Cantonese Opera

Using Stage Movement

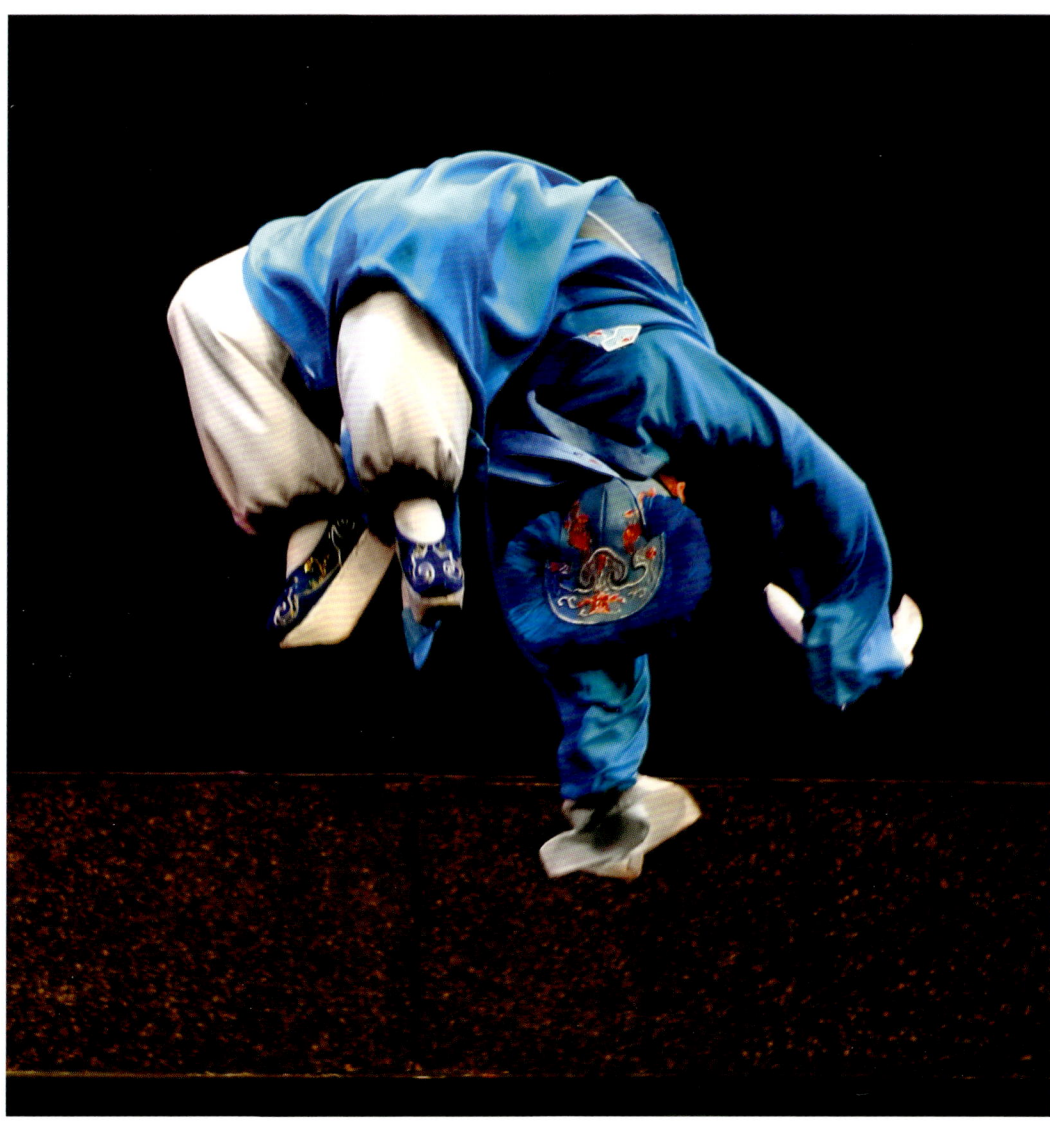

Photo 2.14 *Escape from the Golden Mountain Temple*, Cantonese Opera

Certainly, physical skills are an important ingredient of Chinese opera, which incorporates the whole range of performance art from dance to singing, from mime to acrobatics. Acrobatics cross role types. Clowns, painted face characters, warriors, female roles and male roles all have opportunities to display their prowess in different operas. This kind of skill in Chinese opera is called *tanzigong*, or "carpet work", because tumbling and flips are done on a generally bare stage covered only with the performance carpet.

The back flip is a staple of the acrobat on the Chinese opera stage. One spectacular use of the back flip is the opera scene *Escape from the Golden Mountain Temple*, part of *The Legend of the White Snake* story. The young man, Xu Xian, has unwittingly married White Snake, a snake spirit who has incarnated as a beautiful maiden. The Buddhist abbot, Fahai, declaring this an abomination, imprisons Xu Xian in the Golden Mountain Temple to protect him from White Snake. Xu Xian, however, escapes and makes a specular entrance onto the stage in a move called "backward battering the tiger". Without touching the floor with his hands, the actor springs headlong backwards across the stage, flipping himself over and landing on his feet; he thus demonstrates his distress during a perilous escape (see Photo 2.14).

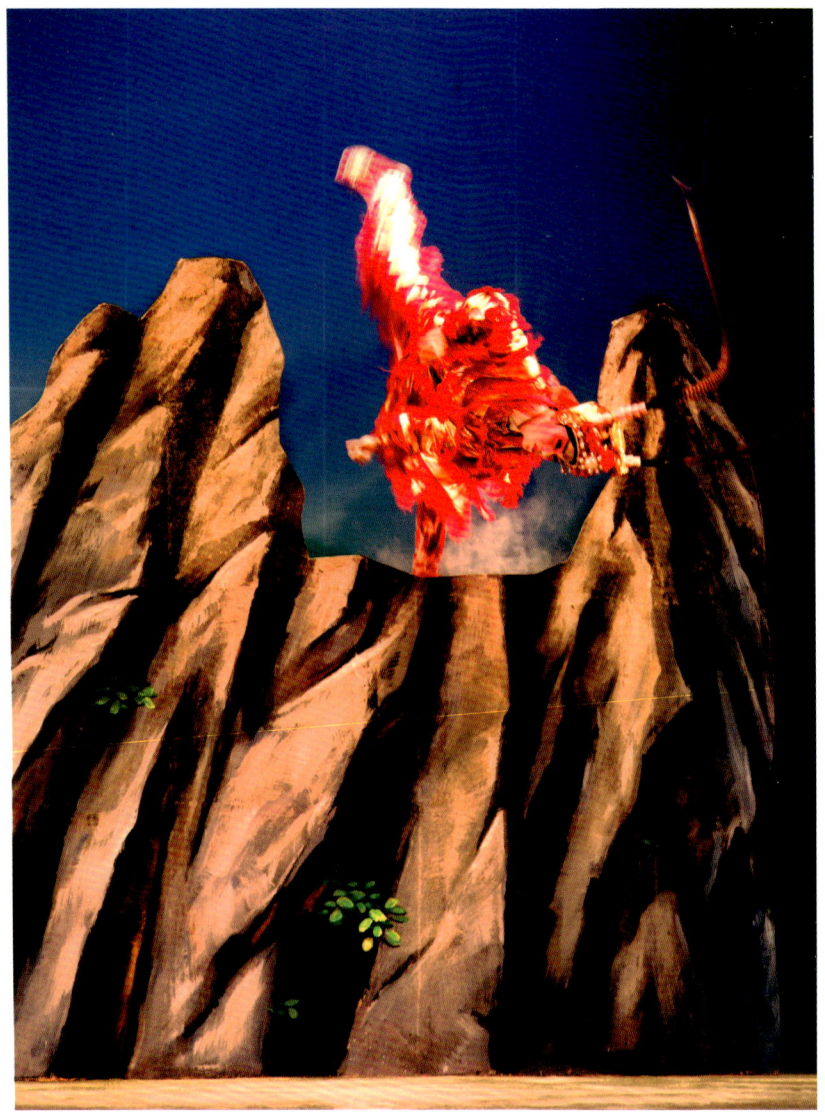

Photo 2.15 *The Eighteen Luohan Pursue the Golden Crane*, Cantonese Opera

Some operas have a number of such acrobatic displays, one after the other. *The Eighteen Luohan Pursue the Golden Crane* is one such opera. The luohan, or arhats, are ascended beings who have achieved Buddhist enlightenment. They are called on to capture the Golden Crane which normally sits before the Buddha, but has fled to take the place of the Golden Eagle Prince in a marriage to a beautiful princess. The Golden Crane in his flight executes a "cloud flip". Normally done from atop several stacked tables, it is also executed from a realistic mountain in more modern productions. The actor leads with his legs, throwing them out over his head as he tumbles from a great height to land on his feet on the stage below (see Photo 2.15).

The luohan discover that the Golden Crane is not easily captured. One of them is struck to the ground and rolls across the stage in a "tiger roll" while the Golden Crane leaps through the air over him (see Photo 2.16).

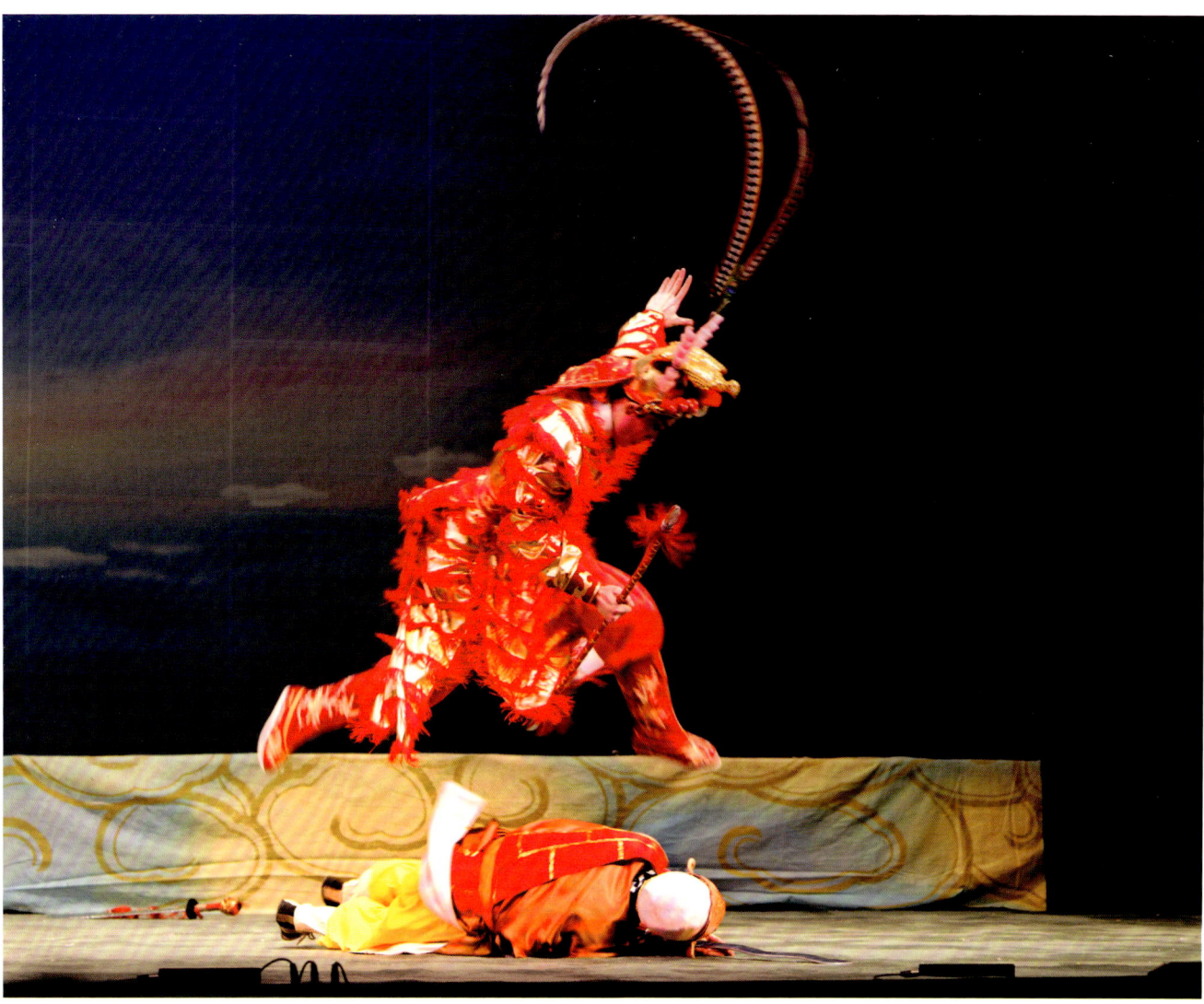

Photo 2.16 *The Eighteen Luohan Pursue the Golden Crane*, Cantonese Opera

The action becomes tense as each of the luohan attacks the Golden Crane in an attempt to catch the wayward bird. They flip and somersault across the stage one after another, but the Golden Crane avoids them all (see Photo 2.17).

Acrobatics are commonly used in a class of Chinese operas called *wuxi* or military opera. The opera *Phoenix Terrace Fortress* is one example. The insurgent Guo Yanwei leads his forces against the court in the Northern Han dynasty (951–979). To get there, he must fight his way through the Phoenix Terrace Fortress, which is protected by the general Murong Yanchao, a formidable fighter. But the general has taken ill and cannot come out to battle. To save the dynasty, his wife, Zhang Xiuying, dons armour and heads out to fight the invaders. The battle is spectacular as she shows that she herself is an able warrior. She fends off the enemy fighters who execute the *gaomao*, or high somersault, over her head. The acrobatic soldier jumps and flies directly above her, hits the ground rolling, stands up and runs off all in one smooth and electrifyingly executed move (see Photo 2.18).

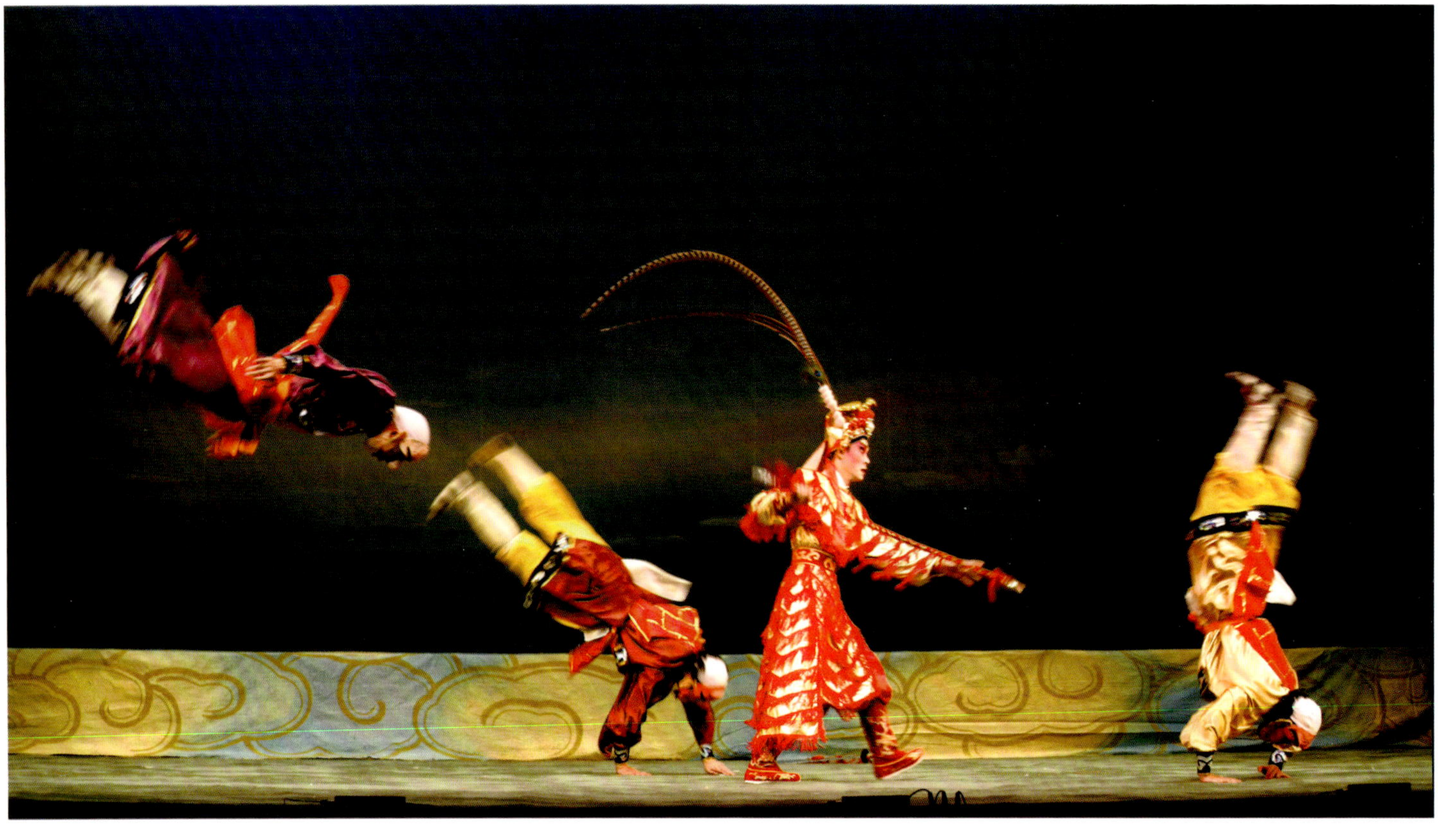

Photo 2.17 *The Eighteen Luohan Pursue the Golden Crane*, Cantonese Opera

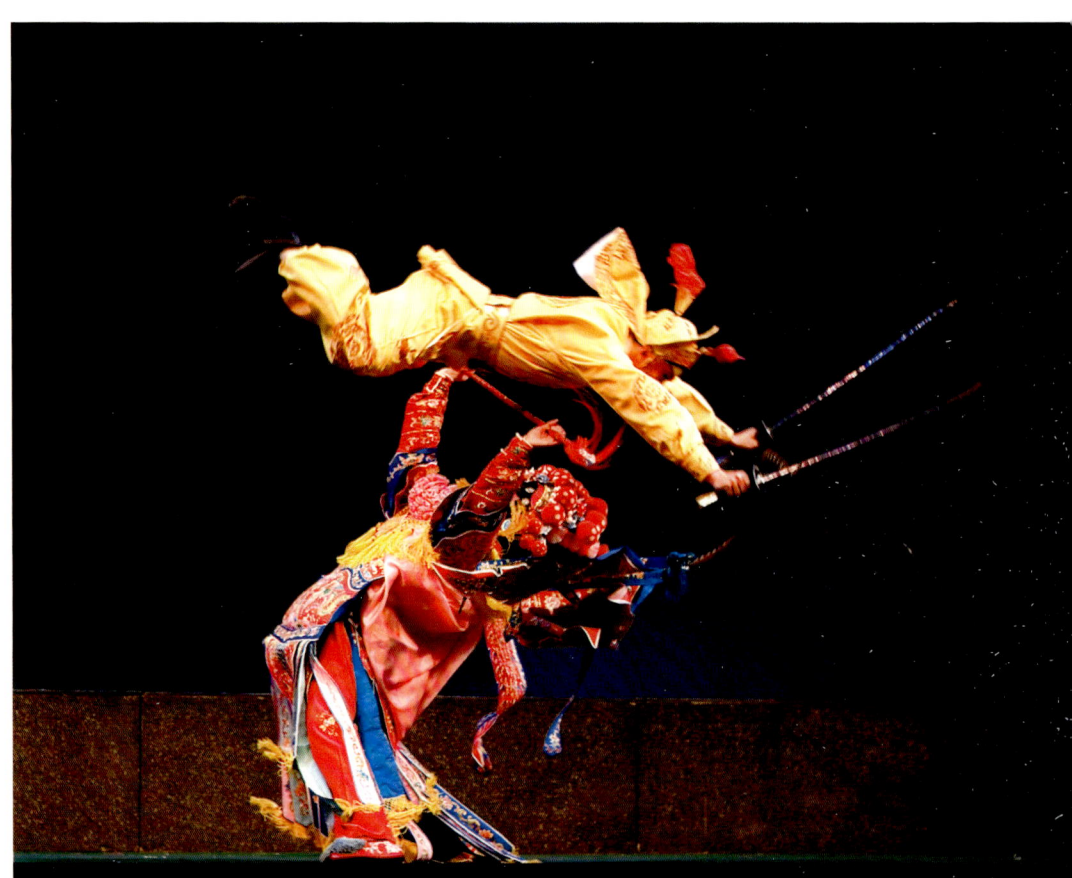

Photo 2.18 *Phoenix Terrace Fortress*, Cantonese Opera

Using Stage Movement

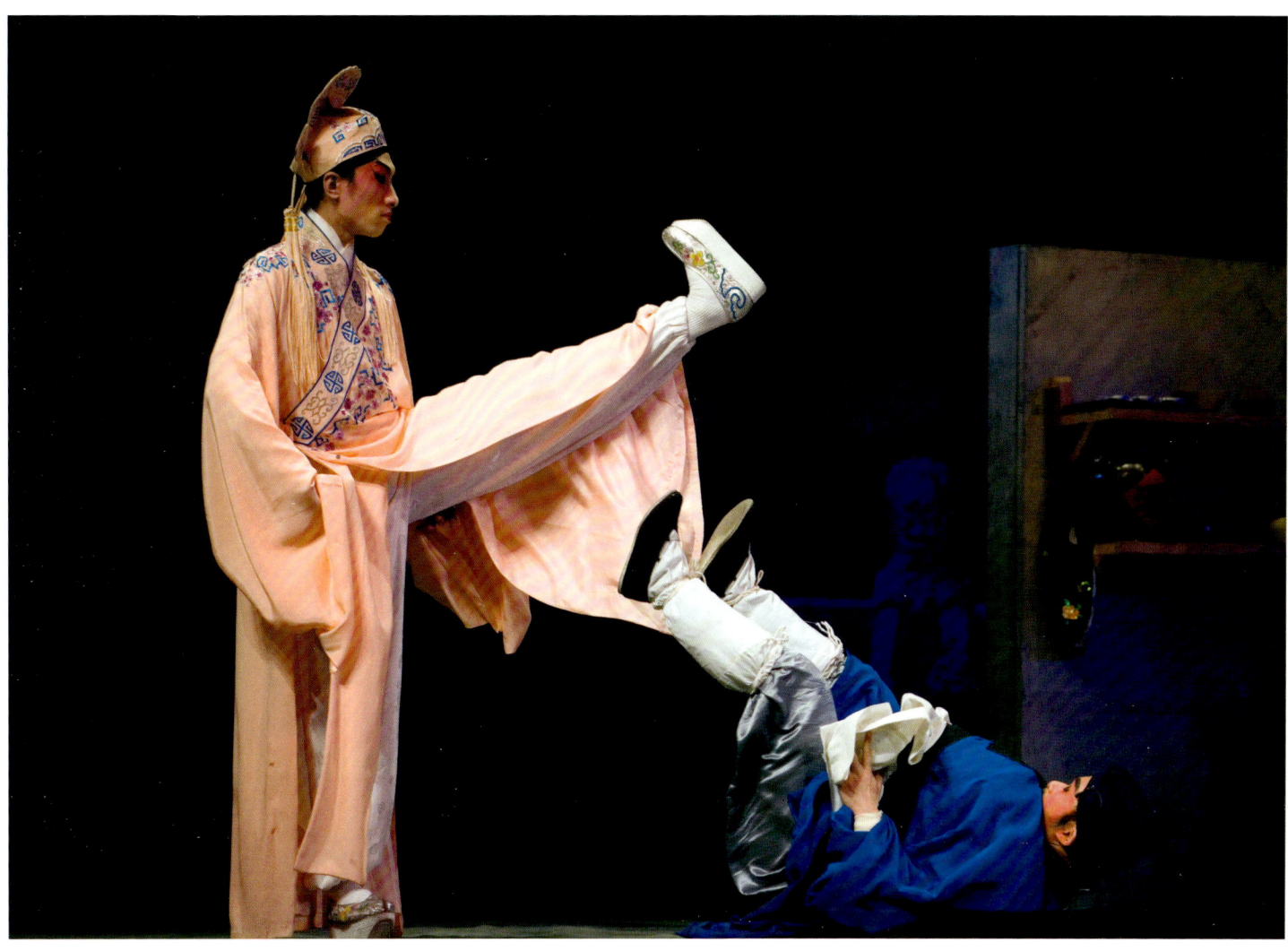

Photo 2.19 *Wu Song*, Cantonese Opera

Acrobatics on the Chinese stage are elegant, and appreciated for the ease in which the actor incorporates them into the action of the play. In the opera *Wu Song* the cuckolded husband, Wu Dalang, somersaults backwards on the stage after a strikingly beautiful kick from the evil Ximen Qing. That actor kicks his leg high while maintaining a perfectly straight posture. Wu Dalang is knocked back, and Ximen Qing quickly brings his leg back (see Photo 2.19).

Yet another striking acrobatic pose is executed by the young man's role in the opera *The Haunting of Zhang Sanlang*. The maiden Yan Xijiao has come back from the grave looking for her lover; she is determined to bring him with her to the underworld so that they can be together again there. As she pursues him, Zhang Sanlang is stunned and collapses. In a move called the "stiff corpse fall", his body stiffens like a board and he falls back perfectly straight until he hits the ground, indicating that he is either stunned or dead. The fall is both beautiful and terrifying to watch (see Photo 2.20).

Physical displays like these are high points in Chinese opera just as much as beautiful singing is. They are further demonstrations of the actor's craft which lies at the centre of Chinese theatre.

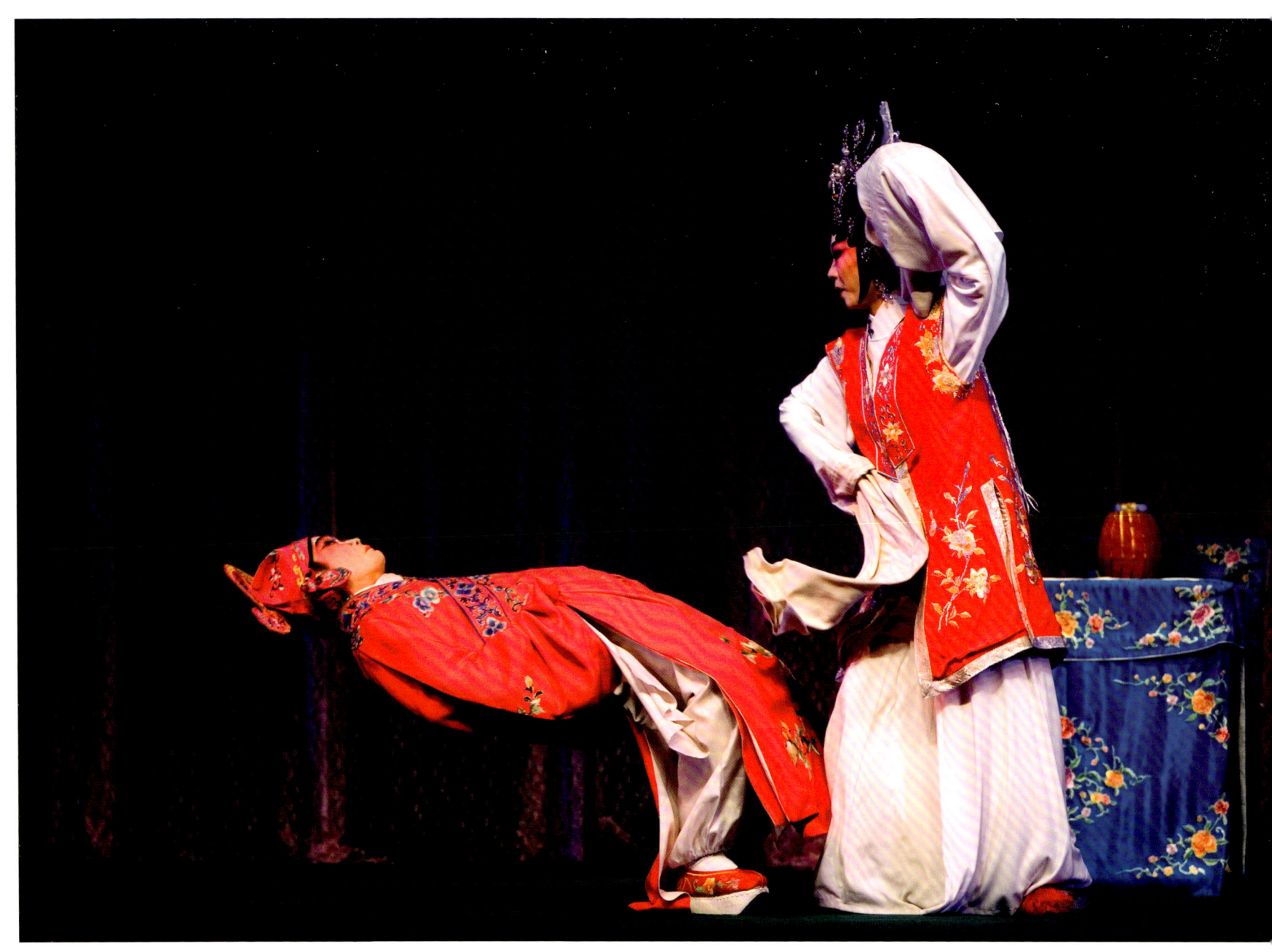

Photo 2.20 *The Haunting of Zhang Sanlang*, Cantonese Opera

Poses

CHINESE OPERA ACTING is larger than life with exaggerated gestures, costumes and stylized props. The stylized pose, or *liangxiang*, is an important feature of Chinese performing arts. It brings in an element of sculpture, suspending the moment in time for the admiration of the audience. Actors will in the midst of the opera strike momentary poses that elegantly express the event or the feeling of the moment. They also often strike a pose upon entering the stage or just before leaving it.

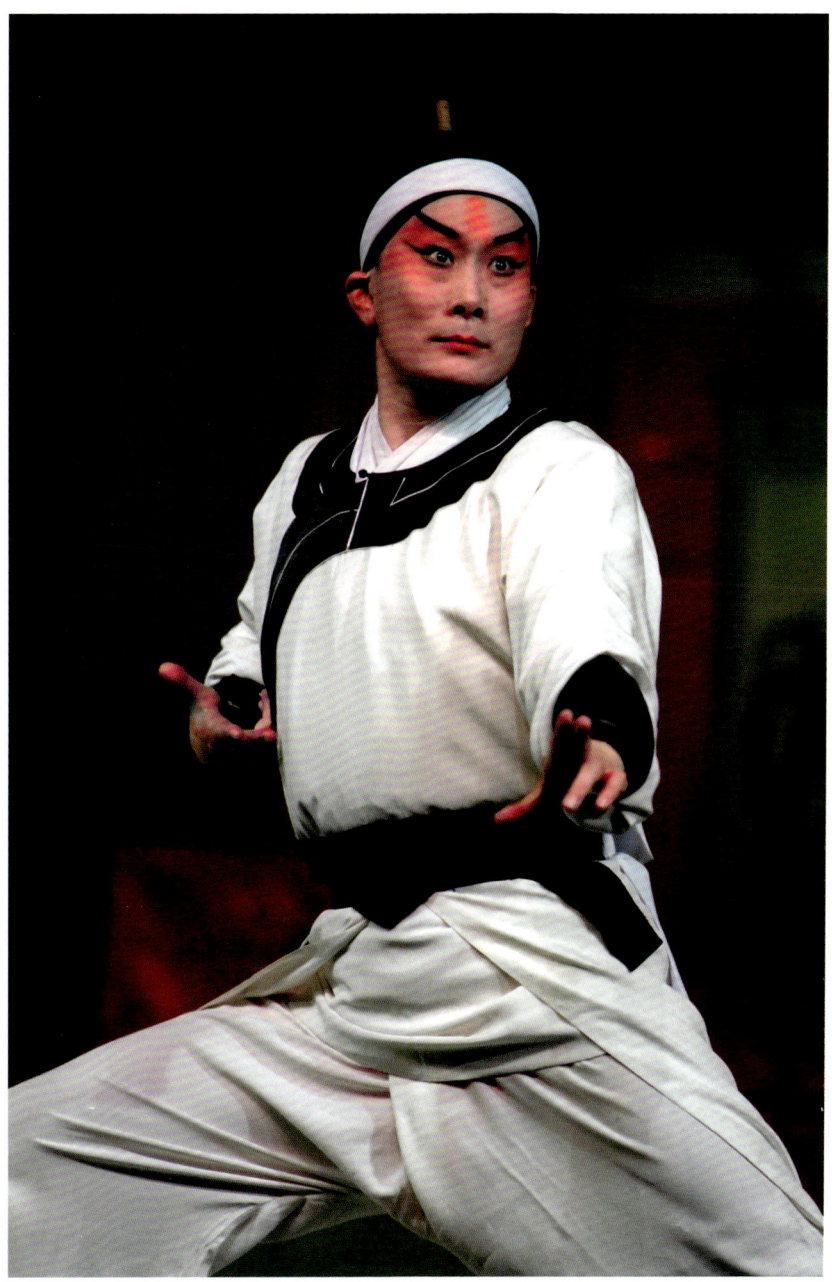

Photo 2.21 *Burning the Camps*, Hebei Clapper Opera

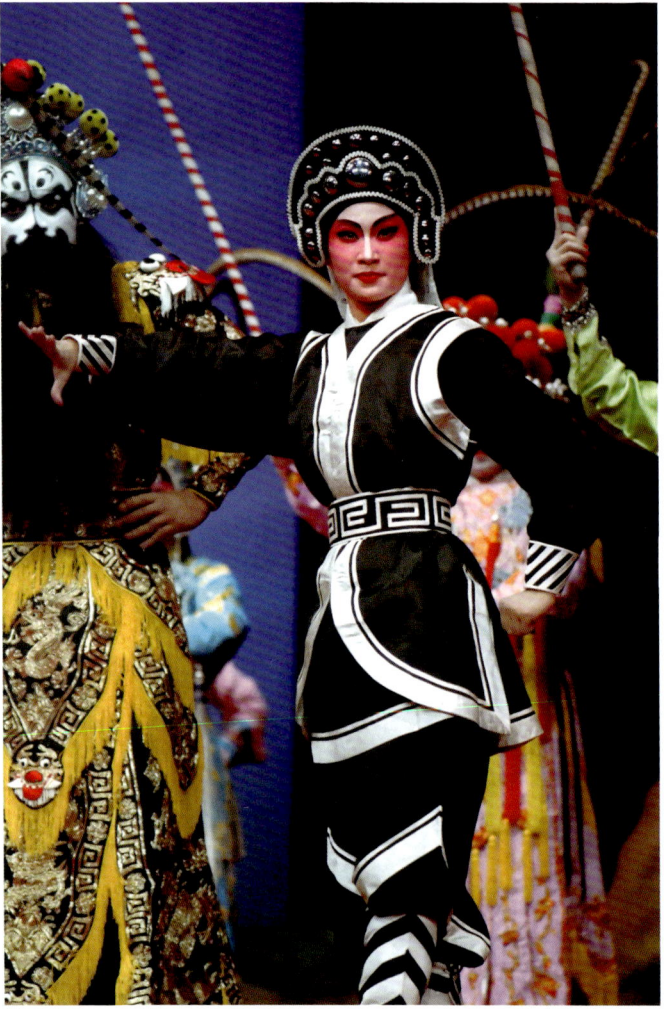

Photo 2.22 *Women Warriors of the Yang Family*, Cantonese Opera

"Mountain shoulders" is a basic pose in Chinese opera that indicates determination, readiness to fight, and military prowess. In the case of the warrior role shown below, one hand, clenched in a hammer fist, rests on the waist, while the other arm, palm extended outwards, rises to extend in a semi-circle from the shoulder (see Photo 2.22). Different roles, however, require different positions for "mountain shoulders", depending on the age and function of the character.

In a Peking opera, the old general Zhao Yun holds his armour in a typical military pose, demonstrating spirit, discipline and severity. He listens soberly to the judgement on the commander who lost a strategic location by disregarding careful advice and through reckless pride. The commander must now pay with his life (see Photo 2.23).

In *The Battle of Baqiu*, General Zhou Yu fights against many warriors of the Three Kingdom's great general Liu Bei. He is unable to defeat his enemies and flees for his life. Finally, he must face the legendary warrior Zhang Fei, but Zhou Yu's horse stumbles. Zhang Fei raises his left leg high, pressing the advantage with his spear as Zhou Yu sinks to the stage, stretching out his legs in a split. In a remarkable stage move, the actor then jumps to his feet from the stage floor as the horse regains its balance (see Photo 2.24).

Photo 2.23 *The Execution of the Commander*, Peking Opera

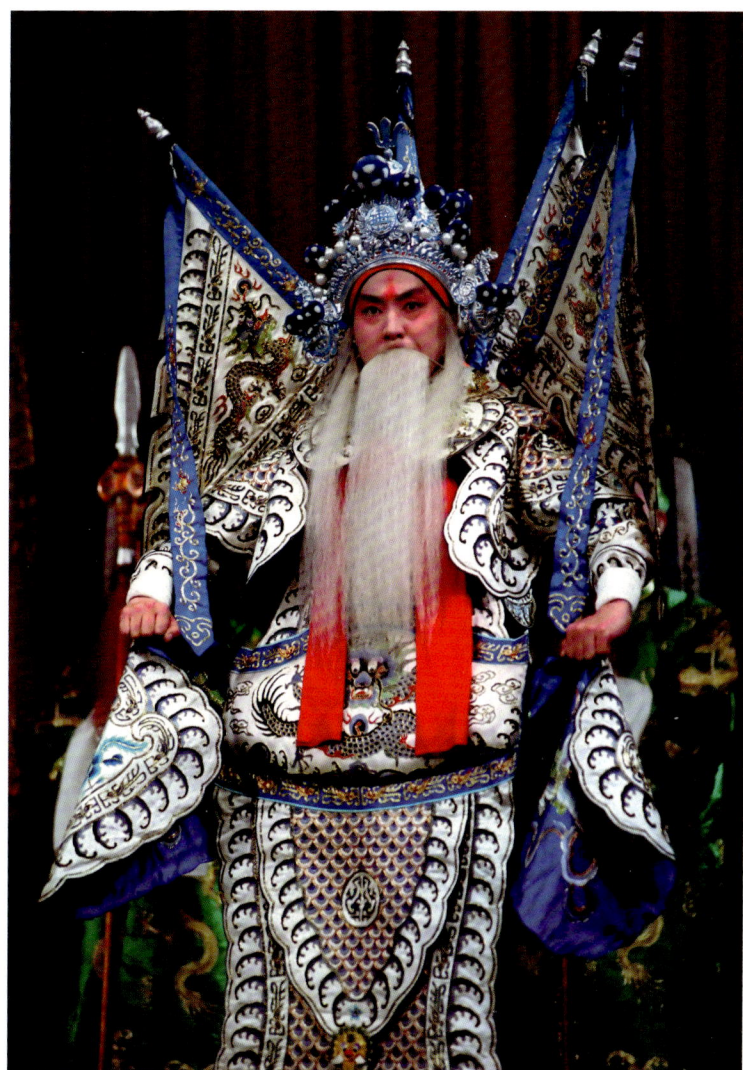

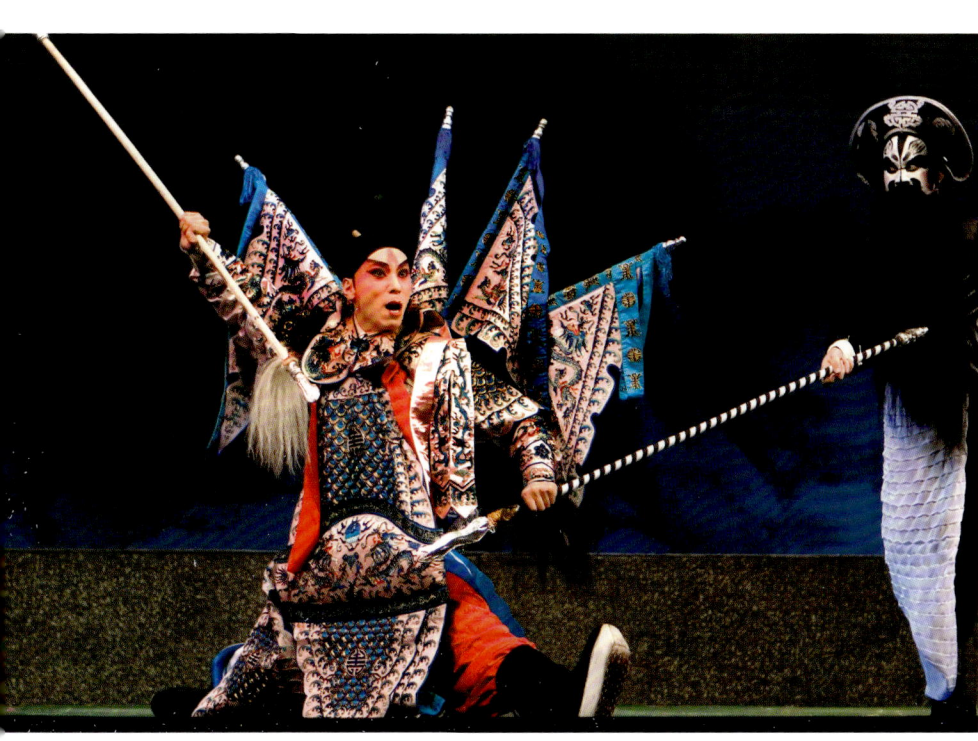

Photo 2.24 *The Battle of Baqiu*, Cantonese Opera

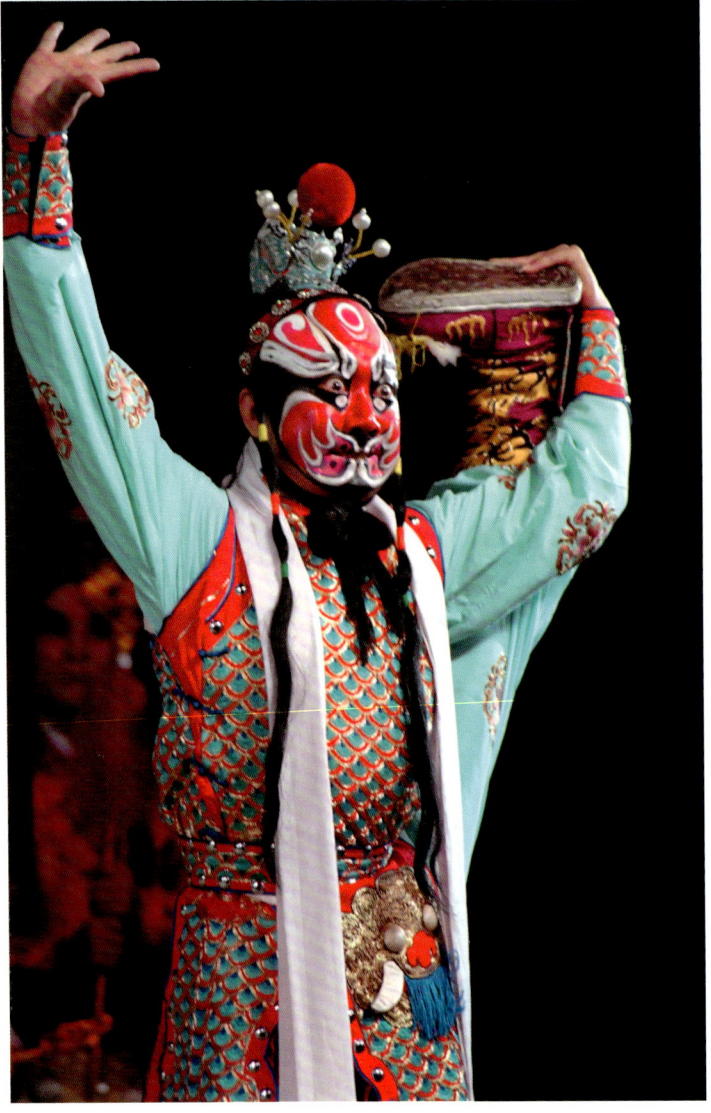

Photo 2.25 *The Cosmic Belt*, Ping Opera

Some poses indicate superior martial skills. Qin Ying fished in the imperial pool at Golden Water Bridge and killed a palace official in a dispute. As punishment he is to be sent off to war, leading the troops. Qin Ying demonstrates his prowess by striking a pose called "pedalling heaven" or "leg twist". He raises his leg straight upward, pulling it behind his arm while grabbing the back of his foot so that the sole faces directly upward (see Photo 2.25).

Another similar pose makes a dramatic impression in the opera *Twice-Locked Mountain*. The formidable warrior maiden Liu Jinding engages in combat with the young, handsome general, Gao Junbao. After a fierce battle, she takes up the "board leg pose". Standing straight on her right leg, she lifts her left leg high, grabbing the back of her foot with her right hand bringing it to her ear. Her determined gaze is fixed in front of her. Her left hand holds firmly onto her polearm. Used in combat and in choreographed spear play, this pose is dramatic, suggesting both courage and high fighting skills (see Photo 2.26).

Actors will often strike poses in the middle of much action. One such case is the fighting match between the warrior Meng Liang and the housemaid Yang Paifeng. Meng Liang has come to the famous

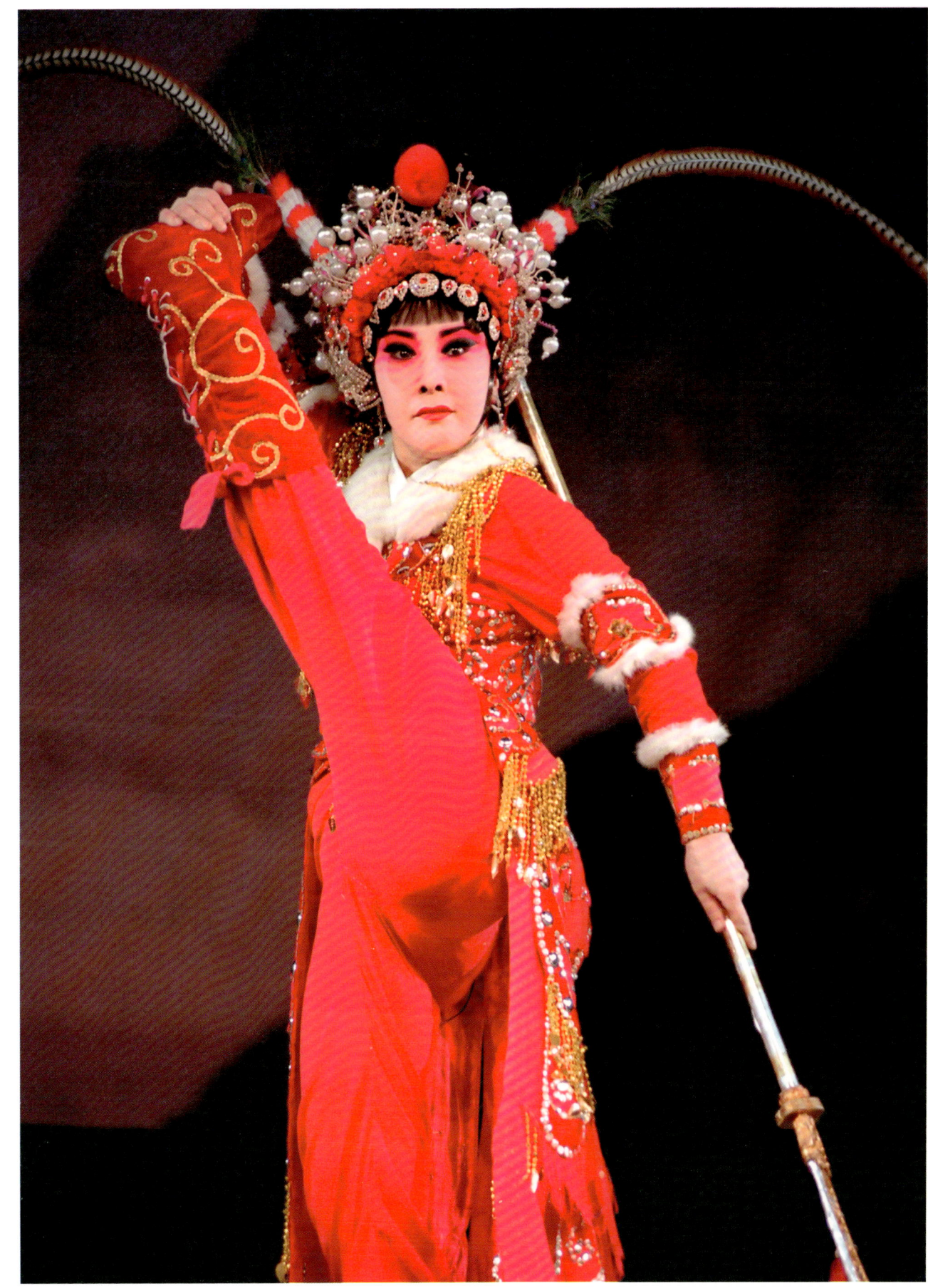

Photo 2.26 *Twice-Locked Mountain*, Longjiang Opera

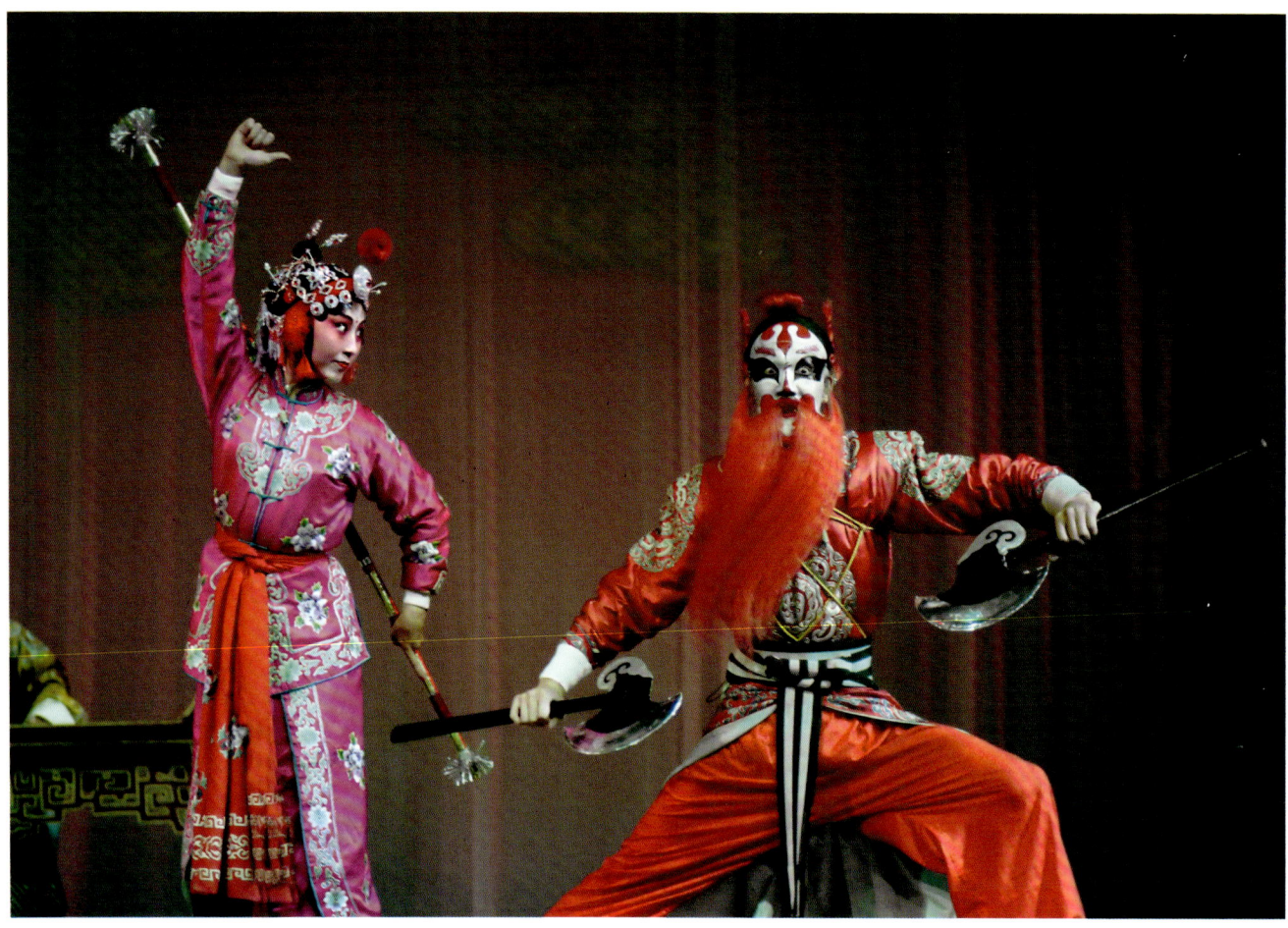

Photo 2.27 *Meng Liang Raises Troops*, Gan Opera

Yang mansion to raise troops against an enemy. The servant girl is determined to prove that she is just as good—in fact better—than any of the male warriors. The sceptical and dismissive Meng Liang puts her to the test and finds that she is indeed unbeatable. In the middle of the fight, accompanied by drums and gongs, the actors freeze in a pose. Yang Paifeng looks on with determination at the frankly stupefied Meng Liang (see Photo 2.27).

The great general Guan Yu, later deified as Guan Gong, flourishes his great polearm in battle, accompanied by great drumming and clanging of gongs. He swings it behind him against his back, the powerful blade facing upward, and strikes a momentary pose that wins the admiration of the audience (see Photo 2.28).

Lu Wenlong has defeated general after general including the powerful Yue Yun. In a moment of self-satisfaction and bravado, he takes the pose "back crossed double spears" (see Photo 2.29). This pose is used by both male and female warriors to demonstrate their agility and skill with weapons.

Photo 2.28 *Cao Cao, Guan Yu and Diaochan*, Hui Opera

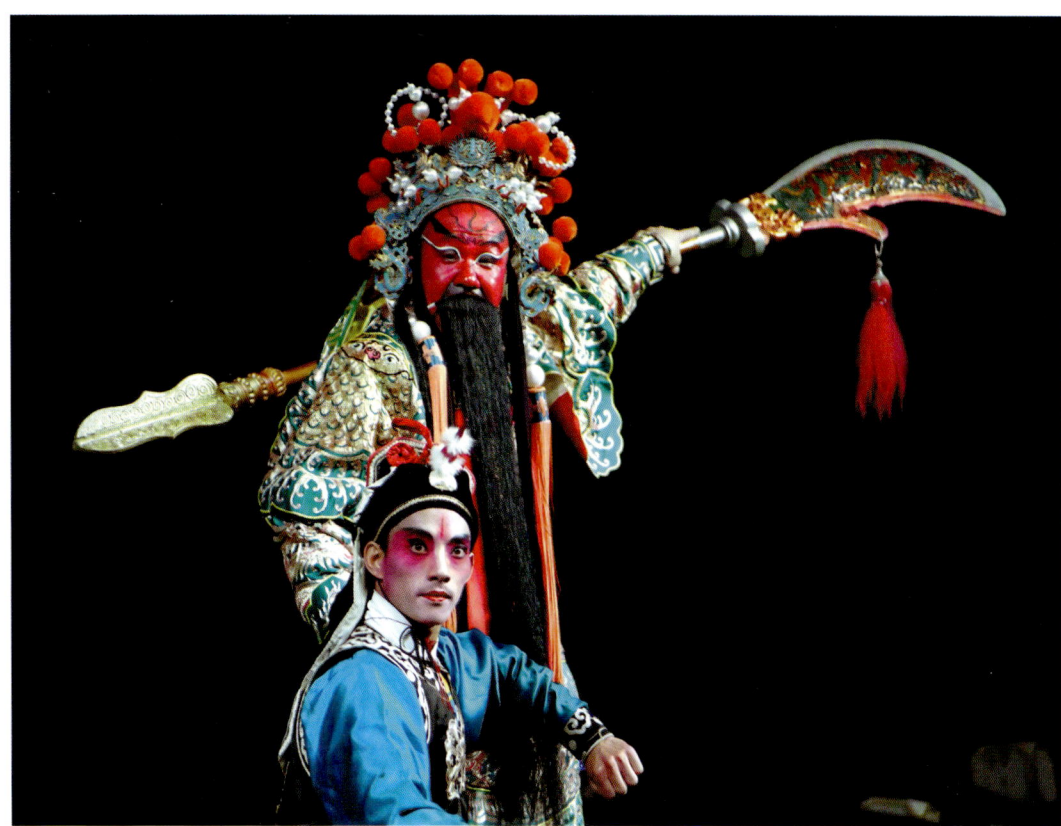

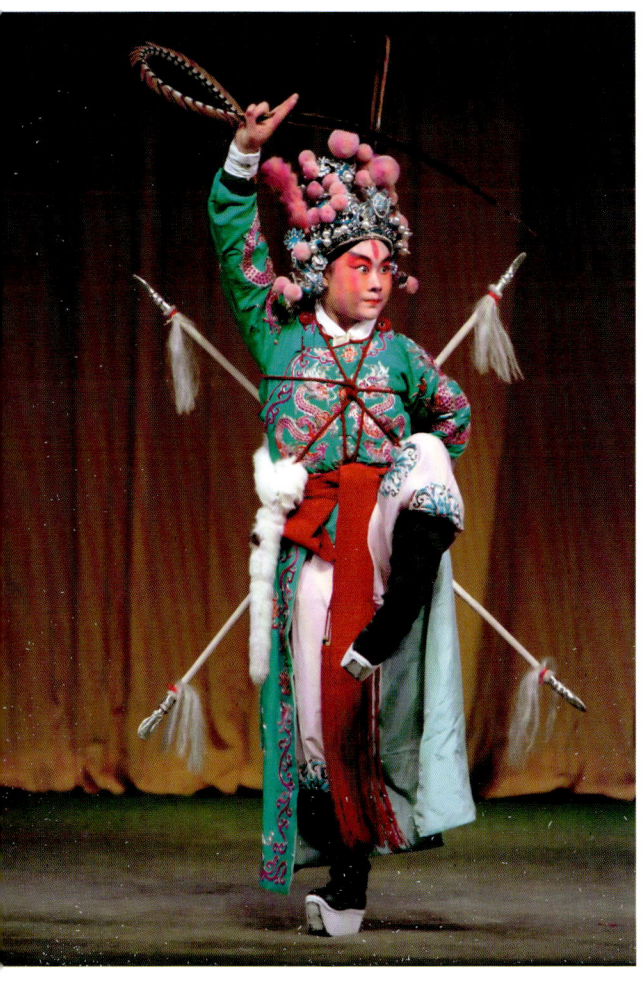

Photo 2.29 *Lu Wenlong and His Double Spears*, Hebei Clapper Opera

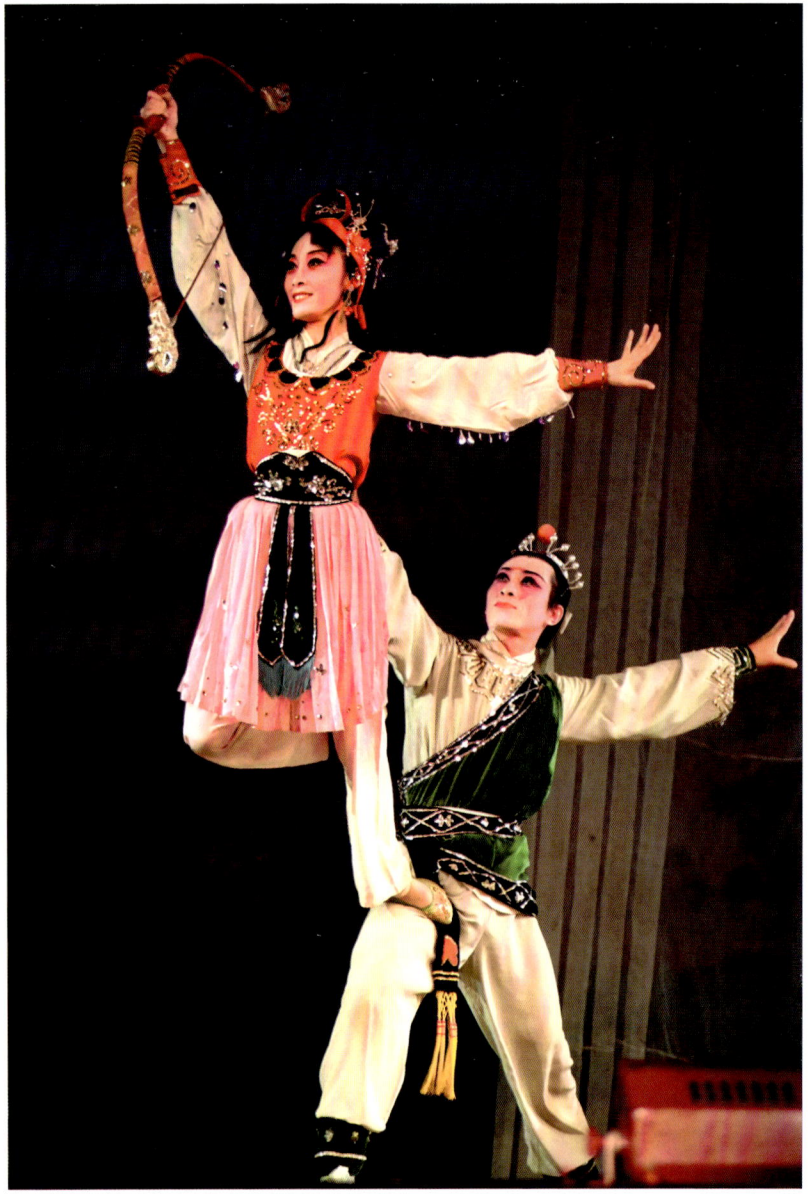

Photo 2.30 *The Romance of the Iron Bow*, Longjiang Opera

Special Moves

ACTORS ALSO MAKE use of special dramatic moves as they tell the story of the opera. These moves are a stylized lifting up of the opera's action to the realm of poetic movement. These moves are named for what they evoke in a similar way to how kungfu or tai-chi moves are named. The moves can be used in different situations.

One of these moves is aptly named "exploring the sea". The actor bends forward over the stage while sweeping both arms out and raising the left leg high. Looking straight down as if searching the depths of the sea, the actor strikes a dramatic pose. The young maiden Lian Jinfeng uses this pose when she dives into the sea and discovers a giant oyster. She is determined to get the precious pearl within it as she wants to repay a debt of kindness and knows that this pearl will make the perfect gift. After a fierce

Using Stage Movement

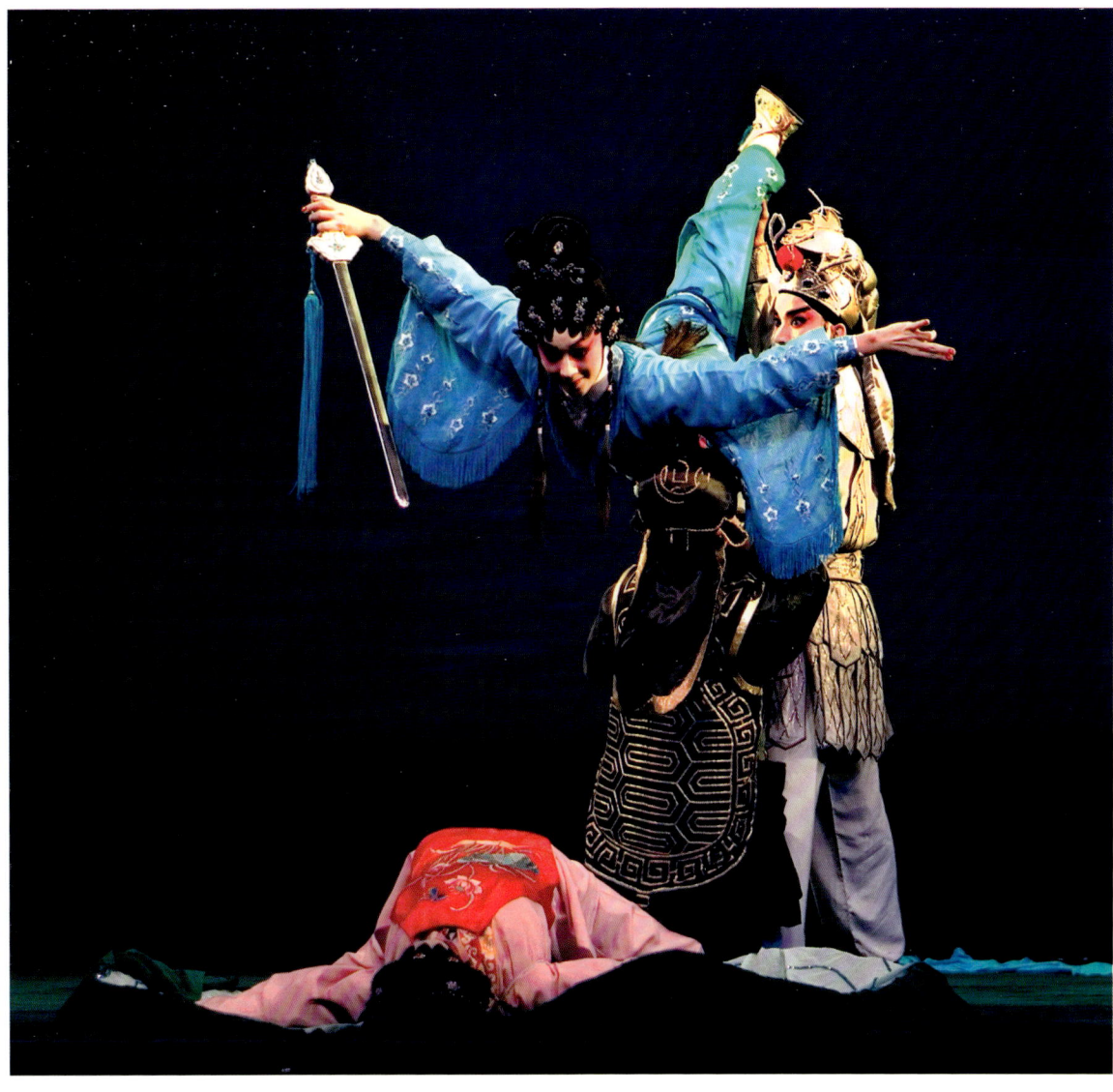

Photo 2.31 *Lian Jinfeng*, Cantonese Opera

battle with various sea creatures, she assumes the pose directly above the oyster, her sword extended, ready for the final strike. The oyster lies defenceless beneath her (see Photo 2.31).

In *The Haunting of Zhang Sanlang*, mentioned earlier, Zhang Sanlang uses the same move when he discovers the ghost of the beautiful Yan Xijiao. She falls straight-backed to the floor in a rigid pose known as "board waist" while Zhang Sanlang holds a lantern over her, taking up the "exploring the sea" position. Rather than looking into the water like Lian Jinfeng, he looks down upon the ghost, carefully inspecting her to see if she indeed is the same beauty that he had known in life (see Photo 2.32).

The great general Gao Chong in the famous opera *Tilting the War Carts* heroically fights against the enemy who in a desperate attempt to stop his advance sends war cart after war cart down the mountain to crush him. The general tilts each cart over with his spear, but in the process exhausts himself and his horse, so that both die on the mountain slope. The actor depicts the moment of exhaustion in a special move called "shooting the wild goose". Bending backwards so that his body is parallel to the stage, he

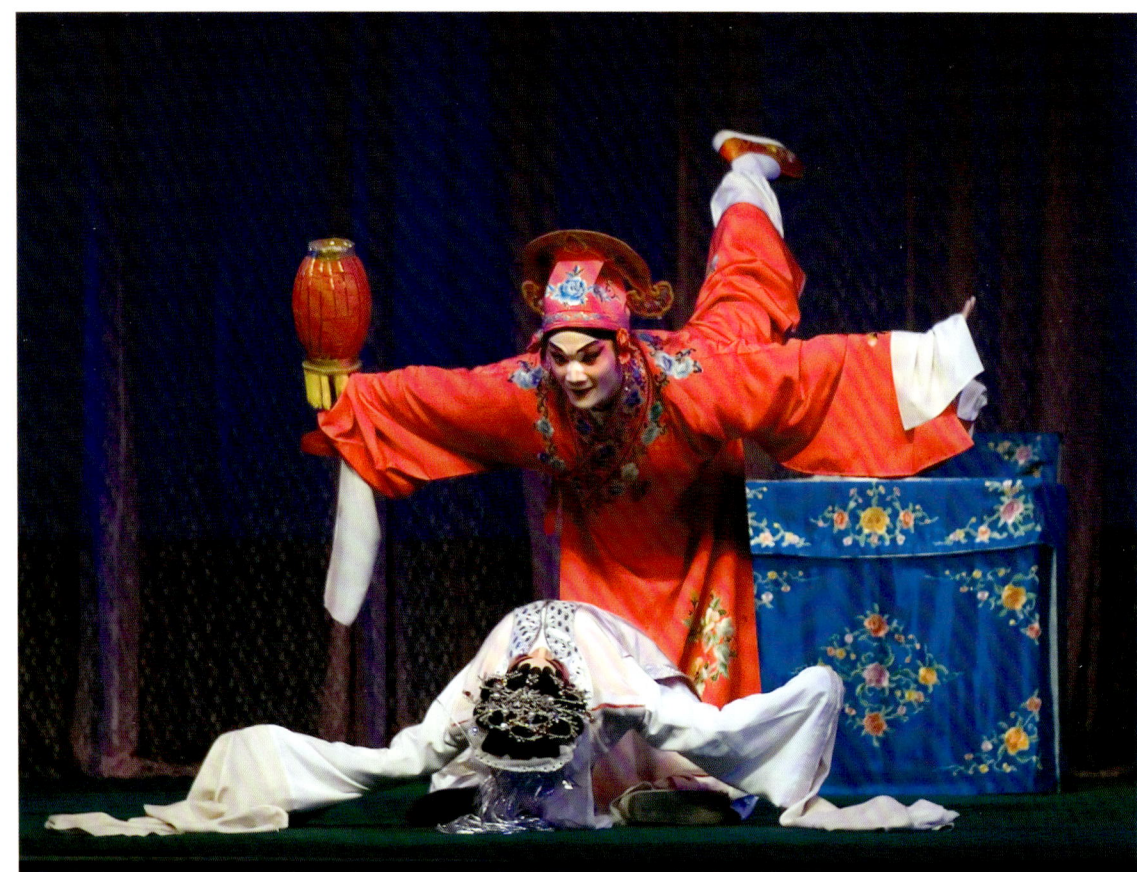

Photo 2.32 *The Haunting of Zhang Sanlang*, Cantonese Opera

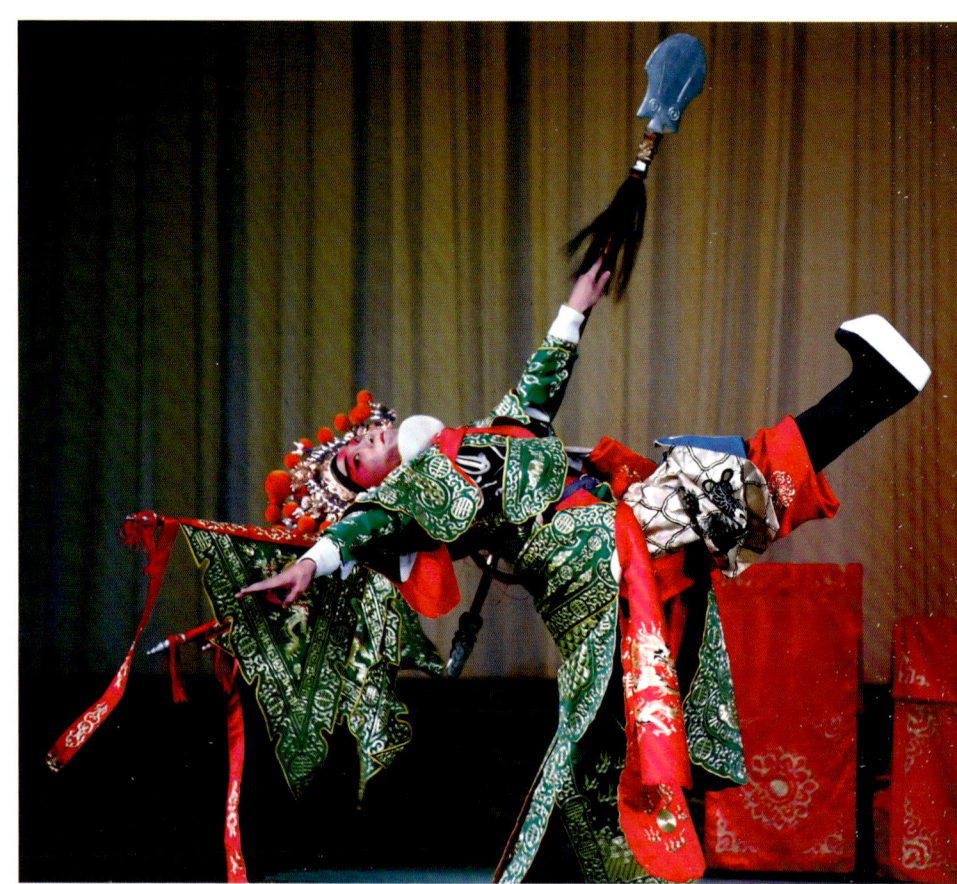

Photo 2.33 *Tilting the War Carts*, Peking Opera

Using Stage Movement

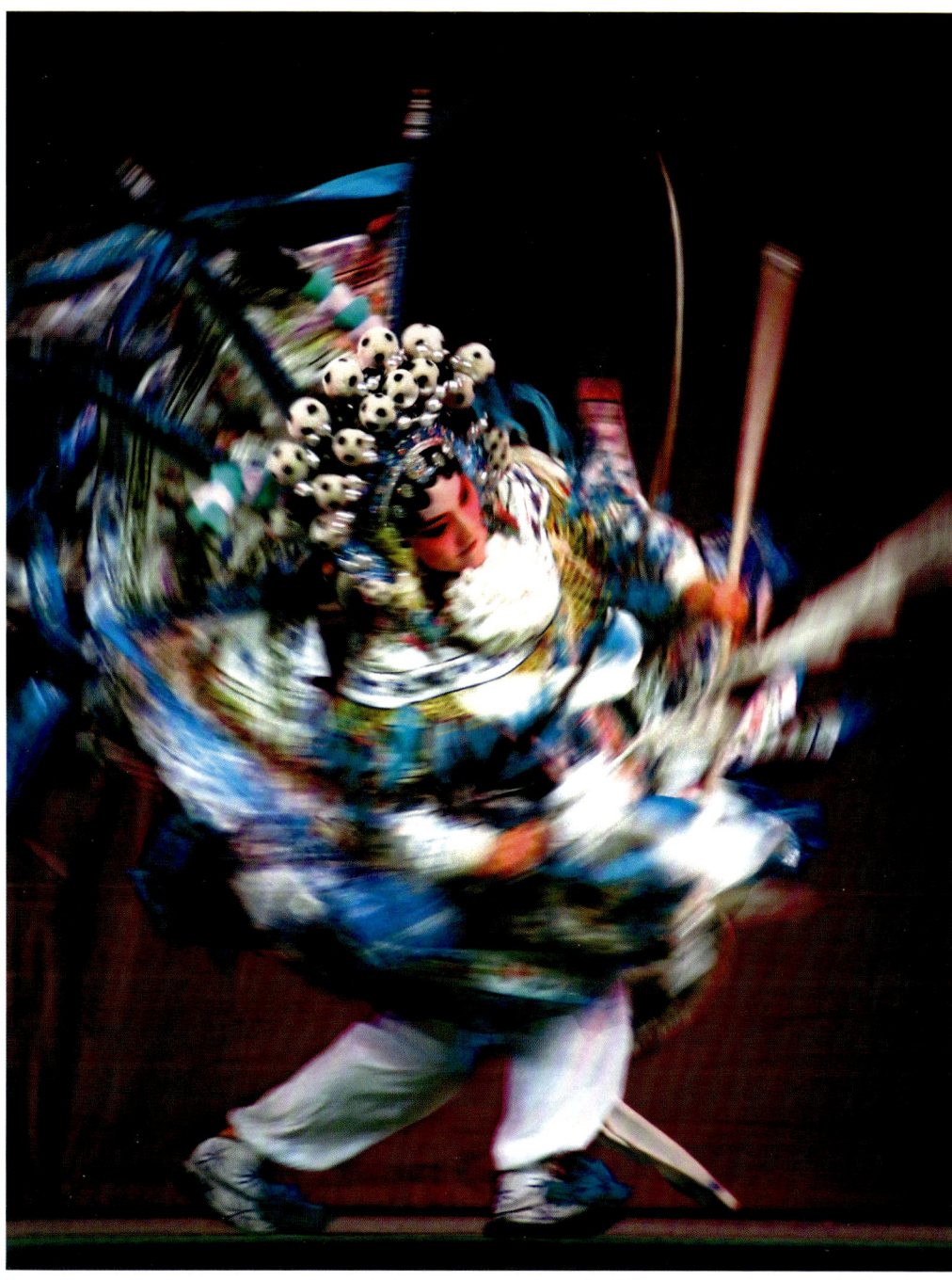

Photo 2.34 *Selecting a Horse for War*, Gan Opera

stretches out his arms and circles his left leg high into the air (see Photo 2.33). In a military play, this action indicates a horse driven beyond its limits, or sliding down a slope.

The female warrior, Mu Guiying, uses a special move to mount her horse. She has assumed the role of commander of the army after her husband, the general, is killed in battle. Determined to defeat the enemy invading the Song dynasty (960–1279), Mu Guiying chooses the fiercest horse in the stable. She mounts the house in a spectacular spin, demonstrating both the spirit of the horse and her own superior horsemanship (see Photo 2.34).

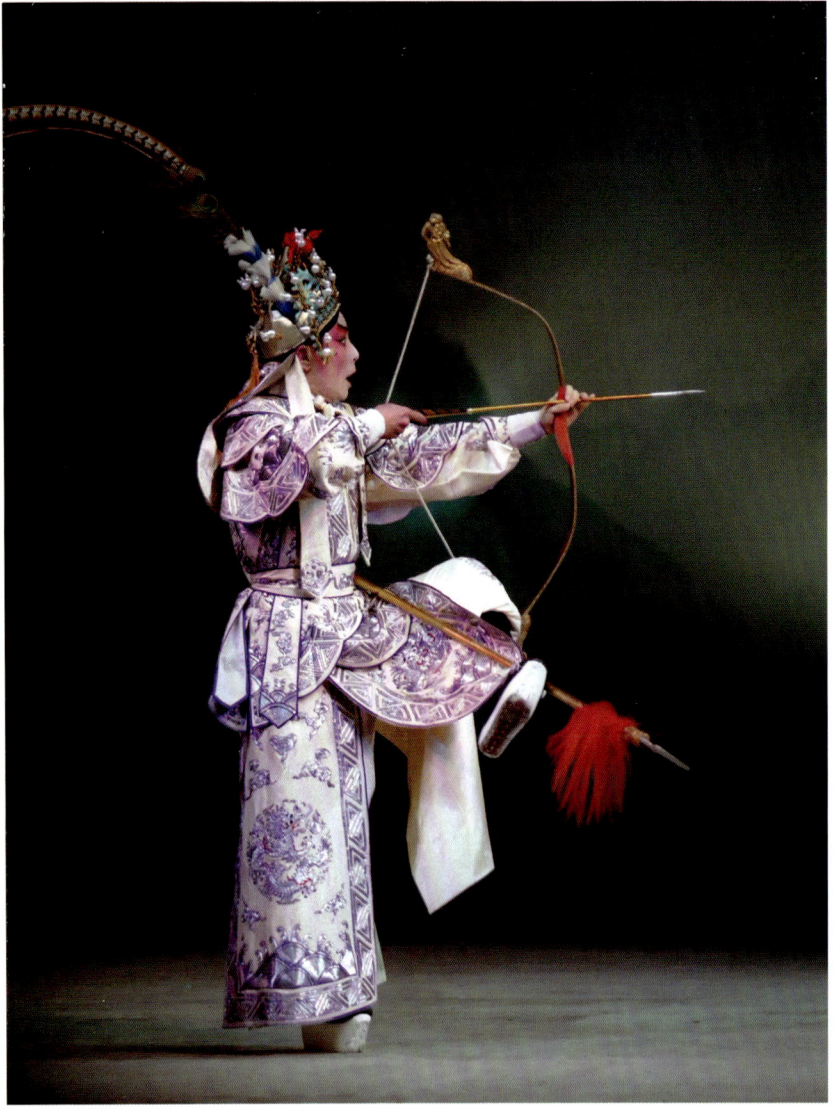

Photo 2.35 *Xue Dingshan Thrice Angers Fan Lihua*, Cantonese Opera

When Xue Dingshan sees a ferocious tiger, he immediately grabs his bow and arrow while elegantly suspending his spear on his leg as he prepares to shoot (see Photo 2.35).

Poses and special moves such as these are features of Chinese opera that, like stylized singing, costumes and props, heighten the artistry of the story telling.

Playing the Dwarf

PAINTED FACE CHARACTERS in Chinese opera use thick-soled boots as a way to make themselves larger than life. Sometimes, though, they are actually smaller. Various operas call for the actors to perform the role of a dwarf. Rather than use a child or a small adult, Chinese opera traditionally expresses the idea of being small through the stage skill of the actor. This technique is called "playing the dwarf". The actor squats low, raises his heels and walks on his toes to convey the effect of being very short.

Using Stage Movement

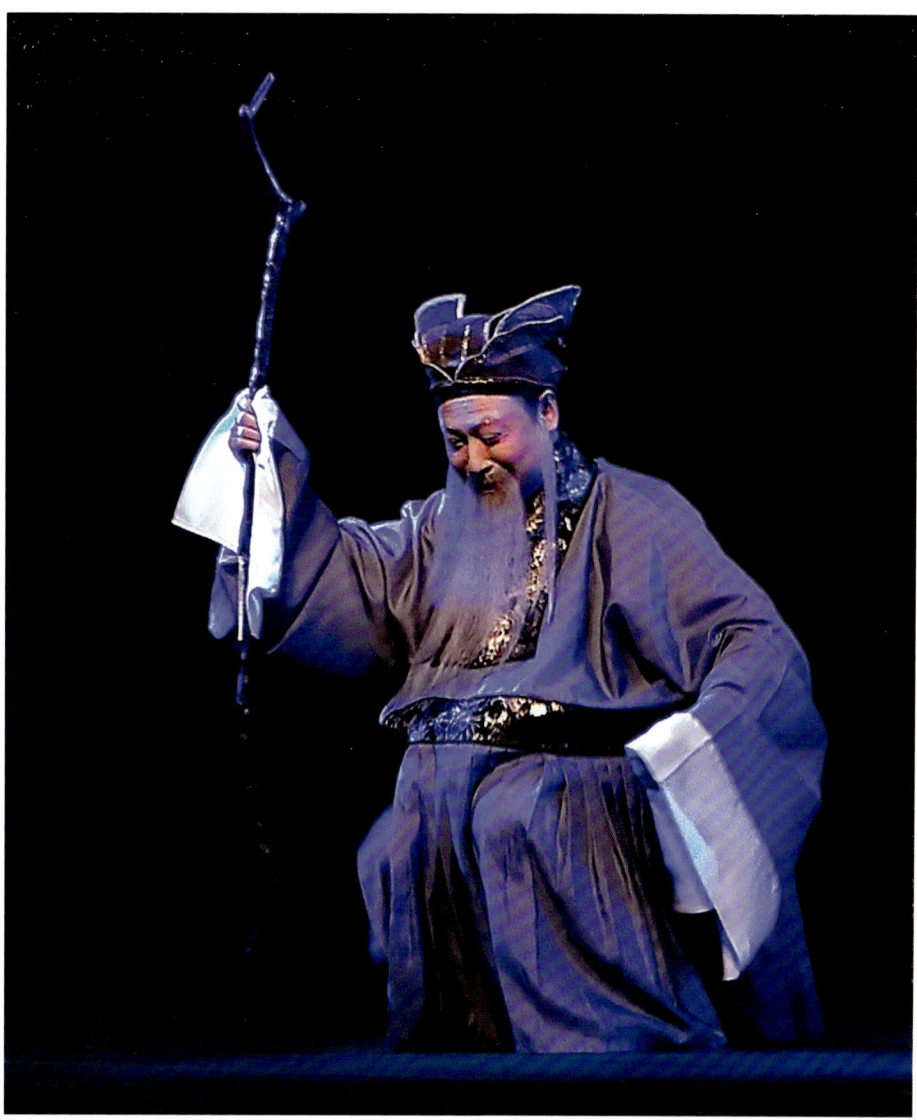

Photo 2.36 *The Story of the Red Plum*, Cantonese Opera

The classic novel *The Legend of the Water Margin*, sometimes known as *All Men Are Brothers*, has provided source material for many operas. It concerns a band of Song dynasty outlaws, comparable to Sherwood Forest's Robin Hood and his merry men. One of these outlaws, Wang Ying, leads a raid on Hu village. Wang Ying's nickname is "Short-legged Tiger" because he is both a dwarf and a fierce fighter. Crouched low, preparing to walk on his toes, he adjusts his armour, one of a series of stage actions called *qiba* that denote preparing for war (see Photo 2.37).

Not only do actors "play the dwarf" as human warriors, but they play it also for magical and spiritual beings as well. In *Eighteen Luohan Pursue the Golden Crane*, mentioned earlier, the errant Golden Crane, who is bent on mischief in the mortal world, suddenly finds himself attacked by a tall luohan on one side, and a dwarf luohan on the other. Both luohan are trying to bring the crane back to their world. To perform the short luohan, the actor not only has to "play the dwarf", but demonstrate fighting skills at the same time (see Photo 2.38).

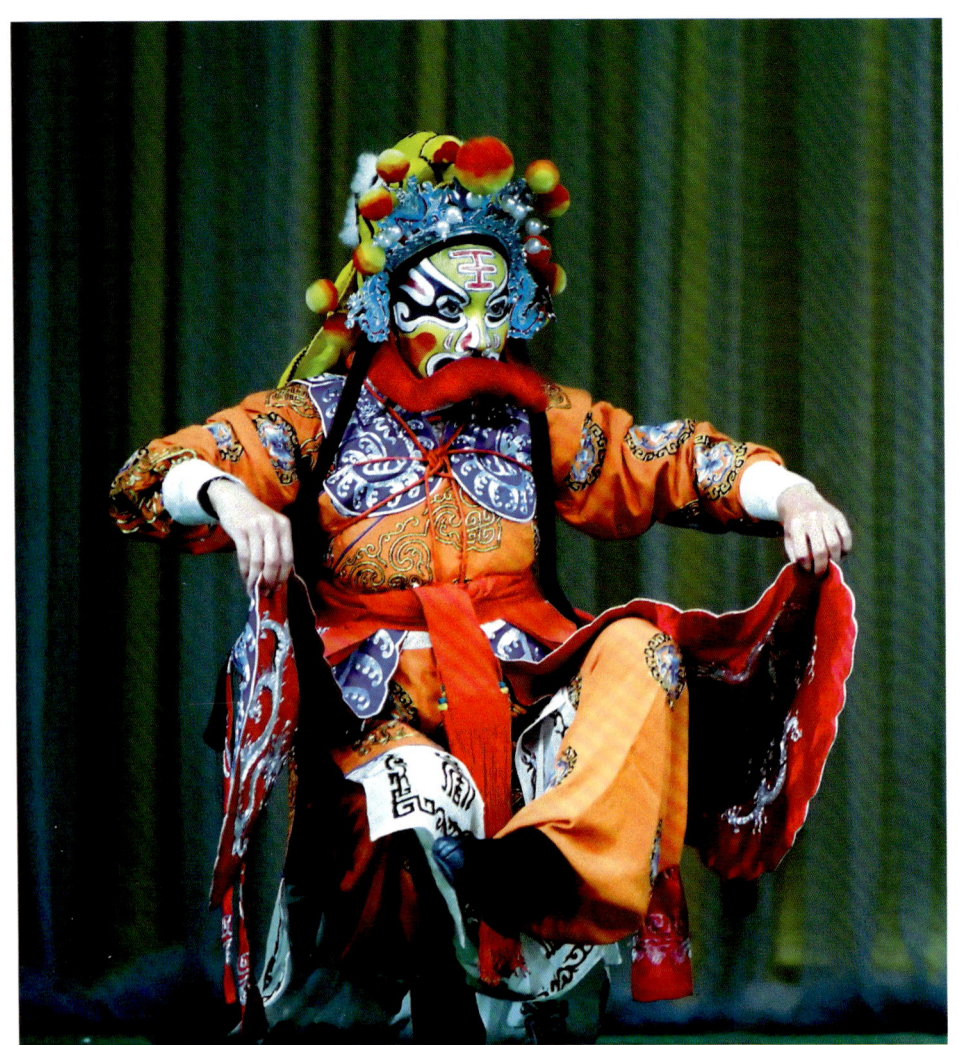

Photo 2.37 *Raid on Hu Village,* Peking Opera

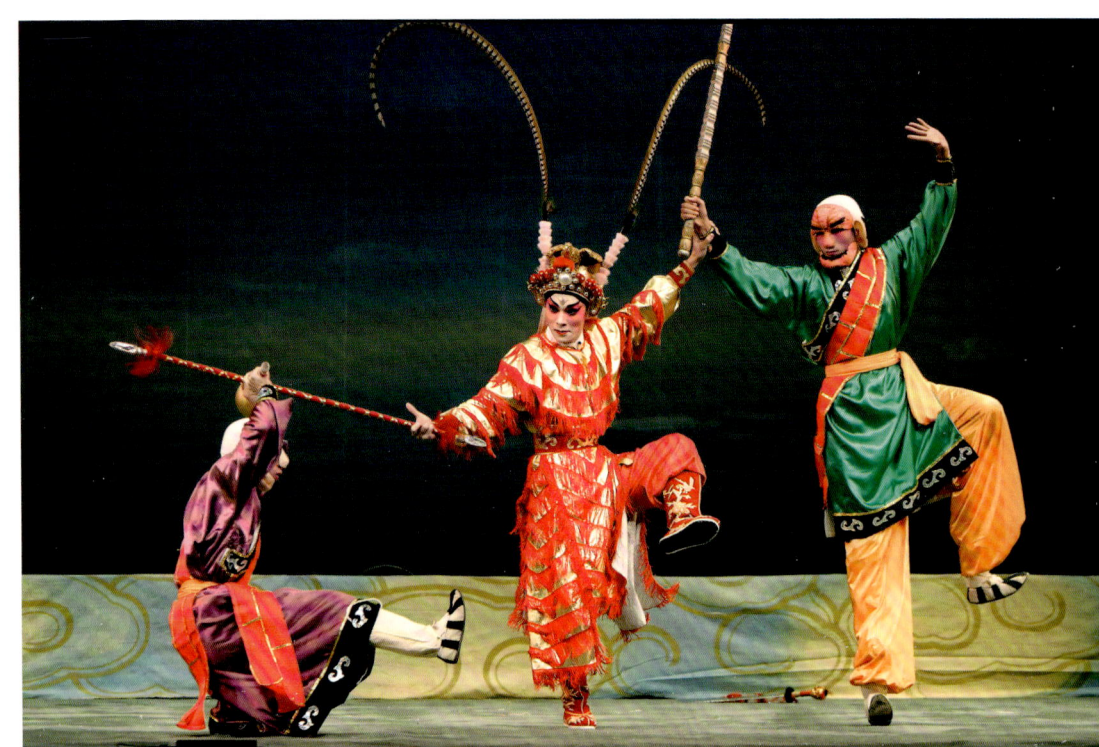

Photo 2.38 *The Eighteen Luohan Pursue the Golden Crane,* Cantonese Opera

Using Stage Movement

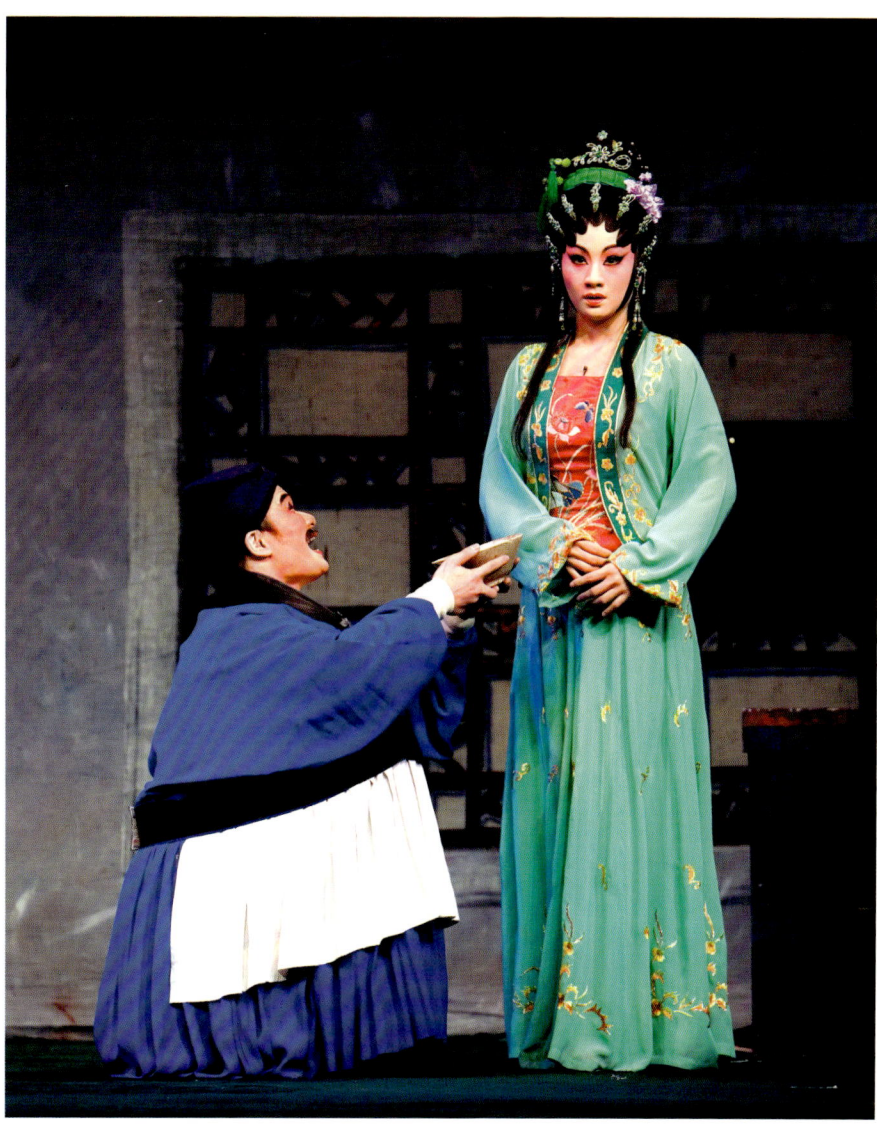

Photo 2.39 *Kneading the Dough, Cantonese Opera*

"Playing the dwarf" is used for roles other than the painted face or the magical being. In the opera named after the famous hero Wu Song, the beautiful but ruthless Pan Jinlian finds herself in an arranged marriage that she detests. Her mistress, jealous of Pan Jinlian's beauty, has married her off to Wu Song's brother, Wu Dalang. As handsome, tall, and vigorous as Wu Song is, his brother is the opposite. He was born an ugly dwarf. The actor who plays Wu Dalang crouches and walks on his toes while Pan Jinlian plans her freedom (see Photo 2.39).

The general principle in Chinese opera is to suggest rather than realistically represent. That suggestion is the work of the actors, who must develop skills beyond singing, delivering lines or performing a role. They also employ a wide range of physical skills like "playing the dwarf". Actors who play the dwarf must be prepared to take the position for considerable period of times demonstrating not only their skills, but their stamina.

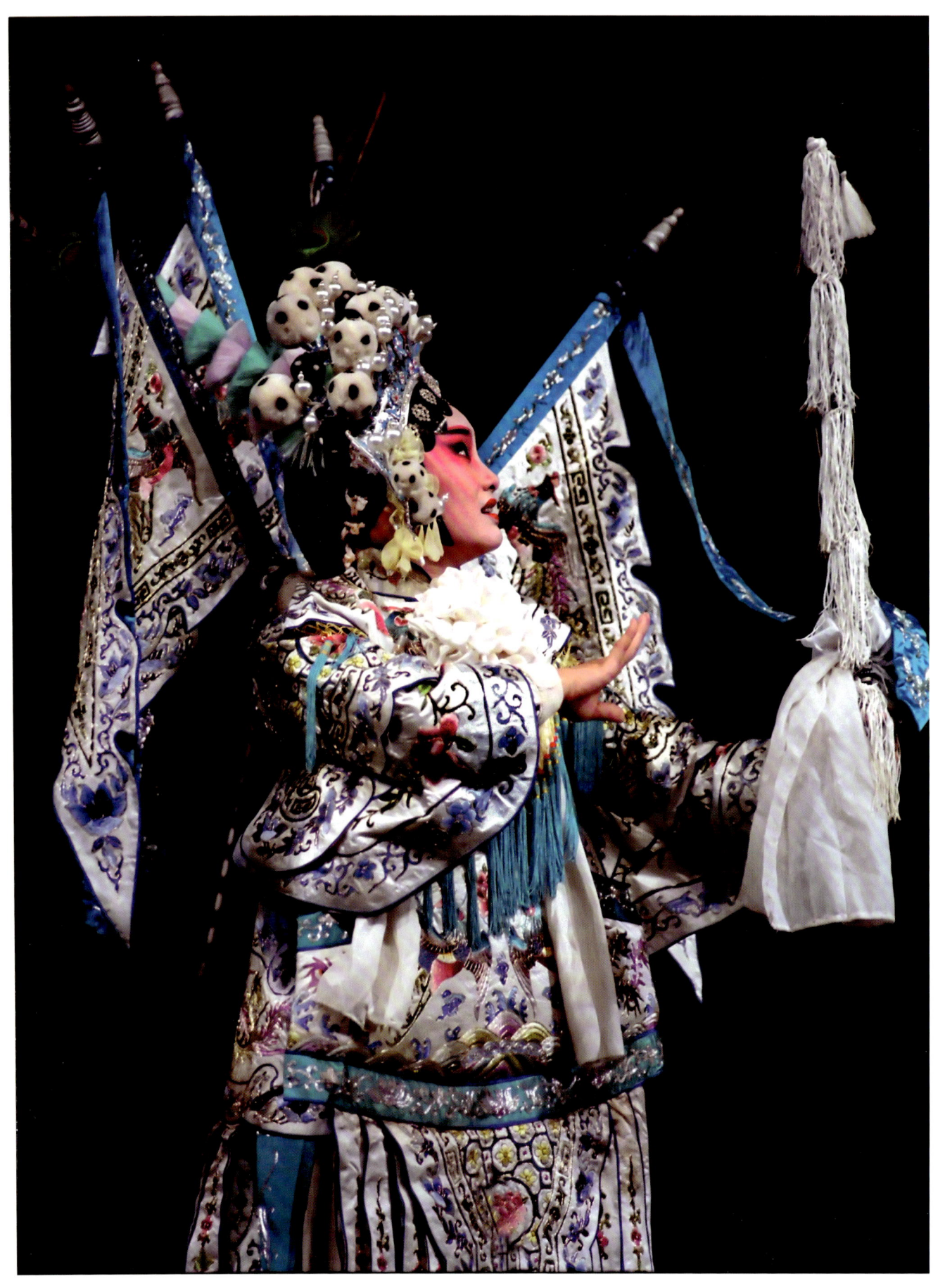

Photo 3.01 *Selecting a Horse for War*, Gan Opera

Chapter 3

Using Props

Horsewhip

Chinese drama has from the beginning called for horses on the stage. Sometimes, this would be for a solitary rider on a long journey. At other times, it might be for several mounted generals on a battlefield. The problem in each case is how to bring the familiar reality of riding a horse into a theatre, teahouse or banquet hall. Other dramatic traditions have used hobbyhorses and various costumes to solve the problem. The Chinese theatrical solution is not to present the horse itself but instead to evoke it through what was most associated with horseback riding, the horsewhip. Over time, this prop became a stylized flexible cane with several tassels and a finger loop at the end. The tip indicates the horse's head. Using the stage horsewhip is one of the basic skills of the opera stage and is required of most role types. By manipulating it, the actor demonstrates mounting, dismounting, riding, and even leading a horse. The horse itself becomes present as the actor executes the stylized movements and positions.

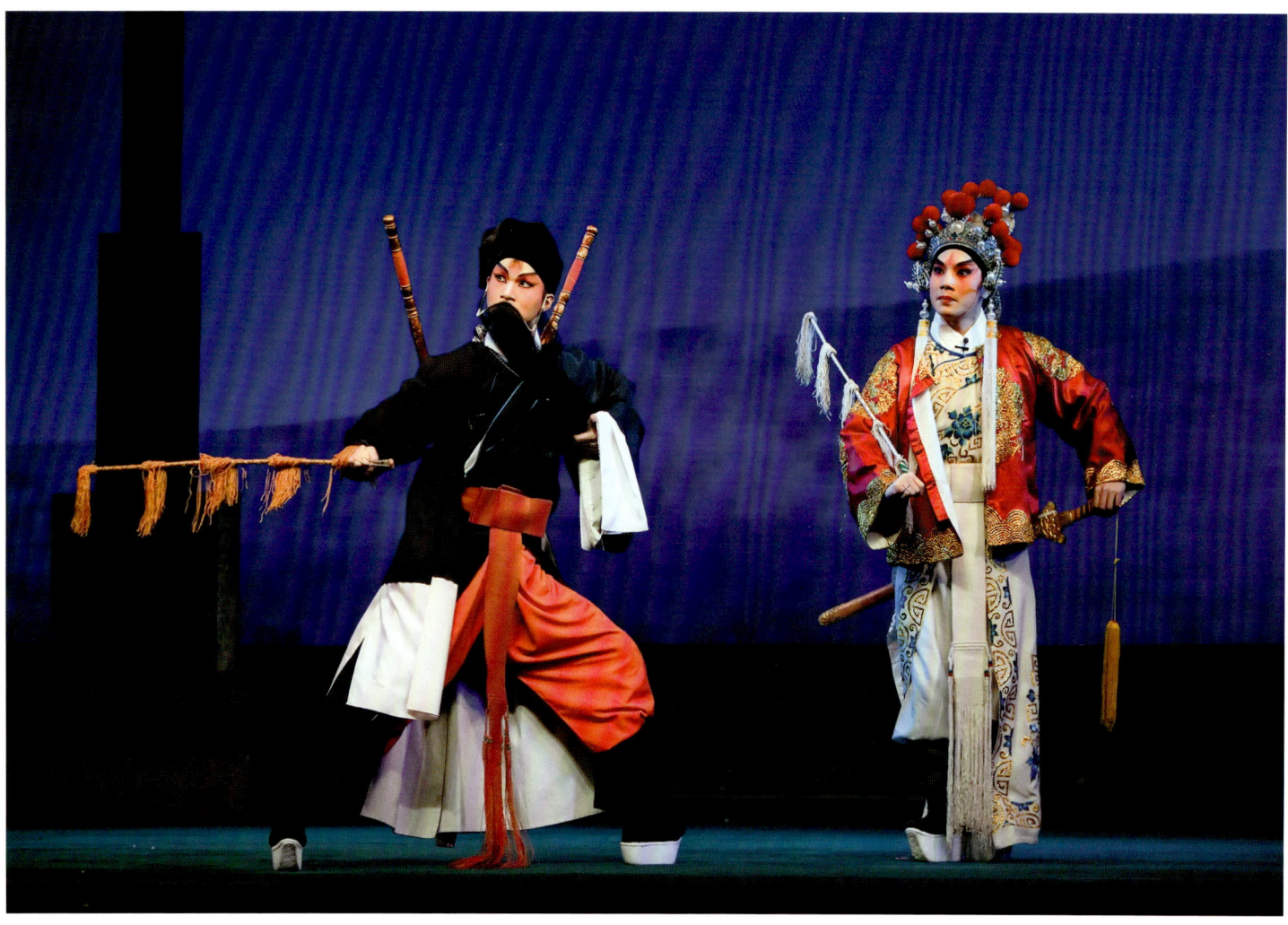

Photo 3.02 *Qin Qiong Observes the Troops*, Cantonese Opera

When an audience sees the horsewhip hanging from the actor's hand, they know that the character is not yet on the animal. A series of stylized moves that includes pulling back the whip across the body, lifting the leg, miming the grabbing of reins, and finally extending the horsewhip horizontally indicates that the actor has mounted the horse. Waving the horsewhip as the actor walks in a circle on the stage indicates the journey, called *tangma* or "horse ride". Miming hanging two loops of the horse's reins on a tree branch, and either dropping the whip on the stage, or hanging it down from the fingers indicates that the ride is over and that the rider has dismounted.

The horse is also established through the mime, and sometimes acrobatics, of a horseman or groom. This character deftly mimes leading the horse out by the reins, coaxing and sometimes struggling with it when it is frightened or in a bad temper. In some cases, both the rider with the whip and the groom establish the animal.

Photo 3.03 *Qin Qiong Observes the Troops*, Cantonese Opera

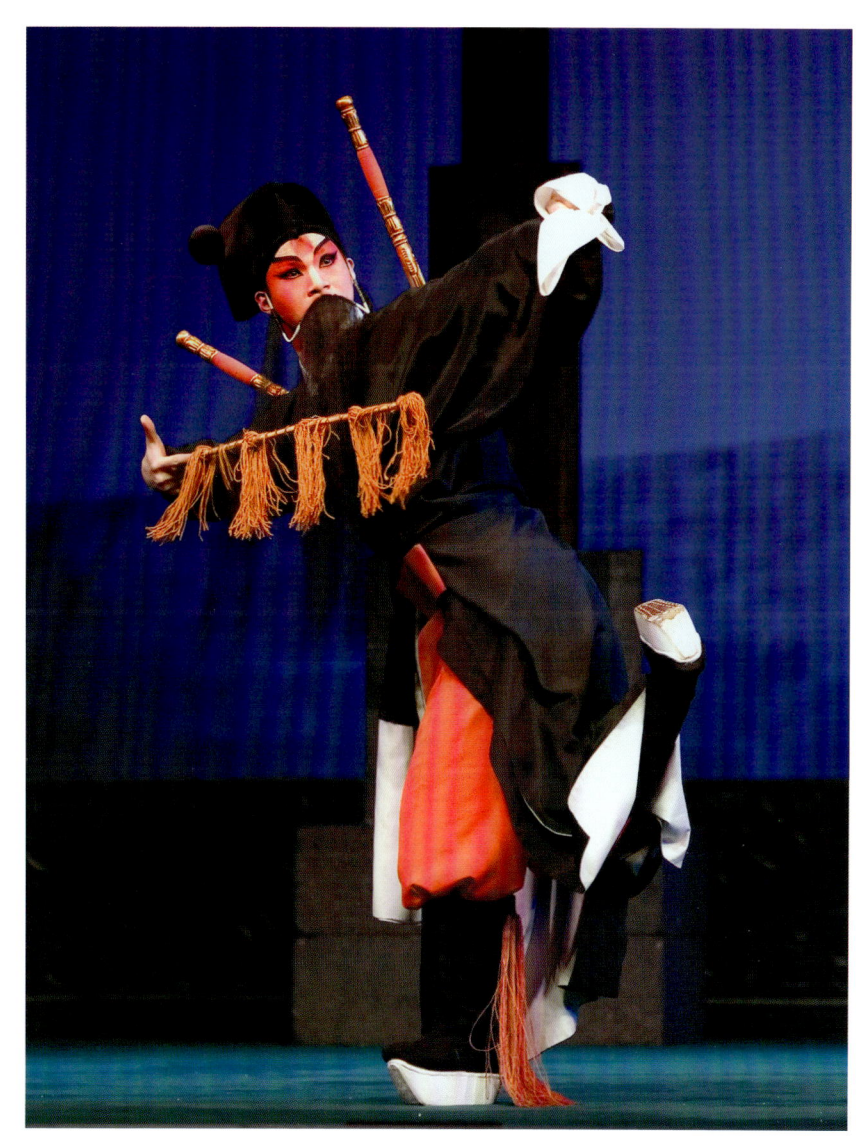

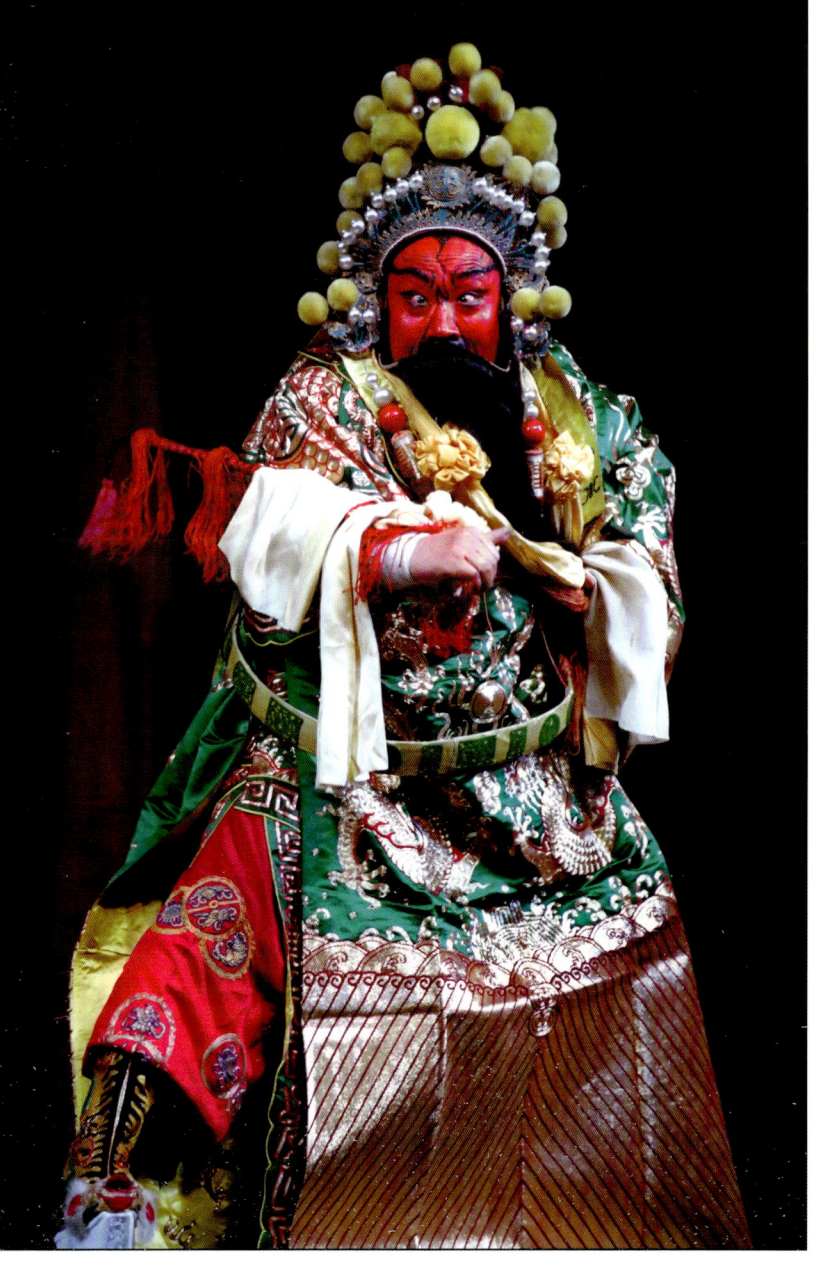

Photo 3.04 *Green Stone Mountain*, Peking Opera

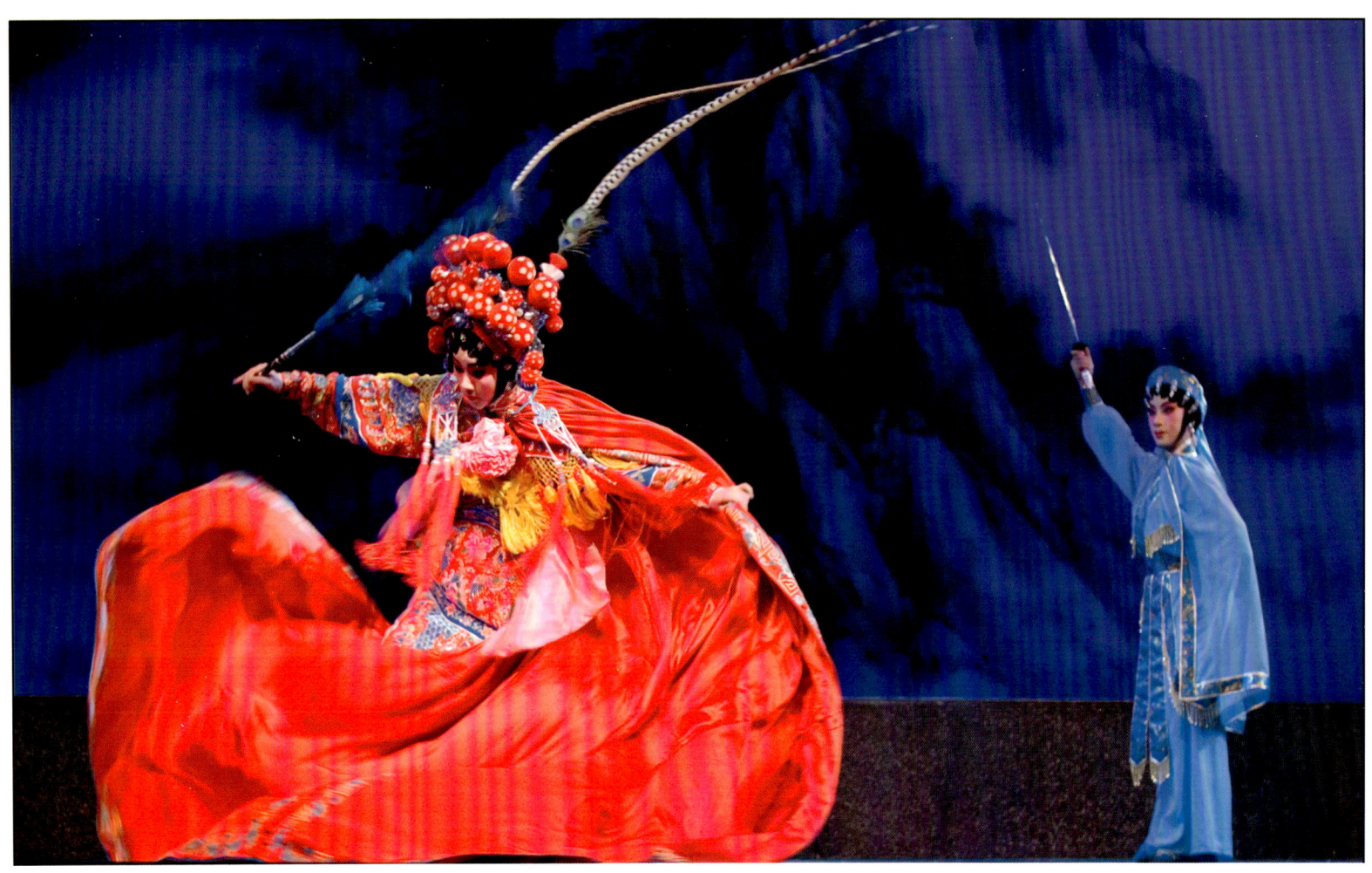

Photo 3.05 *Phoenix Terrace Fortress*, Cantonese Opera

Generally, riders indicate a leisurely pace by gently swaying their horsewhips up and down as they cross the stage. In *Qin Qiong Observes the Troops*, General Qin and the warrior Luo Cheng ride out together to survey the enemy (see Photo 3.02).

The actor can also indicate a fast gallop. Later in the same opera, Qin Qiong rides briskly. His movements are quick and he waves the horsewhip rapidly. He suddenly changes direction, a fact denoted by the front tip of the horsewhip (see Photo 3.03).

Actors invoke an aggressive pace by grasping the reins tightly, tilting the body forward, and waving the horsewhip vigorously. The legendary hero Guan Yu, now revered as a god, uses this technique as he races to Green Stone Mountain to capture the nine-tailed fox (see Photo 3.04).

In another opera, the wife of a sick commander takes his place on patrol on a wild and cold night. Zhang Xiuying circles the stage waving her horsewhip rapidly as she gallops as fast as she can. Her long cape flows behind her as she twists her body, establishing the wind and cold of the night (see Photo 3.05).

Using Props

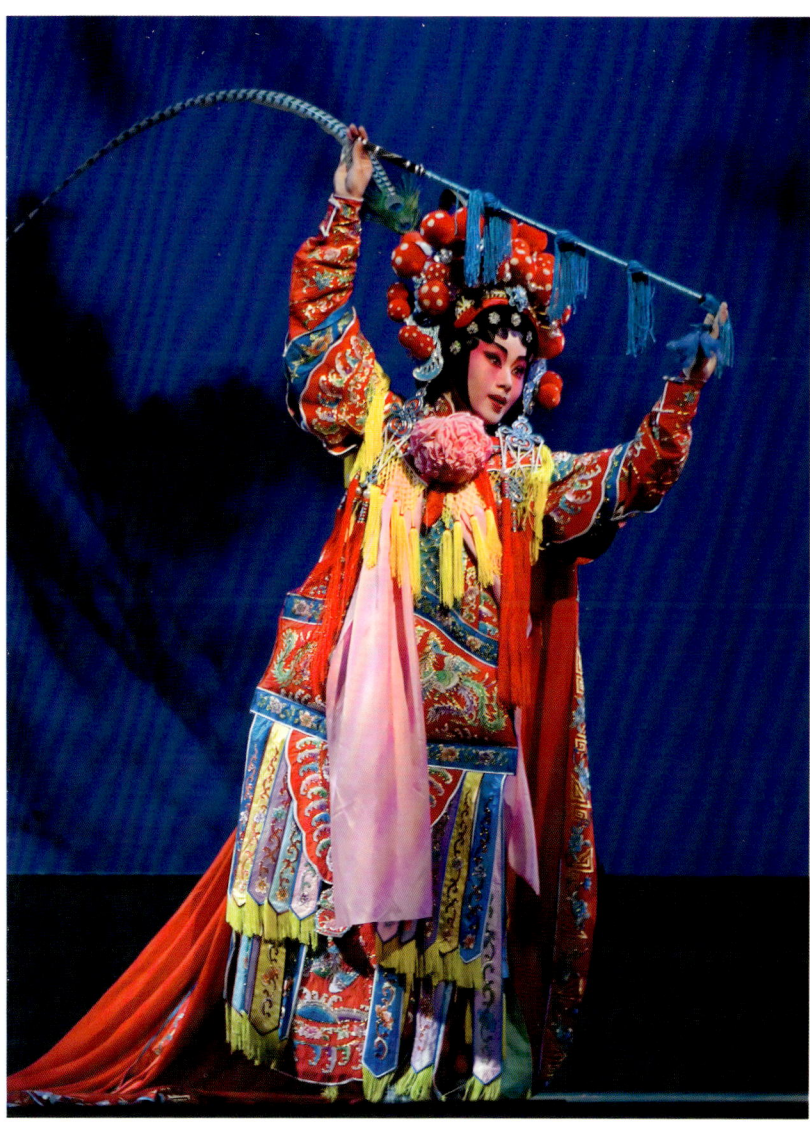

Photo 3.06 *Phoenix Terrace Fortress*, Cantonese Opera

As Zhang Xiuying patrols the city, she rides into dense brush. She uses her horsewhip to push back the low tree branches (see Photo 3.06).

The female warrior Yang Bajie also demonstrates a rapid gallop in the opera *Blocking the Horse*. Dressed in men's clothes, she has gone on a secret mission to obtain crucial military intelligence about the invaders. Having learned what she needs to know, Yang Bajie rides back as fast as possible with the news. She needs to ride down a mountain slope. To evoke this idea, her right hand holds the whip high as her left hand mimes holding the saddle (see Photo 3.07).

As she continues her journey, she urges her horse onward, pushing it to its limits. Her right hand holds the horsewhip out horizontally while the tip rises up and down. This movement describes the repeated whipping of the horse to make it go faster and faster. Her left hand holds the reins, signalling the horse to go even faster (see Photo 3.08).

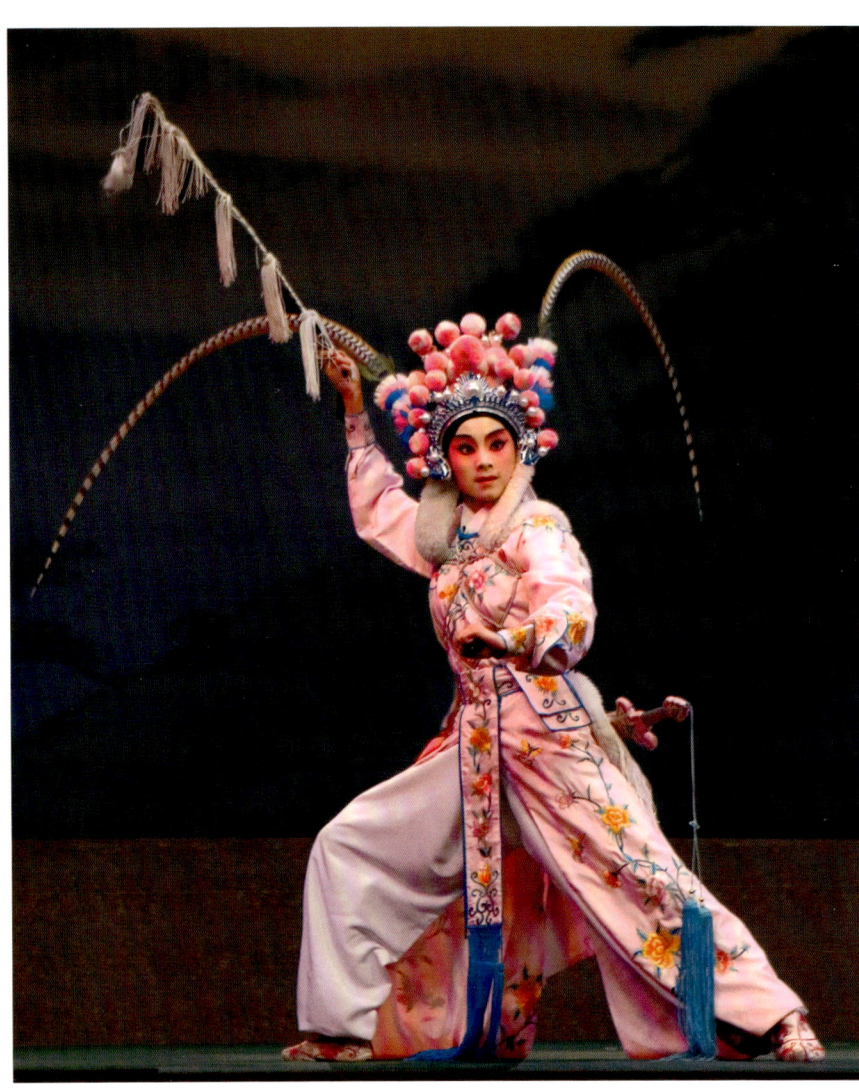

Photo 3.07 *Blocking the Horse*, Cantonese Opera

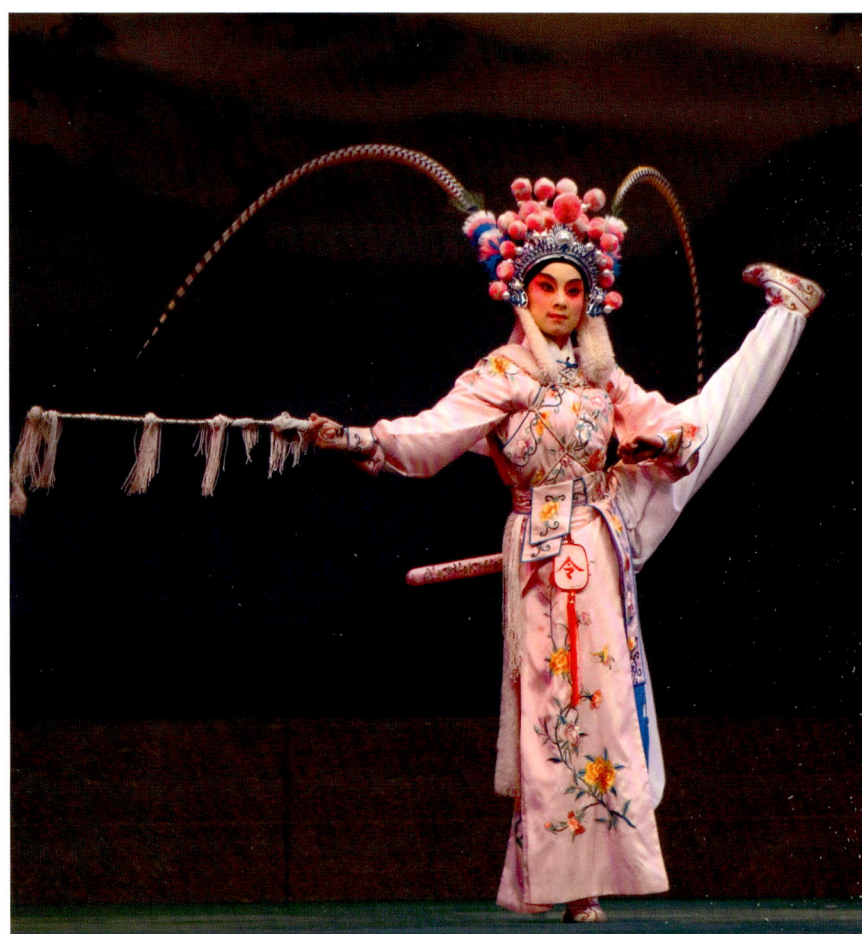

Photo 3.08 *Blocking the Horse*, Cantonese Opera

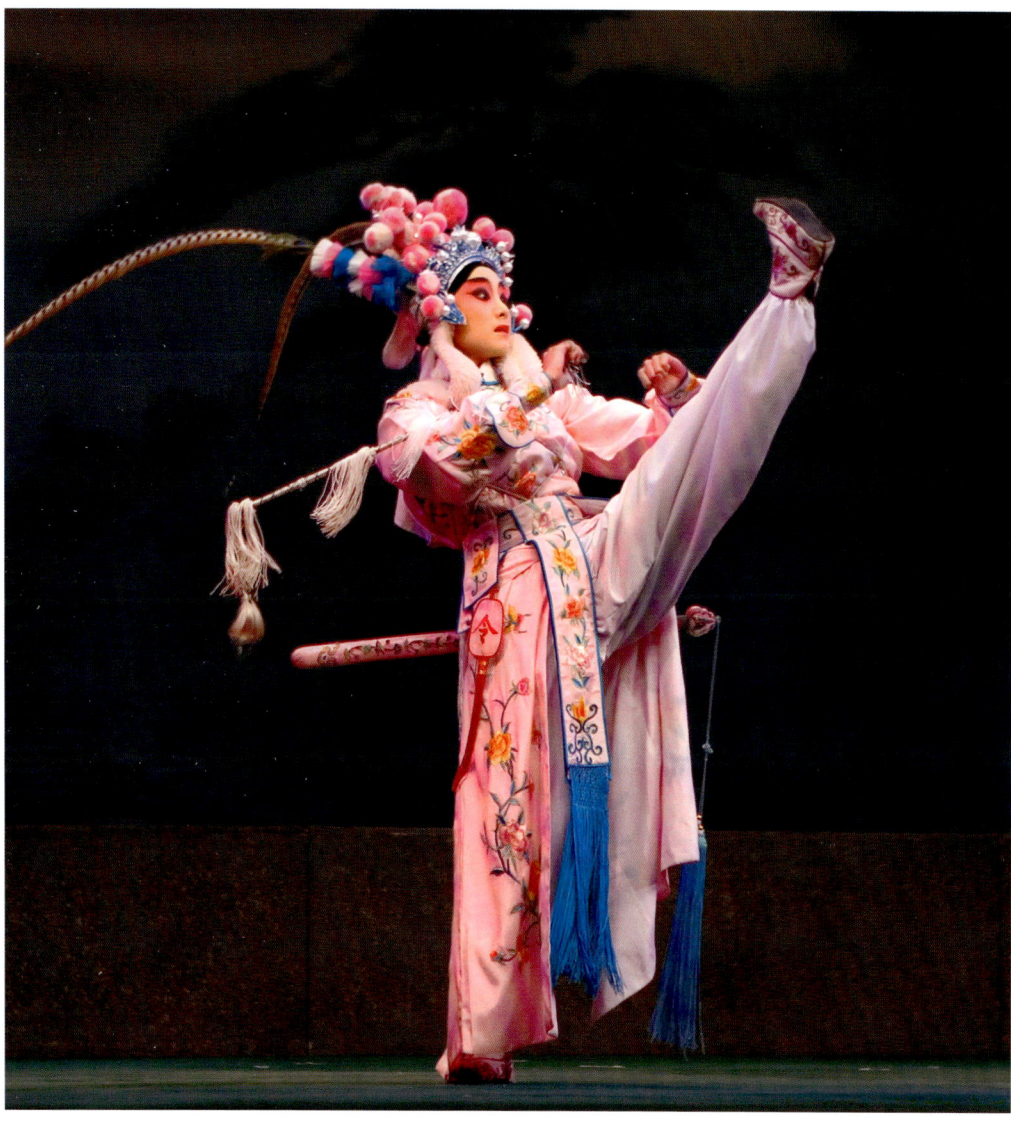

Photo 3.09 *Blocking the Horse,* Cantonese Opera

She holds the reins tightly, urging the horse to go ever faster. The quick gallop is accompanied by fast and furious percussion; she kicks her leg, bends forward, and spins her body as the horse flies over the difficult terrain. Finally, at the end of this series of quick moves, mime and acrobatics, she strikes a dramatic riding pose for the audience (see Photo 3.09).

Other characters can interrupt galloping horses in a different way. Yang Bajie is equipped with a travel pass to spy on enemy forces. Jiao Guangpu blocks her return. He desperately wants to return to his country, but needs to steal her pass to get back. He forcibly grabs the horse's reins, bracing himself against the animal. The actor stretches out her horsewhip, arches her back and raises her right leg in a position known as "exploring the sea" to portray the sudden stop (see Photo 3.10).

Several riders can ride together in a group "horse ride" as in the opera *Cao Cao and Yang Xiu*. General Cao Cao's horse becomes frightened and steps into a forbidden field. Such a transgression requires the rider to make amends, usually with his head, but since it is Cao Cao, simply with a lock of hair (see Photo 3.11).

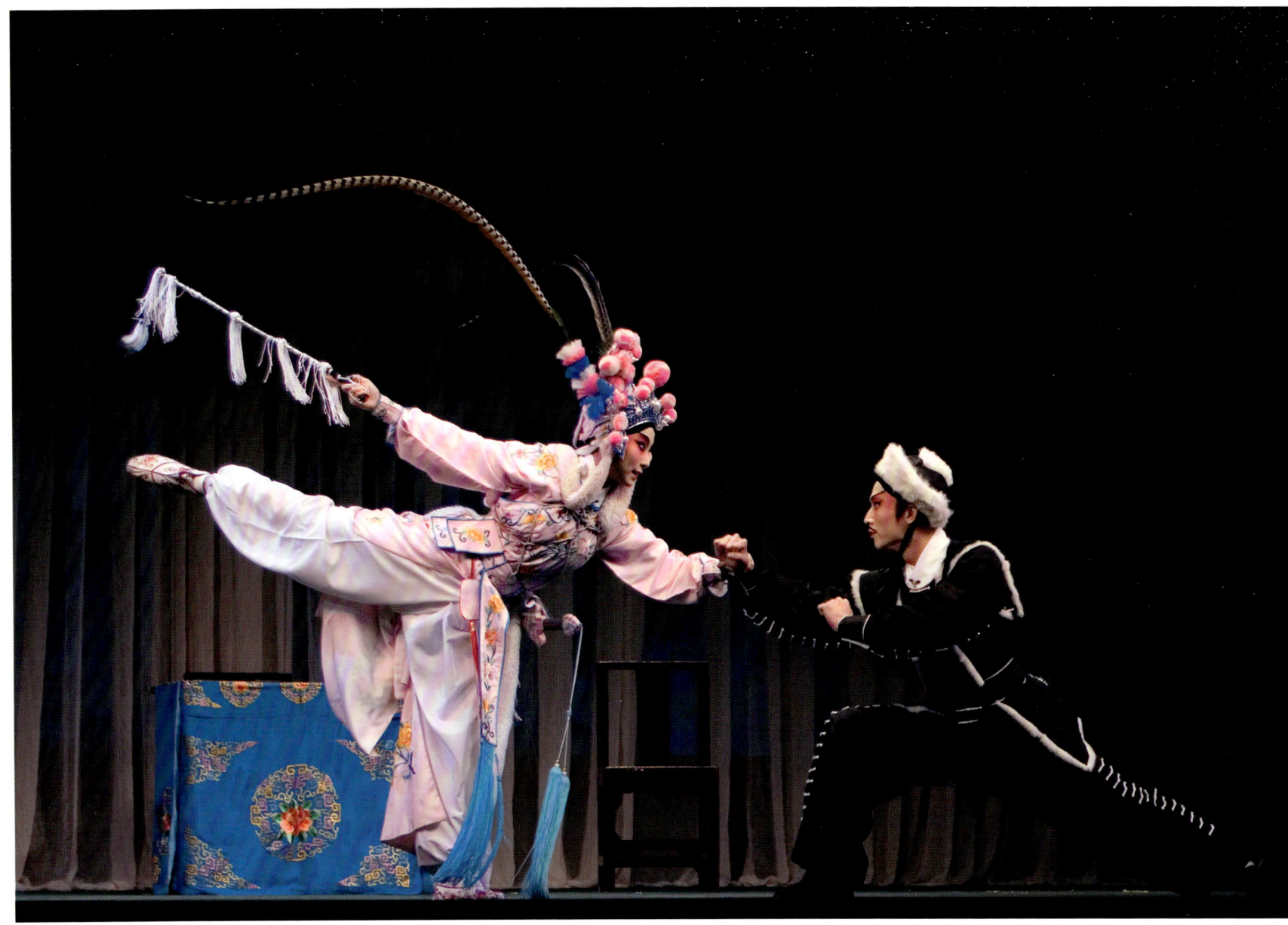

Photo 3.10 *Blocking the Horse,* Cantonese Opera

Using Props

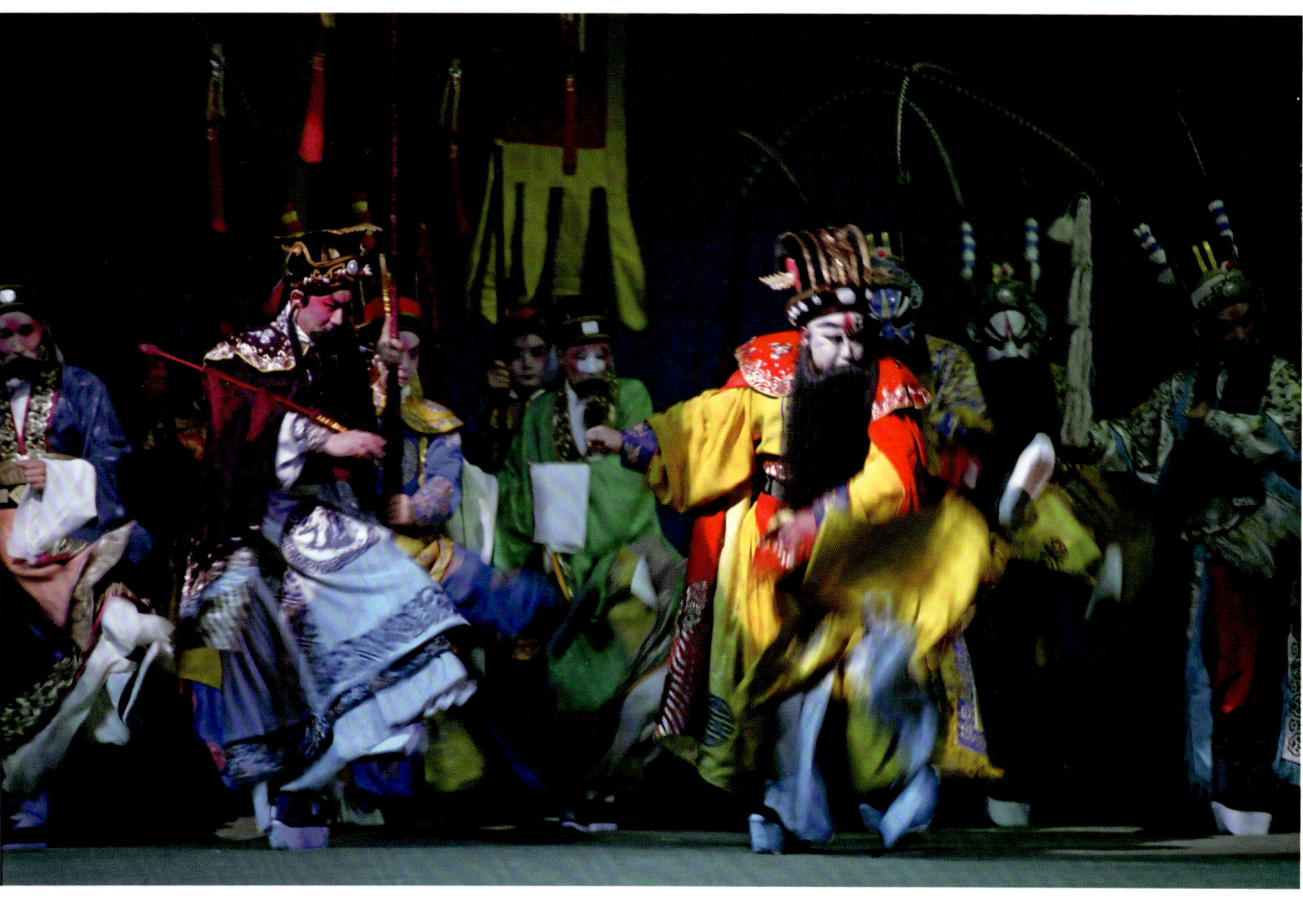

Photo 3.11 *Cao Cao and Yang Xiu, Peking Opera*

In fact, an army can circle a stage waving their whips. Alternately, in a prolonged chase, they can exit the stage on the audience's right and re-enter it on the left, continuing to wave the horsewhip to indicate a long, continuous ride.

Holding the horsewhip high and vertically indicates that the character has stopped the horse at a particularly dramatic moment. One such instant is when the palace beauty, Wang Zhaojun, stops her horse to look back with a heavy heart on the homeland she is leaving. She has been sent as a gift to the northern barbarian tribes to cement peace. Her right hand lifts the horsewhip high, indicating that she has paused in her ride and is looking into the distance, yet her left hand holds the reins as she knows she must continue the journey for the good of her country (see Photo 3.12).

After casting one last fond glance back at her homeland, she urges her horse forward, resigned to her destiny (see Photo 3.13).

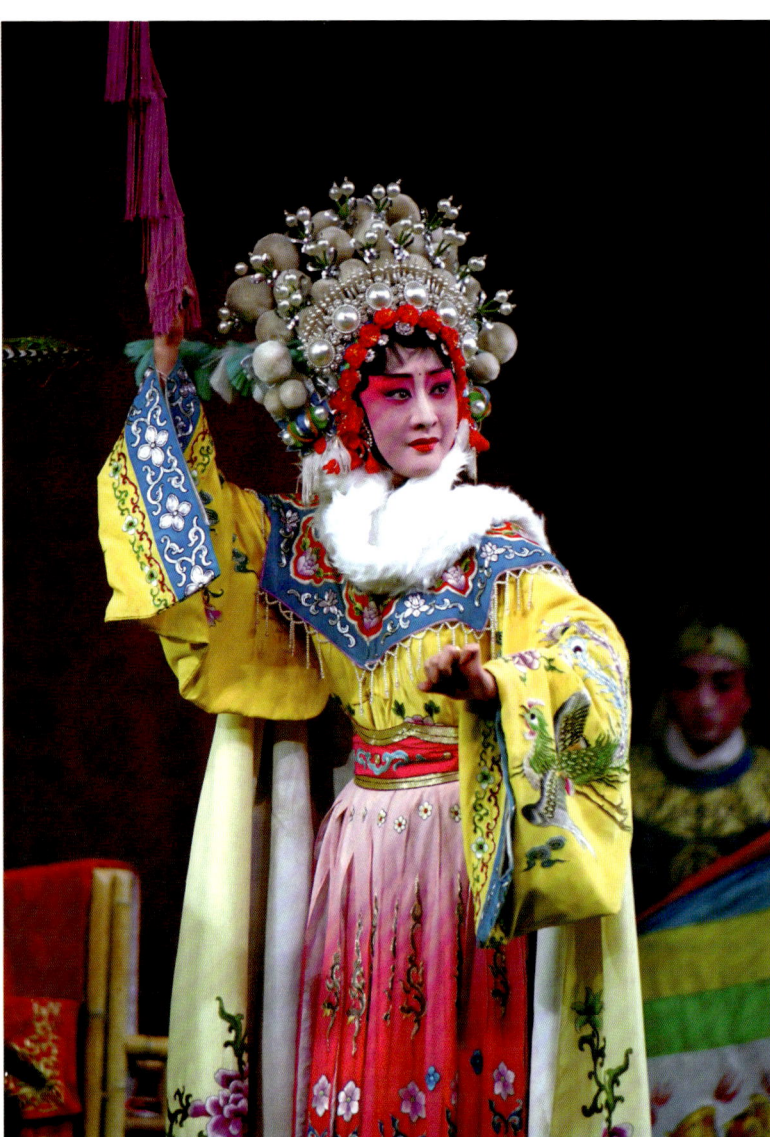

Photo 3.12   *Wang Zhaojun Leaves Her Homeland*, Sichuan Opera

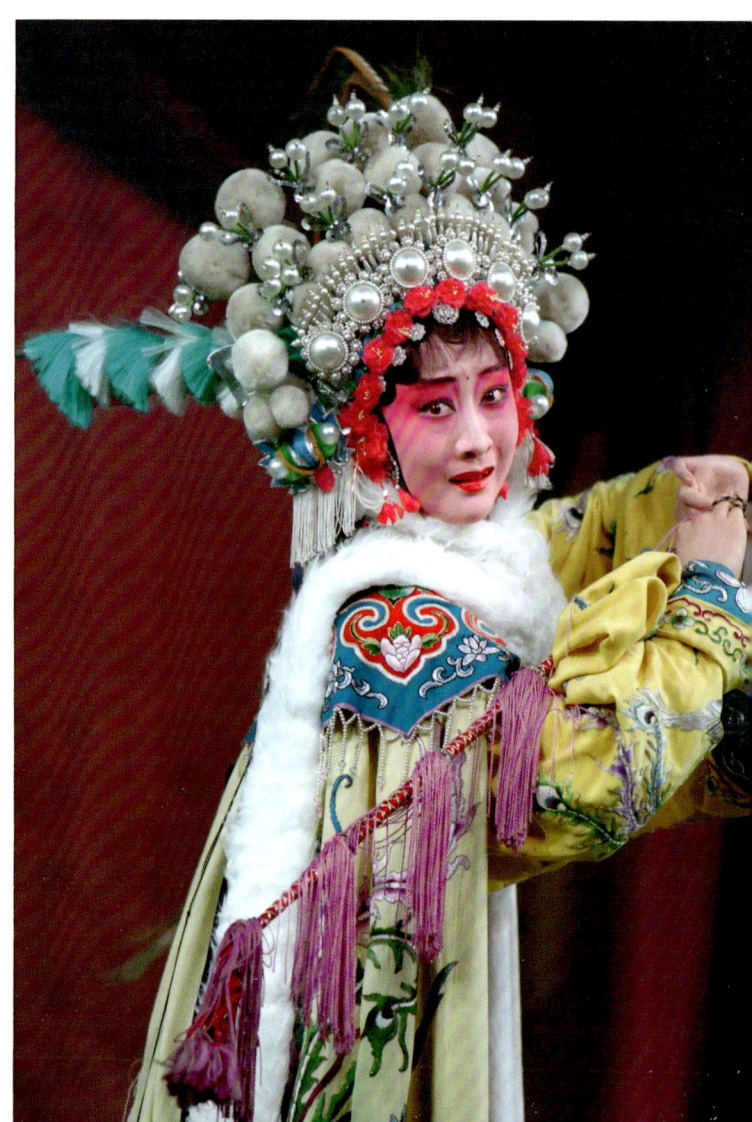

Photo 3.13   *Wang Zhaojun Leaves Her Homeland*, Sichuan Opera

Using Props

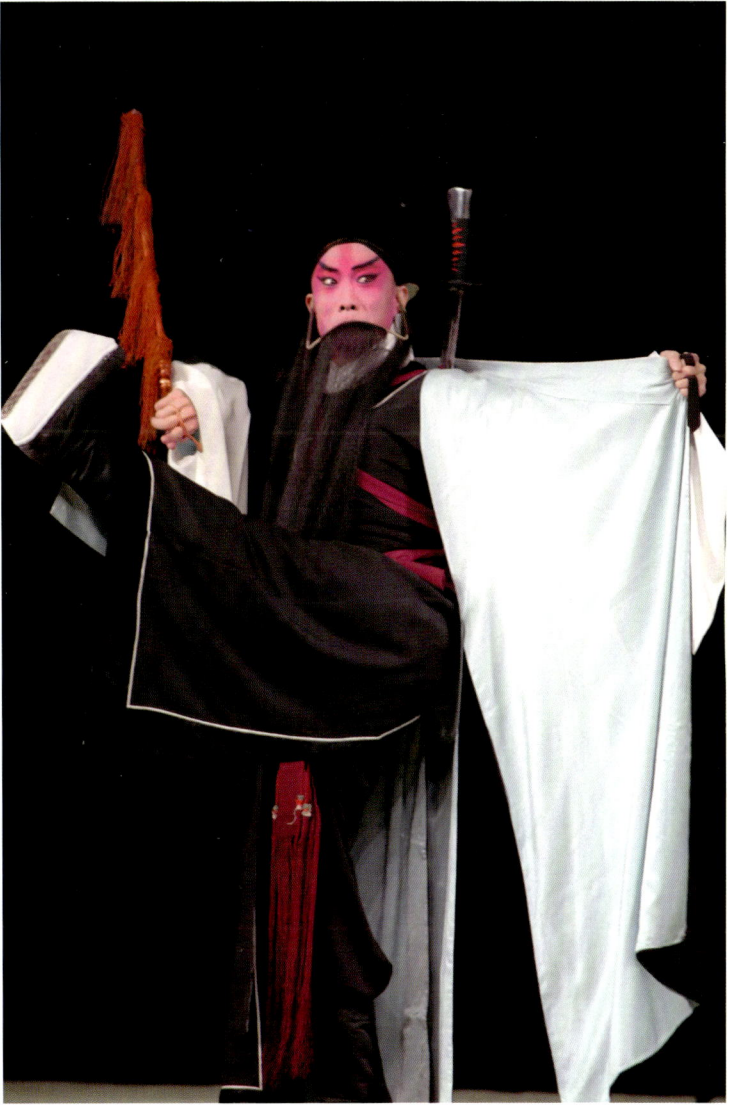

Photo 3.14 *Cleaning Out the Bandit's Lair*, Peking Opera

Similarly, the warrior He Tianbao, riding in the dark, bandit-infested mountains, suddenly pulls his horse to a stop when he hears a suspicious noise. His horsewhip is held vertically, his coat is opened, and his leg is lifted in a T position, all indicating that he has quickly halted the horse in its tracks (see Photo 3.14).

One of the most colourful and exciting performance moments in a Chinese opera is when the horse is established both through the use of a horsewhip and a horse groom. This actor, a skilled acrobat, dives onto the stage accompanied by much percussion before the rider appears. After a series of somersaults and turns, he mimes pulling on the reins of the horse to show that he is controlling a highly spirited horse. With the groom holding the horse steady, the rider then mounts and continues establishing the horse through the use of the horsewhip (see Photo 3.15). The horse groom can accompany the rider on long journeys and is sometimes paired with the legendary figure Guan Yu or the princess Wang Zhaojun.

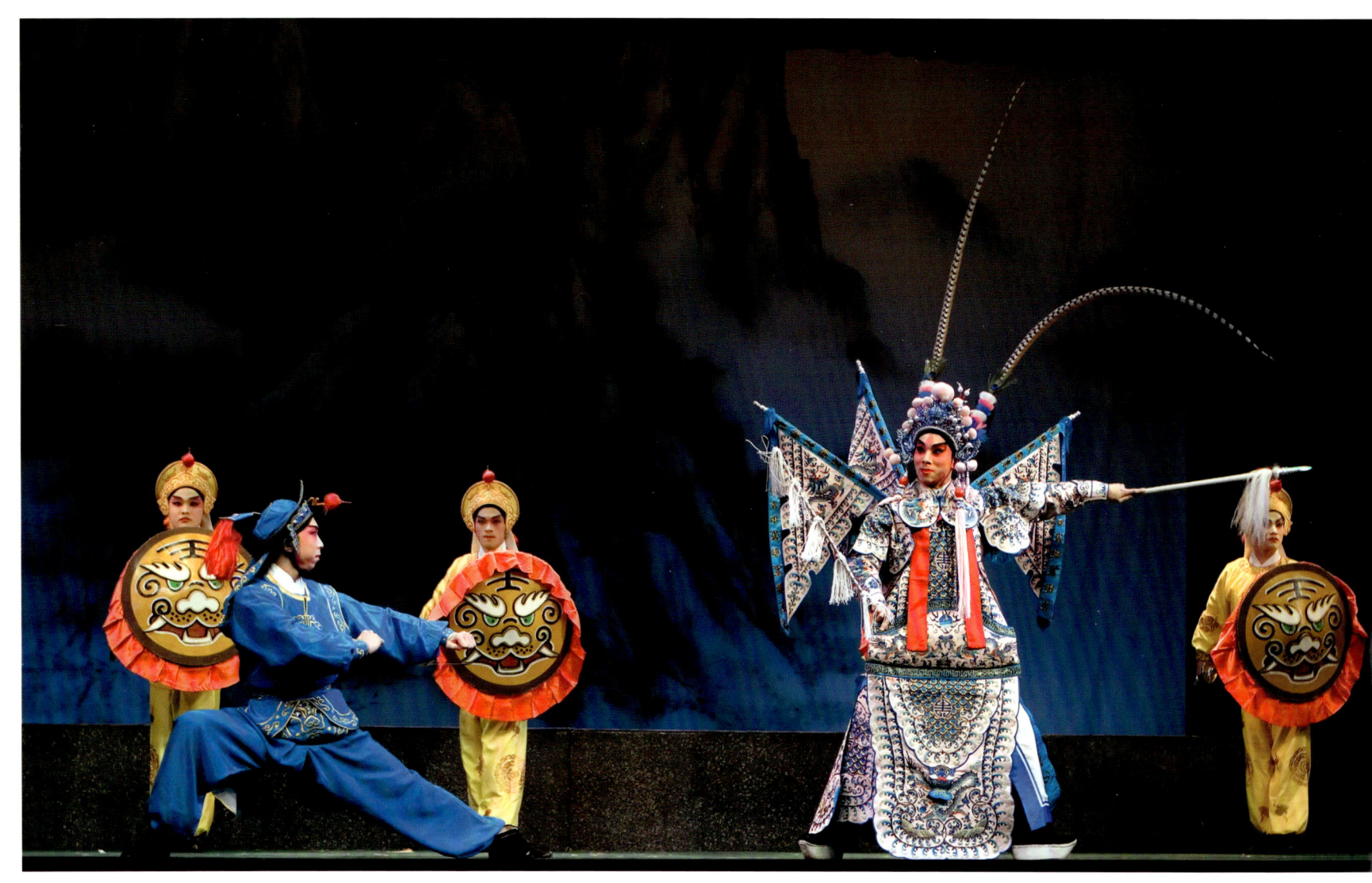

Photo 3.15 *The Battle of Baqiu,* Cantonese Opera

Fan

THE FAN IS an elegant prop used widely not only in the opera, but in all kinds of performance art in China. The cross-talk comedians and southern story-telling masters, for example, regularly use a fan; it becomes an axe, a plate, a sail—whatever the narrative calls for. Chinese dancers use fans for a variety of effects and stage patterns. In opera, different characters use different types of fans depending on their state in life and personality. The round, embroidered fan is used by the young woman, often the coquette. The large folding fan is used by scholars and high officials. They employ it in composed slow waves to show that they can take their leisure—or to fold and point when giving orders. The large feather fan is used by characters known for their high intelligence like the legendary master of strategy in the Three Kingdoms, Zhuge Liang. Like the long water sleeves, the fan gives the actor the ability to make visible large, extended movements that express emotional states and communicate meaning.

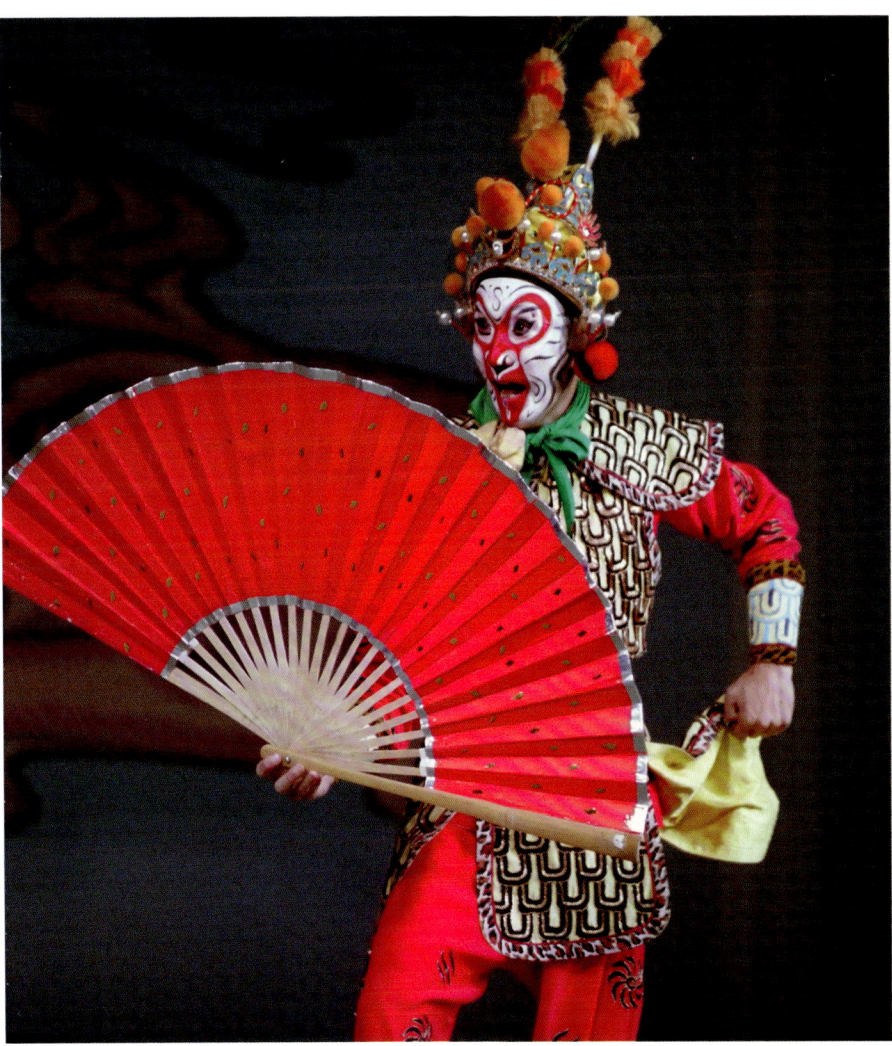

Photo 3.16 *Wreaking Havoc in Heaven*, Peking Opera

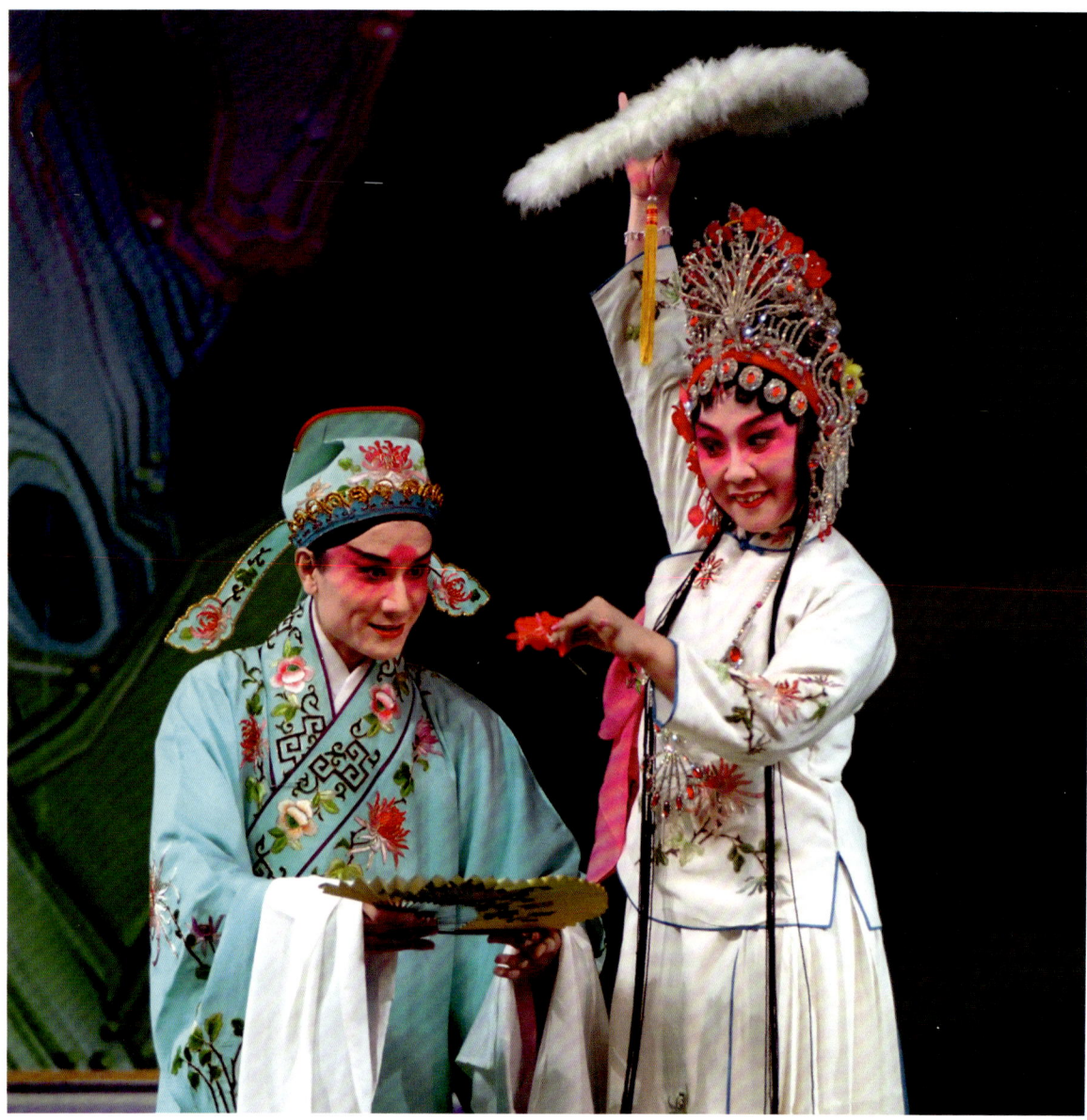

Photo 3.17 *The Flower Matchmaker*, Ping Opera

Love stories commonly use fans to show interplay between young lovers. In *The Flower Matchmaker*, the young man, Jia Junying, has agreed to represent his cousin and meet the maiden, Zhang Wuke, in the back garden. He has been commissioned to arrange a marriage between the lovely girl and someone else. When they meet, however, they instantly fall in love and pledge their love to each other instead. They use their fans to demonstrate this change of affection. Holding her fan high, Zhang Wuke drops a flower as a token and promise of her love. Jia Junying holds out his fan as a tray to receive the blossom, which now has become the true matchmaker (see Photo 3.17).

In another case of love at first sight, the beautiful Zhao Cuihua meets the handsome Sanbao while taking a spring walk. Zhao Cuihua uses two feminine, frilly silk fans, one open and one closed, tilting her body and looking coyly aside, as she flirts with the young man. She points with a folded fan, while demurely hiding behind the fully open one (see Photo 3.18).

Using Props

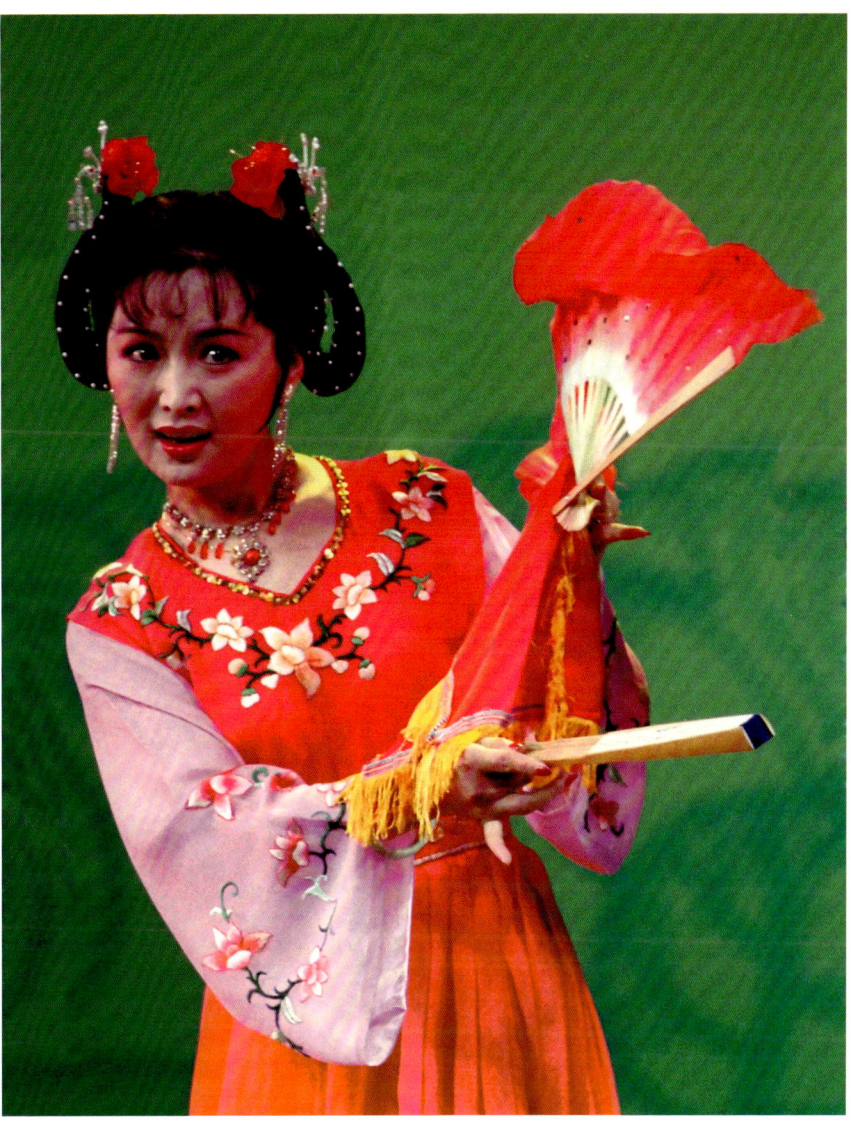

Photo 3.18 *A Spring Stroll*, Huangmei Opera

The most famous of all Chinese love stories, told over and over again in dozens of different opera styles, is the romance of Liang Shanbo and Zhu Yingtai. Zhu Yingtai, a lovely maiden, is insistent that she be allowed a good Confucian education at the academy. The academy is only open to men, and so she disguises herself as a young scholar and attends classes for three years where she forms a friendship with the young man, Liang Shanbo. When the time comes for her to return home, Liang Shanbo escorts her part of the way, passing eighteen crossings. All along the way, Zhu Yingtai tries, unsuccessfully, to hint that she is actually a young woman who is in love with him. Each of them, dressed as young Confucian scholars, holds their folding fans, using them in refined conversation (see Photo 3.19).

Later, having discovered who Zhu Yingtai is, Liang Shanbo sets out to find her and propose marriage. He traces the same route that they have walked together, remembering the hints that he had not understood at the time. Liang Shanbo holds the open fan close behind his back, indicating both his great joy and that he is now in a hurry to get to his destination (see Photo 3.20).

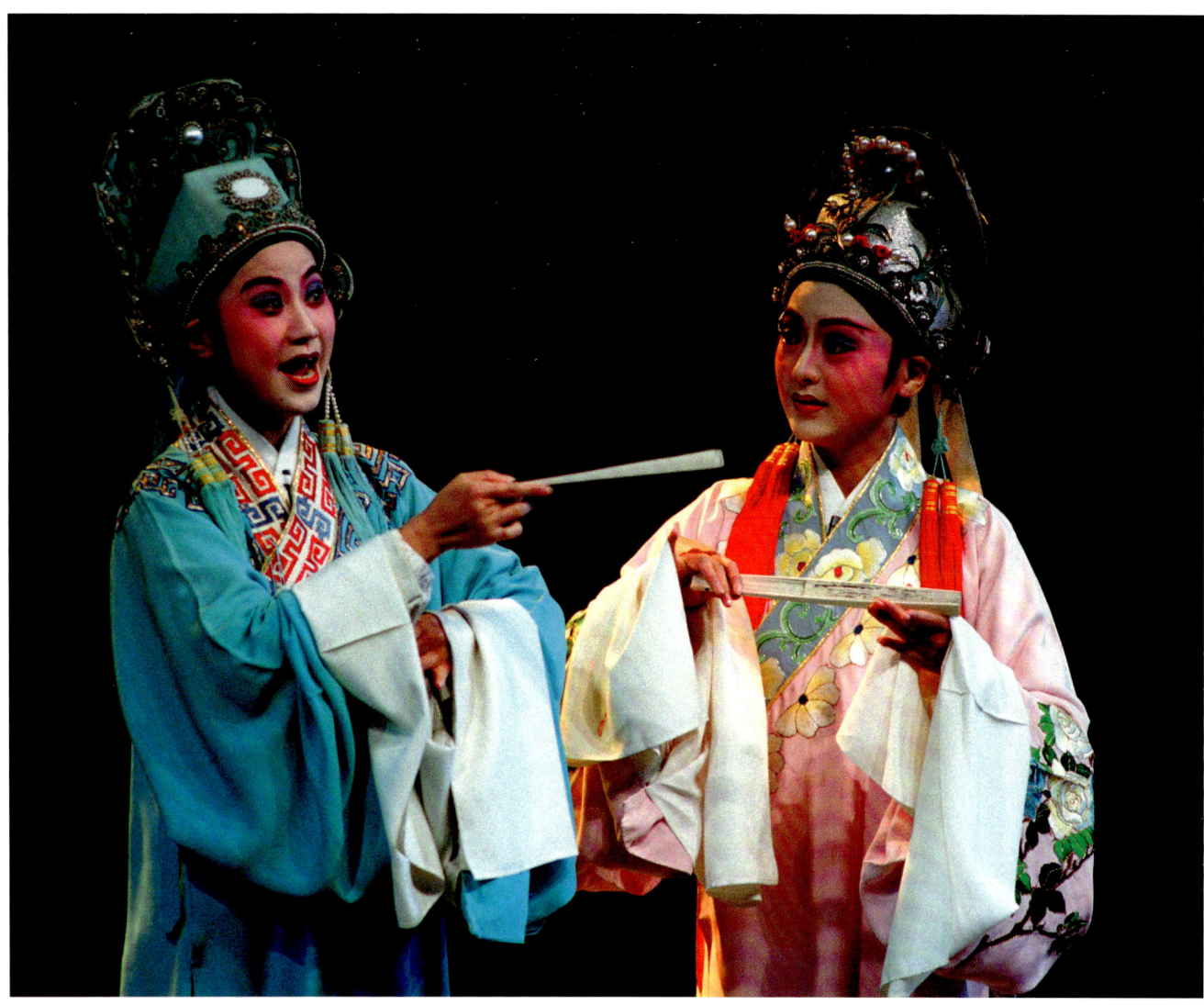

Photo 3.19 *The Eighteen Crossings*, Yue Opera

"The Romance of the West Chamber" is another love story that has been presented in various opera forms since the twelfth century. The story, first written in the eighth century during the Tang dynasty (618–907), tells of the beautiful Cui Yingying, who has stopped at a Buddhist monastery with her mother in mourning for her recently deceased father. The young scholar, Zhang Junrui, has also come to the monastery for peace and quiet to study. The two fall madly in love despite the strong objections of Cui Yingying's mother. The lovers have to meet secretly in the garden with the help of Cui Yingying's maid. In one scene, using the round, embroidered fan of the elegant young woman, Cui Yingying waits in the moonlit garden for her beloved, always holding the fan close to her cheek (see Photo 3.21).

The fan has many uses apart from love scenes. One of the most celebrated scenes for the female role in the Peking opera is *The Intoxicated Concubine*. This scene was one of the specialties of the great twentieth-century female impersonator, Mei Lanfang. In the scene, the famous Tang-dynasty concubine of the emperor Minghuang drinks excessively to forget her disappointment that the emperor seems to

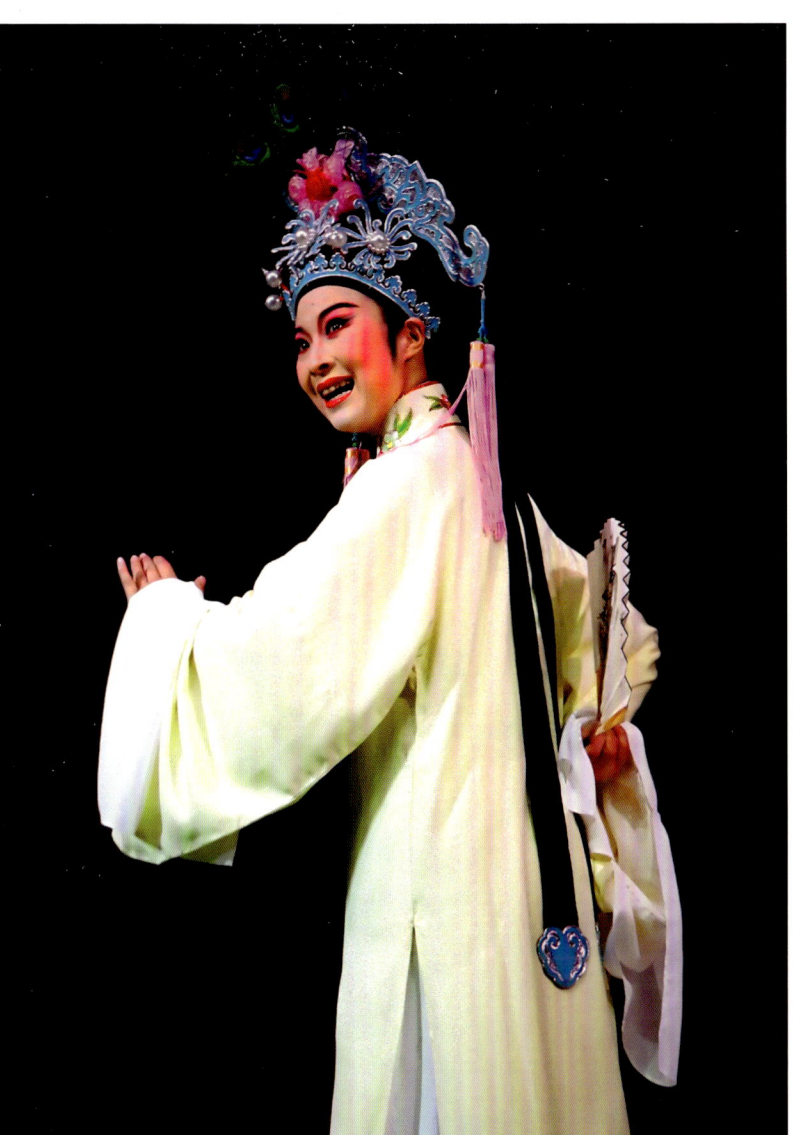

Photo 3.20 *The Eighteen Crossings*, Yue Opera

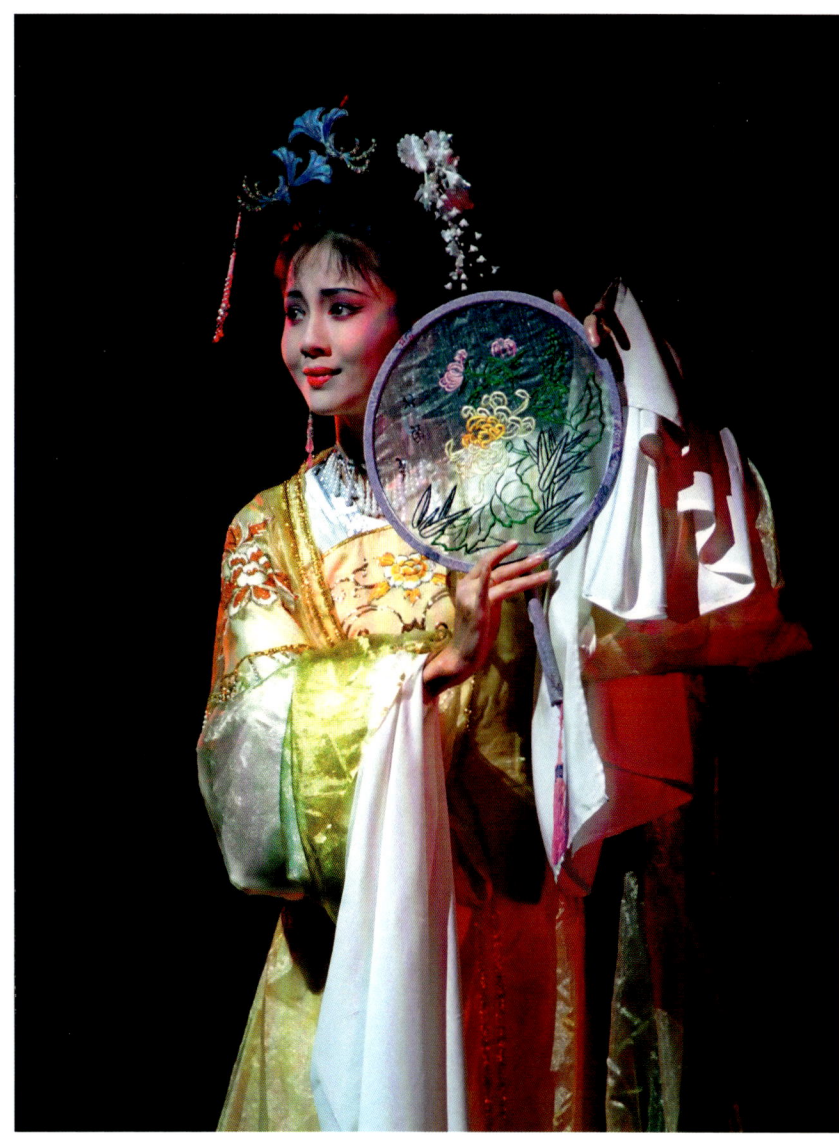

Photo 3.21 *The Romance of the West Chamber*, Yue Opera

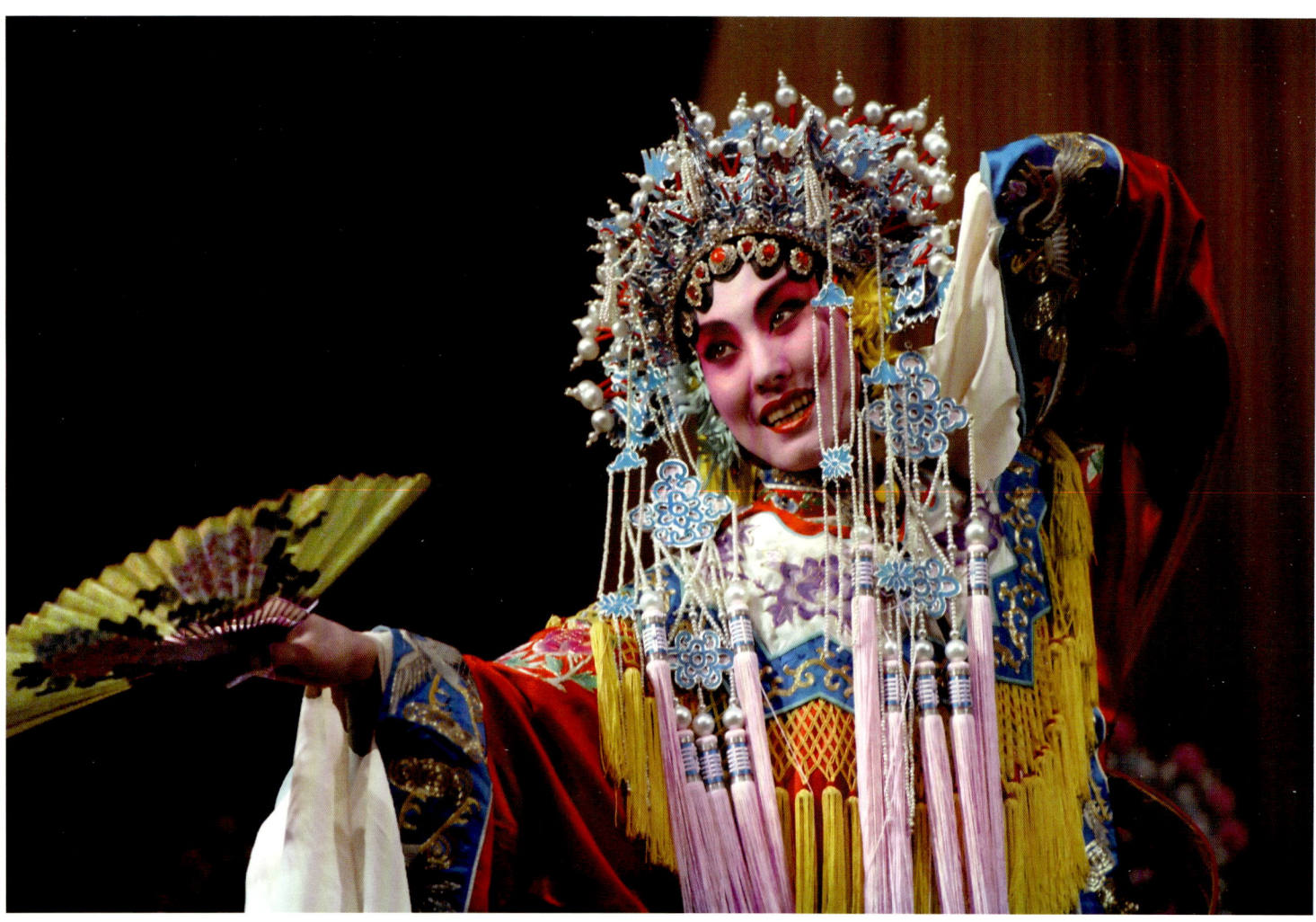

Photo 3.22 *The Intoxicated Concubine*, Peking Opera

have replaced her with another woman. As she drinks, she begins to move in an elegant, yet drunken manner, bending over backwards. All the while, she uses her fan in exquisite, delicate movements, demonstrating her drunkenness and dreamlike state (see Photo 3.22).

Maidservants also use the fan to express their feelings. Mei Ying serves her mistress, Huang Guiying, who is despondent that her engagement to the young, handsome Li Yangui has been broken off by her family. Li Yangui's family, once officials, have lost everything. Mei Ying, upon meeting the young man, who is now reduced to selling water, thinks of a plan to reunite the couple. She holds her fan above her shoulder in delight as she contemplates what is to come (see Photo 3.23).

Young women in Chinese opera do not always use fans to be demure, to flirt, or to show how refined and delicate they are. They can show quite different emotions. The villainous Sun Erniang is fierce and murderous. She regularly drugs guests in her inn, then robs and murders them, serving their flesh in dumplings to other guests, similar to Mrs. Lovett in England's story of Sweeny Todd. In the

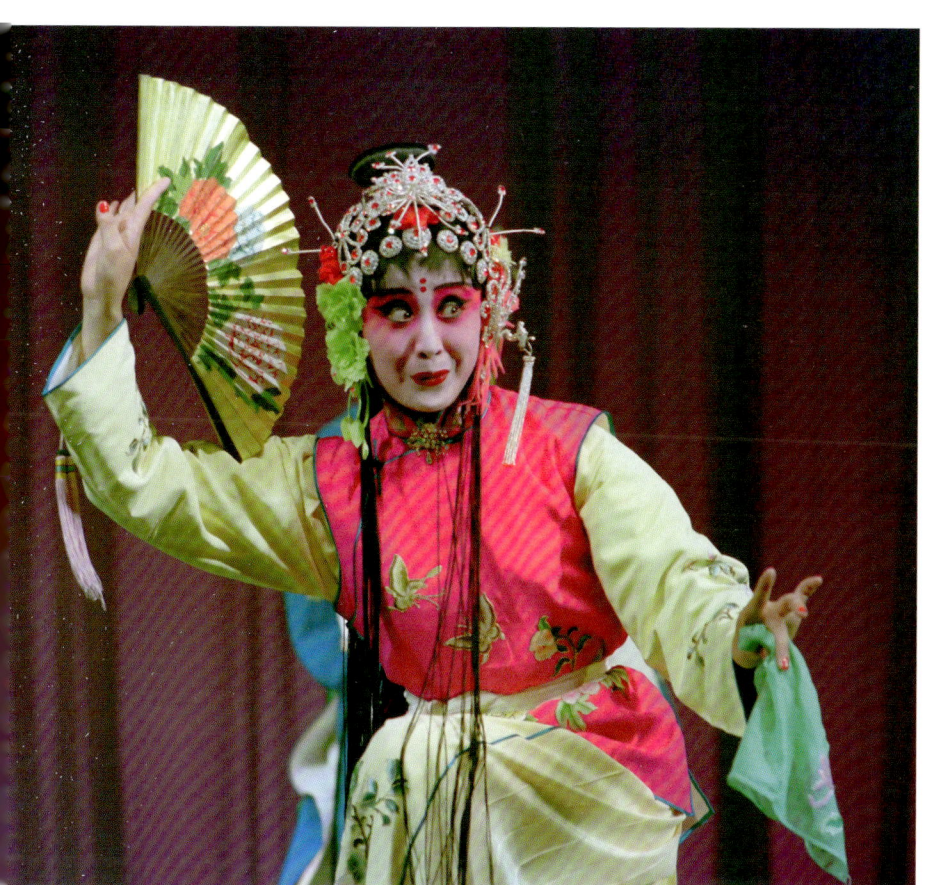

Photo 3.23 *Selling Water*, Peking Opera

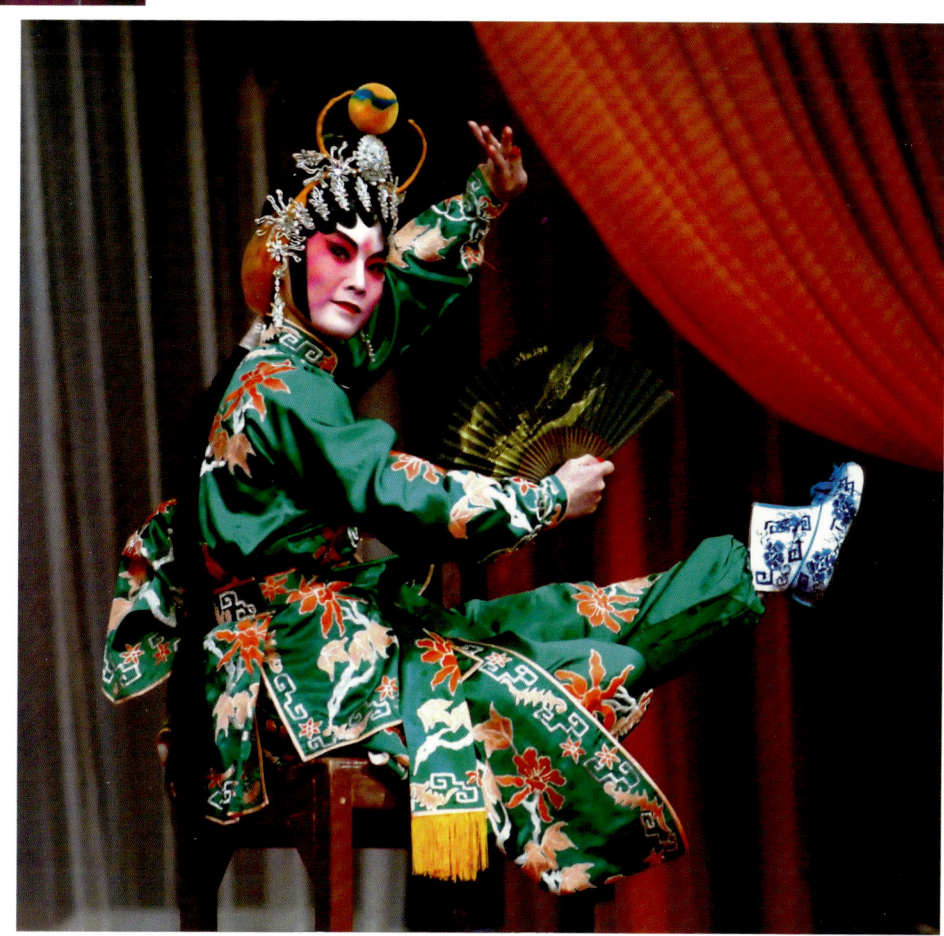

Photo 3.24 *Wu Song's Tavern Fight*, Cantonese Opera

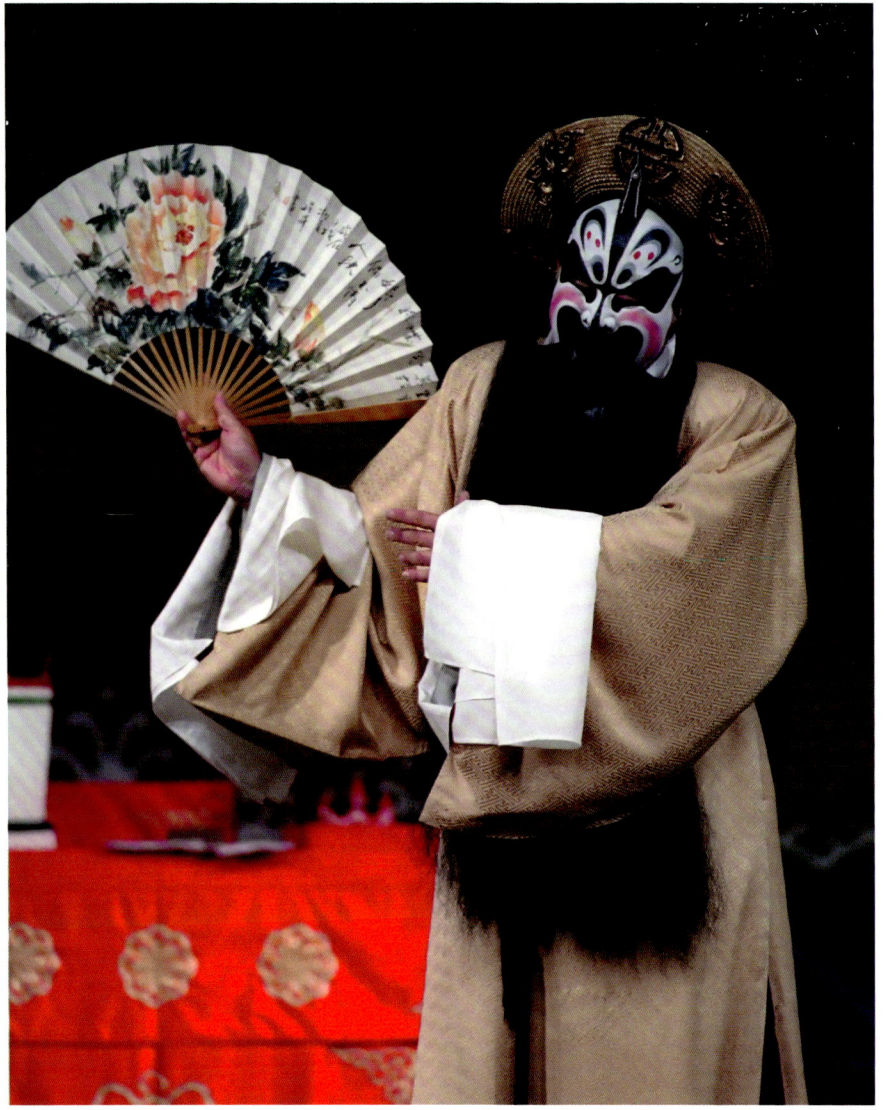

Photo 3.25 *Zhang Fei Honours the Sage Magistrate*, Peking Opera

opera *Wu Song's Tavern Fight*, Sun Erniang, in a fit of delight and pride at her extraordinary fighting skills, cleverness, and villainy, leaps upon a chair, holding her fan in a brash and bold manner to demonstrate how satisfied she is with herself (see Photo 3.24). She does not know, however, that she is about to meet her match in the great hero, Wu Song.

In another opera, a famous warrior from the great novel *The Romance of the Three Kingdoms*, Zhang Fei, uses a large fan to show another side of his character. Known as a rough, brusque fighter, Zhang Fei is loud and rude even to officials. However, when he learns of how one of these officials, Pang Tong, deals justly with people and is not only fair but compassionate, Zhang Fei decides he must make amends for his past rude behaviour to this good official. He dresses up in clothes suitable for a visit to a magistrate. He completes the image of a gentleman by holding a large fan, which he waves slowly to show composure and his respect for Pang Tong. The fan reveals that this rough character actually has another side to him; that he is a diamond in the rough (see Photo 3.25).

Handkerchief

ACTORS IN CHINESE opera make the most of props associated with their roles. For women, mostly young maidens, one such prop is the handkerchief. The handkerchief, like long sleeves, makes it possible to portray interior emotional states in a visible way on the opera stage. The young maiden uses her handkerchief to signal how she feels: embarrassed, shy, playful and joyous.

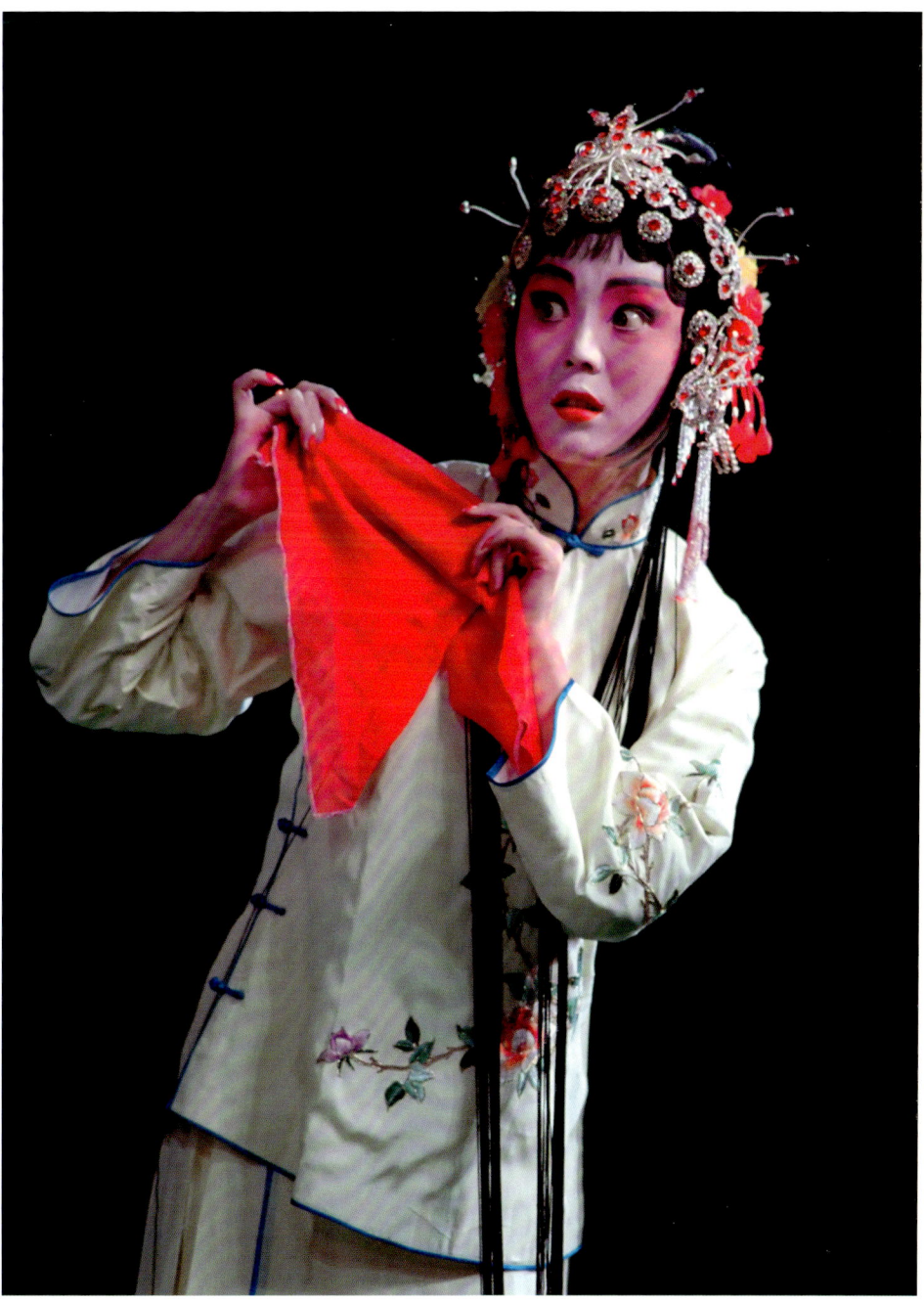

Photo 3.26 *The Sisters Switch Marriages*, Lü Opera

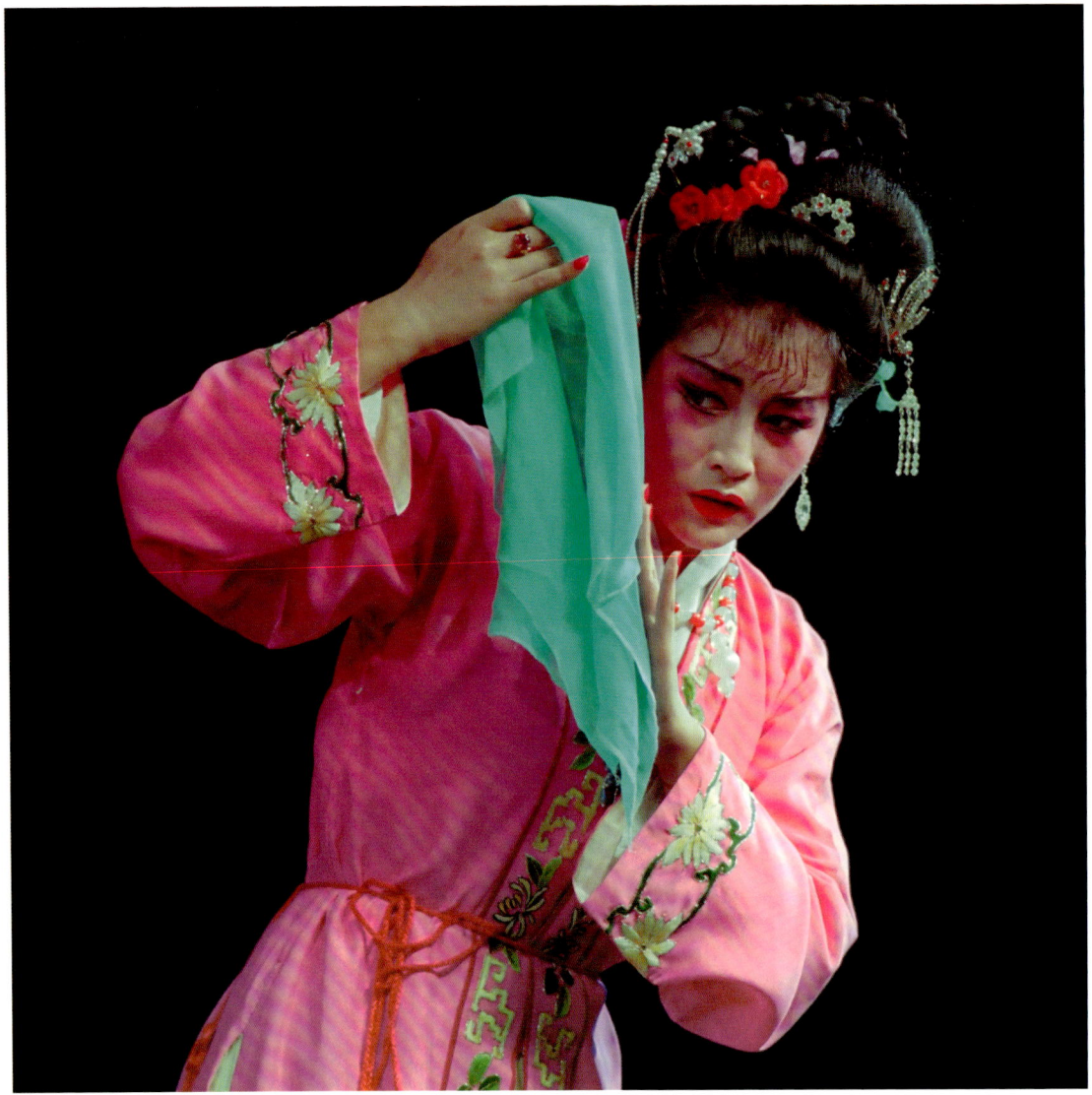

Photo 3.27 *Borrowing at New Year*, Lü Opera

On Chinese New Year's eve, the young maiden Aijie discovers her betrothed, the destitute Wang Hanxi, hiding in her embroidery room. He has come to ask her father for a loan. In girlish embarrassment and modesty, Aijie hides behind her handkerchief (see Photo 3.27).

The handkerchief also indicates a demure maiden. Zhao Cuihua, a young girl, takes a spring walk. Along the way, she runs into the young scholar Sanbao. It is love at first sight. She cannot take her eyes off him, but as a shy and proper maiden she cannot look directly at him either. Consequently, she peers out from her handkerchief, covering the smile that she cannot help and the flush in her cheeks (see Photo 3.28).

A young maiden can also be embarrassed by the attentions of a handsome young man. The lovely Qiuxiang is a maid in a wealthy family. She is amazed to be courted by the famous Ming scholar and painter, Tang Bohu. She is so flustered by his attentions and so moved by his persistent affection that she does not know how to react. Part of her wants to refuse him, but part of her wants to accept his love. What can she do, except hiding behind her sleeves and her handkerchief (see Photo 3.29)?

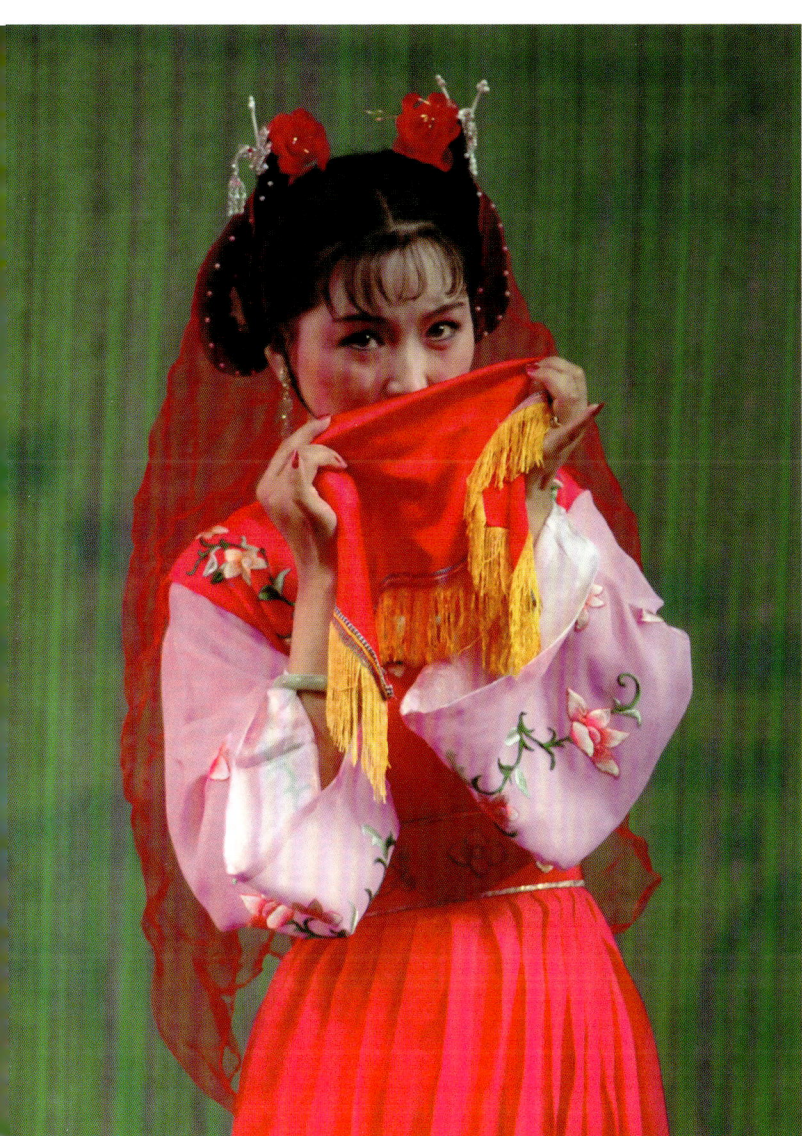

Photo 3.28 *A Spring Stroll*, Huangmei Opera

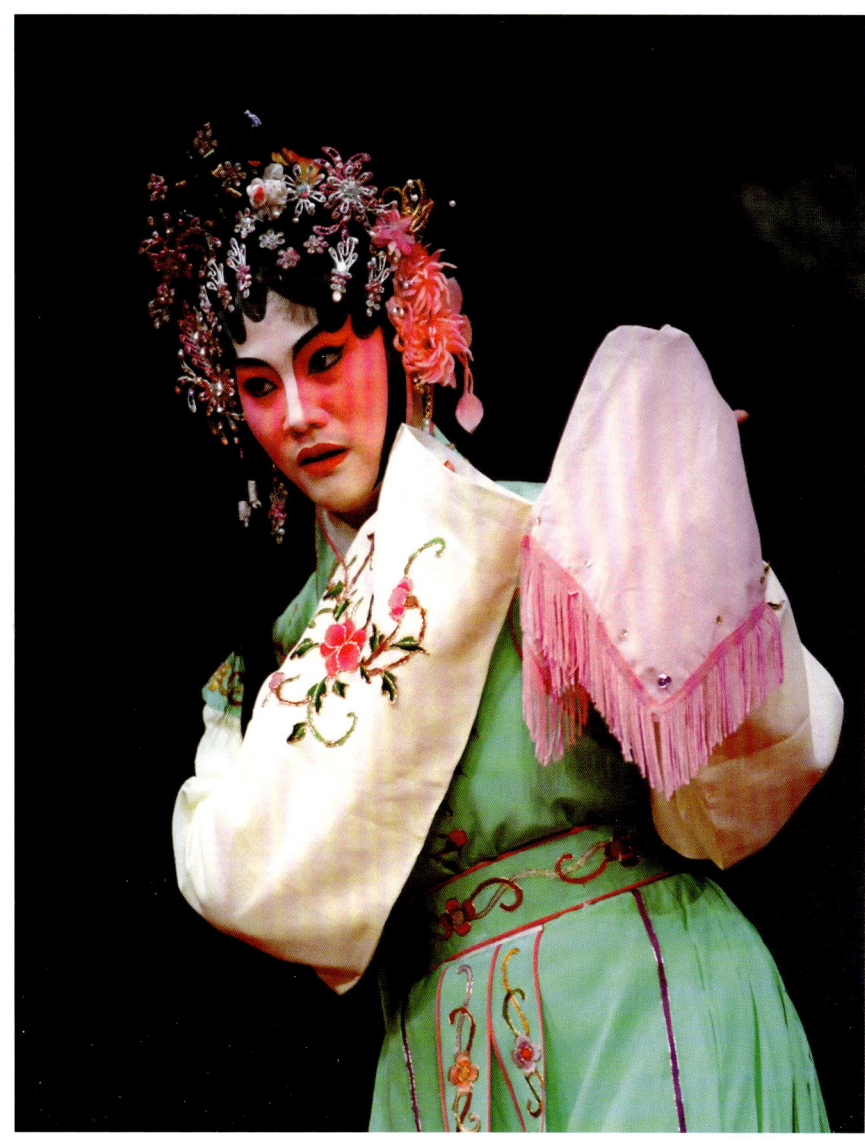

Photo 3.29 *Choosing Qiuxiang*, Cantonese Opera

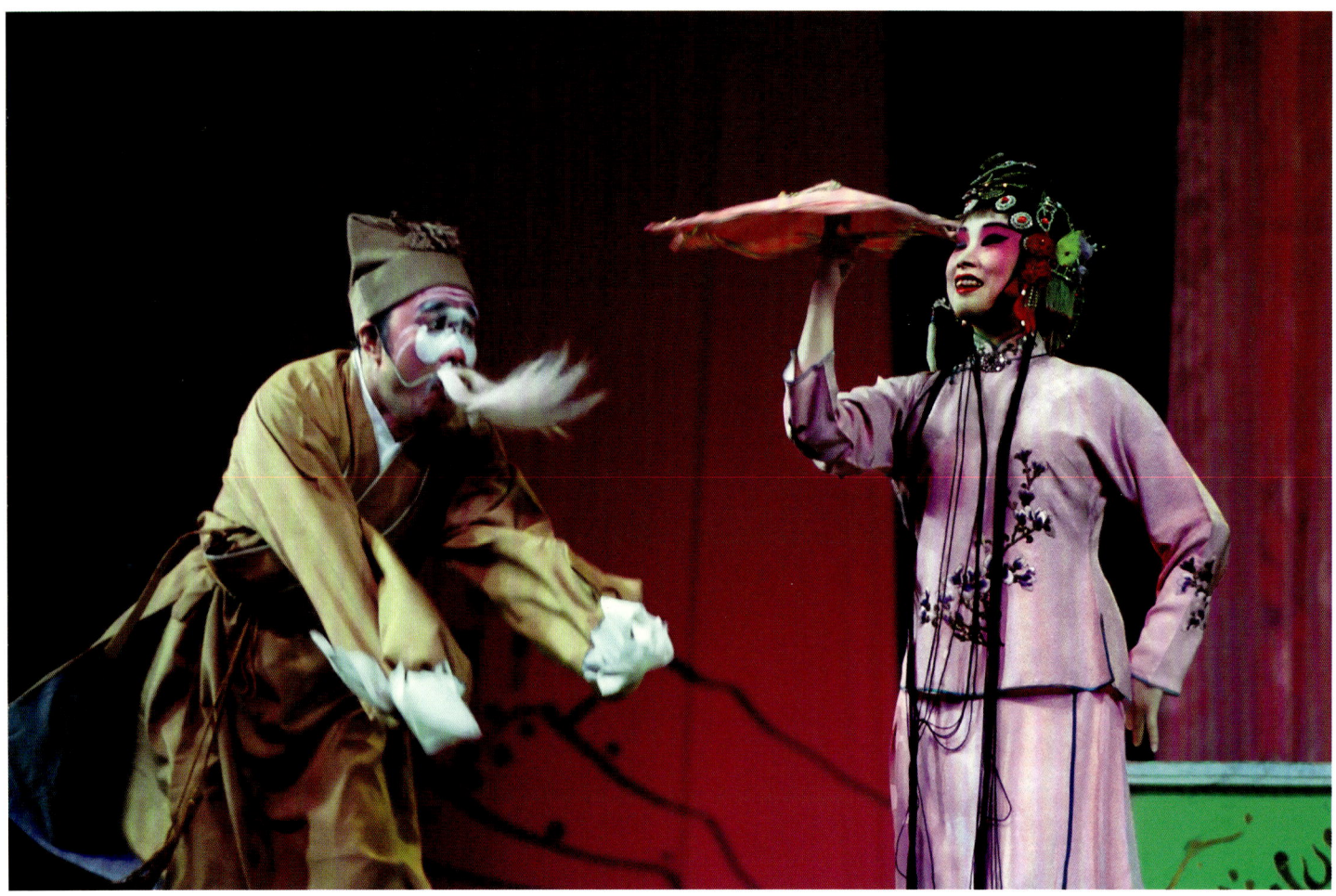

Photo 3.30 *The Joyous Return*, Huangmei Opera

The young maiden does more with a handkerchief than simply hide behind it. She can also manipulate it in a number of ways to show joy. When Cui Xiuying hears that her fiancé has not only won top awards at the imperial exams, but is on his way home to her, she cannot contain her delight. She extends the palm of her right hand upward with her handkerchief lying across her fingertips. With a flick of her wrist, she sets the handkerchief in motion spinning counter-clockwise. Her second finger supports its centre and keeps it moving. The handkerchief used in this flat rotation is weighted at the corners, sometimes with tassels, so that it has just the right inertia to spin. Her old servant watches, sharing in her joy by shaking his beard (see Photo 3.30).

Handkerchiefs are also spun vertically. Ye Hanyan is about to see the man she loves. Full of joy and expectation, she grabs her handkerchief, stretches it between two hands, and then, tossing it in the air, begins flicking it around her wrist. She effortlessly moves her hand out and back to the centre to keep it in motion so quickly that it rotates vertically (see Photo 3.31).

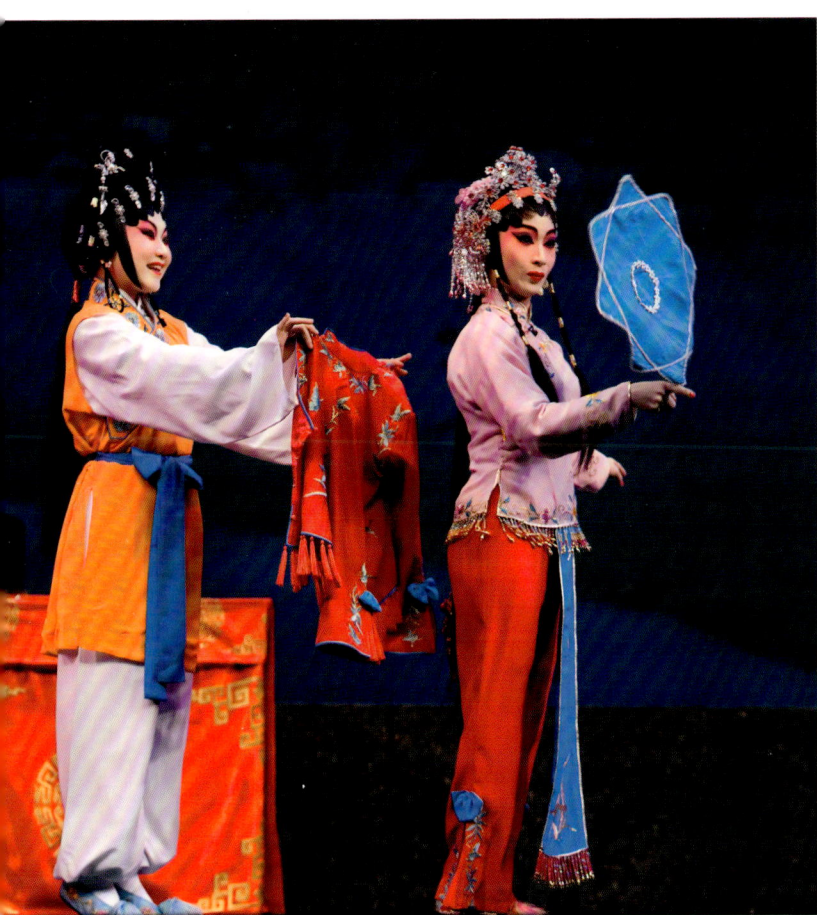

Photo 3.31 *Hanging a Painting*, Cantonese Opera

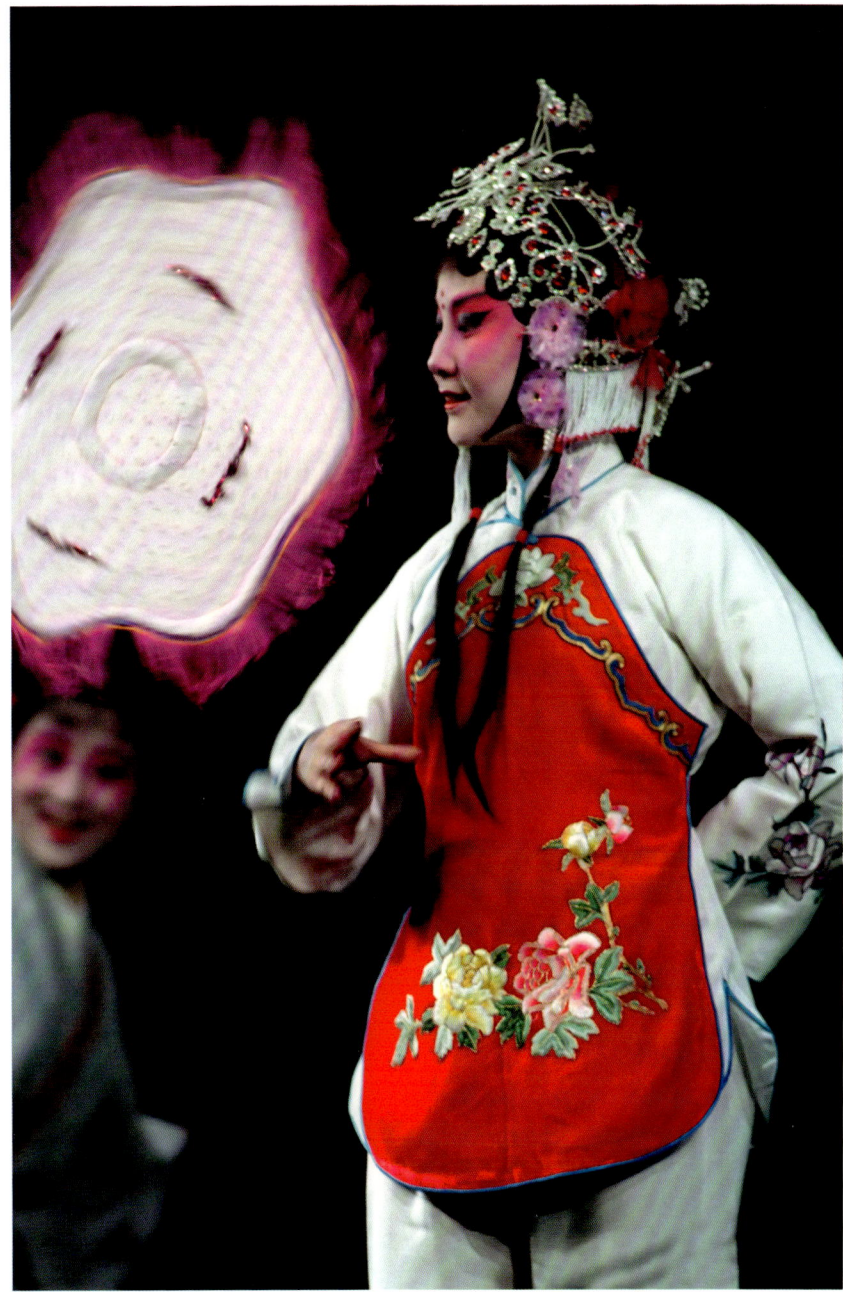

Photo 3.32 *Crossing Wits*, Hui Opera

Chinese Opera: The Actor's Craft

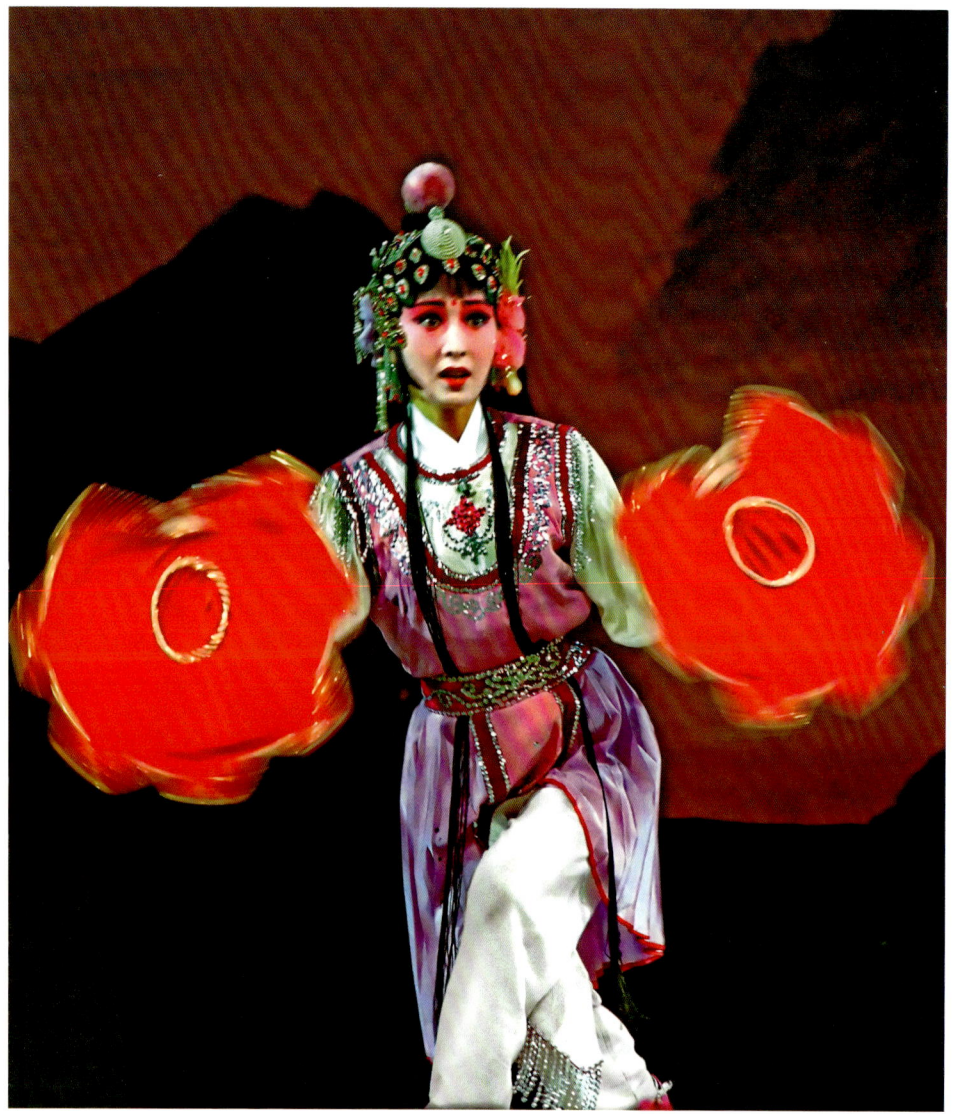

Photo 3.33 *Twice-Locked Mountain*, Longjiang Opera

This vertical rotation can be combined with other skills like shifting the twirling handkerchief from one hand to the other. White Peony, a young maiden running an apothecary, demonstrates these skills after she outplays the immortal being Lü Dongbin, who has tried to trick her by ordering bizarre medicines. Lü Dongbin, unable to best her, has had to leave. White Peony demonstrates her delight by twirling her handkerchief vertically, casting it up in the air and catching it to keep it going (see Photo 3.32).

In the opera *Twice-Locked Mountain*, the lady Liu Jinding has been in search of her husband. When her servant girl sees that her mistress has indeed found him, she is ecstatic, expressing her joy in a double-handkerchief swirl. Both hands rotate the handkerchiefs vertically, flipping her wrists so quickly that the handkerchiefs build up momentum and swirl about, dazzling the audience (see Photo 3.33).

Opposite
Photo 3.34 *The Fire Phoenix*, Cantonese Opera

Ribbon

Chinese dance has used long ribbons since early imperial times. Rubbings show them used in the Han dynasty (second century BC to fourth century AD). They were a popular feature of dance in the Tang dynasty. Ribbons add colour and spectacle to the opera stage by infusing the elements of dance and fast-paced movement.

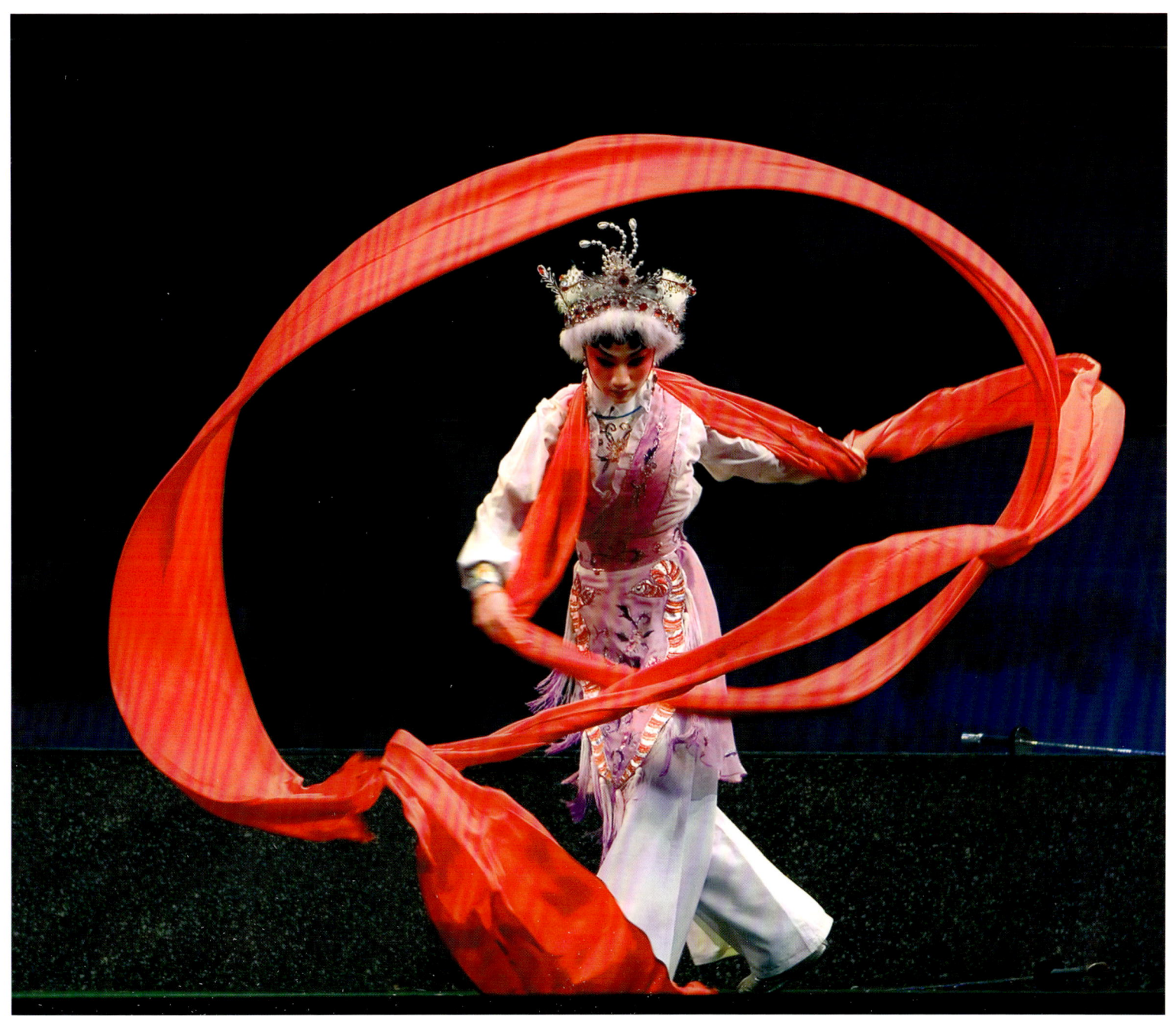

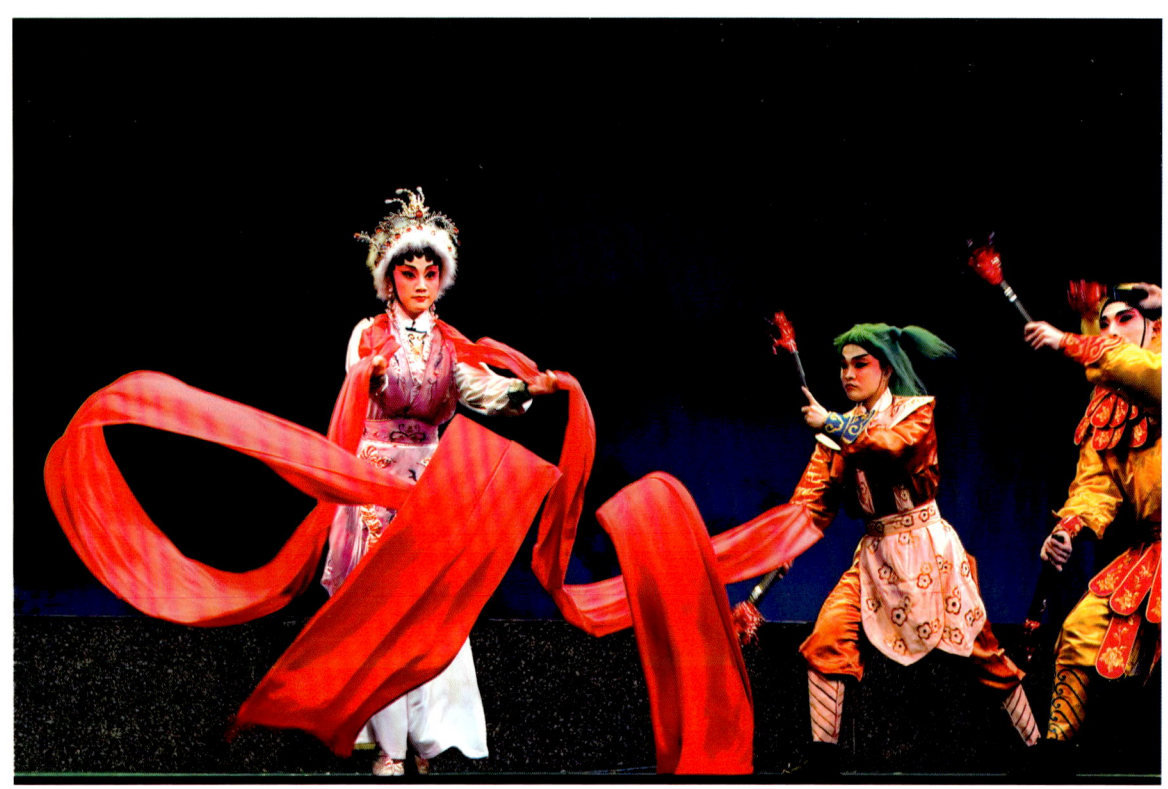

Photo 3.35 *The Fire Phoenix*, Cantonese Opera

Photo 3.36 *The Eight Immortals Cross the Sea*, Peking Opera

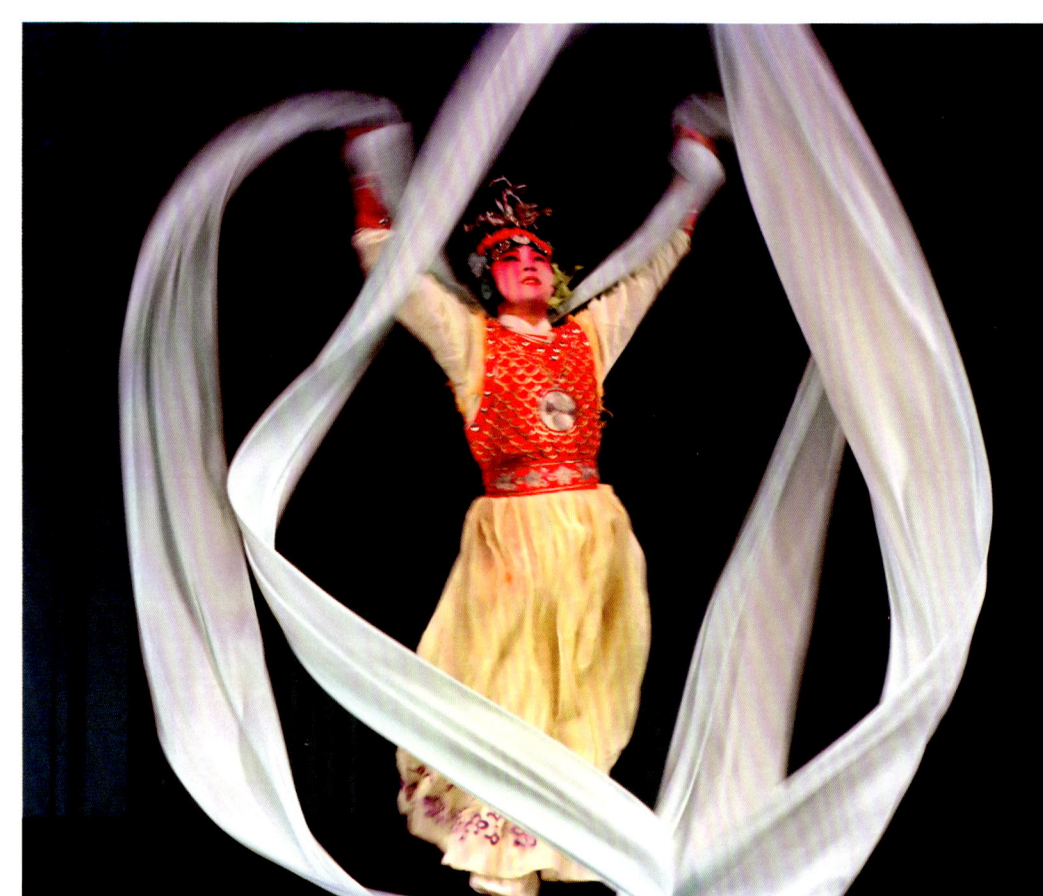

Using Props

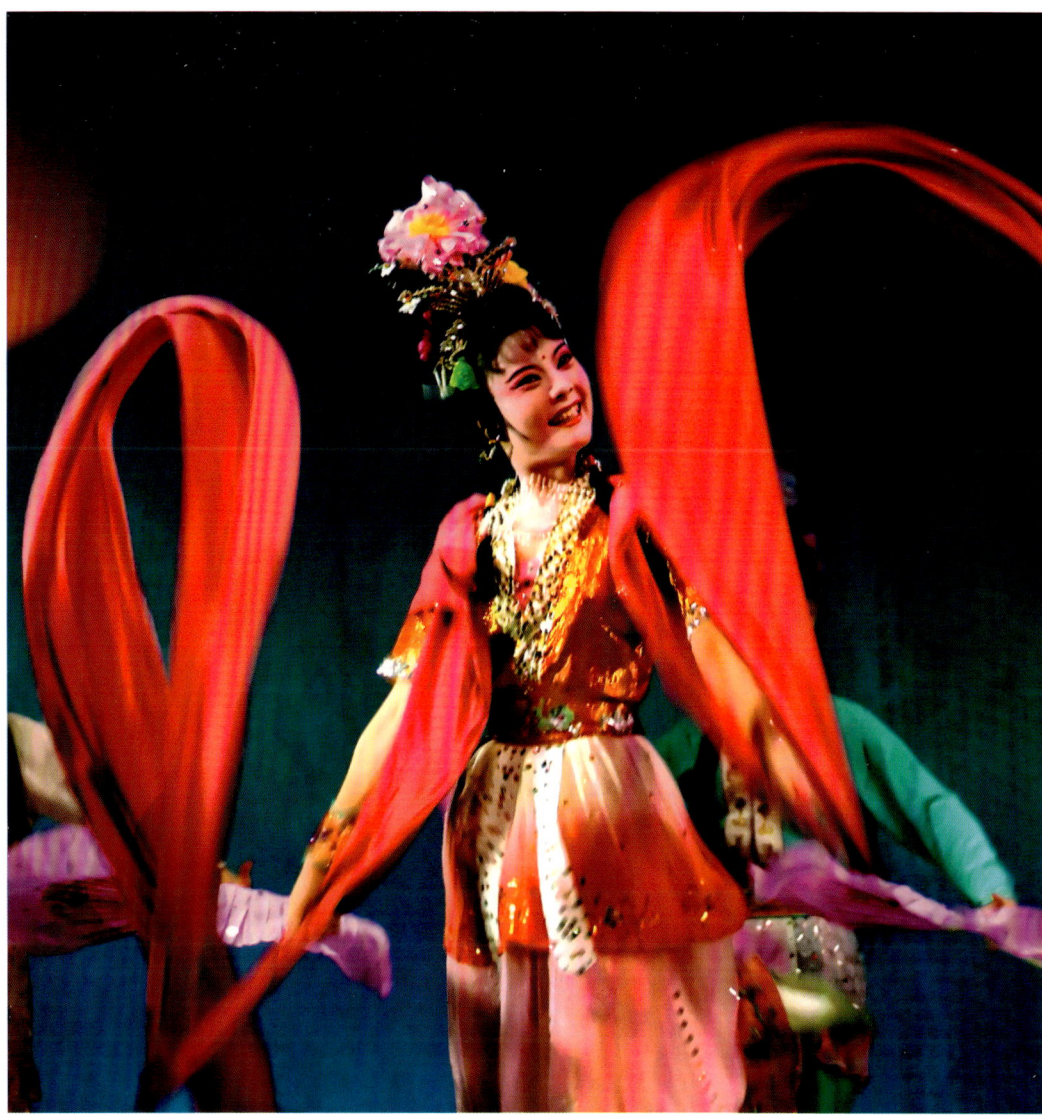

Photo 3.37 *The Hibiscus Fairy*, Sichuan Opera

The ribbons are long pieces of silk ranging from five to twelve feet long. In one method, the dancers wield two separate ribbons by holding onto bamboo sticks sewn into the ends. In another, a single long silk ribbon passes behind the performer's neck. Two sticks are sewn into the ribbon on either side. In both cases, the performer controls the sticks to create colourful swirls, spinning the ribbons in large and small circles, and even enfolding themselves in the twirling ribbons. They can also create dramatic swirls by leaping into the air, thus increasing the size and speed of the loops of silk. The swirling silk gives the impression of floating in clouds, and so ribbons are usually associated with fairies and other magical beings.

The White Crane Fairy finds herself in a contest with the Bald Eagle Fairy, who attacks her with fire. In the midst of the flame, White Crane transforms into a phoenix and stirs up great waves to smash her opponents onto the shore. Her magic power and the waves are symbolized in the flowing red ribbons that the White Crane Fairy deftly handles (see Photo 3.35).

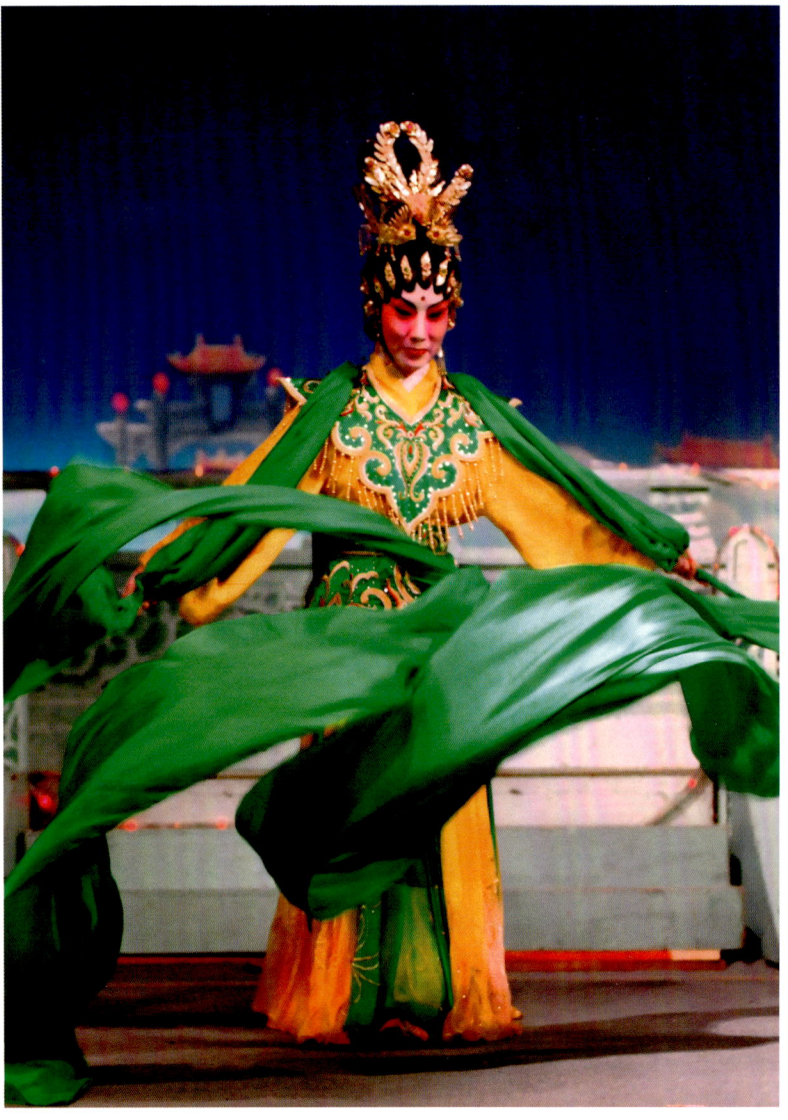

Photo 3.38 *The Red Peony Fairy*, Cantonese Opera

The Goldfish Fairy also uses ribbons in battle. One day, the legendary eight immortals, drunk after a banquet, make sport of the Goldfish Fairy. She cannot abide their impudence and defeats them all in a fantastic display of magical prowess. She whirls her ribbons dramatically to demonstrate her great power, stirring up the waves of the Eastern Sea (see Photo 3.36).

Another fairy makes use of the ribbons, but not for battle. The Hibiscus Fairy wants to reward a fairy child who spoke up for her in an argument with the heavenly queen and was changed into a human being as punishment. The fairy child has incarnated on earth as the scholar Chen Qiulin. Knowing his love for flowers, the Hibiscus Fairy descends into his garden. She uses her ribbons in a dance to describe a garden in full bloom (see Photo 3.37).

The Red Peony Fairy uses ribbons to dance and express her great freedom and joy in heaven, where she has cultivated her magical powers (see Photo 3.38). Little does she know that offending the heavenly empress will soon mean her death. However, she will be brought back to life with magic dew given by the Goddess of Mercy.

Using Props

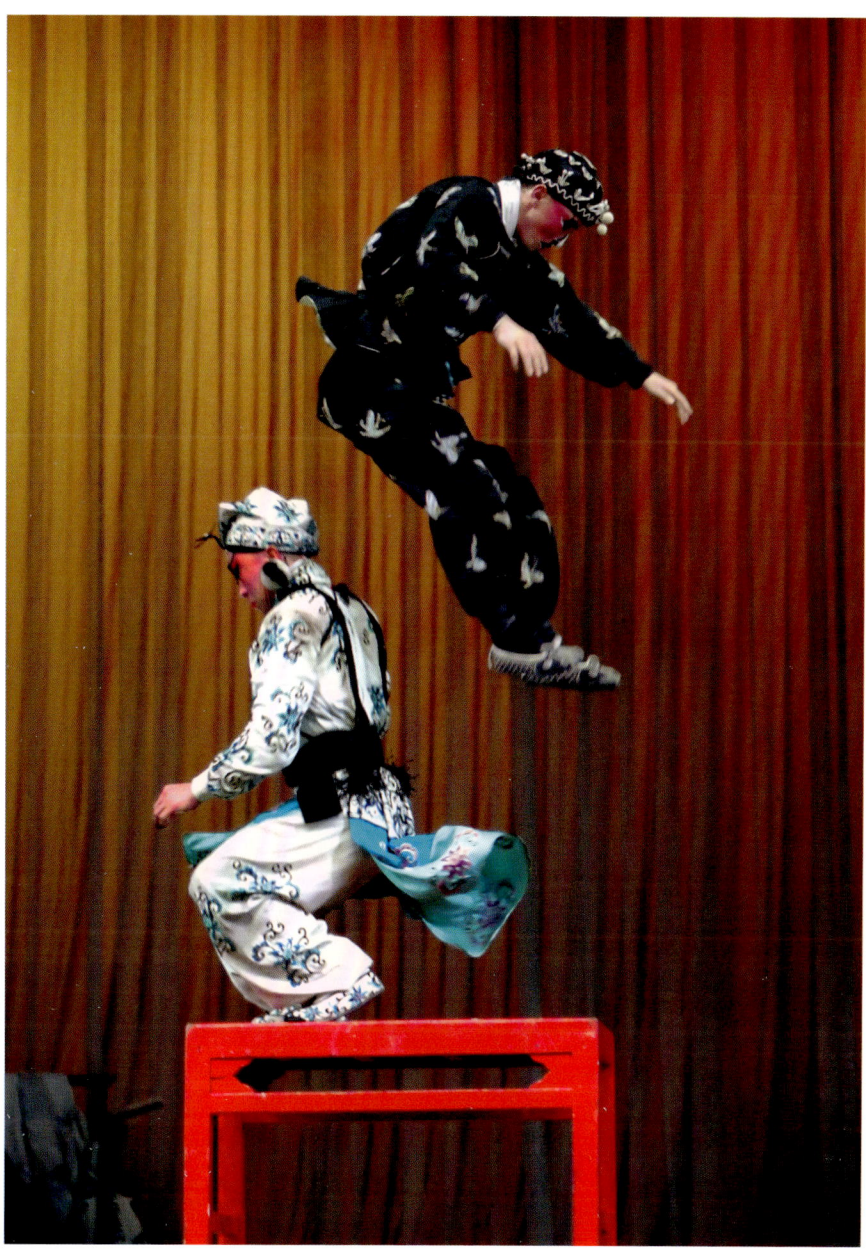

Photo 3.39 *Inn at the Crossroads,* Peking Opera

Table and Chair

The traditional Chinese opera stage is normally bare. Sets and backdrops, along with special effects and lighting, are more recent additions. The norm has been to focus on the actors and their skills rather than on a set designer's concept. Although there are variations from one opera form to another, audiences are used to an empty, carpeted stage, which becomes countryside or town depending on the demands of the story.

If that story should take the audience inside a building, to a courtroom, household or palace, the audience expects to see a table with one or two chairs placed beside it. The positioning of these chairs can indicate different situations. When placed on either side of the table, they indicate the living room

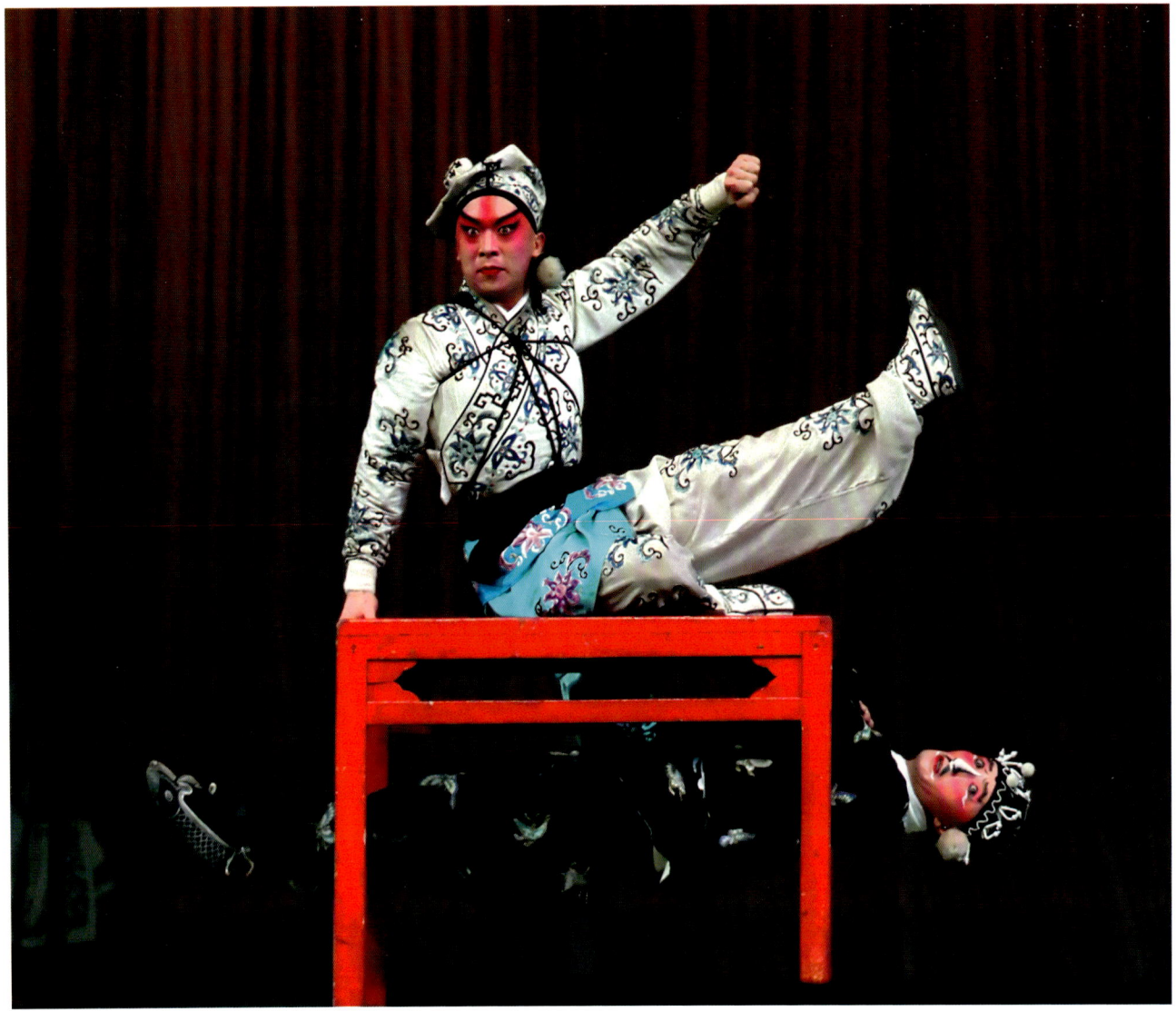

Photo 3.40 *Inn at the Crossroads*, Peking Opera

of a house. When placed behind the table, it can indicate a magistrate, a judge or even an emperor. Some plays make more creative use of this stage furniture. When a chair is placed on top of the table, it indicates a high place like a mountaintop. Chairs and tables can be moved during the opera by stagehands who come onto the stage in a business-like manner and adjust the furniture while the action is still going on. These same stagehands can also remove chairs and tables in full view of the audience when they are no longer required.

Tables and chairs can also be used in the action of the story. One famous example is the Peking opera *Inn at the Crossroads*. In this play, the hero, Ren Tanghui, is at odds with the landlord of a roadside inn. Although the stage is fully lit, the audience understands that this scene is set in the dark of night. Both the hero and the landlord are searching for each other, sometimes with drawn sabres. They are as quiet as they can be, and often discover each other in the dark, but then miss their target. In one particularly dramatic moment, the landlord, Liu Lihua, hangs below the table top. His body pokes out

Using Props

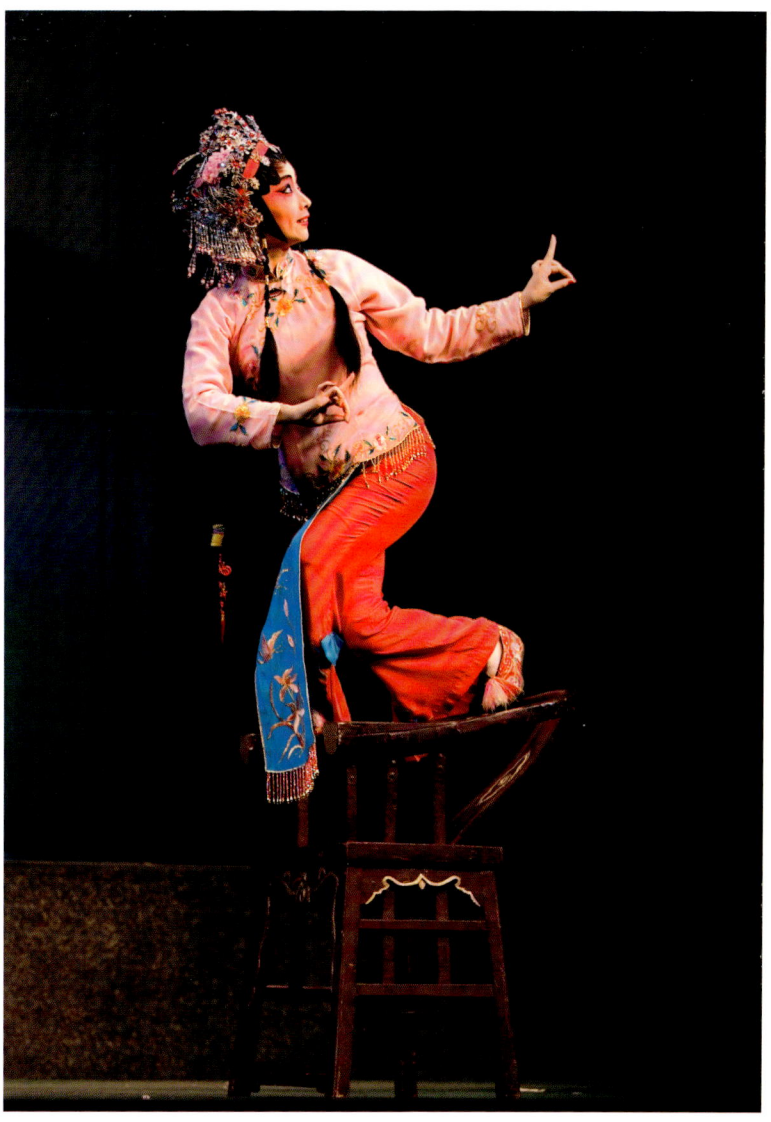

Photo 3.41 *Hanging a Painting,* Cantonese Opera

on both sides, and he looks at the audience with alarm. The hero sits defiantly on top, listening for any sound of where his opponent might be (see Photo 3.40). Both of the actors execute light, fast, precise movements around, on, under and through the table in perfect silence.

Chairs are also used for acrobatics and balancing as part of the story line. The young maiden, Ye Hanyan, in the Cantonese opera *Hanging a Painting*, has learned that she is about to meet the young gentleman who is the desire of her heart. She excitedly prepares the room by decorating it with a hanging scroll painting. Standing on top of the chair, she executes a series of fluid and dexterous moves as she mimes hanging the scroll in mid-air. Jumping onto the very top of the arm rests, she expresses a girlish delight and expectation at the coming of her beau (see Photo 3.41).

Another maiden in another opera, however, uses a chair to express more than girlish delight. Yan Xijiao is actually a ghost. She died still in love with the young man Zhang Sanlang. Determined that death will not separate them, she comes to Zhang Sanlang in his study at night, determined to take him

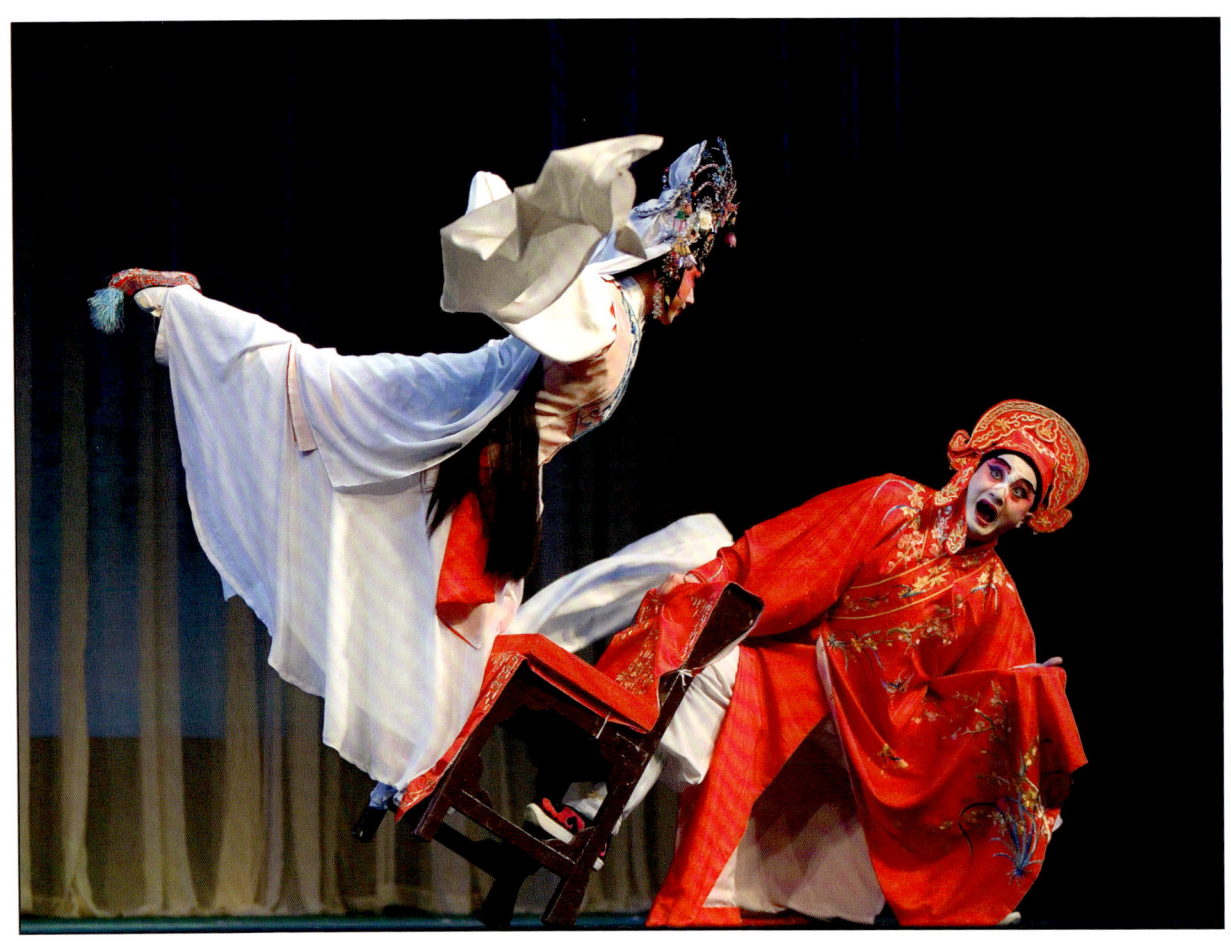

Photo 3.42 *The Haunting of Zhang Sanlang,* Cantonese Opera

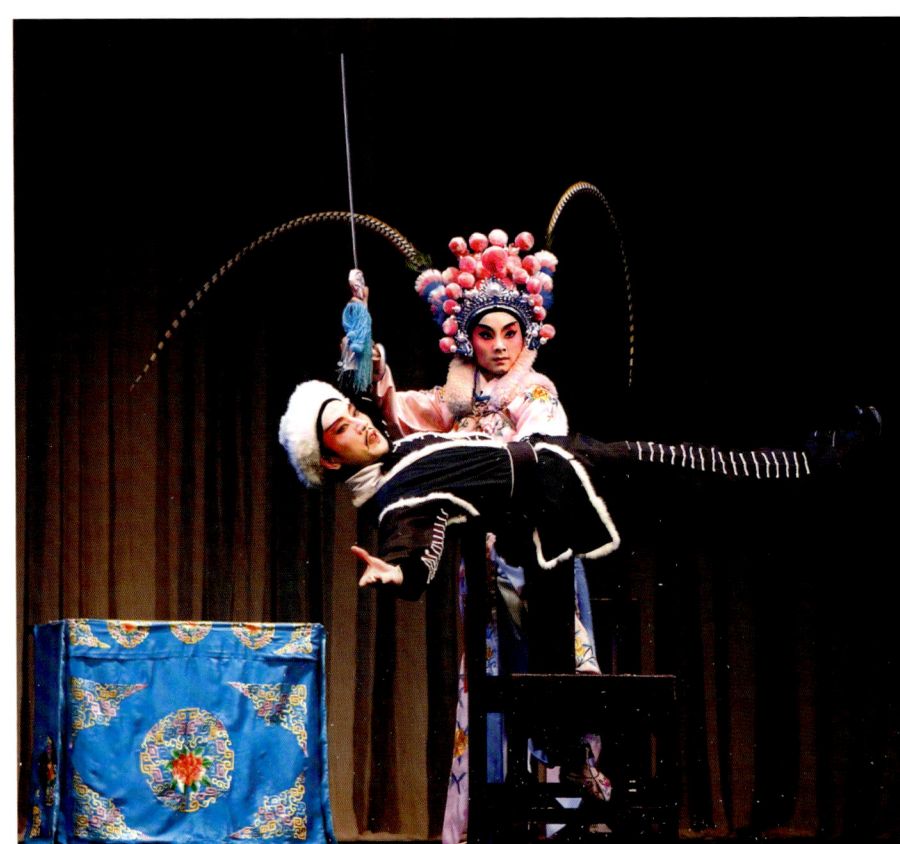

Photo 3.43 *Blocking the Horse,* Cantonese Opera

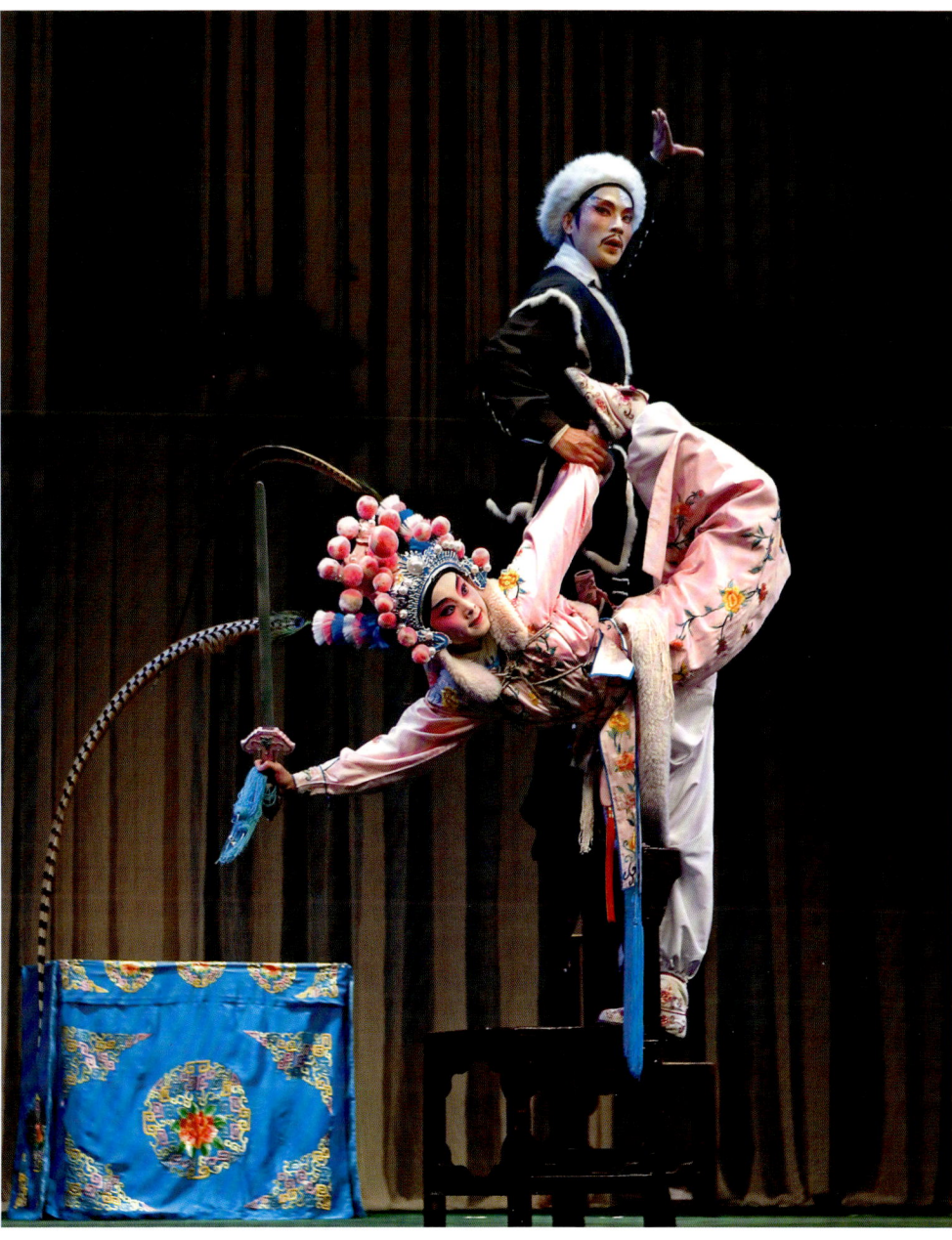

Photo 3.44 *Blocking the Horse,* Cantonese Opera

with her to the underworld so that they might be a ghostly couple there. Zhang Sanlang is terrified at the apparition and at the prospect of going to the underworld. He hides behind the chair of his study, but Yan Xijiao perches on top of it as she resolutely pursues him and eventually carries him off to hell (see Photo 3.42).

A particularly impressive use of the chair is in the opera *Blocking the Horse*. Jiao Guangpu, exiled from his country, runs an inn. When he discovers a traveller from his own land, the maiden Yang Bajie who has disguised herself as a man, he is determined to rob her of her travel pass so that he can go back home safely. A fight breaks out between them in the inn around the table and chairs. At the high point, Jiao Guangpu stretches his body out stiffly while balancing on the backrest of the chair. Yang Bajie braces one foot on the chair as she raises her sword above him (see Photo 3.43).

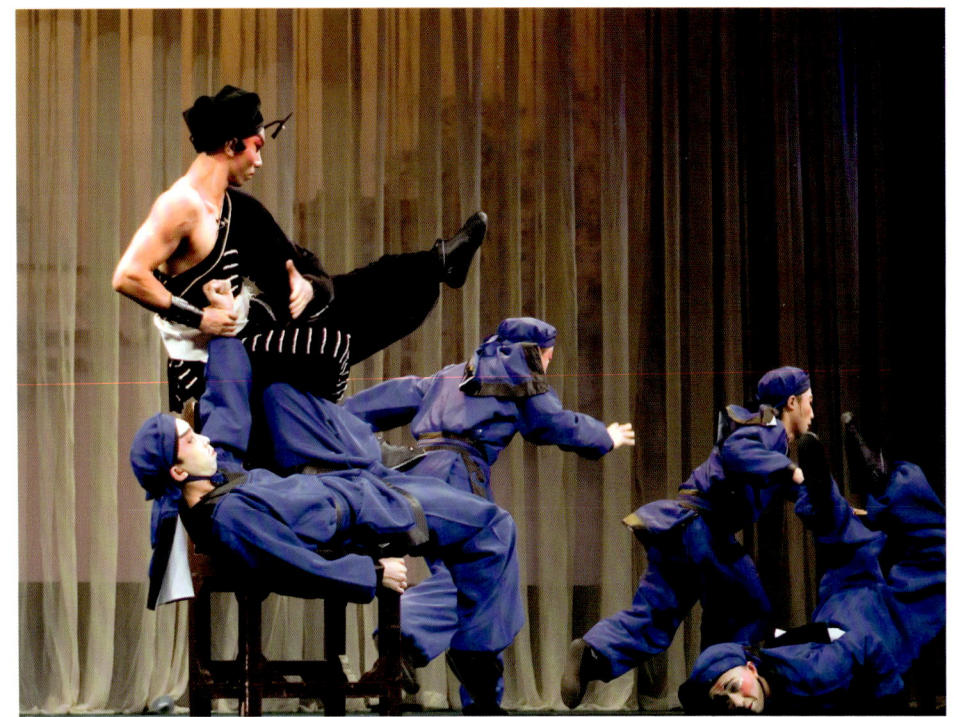 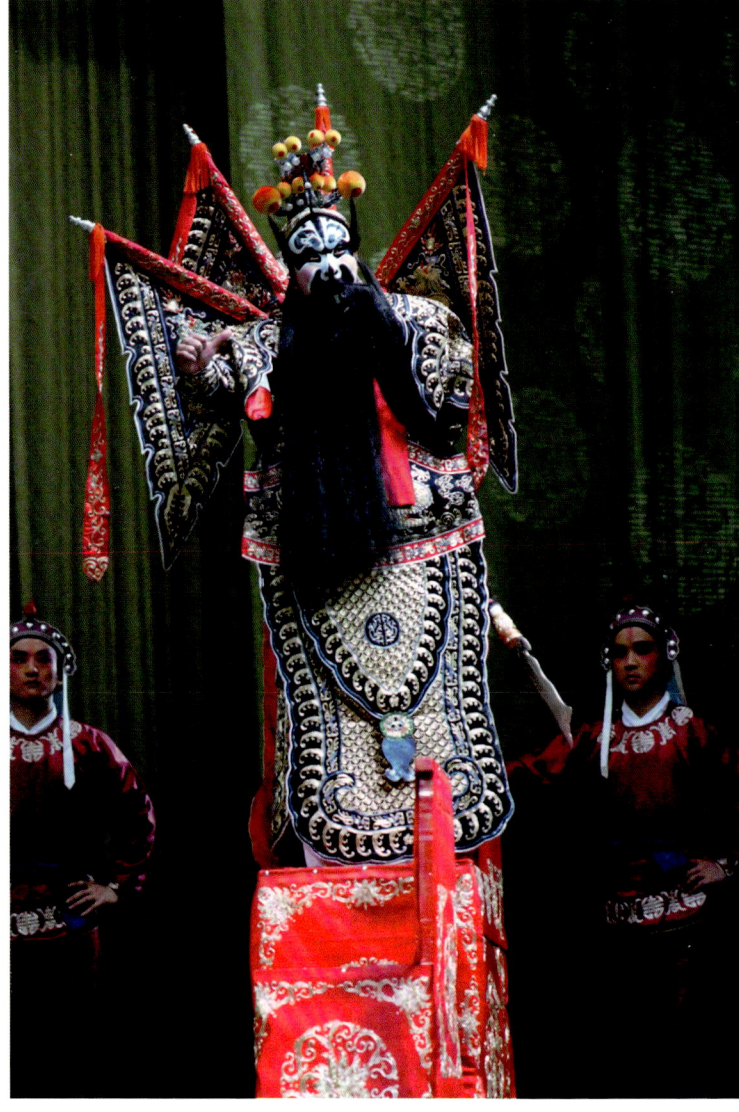

As the fierce fight continues, both Jiao Guangpu and Yang Bajie stand high on the chair as they struggle for possession of the invaluable travel pass. Throughout the contest, both actors demonstrate light, precise acrobatic moves around the chair (see Photo 3.44).

Wu Song is a hero in the great Ming-dynasty novel, *The Legend of the Water Margin*. In one part of this story, Wu Song finds out that his sister-in-law, Pan Jinlian, and her lover, Ximen Qing, have murdered his brother. In a rage, he seeks revenge by attacking them at Lion Tower. He dispatches all the thugs sent against him. While perched on top of a chair, he kicks them out of the way, boxing them with his fists—until he gets to and kills the villainous Ximen Qing (see Photo 3.45).

A chair can be a mountain peak or some other high vantage point. In the military opera *Changban Slope*, the legendary fighter Zhang Fei stands atop a bridge, blocking the way of General Cao Cao's troops. The actor stands on the chair to indicate that he is now in a high place. The chair can also be put on top of a table to emphasize the effect (see Photo 3.46).

Above, left
Photo 3.45 *Lion Tower*, Cantonese Opera

Above, right
Photo 3.46 *Changban Slope*, Peking Opera

Cloud Whisk

When a Chinese opera audience sees a character enter the stage holding a large handle with a horse tail at the end, they recognize a stage prop called the cloud whisk. That prop tells them something about the character carrying it because it is used primarily by supernatural beings like Taoist immortals and religious characters like Buddhist nuns. Originally called a fly whisk, its function was to scatter flies rather than swat them. The use of the whisk to respect life gives the cloud whisk its identification with religion. Consequently, it is sometimes referred to as the dust whisk because it scatters the dust of the mortal world.

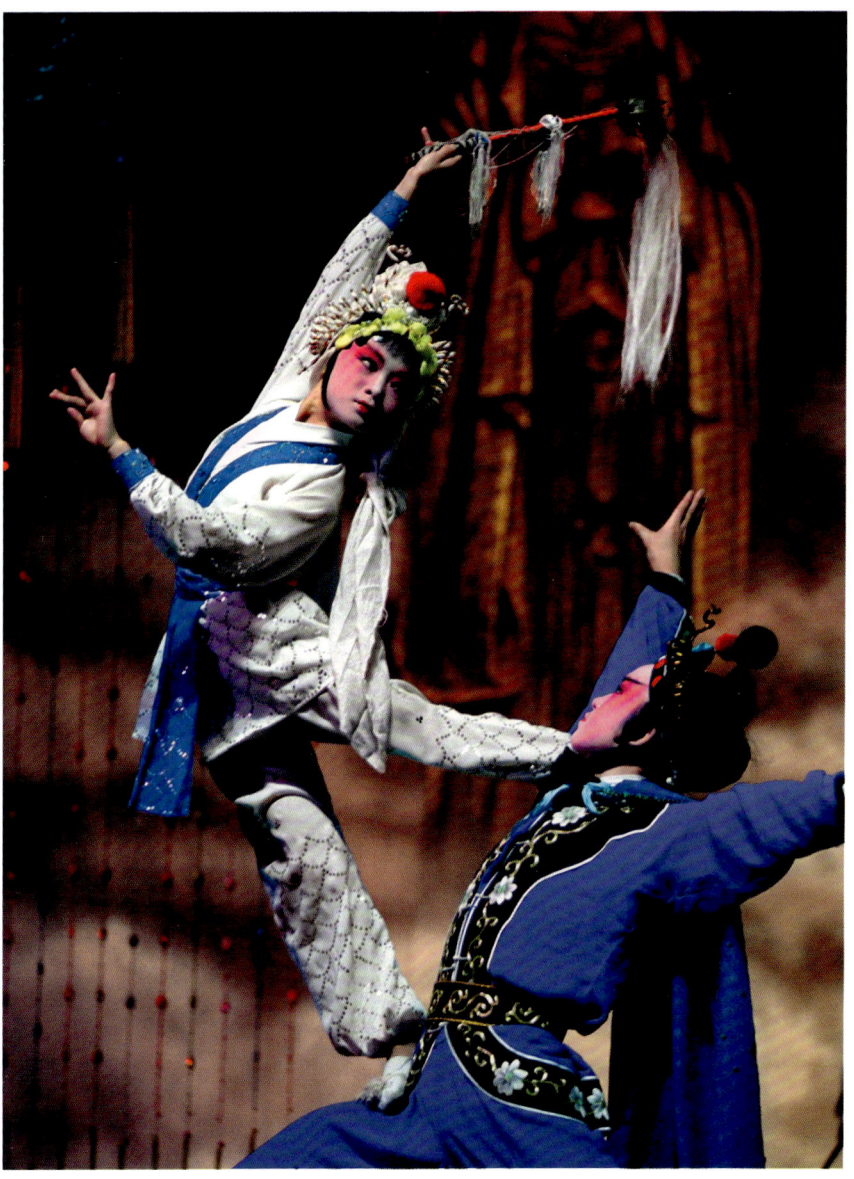

Photo 3.47 *Flooding the Golden Mountain Temple*, Sichuan Opera

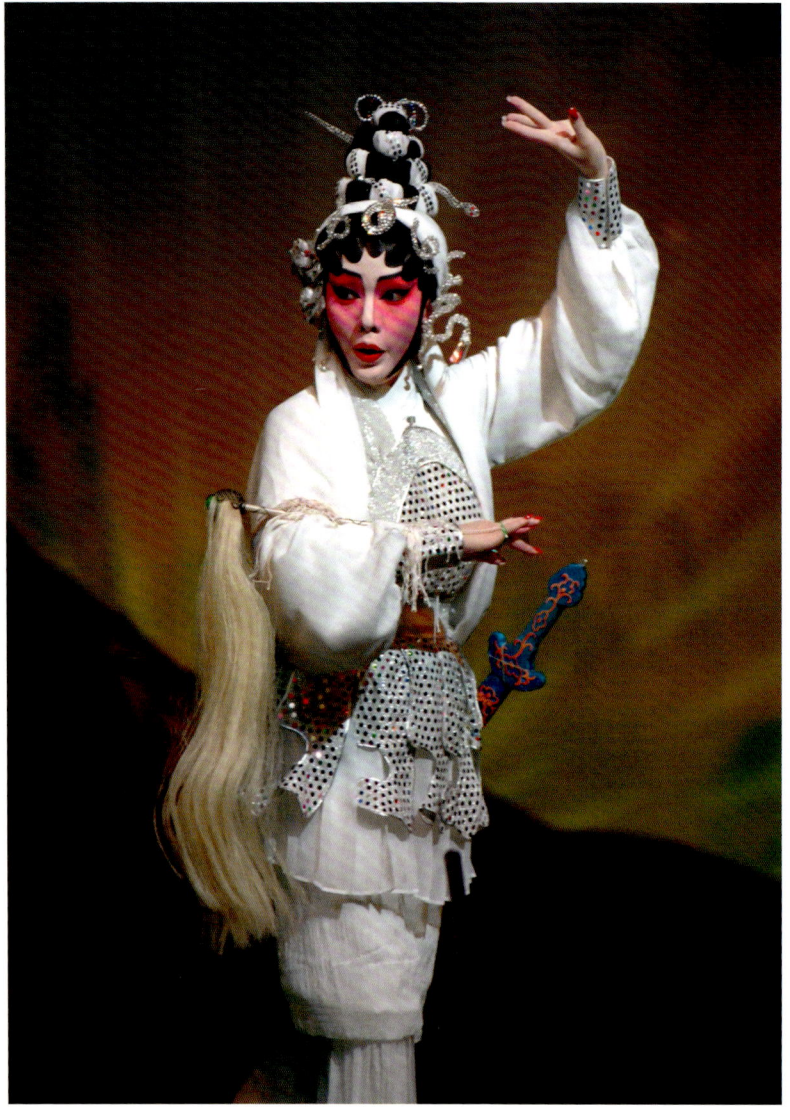

Photo 3.48 *The Legend of the White Snake*, Cantonese Opera

Actors use the whisk in a number of conventions which elegantly express meaning. One of these moves is used in *The Legend of the White Snake*. A snake spirit, White Snake, incarnated as a beautiful woman and married a handsome young man. On one occasion, he sees her original form and collapses in fright. White Snake knows that the only way to resuscitate him is to obtain a medicinal grass from the top of a fairy mountain. Arriving on the mountain, she uses a move called "embrace the whisk" to indicate that she is looking about at a distance. The whisk rests across her right arm and is held fast by her ring finger. Her left hand circles up, palm outward, while she gazes out into the expanse, searching for the fairy grass that will save her husband (see Photo 3.48). Challenged by two spirits of the mountain, she asks for the life-giving herb, and when refused, enters into battle.

Another magical being, Lü Dongbin, the immortal mentioned above, also carries a cloud whisk when he descends to earth to play tricks on an unsuspecting shop girl in a Chinese pharmacy. He decides to teach her a lesson when she claims that her shop has every kind of medicine that can be found. He

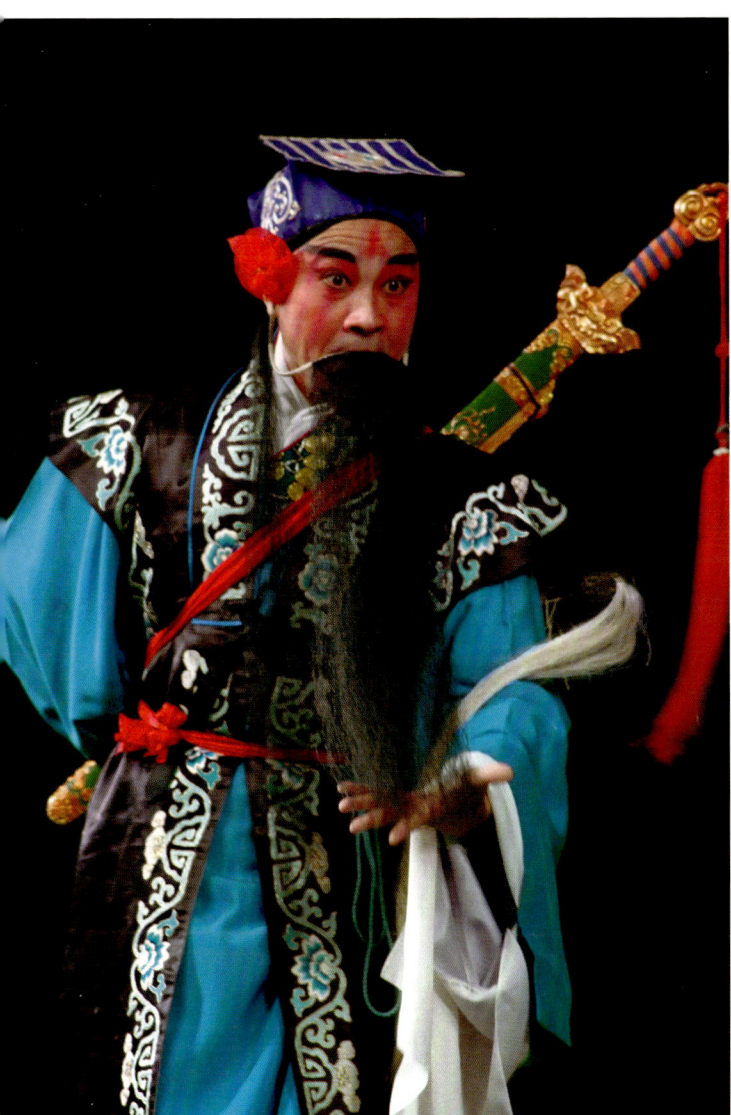

Photo 3.49 *Crossing Wits*, Hui Opera

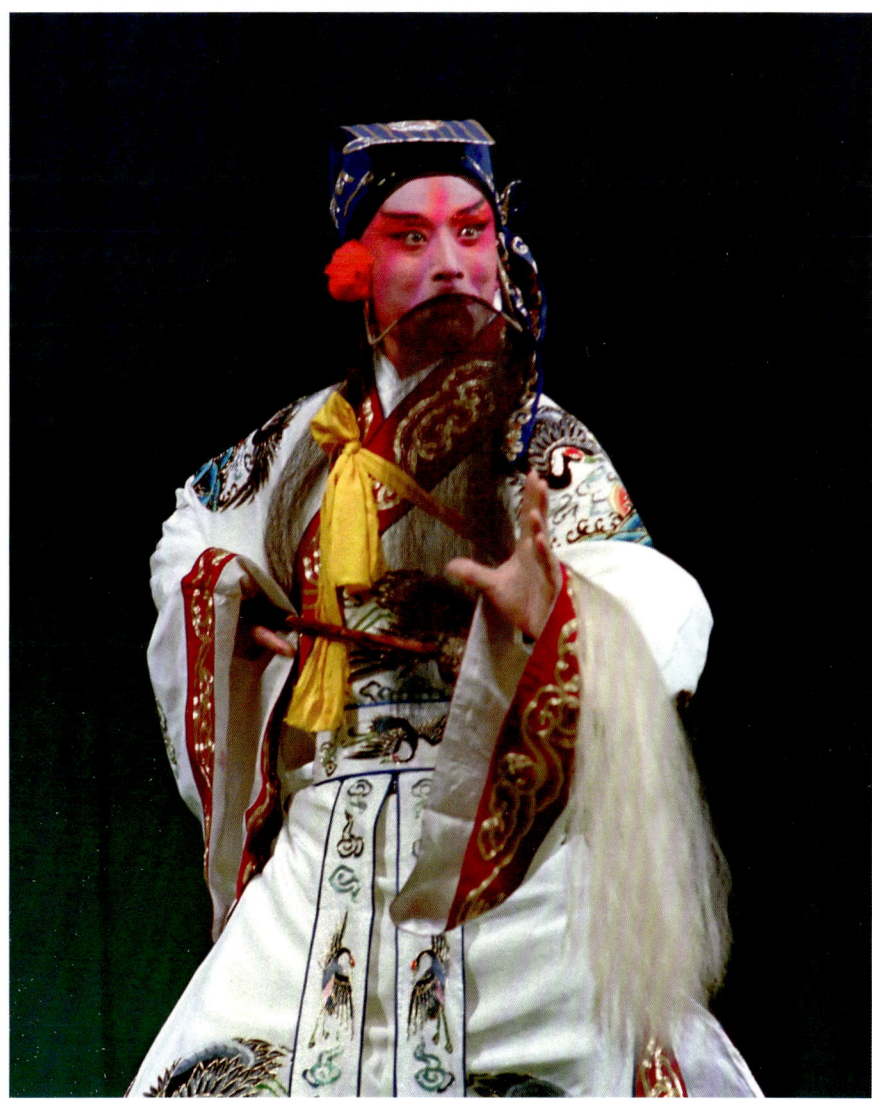

Photo 3.50 *The Eight Immortals Cross the Sea*, Peking Opera

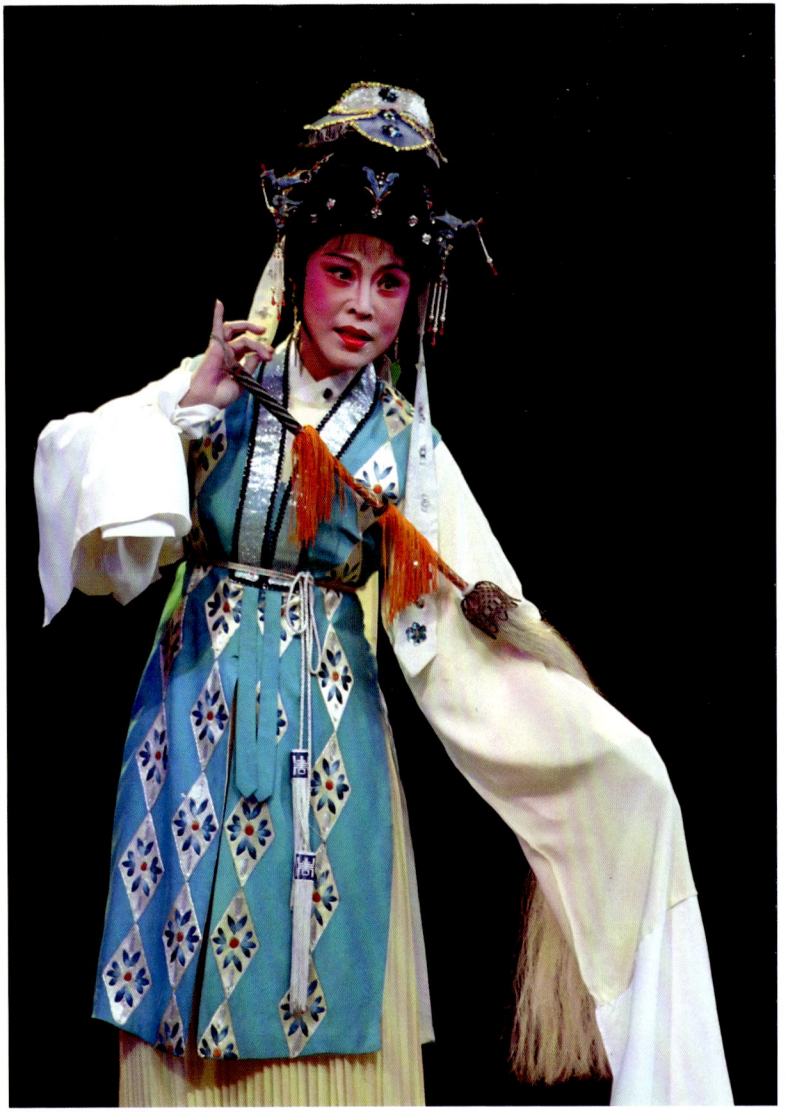

Photo 3.51 *Finding Mother in a Convent*, Yue Opera

begins to order up exotic, strange medicines and herbs of which no one has ever heard to confuse and frustrate her. Lü Dongbin uses the cloud whisk in a move called the "back whisk" to show his confidence as he plays his trick. Holding the whisk directly behind his back, he flips up the horse tail until it rests on his left arm (see Photo 3.49).

In another opera, *The Eight Immortals Cross the Sea*, Lü Dongbin appears on the shore of the Eastern Sea with seven other immortals returning from a grand banquet in heaven. The sea is rough, and each uses their magic powers to cross it. Lü Dongbin holds out his cloud whisk, establishing his identity (see Photo 3.50). He expects the Goldfish Fairy, who lives in the sea, to submit to their authority, but finds he is badly mistaken and has a formidable opponent in her.

Whereas White Snake and Lü Dongbin are magical beings, Zhizhen is human. She is a Buddhist nun who has been in the convent for more than eighteen years. As a young girl, she fell in love with a young scholar and found herself with child. Not knowing what to do, she abandoned the child on the

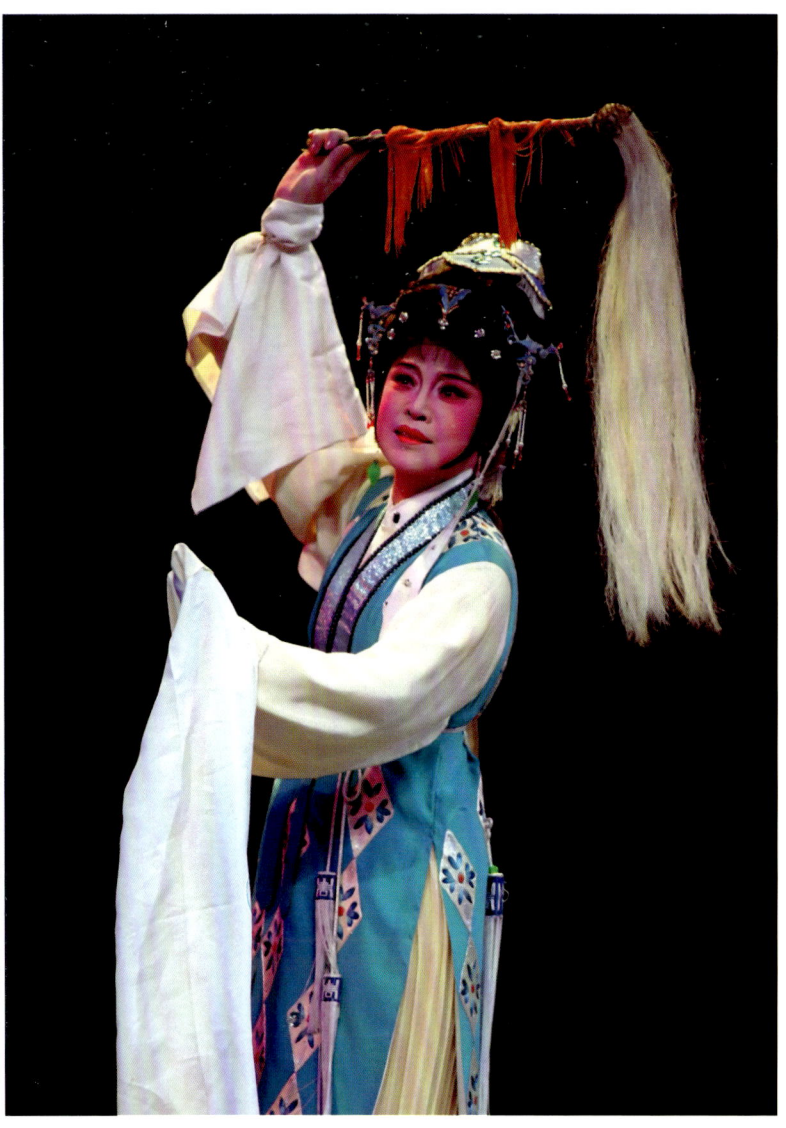

Photo 3.52 *Finding Mother in a Convent*, Yue Opera

side of the road to be adopted by a kind-hearted passer-by. She fled and entered the convent. Eighteen years later, that child is now a young man and is in search of his birth mother. Zhizhen does not dare to reveal that she knows who he is, and uses the cloud whisk in a number of ways that demonstrate her conflicted feelings. In one move, she flips the whisk high and lets the horse tail fall over her extended left arm (see Photo 3.51).

Later, she extends her long water sleeve while holding the cloud whisk over her head, the horse tail hanging down behind her (see Photo 3.52).

Monks, too, carry the cloud whisk, both sincere ones and not so sincere ones. Lu Zhishen is a lusty, hard-drinking hero and outlaw. Hiding out in a monastery, he has taken on the role of a monk. He is known and loved by Chinese opera audiences for his loyalty, superior fighting skills and love of good wine. In one particular bout of drinking during which he causes an uproar at the monastery, he performs

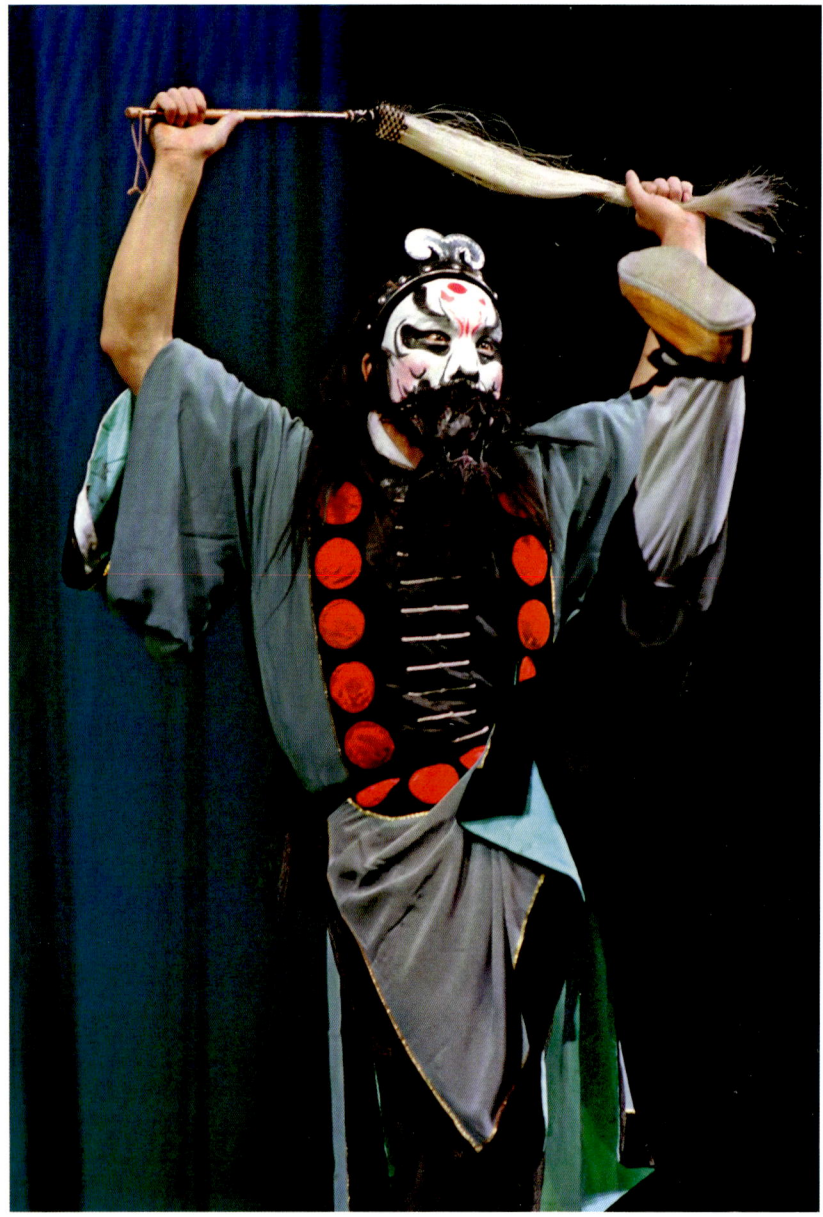

Photo 3.53   *The Drunken Monk*, Peking Opera

a dance-like movement that culminates in the "umbrella whisk". He flips the cloud whisk over his head, catches the horse tail in his left hand and poses, executing a high kick (see Photo 3.53).

Unlike the horsewhip or the fan, each of which has its own function, the cloud whisk in Chinese opera is primarily a stage tool for the elegant execution of movement. Actors manipulate the beautiful flowing horse tail in moves and poses, incorporating it into the action of the play.

Paddle and Boat Pole

Several Chinese operas call for boats on the stage. The question is how to represent both the boat and the movement across water. The Chinese solution is a combination of representative props and mime. The actor implies the whole by using the part, an essential element in Chinese stagecraft.

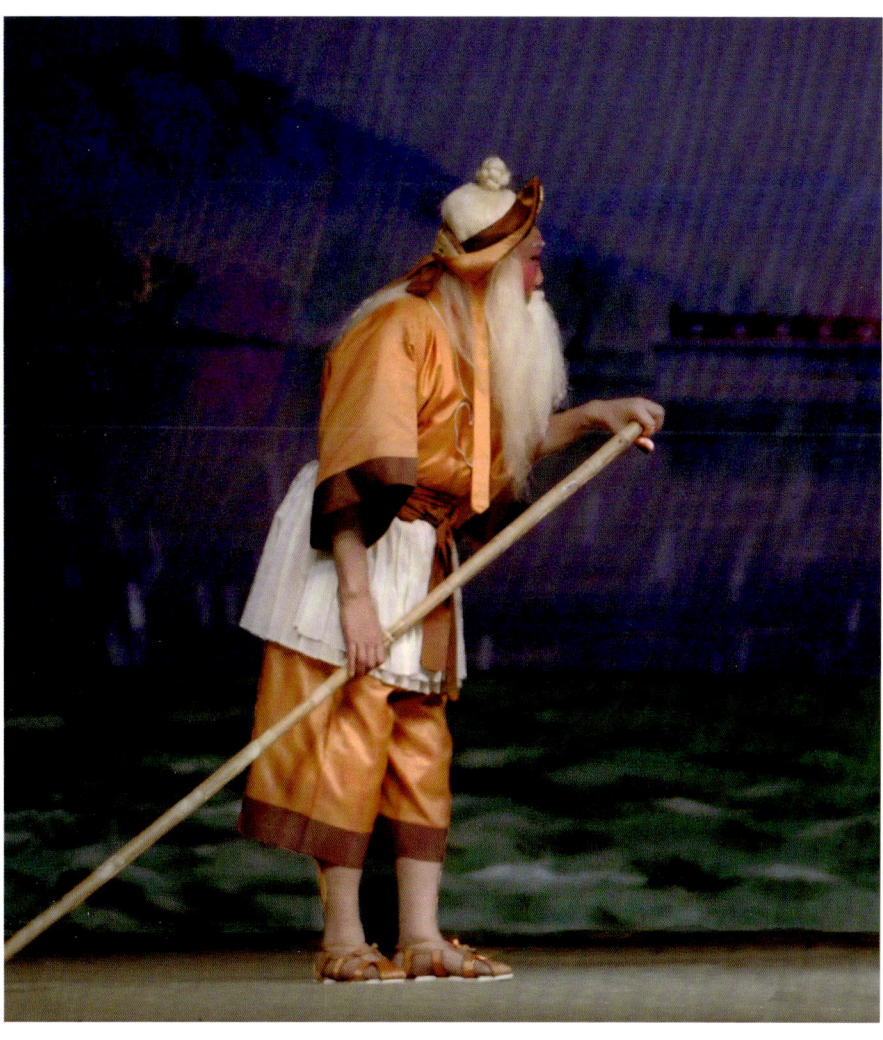

Photo 3.54 *The Legend of the White Snake*, Cantonese Opera

Actors can evoke large boats by arranging themselves with large paddles or oars on both sides of the imaginary craft. To complete the effect, another actor stands at the back with the rudder. As the waves rock the boat on its journey, the actors on one side crouch down, while the actors on the other side rise up. This rising and falling continues in a back-and-forth motion to demonstrate both the boat and its movement (see Photo 3.55).

Another traditional way to propel a small boat is the boat pole. In the popular opera *The Legend of the White Snake*, the snake spirit, in human form, wants to marry the young gentleman Xu Xian. While on a boat ride on the beautiful West Lake, she calls down a storm so that she can take advantage of his umbrella. An old boatman stands at the back of the craft, moving the small boat with his pole (see Photo 3.56).

When the abbot of the Golden Mountain Temple learns that White Snake has, in fact, married Xu Xian, he decides to take matters into his own hands. In order to protect Xu Xian from an unnatural marriage, the abbot tricks him into coming to the temple. Once there, the monk holds Xu Xian so that White Snake cannot get at him. White Snake and her ally Green Snake head to the temple by boat in an effort to rescue Xu Xian. White Snake holds the paddle as she brings her boat closer to the mountain (see Photo 3.57).

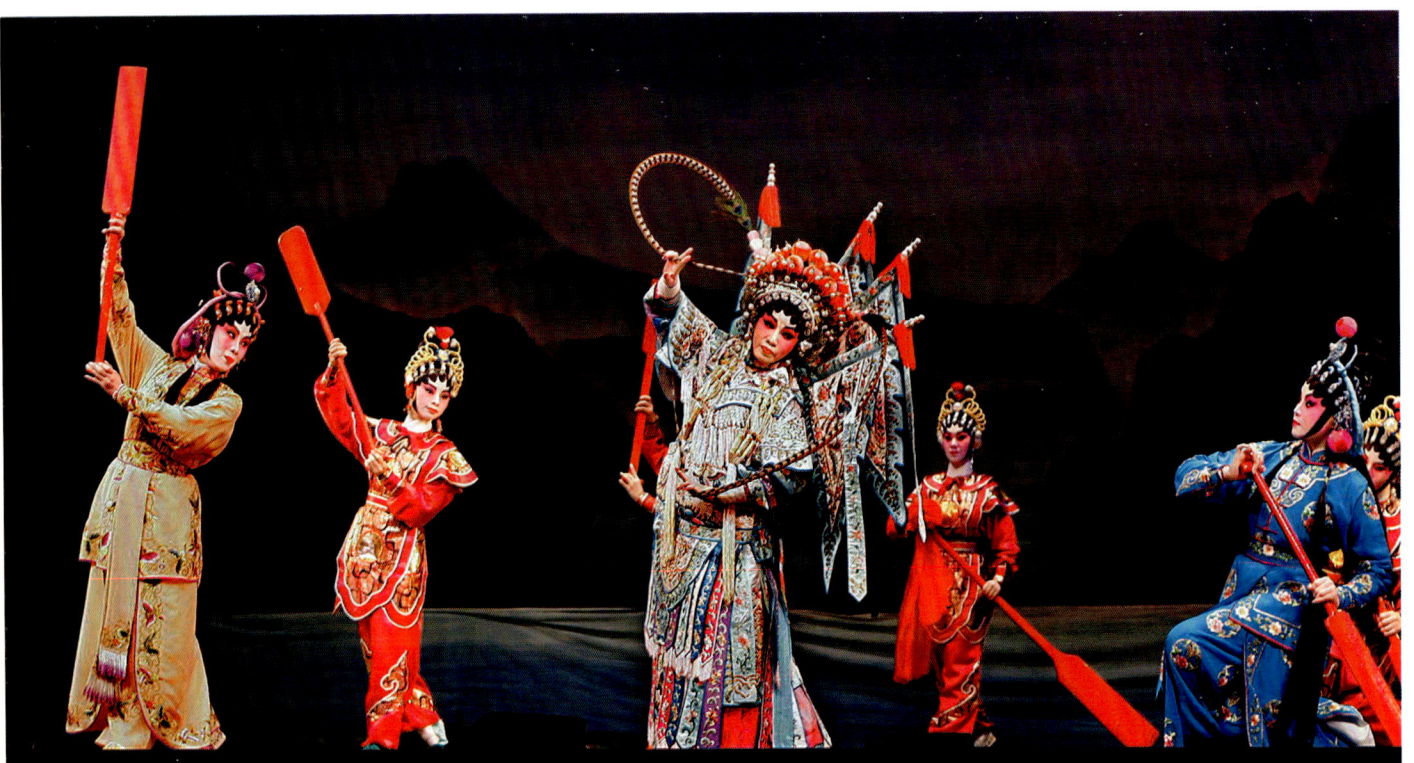

Photo 3.55 *The Dragon Phoenix Battle*, Cantonese Opera

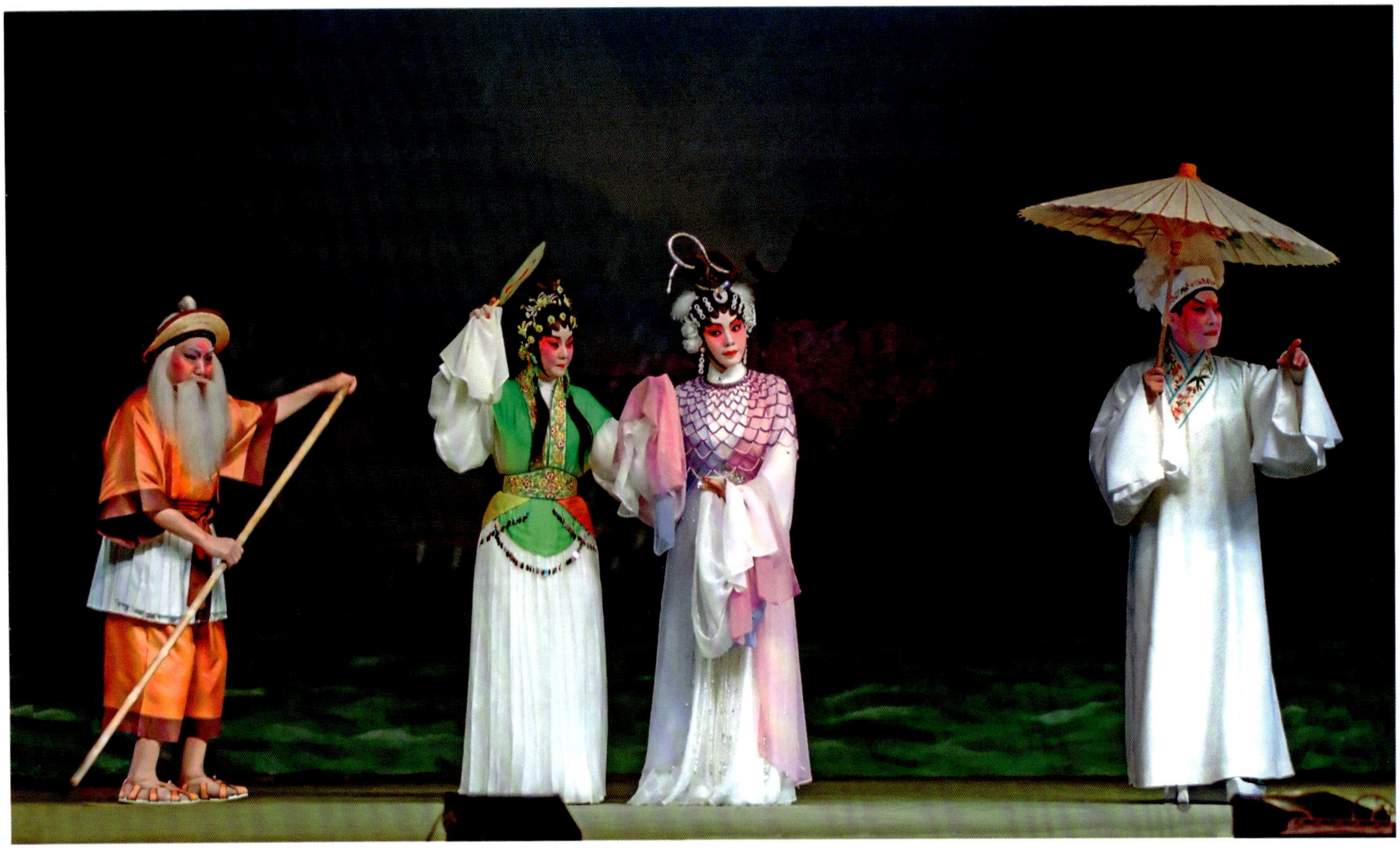

Photo 3.56 *The Legend of the White Snake*, Cantonese Opera

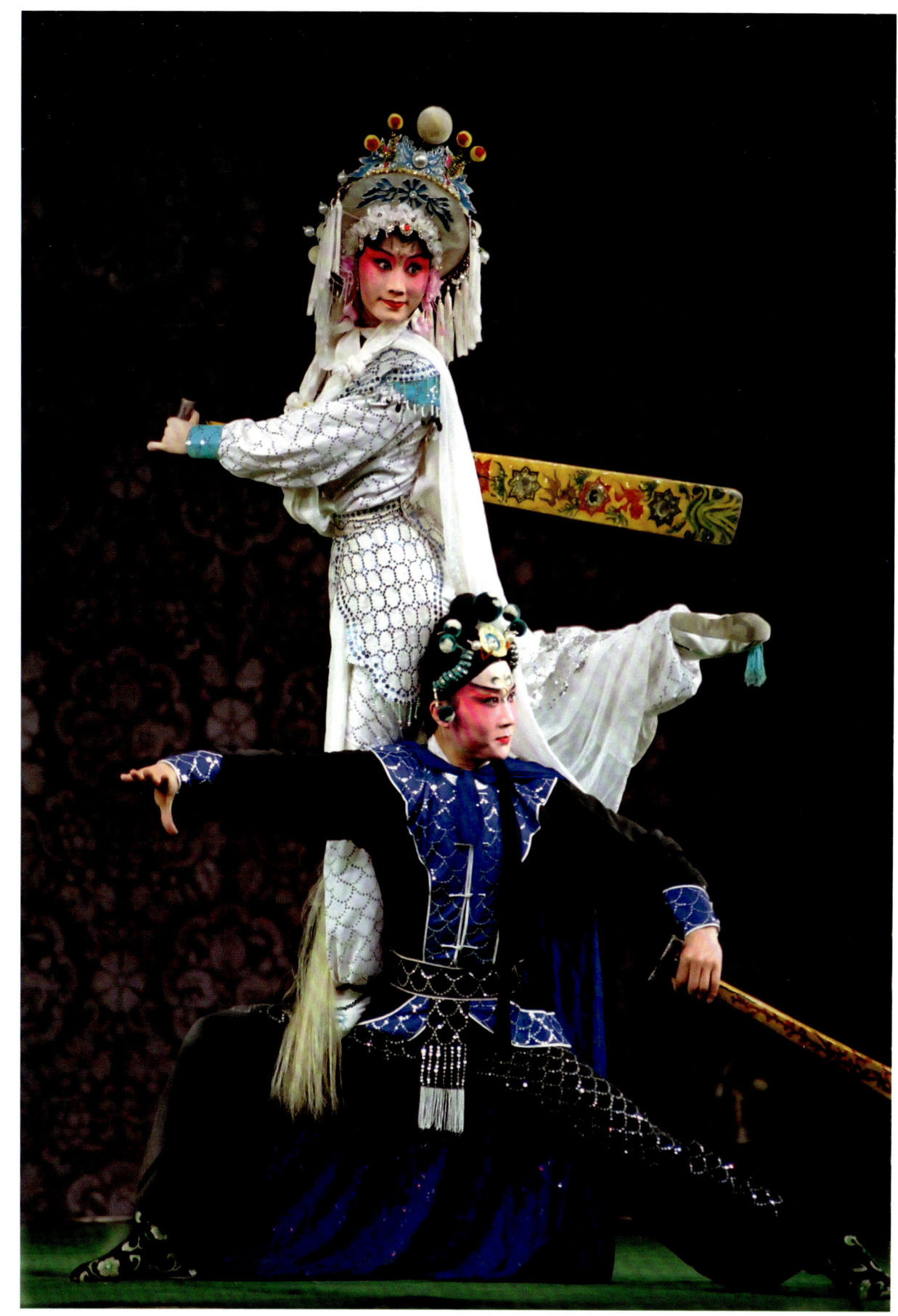

Photo 3.57 *The Legend of the White Snake*, Sichuan Opera

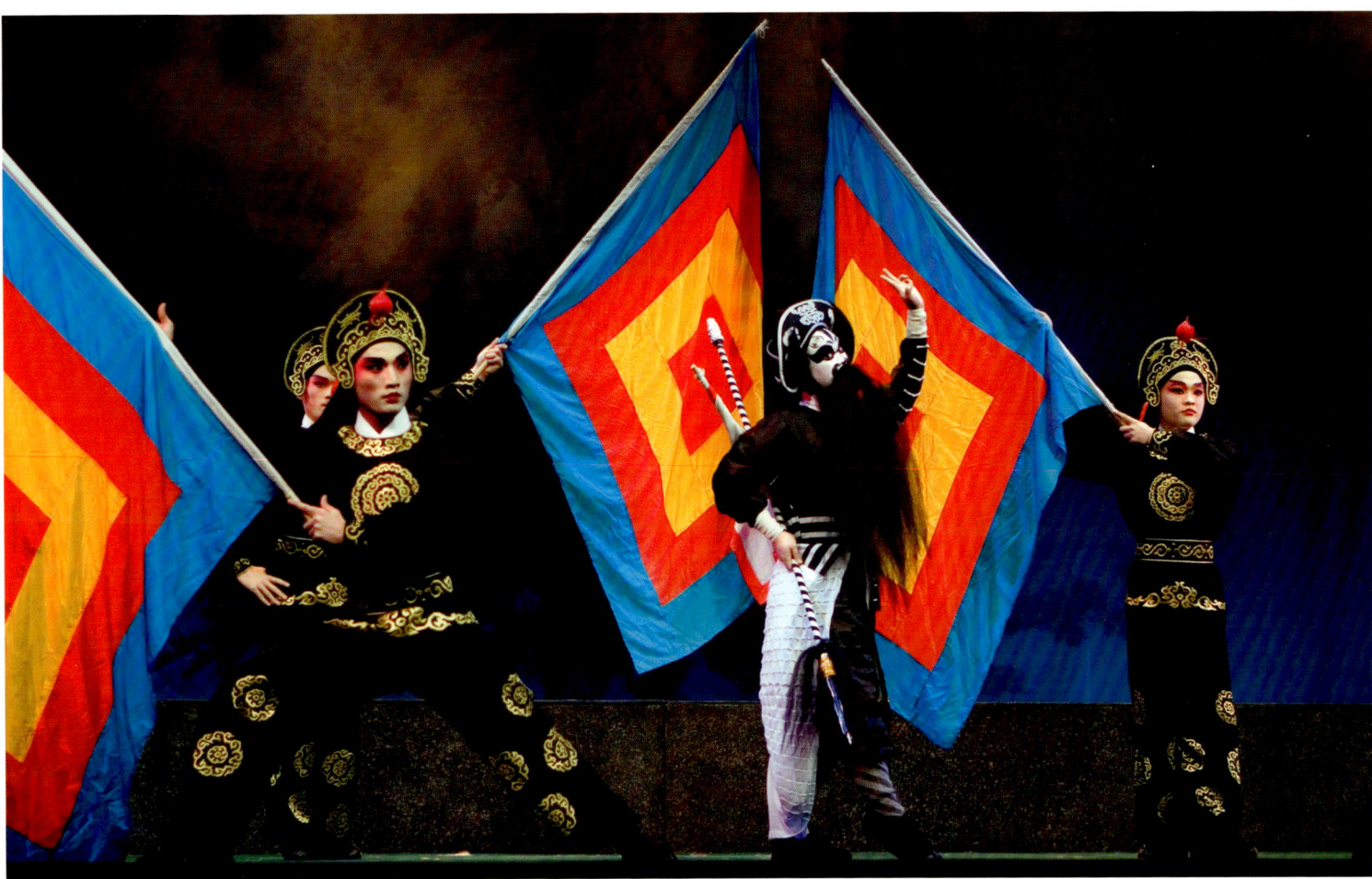

Photo 3.58 *The Battle of Baqiu*, Cantonese Opera

Flag

FLAGS ADD COLOUR and excitement to the opera stage. Actors use them in battle and acrobatics. They wield them to symbolize storms, and even vehicles. Their portability, colour, and clarity make them ideal props to serve a wide range of purposes.

One of the most common purposes is military. A command flag indicates orders to lead the troops. It is a white flag with a single Chinese character "command" written large in the middle. In the opera *Splendour Tower*, the warrior Li Cunxiao carries such a flag to lead his soldiers against the enemy camp. Other flags held by his troops wave behind him (see Photo 3.59). These are flying tiger flags, indicating valiant and ferocious fighters. Flying tiger flags use four squares of bold colours, red, blue and yellow, enclosing each other. A white square sits in the centre with the image of a tiger and flame indicating the power of the army. There are normally four to eight flags waving on the stage as the battle begins.

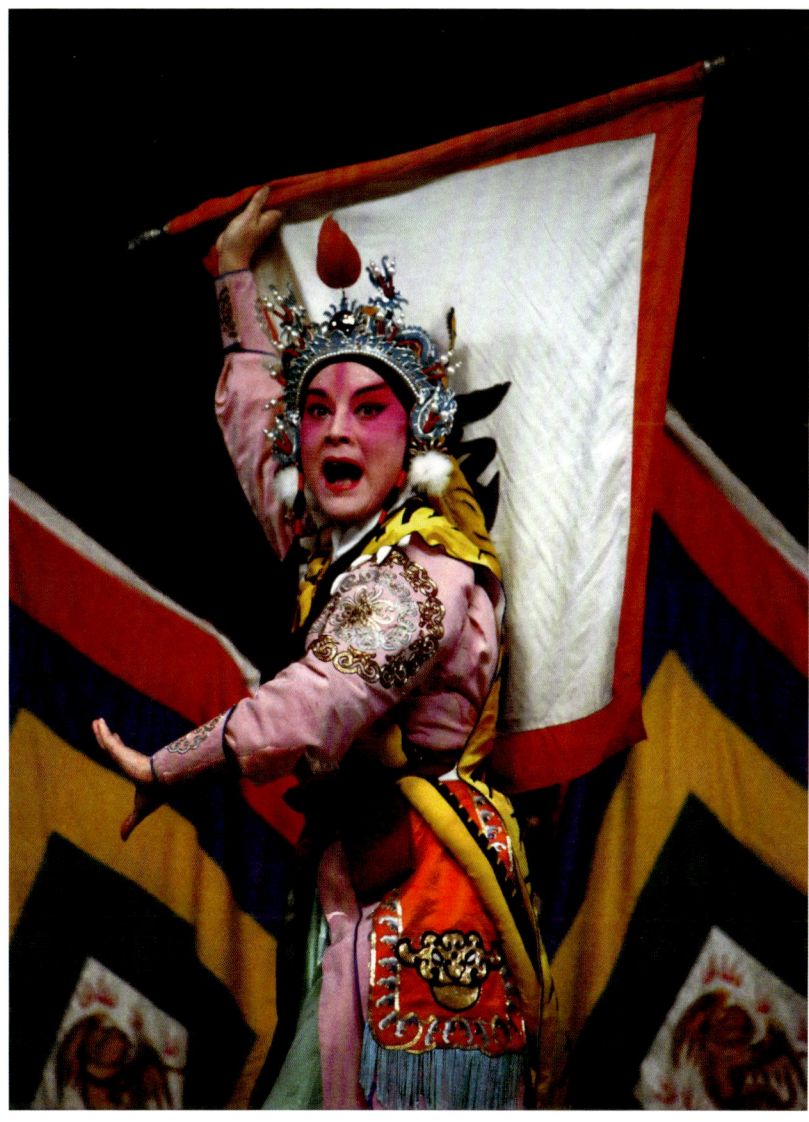

Photo 3.59 *Splendour Tower,* Kunqu Opera

Magical beings also use the command flag. In one opera, Wave Walker, a fairy, prepares to go to war with heavenly spirits. She holds her command flag to lead her sea troops into battle. Behind her, her female warriors hold sea-green water flags; these represent the various kinds of sea life in her aquatic army (see Photo 3.60).

In addition to the flying tiger flags, stage fighters also carry the moonlight flag. These large flags are a series of concentric squares: red, green, yellow and white. Actors walk about the stage waving them vigorously signifying that the general is about to make his entrance (see Photo 3.61).

Flags can also be used in war to stand for more than concepts. They can also represent something as concrete as a war cart. When an actor carries flags with a wheel design, the opera audience know they are now looking at some kind of cart. In the military opera *Tilting the War Carts* the general Gao Chong pursues his enemy up a mountain. In a desperate attempt to block his way, the enemy pushes down war cart after war cart behind them. The heavy war cart is accomplished on stage by an actor holding

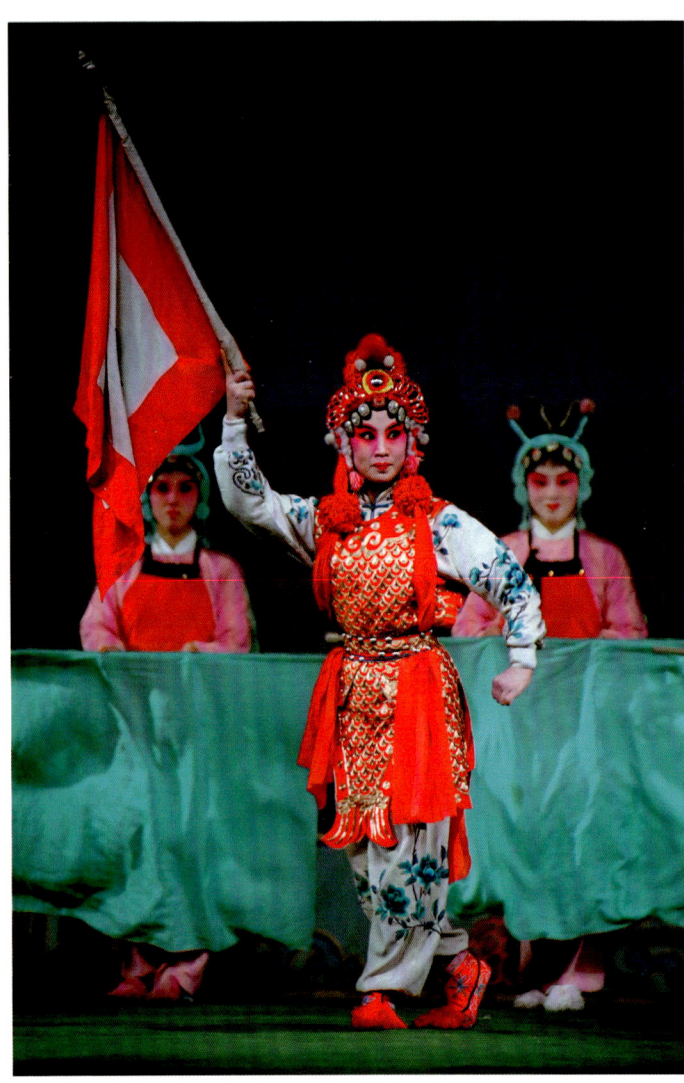

Photo 3.60 *Bringing the Magic Pearl Over the Rainbow Bridge*, Peking Opera

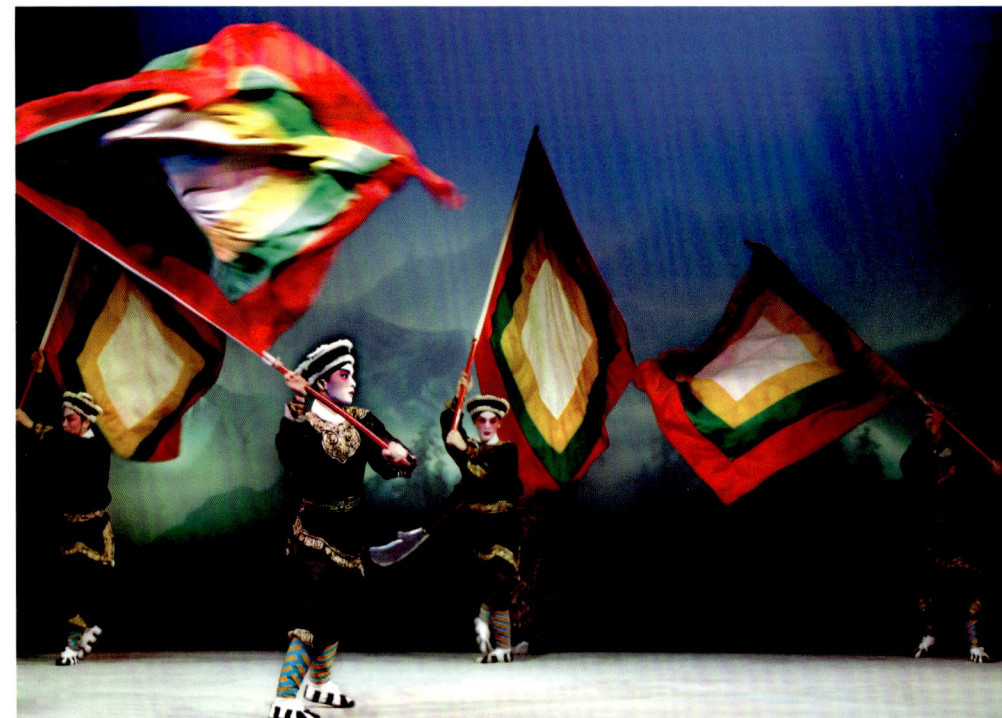

Photo 3.61 *Xue Dingshan Thrice Angers Fan Lihua*, Cantonese Opera

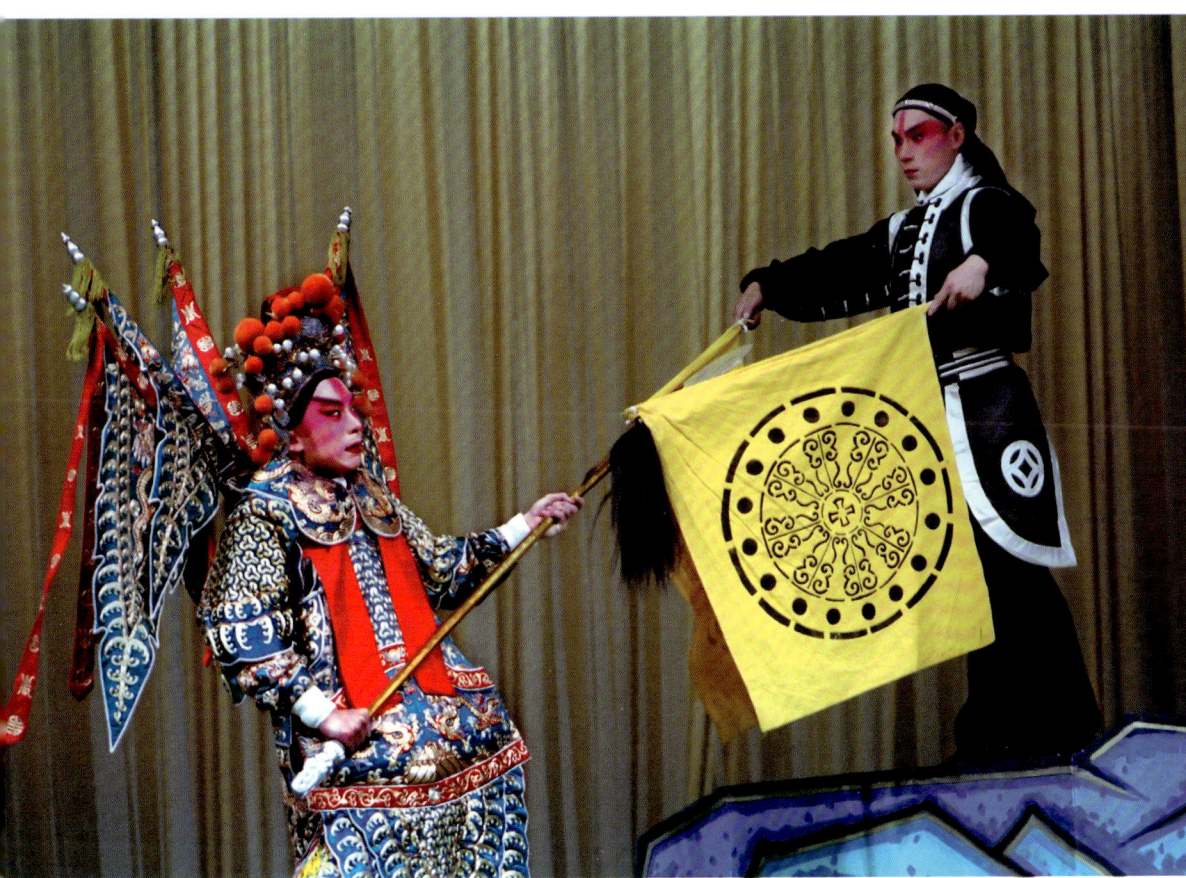

Photo 3.62 *Tilting the War Carts*, Peking Opera

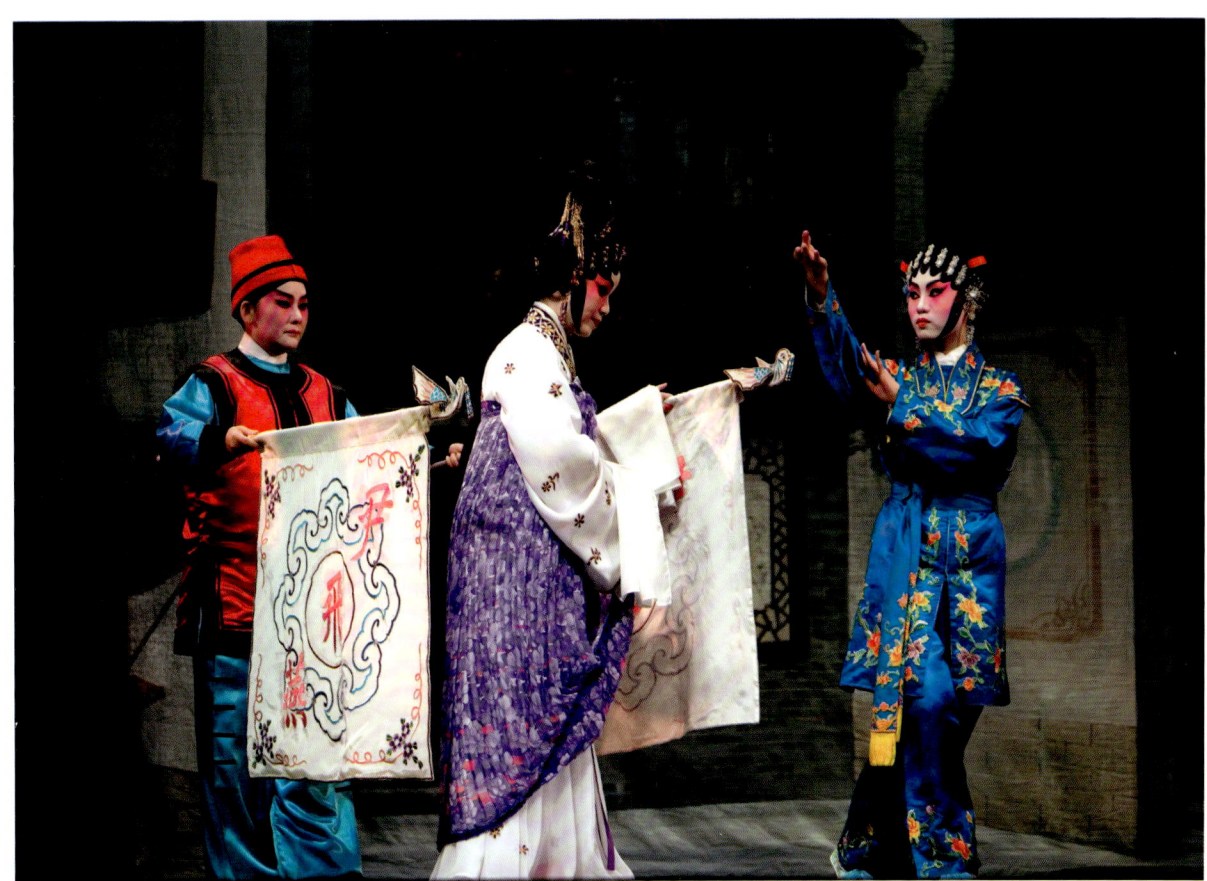

Photo 3.63 *Worshipping the Moon*, Cantonese Opera

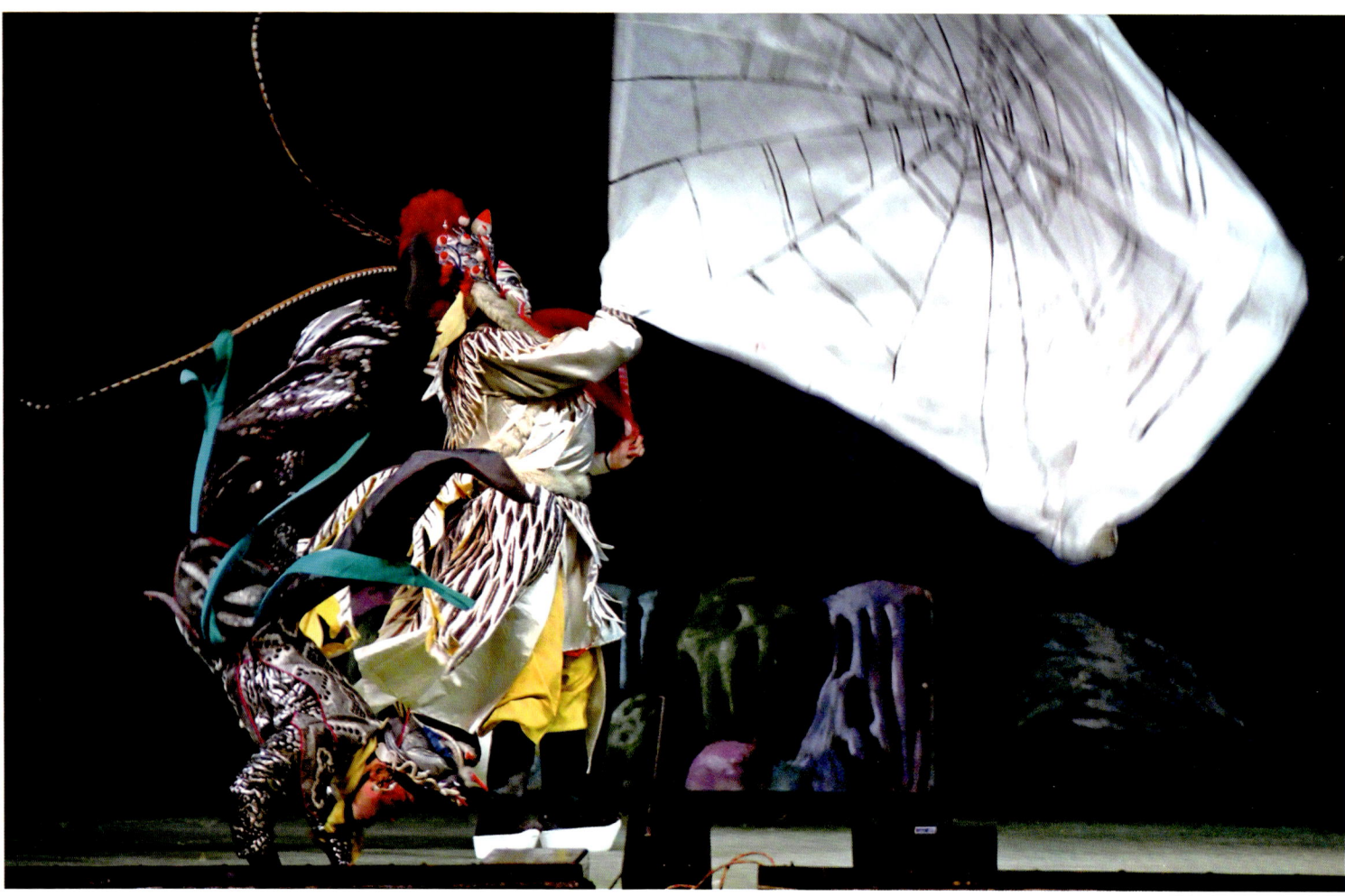

Photo 3.64 *The Cave of Spiders*, Peking Opera

out two flags horizontally so that the wheel designs suggest cart wheels on the road. Gao Chong angrily tilts the sliding carts running towards him using his big spear (see Photo 3.62). He succeeds in tipping the first carts with ease, but needs more strength to tilt over the following carts. Finally, both he and his exhausted horse are crushed by the twelfth cart.

Flags can also suggest a normal passenger carriage. In *Worshipping the Moon*, the young maiden Wang Ruilan descends from her carriage. The carriage is established by an actor holding out two flags with decorative wheel designs, and a servant girl who mimes holding open a curtain that covers the entrance (see Photo 3.63).

Flags can also suggest the fantastic. The Monkey King protects the monk Xuanzang on his mission to India to get the Buddhist scriptures and bring them back to China. Several operas take stories from the classic novel *Journey to the West* to tell tales of various demons and monsters who threaten the travellers along the way. One of these creatures, a spider spirit, attacks the Monkey King in her cave. She uses a flag with a web design to demonstrate the casting of her web over her prey (see Photo 3.64).

Cloud

Heavenly beings regularly descend to earth in clouds, or battle other heavenly beings among the clouds. To establish clouds, Chinese opera uses cloud boards. These are made of plywood and are usually manipulated by stage extras. The first time White Snake and Green Snake descend to the mortal world in human form, they ride on clouds held up behind and stretched across in front of them (see Photo 3.66).

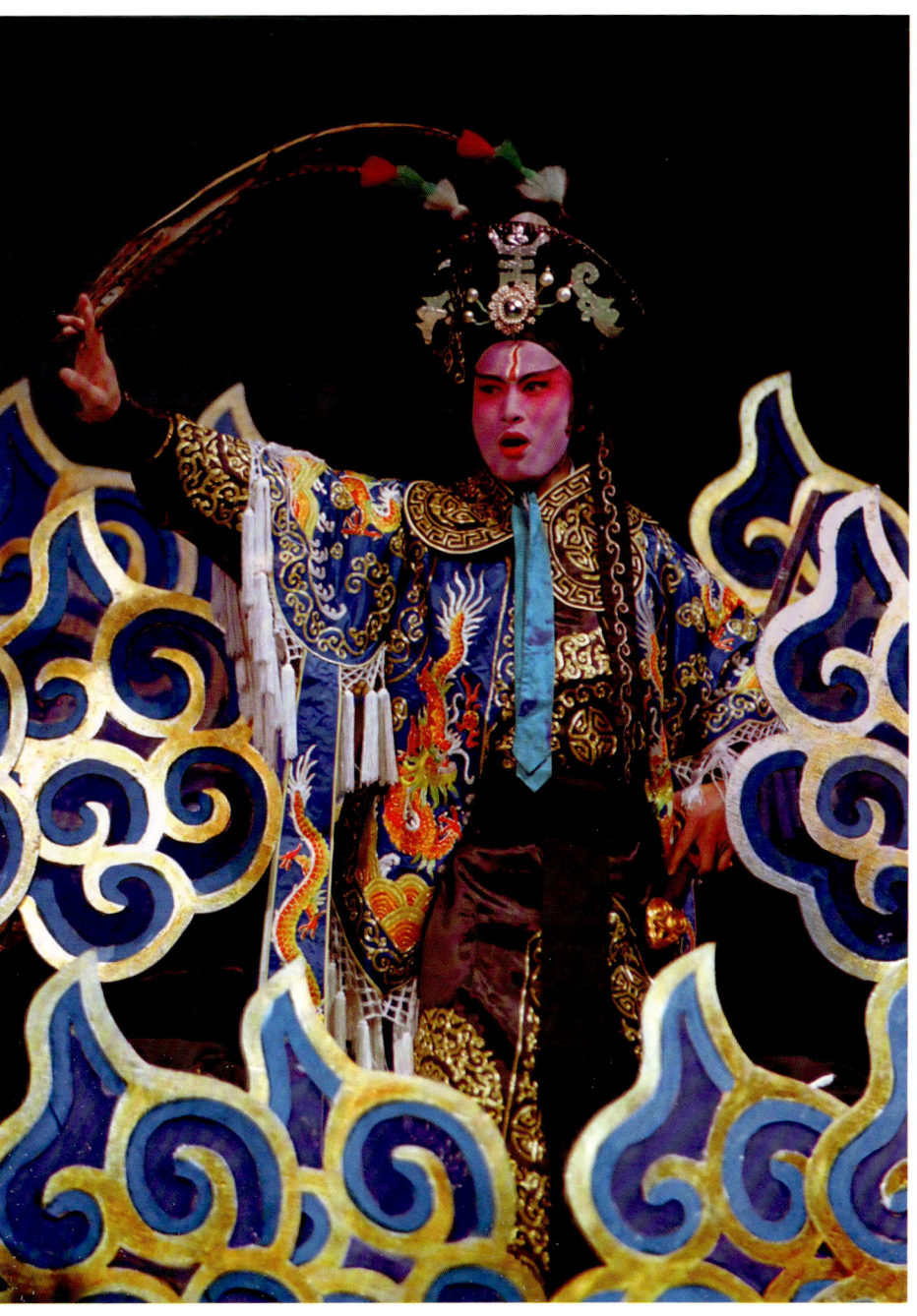

Photo 3.65   *The Legend of the White Snake*, Sichuan Opera

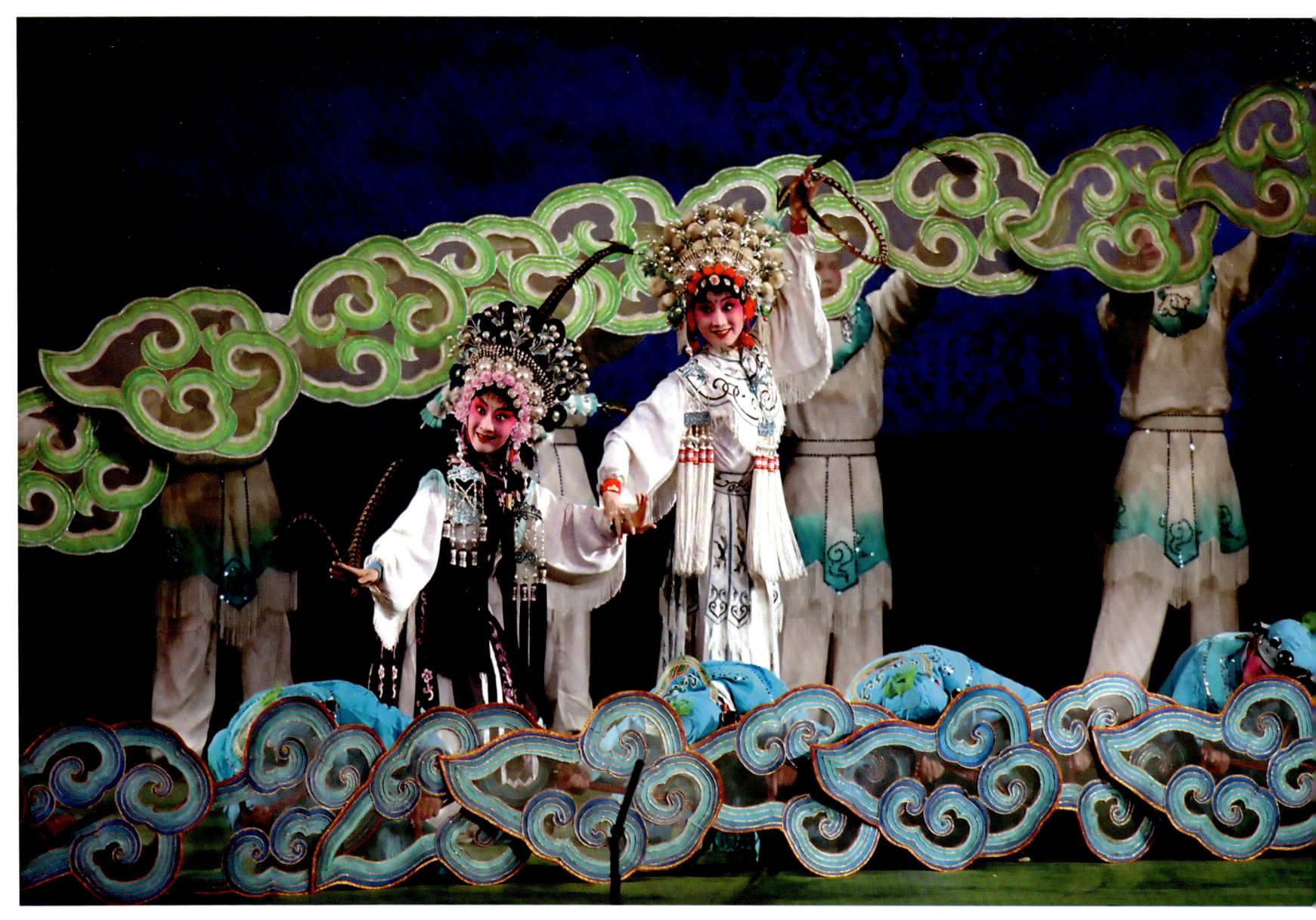

Photo 3.66 *The Legend of the White Snake*, Sichuan Opera

Using Props

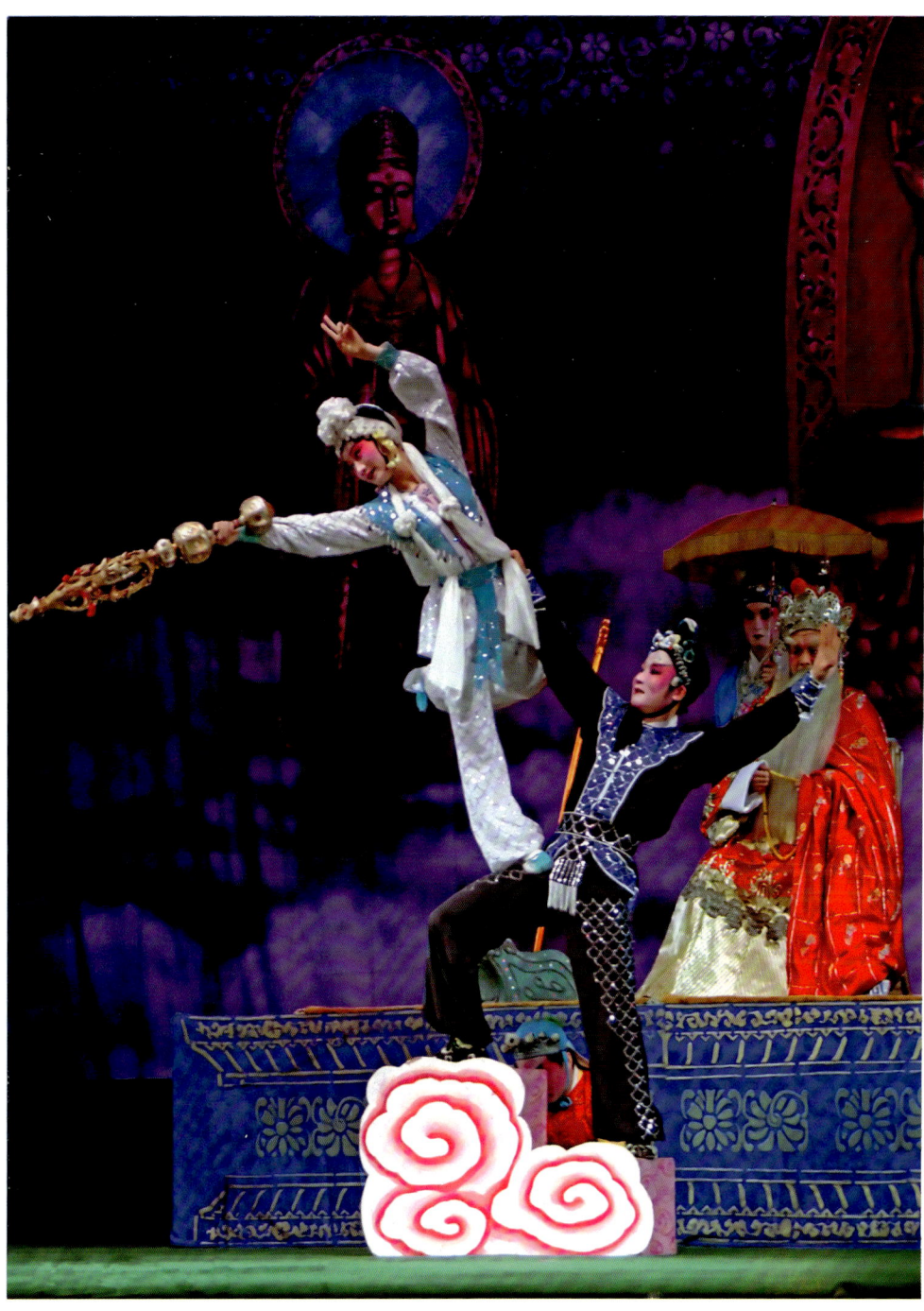

Photo 3.67 *The Legend of the White Snake*, Sichuan Opera

During the battle at the Golden Mountain Temple with the heavenly forces called down by the abbot Fahai, White Snake and Green Snake show that they are fighting the Buddhist forces in the sky by standing on a decorated cloud platform (see Photo 3.67).

The Chinese opera stage solves the theatrical problem of bringing something larger on the stage by evoking it through representative props. Horses, houses, carts, boats, clouds or armies become believable through the actors' skills in using these props and mime. Fans, ribbons, handkerchiefs, and even horsewhips can also be used to make action and emotional states visible to the audience.

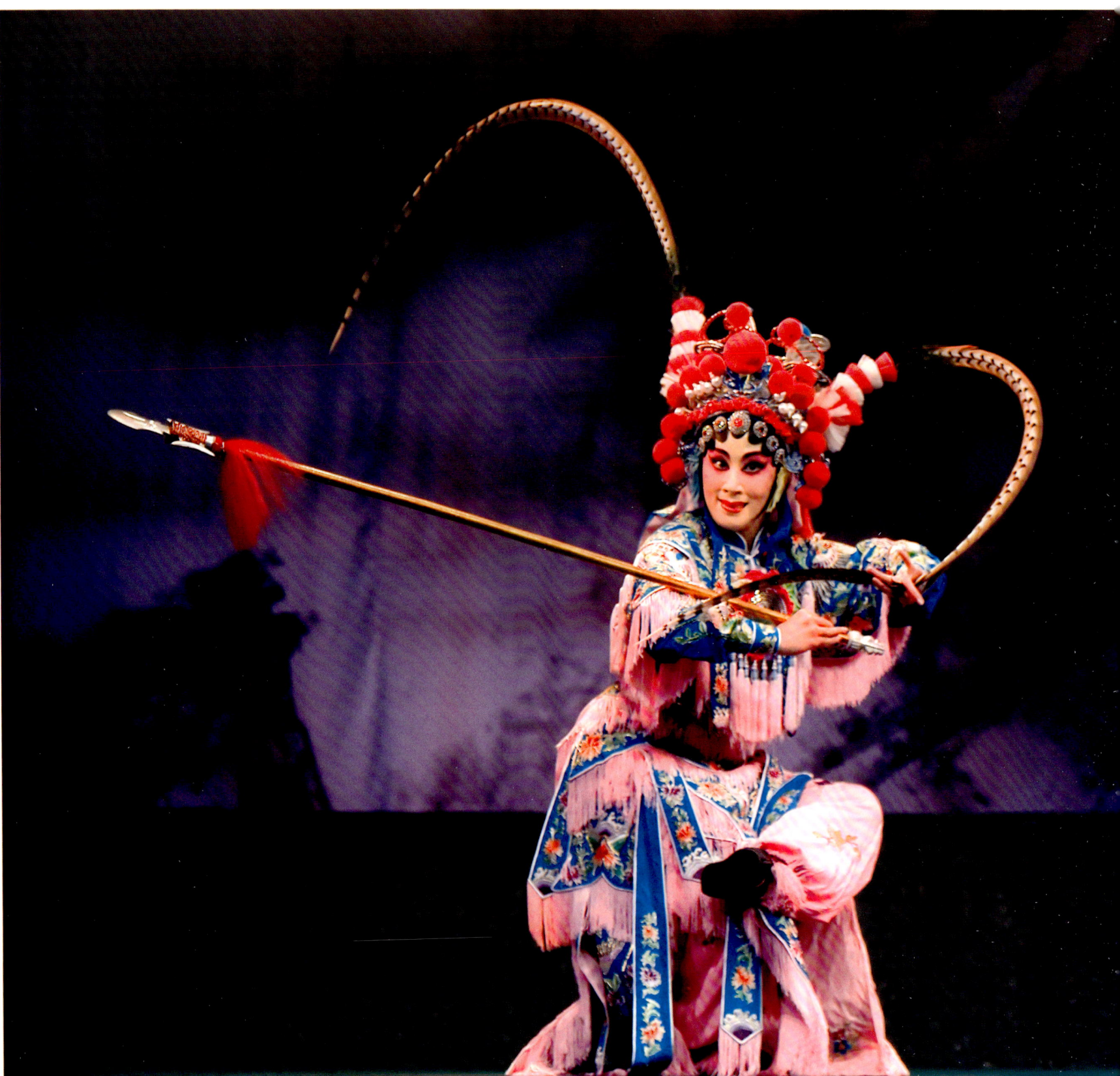

CHAPTER 4

Using Weapons and Skills for Stage Fighting

Opposite
Photo 4.01   *Raid on Hu Village,* Cantonese Opera

Spear

THE CHINESE STAGE becomes a battlefield in many operas. Great generals, heroes, villains and warrior maidens fight with a variety of weapons in carefully choreographed scenes requiring a high level of skill. One of the most common weapons used in these scenes is the spear. This weapon is light, long and flexible, ideal for combat with more than one adversary. Actors will parry, thrust and toss their spears through the air in a variety of ways that require not only manipulation of the weapon, but acrobatic skills as well.

There are different kinds of spears. The male warrior role regularly uses the long spear, which has a sharp blade at the head decorated with a tassel. The actor wields this weapon by holding it firmly at its end to get the maximum reach. A general, like Zhao Yun, wears full armour and is equipped with battle flags. He fights several armed warriors while mounted on horseback (see Photo 4.02). As the actor needs to manipulate the spear, he does not in this case carry the horsewhip that would normally signify the horse.

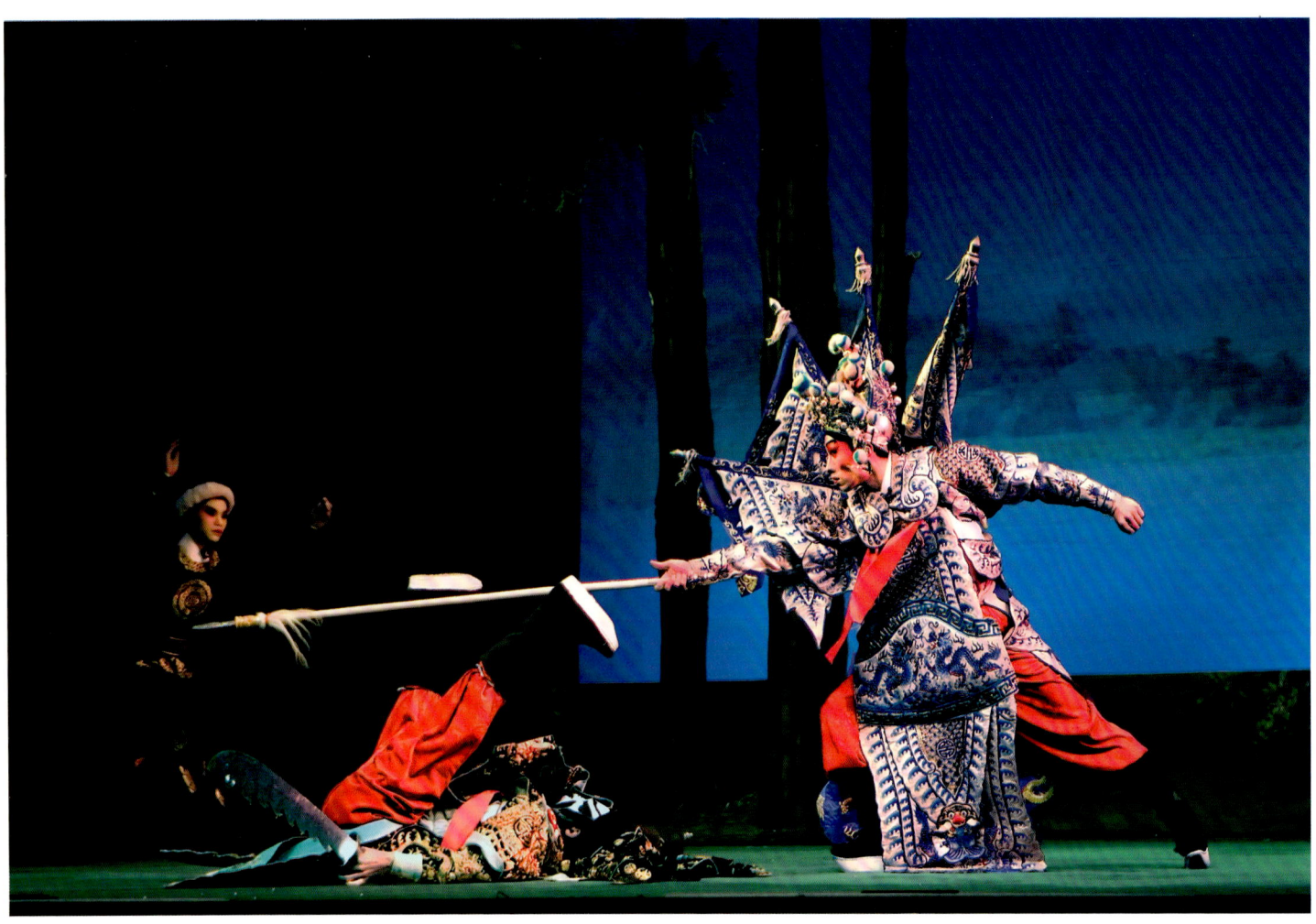

Photo 4.02 *Changban Slope,* Cantonese Opera

Female warriors often use the double-headed spear. This weapon is shorter than the male warrior's long spear, but has the advantage of a sharp blade at each end along with accompanying tassels. The warrior maiden Zhang Xiuying uses such a weapon to successfully fight off two soldiers with long spears in the opera *Phoenix Terrace Fortress* (see Photo 4.03).

Aside from warriors and generals, magical beings often use spears in battle as well. This kind of fighting, called *dachushou*, elevates the battlefield combat into a display of supernatural power. The spear, in particular, flies through the air of its own accord to attack immortals or magical beings, who use their own special powers to defend themselves. In one opera, *The Nine-Tailed Fox Fairy*, the Fox Fairy, an exceptional warrior, has fallen in love with a mortal and so refuses the advances of another fox spirit. Enraged at her rejection of him, he sends spirit warriors to capture her and bring her back. The Fox Fairy uses her feet to fend off the spirits that have encircled her (see Photo 4.04).

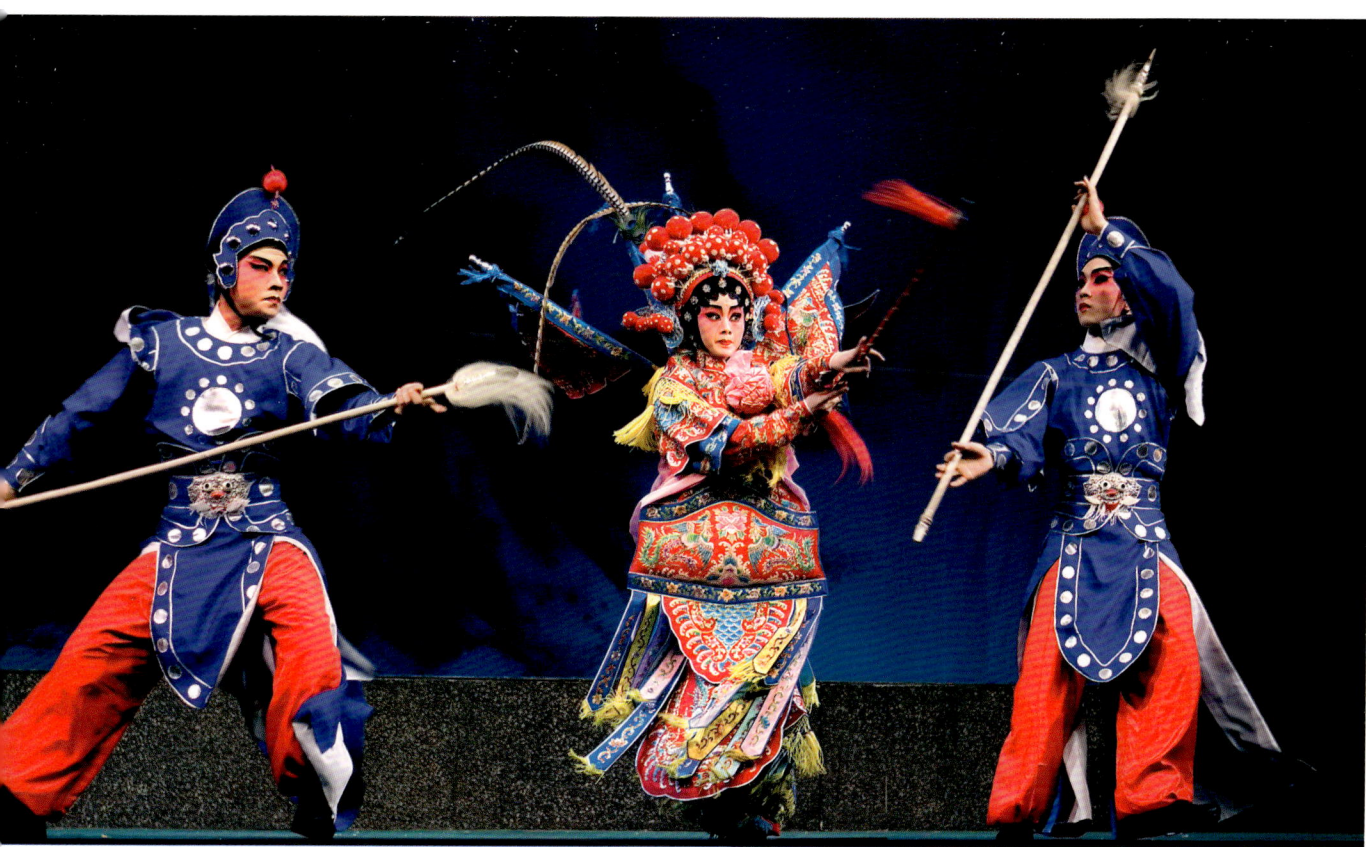

Photo 4.03 *Phoenix Terrace Fortress*, Cantonese Opera

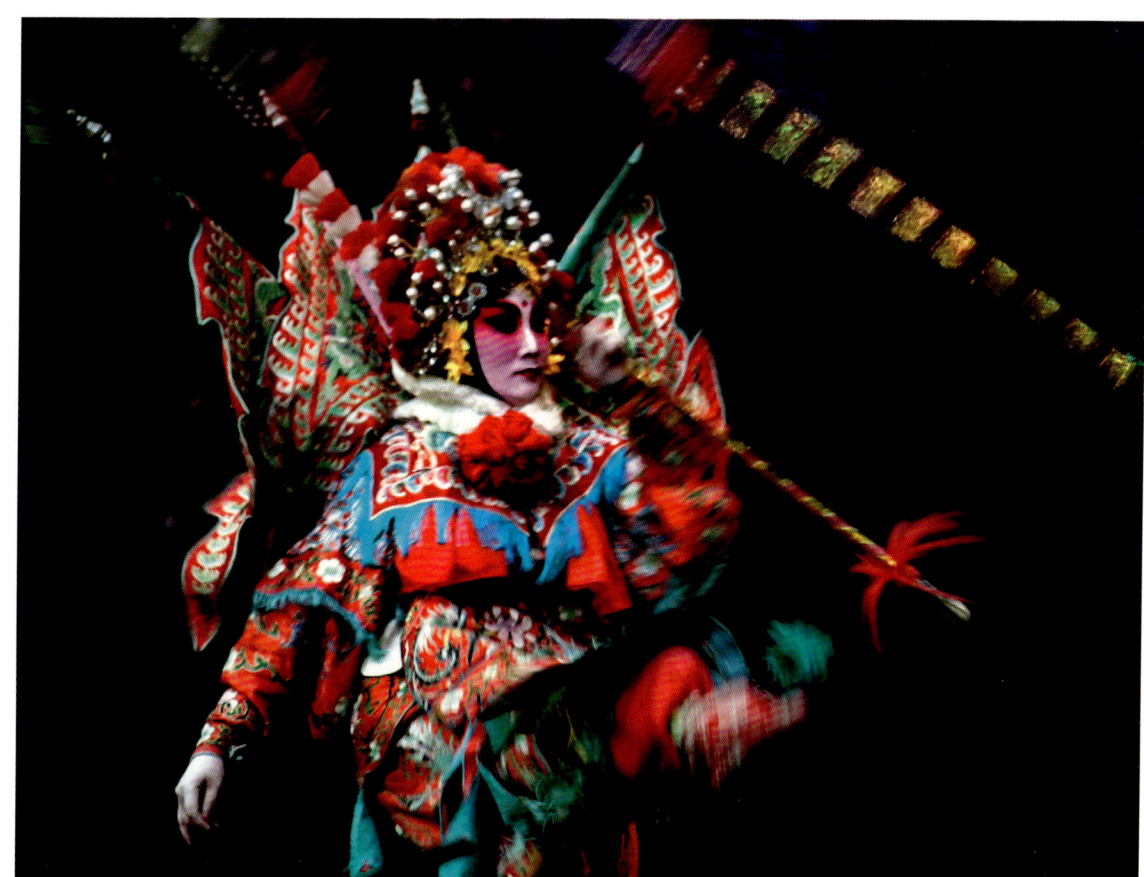

Photo 4.04 *The Nine-Tailed Fox Fairy*, Sichuan Opera

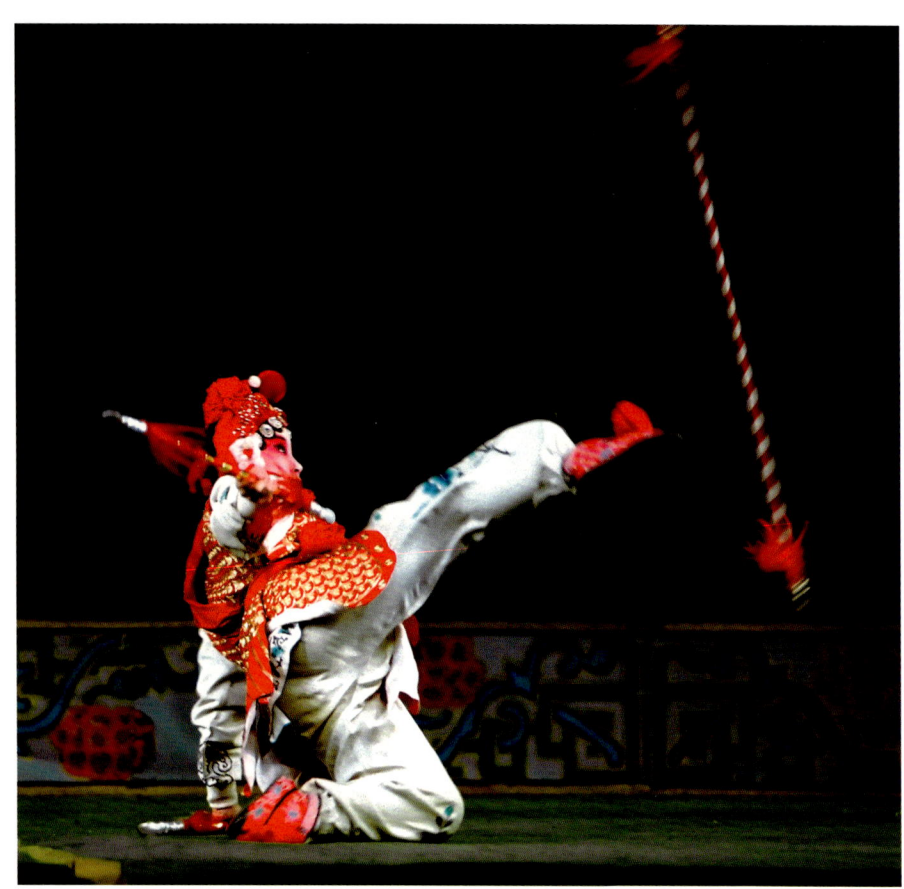

Photo 4.05 *Bringing the Magic Pearl Over the Rainbow Bridge*, Peking Opera

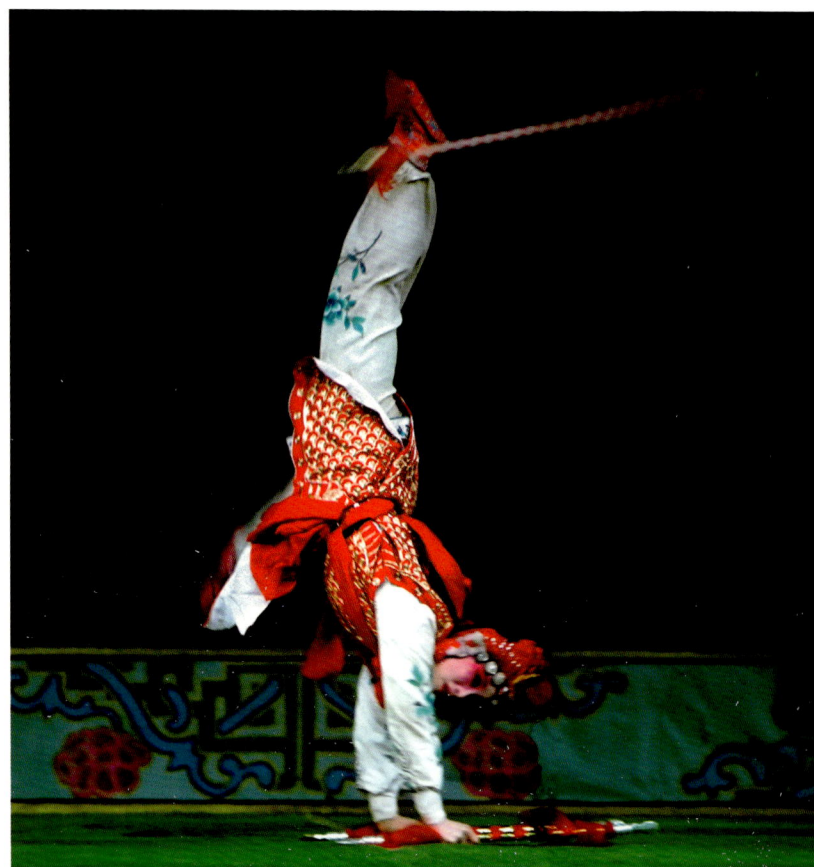

Photo 4.06 *Bringing the Magic Pearl Over the Rainbow Bridge*, Peking Opera

Using Weapons and Skills for Stage Fighting

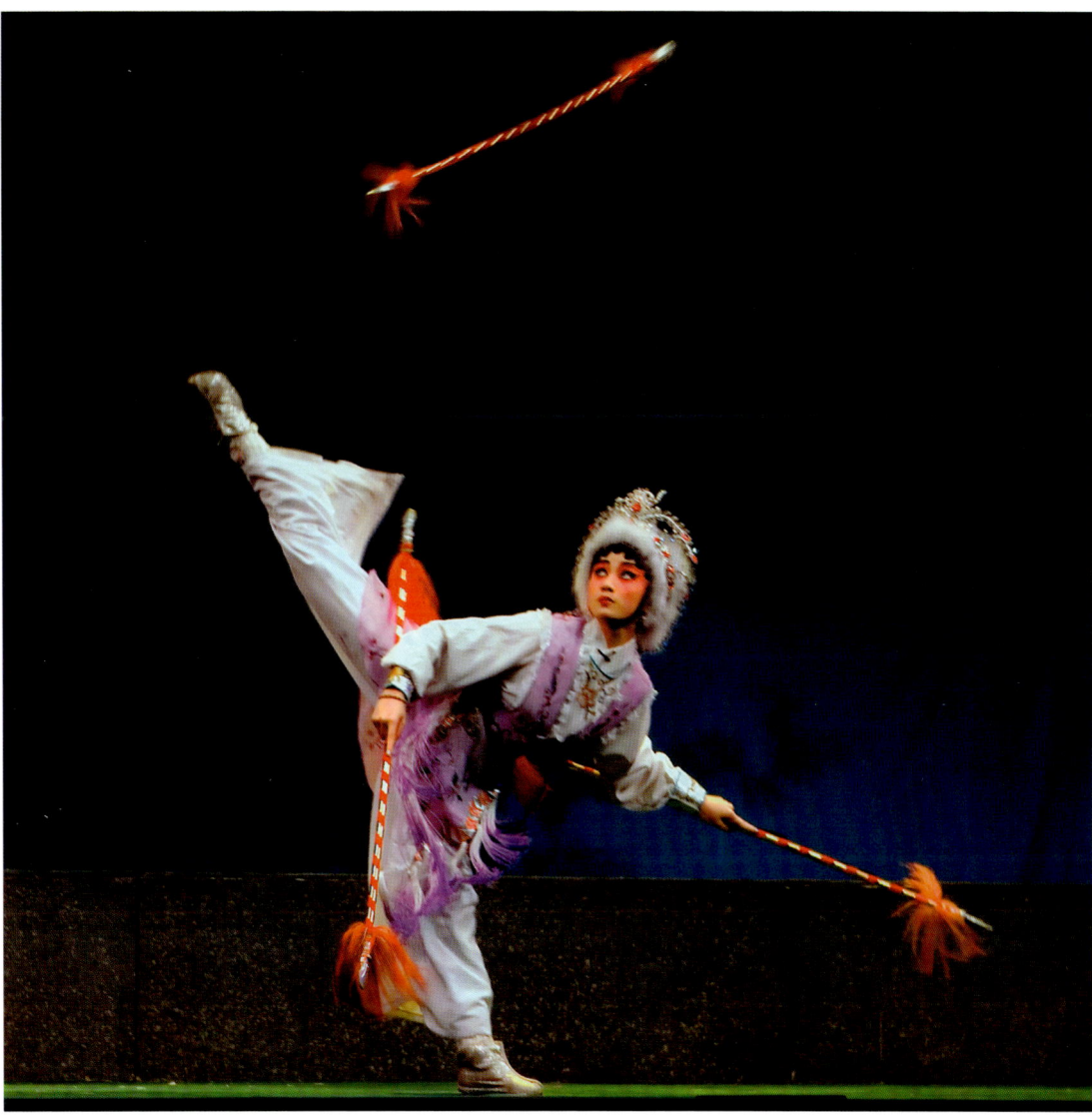

Photo 4.07 *The Fire Phoenix,* Cantonese Opera

The story of a spiritual being's forbidden love for a human being and the resulting battle recurs in several other operas. Wave Walker, a fairy who has also fallen for a mortal, is on her way over a rainbow bridge with a gift of a pearl. She is intercepted, however, by powerful forces dispatched by the Jade Emperor of Heaven. The warrior maiden role who plays the fairy must use a wide range of skills to fend off the attack, including blocking spears with her feet and hands while wielding her own weapon (see Photo 4.05).

Wave Walker, in the midst of battle, fends off a flying spear with her feet while standing on her hands (see Photo 4.06).

The White Egret Fairy, in yet another magical opera, must protect her home from attacking demons. The supernatural powers and magical weapons of both the fairy and the demons are expressed through a fast-paced interchange of weapons. The White Egret Fairy wields two spears while tossing back flying spears with her foot (see Photo 4.07).

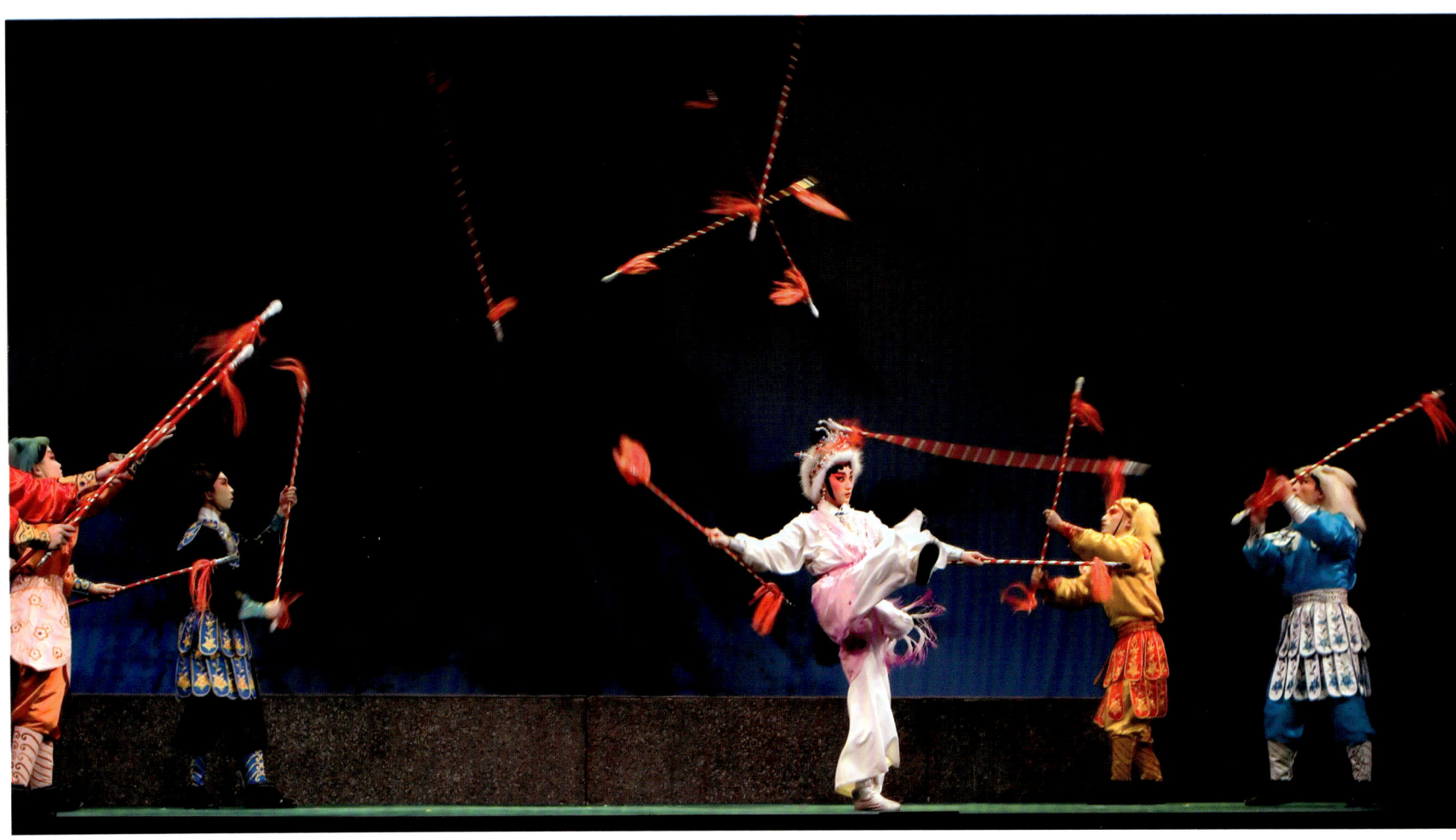

Photo 4.08 *The Fire Phoenix*, Cantonese Opera

The battle becomes heated as she is surrounded by demons who toss spear after spear at her, each of which is deflected back to them as they are juggled by the actress on stage in an impressive display of stage-fighting technique (see Photo 4.08).

One of the most spectacular battles using spears appears in the opera *The Eight Immortals Cross the Sea*. After a banquet with much drinking, the immortal Lü Dongbin decides to play a trick on the Goldfish Fairy. This ends in a violent, and heart-stopping, battle between her and the heavenly banquet guests The Goldfish Fairy fights with two spears as the warriors attack. At the height of the battle, the Goldfish Fairy uses the back of her right leg to deflect a flying spear in a move called "kicking the spear" (see Photo 4.09).

The intensity of the attack grows until the Goldfish Fairy finds herself fending off multiple flying spears from all directions in a breath-taking, split-second display of stage-fighting technique.

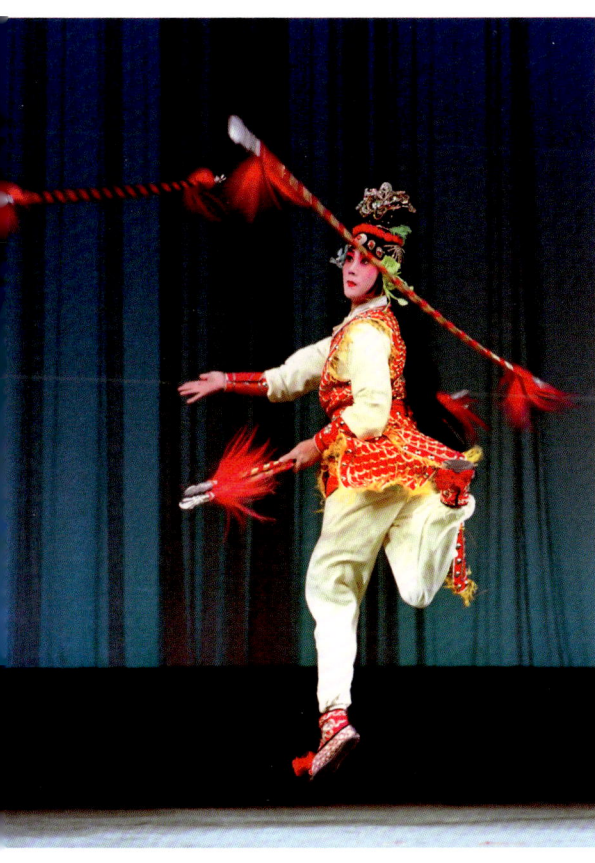

Photo 4.09 *The Eight Immortals Cross the Sea*, Peking Opera

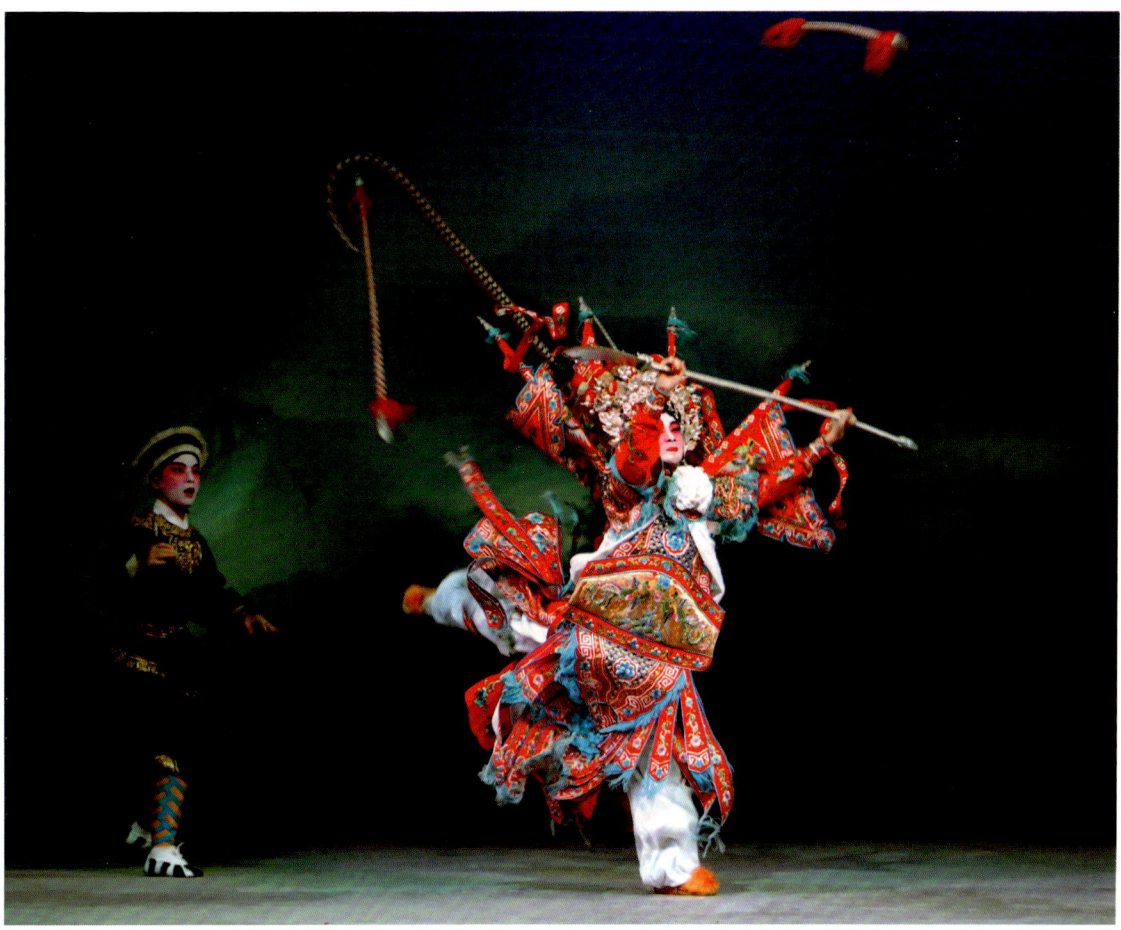

Photo 4.10 *Xue Dingshan Thrice Angers Fan Lihua*, Cantonese Opera

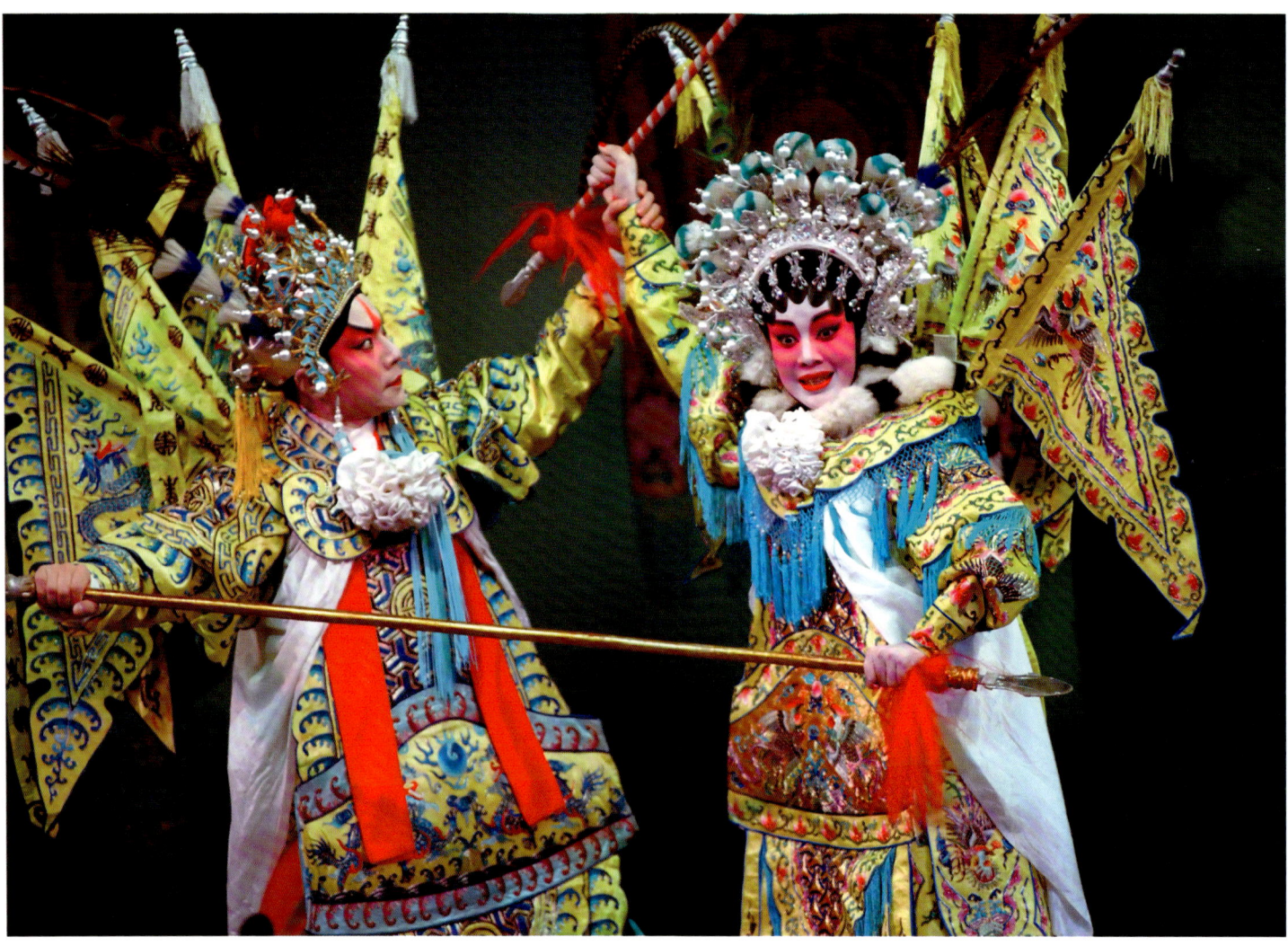

Photo 4.11 *Xue Dingshan Thrice Angers Fan Lihua*, Cantonese Opera

Acrobatic qualities are profiled in the opera *Xue Dingshan Thrice Angers Fan Lihua*. The warrior maiden Fan Lihua has occupied a mountain and set up a base. She goes to meet the forces of the Tang empire, commanded by Xue Dingshan, who in fact is destined to be her husband. Although she wears heavy armour and battle flags, the actress must be light on her feet and dexterously fend off the attacking soldiers. She blocks the spears using her feet, her own polearm (see Photo 4.10), and, in the case of one celebrated actress, Guan Sushuang, the battle flags on her back as she fights off several soldiers at the same time.

Later, she encounters Xue Dingshan in hand-to-hand combat on the battlefield. He uses his long spear and she fights with her double-headed spear. They lock weapons in a move only used in the middle of a stage battle. For a moment, they come to a standstill, expressing something deep between them. Fan Lihua's face expresses the love that she has begun to feel for this talented marshal (see Photo 4.11).

The spear is a stage prop that allows both close-quarter fighting and expanded action as the weapons fly across the stage. They become opportunities to expand a battle through a display of acrobatics and skill that make such scenes unforgettable.

Mace

THE MACE WAS a fearsome weapon in ancient times. It was a heavy mallet or hammer shaped like a melon. For this reason, warriors who fought with it were sometimes called "Golden Melon Warriors". What made the mace so formidable was its weight. Deftly handled, it could deliver devastating blows to an enemy. Like other weapons that appear on the Chinese opera stage, the mace comes in different forms. The long-handled mace is a single weapon which takes much strength to wield. Yet another kind, the chain mace, has chain links at the handle. The most common kind that opera audiences see in stage fighting is the double short-handled mace. The actor using these weapons wields them at a closer range than the long-handled mace.

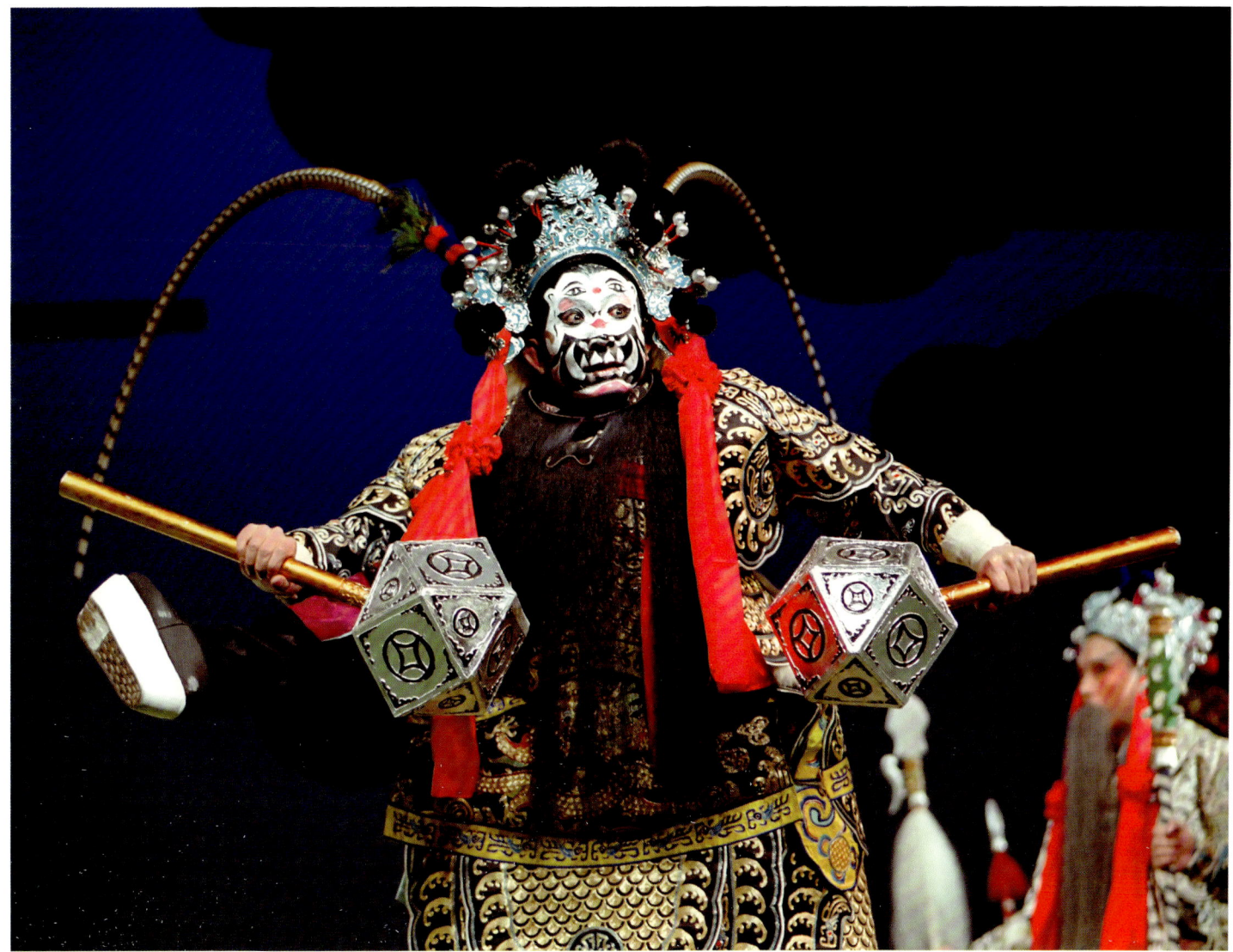

Photo 4.12 *Wreaking Havoc in Heaven*, Peking Opera

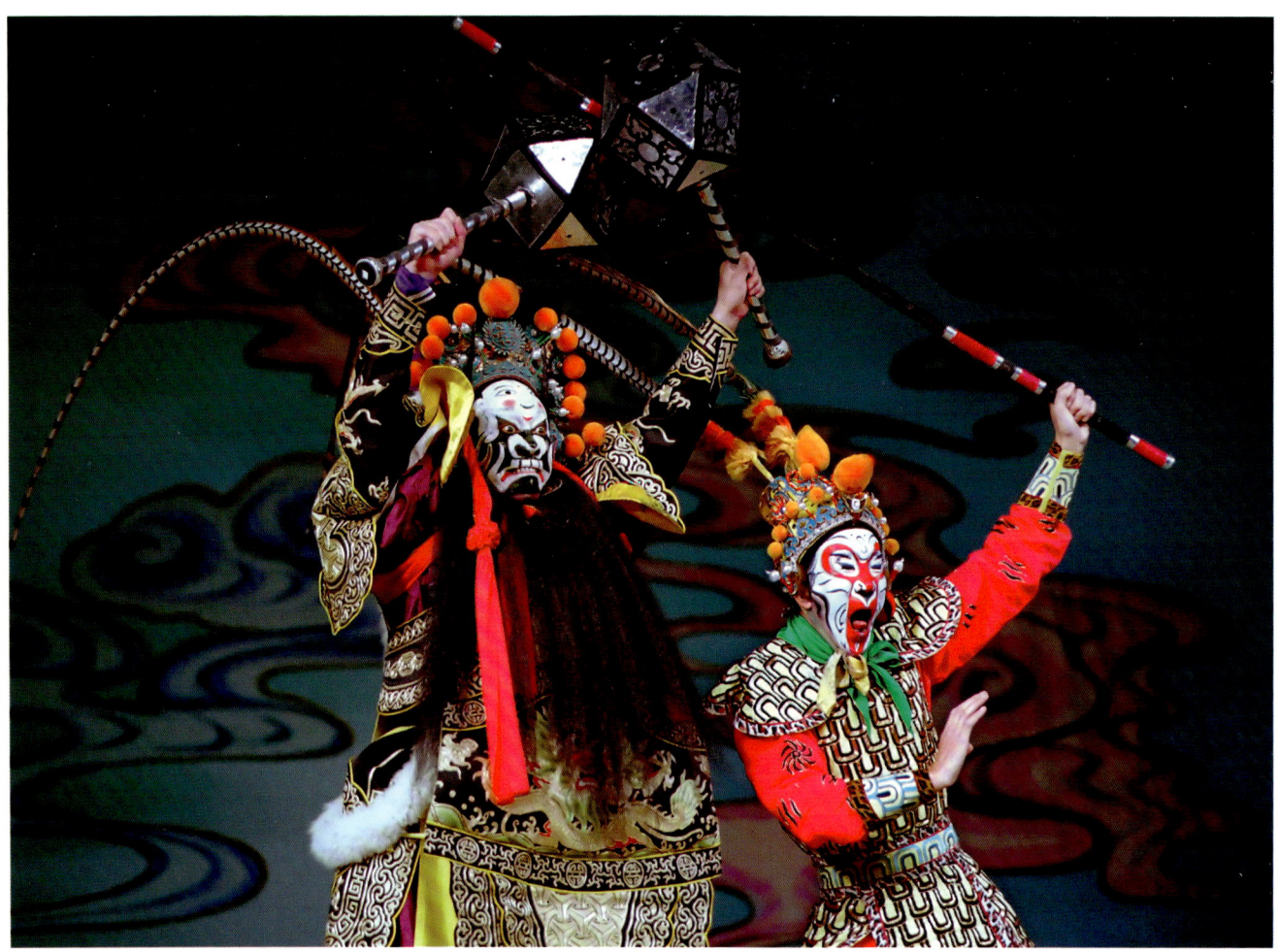

Photo 4.13 *Wreaking Havoc in Heaven*, Peking Opera

The mischievous Monkey King, Sun Wukong, in the acrobatic and comic opera *Wreaking Havoc in Heaven*, encounters a powerful heavenly being who comes against him wielding the double short-handled maces, normally a terrifying spectre. The Monkey King laughs it off and teases his opponent, who misses him at every blow (see Photo 4.13).

There are a number of defences against the double maces. Yue Yun, son of the famous Song general, Yue Fei, comes against Lu Wenlong wielding double maces. Lu Wenlong, raised by the enemy of Song, matches each blow using his twin spears, blocking each of the heavy maces before they strike him (see Photo 4.14).

Actors do not just fight with maces. They also use them to strut their victories. One common stage technique is to juggle them. The general Pei Yuanqing is delighted with himself at having defeated the enemy. He skilfully juggles the double maces after his battle, showing off his skills and his pride (see Photo 4.15).

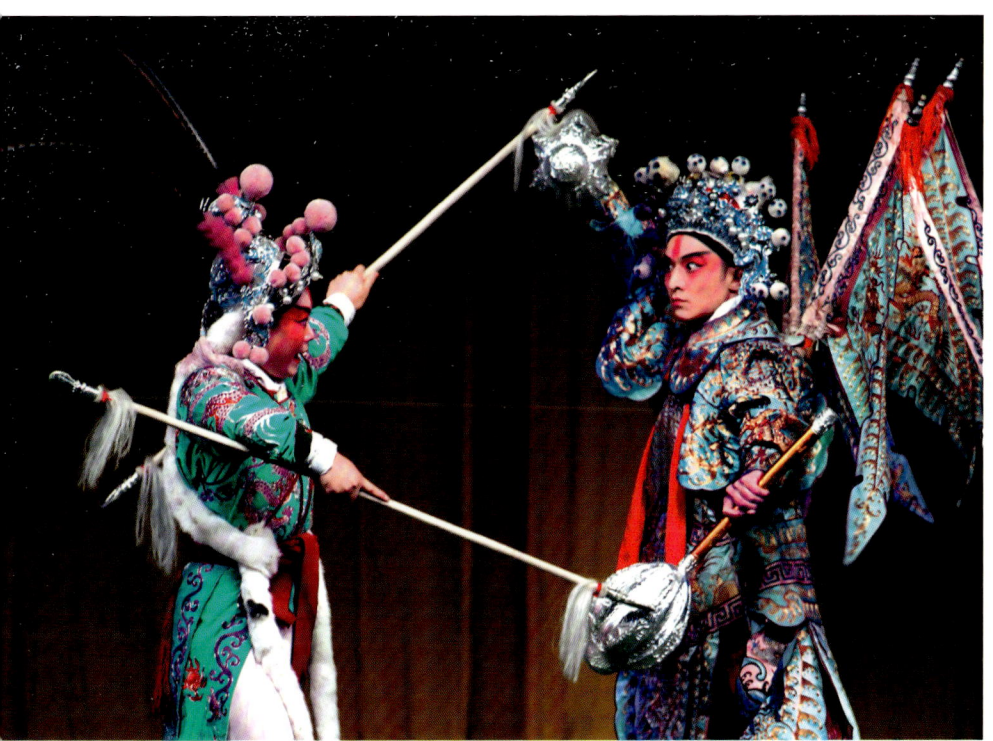

Photo 4.14 *Lu Wenlong and His Double Spears*, Hebei Clapper Opera

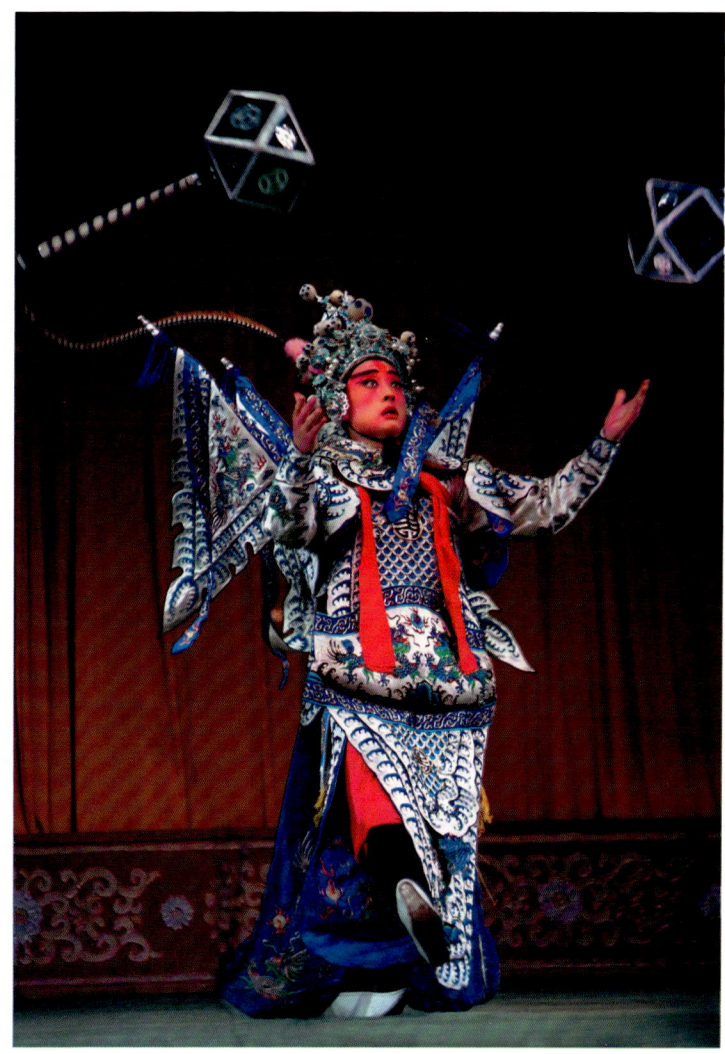

Photo 4.15 *The Burning of Pei Yuanqing*, Hebei Clapper Opera

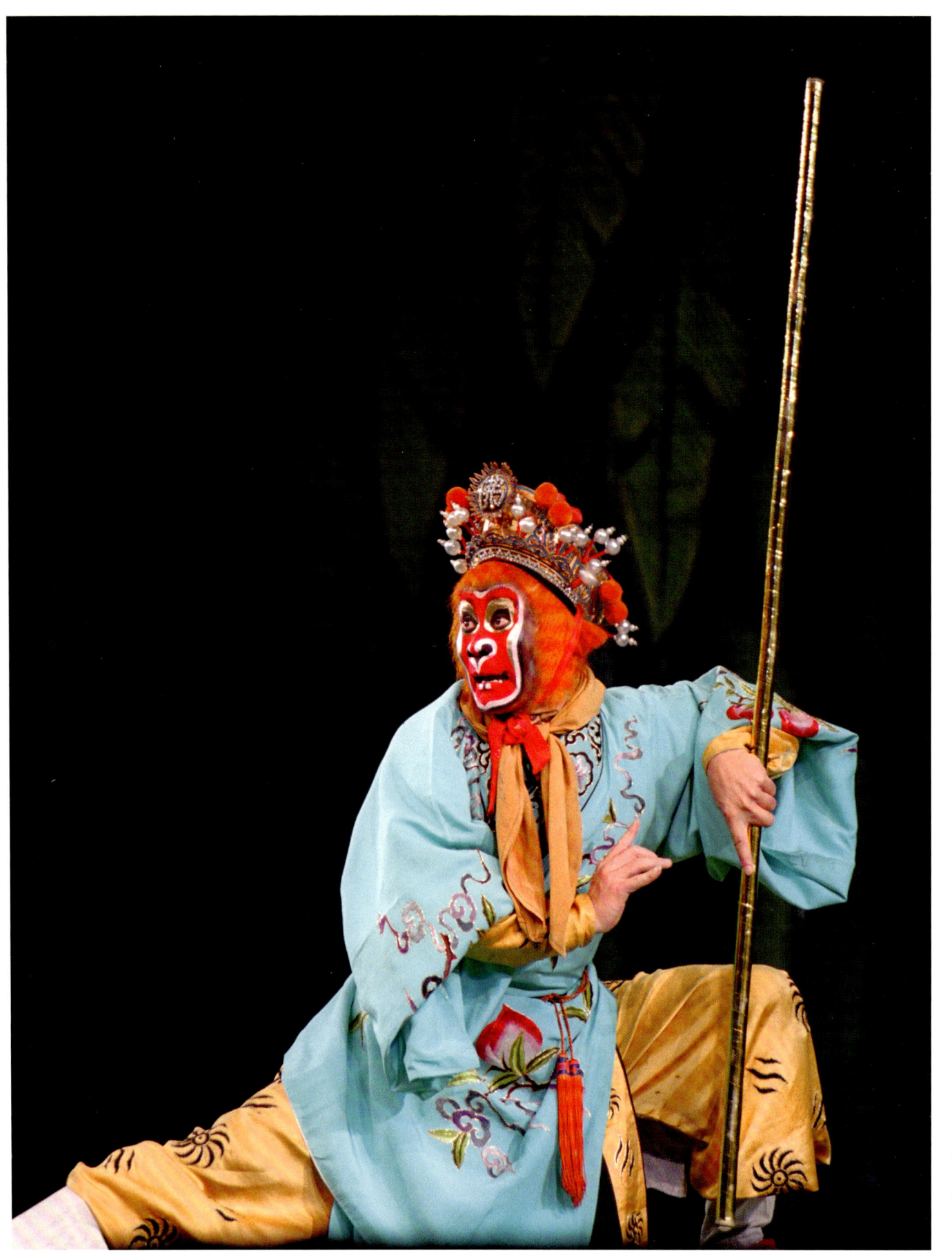

Photo 4.16 *Monkey King Steals the Magic Fan*, Shao Opera

Quarterstaff

THE QUARTERSTAFF IS an elegant weapon. It makes its most common appearance in operas that tell stories from the famous novel, *Journey to the West*. This novel describes the monk, Xuanzang, who journeys to India to get the Buddhist scriptures to bring back to China. He is accompanied along the way by Pigsy, Sandy and the beloved Monkey King. The Monkey King's weapon is the quarterstaff. It is not, however, just any quarterstaff, but a magical one taken from the watery abode of the Dragon King of the Eastern Sea. This quarterstaff is immensely heavy and powerful. Its magic lies in the fact that it can change its size. The Monkey King regularly makes it as small as a needle and carries it behind his ear until he needs it.

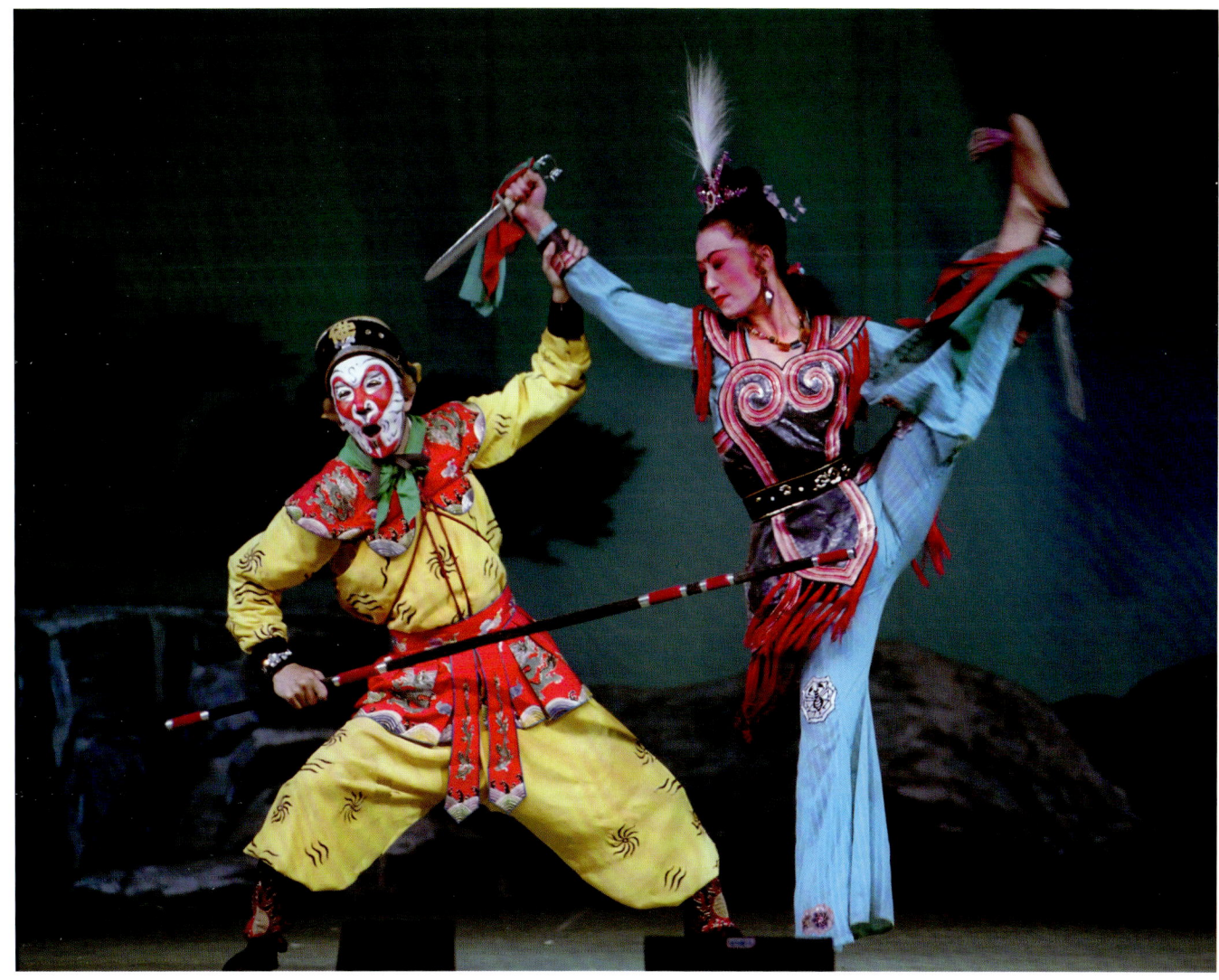

Photo 4.17 *The Cave of Spiders*, Peking Opera

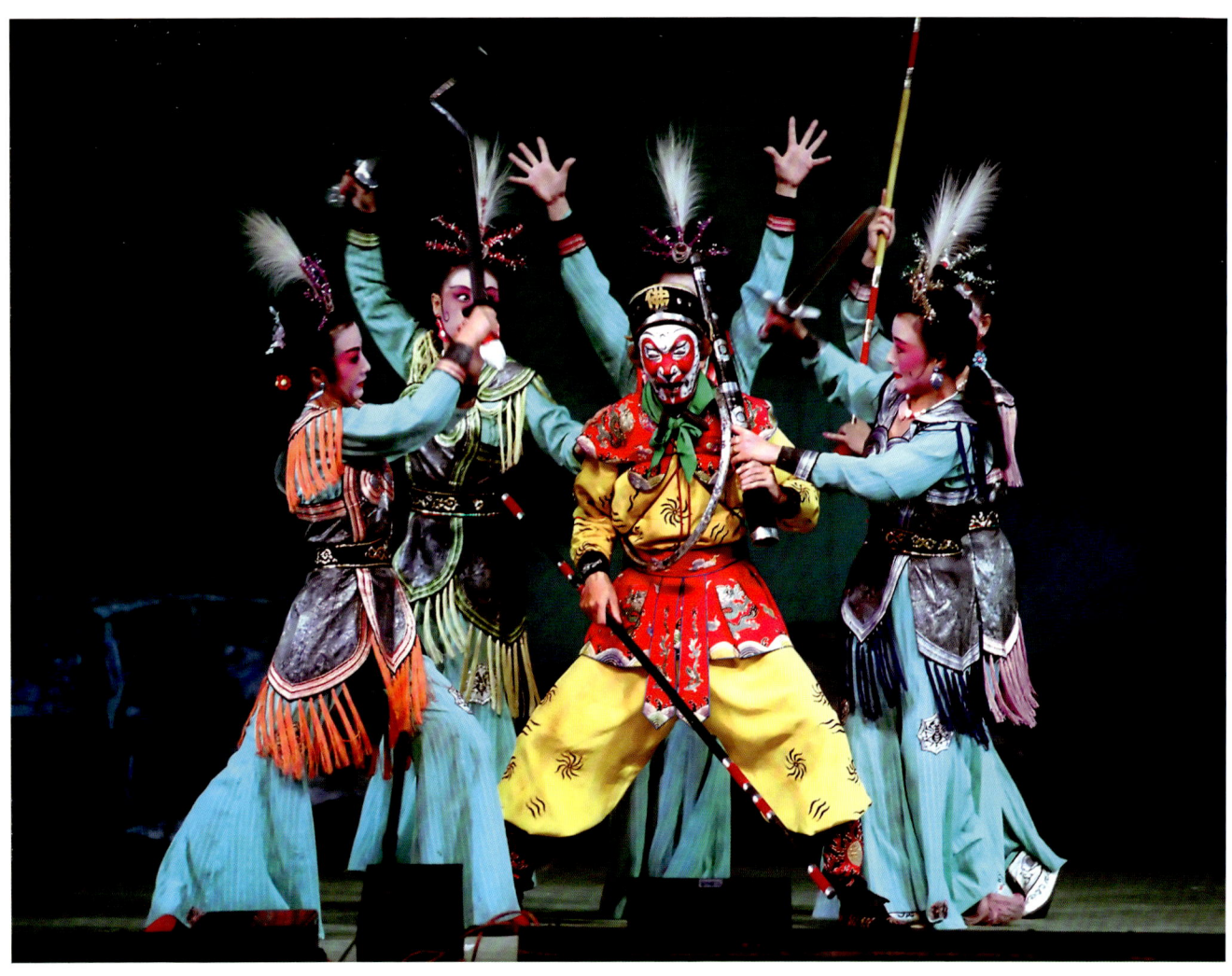

Photo 4.18 *The Cave of Spiders*, Peking Opera

Many perils await the travelling band as they journey to the west. One of these perils is the deadly trap by the Queen of Spiders and her female warriors, who try to seduce the holy monk and his companions. The Monkey King comes to the rescue with his mighty Golden Iron Staff. He battles with his quarterstaff in an episode of fierce, yet comic, fighting (see Photo 4.17). These characteristics make a Monkey King opera immensely entertaining.

None of the swords or spears of the spider women are a match for him. None of their weapons can even touch him. He overcomes them all, frees his master, and sets out on the next leg of their journey (see Photo 4.18).

The staff also appears in operas describing earthly battles. The great robber chieftain, Song Jiang, a hero in the classic novel *The Legend of the Water Margin*, sends out his fighter Shi Xiu to scout out Zhu village. When the attack begins, Shi Xiu valiantly uses his spear against a quarterstaff as he breaks through an ambush (see Photo 4.19).

Using Weapons and Skills for Stage Fighting

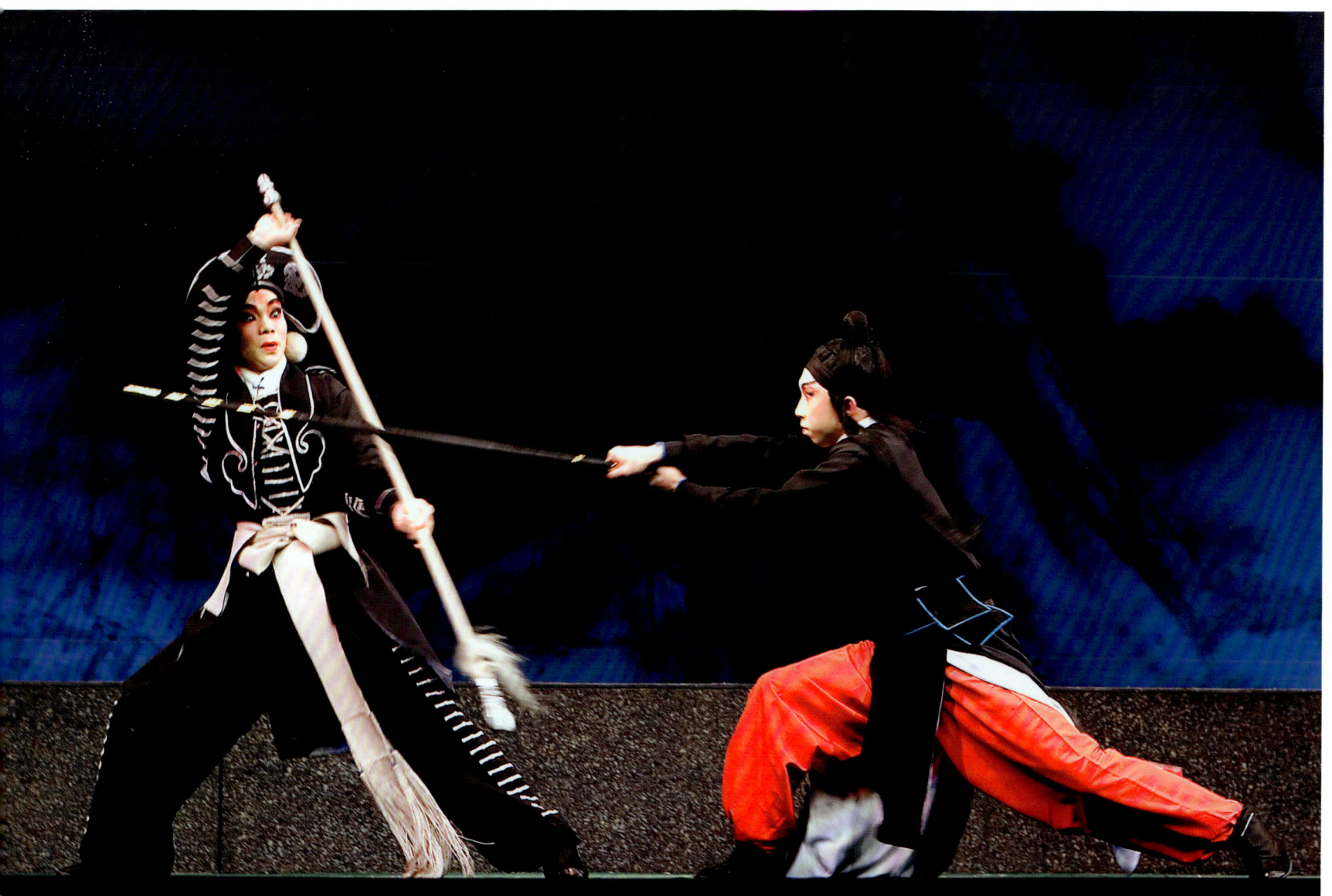

Photo 4.19 *Shi Xiu Scouts Out Zhu Village*, Cantonese Opera

Polearm

ONE OF THE most impressive weapons on the Chinese opera stage is the polearm. The long pole or shaft permits an extended reach. The large blade on the end is used like a battle-axe. This magnificent, larger-than-life weapon has several variations. Among these are the door-splitting blade, the silver-mouthed blade, and the elephant-trunk blade. The shafts are gold, and the blade face is often elaborately decorated. As formidable as the weapon appears, it is not used in violent fighting or acrobatic displays. Instead, the actor wields it slowly to suggest the battle through slow and elegant moves.

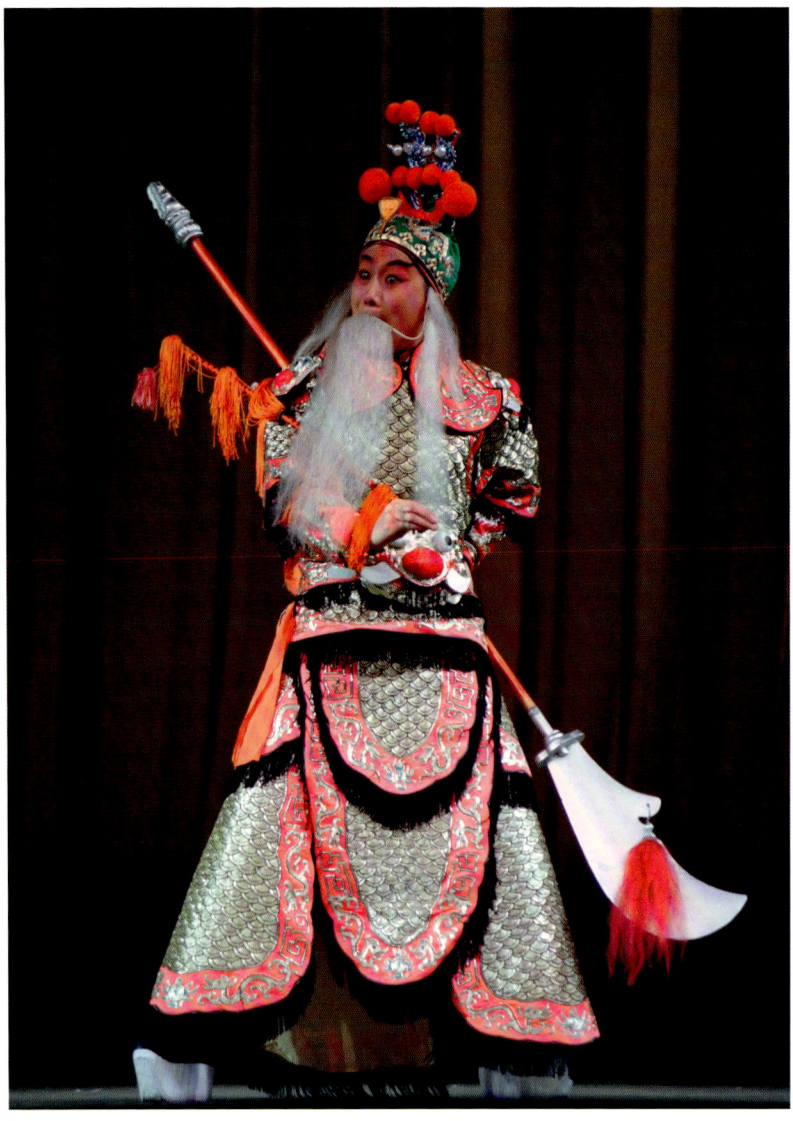

The most famous wielder of the polearm is the legendary general Guan Yu from China's warring Three Kingdoms period. He is instantly recognizable on the stage by his full-face red make-up and by his polearm, which carries a dragon and crescent moon design. It is Guan Yu's signature weapon. His entry on the stage with this weapon is spectacular. Before he steps out, the audience hears a deep powerful beating of drums, signalling that Guan Yu is about to appear. After he walks on the stage to thunderous applause, the drumbeats intensify. Guan Yu makes slow, majestic moves, and takes up several poses to the delight of the audience (see Photo 4.21).

Female warriors and magical female spirits wield their own version of the polearm. Although the shaft is every bit as long as its counterpart for male warriors, the axe-blade is smaller. This weapon is traditionally called the female warrior's blade. The famous female warrior Mu Guiying uses this weapon in the opera *Twice-Locked Mountain* (see Photo 4.22).

Photo 4.20 *Burning the Camps*, Hebei Clapper Opera

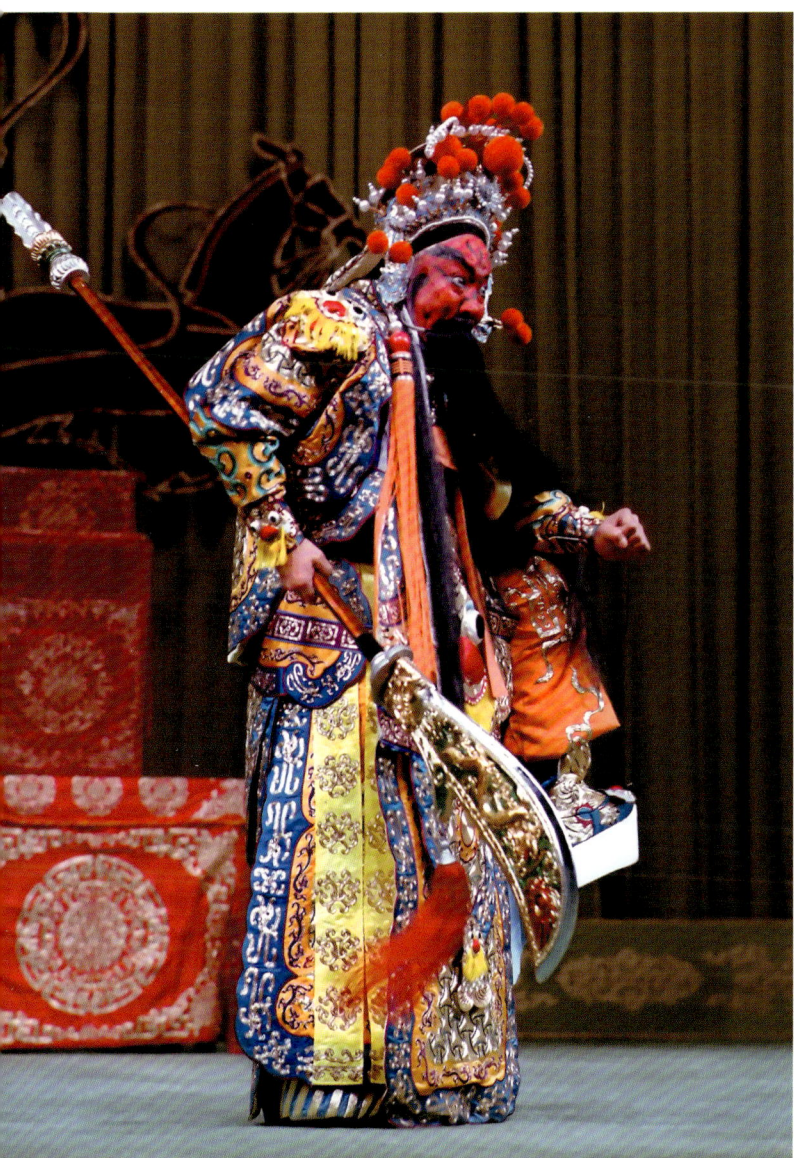

Photo 4.21 *Huarong Pass*, Peking Opera

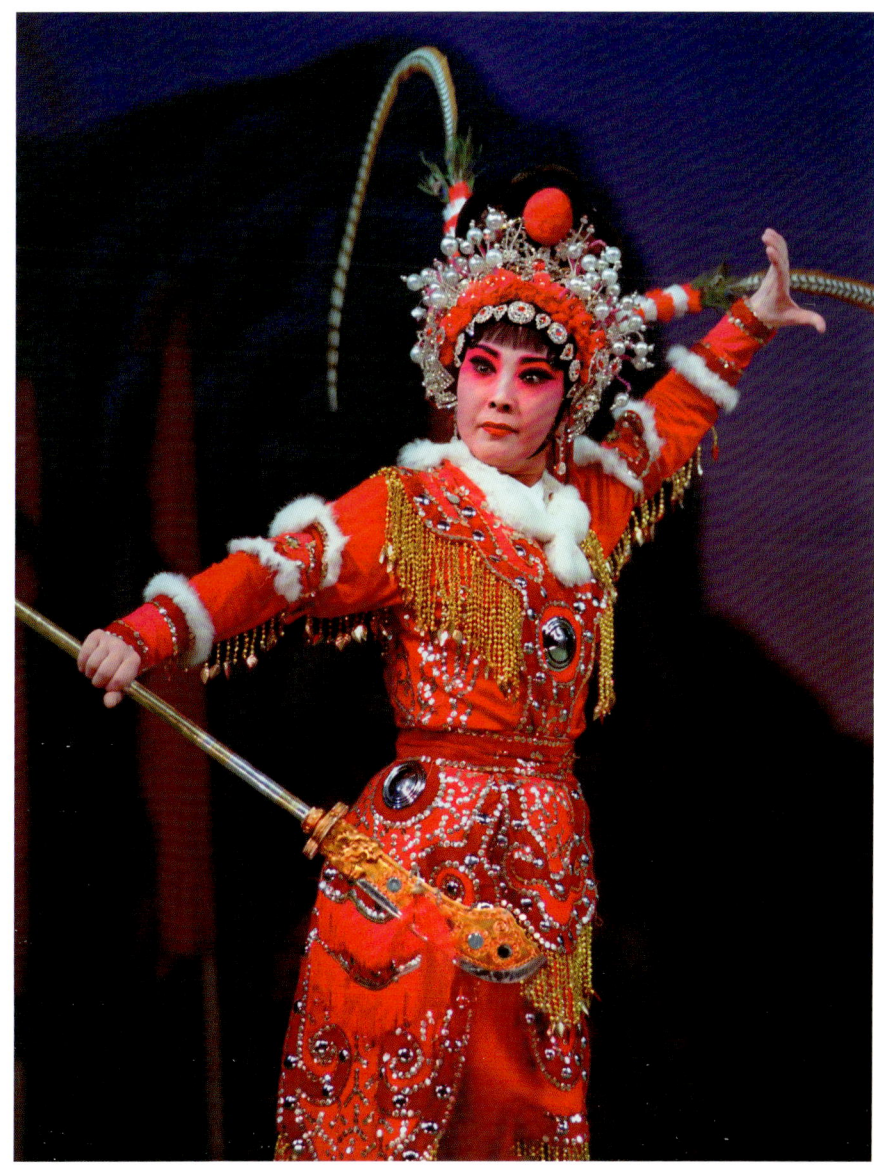

Photo 4.22 *Twice-Locked Mountain*, Longjiang Opera

Sword

THE SWORD IS the most common stage weapon in Chinese opera. It is also one of the most versatile, used both in dance and furious displays of prowess. Different characters use different types of swords. Heroes carry the long straight sword in a decorated sheath. This sword has a brilliant silver blade sharpened on both sides. One particular kind of this sword is the precious sword—an ornamented weapon presented by the emperor as a sign that the bearer has imperial authority to command. Yet another type of the long sword is the double sword used by women fighters and dancers. Carried together, one on top of the other, appearing at first as a single sword, they can be separated so that the female character wields one in each hand.

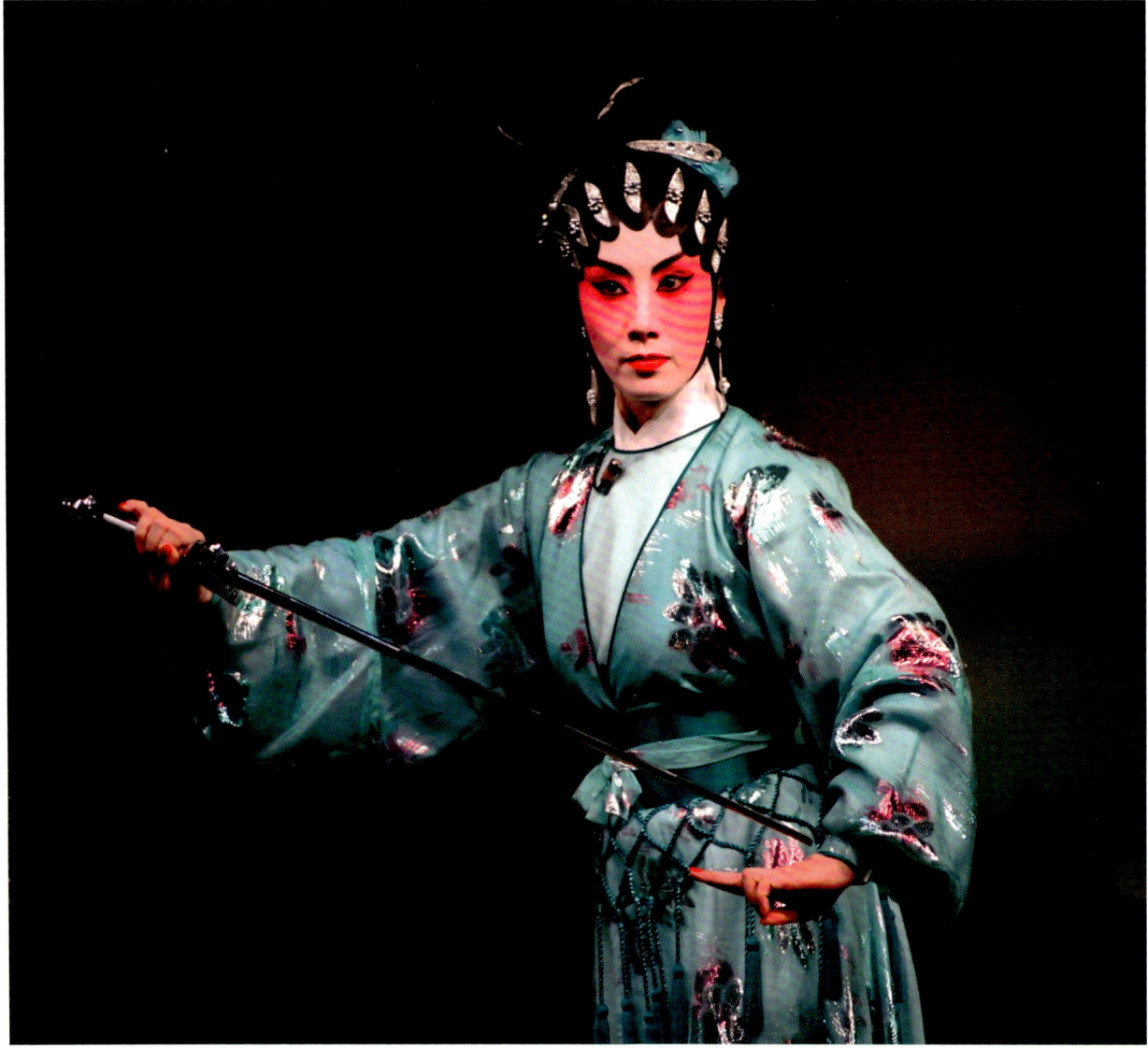

Photo 4.23 *The Red Peony Fairy*, Cantonese Opera

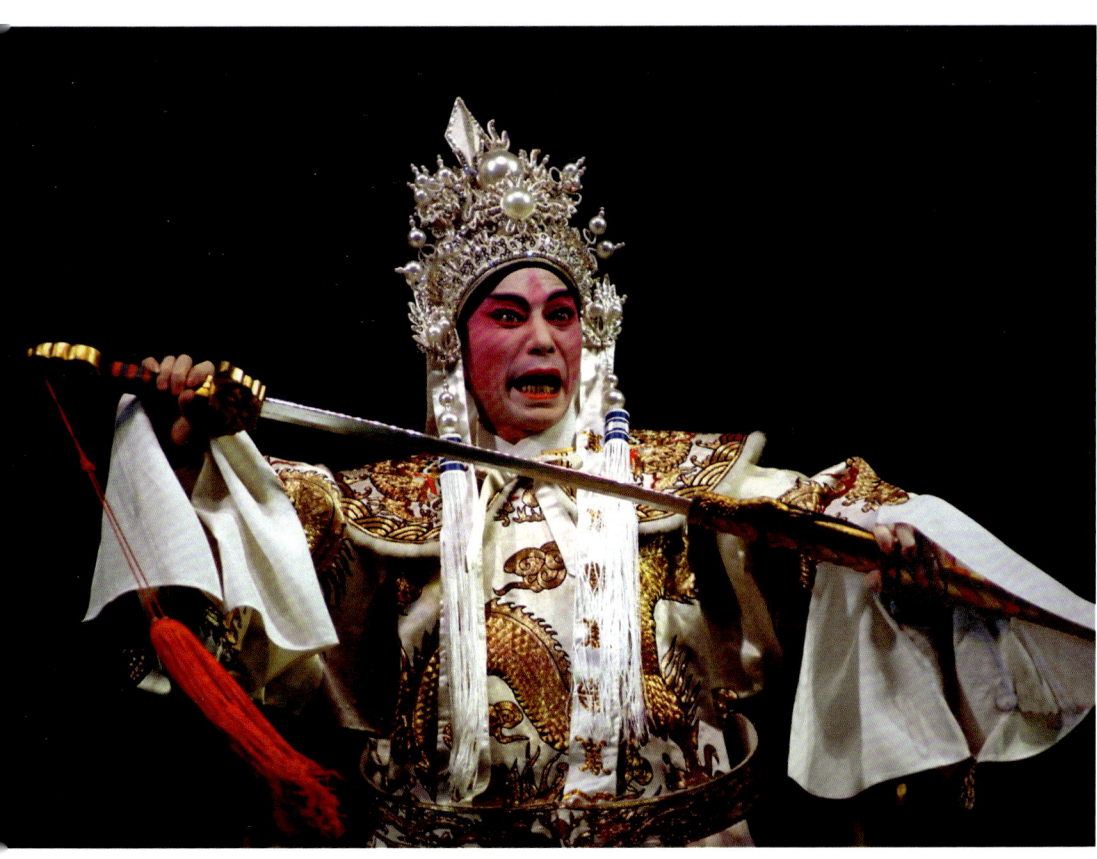

Photo 4.24 *Yuan Chonghuan,* Cantonese Opera

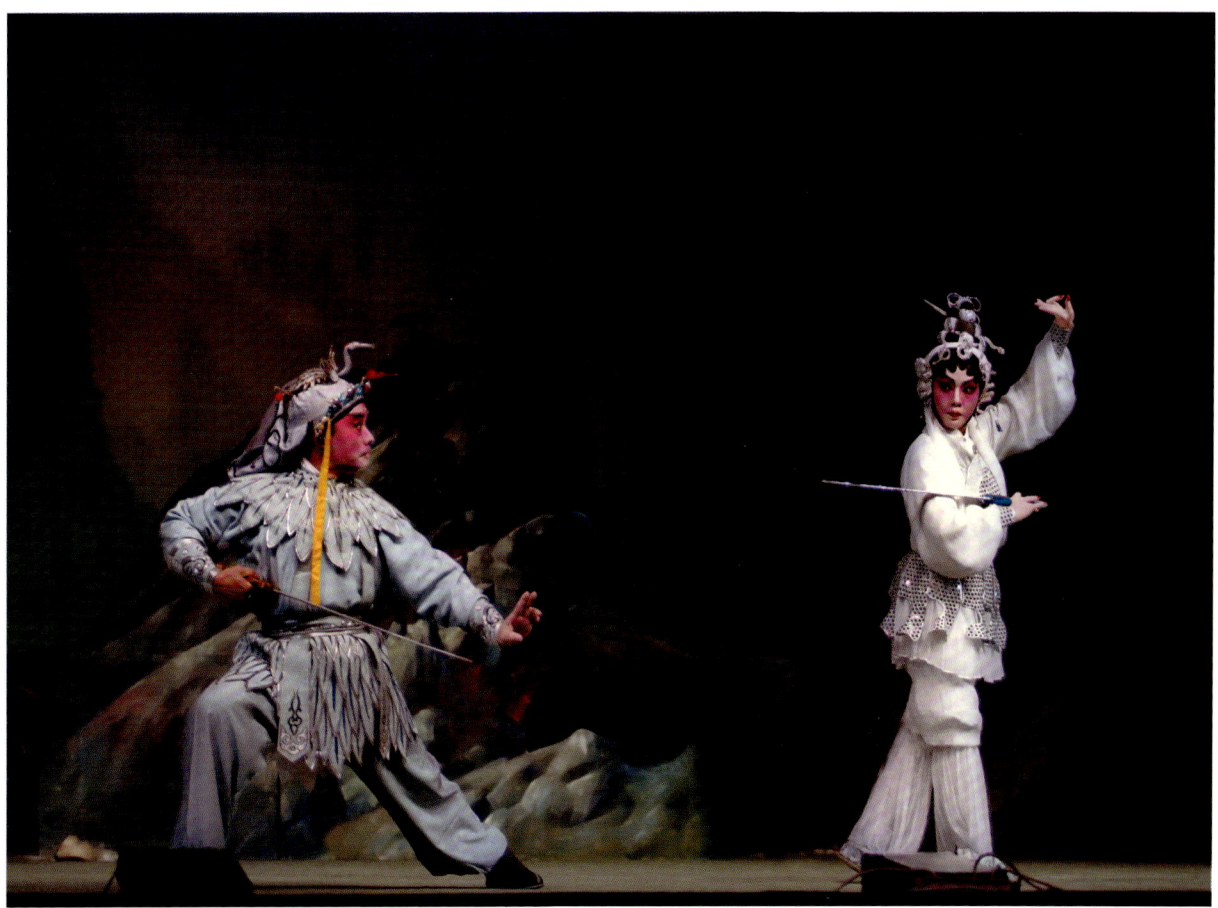

Photo 4.25 *The Legend of the White Snake,* Cantonese Opera

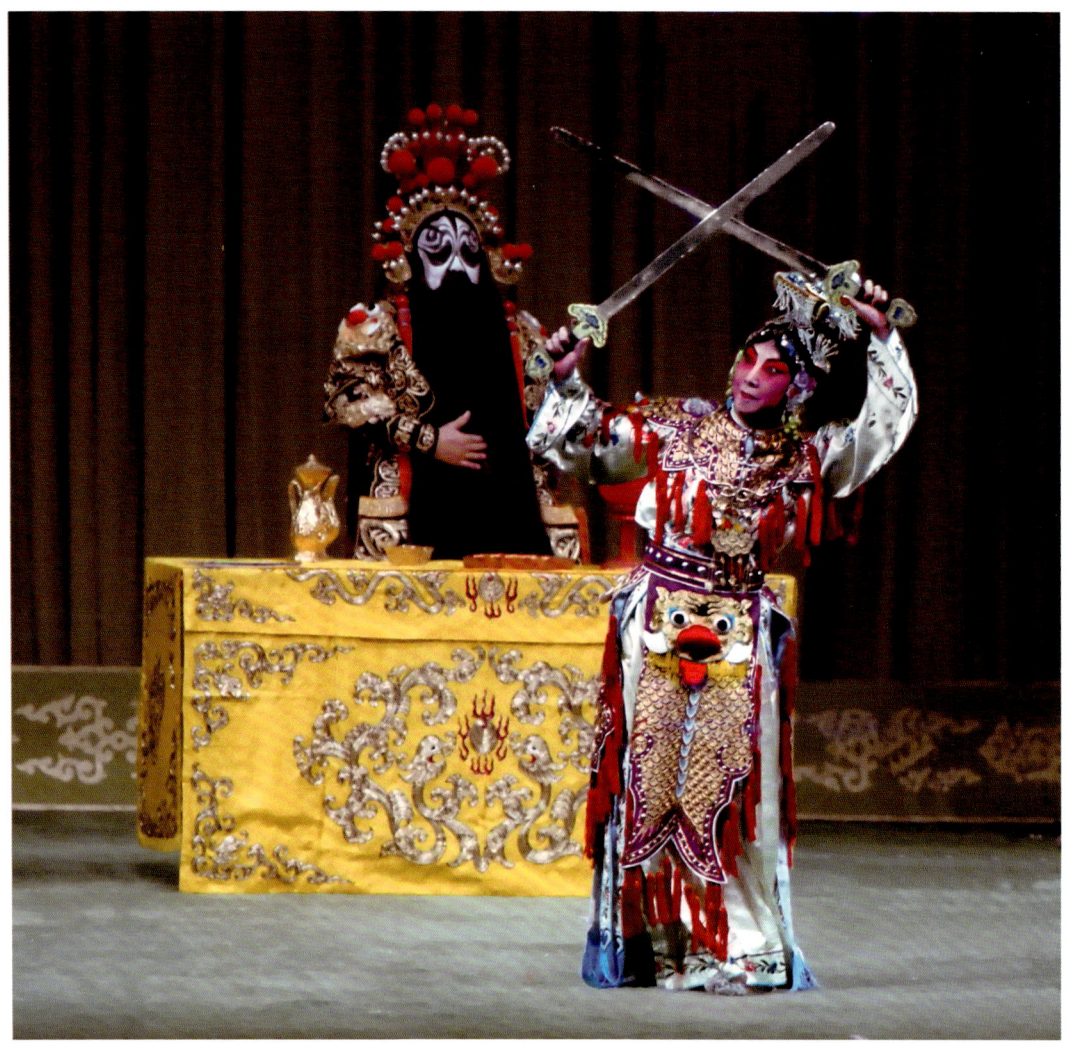

Photo 4.26 *Farewell, My Concubine*, Peking Opera

General Yuan Chonghuan is charged with protecting the northeast of China in the final years of the Ming dynasty from the Manchu invaders. He has had great success and plans to settle the borders within five years. The emperor presents him with a precious sword, giving him imperial authority to command (see Photo 4.24). Despite his great success, the Manchu's Qing dynasty will eventually replace the Ming.

Women fighters also carry swords on the opera stage. The White Snake spirit, incarnated as a beautiful woman, must fight deer and crane spirits in order to obtain a magical herb to cure her human husband. She faces the crane spirit first. She raises her left arm, pointing back with her fingers and resting the sword in her right hand across her elbow in a pose that indicates readiness for battle (see Photo 4.25).

Farewell, My Concubine is a showpiece for the female role. It was a signature role for the great twentieth-century female impersonator, Mei Lanfang. In a story drawn from Chinese history, King Xiang Yu of Chu has been surrounded by Liu Bang's troops, who employ a unique strategy—singing sorrowful songs from Chu that cause Xiang Yu's troops to lose heart and desert. The king's concubine tries to lighten his heart by performing a skilful dance with double swords (see Photo 4.26).

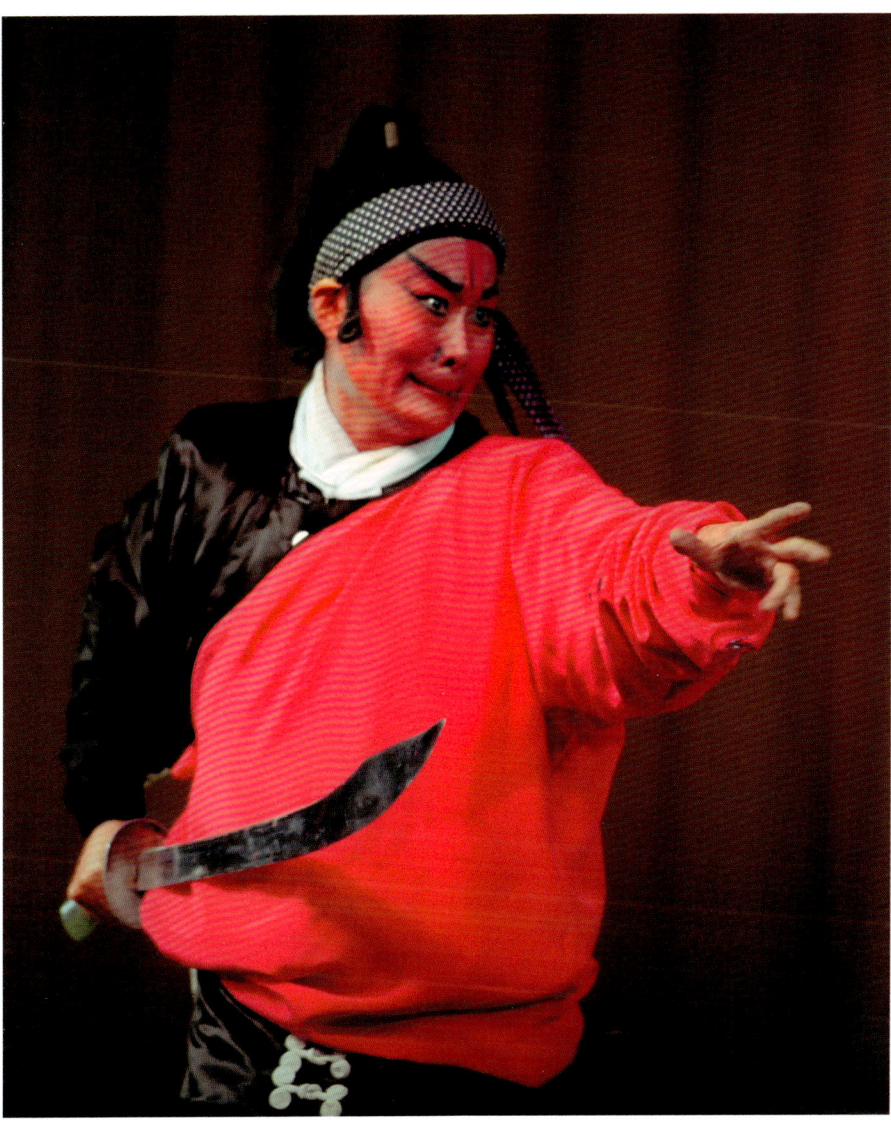

Photo 4.27 *Wu Song's Revenge*, Hebei Clapper Opera

Sabre

FOOT SOLDIERS AND bandits often use the sabre. This weapon has a curved blade sharpened only on one side. It is usually worn at the waist or on the back through a belt and used in fast, close fighting. A cousin to the sword, the sabres permit wide sweeps used by acrobatic fighters in mime and stage battles.

He Tianbao is on a mission to scout out a bandit base on Fu Mountain where his martial arts disciple, Lu Zhiyi, was murdered. He suddenly finds himself surrounded by bandits all wielding sabres. Each tries to find the other as they fight in darkness (see Photo 4.28).

In the famous Peking opera *Inn at the Crossroads*, the traveller Ren Tanghui and the innkeeper Liu Lihua wield sabres in silence in the dark. The stage lights are at full glare, but the audience is aware that the characters in the opera cannot see each other as they mime their way through a pitch-dark night. The sabres brush by their heads, narrowly missing, as the two probe the darkness. Sometimes, they stumble against each other. At other times, they briefly engage in battle, but then lose each other in the darkness and silence (see Photo 4.29).

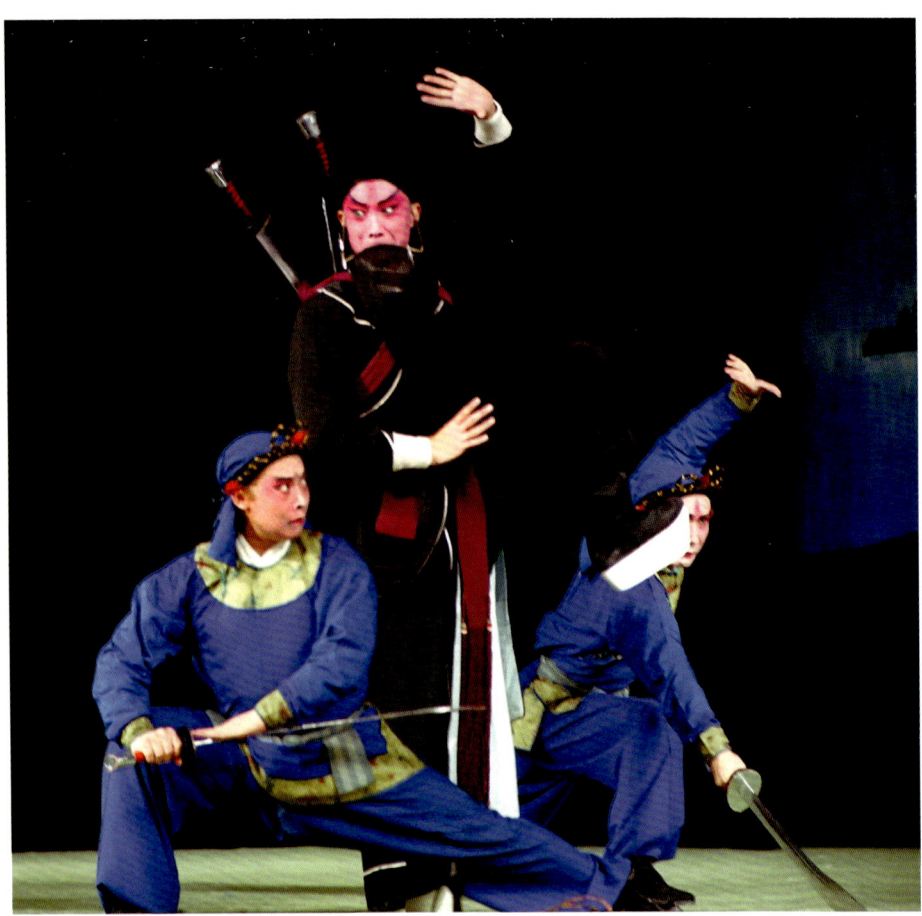

Photo 4.28 *Cleaning Out the Bandit's Lair*, Peking Opera

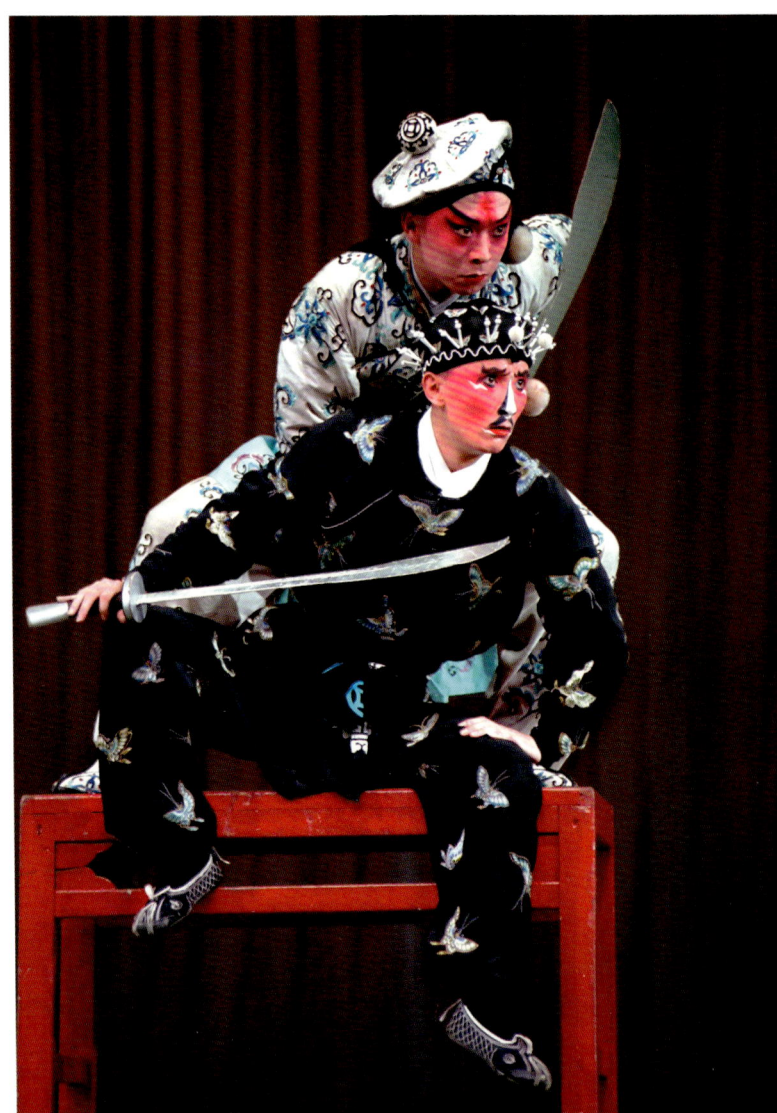

Photo 4.29 *Inn at the Crossroads*, Peking Opera

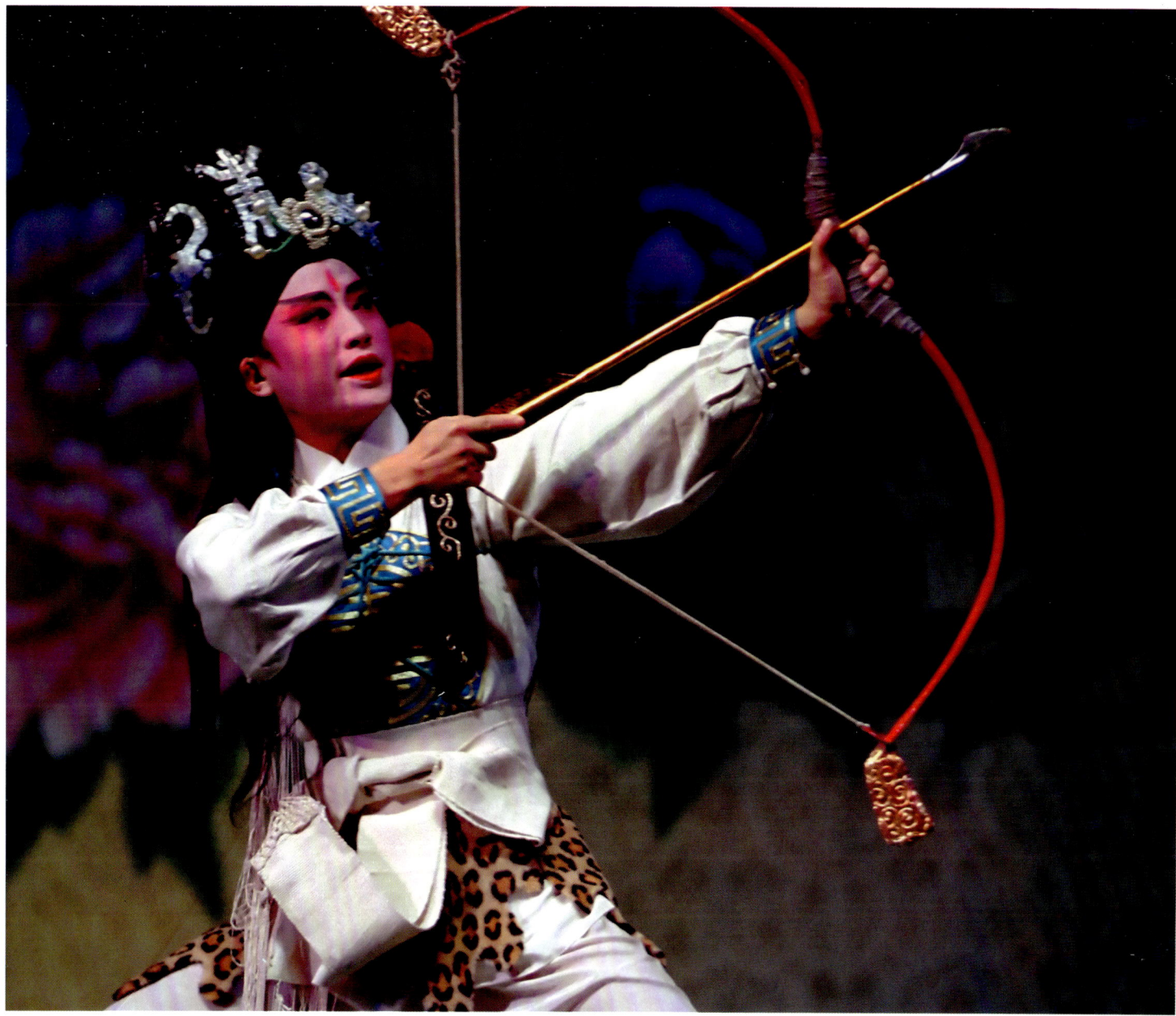

Photo 4.30 *Hua Rong Shoots the Hawk*, Sichuan Opera

Bow and Arrow

THE BOW AND arrow also makes its appearance on the Chinese opera stage, usually in hunting scenes. The bow and arrow on the Chinese stage is fully functional as actors deftly shoot arrows off into the wings.

In one opera, Xue Dingshan goes out hunting for pleasure and has the good fortune to find the great white tiger. He deftly draws his bow, aims and hits his target, killing the ferocious beast (see Photo 4.31). What he did not know, however, is that the White Tiger spirit was, in fact, his own father. His joy turns to sorrow when the wounded, dying beast turns back into his father's form.

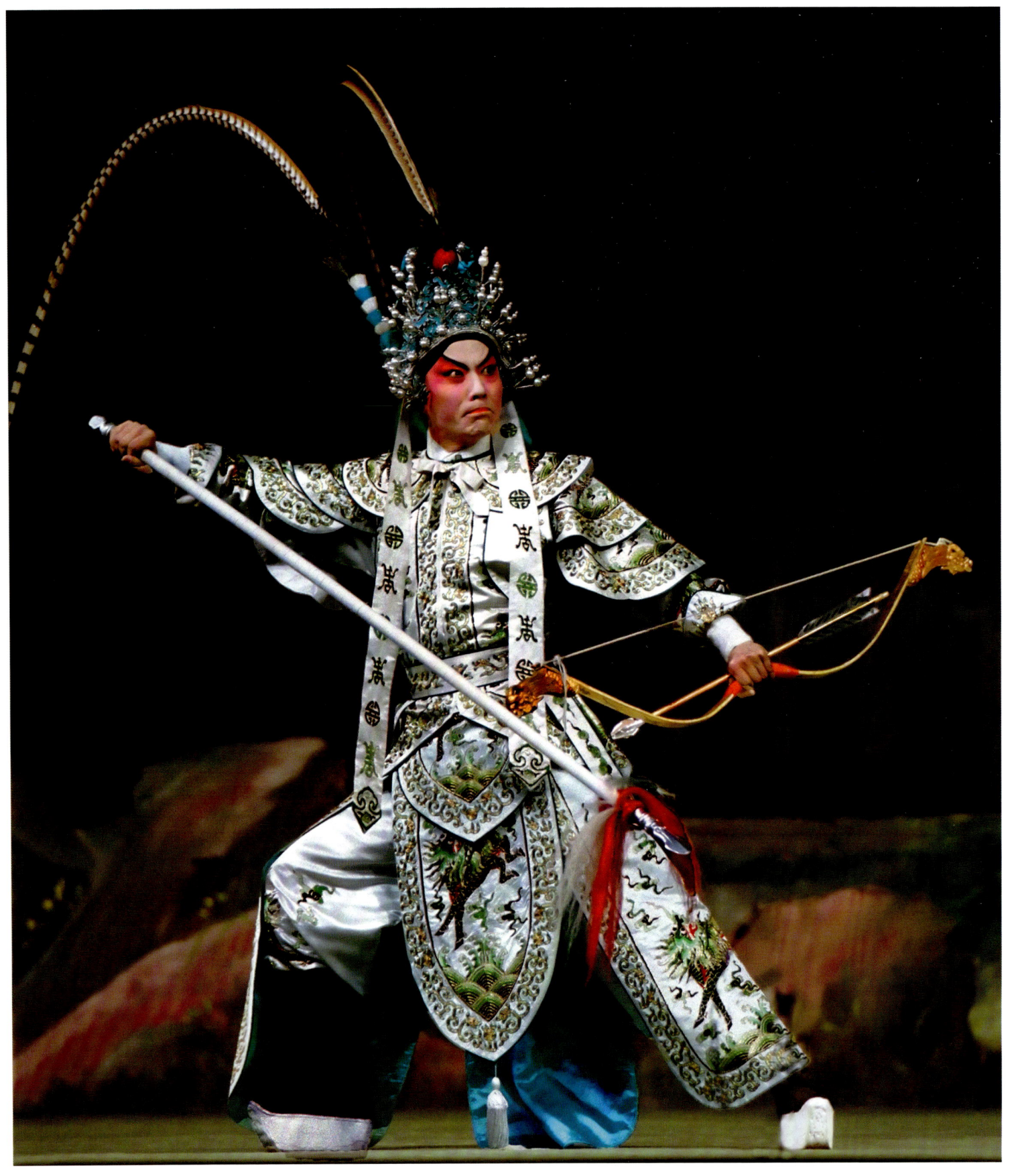

Photo 4.31 *Xue Dingshan Thrice Angers Fan Lihua*, Cantonese Opera

Using Weapons and Skills for Stage Fighting

In another opera, the bow and arrow becomes a test of true love. The great martial arts master Chen Yong declares to his daughter on his deathbed that he has provided a test for her future husband. Only a man who can bend the ancestral bow is worthy of her. Only such a man can become part of their family. His daughter, Xiuying, and her mother run a tea house after Chen Yong dies. One day, a handsome youth, Kuang Zhong, comes to drink tea, but is mesmerized by the beautiful bow. He cannot keep his hands off it. He picks it up and bends the bow three times. Xiuying sees this and instantly gives her heart to him. The couple take a series of beautiful poses with the bow, expressing their love (see Photo 4.32).

Photo 4.32 *The Romance of the Iron Bow,* Longjiang Opera

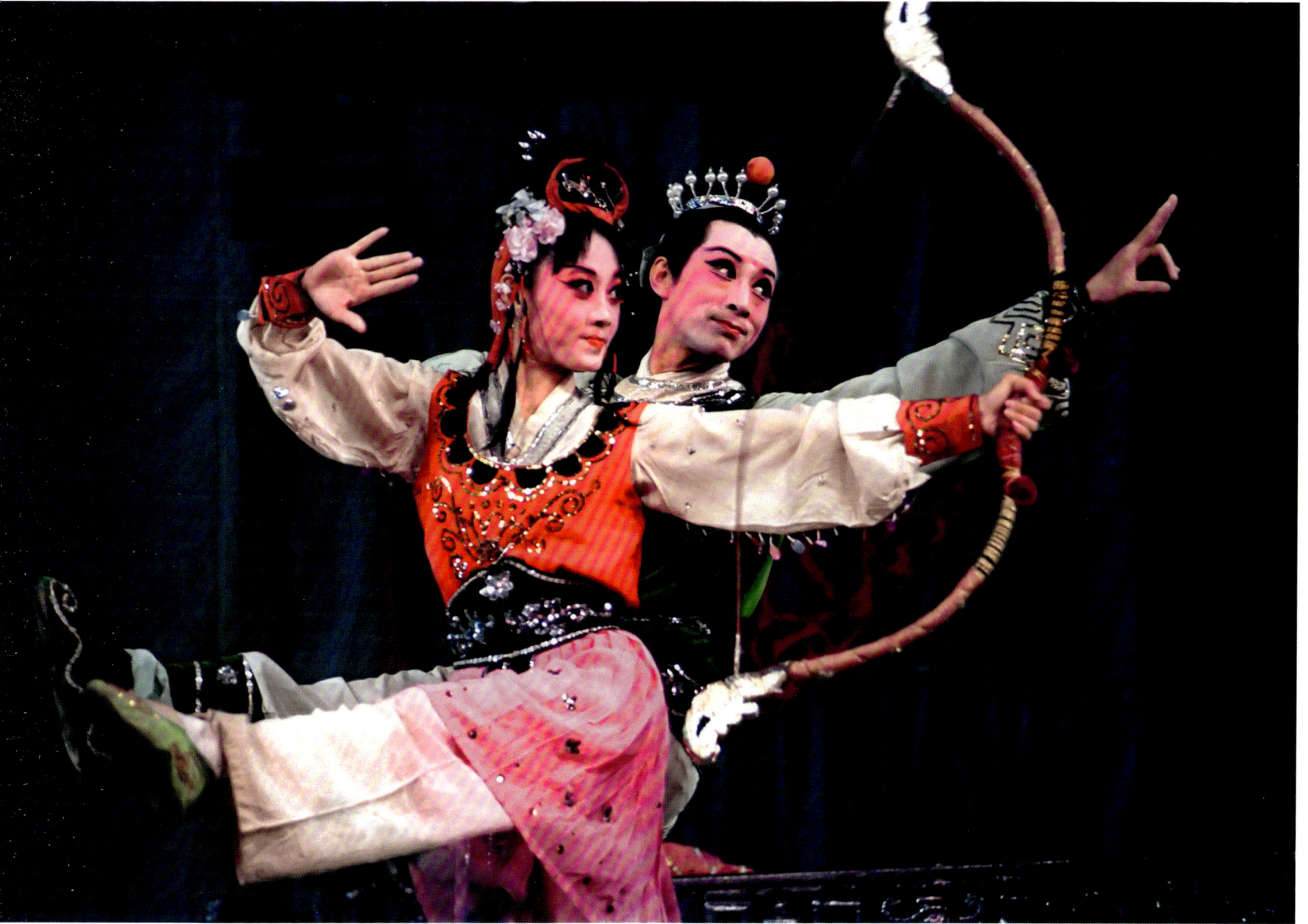

Special Weapons

CERTAIN WEAPONS ON the stage denote individual characters. Just as a particular costume is associated with a Western superhero, these weapons identify these stage heroes. Guan Yu, or Guan Gong, has his massive polearm. The Monkey King, Sun Wukong, has his Golden Iron Staff that no one can lift but him. Others have their own unique weapons.

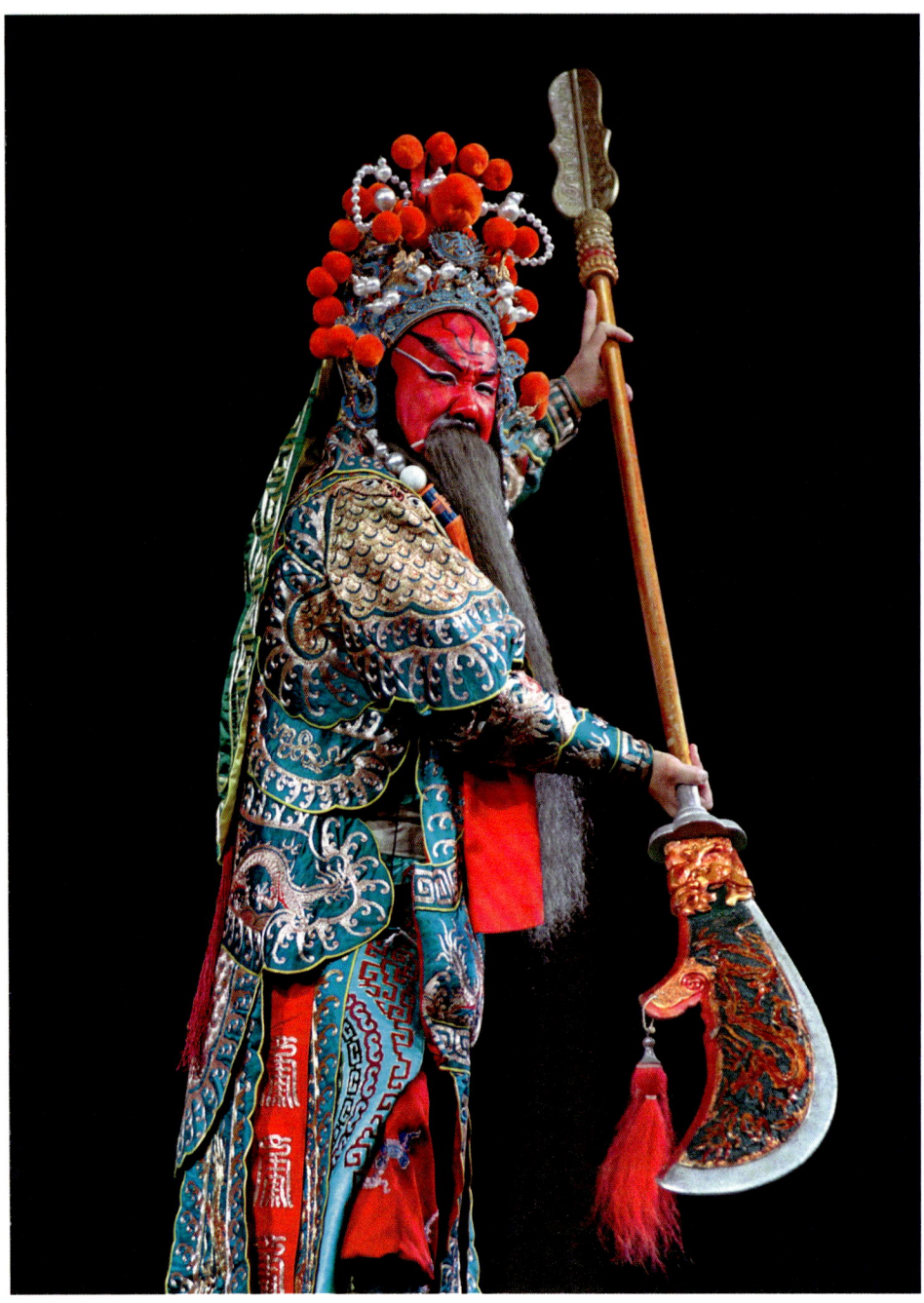

Photo 4.33 *Drowning the Enemy Troops*, Anhui Opera

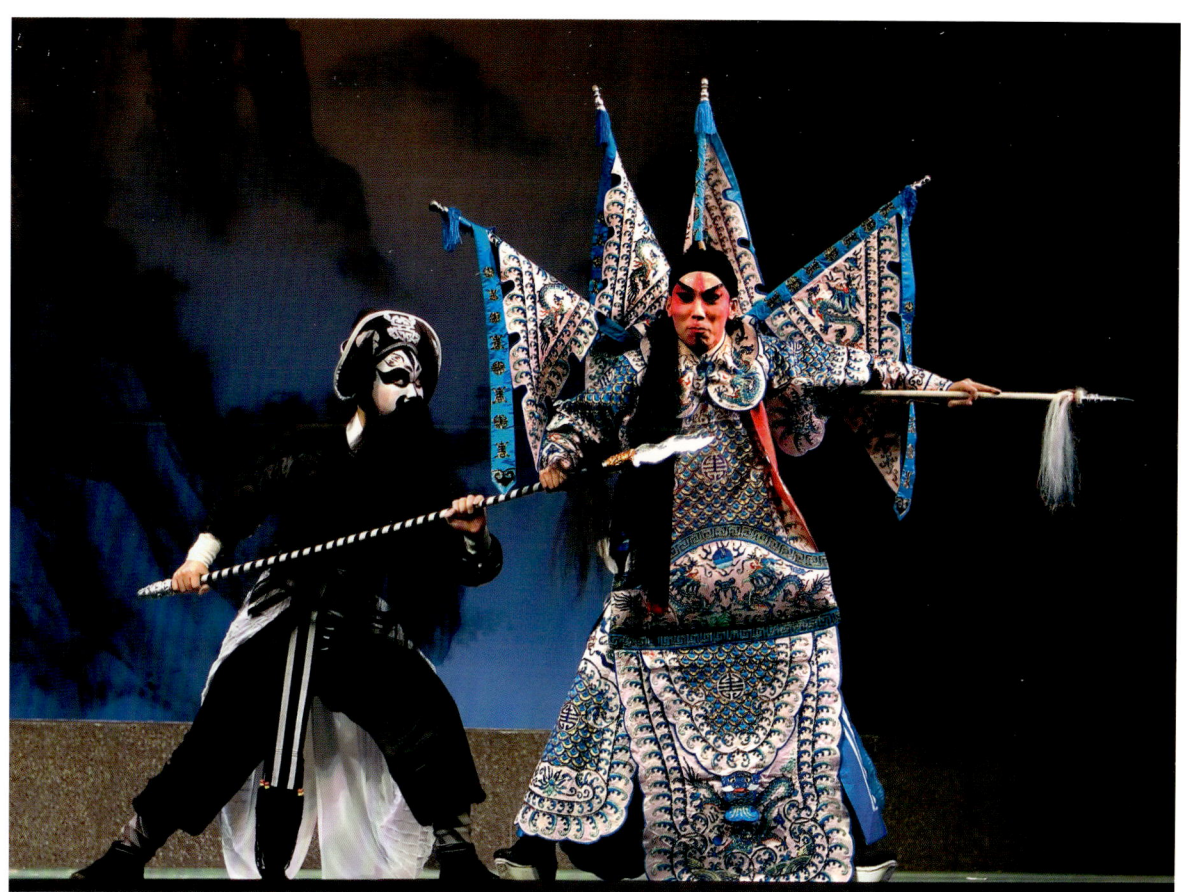

Photo 4.34 *The Battle of Baqiu*, Cantonese Opera

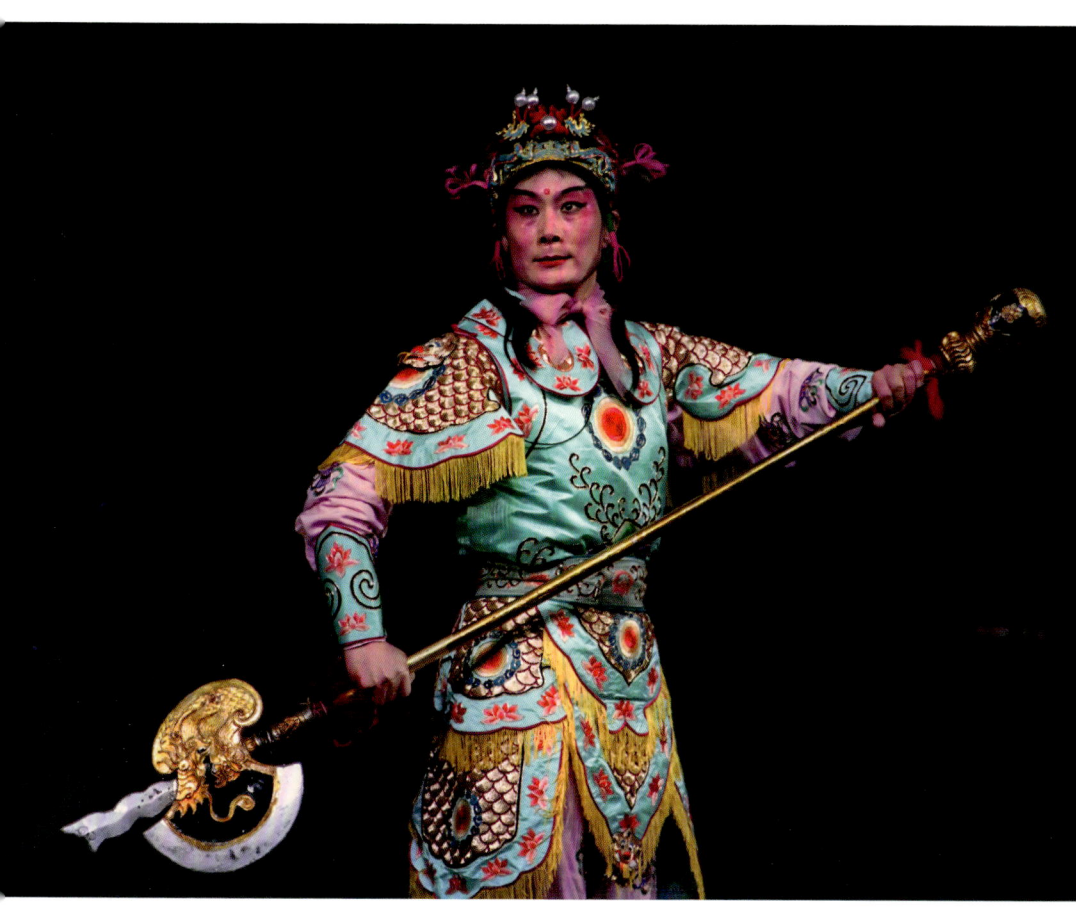

Photo 4.35 *The Magic Lotus Lantern*, Hebei Clapper Opera

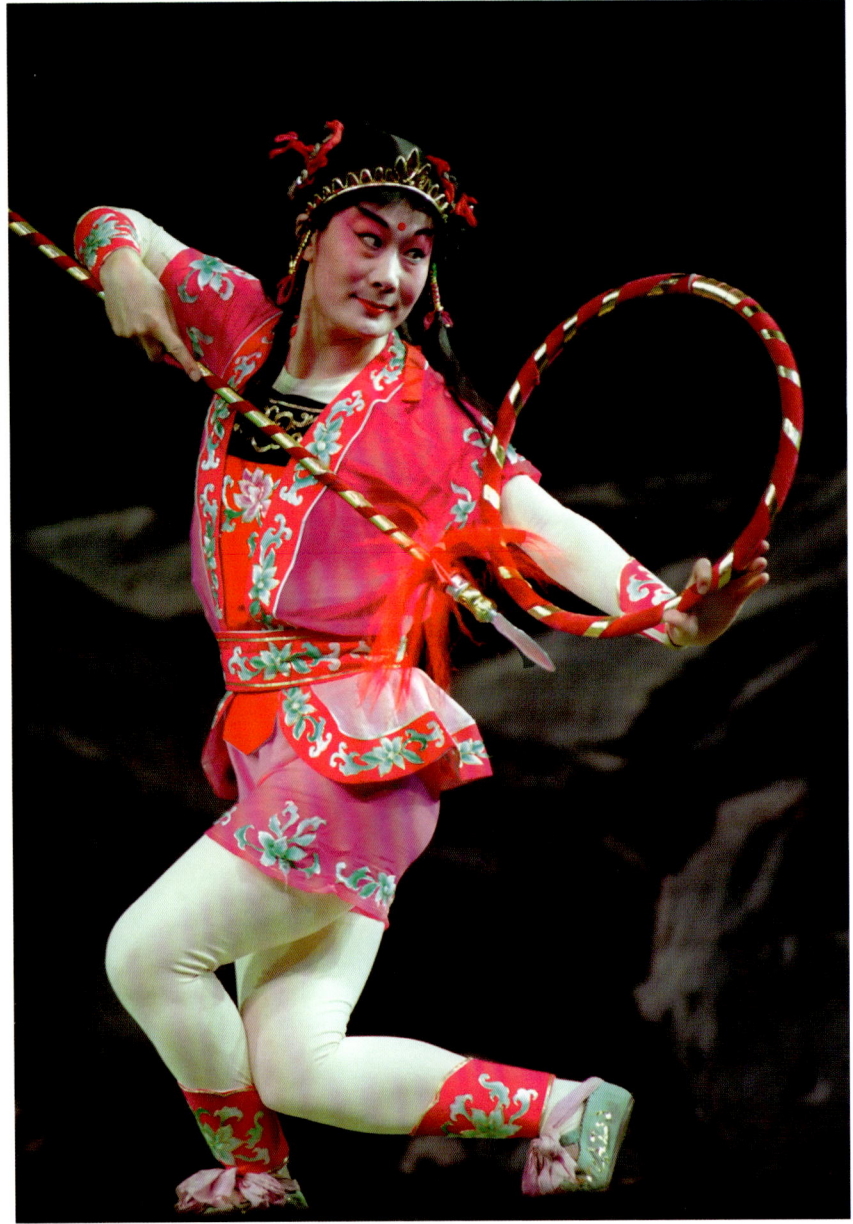

Photo 4.36 *Wreaking Havoc in the Eastern Sea*, Hebei Clapper Opera

Three heroes swore brotherhood in a peach orchard in China's legendary Three Kingdom's period. One of them was Guan Yu, the other was Liu Bei, and the last was the fiery Zhang Fei. Guan Yu's polearm has been described already. Zhang Fei had his light, quick Snake Spear. That weapon differs from the ordinary spear in that it has a long, curving, snake-shaped blade at the end (see Photo 4.34).

Chenxiang wields a long-handled axe as his signature weapon. He is the son of a wayward fairy who incarnated as a human and fell in love with a mortal. Having learned powerful fighting skills from a heavenly being, he is on a mission to rescue his mother, who was imprisoned by the mystical power of the Magic Lotus Lantern for her transgression. When he finds her buried beneath a great mountain, he uses his mighty axe to split the mountain apart. Thus, his weapon has become known as the Mountain-splitting Axe (see Photo 4.35).

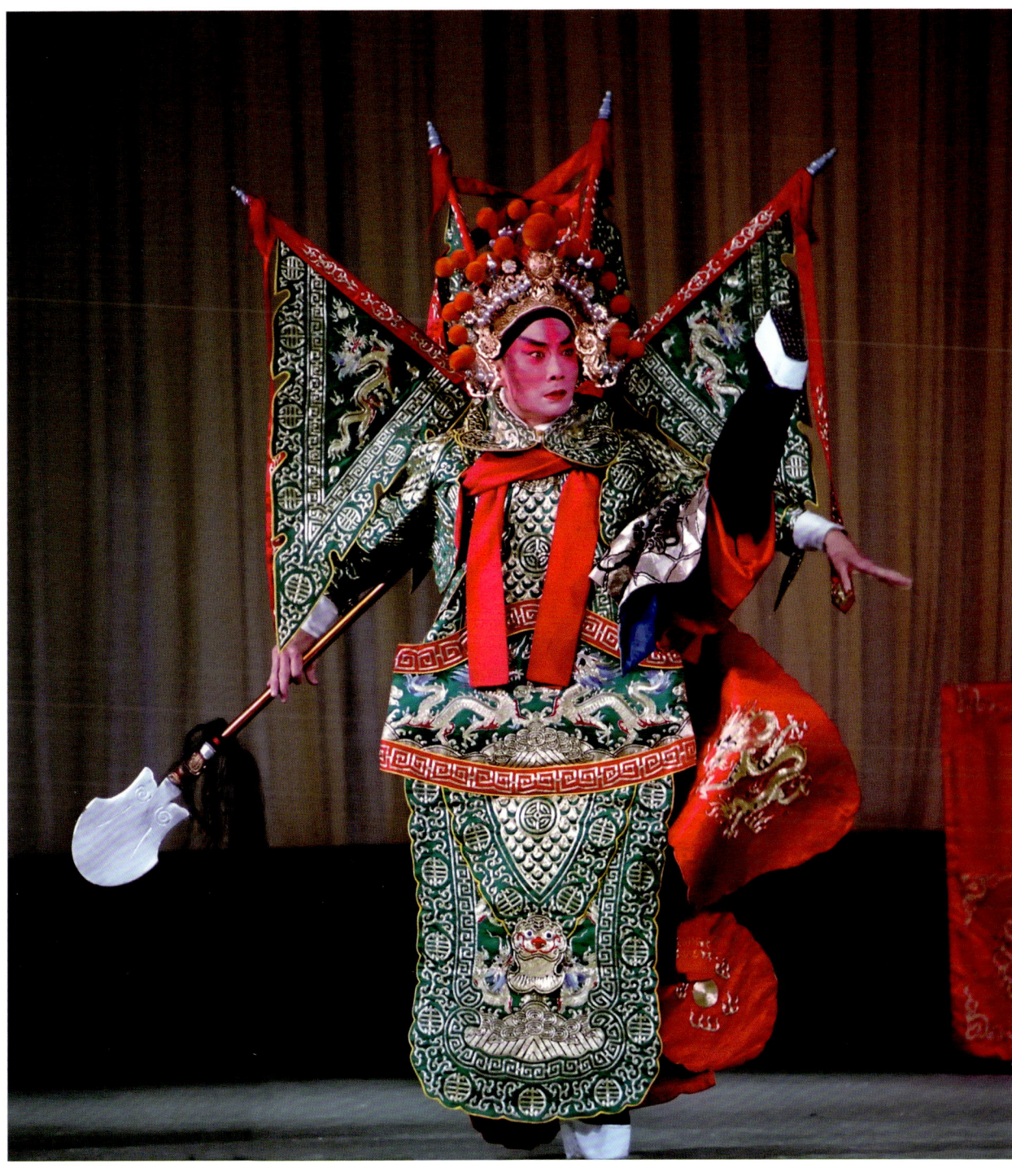

Photo 4.37 *Tilting the War Carts*, Peking Opera

Another mythical being, Nezha, was born in a miraculous way. The young boy soon displays supernatural powers and fights dragons and other powerful beings with his Sharp Fire Spear and his Cosmic Circlet (see Photo 4.36).

The Song dynasty faced invaders from the north. In *Tilting the War Carts*, General Gao Chong uses his signature weapon, a spear with a large sharp blade, to turn over the war carts sent down the mountain by the enemy (see Photo 4.37).

Preparing for Battle

Chinese opera lore has it that in a Ming-dynasty classical opera an actor performed a series of moves getting his armour ready before battle. The opera tells the story of Xiang Yu, the Hegemon King, and his favourite concubine, Yu Ji. Xiang Yu's camp has been encircled by the enemy. There is no way out except to try a desperate escape. Yu Ji kills herself so as not to burden her beloved lord with the care of her safety. The scene is called "The Hegemon Rises" or *Qiba*. This series of moves, which denotes checking the armour in preparation for battle, became a standard performance skill in Chinese opera. Embellished and refined over the years, the series is still called *qiba* after the original scene. There are several sets of *qiba*. Among them, the male character *qiba* and female character *qiba* are fundamental.

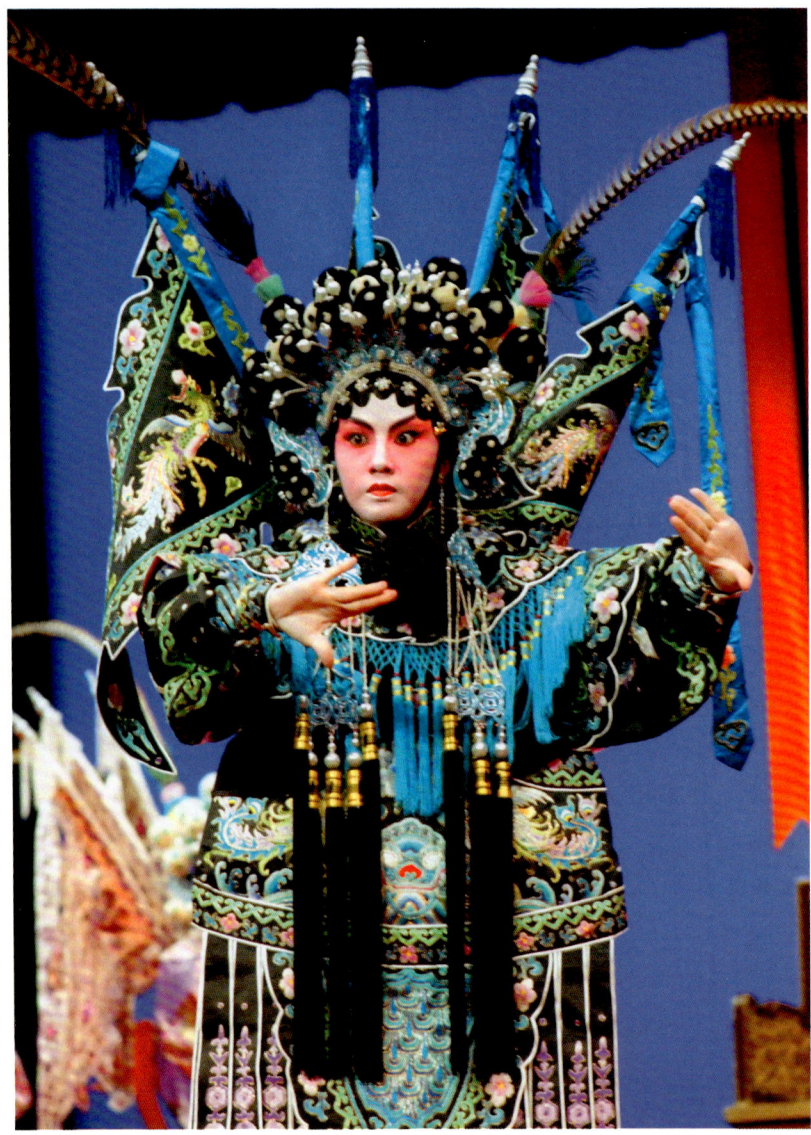

Photo 4.38 *Women Warriors of the Yang Family*, Cantonese Opera

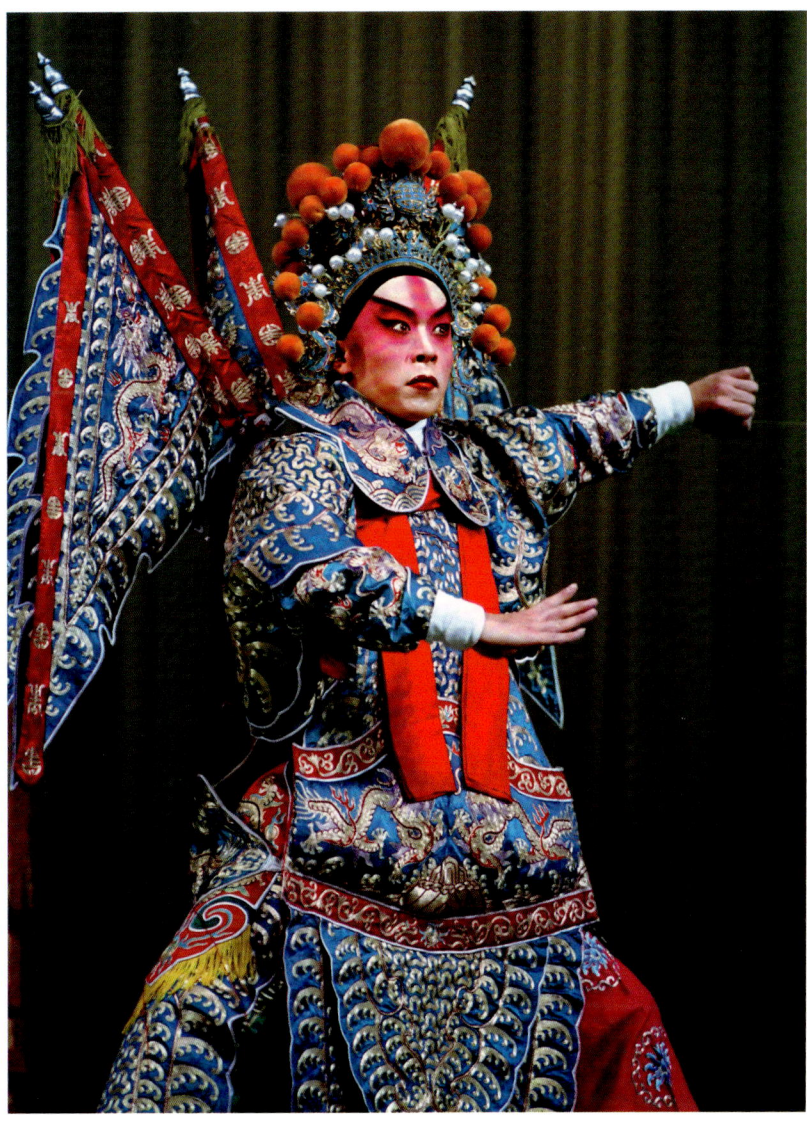

Photo 4.39 *Tilting the War Carts*, Peking Opera

Male Qiba

In *Tilting the War Carts*, Gao Chong prepares for battle against his enemy. It will be a heroic battle that will in the end cost him his life. The character enters the stage with a flourish, raising his leg and lifting up his armour with both hands. He poses to indicate his courage and readiness to fight. Stepping forward, he checks his boots, bends his legs in a squatting horse position, and extends his arms in the double mountain shoulder pose. He shakes his armour and the command flags on his back, raises his hands to check his helmet, then circles his hands in a move called "cloud hands" to tighten his breast plate. Taking a step, he lifts his armour, and takes another pose. One hand makes a fist, ready to fight, while the other hand is open, palm facing the stage. Finally, in a move called "Waiting for the Command", he steps forward ready to fight, awaiting the moment for battle. In some *qiba*, the character will raise his right hand, while his left hand lifts his armour (see Photos 4.40, 4.41 and 4.42).

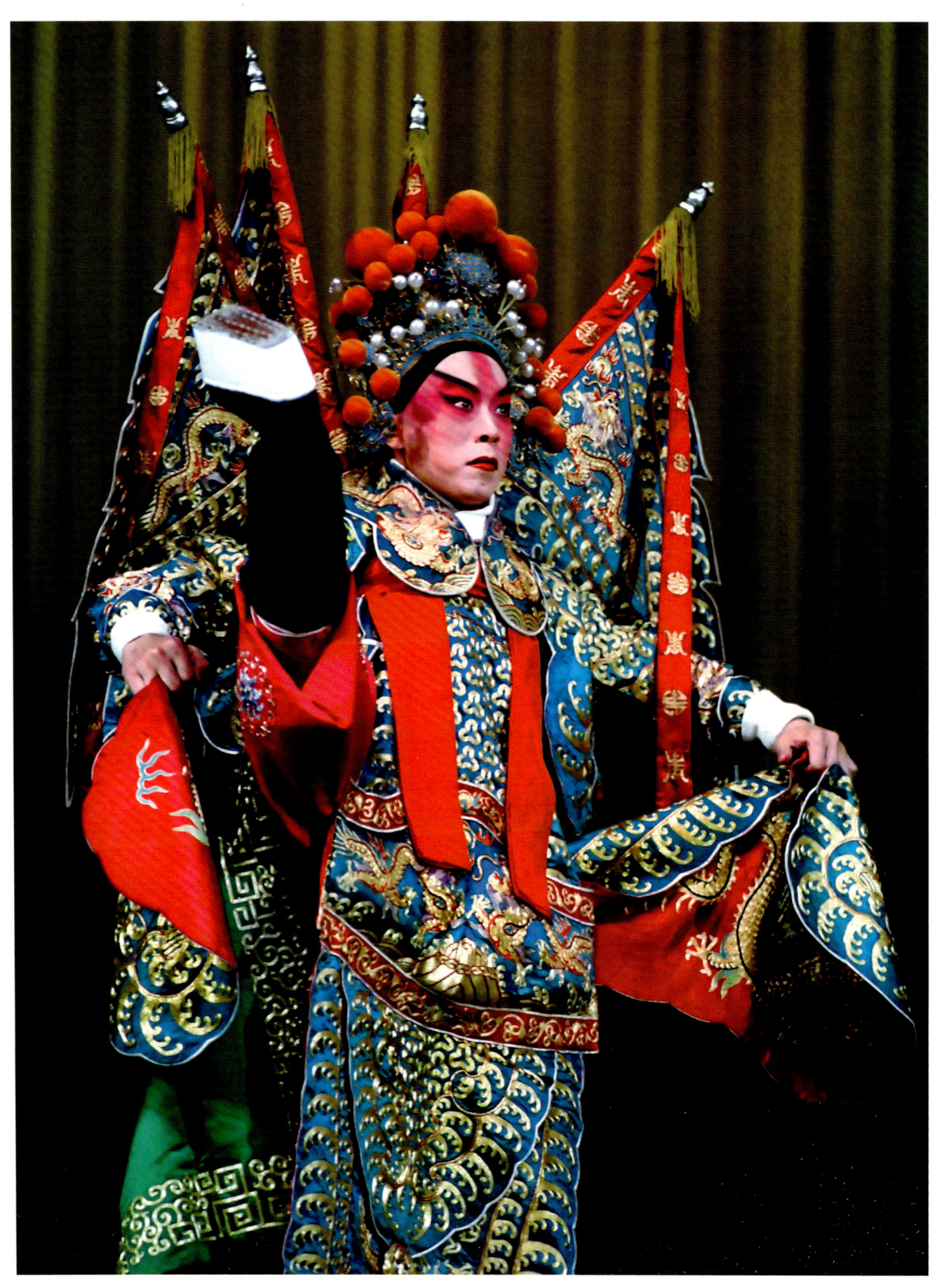

Photo 4.40 *Tilting the War Carts*, Peking Opera

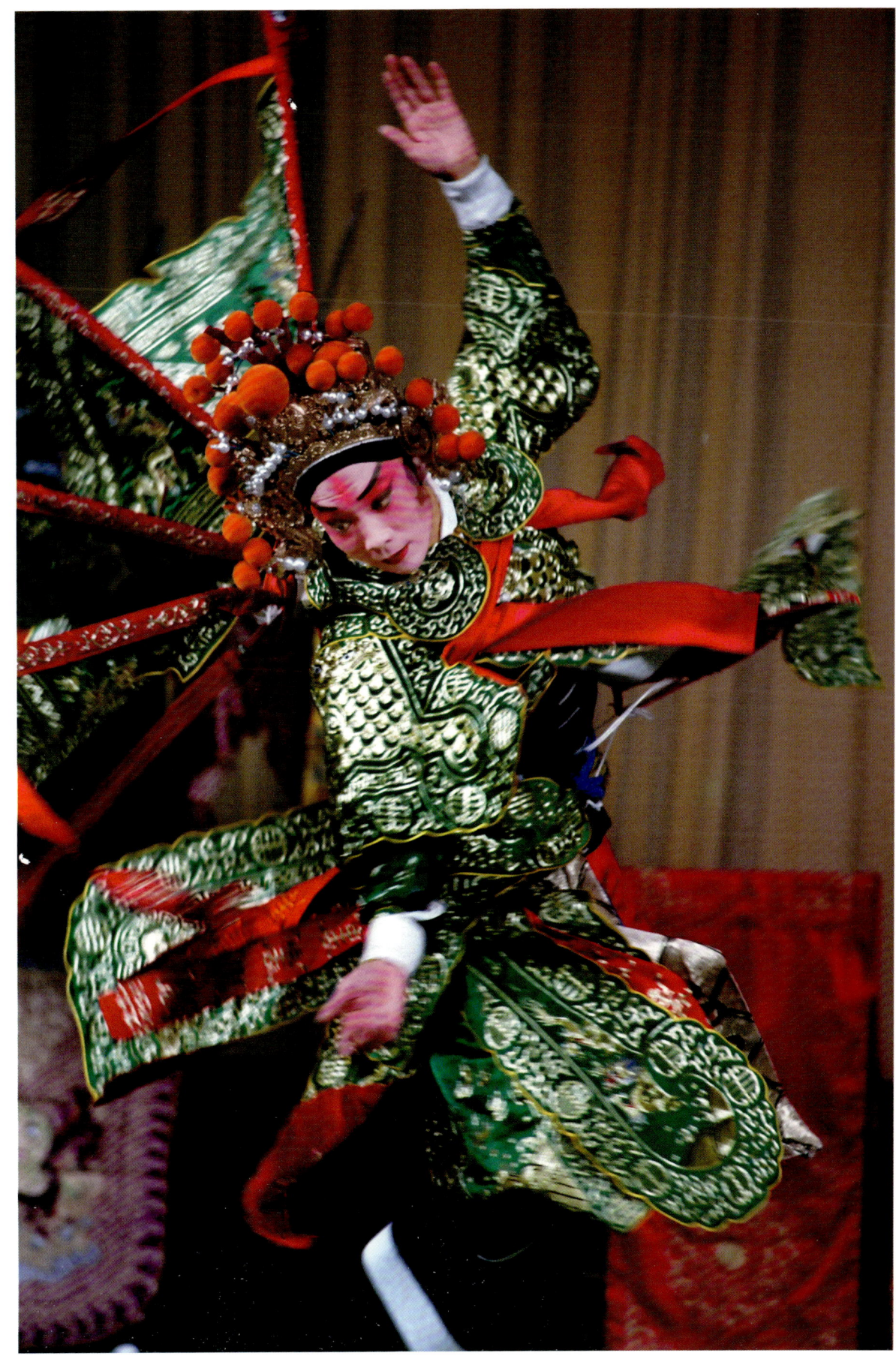

Photo 4.41 *Tilting the War Carts,* Peking Opera

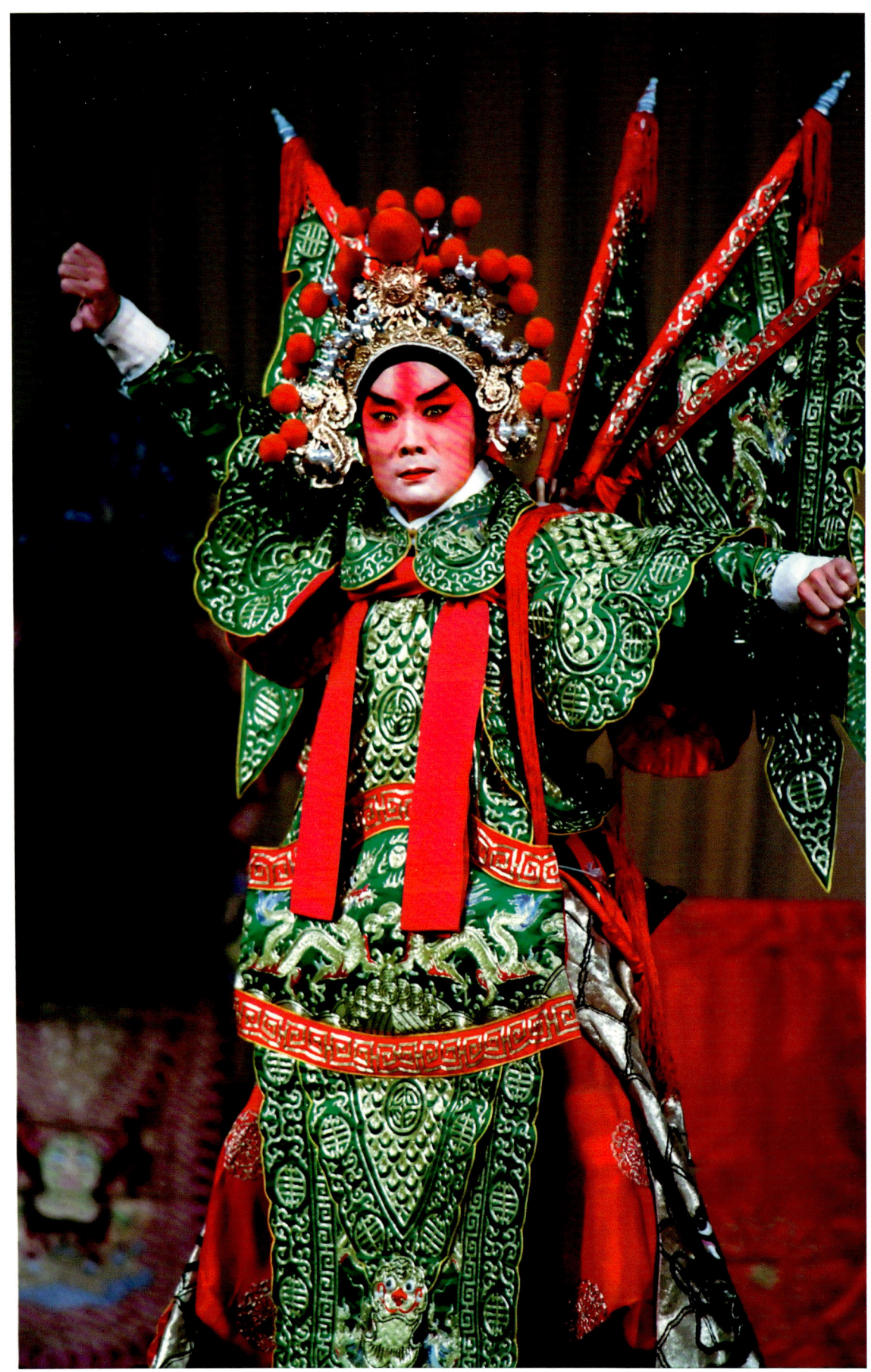

Photo 4.42 *Tilting the War Carts*, Peking Opera

Female Qiba

FORMIDABLE FEMALE WARRIORS are commonplace on the Chinese opera stage. One of these, Hu Sanniang, is skilled at martial arts. She has married into the Zhu family, cementing an alliance between the two villages. One day, while practising her kungfu in the garden, she hears that the famous Liang Mountain bandits are attacking. She leads her female fighters out to war and captures one of their leaders, Wang Ying.

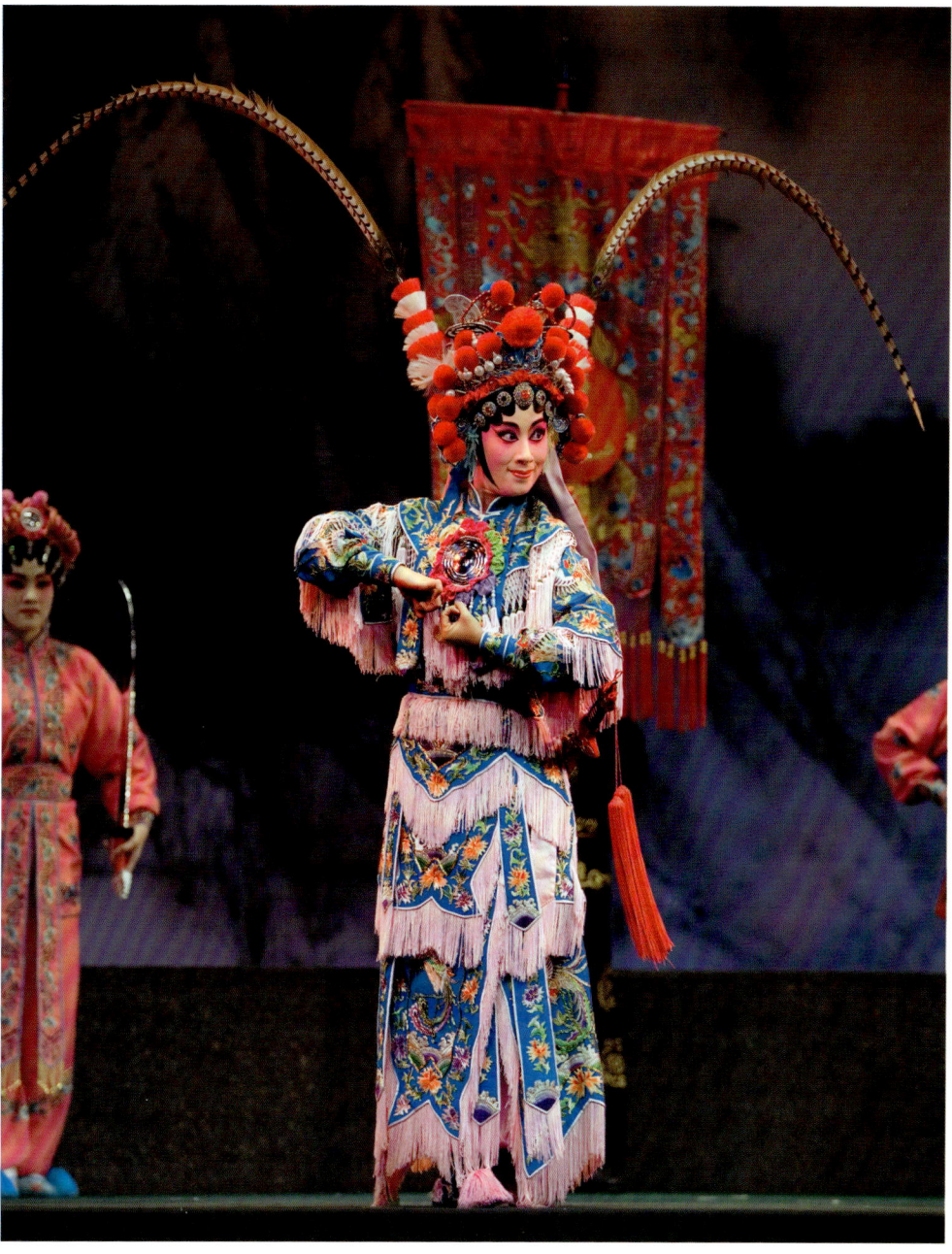

Photo 4.43 *Raid on Hu Village*, Cantonese Opera

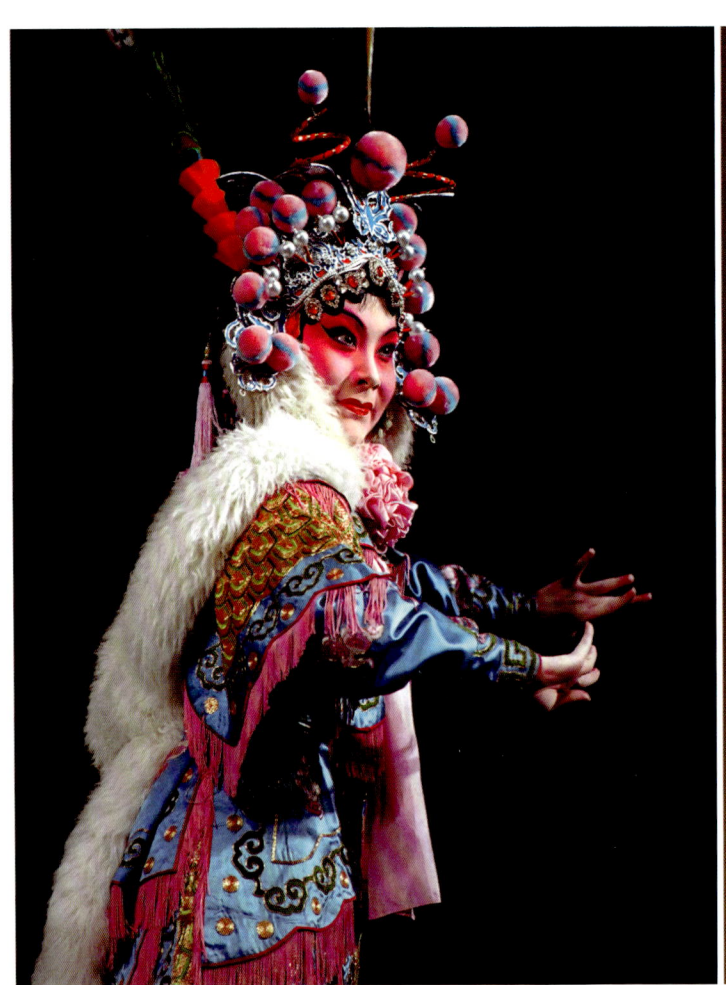
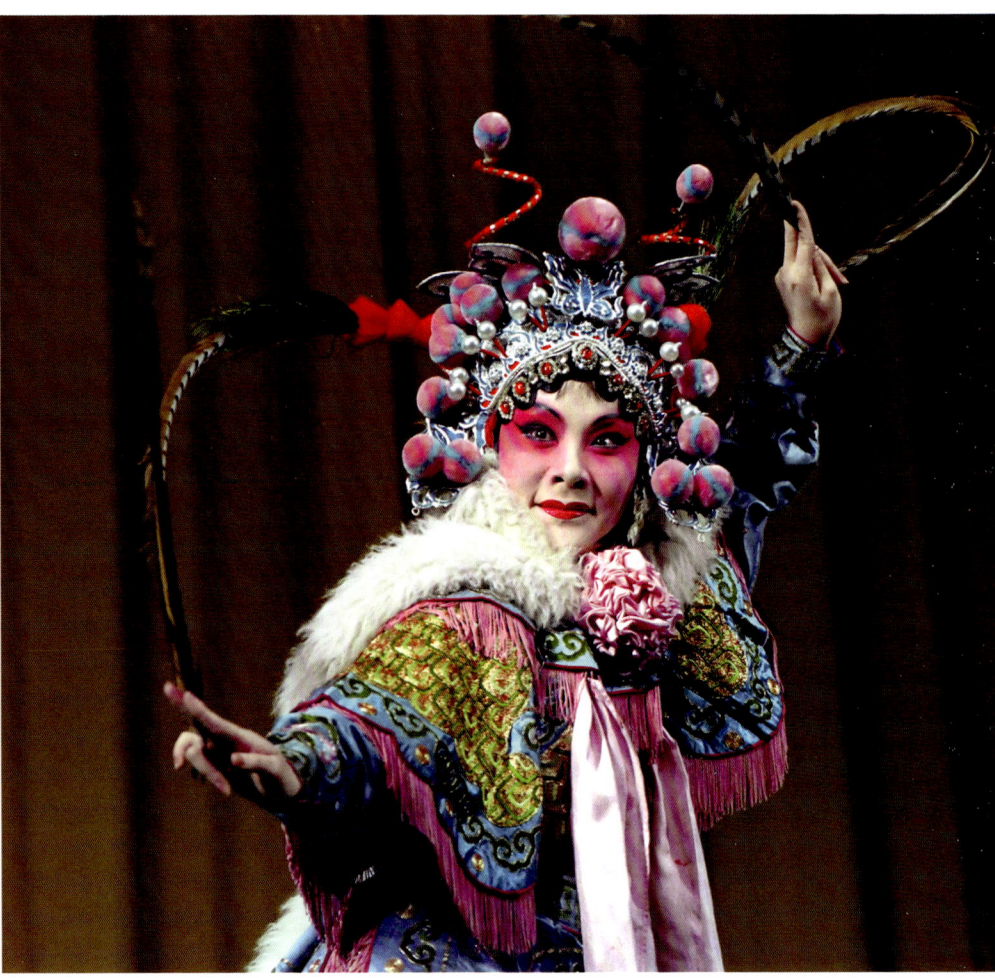

As a female warrior, she has her own *qiba*. Holding her armour and grabbing her weapons, she enters the stage accompanied by vigorous drumming and the clanging of gongs. She clasps her sword hilt with her left hand and holds the pheasant tail on her headdress with the other, twisting it and then releasing it to snap it back into place. Carefully checking her armour with her hands, she grasps her sword hilt again. Crossing her legs and squatting, she brings both pheasant tails forward in front of her.

Hu Sanniang then performs a series of quick moves: trying out her boots, swaying her waist, and grabbing both of the pheasant feathers as she turns her body in a low backward bend. The female warrior, like her male counterpart, then adjusts her helmet and tightens her armour. After that, she takes a finishing pose, preparing to give orders for the attack (see Photos 4.44, 4.45 and 4.46).

Qiba combines mime, dance and acrobatic skill in a series of moves that demonstrate an actor's precision and artistic flare. It sets the scene for the drama that is to follow.

Above, left
Photo 4.44   *Raid on Hu Village*, Peking Opera

Above, right
Photo 4.45   *Raid on Hu Village*, Peking Opera

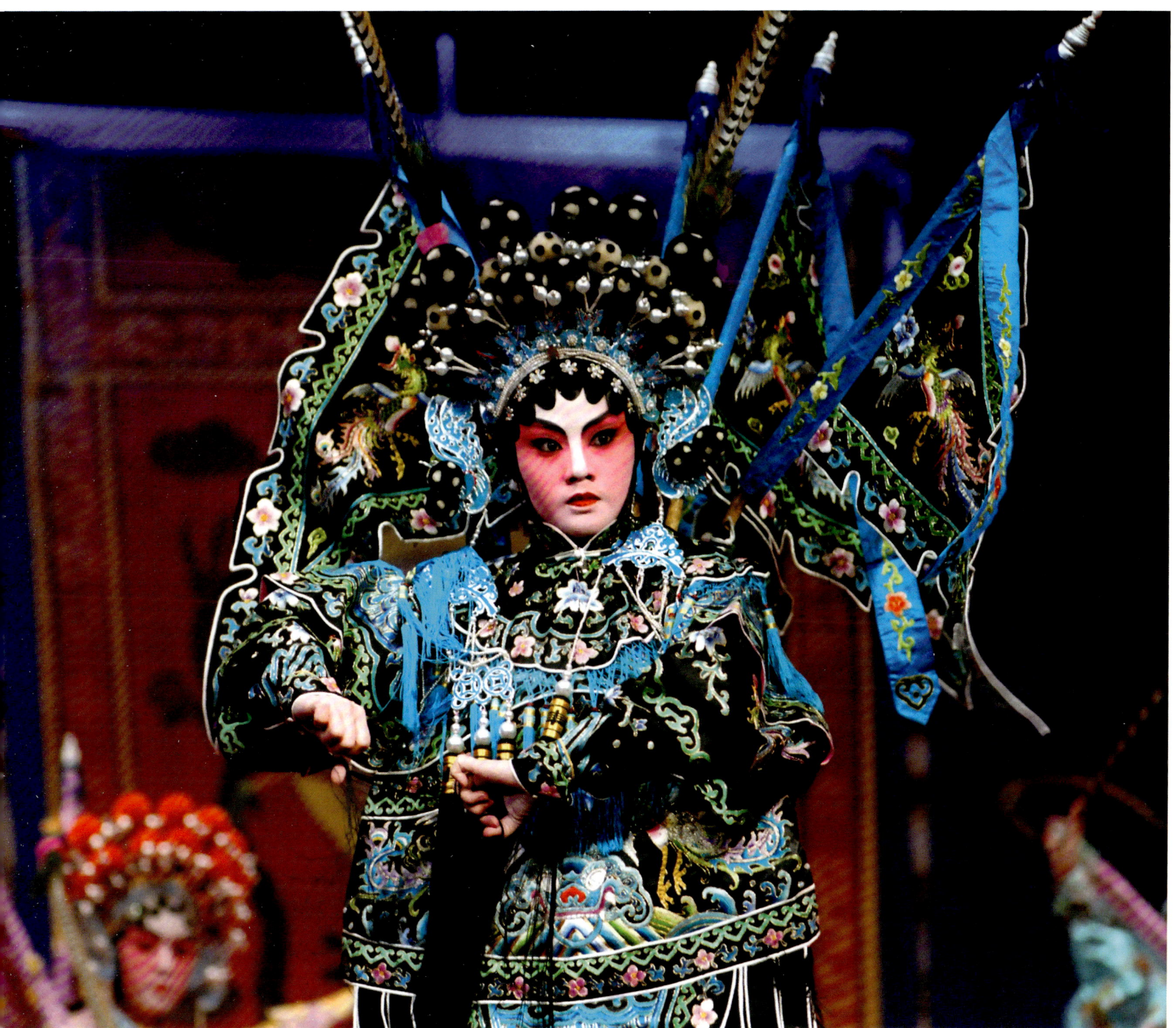

Photo 4.46 *Women Warriors of the Yang Family*, Cantonese Opera

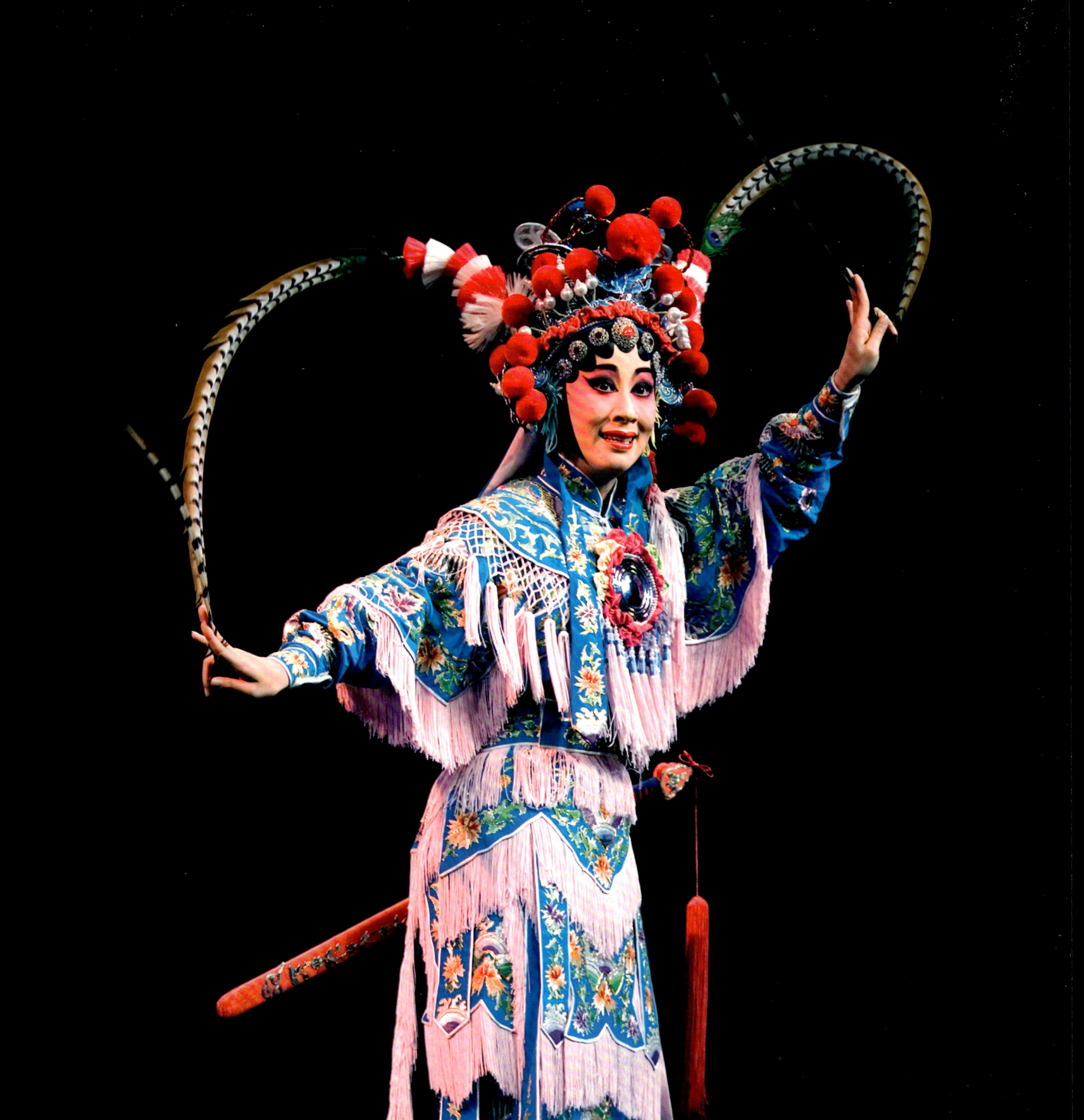

CHAPTER 5

Using Costumes

Opposite
Photo 5.01 *Raid on Hu Village,* Cantonese Opera

Pheasant Tails

THE MALE, FEMALE, painted face, and clown roles in Chinese opera all use pheasant tail skills for particular characters. The young man's role even has a particular subcategory role type for it. These actors play heroic, and sometimes fierce, characters, who enter the stage with two long pheasant tails attached to their headdresses. These feathers can be as long as six feet. They are more, however, than just dramatic additions to the costume. They are also tools that the actor manipulates to express a wide range of emotions from joy to anger, from thoughtfulness to determination. The actors use two fingers of each hand to hold and bend the tails in various poses both in front of and behind themselves. They even clench the feathers in their teeth. The feathers instantly spring back when released and thus permit the actor to demonstrate both graceful and striking poses. Originally the mark of warriors from distant places, pheasant tails have come to be used by many characters, including spirits, who often pair the feathers with fox tails on their headgear. This technique is found in most opera styles.

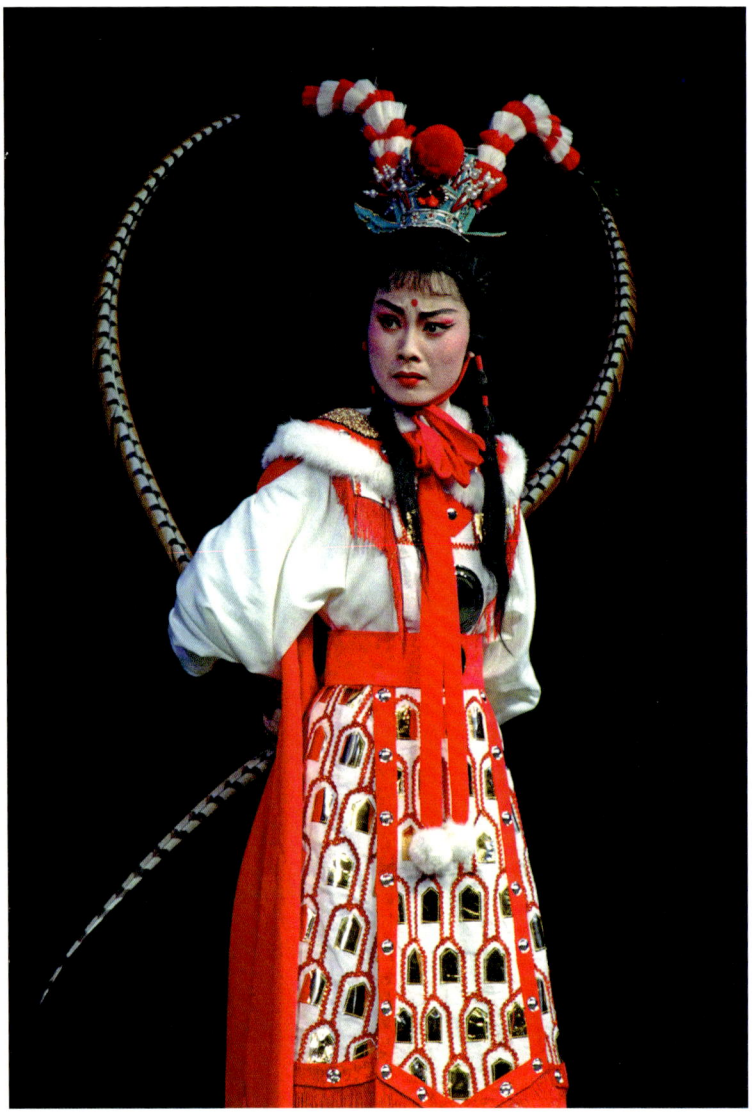

In one opera, the actor shows his changing internal state through his use of the pheasant tail feathers. The young man, Liu Chengyou, played by a woman in Yue opera tradition, comes across a woman, Li Sanniang, while stopping at a well during a hunt. As they talk, they begin to suspect that they are actually mother and son, separated for over sixteen years. This growing awareness is demonstrated by Liu's manipulation of the large pheasant tails on his headdress while he listens to Li Sanniang. First, he grabs both feathers and bends them down behind his back in a pose of attentive listening (see Photo 5.02).

But as he hears more of her story, he expresses first surprise and then growing agitation by circling and raising one feather with his left hand, and extending the other feather downward in front of him with his right hand (see Photo 5.03).

In other operas, bending the pheasant tails can also express delight. A white eel cultivated itself through much spiritual practice and developed into a fairy. She lived for a long time in a fairy cave without ever visiting the human world. One day, deciding it was time to see where humanity lived, she travelled

Photo 5.02 *The Story of the White Rabbit*, Yue Opera

Opposite
Photo 5.03 *The Story of the White Rabbit*, Yue Opera

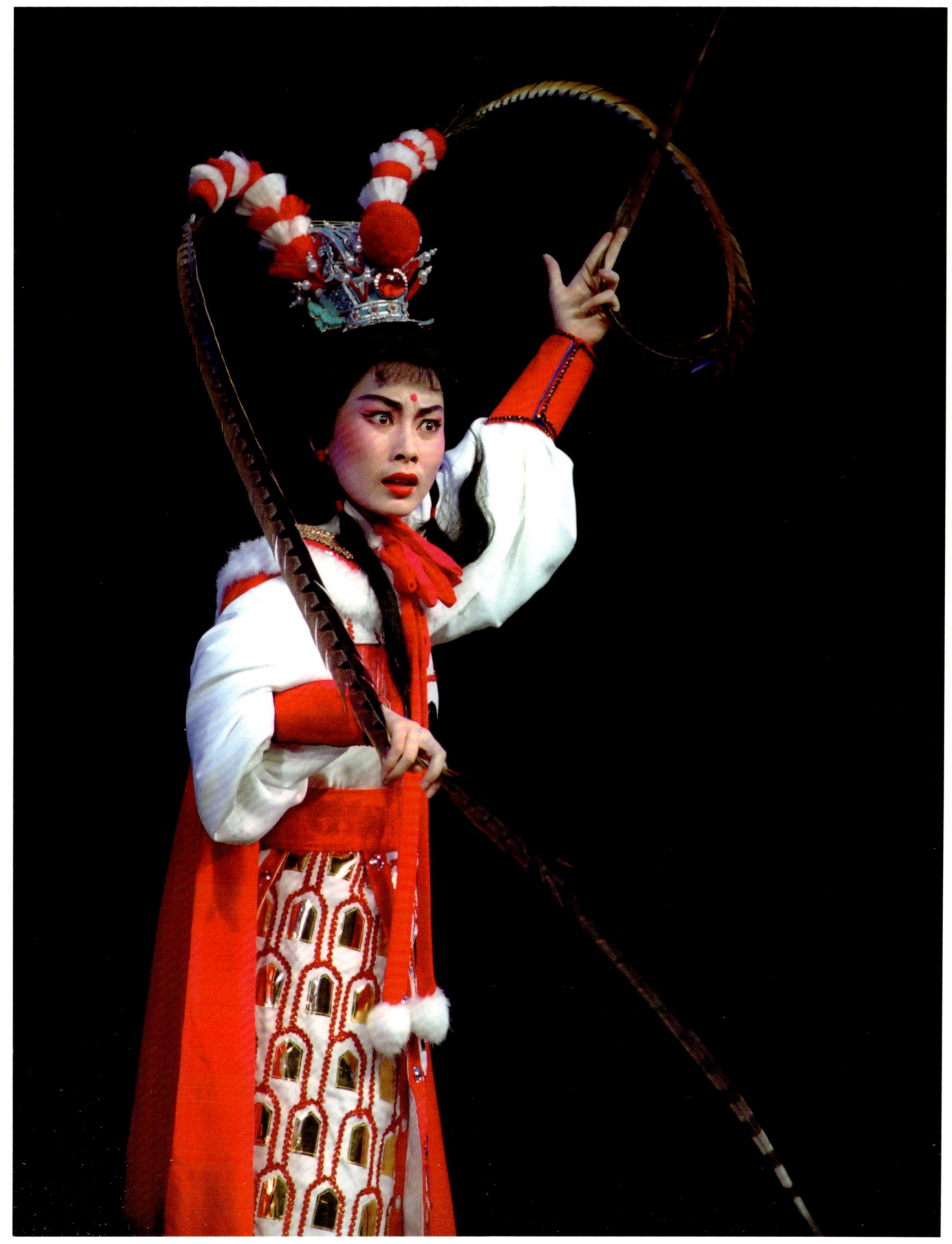

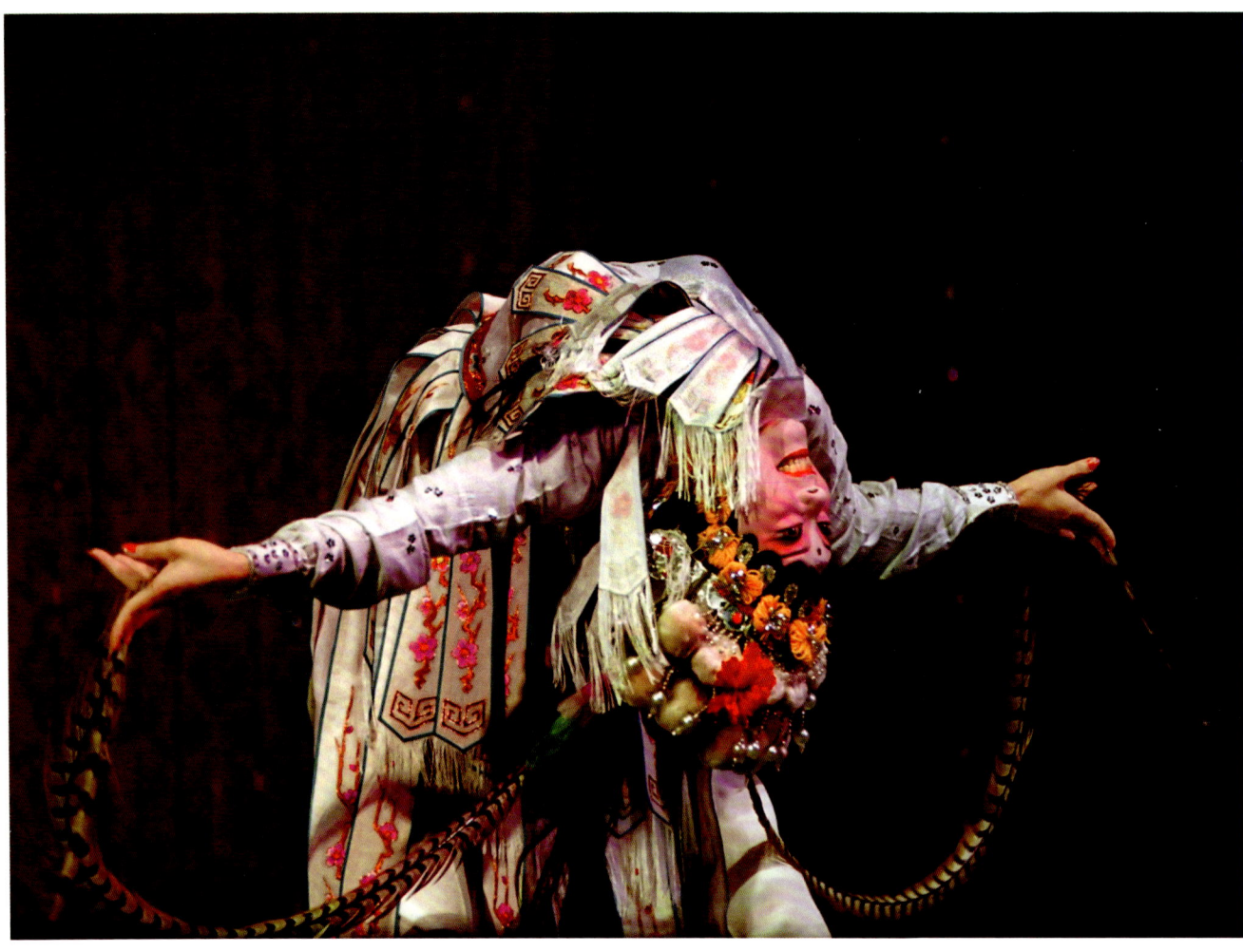

Photo 5.04 *Delights of the Mortal World*, Sichuan Opera

in a fairy boat to our world. Once here, she is amazed at the beauty and marvels she sees. Intoxicated with delight, she arches backward, bending her waist. She grabs the pheasant tails between the second and third fingers of each hand, extending them to either side in a gesture of pure joy (see Photo 5.04).

The beloved Monkey King character also makes use of pheasant tails to express his feelings. While frolicking with his monkey clan on the Mountain of Flowers and Fruits, he learns that his master, the monk Xuanzang, has been captured by the White-Boned Demon. He grabs both pheasant tails, bending one up and the other down taking a pose of defiance and bravery as he determines to go and do battle (see Photo 5.05).

The pheasant tails can express very different emotions from joy to bravado. They can also express the vitality of evil. One of the great villains of the Chinese opera stage is Prince Yang Guang, son of the founder of the Sui dynasty (581–618). Pretending to be concerned for his father's illness, he was, in fact, eager for the emperor to die so that he could take over. His ambitions were not hidden for long; he drove his father to an early grave and struggled with his own mother for the crown, resulting in her death, too.

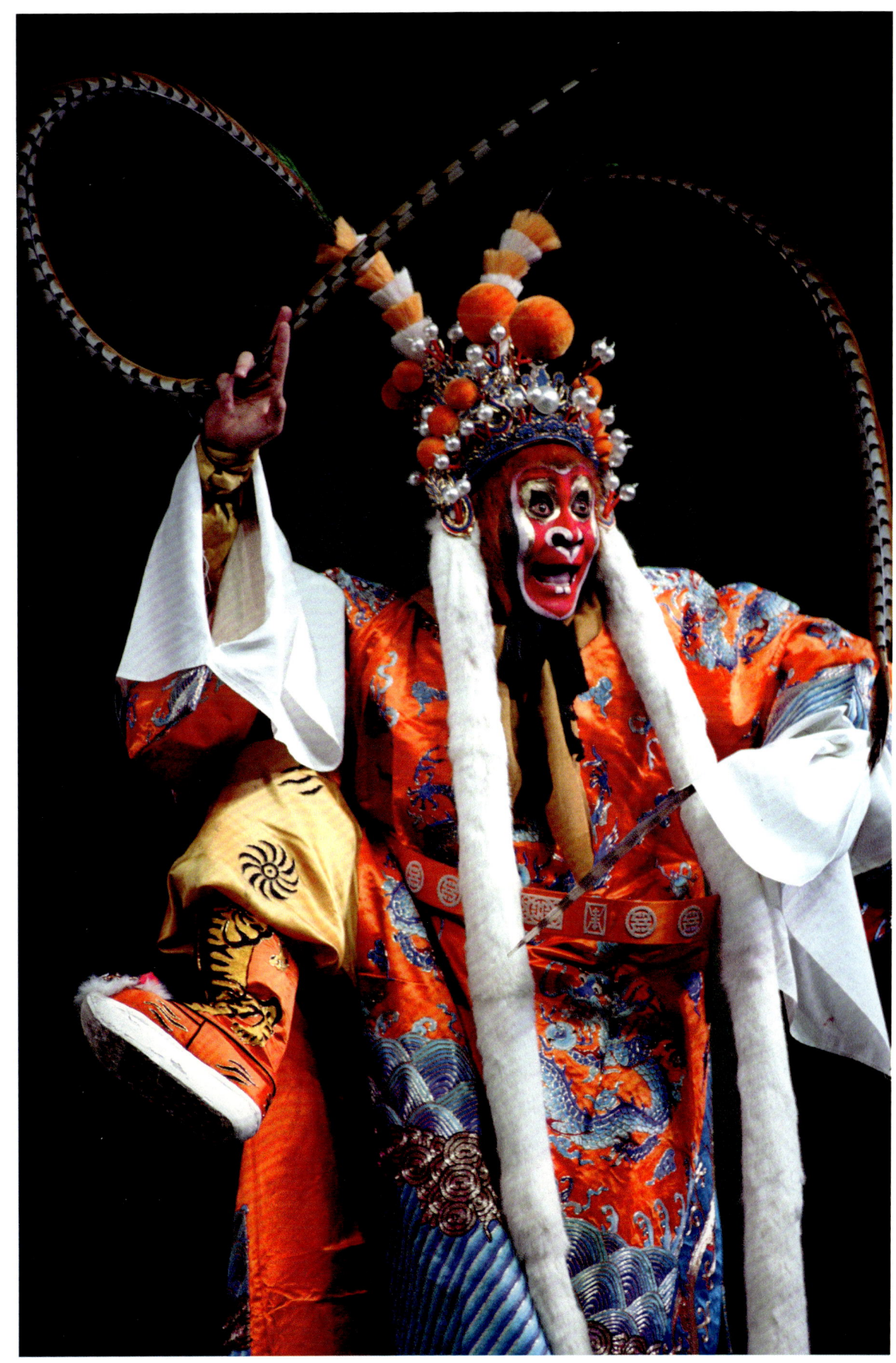

Photo 5.05 *Monkey King Battles the White-Boned Demon*, Shao Opera

Photo 5.06 *Wresting the Dragon Throne*, Sichuan Opera

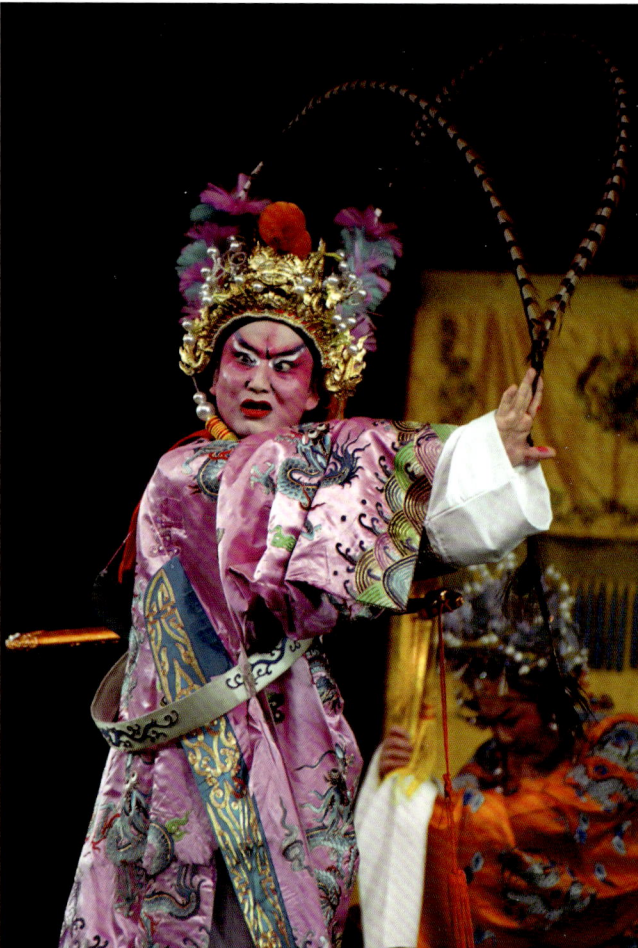

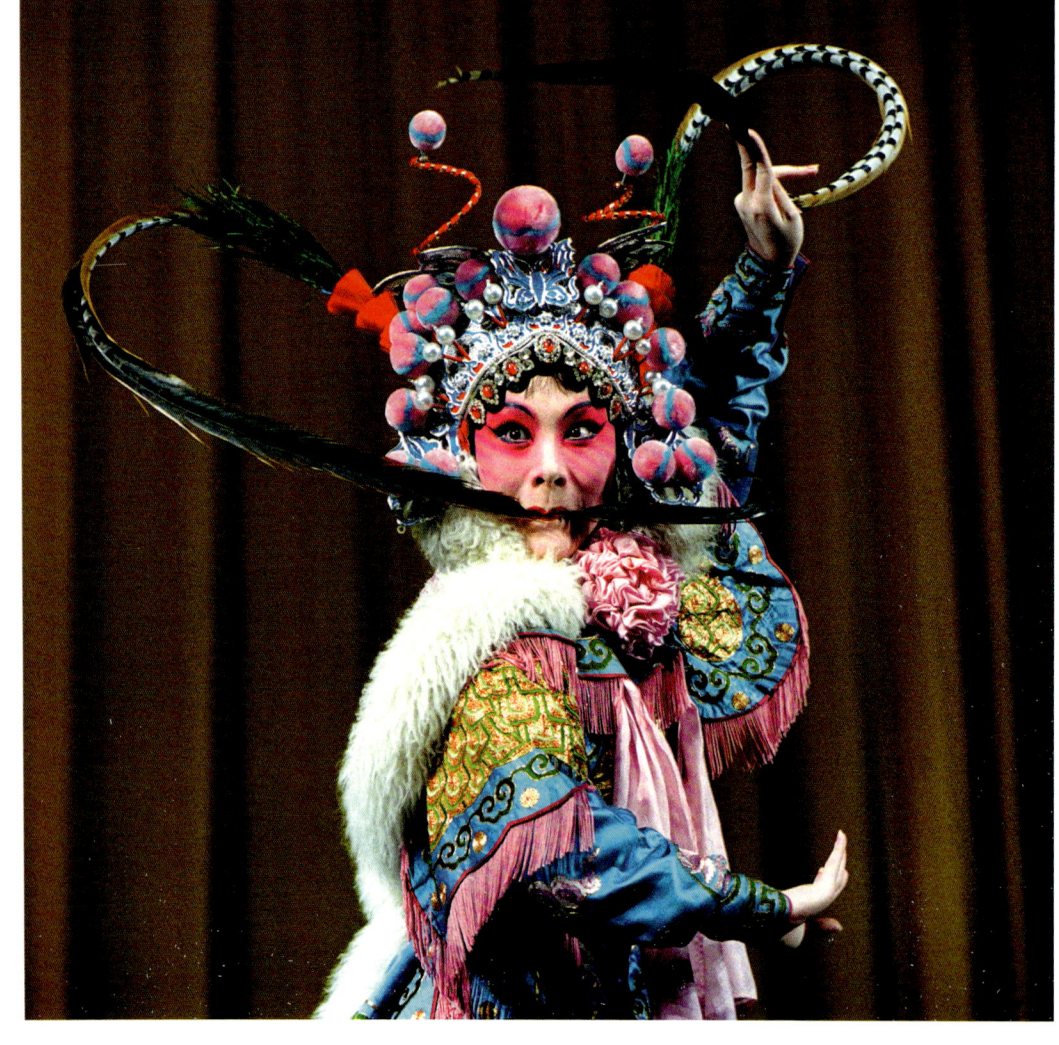

Photo 5.07 *Raid on Hu Village*, Peking Opera

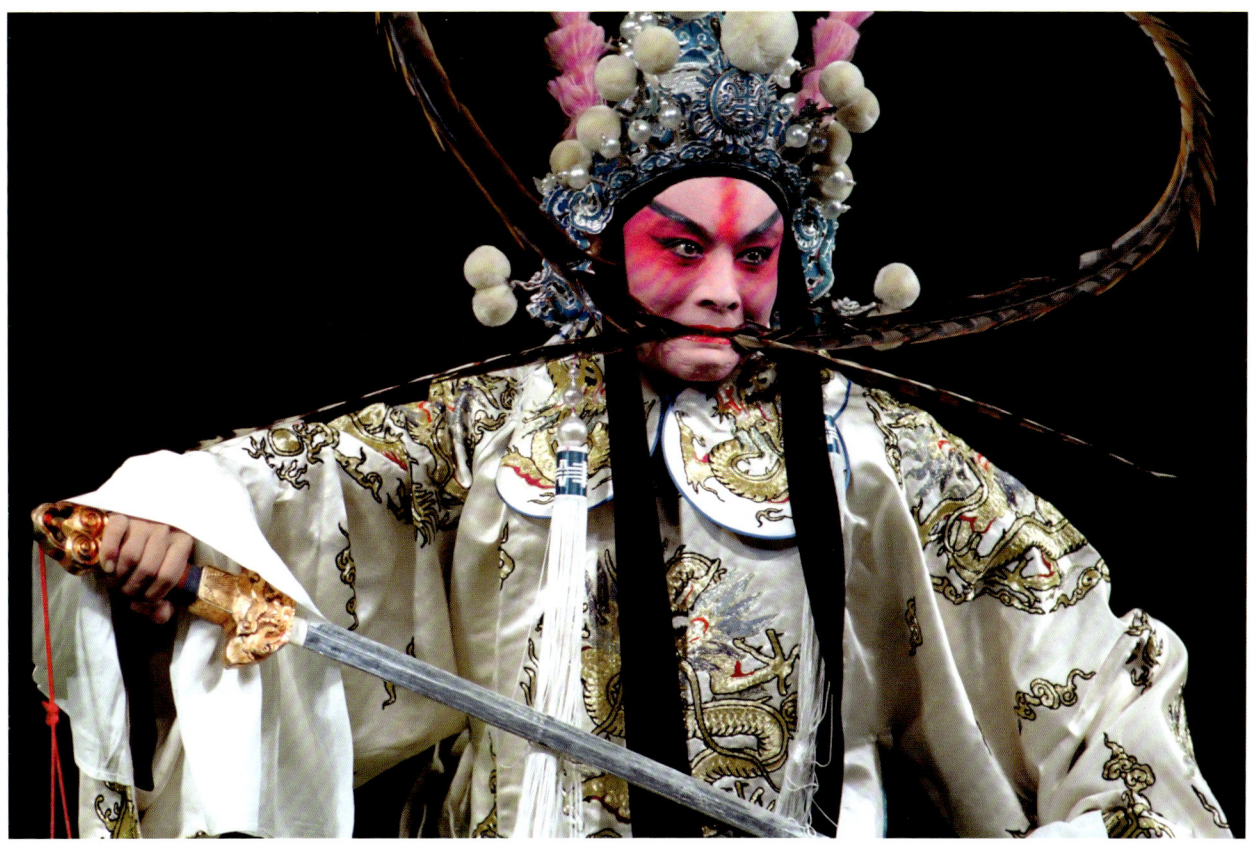

Photo 5.08 *Meeting at the Riverside*, Anhui Opera

In the Sichuan opera, *Wresting the Dragon Throne*, the make-up of Prince Yang Guang changes as his ambition becomes more aggressive. After the death of his parents, he grabs the pheasant tails between his fingers, thrusting them forward in a gesture of exaggerated cruelty and violence (see Photo 5.06).

Actors also use their mouths to clamp down on the pheasant tails to show determination. Song Jiang, the leader of a band of robbers, is to China as Robin Hood is to England. He sent one of his band, Wang Ying, to lead an attack against Hu village. The warrior maiden of the village decides to go out and defend her people. Before setting out, she strikes a dramatic warrior pose, and to show her fixed determination, she grabs one feather above her head with her left hand, while clenching the other in her mouth (see Photo 5.07).

Another character in a different opera also shows his determination by clenching both pheasant feathers in his teeth. The night before the greatest battle in ancient China, the Battle of Red Cliff, General Zhou Yu invites Liu Bei, leader of a small army, to come see him on the pretence of discussing strategy against their common enemy, Cao Cao. His real intention, however, is to murder his rival once in his grasp. Having set his mind to his plan, Zhou Yu holds his sword and expresses his determination by biting down on the crossed pheasant feathers (see Photo 5.08).

Headgear

CHARACTERS WEAR A wide variety of headgear in Chinese opera. These headgear identify rank and function. They are also used, as are so many other parts of the costume, to express feelings.

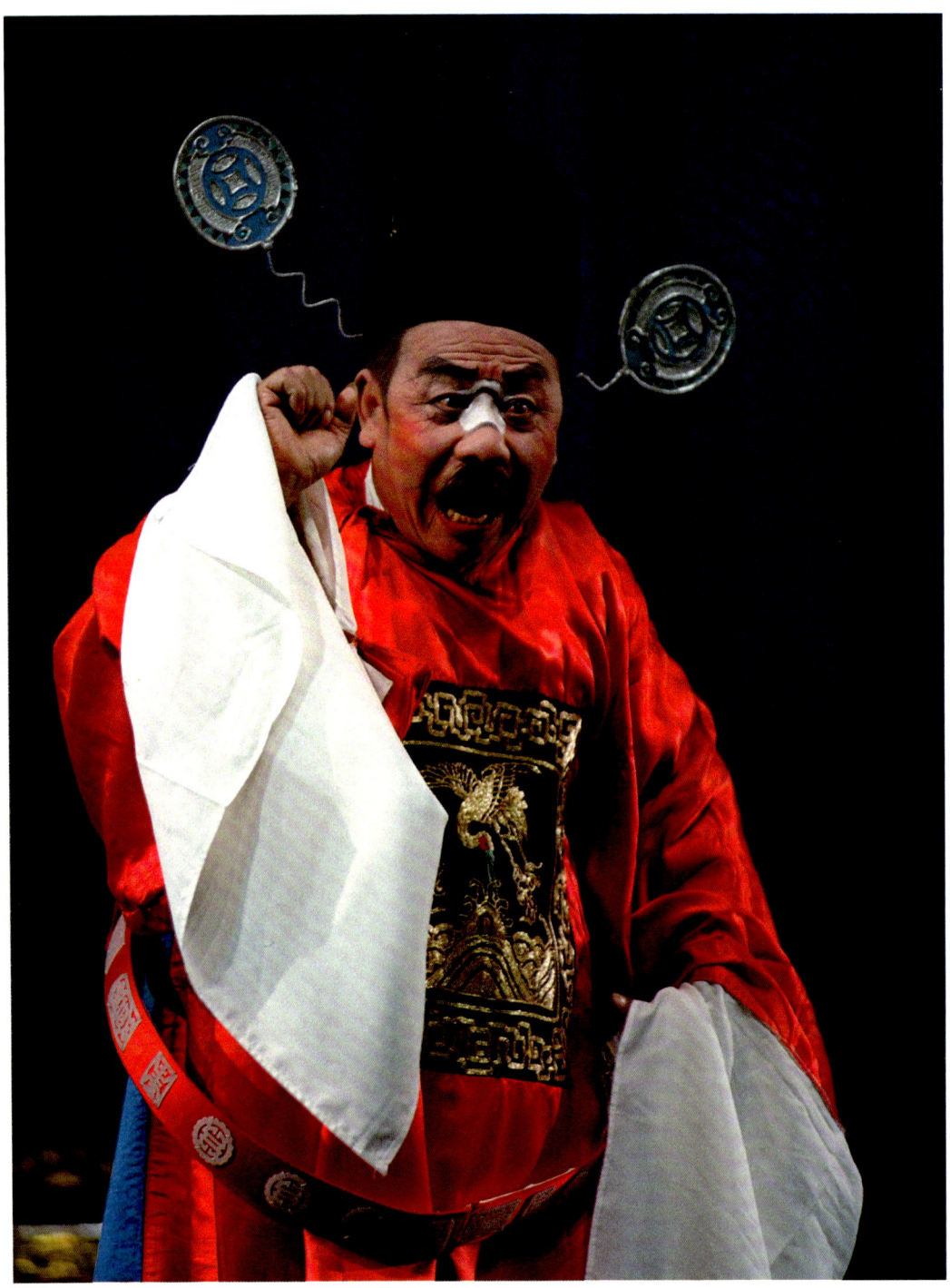

Photo 5.09 *The Trial of Chen San*, Gaojia Opera

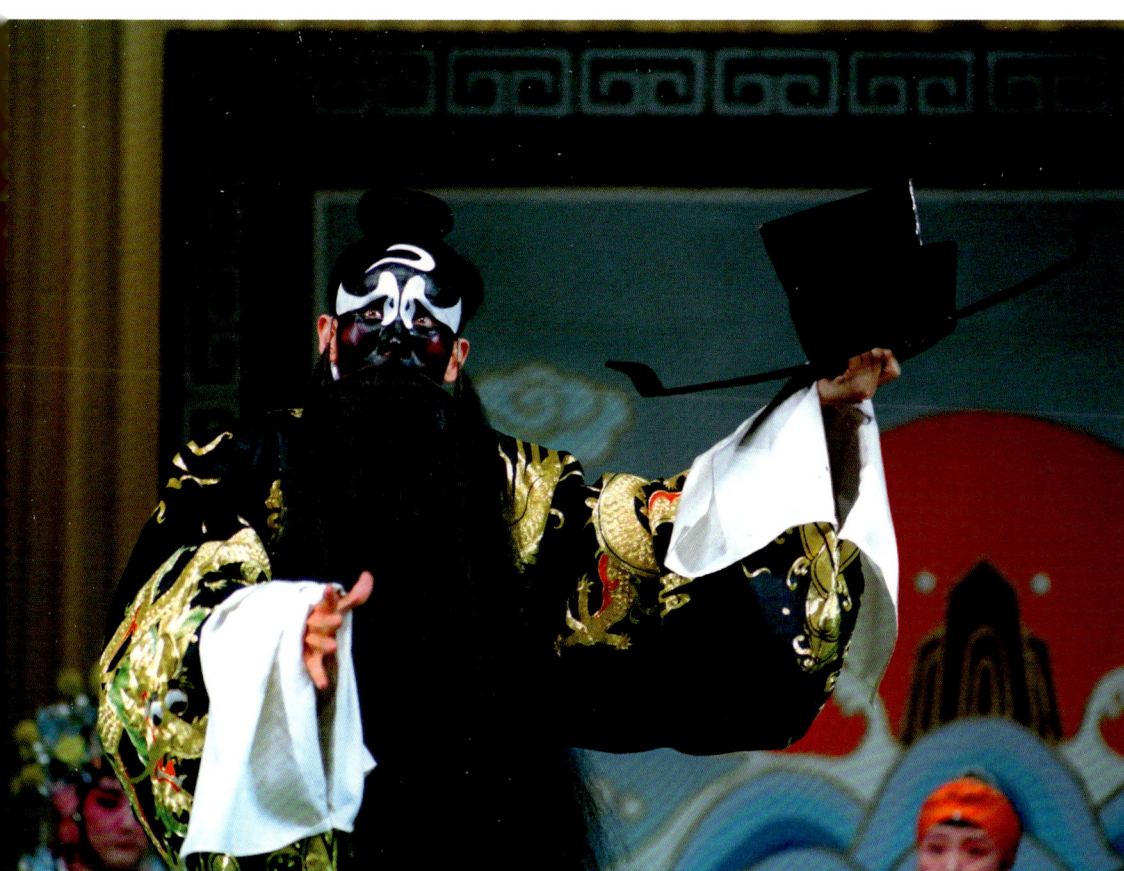

Photo 5.10 *The Beheading of a Wicked Husband*, Peking Opera

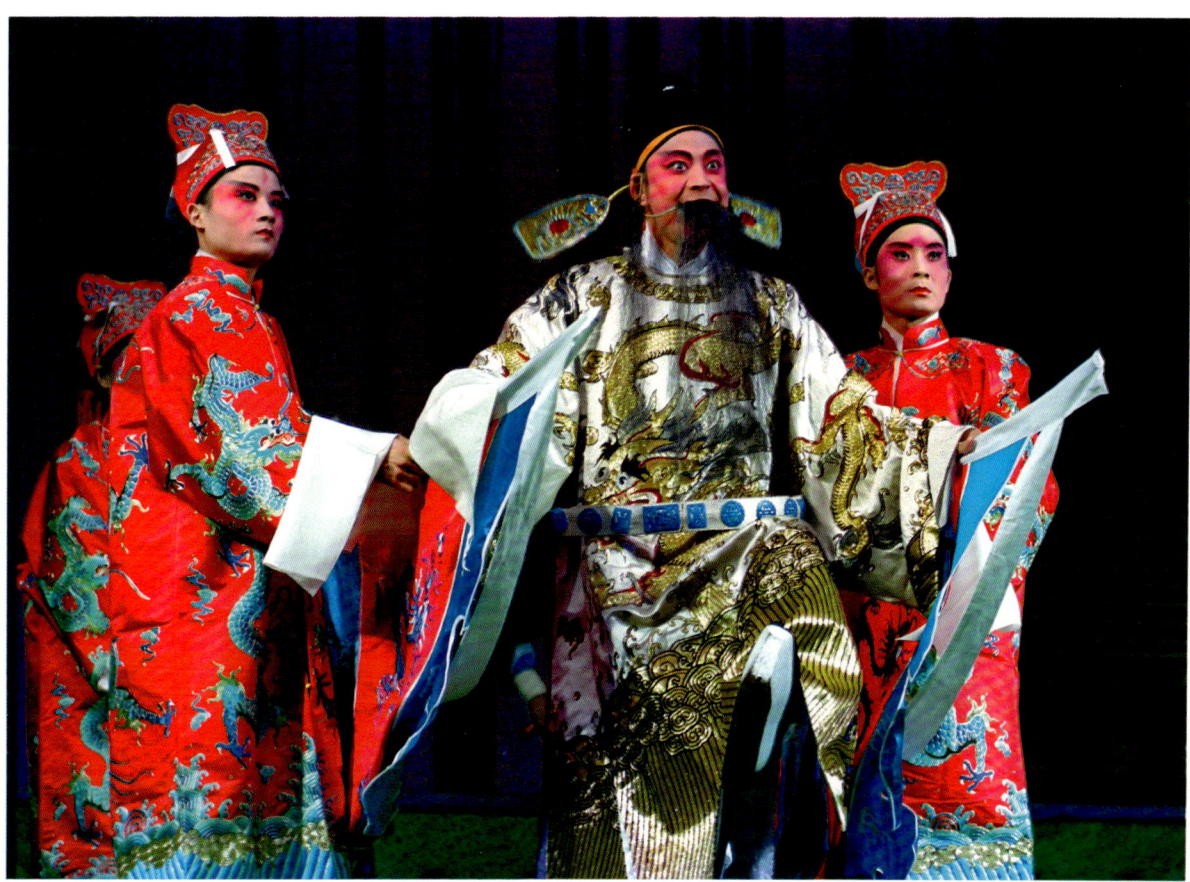

Photo 5.11 *The Story of the Perfumed Sachet*, Yu Opera

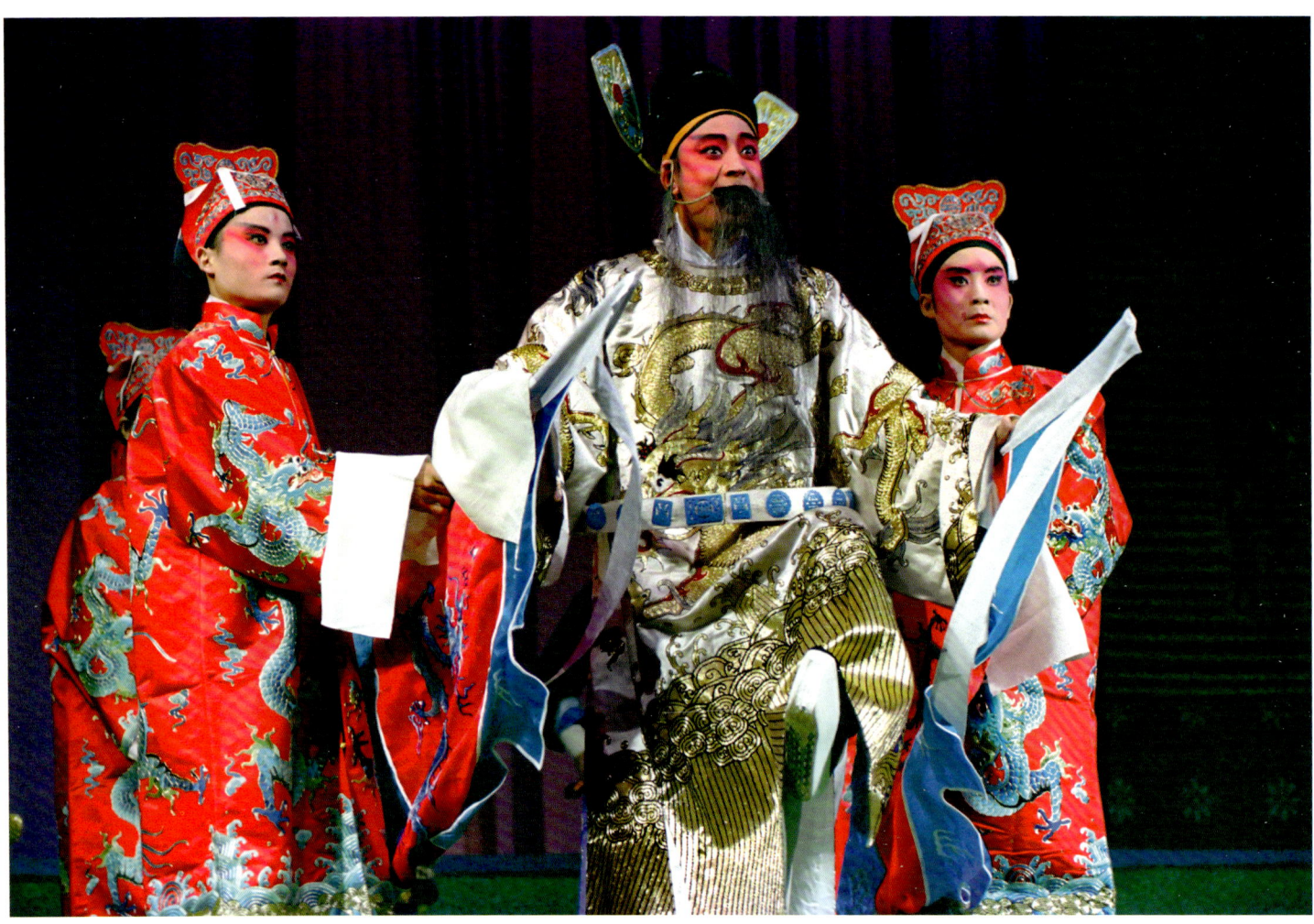

Photo 5.12 *The Story of the Perfumed Sachet*, Yu Opera

The beloved Judge Bao from the eleventh-century Song dynasty can be counted upon in Chinese opera to bring impartial justice and to right the wrongs of the downtrodden. In one opera, he removes his official's hat and holds it out in a gesture that the opera audience reads as determination. He has heard a terrible story of an abandoned wife and child who demand justice. Even though the culprit abandoned them to marry into the imperial family, Judge Bao expresses his determination to pursue the truth no matter what (see Photo 5.10).

In another opera, Zhou Ding has adopted a young scholar. Happy with the news, Zhou Ding rides in his chariot, which is symbolized by the two servants carrying flags on either side of him. The audience sees how happy and satisfied Zhou Ding is through the movement of his official's cap (see Photo 5.11). Without moving his head, the actor causes the wings on his cap to move back and forth, and up and down (see Photo 5.12). Sometimes, the actor moves one wing while keeping the other still.

Chinese opera costumes are extensions of the actors. They become the larger movements of their body and through skilful manipulation communicate emotions to the audience.

Hair

Hair and Male Roles

Just as Chinese actors use long sleeves to express emotion and punctuate a scene with dramatic action, they also use long tresses. The waving sleeves are called "water sleeves" because they evoke flowing water. In the same way, long tresses are called "water hair" because they serve the same function. Normally, a general wears his helmet, and a young student wears his scholar's cap. When the character appears on the stage bare-headed, with dishevelled hair hanging over his shoulders, the audience has been told there is something wrong. The character is in distress.

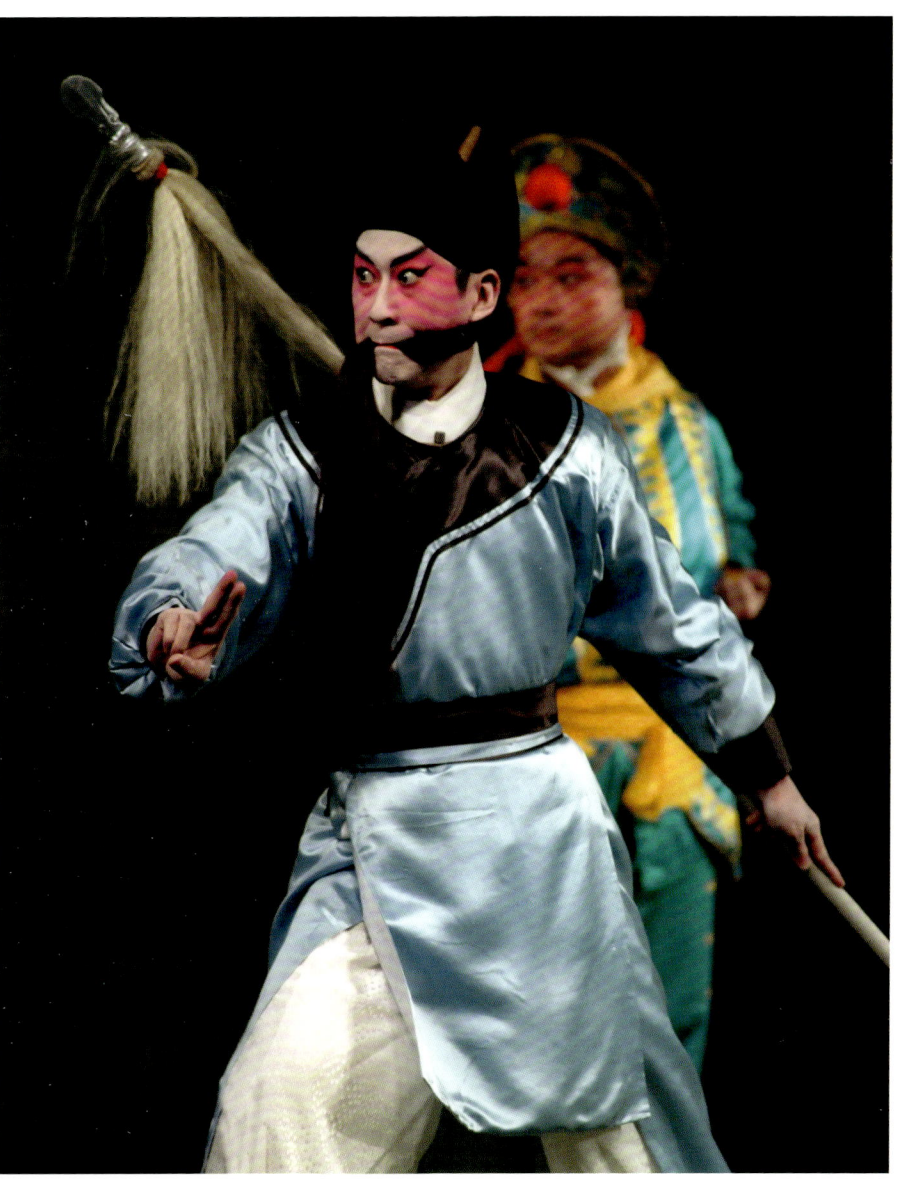

Photo 5.13 *The Merciless Sword,* Cantonese Opera

Photo 5.14 *The Story of the Perfumed Sachet*, Yu Opera

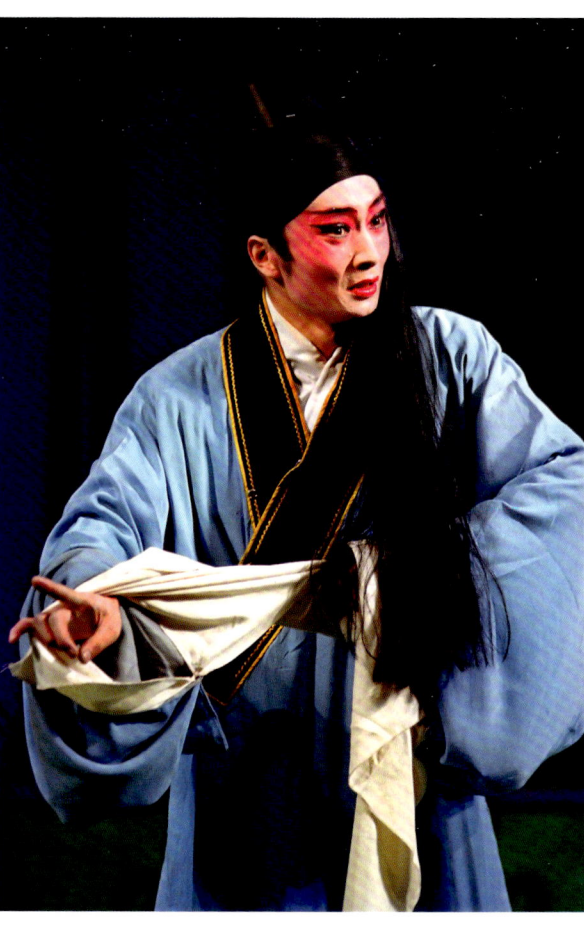

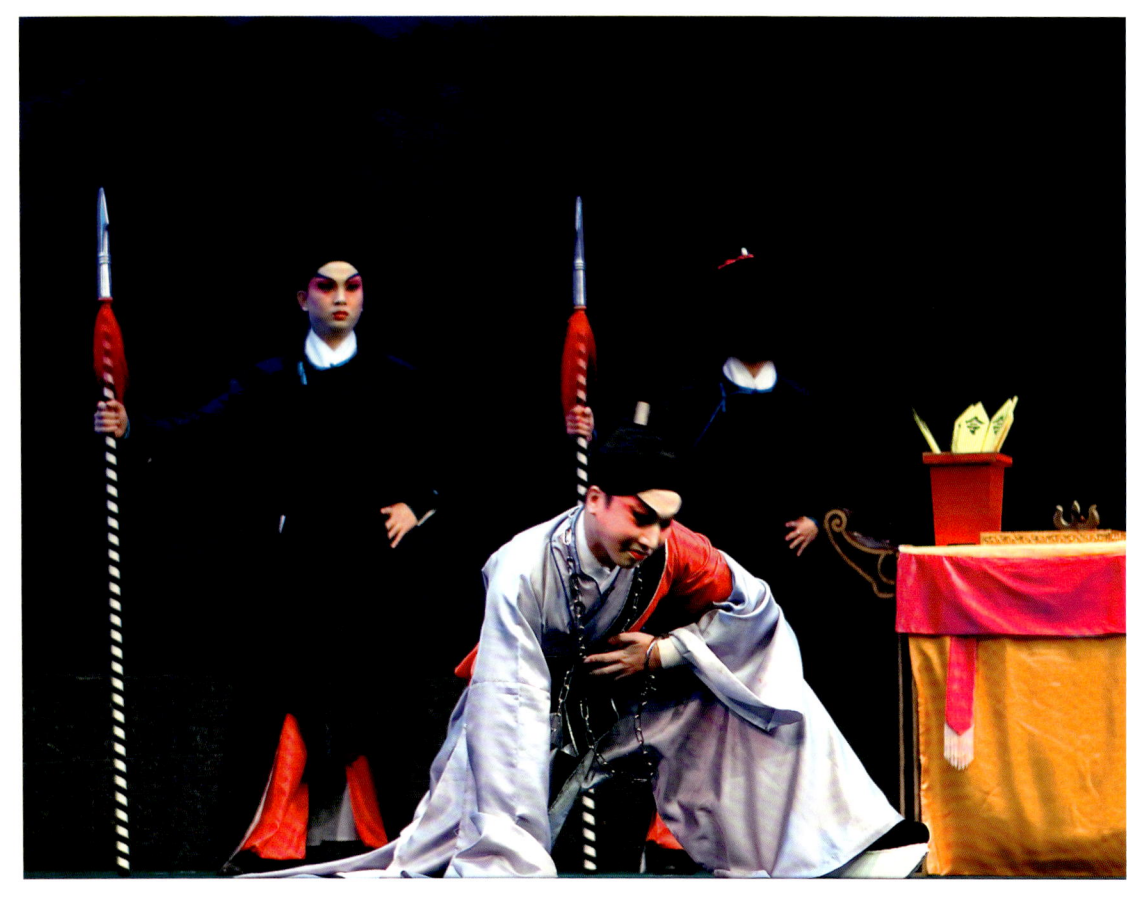

Photo 5.15 *Accusing the Traitor*, Cantonese Opera

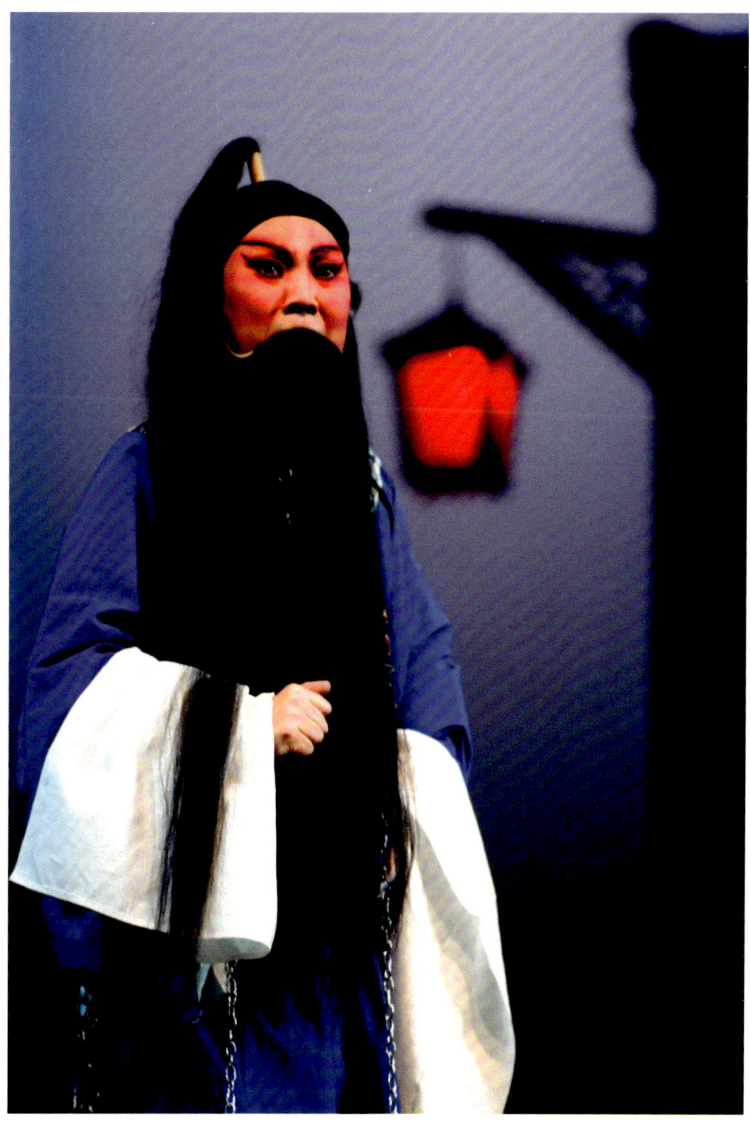

Photo 5.16 *Drawing Lots for Life and Death*, Xiang Opera

In one opera, a poor young scholar, Wang Tiancai, has fallen in love with the beautiful and rich maiden Qian Jin, who pledges herself to him with a gift of a sachet. Qian Jin's parents have other plans for her, however. When they find out about the pledge, the powerful family drives Tiancai away. His hair hangs loose in his despair at having lost his beloved (see Photo 5.14).

Prisoners also have long, loose hair. The appearance of a dishevelled main character formerly well dressed and wearing headgear, but now with long, loose hair, is a dramatic moment. A prisoner can use this long hair to effectively demonstrate distress, or even resistance. In the Cantonese opera *Accusing the Traitor*, Xia Yuanchun has been unjustly arrested. Though chained, he is defiant as he scolds the traitor responsible for his plight, flinging his long hair clockwise in circle after circle (see Photo 5.15).

In *Drawing Lots for Life and Death*, the local magistrate Wang Boxian is up against the wall. The local commander is insistent that the young maiden, Wang Yuhuan, be executed for the drowning of his son. The magistrate knows that she is completely innocent, that in fact the commander's son

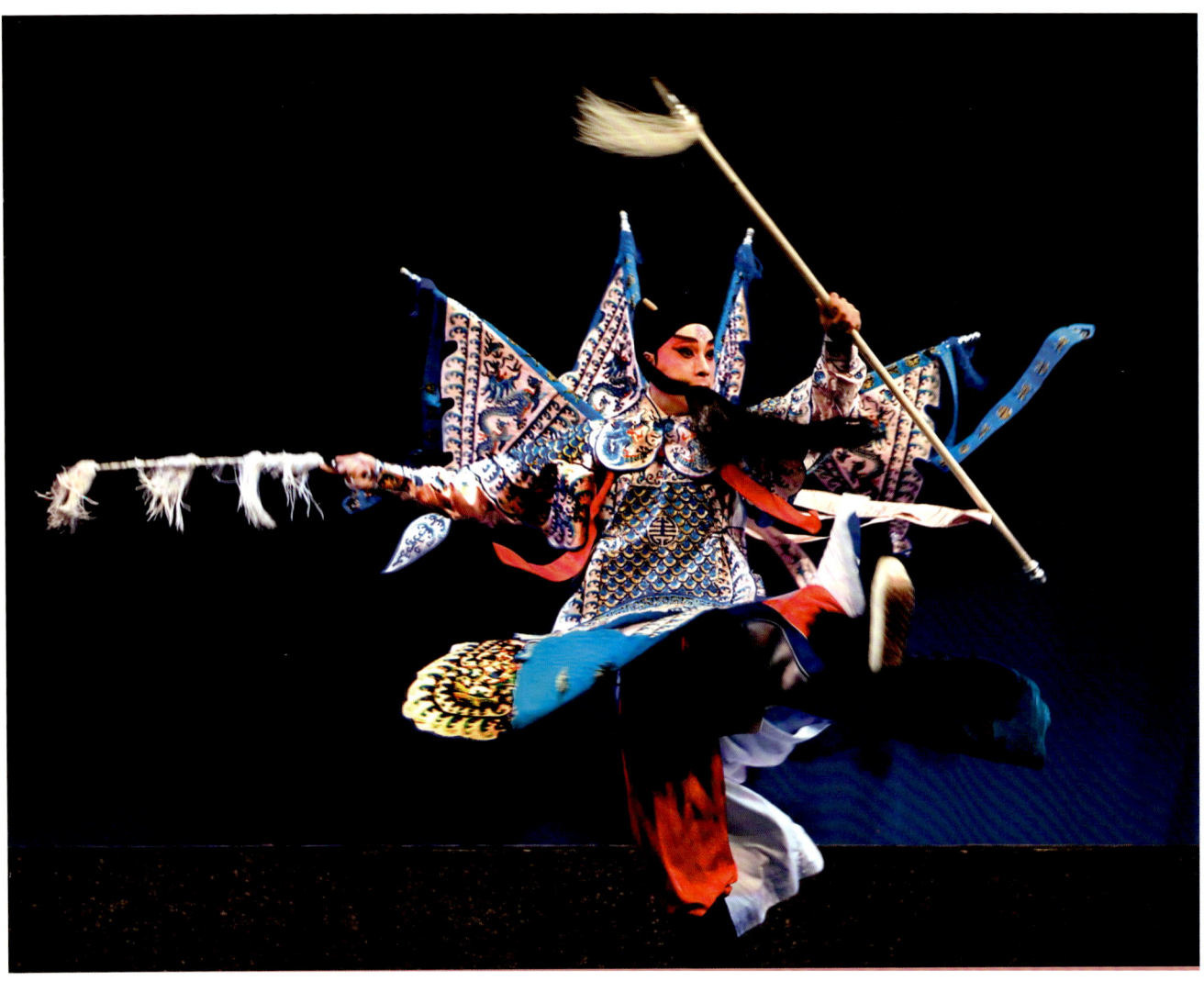

Photo 5.17 *The Battle of Baqiu*, Cantonese Opera

drowned while pursuing her over a bridge, and so defies the commander and sets her free. Later Wang Yuhuan, the magistrate's own daughter, and his adopted daughter draw lots to be executed and thus save the magistrate from the commander's wrath. The commander finds out the deception and arrests the magistrate for not executing Yuhuan. Wang Boxian stands in chains, a prisoner with long dishevelled hair. It is only the fortuitous arrival of the high official Hai Rui, who was famous for his integrity, that saves the day (see Photo 5.16).

Determination is another powerful emotion that, like despair, grief or righteous anger, can be performed on the Chinese opera stage with "water hair". General Zhou Yu has been chased by his enemies until he is cornered at the river's edge. There is nothing for it but to fight the brave fight. He grabs his long hair and grips it in his mouth showing his readiness to fight and his courage (see Photo 5.17). Warrior characters without beards use this method to show their grit and determination.

Using Costumes

Hair and Female Roles

WHILE MALE CHARACTERS may swing their hair and clench it in their teeth, female characters make use of the tresses that hang from either side of their coiffure. The main female role in the opera *Accusing the Husband*, makes use of this technique. Wen Shuzhen has learned that her husband, Gai Liangcai, has tried to murder another young woman pregnant with his child. Outraged, she threatens to expose him, but he throws her in the river to kill her, too. She holds out her tresses thoughtfully, determined to do the right thing, eventually writing a letter in her own blood revealing her husband's crimes (see Photo 5.19).

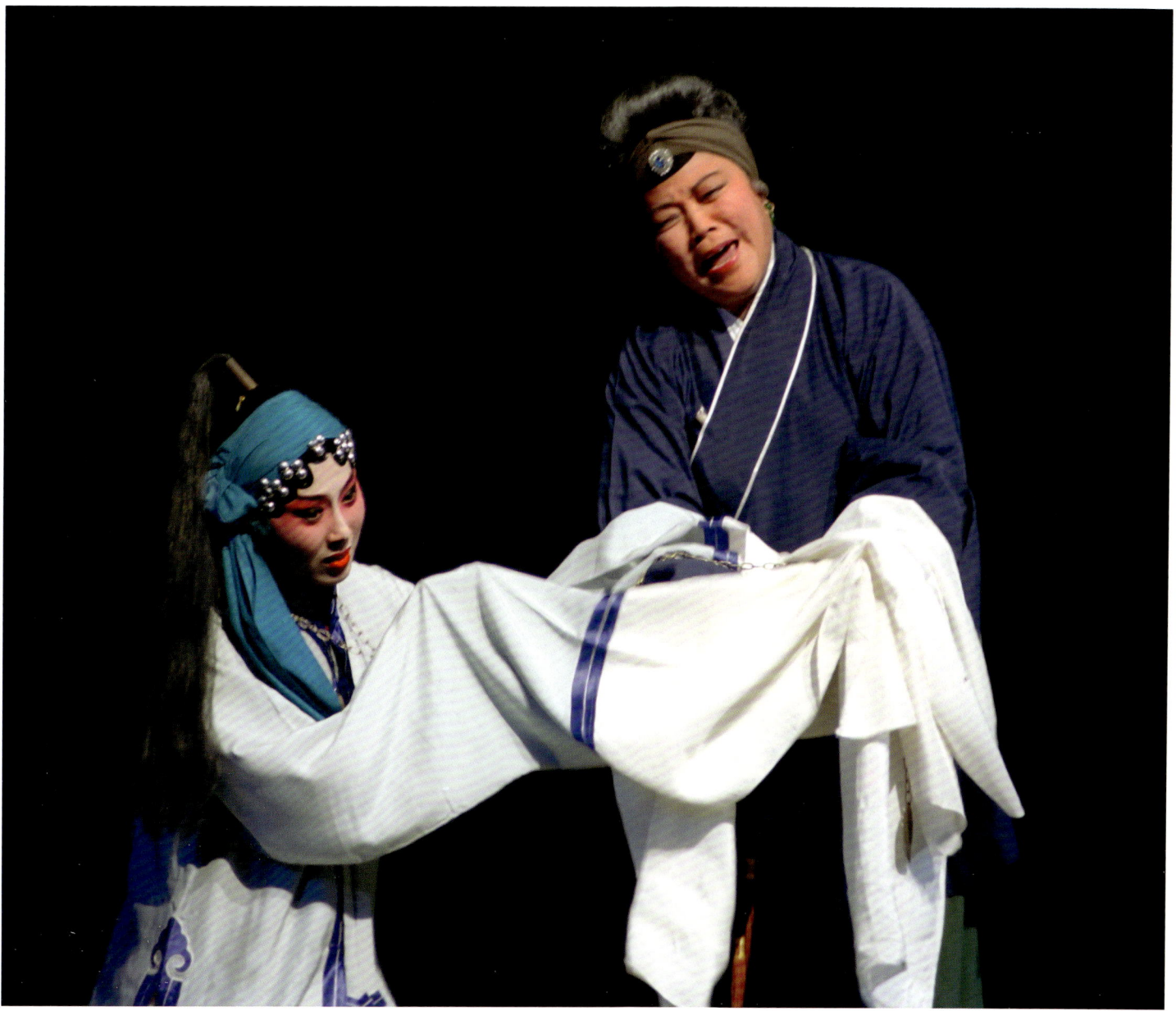

Photo 5.18 *The Grievances of Dou E,* Gan Opera

Photo 5.19 *Suing the Husband*, Chaozhou Opera

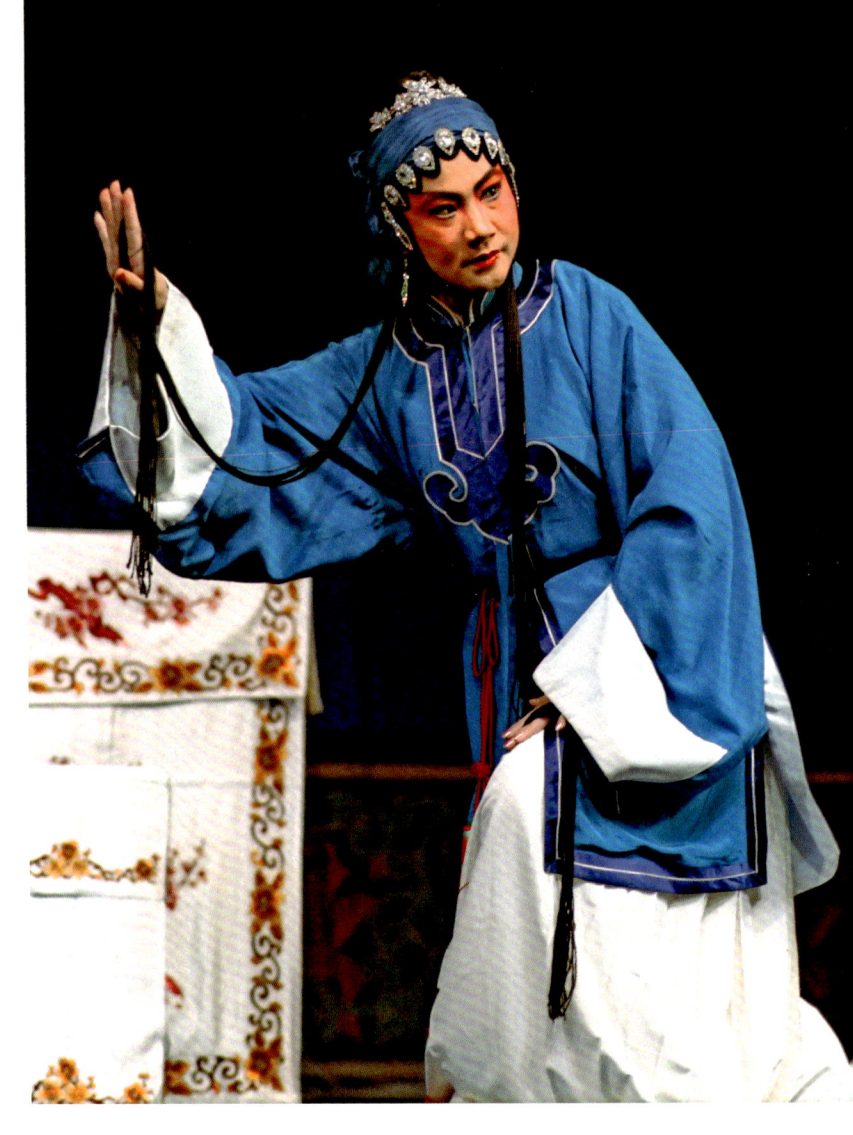

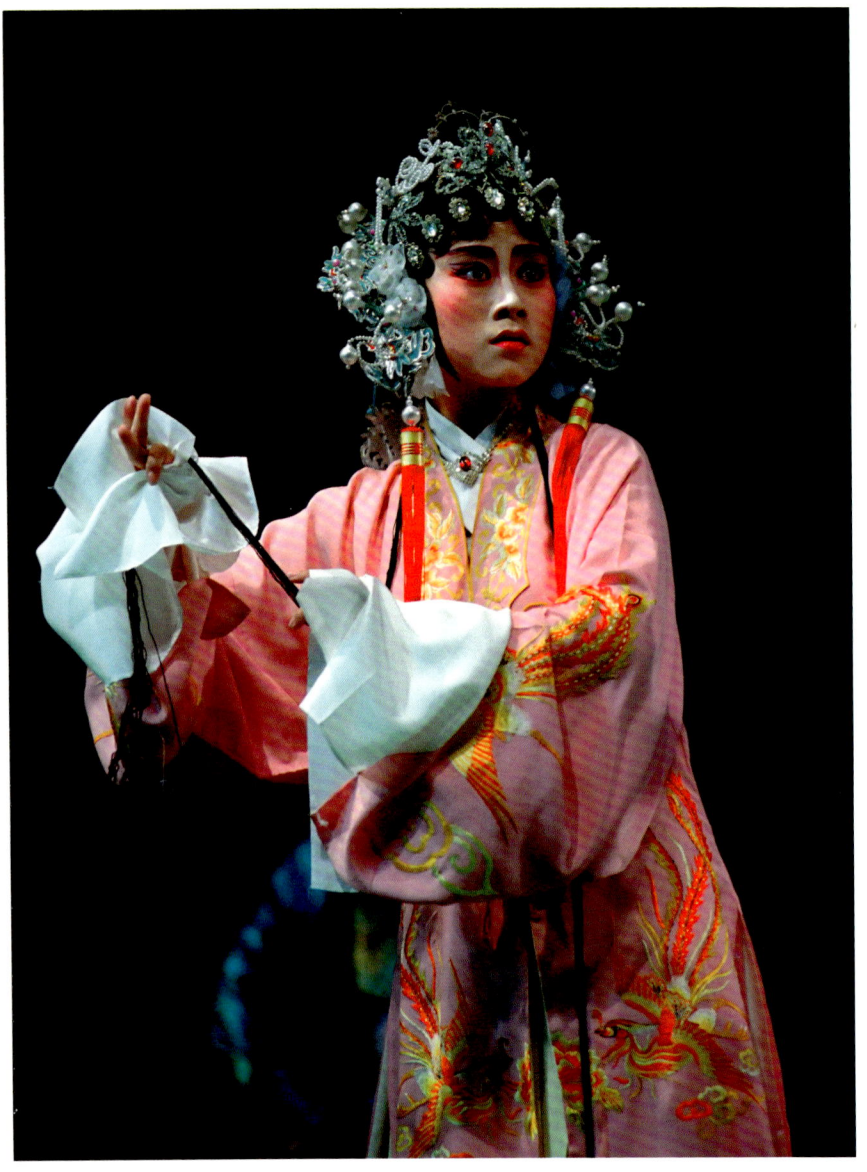

Photo 5.20 *The Trial of Chen San*, Gaojia Opera

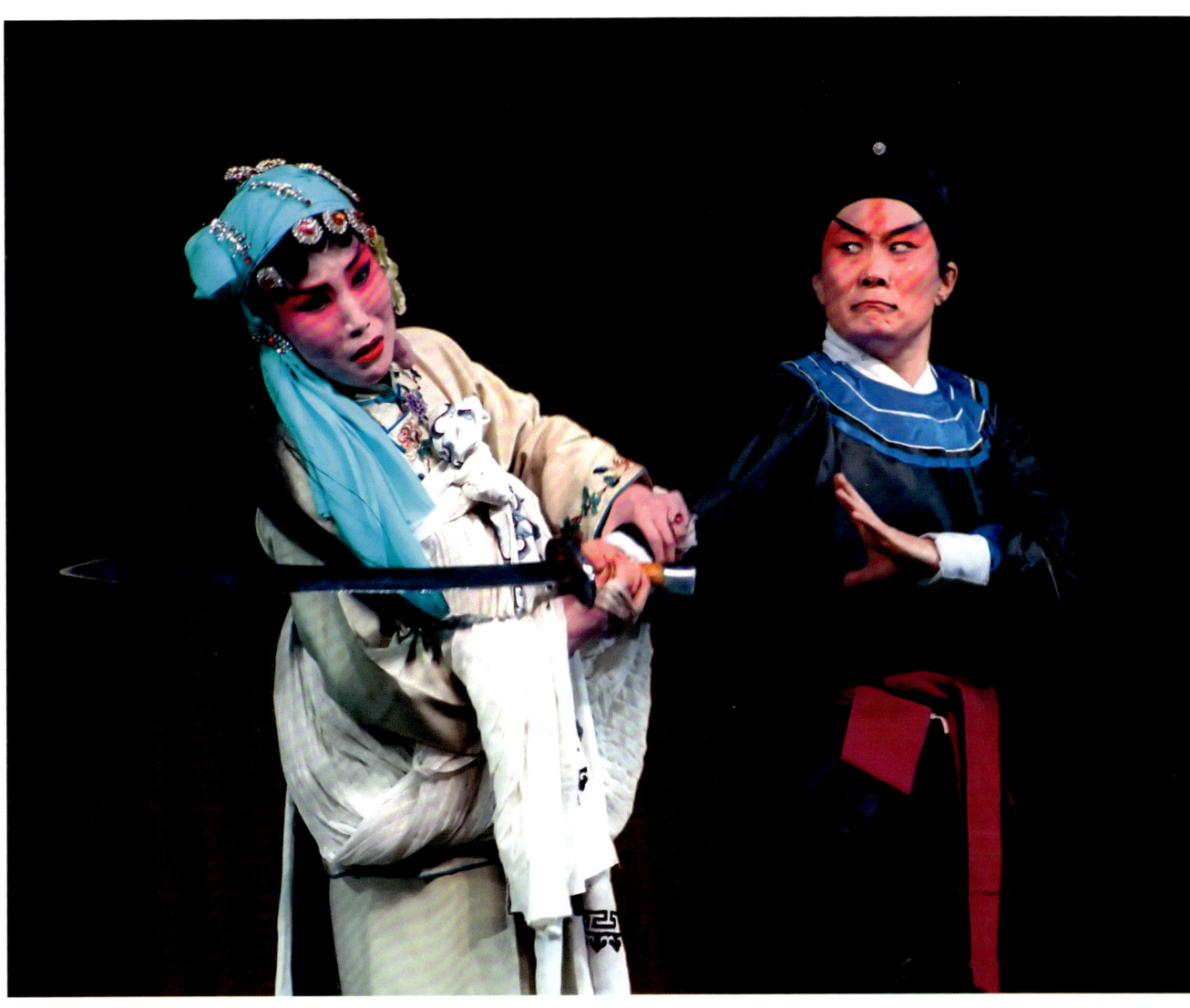

Photo 5.21 *Shi Xiu Slays an Unfaithful Wife*, Hebei Clapper Opera

In another opera, a young woman, Pan Shi, upon learning that her cousin's lover has been falsely accused and sent off to the army in punishment, grabs her tresses, twisting them in surprise and anguish (see Photo 5.20).

A tuft of hair sticking out from the side of a maiden's head can also signify distress, anxiety or emotional imbalance. Pan Qiaoyun has cheated on her husband with a monk. Shi Xiu, her husband's sworn blood brother, takes vengeance by first killing the monk, and then Pan Qiaoyun (see Photo 5.21).

"Water hair" artfully conveys the inner state of characters in clear, dramatic terms recognizable to the Chinese opera audience. Like the use of other costume elements such as sleeves or props such as fans, long hair permits the actor to communicate in familiar stage conventions to move the story forward.

Beards

THE FALSE BEARD is a distinctive part of the costume for many characters in Chinese opera including the painted face, old man, and other male role types. Like high shoes and water sleeves, beards are exaggerated, giving the actors opportunities to use them in dramatic ways. Made from calf tails, the Chinese opera stage beards were originally hung on the face with thin string. This design had some limitations and the beards were shorter than they are now. In more recent times, the beards hang from a stiff copper wire frame which is hung behind the ears and rests just above the upper lip. Beards come primarily in three main colours that are indicative of age: black, grey, and pure white. Special characters in particular plays also sport bright red, purple and even blue beards. Beards come in several designs. A full beard, for example, hangs completely around the face. Another kind is the three-part beard, which has a narrow section for each cheek, and a wide one across the chin. "Beard work" in Chinese opera refers to the skilful manipulation of the beard, tossing it in the air, grabbing it in a dramatic pose, and even blowing it outwards to indicate various emotions.

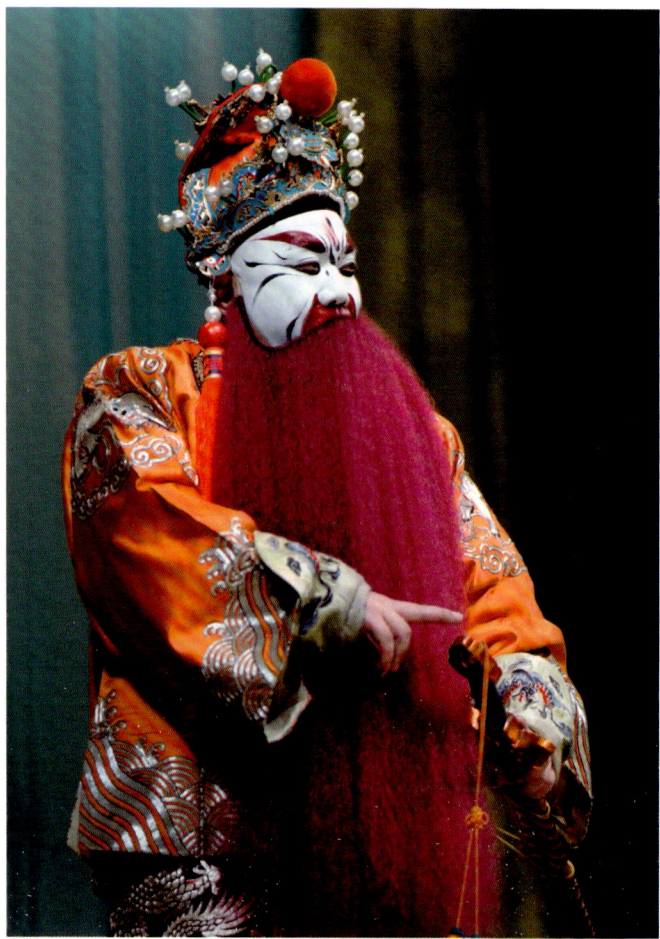

Photo 5.22 *The Marriage of the Dragon and the Phoenix*, Peking Opera

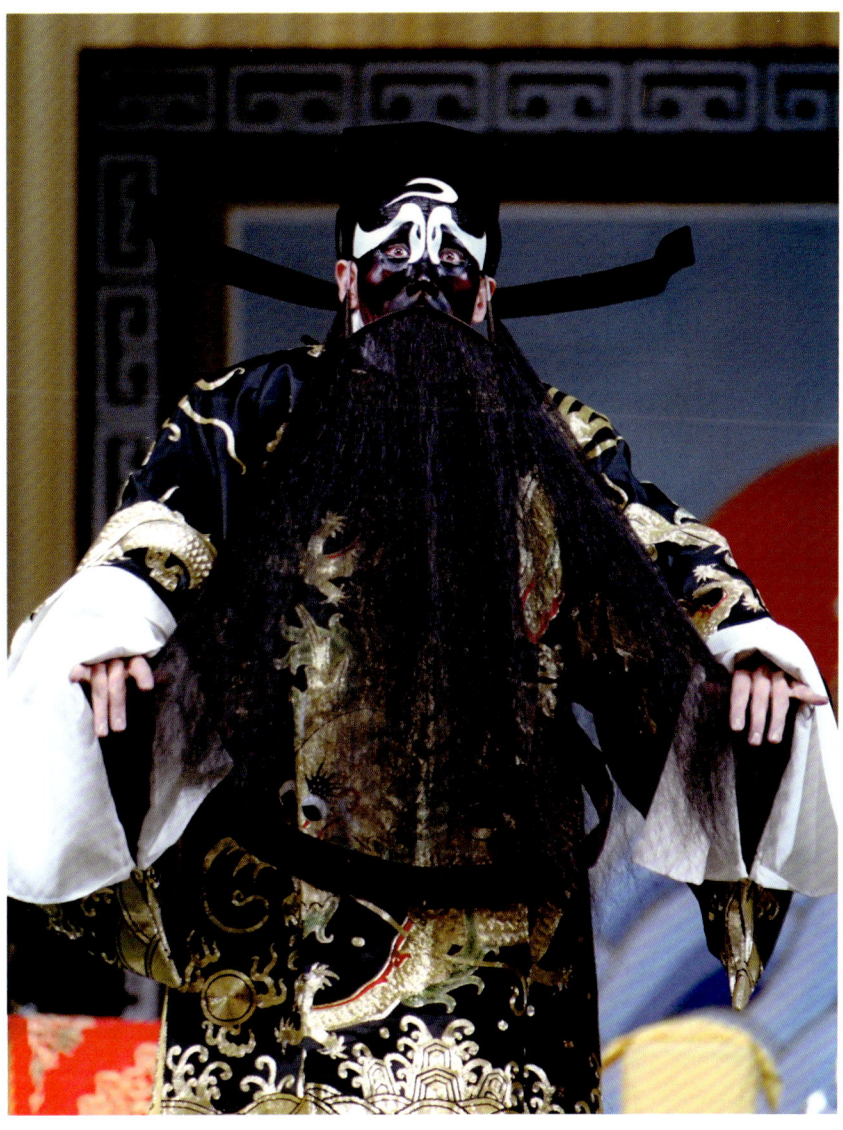

Photo 5.23 *The Beheading of a Wicked Husband*, Peking Opera

Let us return to Judge Bao and his pursuit of justice for the wronged wife and child. The young woman, Qin Xianglian, brings her complaint to the honest judge. She and her young child have been abandoned by her husband, who has married into the royal family. Eager to be rid of his family, the husband had even arranged to have them both killed. When Judge Bao hears this horrific story, he spreads out his beard and grabs both sides in a tight gesture, demonstrating determination to redress this wrong, even if it means going against a member of the royal household (see Photo 5.23).

Holding the beard aside indicates that the character is observing a scene. One example of this beard work may be found in the opera *Drowning the Enemy Troops*. The audience instantly recognizes the red-faced actor as the legendary hero Guan Yu. He and his bodyguard Zhou Cang stand overlooking their enemy, who has been overcome by the flood that Guan Yu has caused by diverting the river. It is now the time for a decisive attack. Guan Yu indicates that he is surveying the scene by grabbing his long black beard and pulling it to his right side (see Photo 5.24).

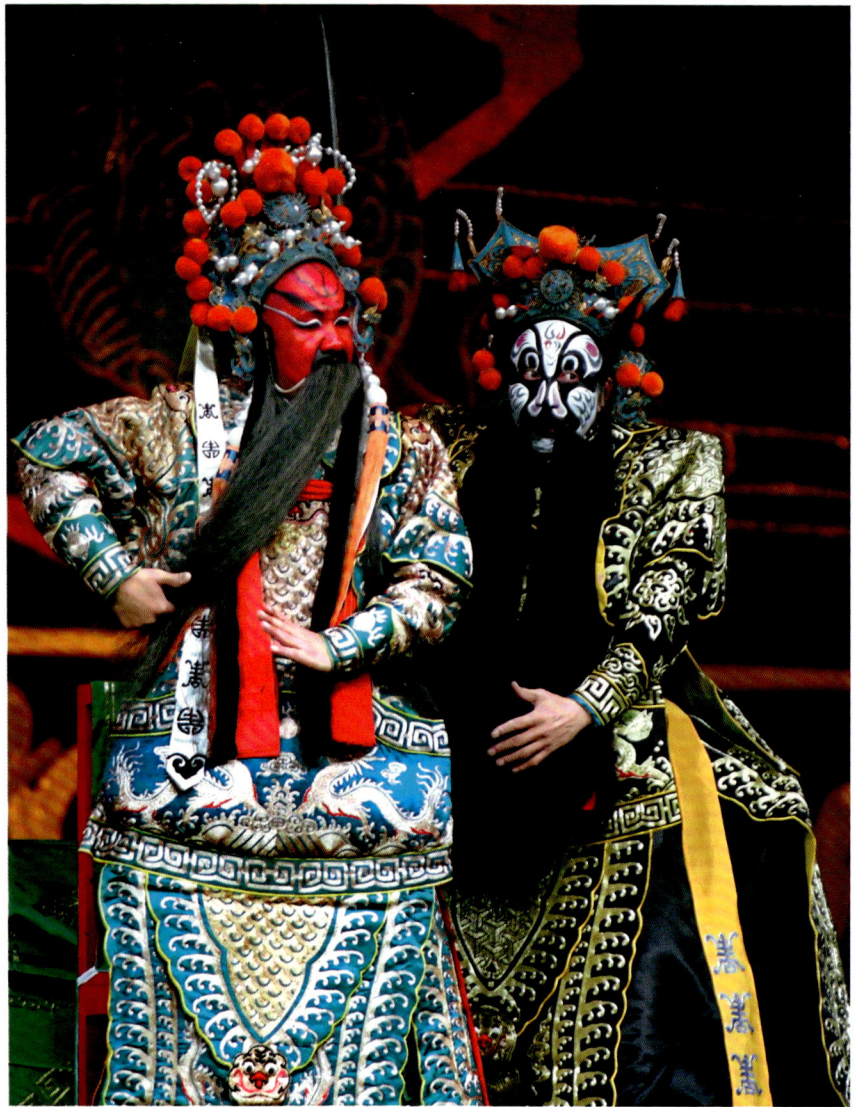

Photo 5.24 *Drowning the Enemy Troops*, Anhui Opera

The same gesture is used by the warrior He Tianbao in *Cleaning Out the Bandit's Lair*. In this story, thieves steal disaster rations meant for an impoverished people and whisk them away to their base camp on Fu Mountain. He Tianbao, outraged at the deed, comes to scout out the camp at night. Holding his beard firmly to his side, he indicates careful reconnoitring of the enemy (see Photo 5.25).

Holding the beard aside can also have a very different meaning. Meng Liang, a military officer in the Song dynasty for the famous Yang family, has come to Tianbo Mansion to get reinforcements because foreign invaders have taken over his country and captured the great general Yang. His red beard and make-up remind the audience of his signature weapon that uses fire in battle. Looking for help, he comes across the housemaid, Yang Paifeng, who is determined to help. She claims to be able to fight, to even be able to best Meng Liang in battle. Meng Liang, however, looks at her, a mere serving girl, with disdain. He exhibits that distain by holding up a strand of his bright red beard, twisting it and pulling it out to the side (see Photo 5.26). Little does he know that not only will this serving girl best him in battle, but she also will defeat the invader and bring General Yang back home safely.

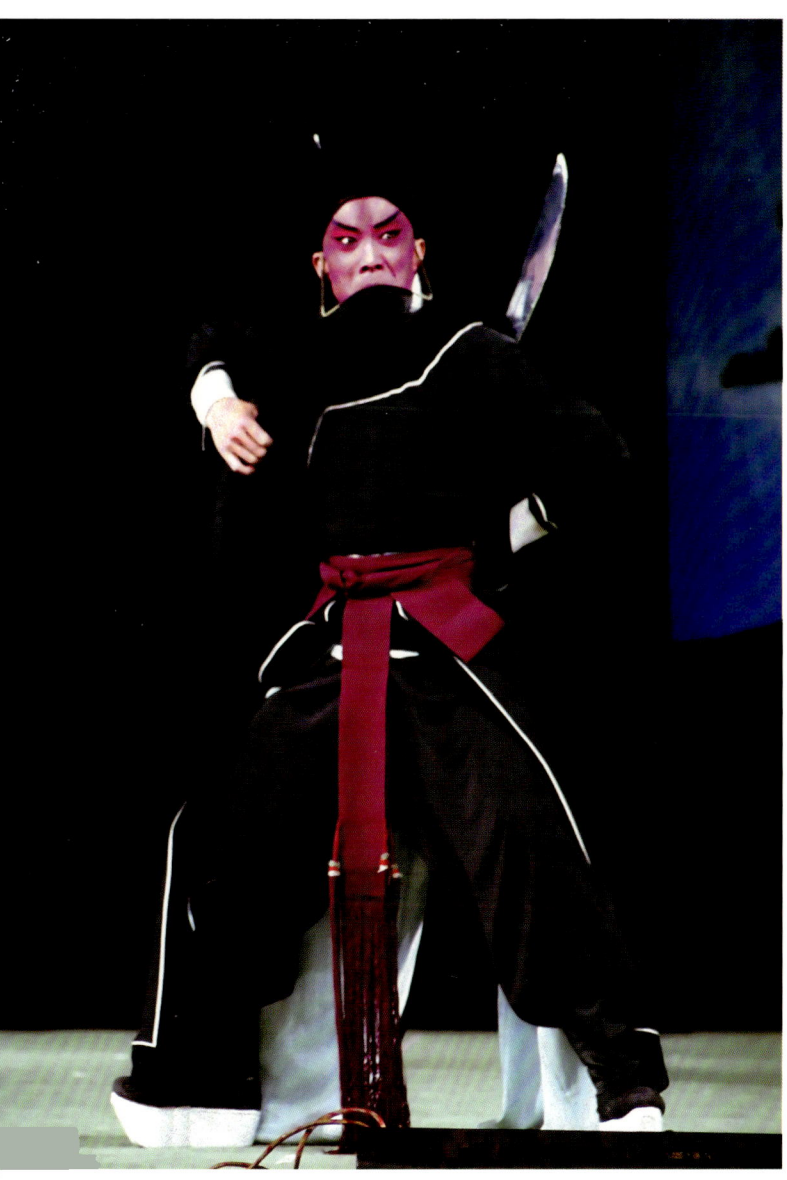

Photo 5.25 *Cleaning Out the Bandit's Lair*, Peking Opera

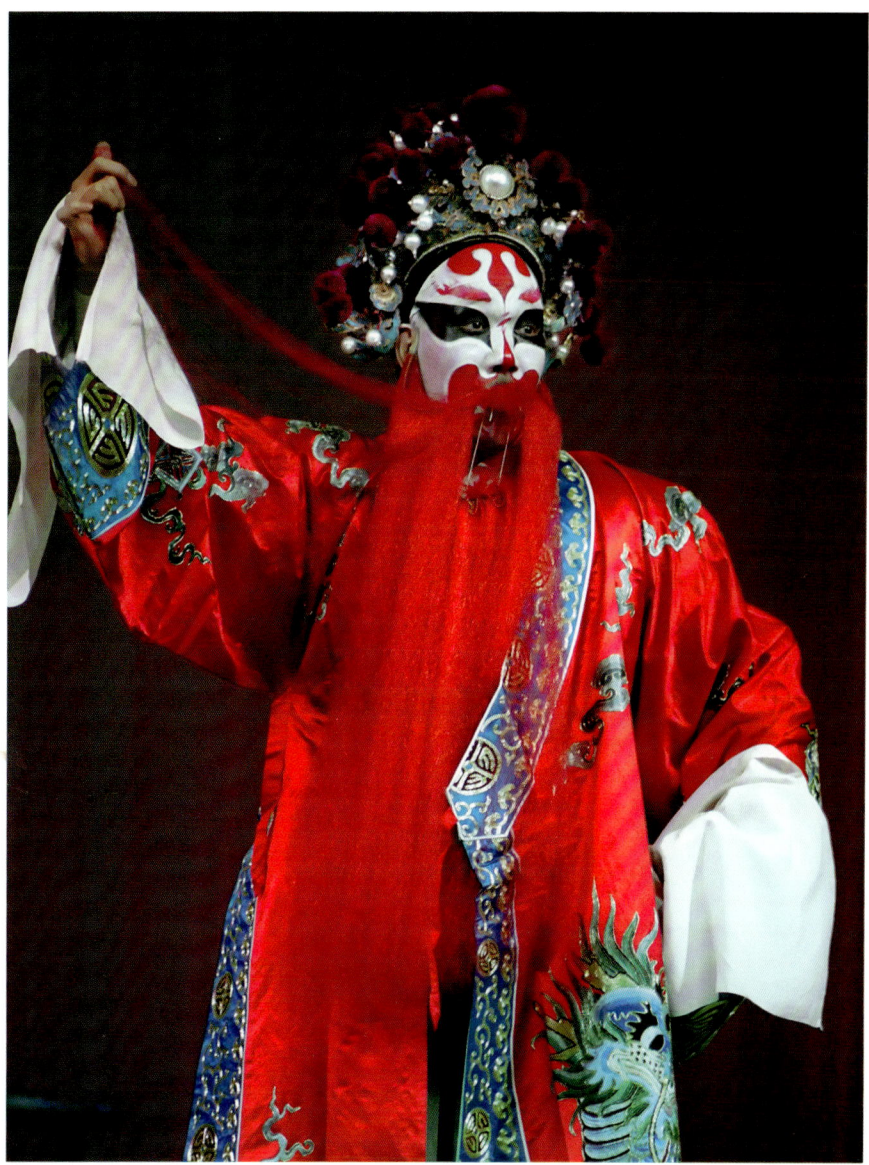

Photo 5.26 *Meng Liang Raises the Troops*, Gan Opera

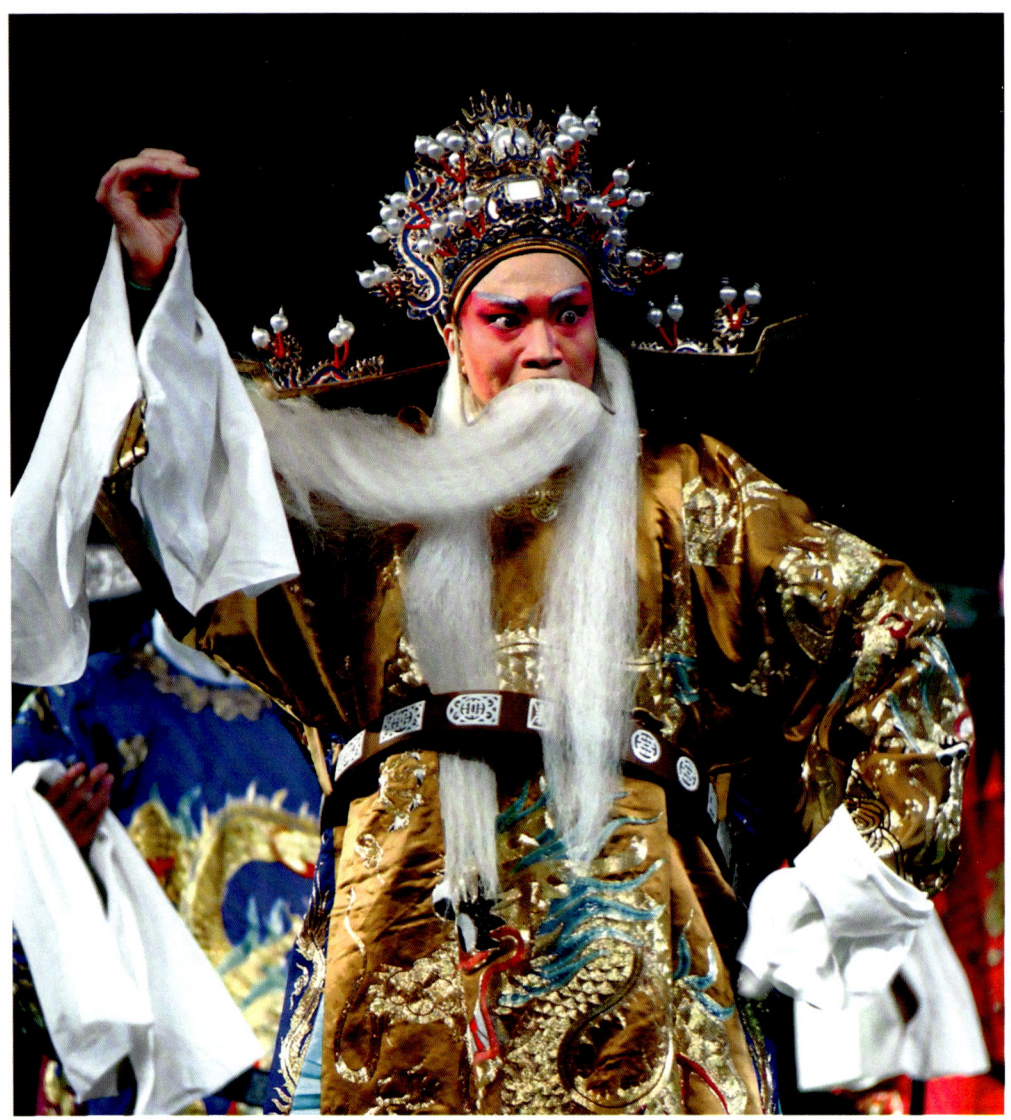

Photo 5.27 *The Prime Minister of Wei*, Shao Opera

In some operas, actors use a series of beard work movements, some connected one after the other. In *The Prime Minister of Wei*, the honest general Yue Yang has been falsely accused of treachery while on the border defending the Wei nation. Prime Minister Zhai Huang just cannot believe this of him because Yue Yang is his protégé. He knows him well and trusts him. But the court is against the prime minister, sure that Yue Yang has betrayed them all. The prime minister throws out his beard in agitation and declares that he will prove Yue Yang innocent, offering his own family as hostages as he goes to the border to investigate the charges himself (see Photo 5.27).

Once at the border, the prime minister, convinced of Yue Yang's innocence, discovers that he has already been sent to prison. The prime minister is distraught at the news and frustrated at the confusing roads, not knowing where to go. He flings out his beard, blowing the whiskers up in a skilful display of agitation, impatience, and exhaustion (see Photos 5.28 and 5.29). Eventually, the trust of the prime minister will be rewarded and Yue Yang will be exonerated as a hero and master strategist.

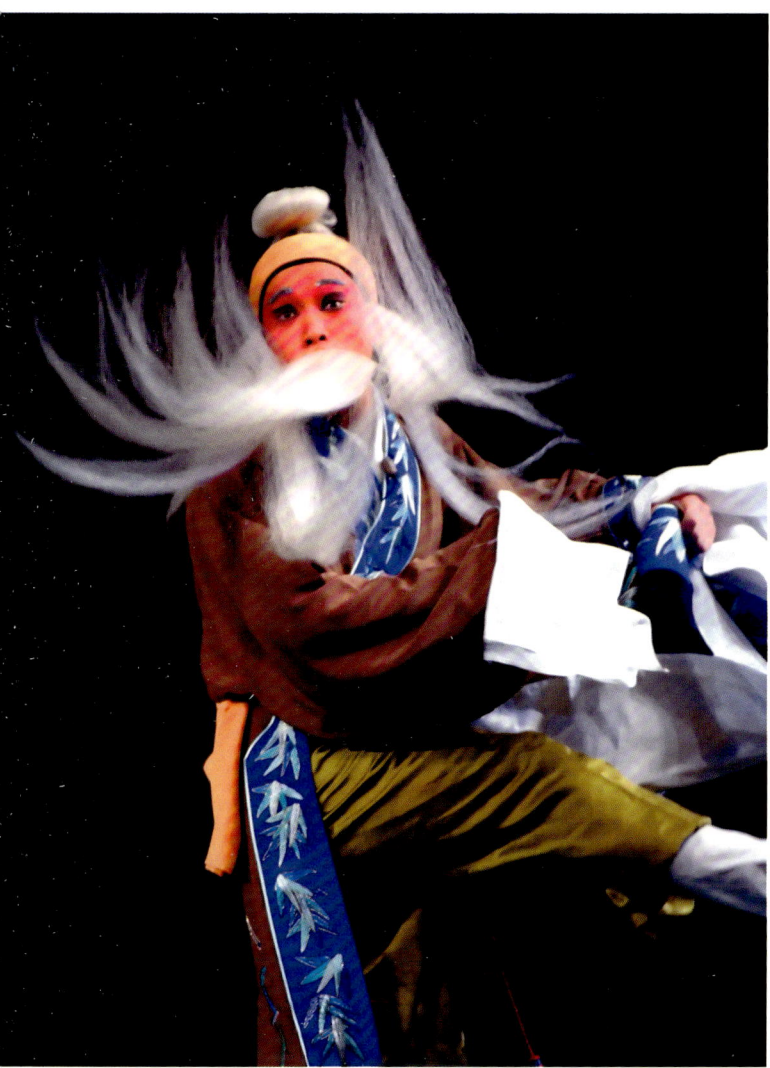

Photo 5.28 *The Prime Minister of Wei*, Shao Opera

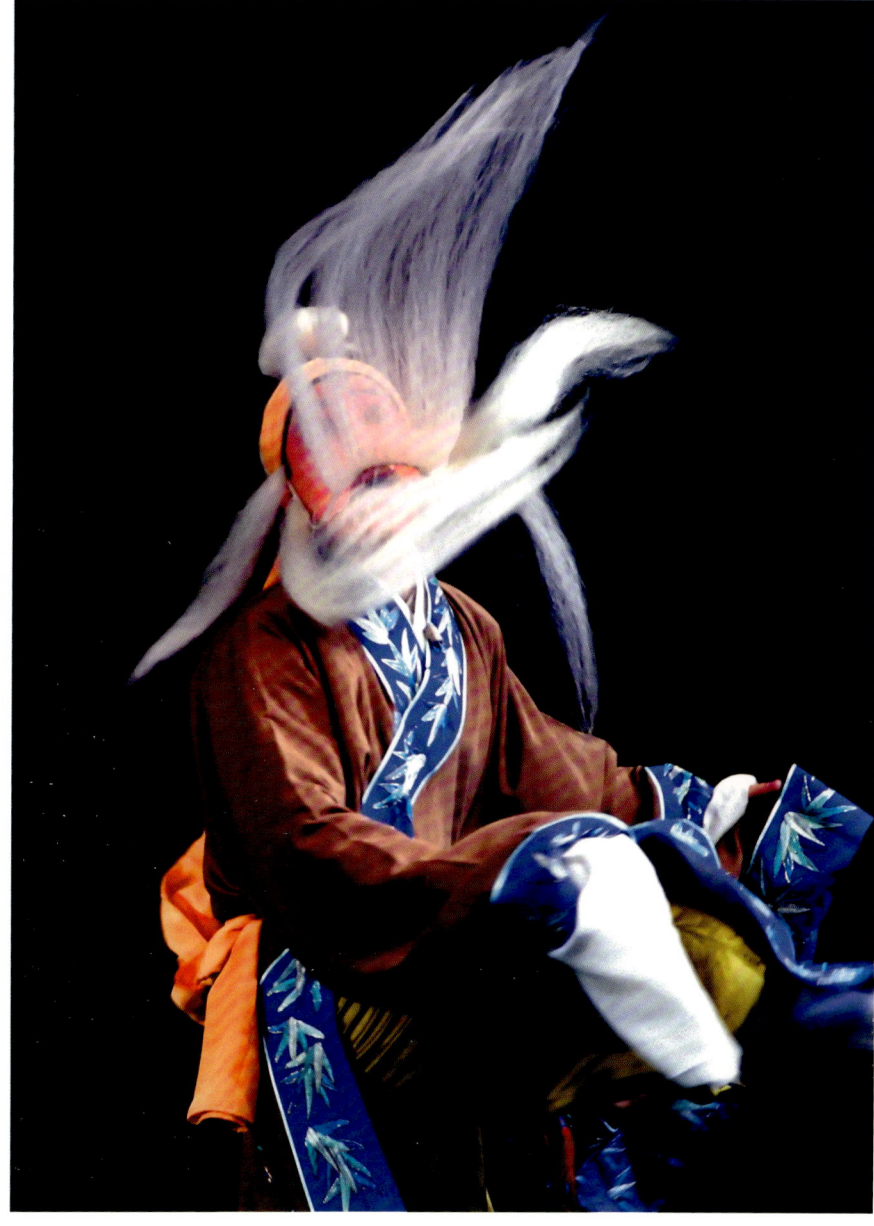

Photo 5.29 *The Prime Minister of Wei*, Shao Opera

Water Sleeves

WATER SLEEVES ARE one of the most distinctive features of Chinese opera costumes. They have a long tradition in Chinese drama and dance. Mastering the use of water sleeves constitutes one of the most important parts of an actor's physical training with costumes. Actors can make their sleeves ripple like a flowing stream, giving them their name. The sleeves are made of light, white silk. Normally about one-third of a metre long, they can be as long as a full metre depending on the opera. They are slit open at the bottom for easier manipulation as the actor needs to be able to fold extended sleeves back upon themselves in a few dexterous moves with the fingers. The longest sleeves are used by the female role, but the male, painted face and clown roles also have their versions of water sleeves.

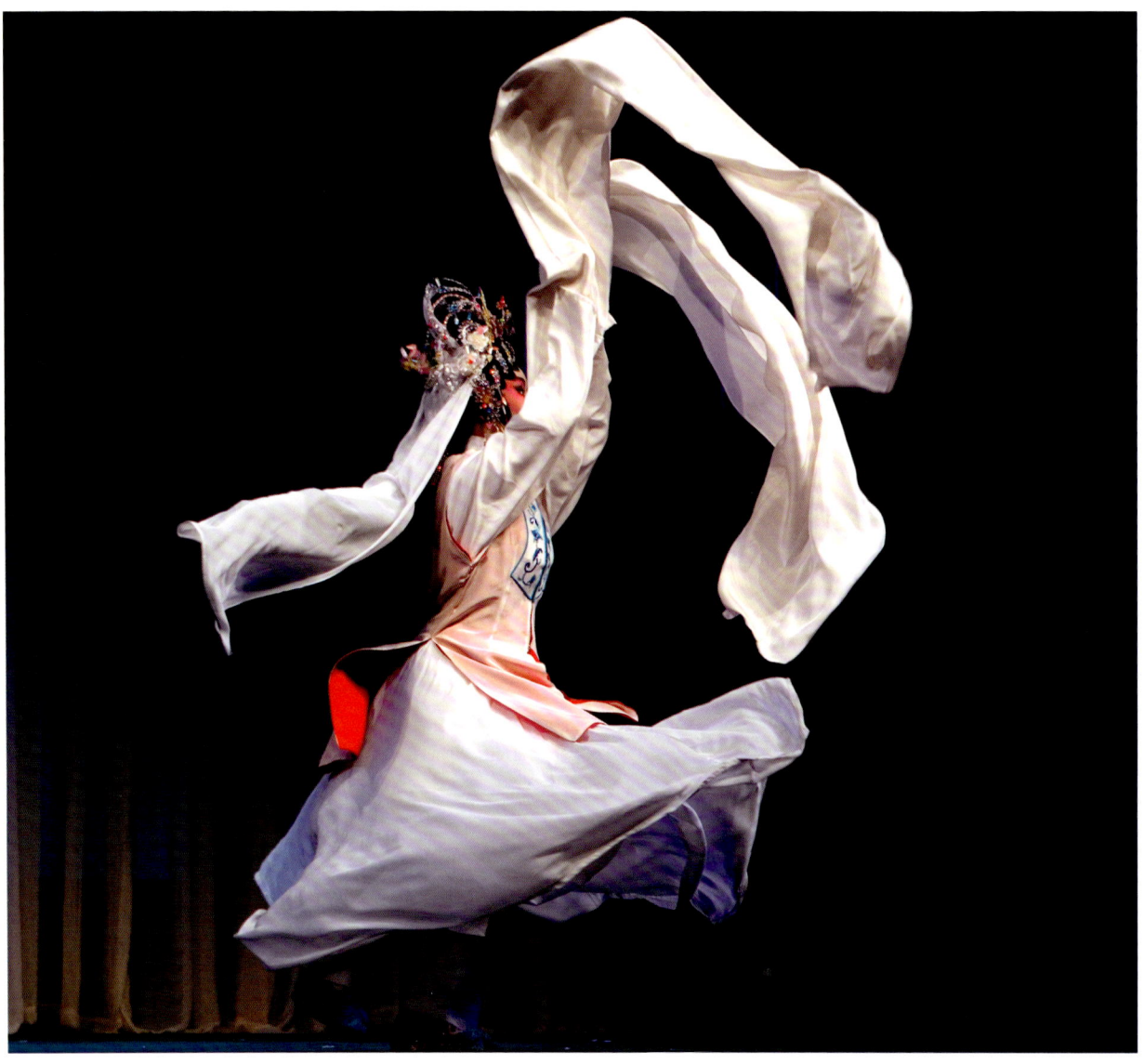

Photo 5.30 *The Haunting of Zhang Sanlang*, Cantonese Opera

Using Costumes

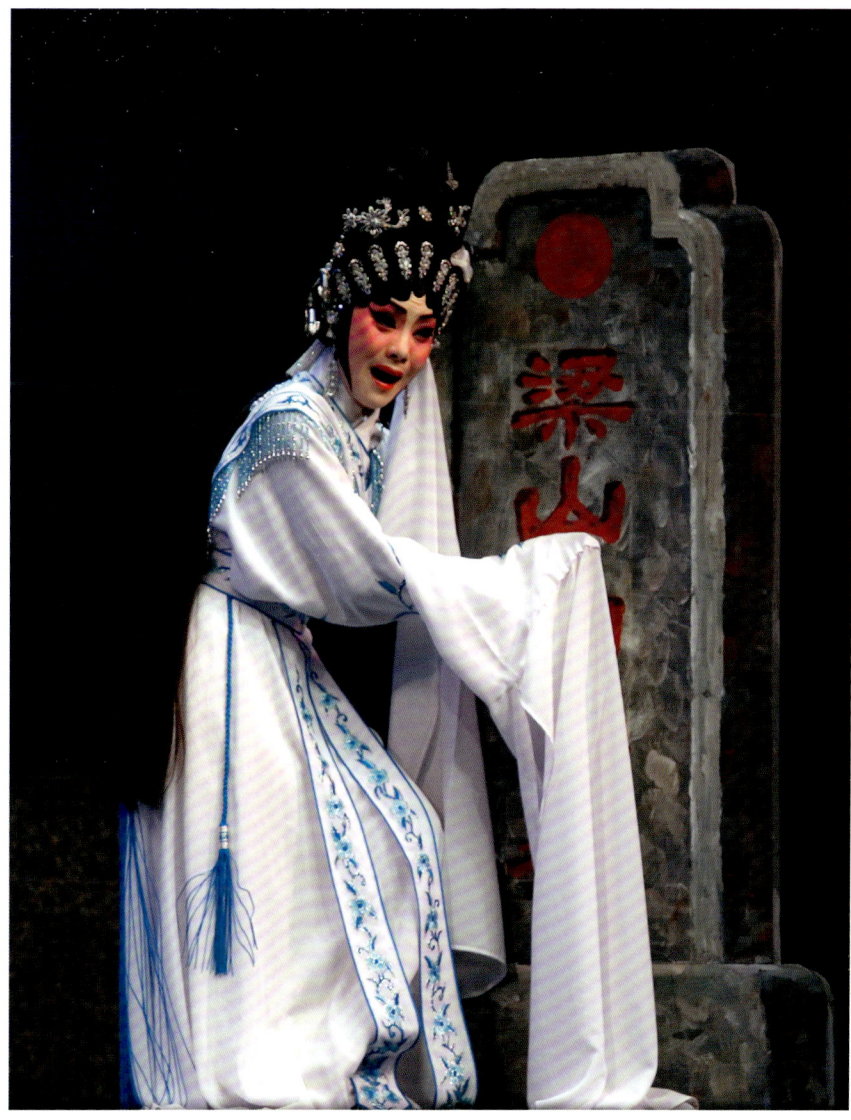

Photo 5.31 *Mourning at the Tomb, Cantonese Opera*

Actors use their sleeves to punctuate their performances in many ways. They can throw out water sleeves as a signal that they are about to sing. Having entered the stage, an actor will often extend the sleeves in a quick gesture and collect them back on themselves in three short moves. The audience knows this action means that the character will now sing. Having come out of a tradition of court dance, water sleeves continue to be used in stage dance and decorative movement. The actor also uses sleeves to express a wide range of emotions. Just as Chinese opera make-up expresses character in a larger-than-life manner, so the water sleeves convey interior emotional states to a large audience.

Water sleeves are often used to express sorrow and distress. Zhu Yingtai, from the famous love story *The Butterfly Lovers*, mourns her beloved at his tomb. Her long water sleeves are extended, hanging from her arms in sorrow like tears (see Photo 5.31).

The concubine Wei Zifu also hangs out her water sleeves in distress. The Han emperor has a new favourite, and now has no time for his former favourite. Yet, her sadness is tempered with hope that sooner or later the emperor will return his affections to her (see Photo 5.32).

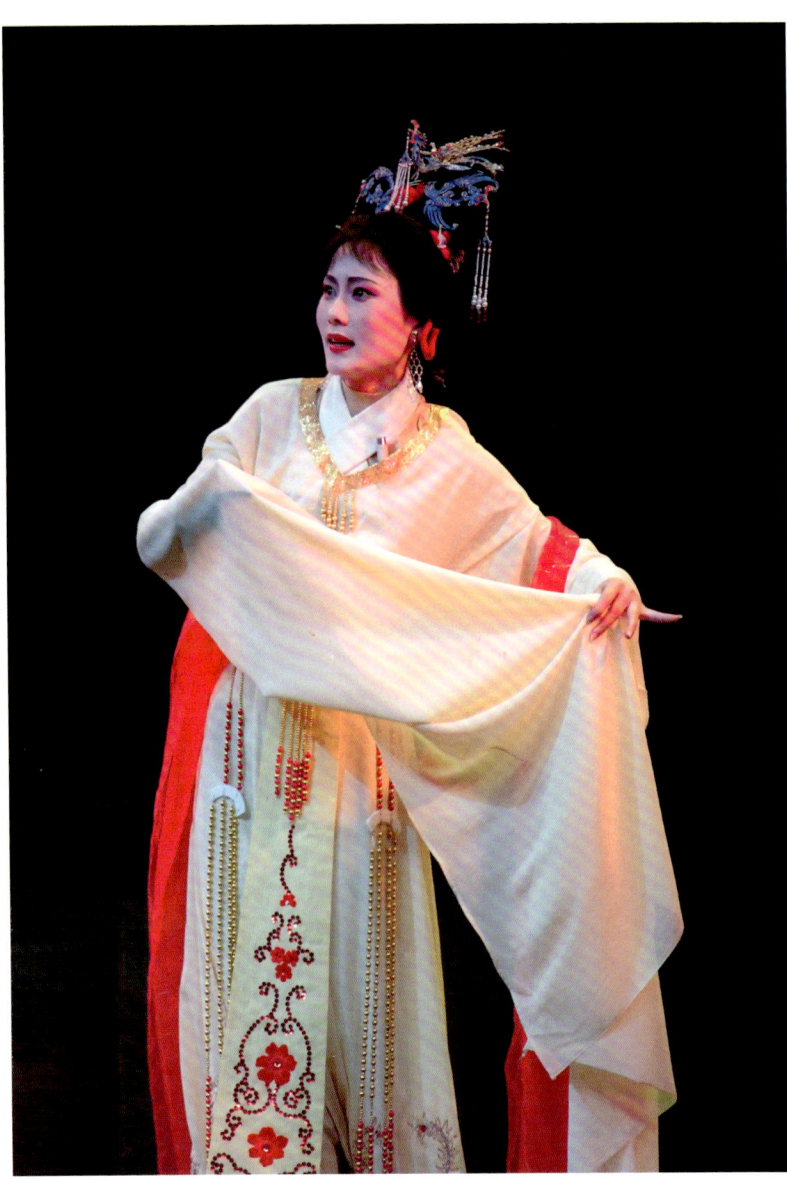

Photo 5.32 *The Romance of Emperor Han Wu*, Yue Opera

Photo 5.33 *The Story of the Purple Hairpin*, Cantonese Opera

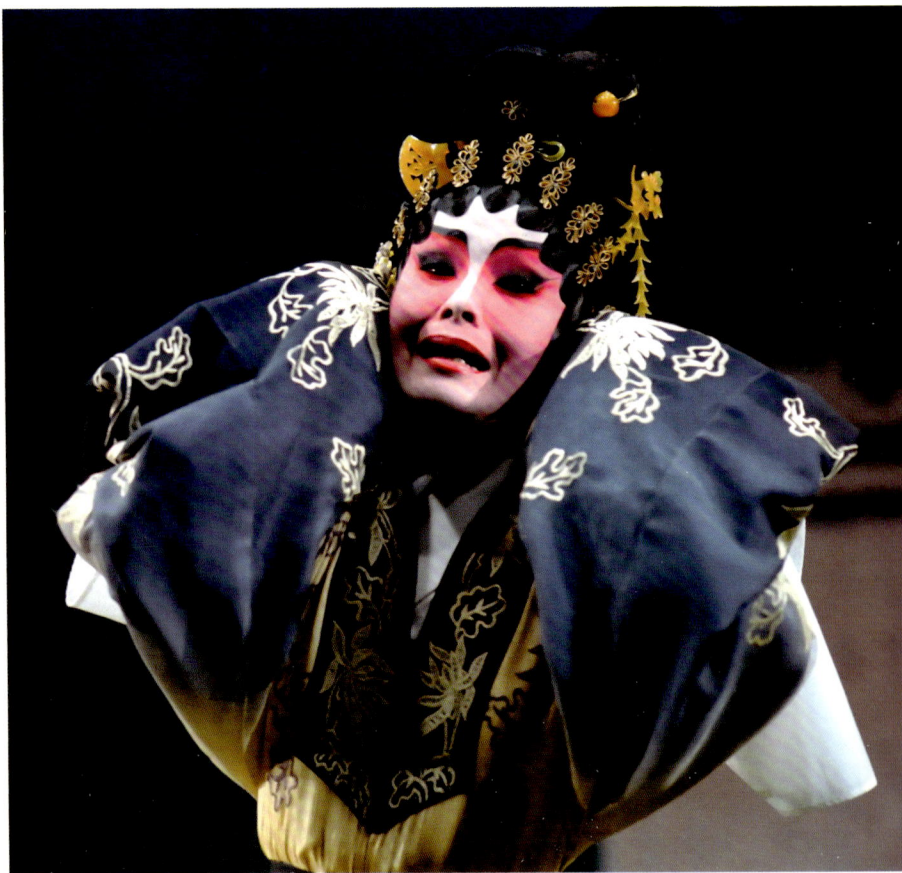

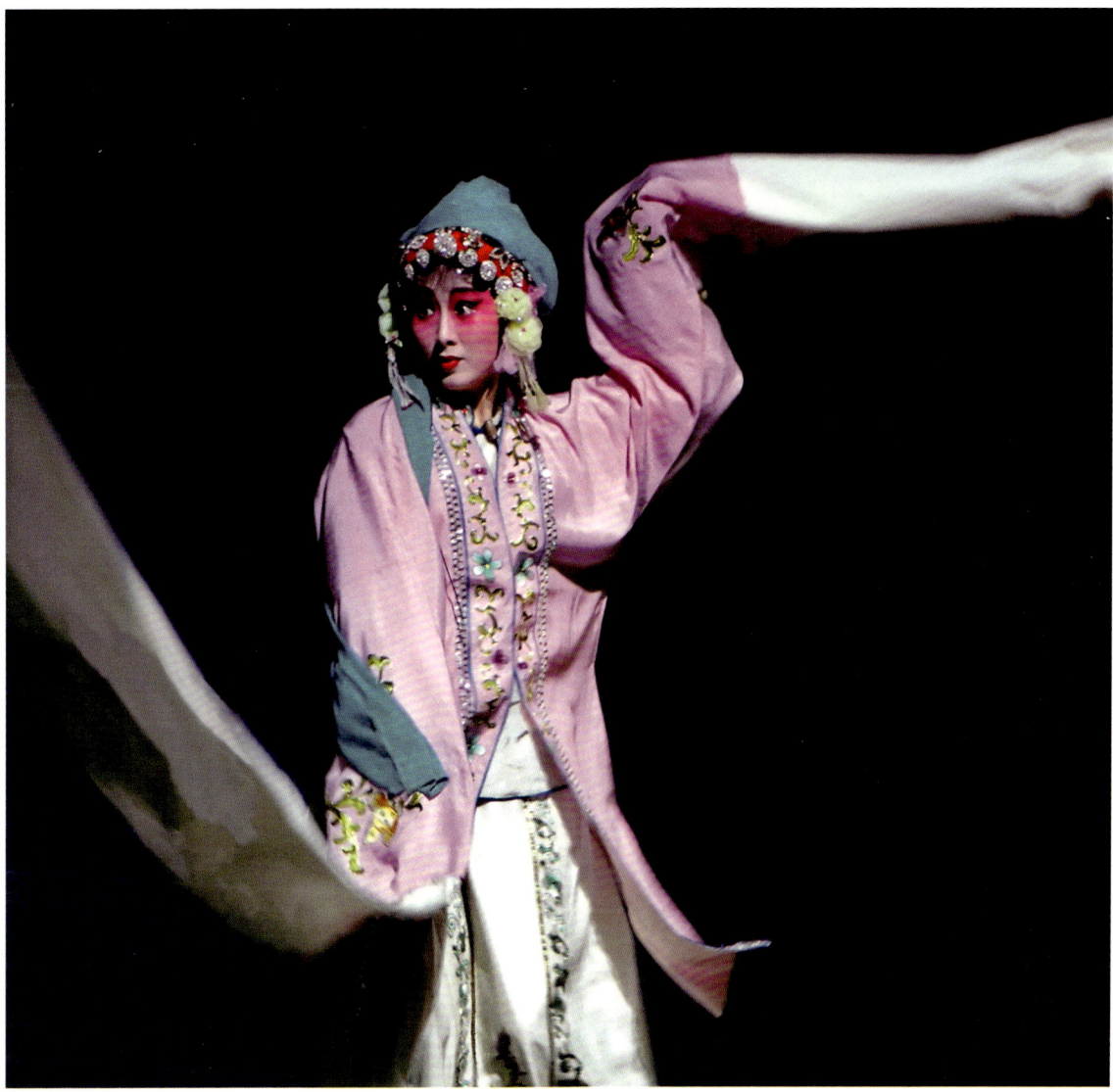

Photo 5.34 *The Story of the Wooden Hairpin*, Gan Opera

In another opera, the young wife Huo Xiaoyu, having learned that her husband has taken another wife, is in distress. Rather than extend her sleeves in sorrow as Zhu Yingtai does at the tomb, she folds them up around her face in deep despair (see Photo 5.33).

Despair can become so extreme that the character's mind is unhinged. This happens to Qian Yulian, who receives a letter from her husband. The letter was altered by a villain to read like a notice of divorce. Qian Yulian throws out her sleeves sharply in different angles, demonstrating her confusion and shock, before she kills herself by jumping into a river (see Photo 5.34).

Actors can also use their water sleeves to express fear in a number of ways. One of these is to extend the sleeve and shake it violently. Su Yu'e, who has plotted with her father to kill the emperor at a feast, throws out her water sleeves in terror when the warrior maiden Liu Guilian spoils the plan and threatens her with a sword (see Photo 5.35).

In another opera, the young woman Wang Guiying returns to the Temple of the Sea God where she and her husband had sworn eternal devotion. She swirls her sleeves in large figure eights at the god in protest at the god's indifference (see Photo 5.36).

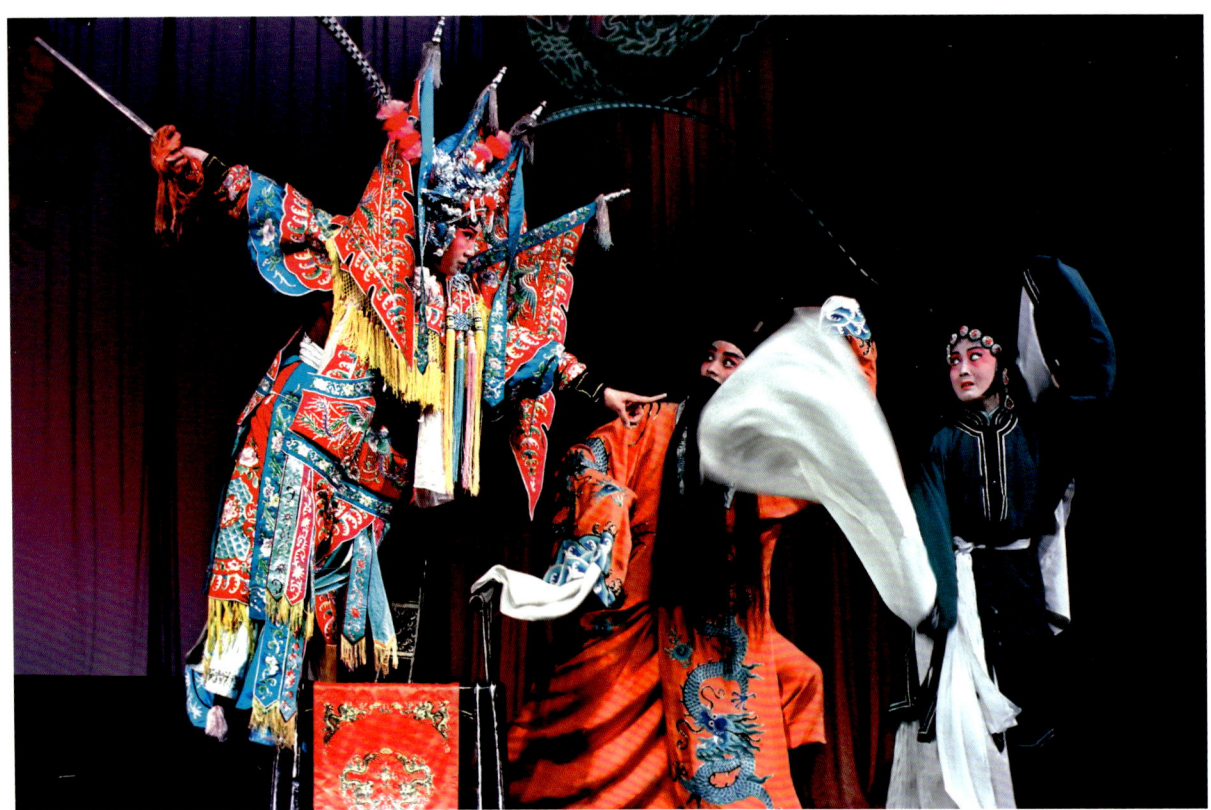

Photo 5.35 *The Killing of the Imperial Concubine*, Jin Opera

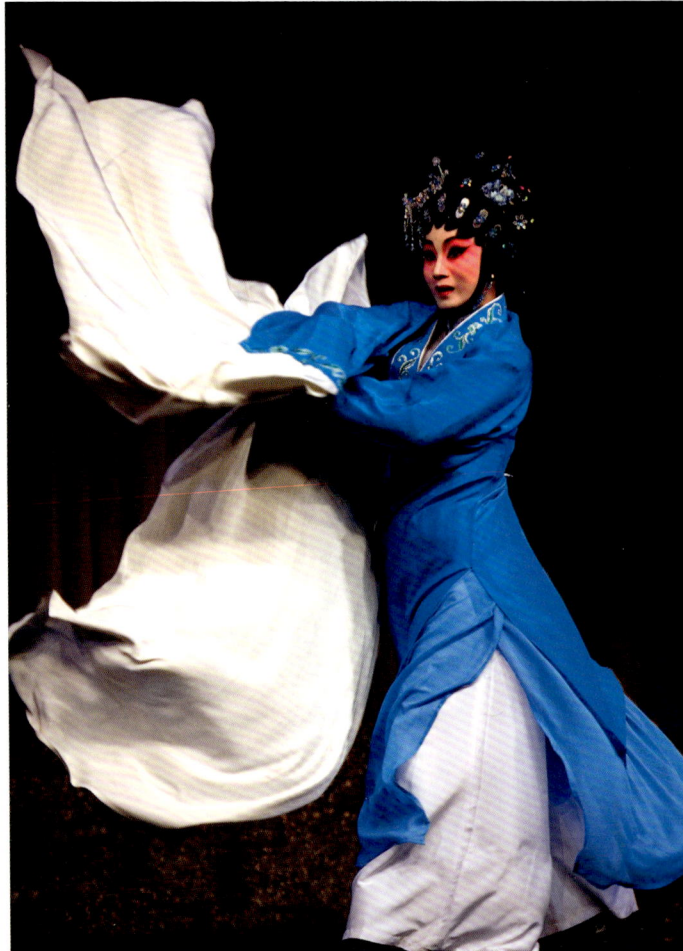

Photo 5.36 *At Odds with a God*, Cantonese Opera

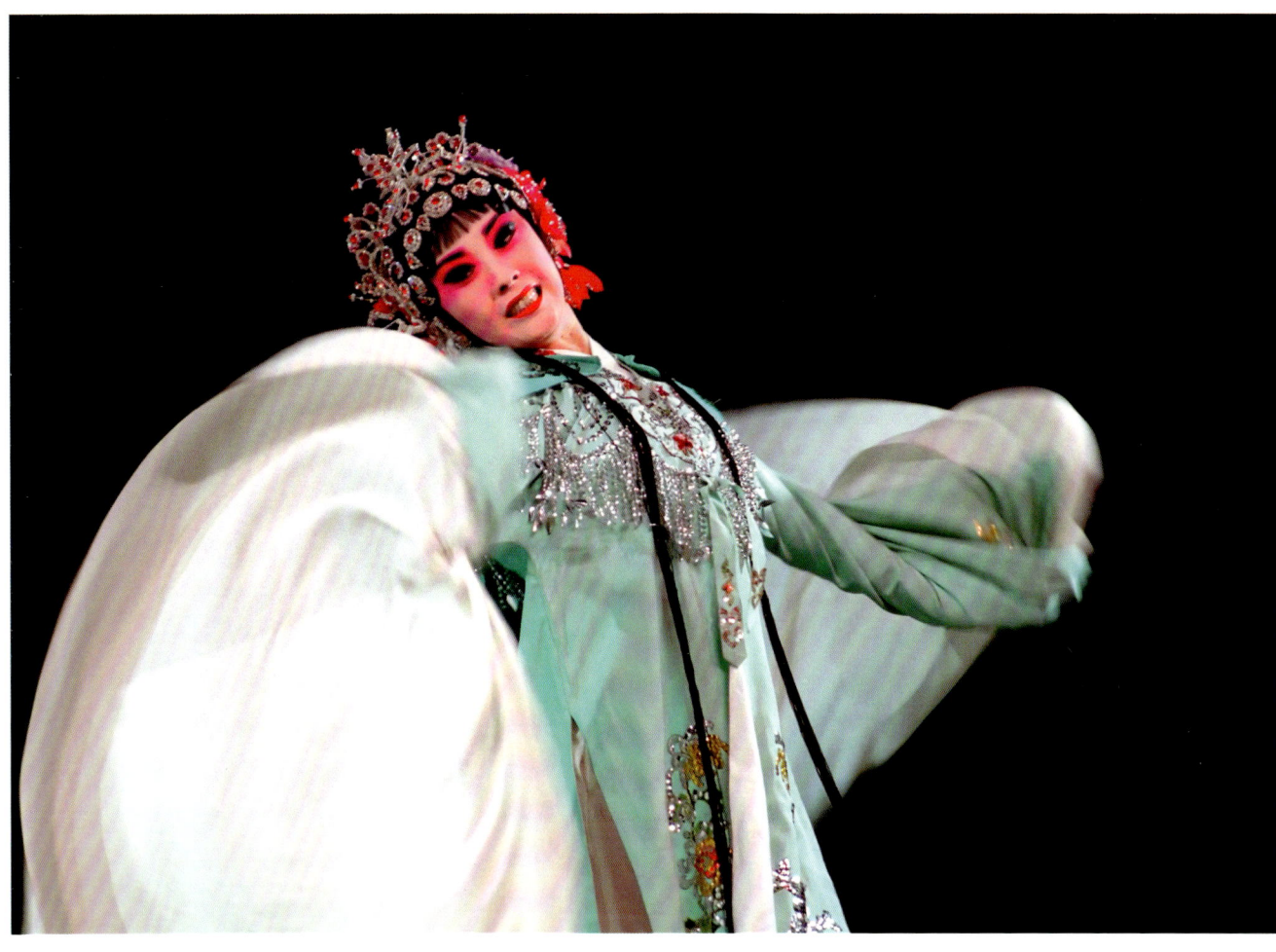

Photo 5.37 *Twice-Locked Mountain*, Longjiang Opera

Just as water sleeves can express sorrow, distress, fear and protest, they can also convey joy. In the opera *Twice-Locked Mountain*, Liu Jinding, who has been unwilling to accept her father's arrangements for a marriage, is delighted to receive permission to choose her own husband. She throws out her water sleeves and then twirls them playfully to show how light-hearted she now feels (see Photo 5.37).

Apart from expressing emotion, water sleeves make for dramatic moments in the action of the story. Judge Bao flips up his water sleeve as he orders the execution of the malicious Chen Shimei, who terribly wronged his wife and children (see Photo 5.38).

Water sleeves can also show magic power. In *The Legend of the Red Plum*, Li Huiniang has returned from the grave to defend her love from an assassination. The actress violently throws out her long water sleeves, symbolizing the discharge of magic power that sends the assassins tumbling head over heels (see Photo 5.39).

Water sleeves add movement, drama and poignancy to an actor's delivery. They are tools to express inner states, to punctuate the action, and to move the story forward. In this way, costume is much more than decoration; it is rather a means of expression.

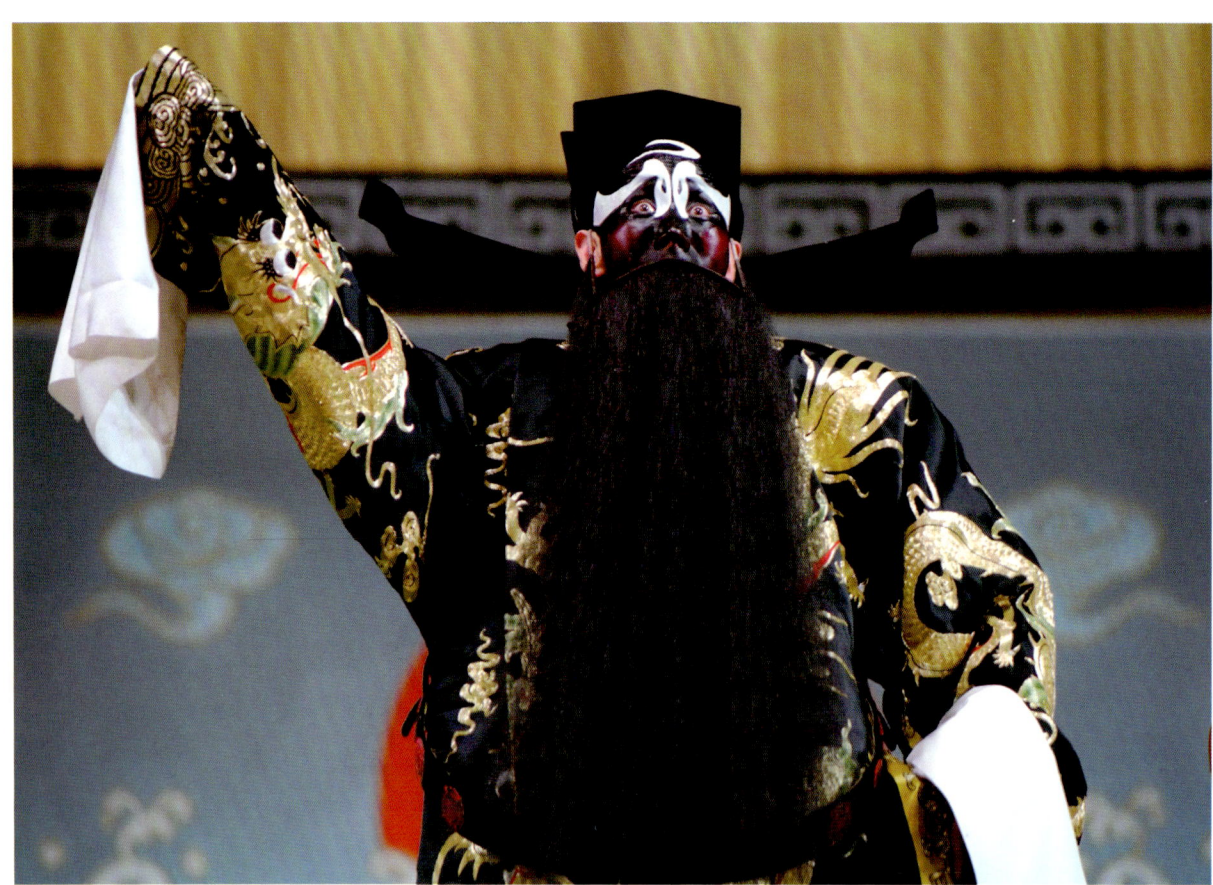

Photo 5.38 *The Beheading of a Wicked Husband*, Peking Opera

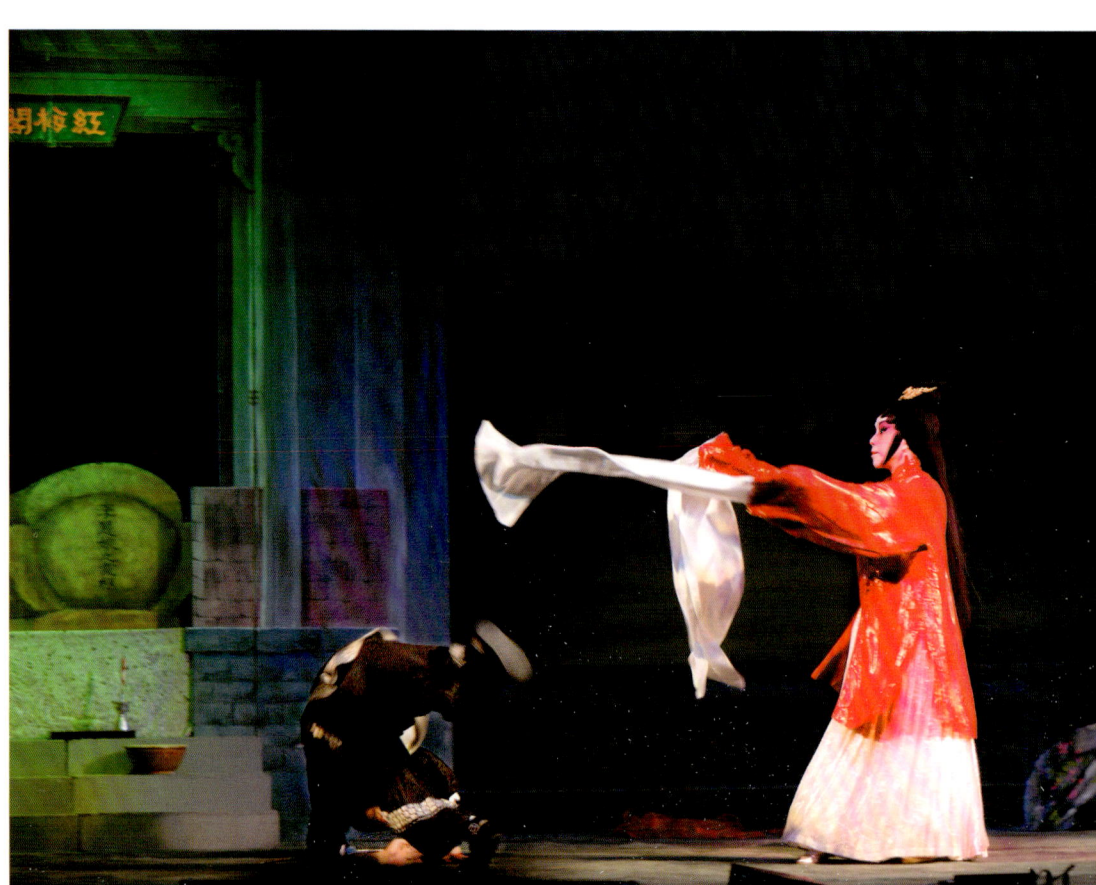

Photo 5.39 *The Legend of the Red Plum*, Cantonese Opera

Outer Robe

Young scholars and officials often wear casual outer robes. These robes usually have wide embroidered collars that come around the neck and cross the front. They also have long white water sleeves, which actors use to express a wide variety of emotions. Actors use these outer robes as they use other parts of their costume in their performances.

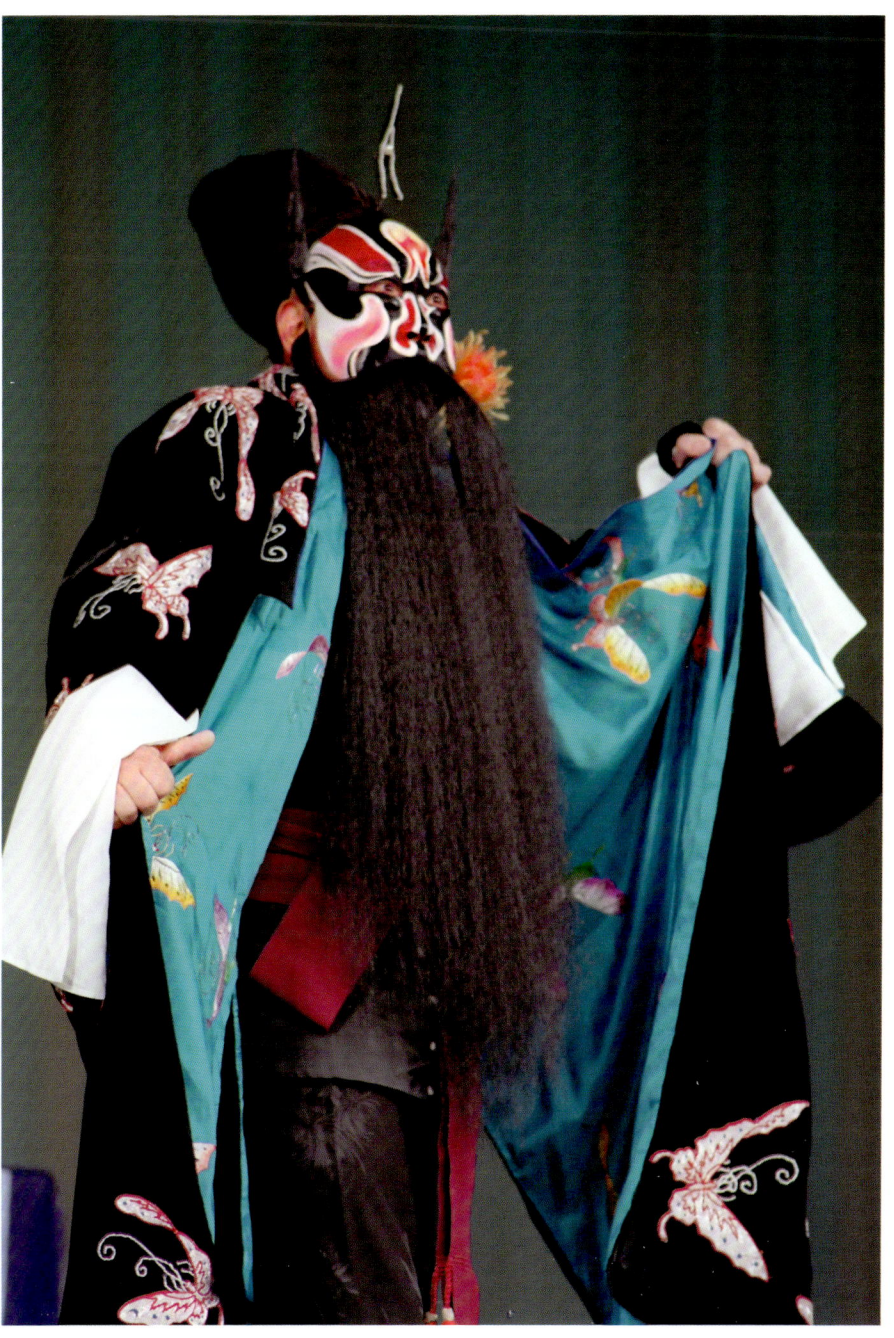

Photo 5.40 *Li Kui Visits His Mother*, Peking Opera

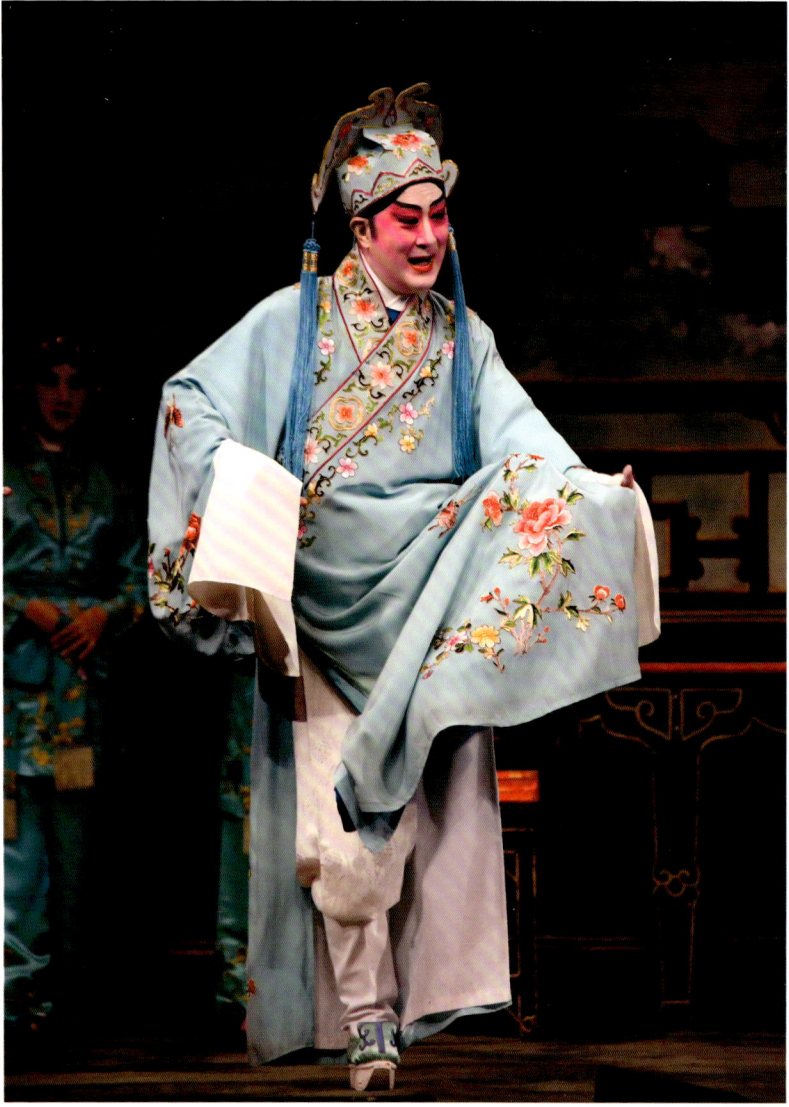

Photo 5.41 *The Butterfly Lovers*, Cantonese Opera

Manipulating the outer robe can help with the illusion of climbing stairs. In the popular love story *Liang Shanbo and Zhu Yingtai*, sometimes called *The Butterfly Lovers*, the young scholar Liang Shanbo has come to the house of his beloved Zhu Yingtai, where he will ask for her hand in marriage. He is full of joy and expectation as he mounts the stairway to the front door. He hikes up the edge of his robe as he takes pronounced steps indicating the climb (see Photo 5.41).

In another opera, the actor indicates that he is about to kneel by stretching the side of his robe out in front of him. The great warrior from the Three Kingdoms period, Zhang Fei, is prepared to offer his apologies to the sage magistrate, Pang Tong, for not having shown the proper respect for his talents. This kind of exaggerated kneeling and lifting up of his robe indicates that this is a solemn gesture of respect (see Photo 5.42).

The opposite of humility is over-confidence. Just as an actor can stretch out his robe to kneel in respect, he can also flare open that robe in a gesture of arrogance. When Meng Liang meets Yang Paifeng, the servant girl wants to show that she is a worthy warrior and could best even Meng Liang. In disdain,

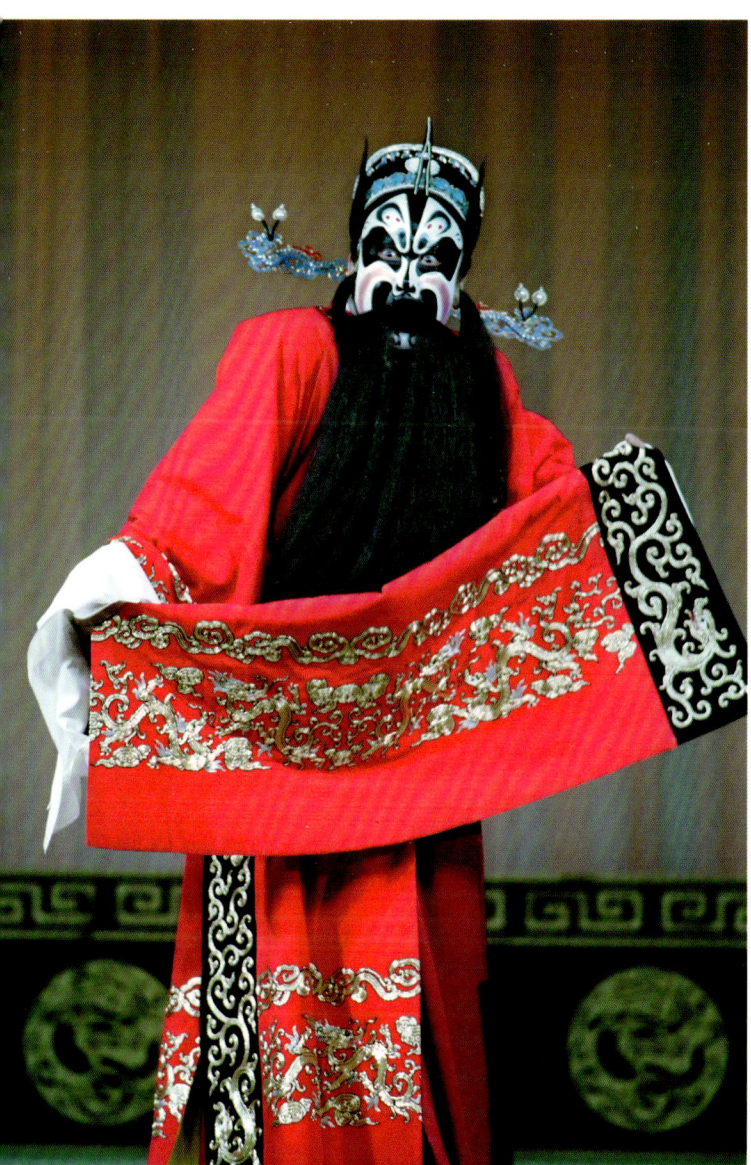

Photo 5.42 *Zhang Fei Honours the Sage Magistrate*, Peking Opera

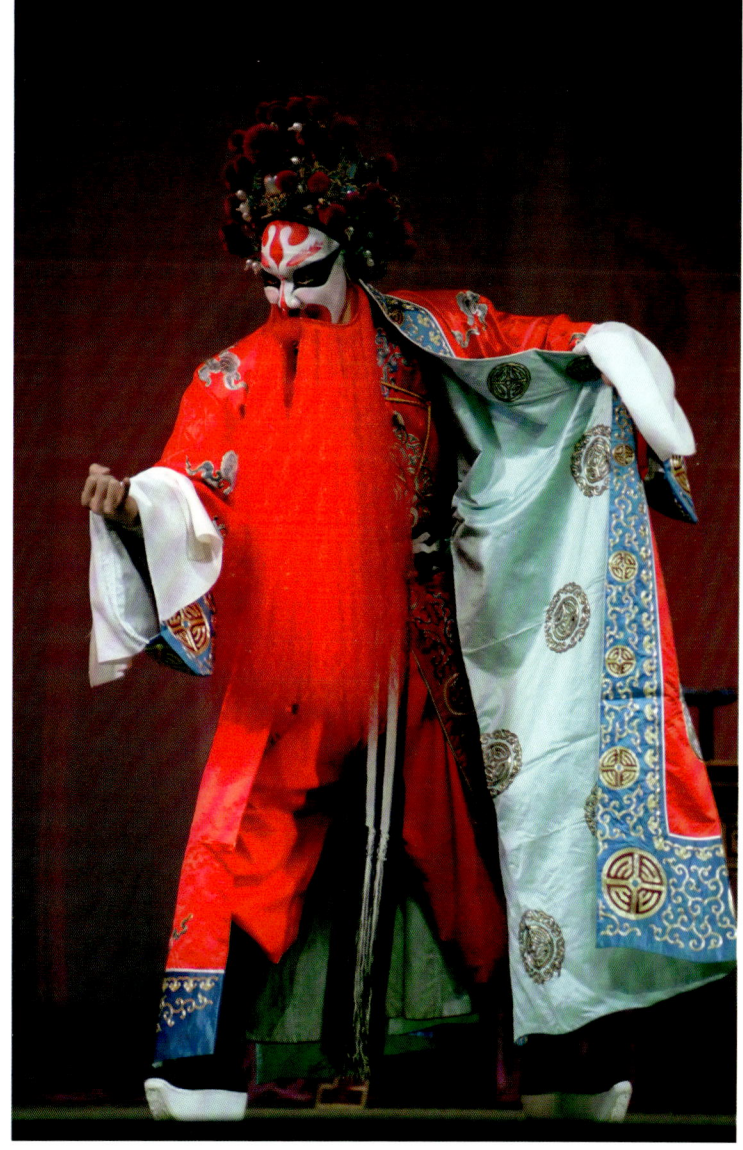

Photo 5.43 *Meng Liang Raises Troops*, Gan Opera

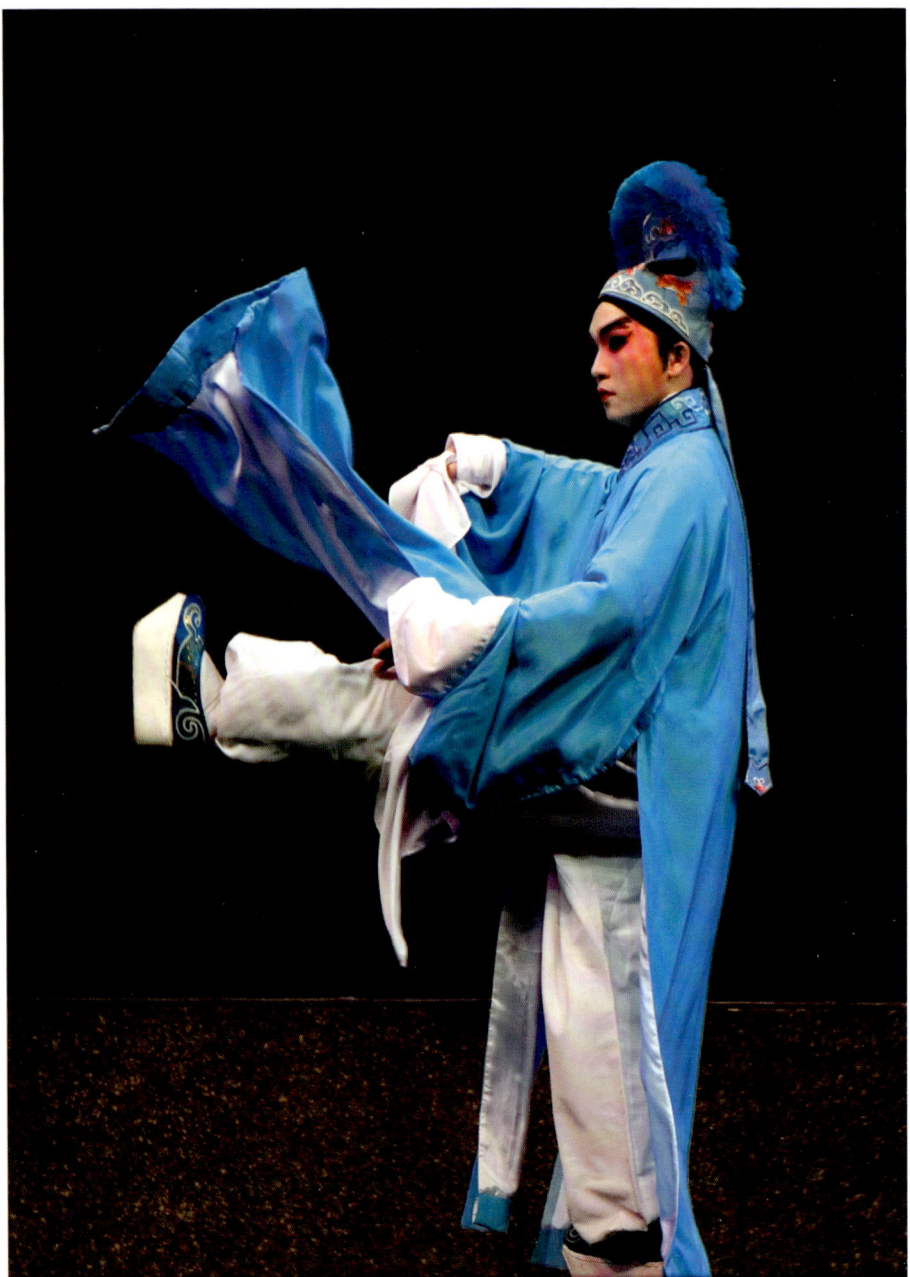

Photo 5.44 *Escape from the Golden Mountain Temple*, Cantonese Opera

assured of his own military prowess, Meng Liang flips open his robe—not knowing that she will indeed defeat him and go on to prove her claim (see Photo 5.43).

Kicking the hem of the outer robe in just the right way shows the audience a character's agitation. Xu Xian uses this technique in *The Legend of the White Snake*. The White Snake spirit, incarnated as a beautiful woman, has tried to defeat the monk Fahai to free her husband, Xu Xian. She has been unsuccessful. Fahai's resources are just too great. Xu Xian, however, makes his escape and runs as quickly as he can back to West Lake to find his wife. Worried that he will be recaptured, his agitation grows. The actor kicks his leg high to fling up the bottom of the outer robe, which gently floats down to be kicked up yet again, so that it is constantly fluttering in the air (see Photo 5.44).

Using Costumes

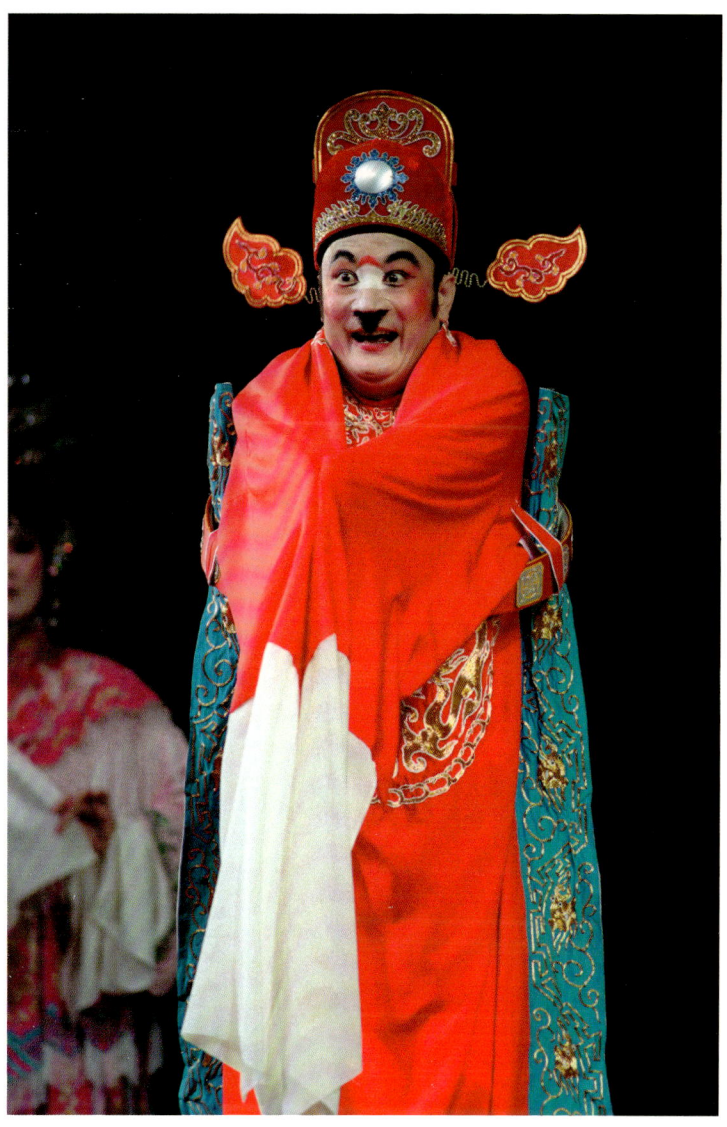

Photo 5.45 *Dr. Happenstance,* Chaozhou Opera

Just as the outer robe can be used to express reverence, humanity, over-confidence and agitation, it can also help an actor express downright fear. Chaozhou opera is famous for its comedies. The clown role holds a very special place in that genre. In one of these operas, *Dr. Happenstance*, the clown experiences a hilarious series of bizarre coincidences until he finds himself mistaken for a doctor charged with healing the emperor's mother. Completely at a loss for what to do, the hapless Dr. Happenstance tries to hide himself in his outer robe, his white sleeves trembling before him (see Photo 5.45).

The slanted python robe is an outer garment that descends from the left shoulder, leaving the right arm free. It indicates that the wearer is going out to battle in a distant place. Prince Lanling wears such a robe. He is so good-looking, however, that he eventually must take to wearing a mask in order to strike terror in his enemies (see Photo 5.46).

The legendary fighter Wu Song from the novel *The Legend of the Water Margin* is outraged to hear that a great bully, Jiang Zhong, has wrested a grove away from its rightful owner. Becoming more

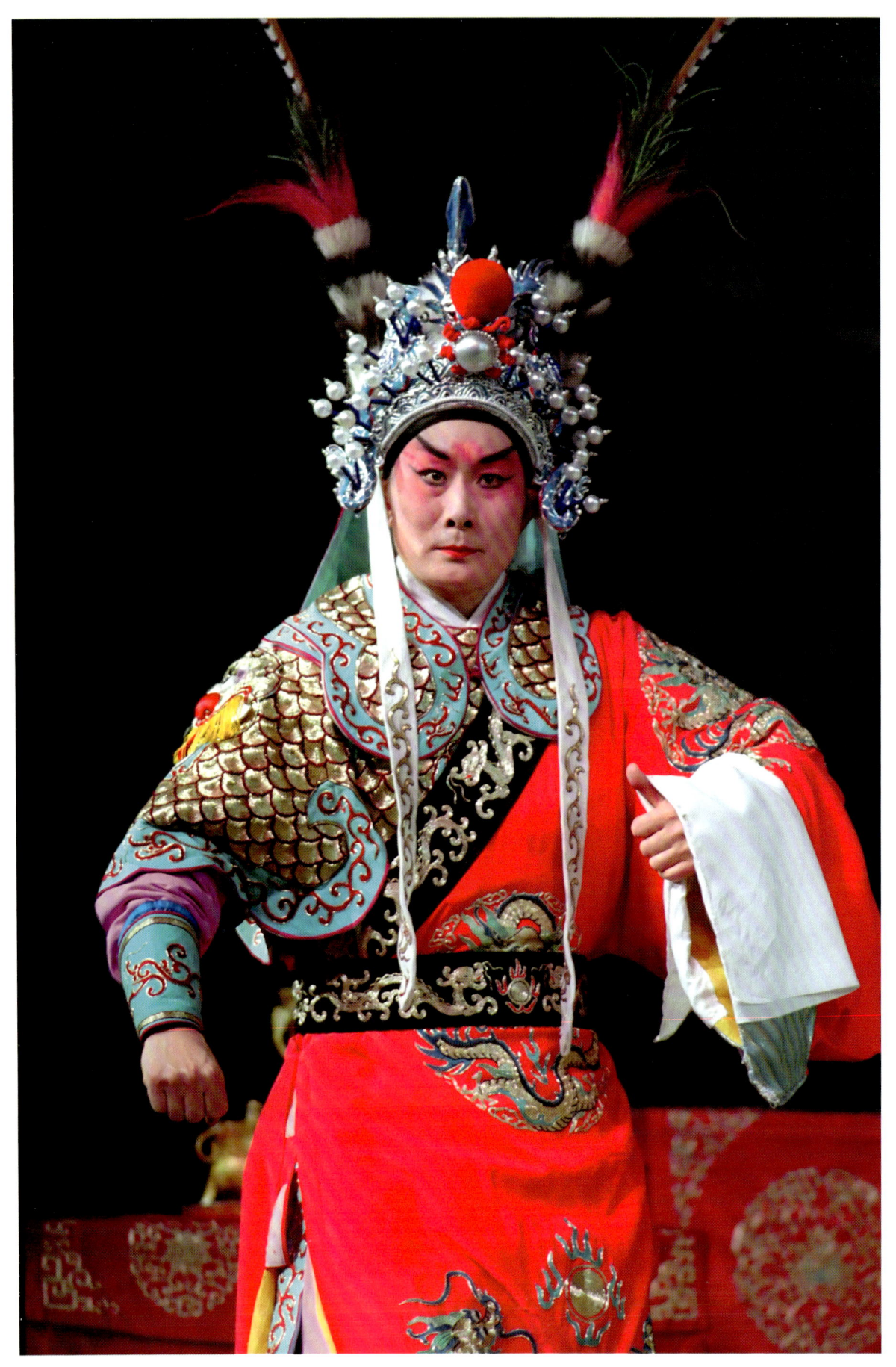

Photo 5.46 *Prince Lanling*, Hebei Clapper Opera

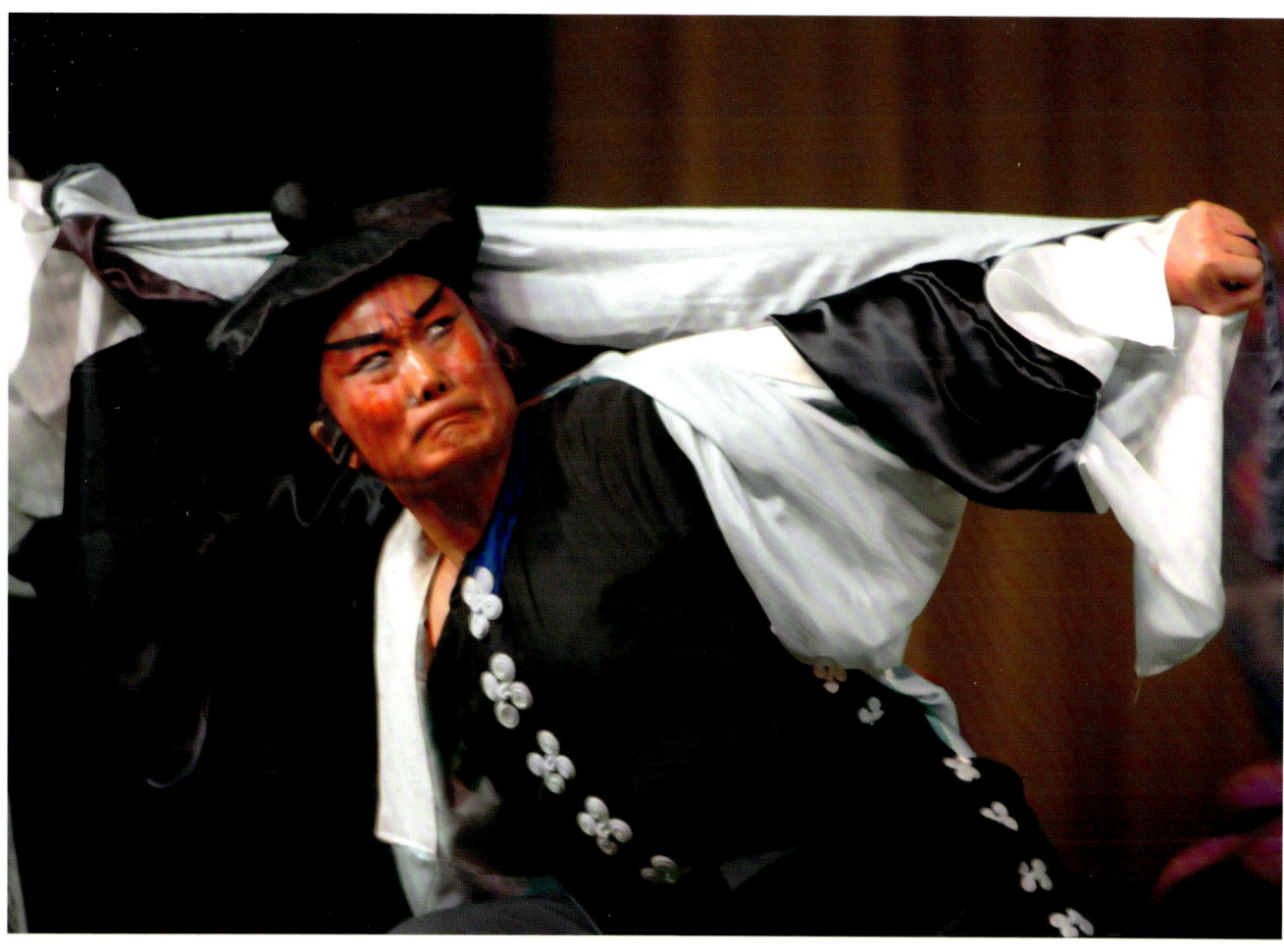

Photo 5.47 *Wu Song's Revenge*, Hebei Clapper Opera

infuriated as he drinks, Wu Song decides to set the injustice right. He twists and turns his outer robe behind him, demonstrating his passion, determination and bravery (see Photo 5.47).

Big Belt

BELTS INDICATE STATUS and can be manipulated as part of the actor's performance craft. Actors wear different styles of belts on the opera stage. The jade belt is a solid hoop that circles the body with a piece of jade at the front. It is worn by male characters with high social standing, usually officials. Another kind of belt is the big belt, a long sash tied around the waist with long, wide, hanging ends. Actors can use these ends in their performances. "Lifting the big belt" is often used when a character first appears on the stage and takes a pose. It is also used to indicate that the character is travelling quickly on a journey, often at night or across difficult terrain.

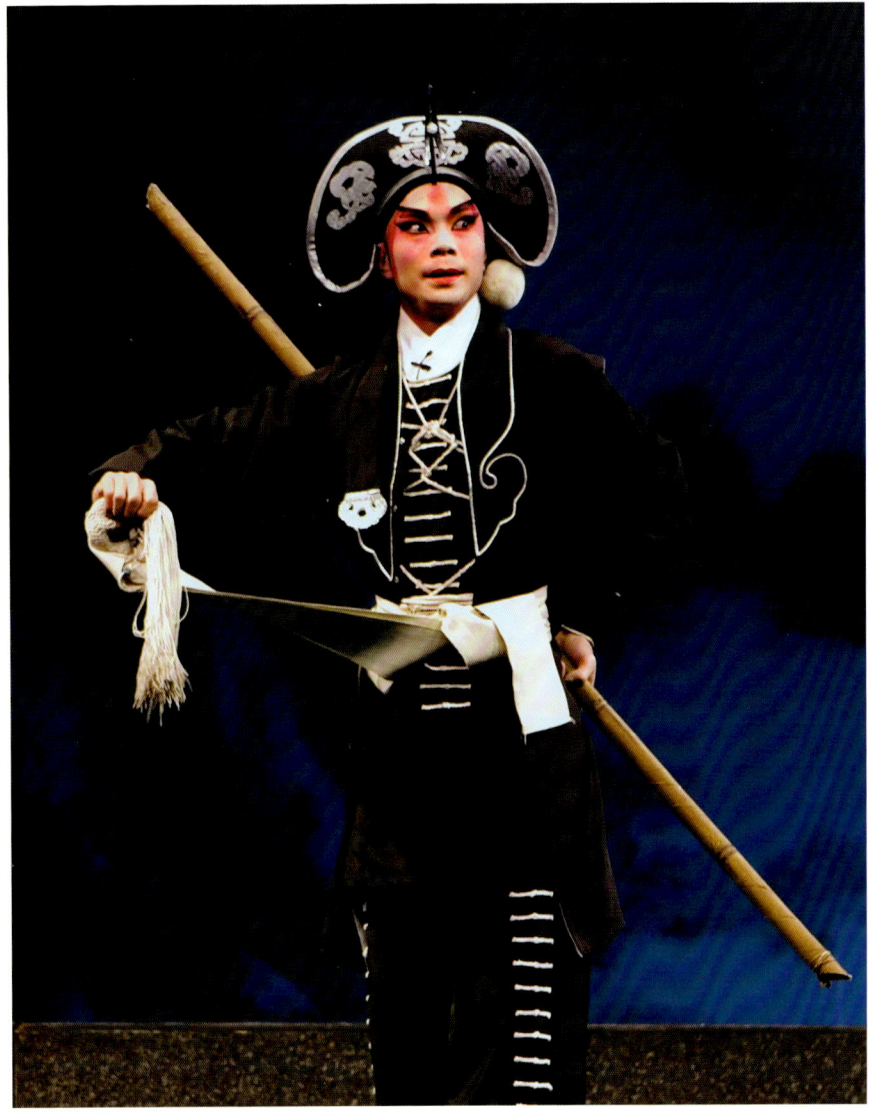

Photo 5.48 *Shi Xiu Reconnoiters a Village*, Cantonese Opera

Shi Xiu is indeed on a journey. He has been expelled from the household of his friend and sworn blood brother, Yang Xiong, after accusing Yang Xiong's wife of adultery with a villainous monk. Determined to set things right, Shi Xiu has killed the monk and obtained the evidence he needs. Sabre in hand and lifting up his big belt, he grimly sets out to present that evidence to Yang Xiong (see Photo 5.49).

Shi Xiu later also kills Yang Xiong's unfaithful wife. In another opera, Shi Xiu, now an outlaw, takes refuge with the famous bandits on Liang Mountain. These bandits are largely victims of injustice and have become as famous as Robin Hood's band of merry men. They send him to find a way around Zhu village, which is blocking the advance of the bandits. Shi Xiu "kicks the belt on the shoulder", indicating that he has taken a big step on this difficult journey (see Photo 5.50).

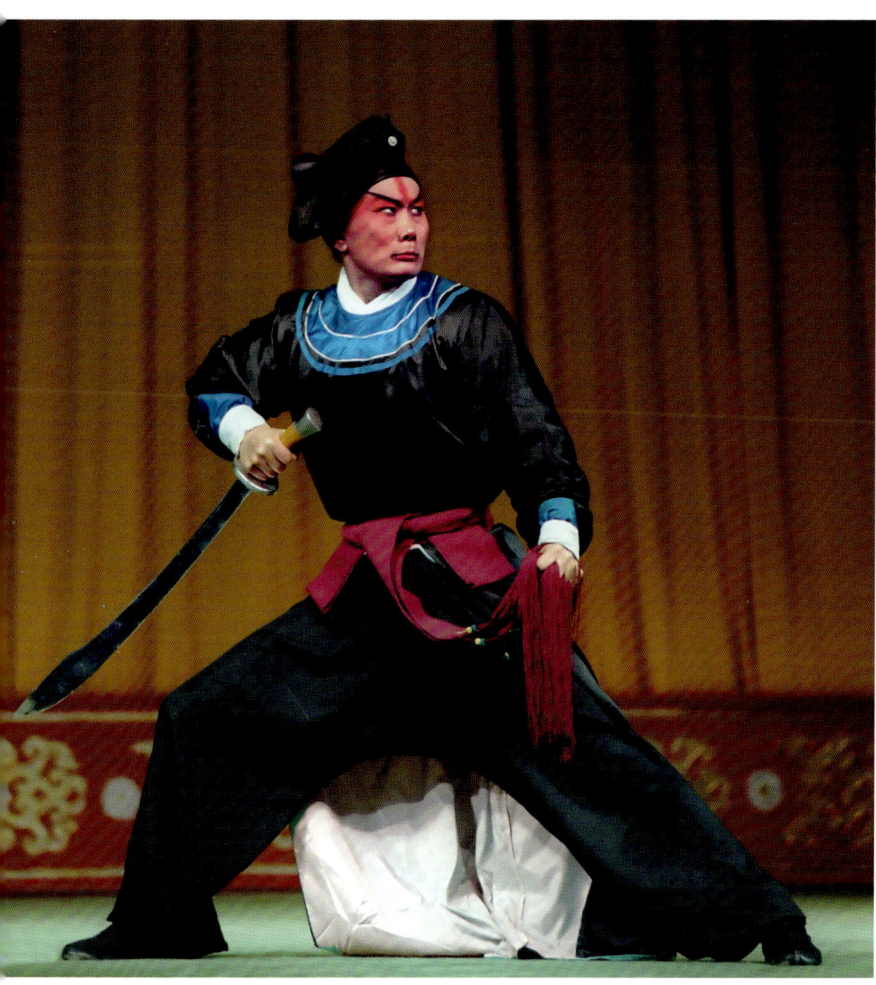

Photo 5.49   *Shi Xiu Slays an Unfaithful Wife*, Hebei Clapper Opera

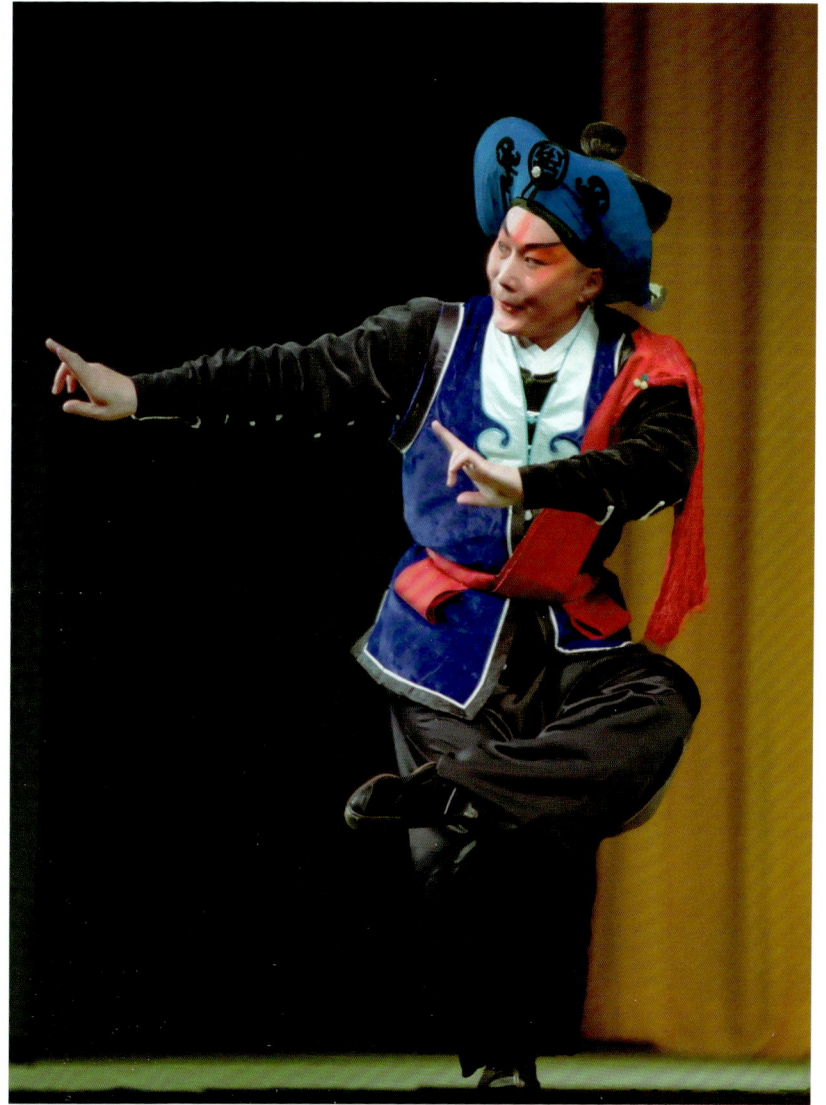

Photo 5.50   *Shi Xiu Reconnoiters a Village*, Hebei Clapper Opera

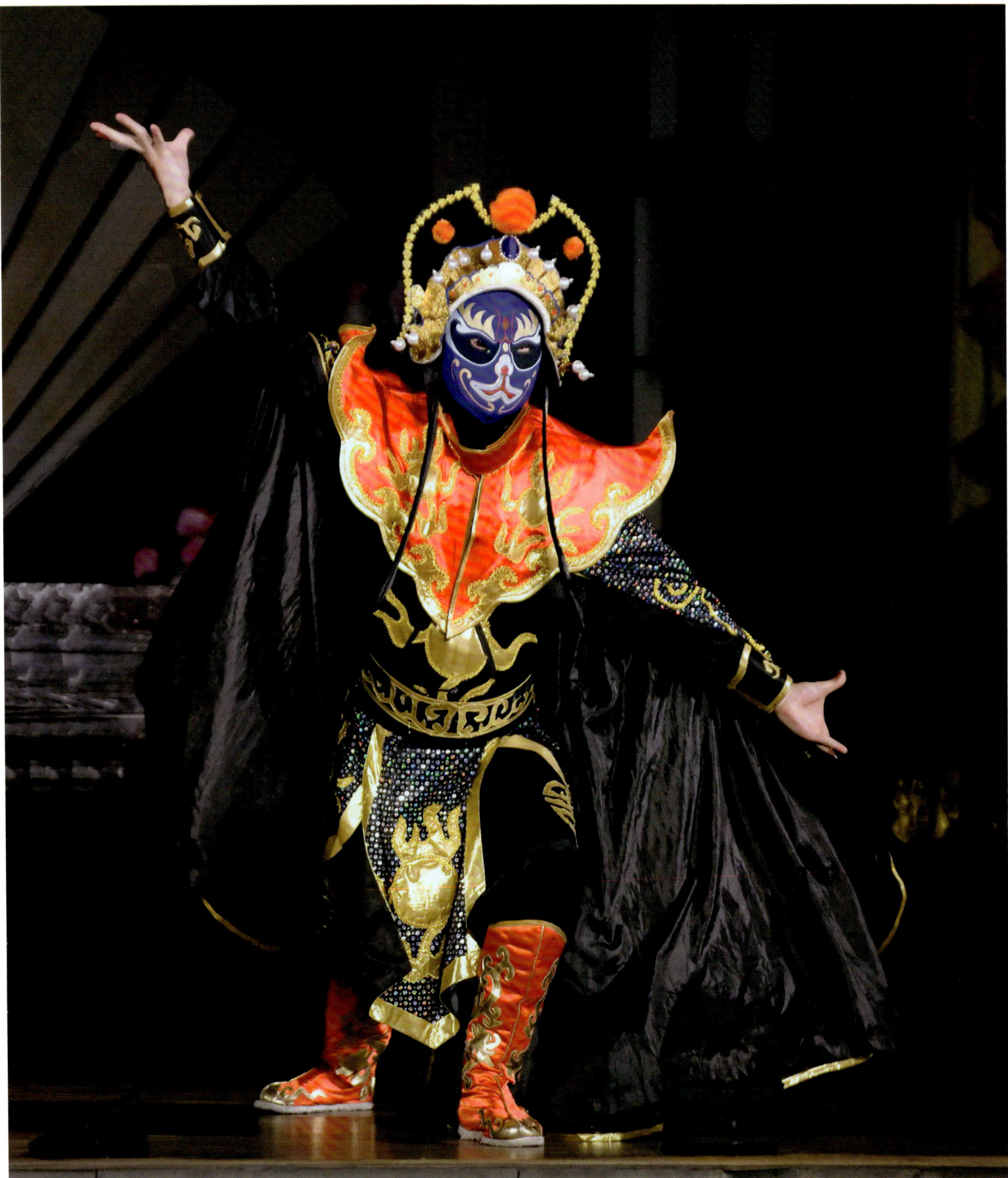

CHAPTER 6

Using Special Skills

Opposite
Photo 6.01 An actor performing face changing in a tea-house in Chengdu, Sichuan Opera

Face Changing

THE SICHUAN OPERA is famous for its tales of the fantastic. Ghosts, demons, and fairies share the stage with emperors, beauties, and heroes. It even has a special role type for female ghosts and fox spirits. The Sichuan opera makes use of special skills to tell these stories. One of the most famous of these is face changing.

Audiences are stunned to see a character change his face in the blink of an eye. These metamorphoses show emotions like sudden terror, or display the ability of magical beings to transform. One of the earliest methods was to blow into a vessel like a wine bowl to spread a gold powder all over the actor's face; the powder would stick to make-up. Another method was to use the fingertips to rub red or black on the face to show a shift in emotion. In one variation of this, "stormy eyes", the actor blackens his eyes to show anger or fear. In the twentieth century, Sichuan opera became famous for yet another face-changing technique. In this method, actors rapidly switch through many silk masks, each with an intricate design. The mechanism for this is considered a national treasure and not discussed openly, but

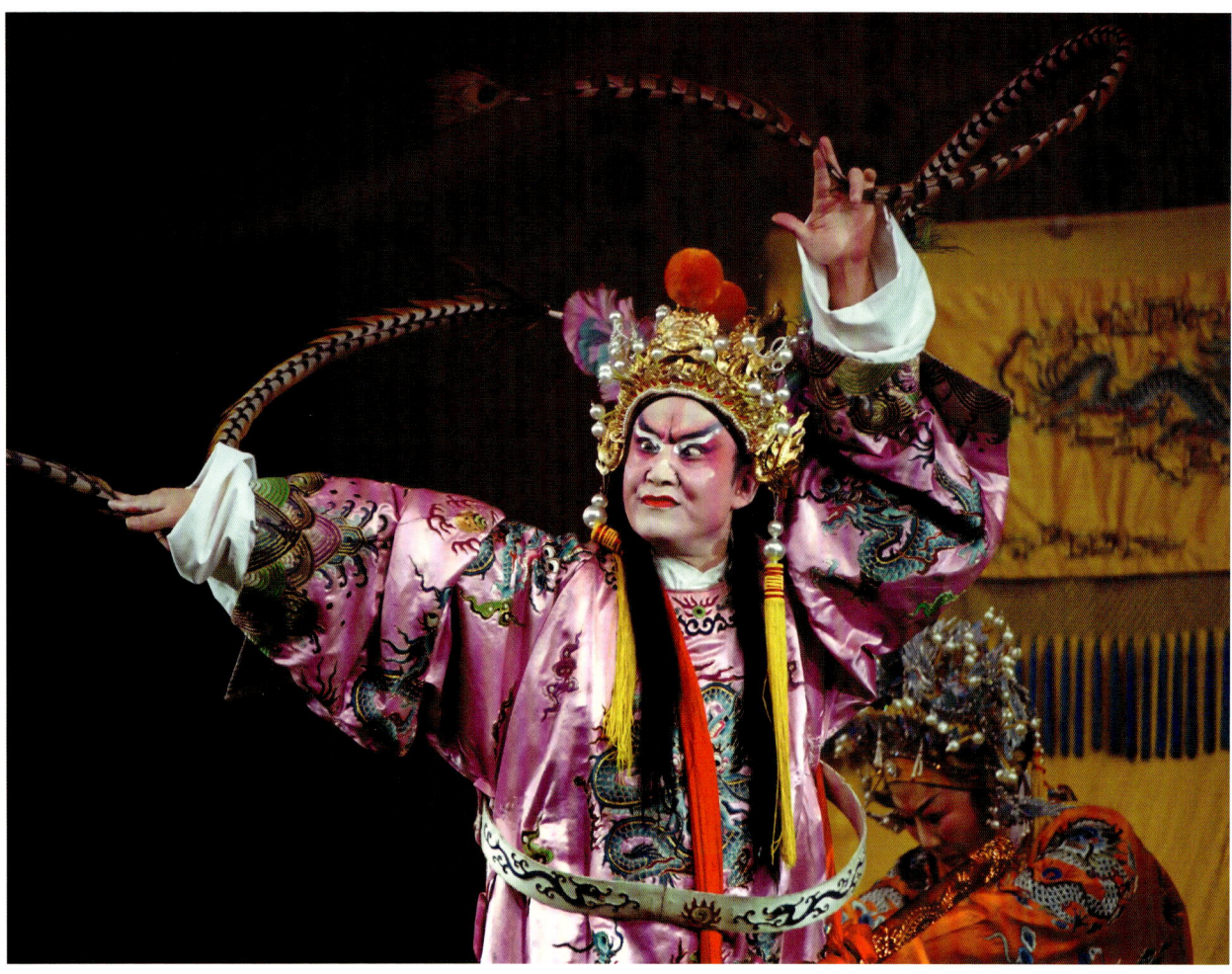

Photo 6.02 *Wresting the Dragon Throne*, Sichuan Opera

has found its way into magic shows and has been the subject of documentaries. The instantaneous and multiple changes are a striking Sichuan opera stage technique.

All of these techniques are still used in the Sichuan opera repertoire. In the play *Wresting the Dragon Throne*, the wicked prince feigns concern for his father's illness, but is eager to take the throne. He reveals his true evil nature to the audience during the story by rubbing white grease paint, used to show villainy, below his eyebrows and on his face (see Photo 6.02).

In another play, the good eunuch Chen Lin uses the same technique to change his face, but this time rubs black paint around his eyes. This indicates his fear as he tries to protect an infant prince from the plotting of a concubine who is suspicious of him (see Photo 6.03).

A simple method of face changing involves a mask that is kept on by biting down with the teeth. The young maiden Yan Xijiao uses this technique in the opera *The Haunting of Zhang Sanlang*. She cannot give up her beau even though she has died. She returns wearing her mask to bring him to the underworld so that they can be a ghostly couple (see Photo 6.04).

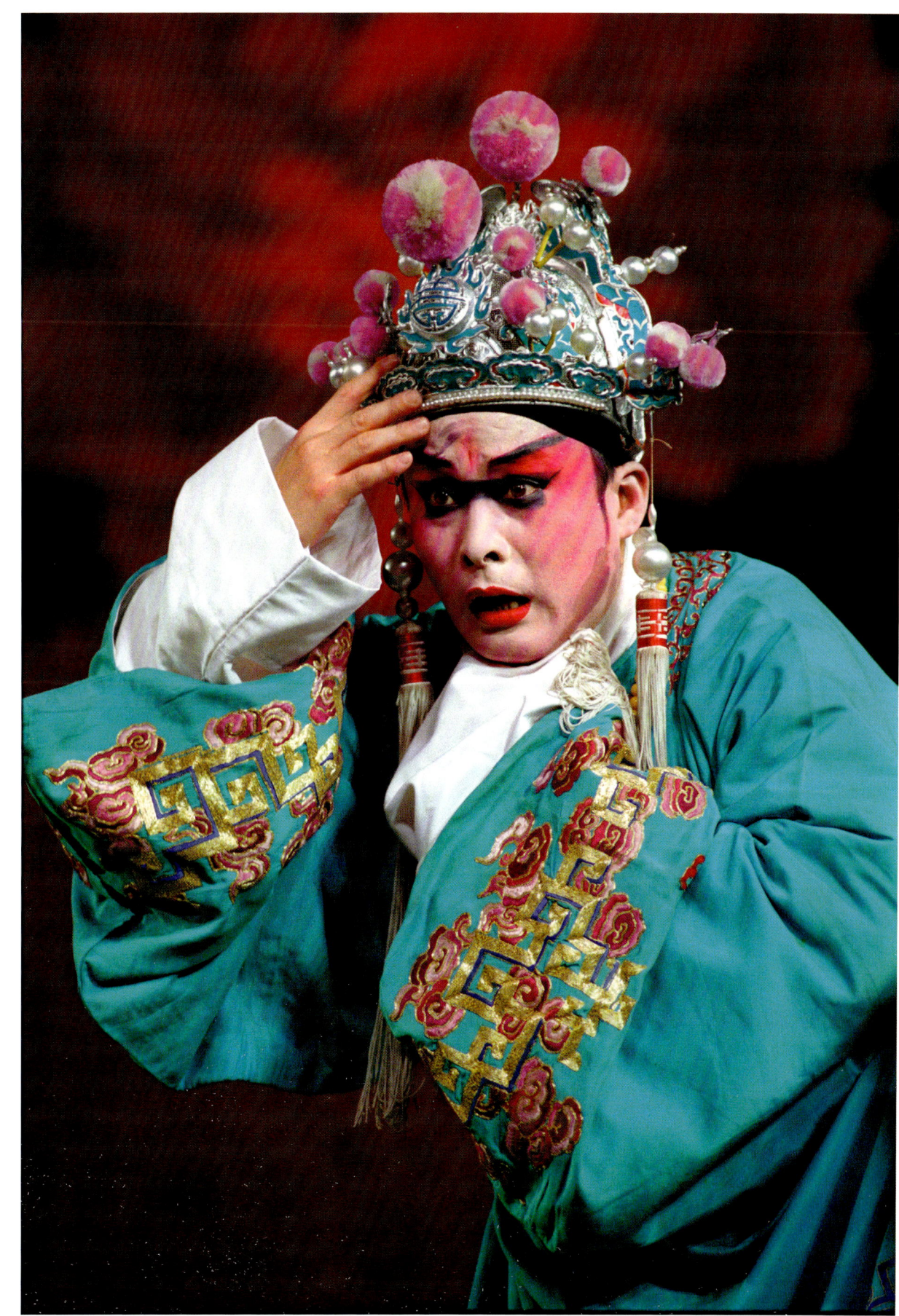

Photo 6.03 *A Palace Interrogation,* Sichuan Opera

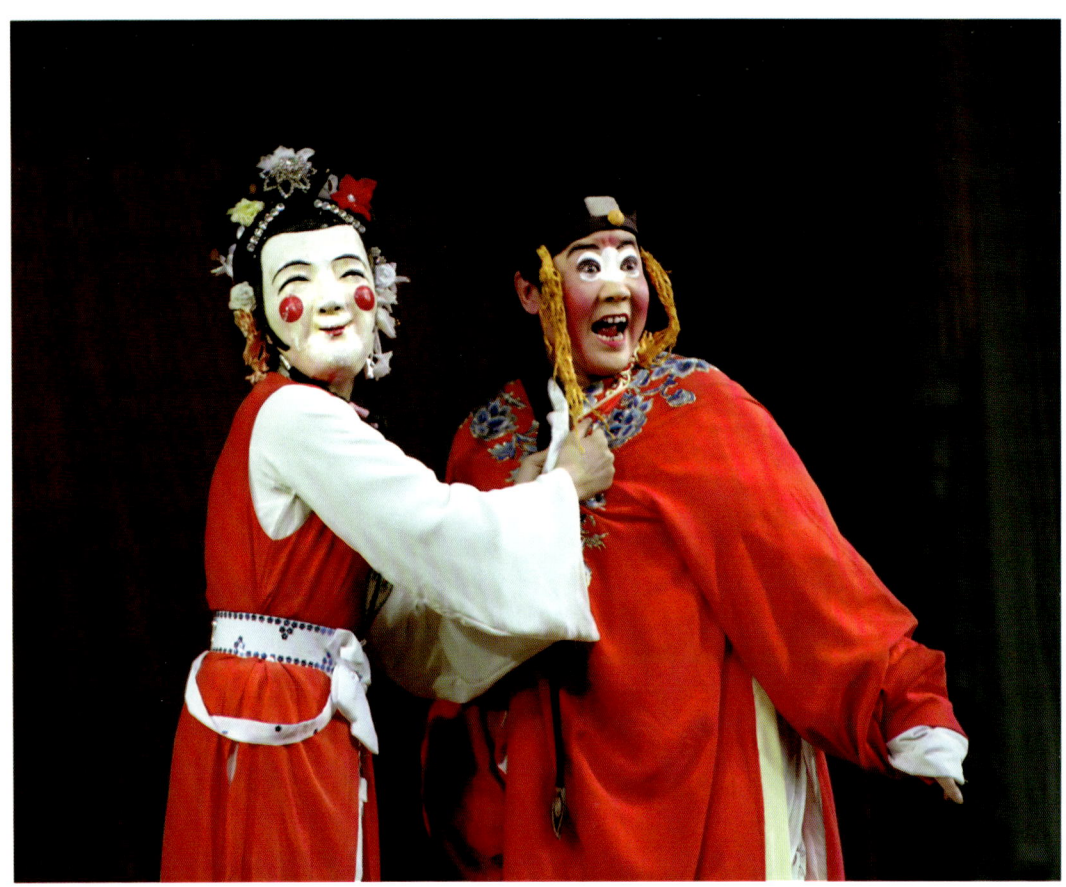

Photo 6.04 *The Haunting of Zhang Sanlang*, Sichuan Opera

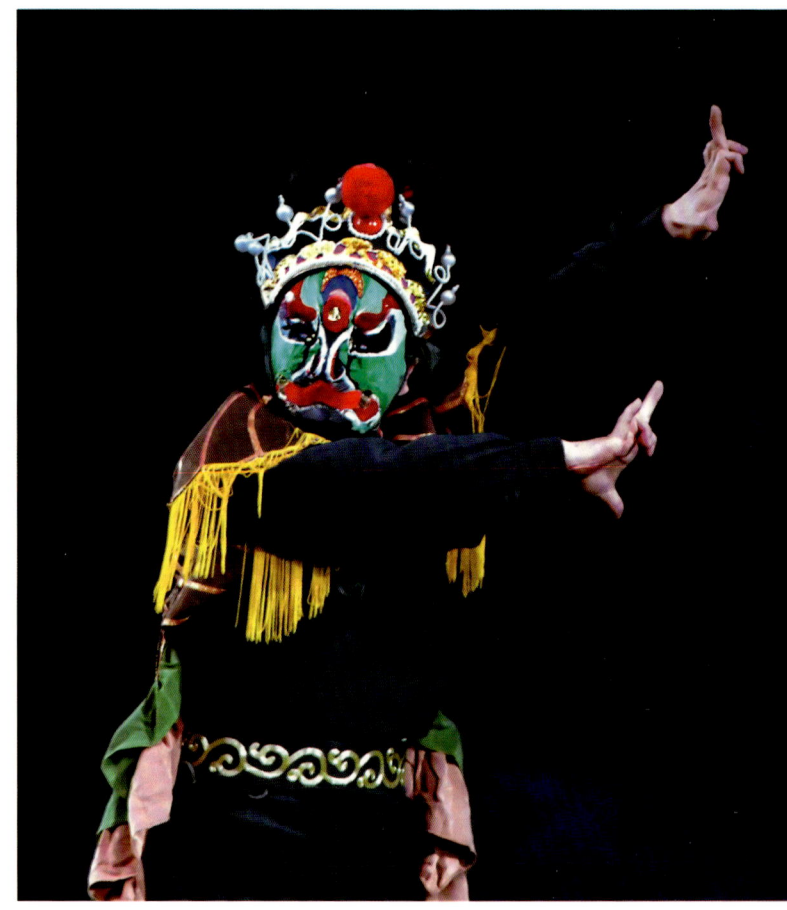

Photo 6.05 *The Legend of the White Snake*, Sichuan Opera

Using Special Skills

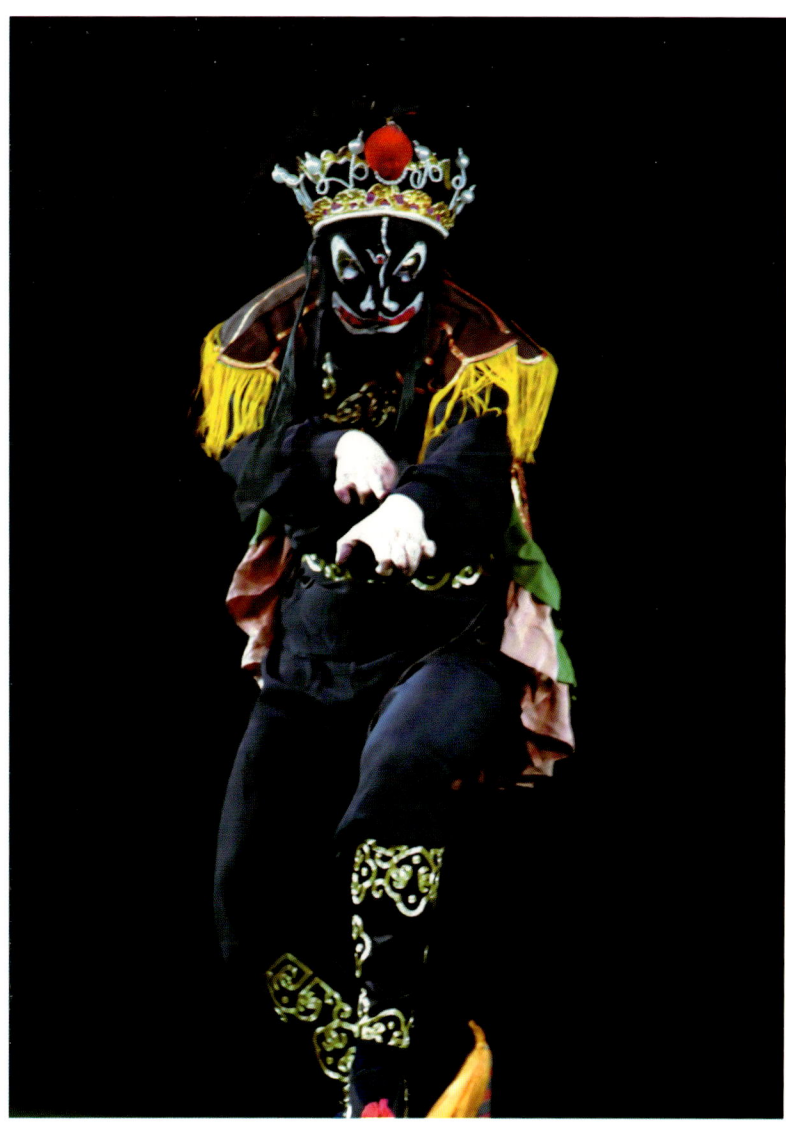

Photo 6.06 *The Legend of the White Snake*, Sichuan Opera

One of the most famous uses of face changing in the Sichuan opera appears in *The Legend of the White Snake*. In this play, White Snake, a snake spirit who has transformed into a beautiful maiden in order to marry a human, is tracked down by heavenly spirits commanded by the Buddhist abbot, Fahai. They are no match for White Snake, so Fahai resorts to a powerful weapon, golden cymbals or *naobo*. They transform into a warrior spirit who repeatedly changes his face as he fights with White Snake (see Photo 6.05).

At first, he tracks her with a black face, white eyes and bloody mouth (see Photo 6.06).

As he pursues her, his face changes in an instant to gold with thick painted eyebrows (see Photo 6.07).

And finally, when he catches up with her, his face changes again in a flash to oily white with pink cheeks and a smile of satisfaction (see Photo 6.08).

The skill of the face changer is dramatic. Rather than an extraneous trick, it is closely bound to the story so that the audience sees inner states or displays of magic power that reveal who these characters really are.

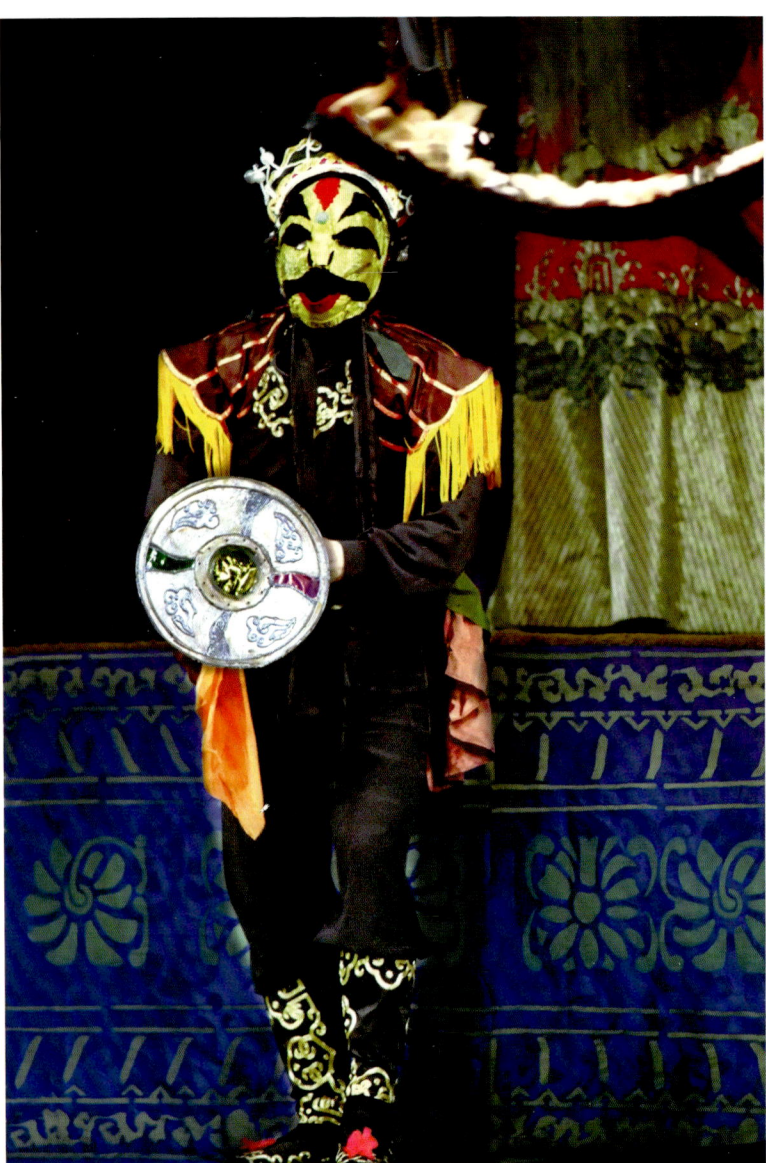

Photo 6.07 *The Legend of the White Snake*, Sichuan Opera

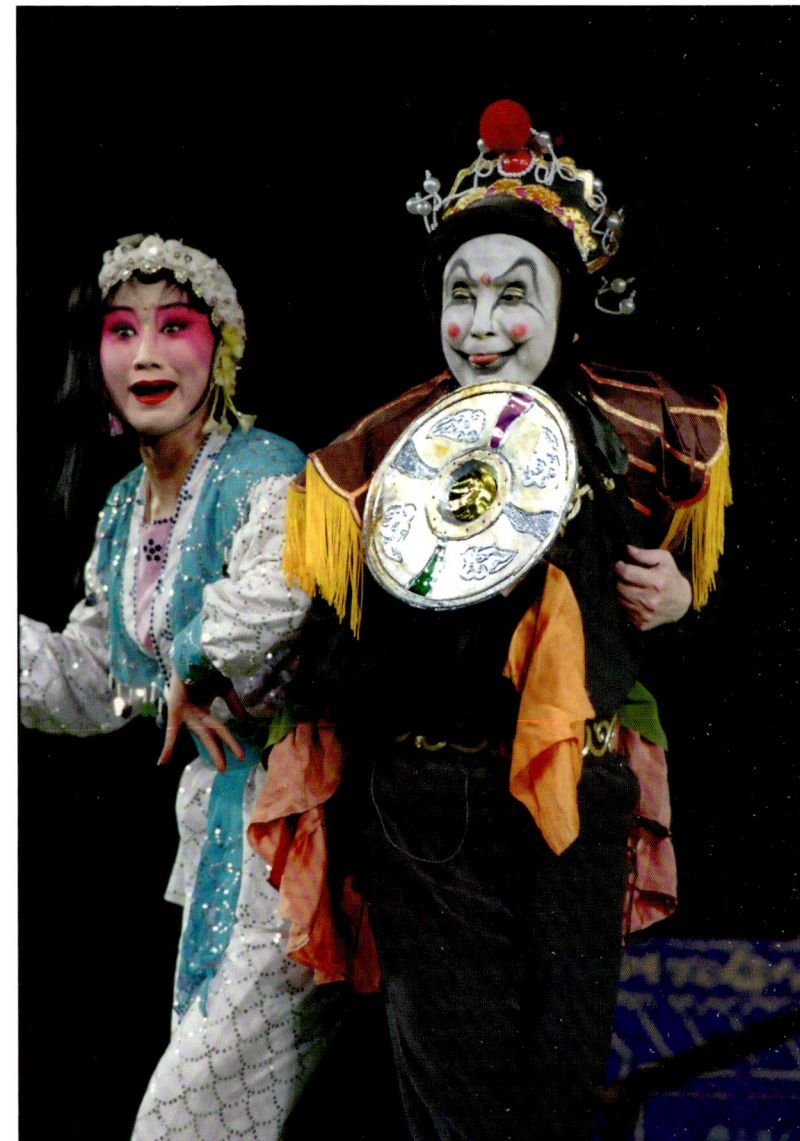

Photo 6.08 *The Legend of the White Snake*, Sichuan Opera

Fire Breathing

MAGICAL AND SPIRITUAL beings demonstrate supernatural power on the Chinese opera stage. One of the most spectacular ways of doing that is breathing fire. Unlike face changing, which is a distinctive feature of the Sichuan opera, fire breathing can be found in several Chinese opera styles. The most common technique requires the actor to hold a paper cone in his or her mouth. That cone is filled with the same powdered resin used for violins; this is mixed with ash. At the right moment, the actor blows out an explosive, short burst of the mixture into an open flame, which then ignites into a large, dramatic flare. Oils, kerosene and even lighter fluid have been used, but resin remains the standard material. Other methods include blowing small specks of materials like sawdust; this creates an entirely different effect resembling sparks. The techniques all take considerable skill and must take into account the costume the performer wears, and if performing outside, the wind. Once mastered, this stage effect is unforgettable.

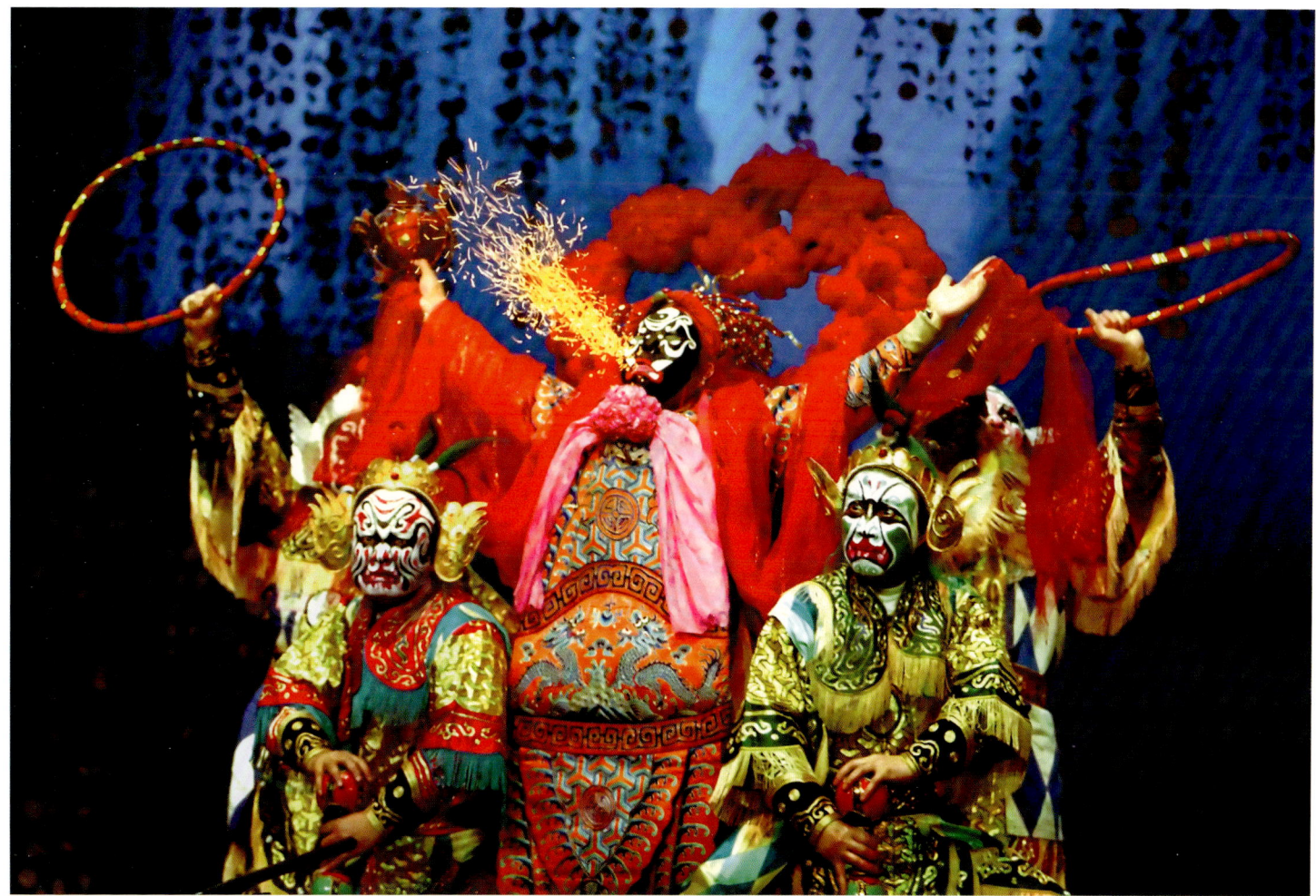

Photo 6.09 *The Nine-Tailed Fox Fairy*, Sichuan Opera

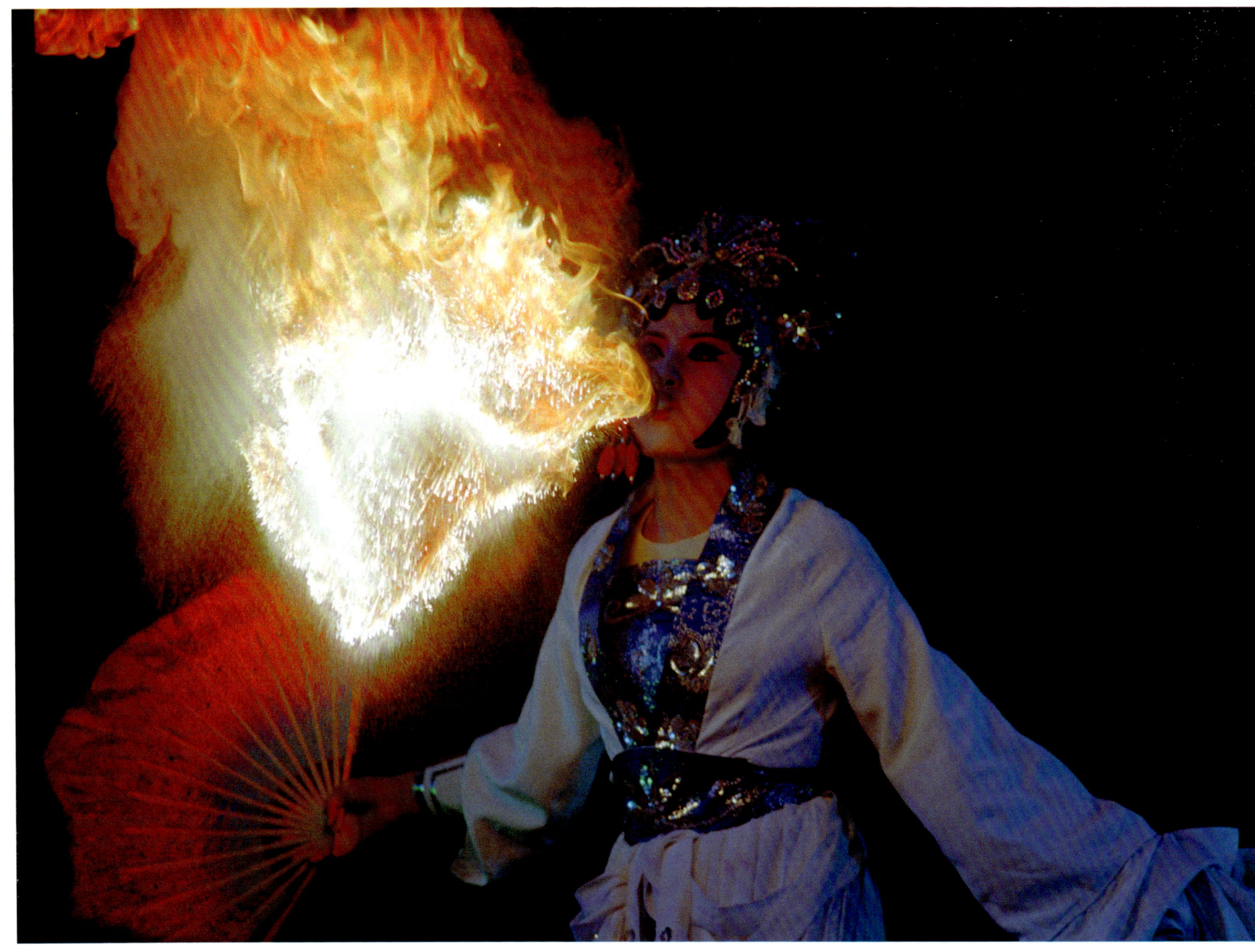

Photo 6.10 *The Sorrow at West Lake*, Qinqiang Opera

Using Special Skills

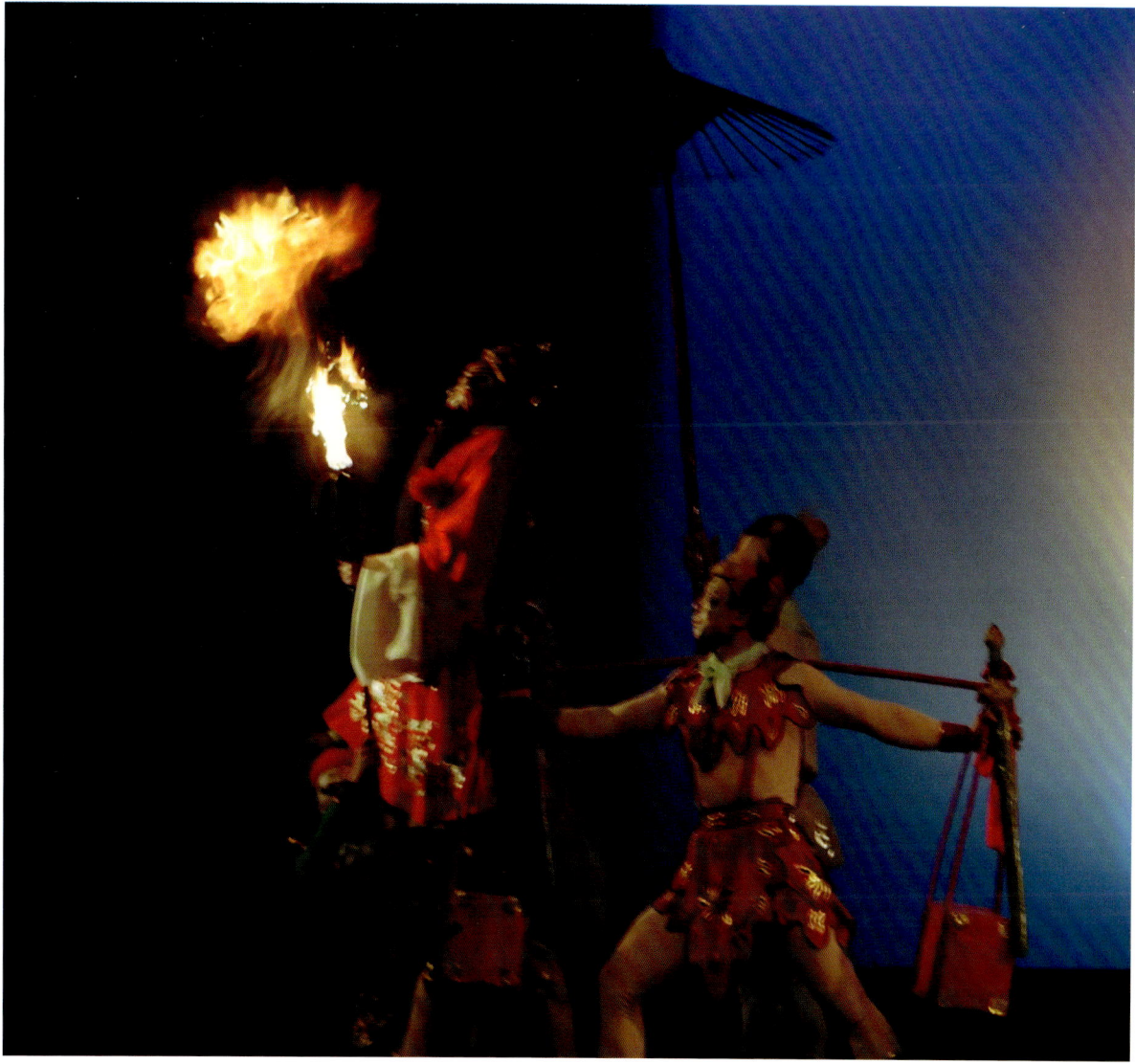

Photo 6.11 *Zhong Kui Arranges a Marriage*, Hebei Clapper Opera

In a famous story told in just about all Chinese opera styles, a young maiden, Li Huiniang, is murdered by a jealous official because of her love for a young scholar. She returns as a ghost with the help of the *Yinyang* Magic Fan to help her beloved, whom the official also plans to murder. At the climax of the opera, Li Huiniang appears in the garden in the dead of night to terrify the would-be assassin by waving her fan and blowing flames from her mouth (see Photo 6.10).

In another ghost story, Zhong Kui is cheated out of the highest honours and a stellar career by a corrupt official. But the next world is more just than this one, and Zhong Kui becomes an official among the ghosts. He leads a band of ghosts into this world to right wrongs and arrange for the marriage of his sister, who was left in poverty, to one benefactor he knew in life. The ghosts must travel a long road from the underworld to his sister's home, and so Zhong Kui leads the way, blowing plumes of fire to demonstrate his new-found power and authority (see Photo 6.11).

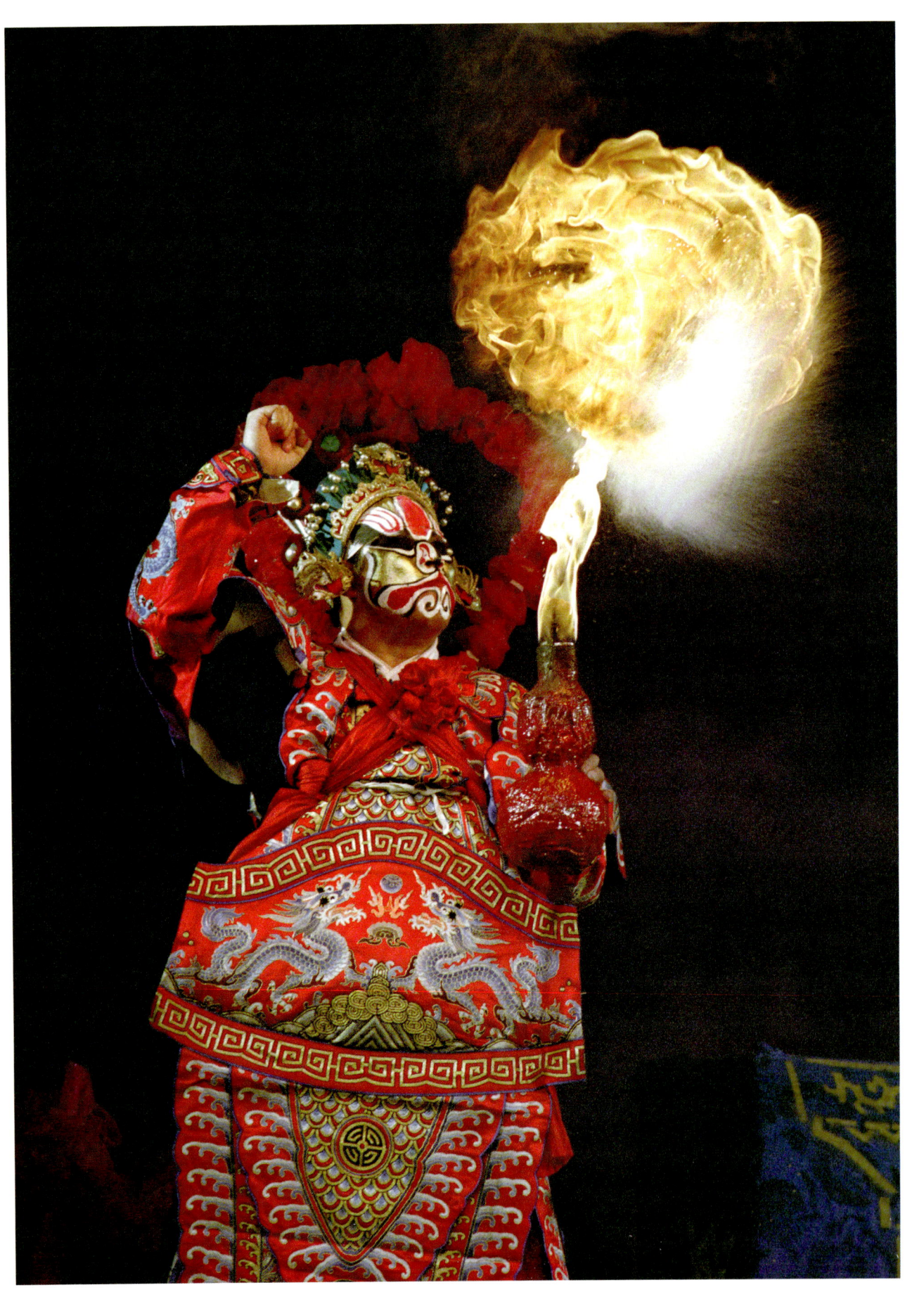

Photo 6.12 *The Legend of the White Snake*, Sichuan Opera

Using Special Skills

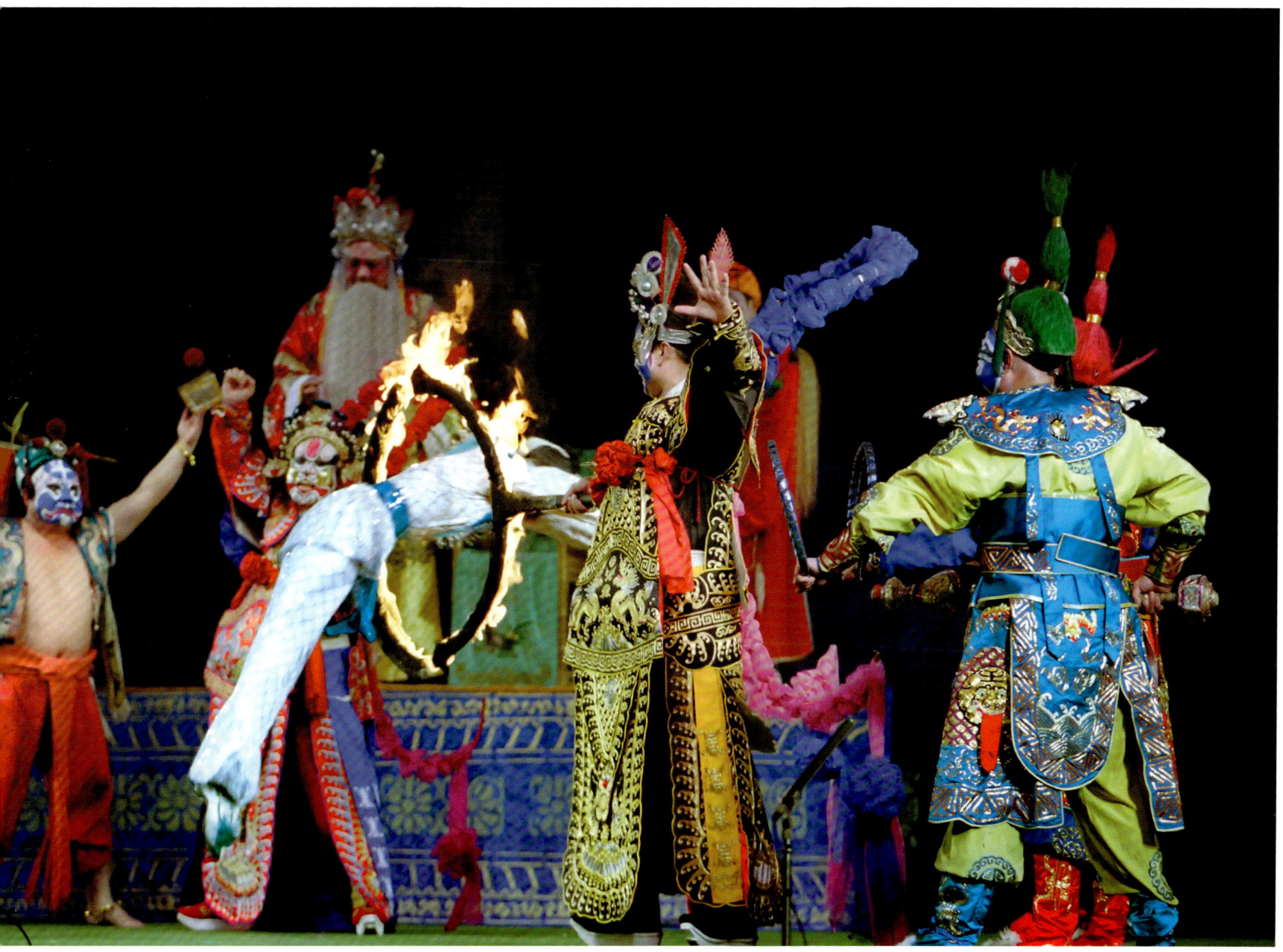

Photo 6.13 *The Legend of the White Snake*, Sichuan Opera

Fire is an important element in *The Legend of the White Snake* as well. In her battle with Fahai, White Snake floods the temple in which Fahai has secured her husband. Fahai in response sends a fire spirit to capture her. This spirit uses a magic gourd as he breathes out his magic fire, but cannot overcome the powerful White Snake (see Photo 6.12).

As the battle continues, the spirits of wind and fire both try to capture White Snake. They spit out fire to create a circle of flame to block her. To their surprise, White Snake jumps through it, escaping them and proving her superior magical skills (see Photo 6.13).

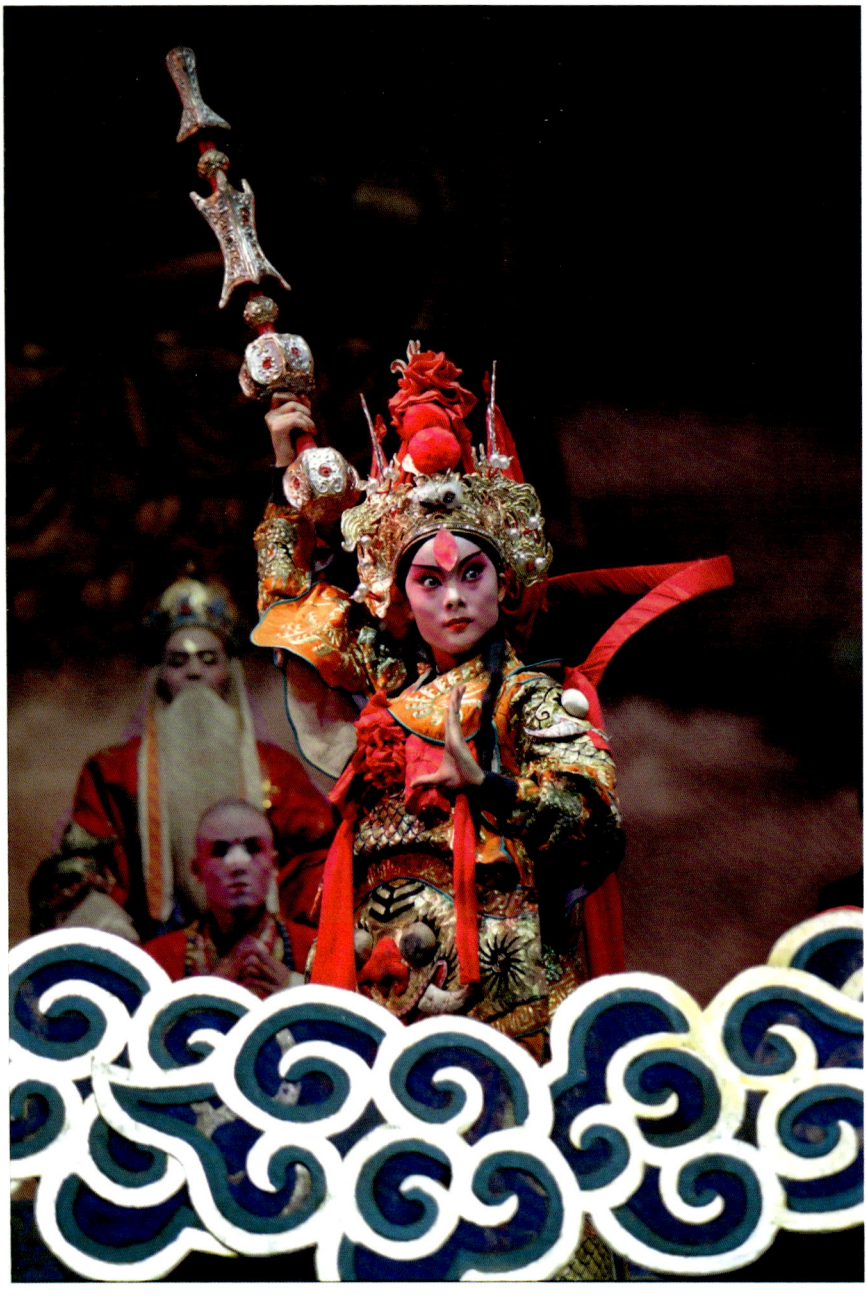

Photo 6.14   *The Legend of the White Snake*, Sichuan Opera

Opening the Eye of Wisdom

THE COSMIC BATTLE between White Snake and Fahai's heavenly legions calls for more than just fire-breathing skills. One effect is called "Opening the Eye of Wisdom". The Eye of Wisdom is the mystical eye of supernatural sight, the sign of a spiritual being. In religious art, it is situated in the middle of the forehead, indicating that the mind is seeing in ways beyond the normal. In *The Legend of the White Snake*, opening that supernatural eye is executed by the spirit Weituo, the first heavenly warrior that the abbot sends against his adversary. Weituo flies on a cloud in search of White Snake, but cannot locate her (see Photo 6.15).

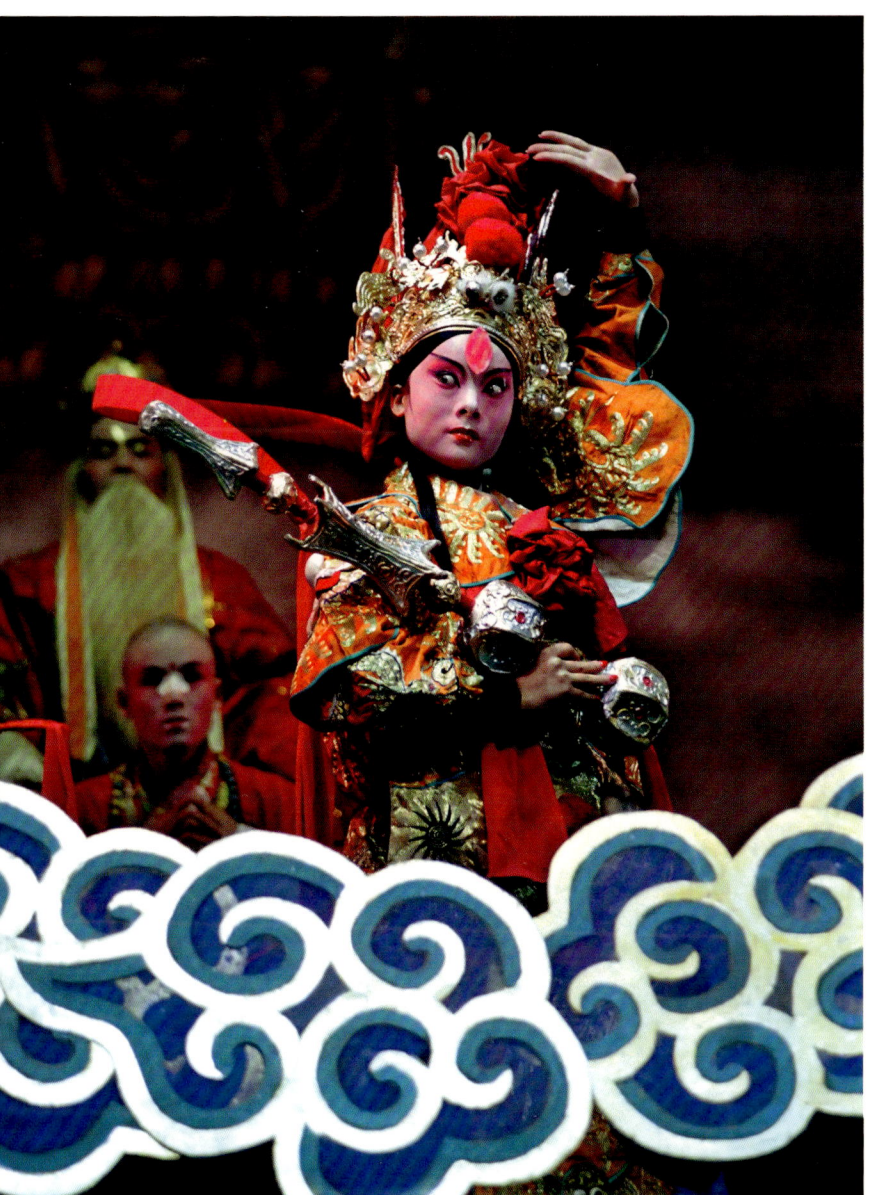

Photo 6.15 *The Legend of the White Snake*, Sichuan Opera

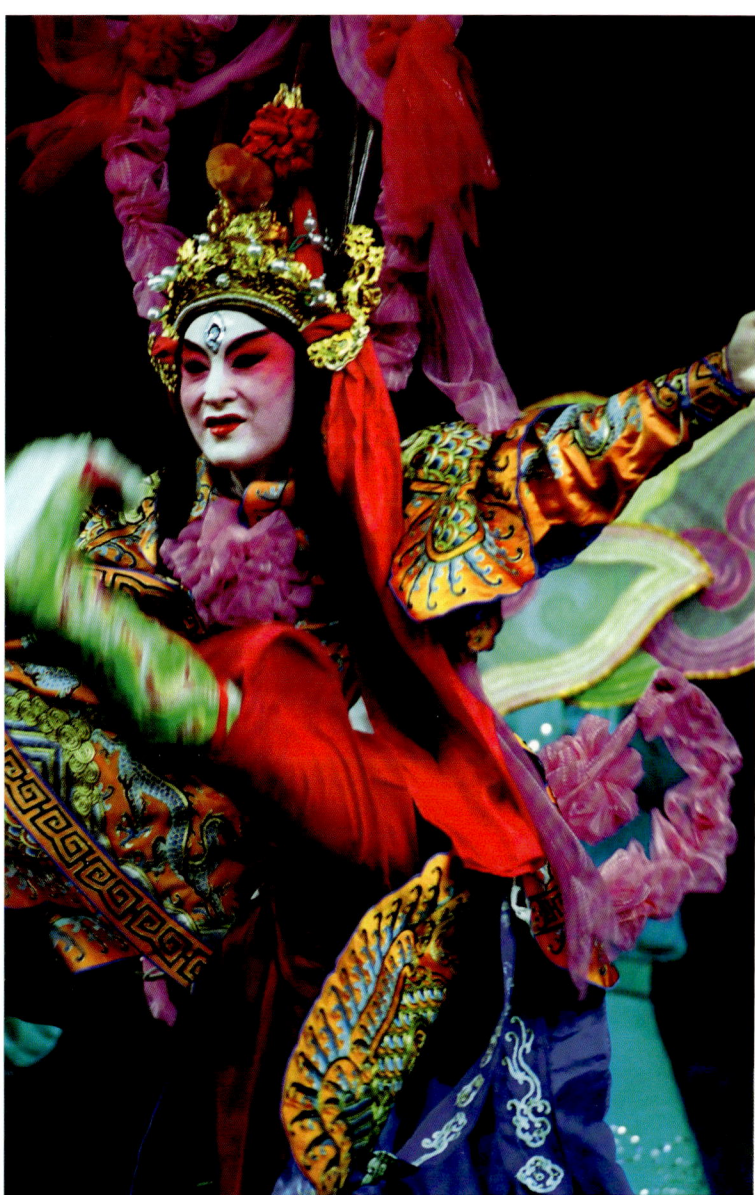

Photo 6.16 *The Legend of the White Snake*, Sichuan Opera

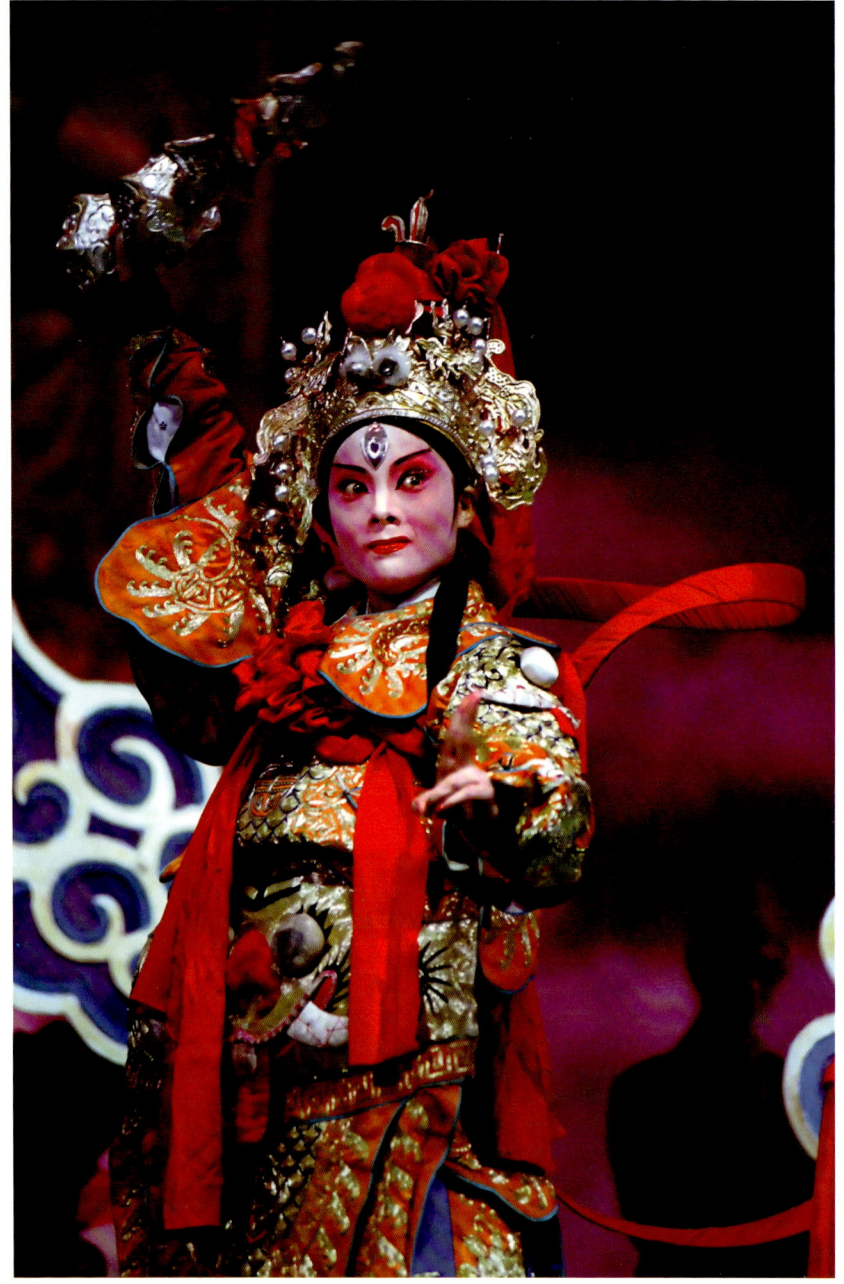

Knowing that he must employ supernatural sight to find his opponent, Weituo cries out, "Let me open my Eye of Wisdom!" and then plants a flying kick on his own forehead (see Photo 6.16). Traditionally, the eye was mounted on the tip of the boot. Current practice is to paste a piece of flesh-coloured paper over the eye on the forehead. When the boot touches the forehead, the glue on the tip of the boot takes the paper away, exposing the third eye neatly in the middle of the forehead (see Photo 6.17). Wide-open, the Eye of Wisdom indicates that Weituo now has special sight enabling him to search out White Snake. The sudden appearance of a third eye on the forehead of the actor is a surprising act that both delights and excites.

Photo 6.17 *The Legend of the White Snake*, Sichuan Opera

Balancing the Oil Lamp

JUST AS HEAVENLY beings make frequent use of special skills, so do clowns. The Sichuan opera has many kinds of supernatural characters, and many kinds of clowns as well. Those clowns can be people of any social standing, from princes to old women.

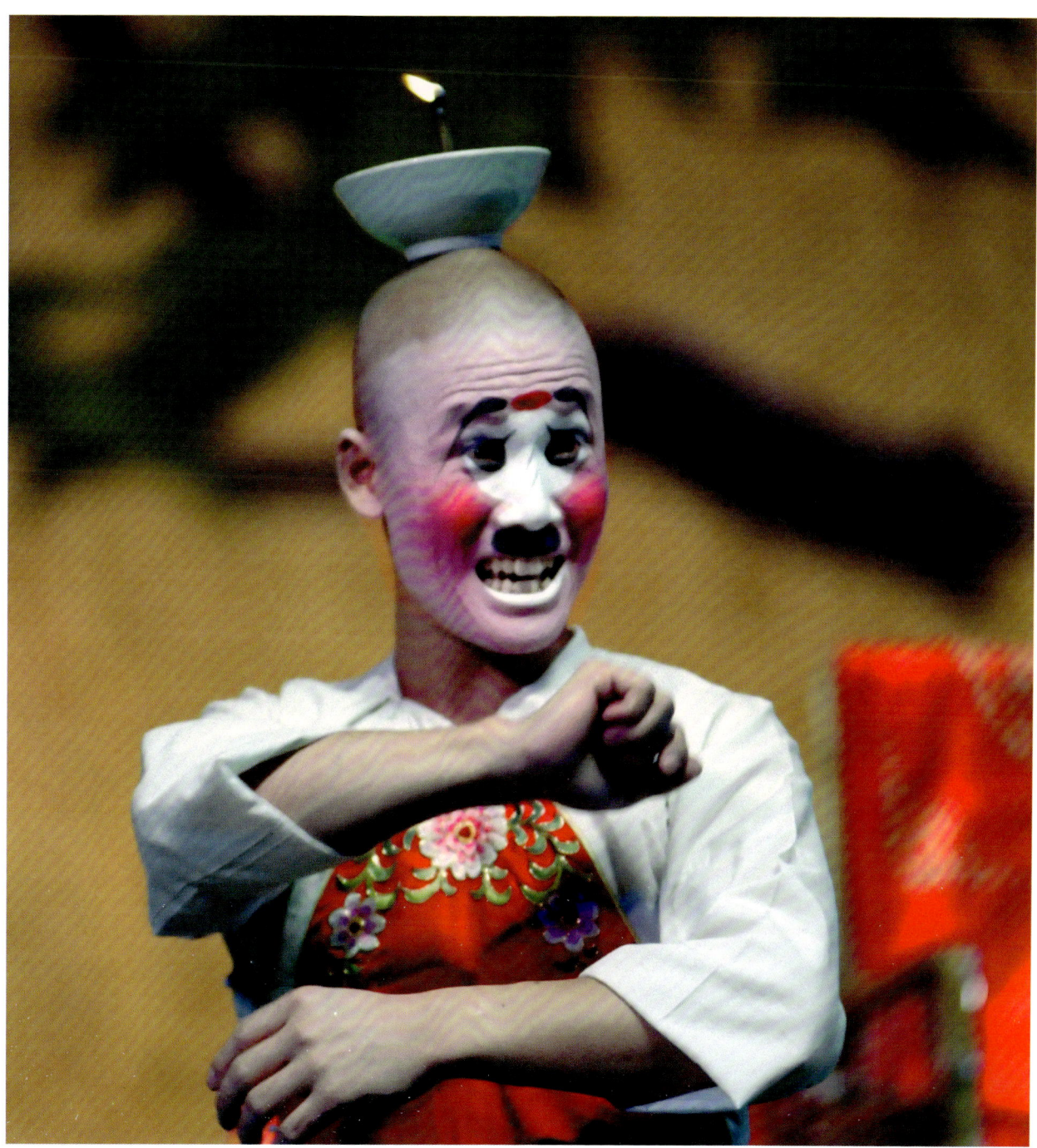

Photo 6.18 *Pi Jin Plays the Fool*, Sichuan Opera

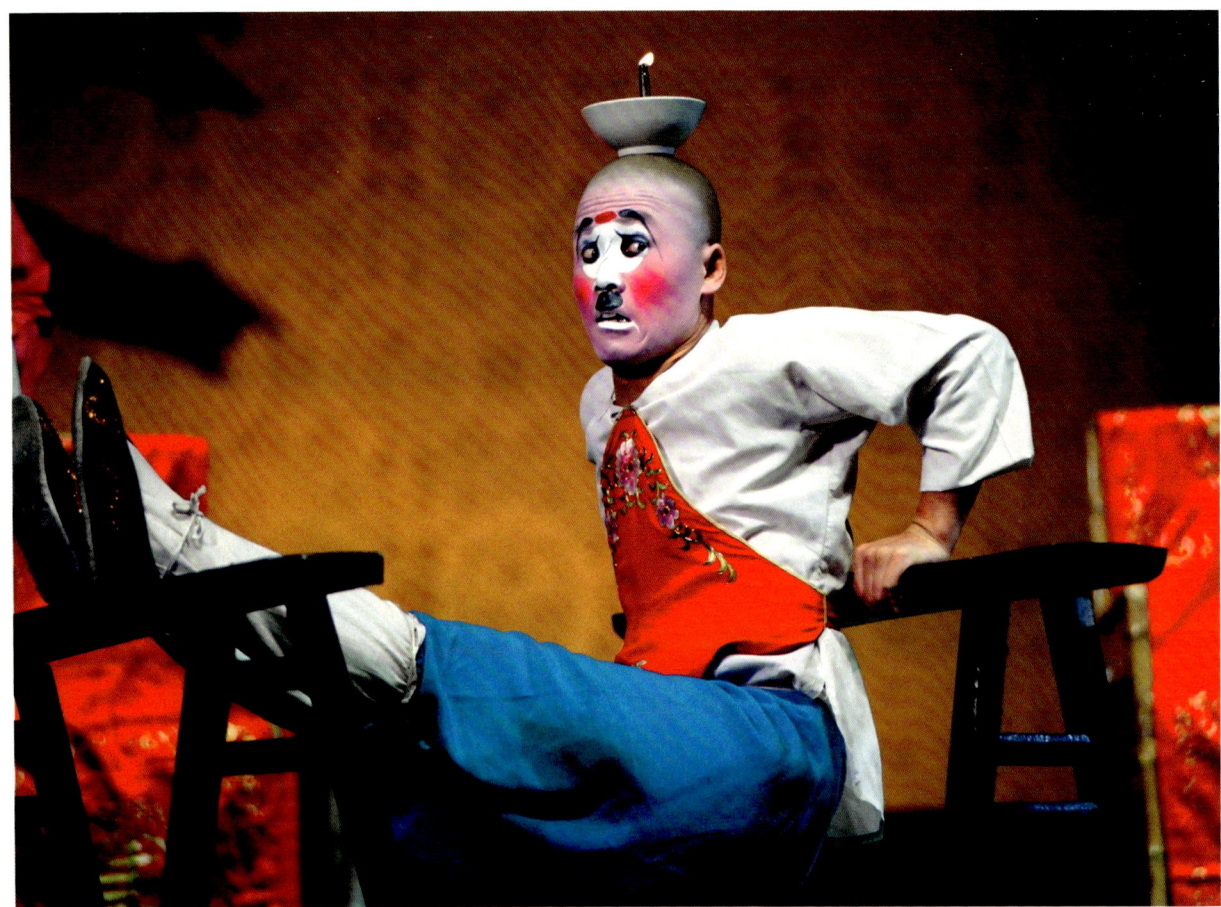

Photo 6.19 *Pi Jin Plays the Fool*, Sichuan Opera

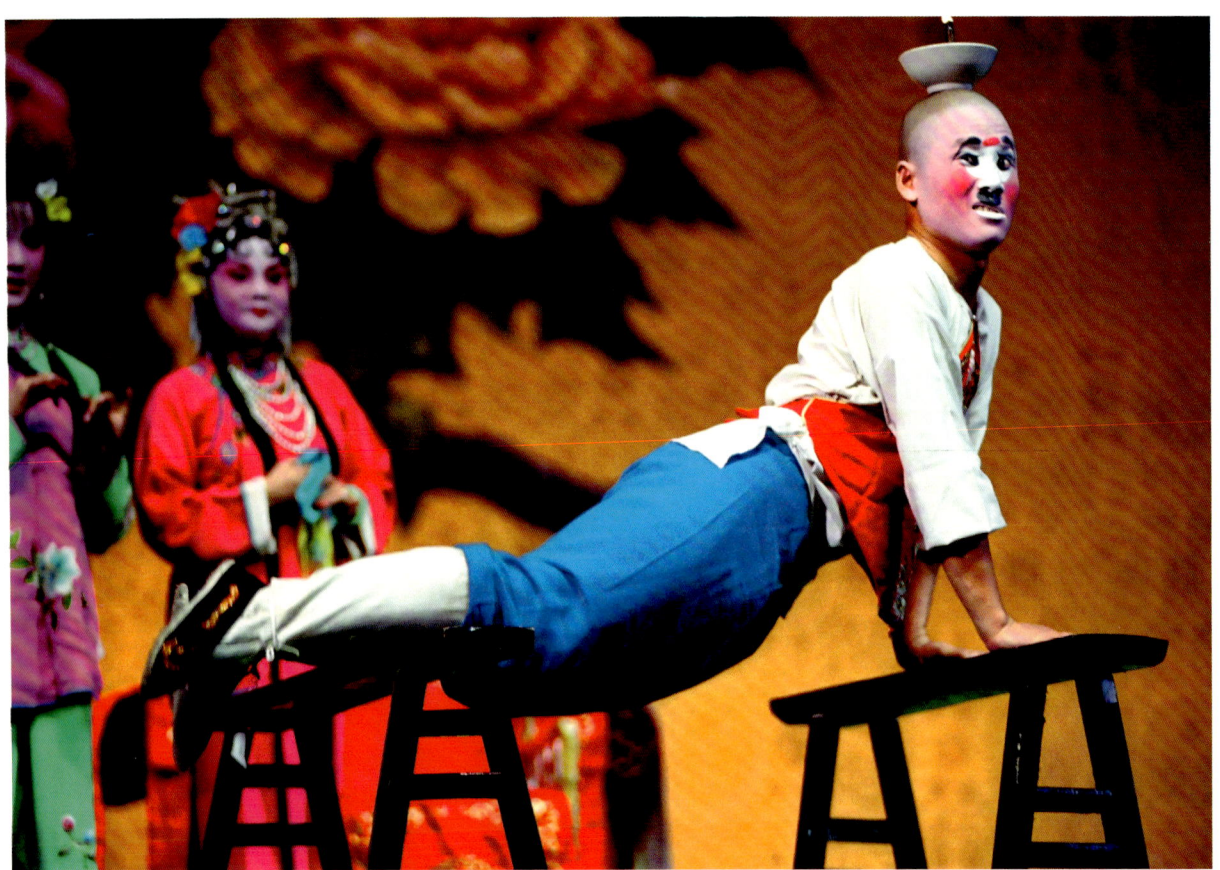

Photo 6.20 *Pi Jin Plays the Fool*, Sichuan Opera

Using Special Skills

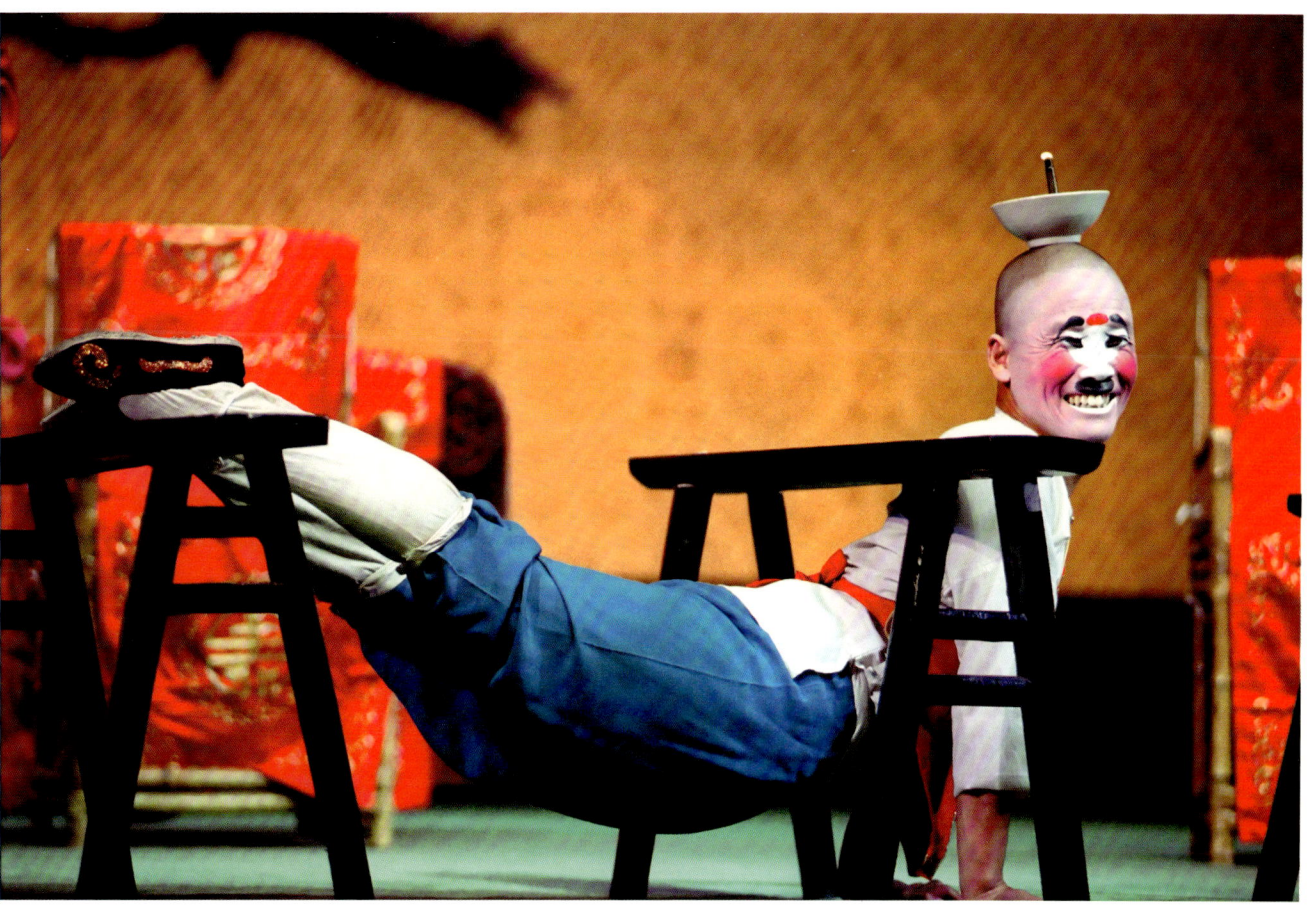

Photo 6.21 *Pi Jin Plays the Fool*, Sichuan Opera

One clown type is the *wawa*, or doll clown, who is very young and very silly. That clown is also highly skilled as is demonstrated in *Pi Jin Plays the Fool*. Pi Jin's wife, sick to death of his foolish, lazy ways, puts him through an impossible series of moves while balancing an oil lamp on his head. First, he is perched between two stools (see Photo 6.19).

Then, on top of the stools, he has to turn his body completely around without dropping the lamp (see Photo 6.20).

Next, he has to stretch through the stools, bending his back and raising his head (see Photo 6.21).

Finally, he has to blow the light out. These are only a few of a very difficult series of moves that the actor executes, demonstrating amazing flexibility, control and balance.

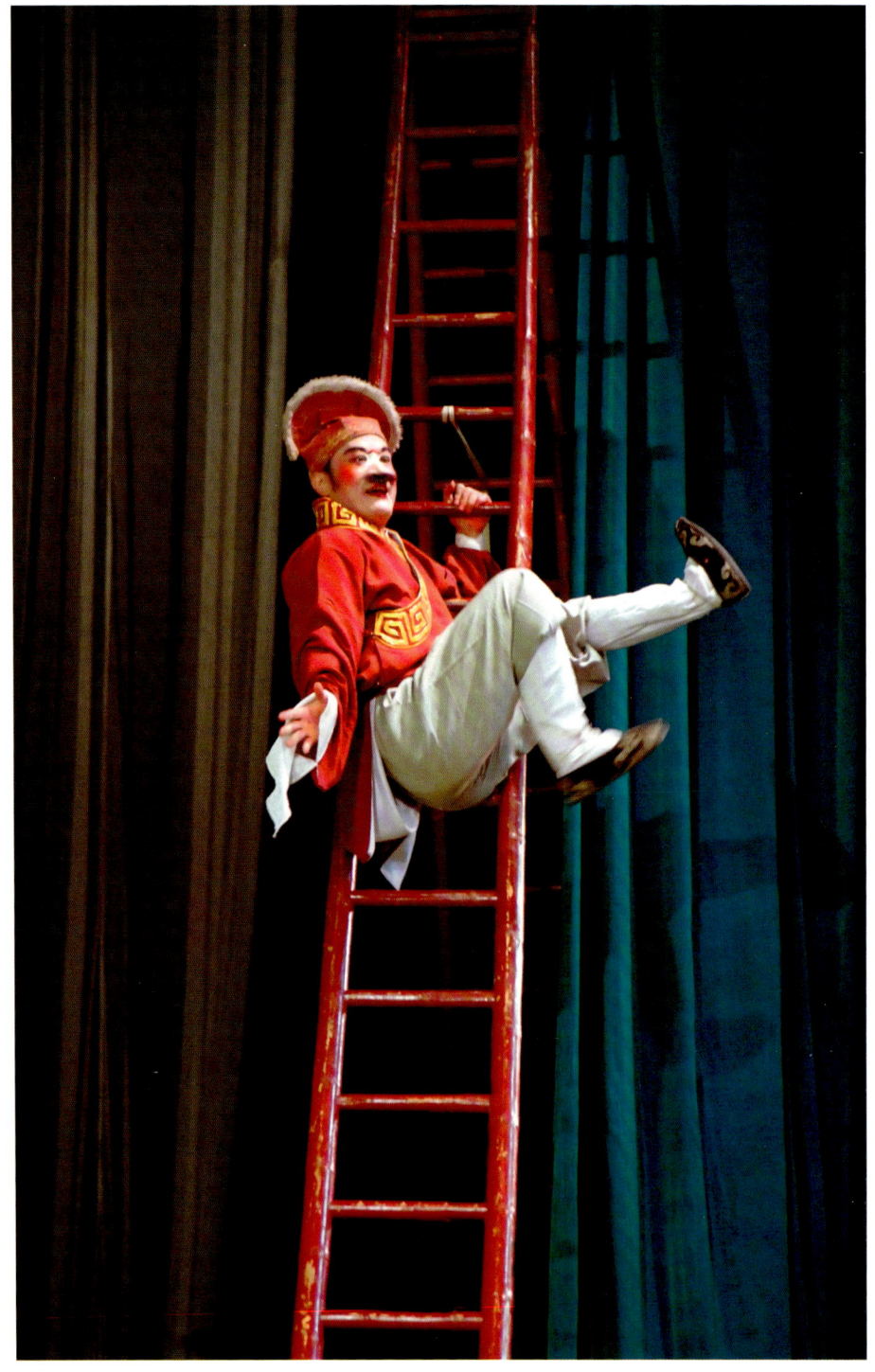

Photo 6.22 *A Woodshed Encounter*, Chaozhou Opera

Ladder Skills

CHAOZHOU OPERA, WHICH hails from the east of Guangdong Province, is another opera style justly famous for its clowns. It, too, has a range of clowns from emperor to beggar. They speak in a local language both expressive and rich in dialect. They are, moreover, known for a range of special skills involving fans, chairs, and especially ladders.

Using Special Skills

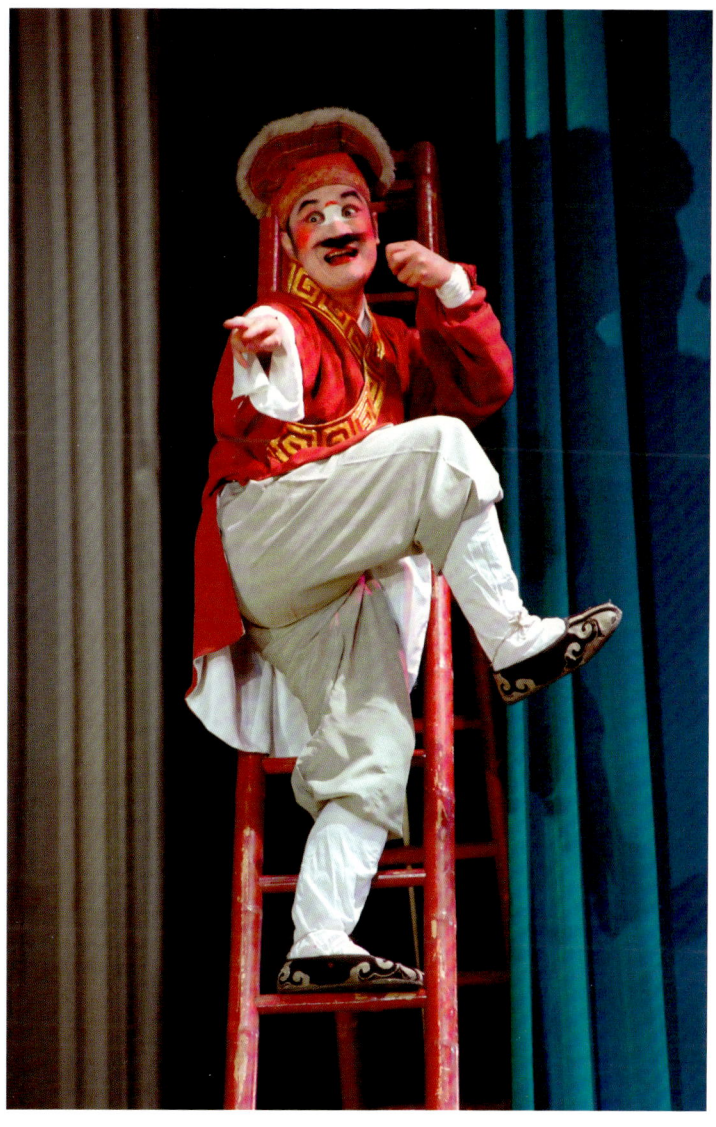

Photo 6.23 *A Woodshed Encounter,* Chaozhou Opera

In *A Woodshed Encounter*, the pedlar Li Laosan sleeps in the woodshed of an old inn. A ghost suddenly appears. Li's terror is the opera's comedy. He scuttles up a ladder, slides down it, hooks around the rungs, and comes down head first in a hilarious, and dangerous, series of moves (see Photo 6.23).

Actors in Chinese opera train for a role type in which they will specialize. Some of those role types, like the spiritual beings and clowns in this section, require not only training in musical and acting skills, but in acrobatic skills as well.

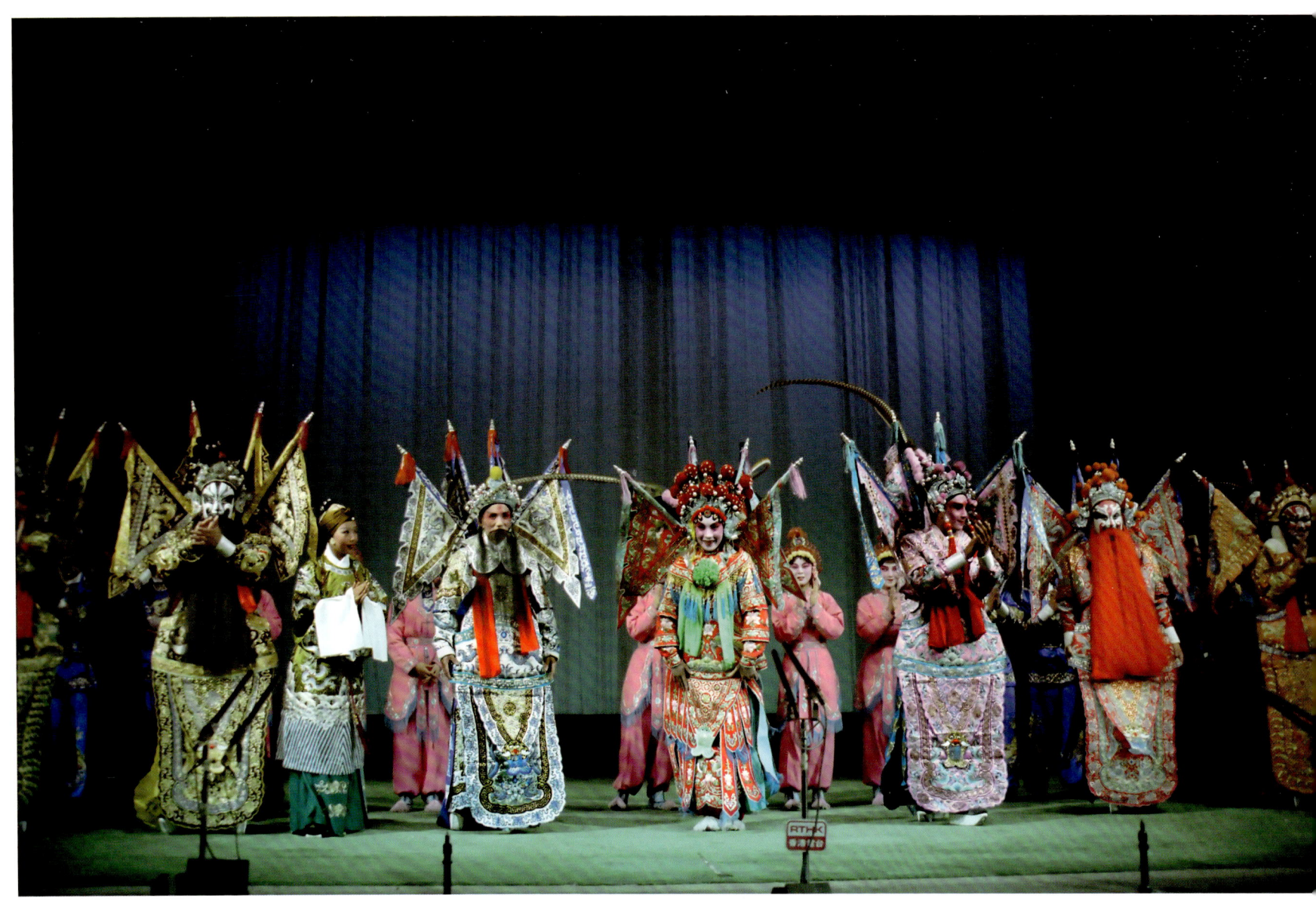

Photo 7.01 *The Warrior Maiden Mu Guiying*, Peking Opera

From the Photographer

The best Chinese opera troupes of various genres from across the country with top-grade actors and actresses visited Hong Kong between 1985 and 1993. This event has great historical significance and became a major part of my life's work. Looking back at it, I believe a performance series like that will probably never happen again. I was fortunate enough to record these operas with my camera, and am pleased to share these images with the reader of this book.

It has been thirty years since I first started taking pictures of the Chinese opera in performance. As an ordinary member of the audience, I took shot after shot using a hand-held camera without flash or tripod so as not to disturb the ongoing performance. My collection of opera photos grew exponentially over those three decades. Most of the images taken before 1993 were with analogue negative film; thus, the colour has faded over time. Some of the film was not well processed and the photos have been lost. I was alarmed at the prospect of losing these invaluable records of opera performances. Thanks to modern technology, I have been able to convert the analogue images to digital images, thus preventing further deterioration. I did the conversion myself—because I only trust myself—but this conversion took me ten years to complete.

I must thank Peter Lovrick, co-author of this book, for his enduring support and patience. Without him this book, as well as our first book, *Chinese Opera: Images and Stories*, would not have come to light. I still owe much gratitude to Kwan Lihuen, who was the first to encourage me to publish my Chinese opera images. My special thanks go to Yuen Siu-fai, Shen Zu'an, He Saifei and Annie Chow Ka-yee for their expert advice all through the project. I also wish to thank my very good friends Cheng Pui-kan, Tang Wai-lam and Lum Tin-wan for their valuable opinions. Last, but not least, I extend my thanks to Cheng Kwok-ho for his Chinese calligraphy on the cover of this book.

From the Writer

The director could not contain himself in rehearsals as he explained this or that aspect of Chinese performing art to an amateur actor. "Chinese opera is wonderful!" he exclaimed. It is. The sense of wonder grows when that new, powerful, evocative language becomes part of our vocabulary. Suddenly, we are no longer missing something, but peering into a rich experience carefully polished through centuries of practice. We see an actor waving a whip and know he is dashing into battle; a woman biting the tresses of her hair and know that she has set her heart as solid as a rock; an official rushing onto the stage without his hat, his hair hanging down, and know that he is in distress; a general climbing upon a chair set on a table, and know that he is atop the mountain, surveying the battleground. These conventions suggest rather than realistically represent. They open the imagination rather than present all that there is so that the audience becomes an active participant in this whole amazing enterprise called the Chinese theatre. It is worth spending time to learn this language. The rewards are endless. Chinese drama brings together the Chinese heart and soul, history and philosophy, music and literature, religion and story-telling, all that is valued and despised by the culture into one package. It is surely one of the best avenues into understanding China's past and what has formed its present. It is surely an intoxicating experience on its own merits.

It is no secret, however, that Chinese opera has fallen onto hard times. Things are not what they were. Once a common feature in towns and villages, teahouses and temples, outdoor and indoor theatres, the opera is less and less attended. It has had to compete first with film and television, then with the internet and digital communication that favours the quick and the fast. It is not an art form for the impatient. Many young people have been cut off for one reason or another from the language of the stage which is the subject of this book. That means that an actor communicates in a performance language that is no longer commonly understood. The delicate movement of an actor's fingers manipulating water sleeves has a hard time competing with special effects in 3D. People are less and less familiar with the old stories.

Chinese opera will, however, make its comeback—probably repackaged, rethought, and represented, but it *will* make its comeback. Several signs of that are already evident. We rediscover the treasures from the past periodically. Sometimes, sufficient time needs to pass to be able to see them afresh so that they are not frozen artefacts that belong to a classical age and have no relevance today. Throughout its history, Chinese opera has connected with the contemporary even if its stories referred to history or legend. That connection will happen again as a new audience becomes acquainted with the language of the stage, its plots, its artistry and the skills of the actors. That might take bold experiments, or might simply emerge as a new trend. New audiences, too, will say, "Chinese opera is wonderful!" Until that time, we have resources like the truly amazing collection of photos of Siu Wang-Ngai. Captured in performance, the images in his photographs are an alphabet of Chinese opera stage language. Beautiful on their own, they also connect us to something else beautiful—the living art of the Chinese opera.

Glossary

back crossed double spears 雙槍後背式
back flip 後翻
back whisk 背帚
backward battering the tiger 倒撲虎
Battle of Red Cliff 赤壁之戰
Battle of Baqiu 巴丘之戰
beard work 髯口功
board leg pose 腿亮相
board waist 板腰
chuanqi 傳奇
circling the stage 跑圓場
cloud flip 雲裡翻
cloud hands 雲手
cloud whisk 雲帚
command flag 令旗
Cosmic Circlet 乾坤圈
cross-talk 相聲
dachushou 打出手
door splitting blade 開門刀
double-headed spear 雙頭槍
elephant trunk blade 象鼻刀
embrace the whisk 抱帚
exploring the sea 探海
Eye of Wisdom 慧眼
face changing 變臉
flying tiger flag 飛虎旗
gaomao 高毛
Golden Iron Staff 金剛棒
Golden Melon Warrior 金瓜將
Jade Emperor of Heaven 玉帝
kicking the belt on the shoulder 踢帶上肩
kicking the spear 踢槍
kungfu (*gongfu*) 功夫
leg twist 側搬腿
liangxiang 亮相

lifting the big belt 拎大帶
luohan 羅漢
moonlight flag 月華旗
Mountain of Flowers and Fruits 花果山
mountain shoulders 山膀
Mountain-splitting Axe 劈山斧
naobo 鐃鈸
opening the Eye of Wisdom 開慧眼
pedalling heaven 朝天蹬
pheasant tail 翎子
playing the dwarf 走矮子
Precious Lotus Lantern 寶蓮燈
Precious Sword 尚方寶劍
qiba 起霸
Sharp Fire Spear 火尖槍
shooting the wild goose 射雁
side step 碎步
side walk 走邊
singing side walk 響邊
Snake Spear 蛇矛槍
stiff corpse fall 硬僵屍
stormy eyes 抹眼
tai-chi (*taiji*) 太極
tangma (horse ride) 趟馬
tanzigong (carpet work) 毯子功
tiger roll 虎滾
umbrella whisk 傘帚
water hair 水髮
water sleeves 水袖
wawa clown (doll clown) 娃娃丑
Wave Walker 凌波仙子
White-Boned Demon 白骨精
wuxi 武戲
Yinyang Magic Fan 陰陽寶扇
Yuan *zaju* 元雜劇

Appendix 1

English Guide to the Photographs

Photo	Opera Type	Opera/Scene Title	Troupe	Character	Performer	Year
1.01	Peking	*Women Warriors of the Yang Family*	Hubei Provincial Peking Opera Troupe	Mu Guiying, Lady She, etc.	Li Chunfang, Zhen Jingxian, etc.	1987
2.01	Cantonese	*A Comedy of Eight Errors*	Hong Kong Youth Cantonese Opera Troupe	Spring Orchid	Cheng Wing-mui	2008
2.02	Liyuan	*Dong Sheng and Li Shi*	Fujian Liyuan Opera Experimental Troupe	Dong Sheng, Li Shi	Gong Wanli, Zeng Jingping	2005
2.03	Cantonese	*Picking Up the Jade Bracelet*	Hong Kong Tuen Mun Cantonese Opera Experimental Troupe	Sun Yujiao	Chan Sau-hing	1981
2.04	Ping	*Picking Up the Jade Bracelet*	Hebei Shijiazhuang Youth Ping Opera Troupe	Sun Yujiao	Liu Fengzhi	1991
2.05	Sichuan	*Pan Jinlian Tempts Her Brother-In-Law*	Chengdu Sichuan Opera Theatre	Pan Jinlian	Chen Qiaoru	1991
2.06	Cantonese	*The Magic Lotus Lantern*	Hong Kong Tuen Mun Cantonese Opera Experimental Troupe	Lingzhi	Hui Chow-hung	1988
2.07	Cantonese	*Women Warriors of the Yang Family*	Hong Kong Tung Sing Opera Troupe	Yang Wenguang, Mu Guiying, etc.	Yu Tung-sing, Yu Ling-lung, etc.	2011
2.08	Cantonese	*Spring Grass Rushes to Court*	Hong Kong Tuen Mun Cantonese Opera Experimental Troupe	Spring Grass	Hui Chow-hung	1985
2.09	Hebei Clapper	*Wreaking Havoc in the Eastern Sea*	Hebei Clapper Opera Troupe	Turtle Magistrate	Li Lishui	1991
2.10	Hebei Clapper	*Lin Chong's Night Flight*	Hebei Clapper Opera Troupe	Lin Chong	Pei Yanling	1992
2.11	Peking	*Cleaning Out the Bandit's Lair*	Shanghai Peking Opera Theatre	He Tianbao	Xi Zhonglu	1992
2.12	Shao	*The Prime Minister of Wei*	Zhejiang Shaoxing Opera Troupe	Yue Yan	Sun Xiaoyan	1991
2.13	Cantonese	*Zhao Yun Hides the Baby Prince*	Guangdong Cantonese Opera Theatre	Zhao Yun	Lu Wenbin (Ma Yilong)	2006
2.14	Cantonese	*Escape from the Golden Mountain Temple*	Guangdong Cantonese Opera Theatre	Xu Xian	Li Zhanping (Sima Xiang)	2006
2.15	Cantonese	*The Eighteen Luohan Pursue the Golden Crane*	Zhanjiang Cantonese Opera Troupe	Golden Crane	Liang Zhaoming	2005
2.16	Cantonese	*The Eighteen Luohan Pursue the Golden Crane*	Zhanjiang Cantonese Opera Troupe	Golden Crane	Liang Zhaoming	2005
2.17	Cantonese	*The Eighteen Luohan Pursue the Golden Crane*	Zhanjiang Cantonese Opera Troupe	Golden Crane, Luohans	Liang Zhaoming (others unknown)	2005
2.18	Cantonese	*Phoenix Terrace Fortress*	Guangdong Cantonese Opera Theatre	Zhang Xiuying	Zeng Xiaomin	2006
2.19	Cantonese	*Wu Song*	Guangdong Cantonese Opera Theatre	Ximen Qing, Wu Dalang	Wen Ruqing, Chen Wencong	2006
2.20	Cantonese	*The Haunting of Zhang Sanlang*	Guangdong Cantonese Opera Theatre	Zhang Sanlang, Yan Xijiao	Huang Chunqiang, Liang Xiaoying	2006
2.21	Hebei Clapper	*Burning the Camps*	Hebei Clapper Opera Troupe	Guan Xing	Pei Yanling	1991
2.22	Cantonese	*Women Warriors of the Yang Family*	Hong Kong Tuen Mun Cantonese Opera Experimental Troupe	Zhang Biao	Chan Bik-ying (Man Kim-fei)	1983
2.23	Peking	*The Execution of the Commander*	Tianjin Youth Peking Opera Troupe	Zhao Yun	Fang Zhigang	1990
2.24	Cantonese	*The Battle of Baqiu*	Guangdong Cantonese Opera Theatre	Zhou Yu, Zhang Fei	Peng Qinghua, Li Yongbin	2006
2.25	Ping	*The Cosmic Belt*	Hebei Shijiazhuang Youth Ping Opera Troupe	Qin Ying	Zhao Xincheng	1991
2.26	Longjiang	*Twice-Locked Mountain*	Heilongjiang Longjiang Opera Experimental Troupe	Liu Jinding	Bai Shuxian	1991
2.27	Gan	*Meng Liang Raises Troops*	Jiangxi Provincial Gan Opera Troupe	Yang Paifeng, Meng Liang	Tu Linghui, Li Weide	1992
2.28	Hui	*Cao Cao, Guan Yu and Diaochan*	Anhui Provincial Hui Opera Troupe	Guan Yu	Zhang Qixiang	1991
2.29	Hebei Clapper	*Lu Wenlong and His Double Spears*	Hebei Clapper Opera Troupe	Lu Wenlong	Pei Xiaoling	1991

English Guide to the Photographs

Photo	Opera Type	Opera/Scene Title	Troupe	Character	Performer	Year
2.30	Longjiang	*The Romance of the Iron Bow*	Heilongjiang Longjiang Opera Experimental Troupe	Kuang Zhong, Chen Xiuying	Zhou Jingkui, Dou Chunfeng	1991
2.31	Cantonese	*Lian Jinfeng*	Guangdong Cantonese Opera Theatre	Lian Jinfeng, Oyster Spirit	Yan Jinfeng, Chen Xiaoxian	2006
2.32	Cantonese	*The Haunting of Zhang Sanlang*	Guangdong Cantonese Opera Theatre	Zhang Sanlang, Yan Xijiao	Huang Chunqiang, Liang Xiaoying	2006
2.33	Peking	*Tilting the War Carts*	Shenyang Peking Opera Theatre	Gao Chong	Chen Qingguang	1987
2.34	Gan	*Selecting a Horse for War*	Jiangxi Provincial Gan Opera Troupe	Mu Guiying	Chen Li	1992
2.35	Cantonese	*Xue Dingshan Thrice Angers Fan Lihua*	Foshan Youth Cantonese Opera Troupe	Xue Dingshan	Yuen Siu-fai	1997
2.36	Cantonese	*The Legend of the Red Plum*	Guangdong Cantonese Opera Theatre	God of Earth	Liang Hengxian	2006
2.37	Peking	*Raid on Hu Village*	Tianjin Youth Peking Opera Troupe	Wang Ying	Shi Xiaoliang	1990
2.38	Cantonese	*The Eighteen Luohan Pursue the Golden Crane*	Zhanjiang Cantonese Opera Troupe	Golden Crane	Liang Zhaoming	2005
2.39	Cantonese	*Kneading the Dough*	Guangdong Cantonese Opera Theatre	Wu Dalang, Pan Jinlian	Chen Yuncong, Cen Fengping	2006
3.01	Gan	*Selecting a Horse for War*	Jiangxi Provincial Gan Opera Troupe	Mu Guiying	Chen Li	1992
3.02	Cantonese	*Qin Qiong Observes the Troops*	Guangdong Cantonese Opera Theatre	Qin Qiong, Luo Cheng	Yan Yuntao, Chen Jiading	2006
3.03	Cantonese	*Qin Qiong Observes the Troops*	Guangdong Cantonese Opera Theatre	Qin Qiong	Yan Yuntao	2006
3.04	Peking	*Green Stone Mountain*	Shenyang Peking Opera Theatre	Guan Yu	Wang Qingyuan	1992
3.05	Cantonese	*Phoenix Terrace Fortress*	Guangdong Cantonese Opera Theatre	Zhang Xiuying	Zeng Xiaomin	2006
3.06	Cantonese	*Phoenix Terrace Fortress*	Guangdong Cantonese Opera Theatre	Zhang Xiuying	Zeng Xiaomin	2006
3.07	Cantonese	*Blocking the Horse*	Guangdong Cantonese Opera Theatre	Yang Bajie	Zhu Hongxing	2006
3.08	Cantonese	*Blocking the Horse*	Guangdong Cantonese Opera Theatre	Yang Bajie	Zhu Hongxing	2006
3.09	Cantonese	*Blocking the Horse*	Guangdong Cantonese Opera Theatre	Yang Bajie	Zhu Hongxing	2006
3.10	Cantonese	*Blocking the Horse*	Guangdong Cantonese Opera Theatre	Yang Bajie, Jiao Guangpu	Zhu Hongxing, Wu Guowen	2006
3.11	Peking	*Cao Cao and Yang Xiu*	Shanghai Peking Opera Theatre	Yang Xiu, Cao Cao	Yan Xingpeng, Shang Changrong	1992
3.12	Sichuan	*Wang Zhaojun Leaves Her Homeland*	Chengdu Sichuan Opera Theatre	Wang Zhaojun	Liu Ping	1991
3.13	Sichuan	*Wang Zhaojun Leaves Her Homeland*	Chengdu Sichuan Opera Theatre	Wang Zhaojun	Liu Ping	1991
3.14	Peking	*Cleaning Out the Bandit's Lair*	Shanghai Peking Opera Theatre	He Tianbao	Xi Zhonglu	1992
3.15	Cantonese	*The Battle of Baqiu*	Guangdong Cantonese Opera Theatre	Zhou Yu	Peng Qinghua	2006
3.16	Peking	*Wreaking Havoc in Heaven*	Tianjin Youth Peking Opera Troupe	Sun Wukong	Shi Xiaoliang	1990
3.17	Ping	*The Flower Matchmaker*	Hebei Shijiazhuang Youth Ping Opera Troupe	Jia Junying, Zhang Wuke	Zhao Lihua, Li Xiurong	1991
3.18	Huangmei	*A Spring Stroll*	Anqing Huangmei Opera Theatre	Zhao Cuihua	Wu Yaling	1993
3.19	Yue	*The Eighteen Crossings*	Shanghai Yue Opera Theatre	Liang Shanbo, Zhu Yingtai	Zhang Ruihong, Chen Ying	1991
3.20	Yue	*The Eighteen Crossings*	Zhejiang Little Flowers Yue Opera Troupe	Liang Shanbo	Fang Xuewen	1986
3.21	Yue	*The Romance of the West Chamber*	Zhejiang Little Flowers Yue Opera Troupe	Cui Yingying	Tao Huimin	1991
3.22	Peking	*The Intoxicated Concubine*	Liaoning Youth Peking Opera Troupe	Yang Yuhuan	Liu Yajun	1986
3.23	Peking	*Selling Water*	Liaoning Youth Peking Opera Troupe	Mei Ying	Guan Bo	1986

Photo	Opera Type	Opera/Scene Title	Troupe	Character	Performer	Year
3.24	Cantonese	*Wu Song's Tavern Fight*	Hong Kong Tuen Mun Cantonese Opera Experimental Troupe	Sun Erniang	Luk Mei-kum	1981
3.25	Peking	*Zhang Fei Honours the Sage Magistrate*	Shanghai Peking Opera Theatre	Zhang Fei	Shang Changrong	1992
3.26	Lü	*The Sisters Switch Marriages*	Shandong Lü Opera Troupe	Zhang Sumei	Gao Jing	1990
3.27	Lü	*Borrowing at New Year*	Shandong Lü Opera Troupe	Aijie	Wang Yuanyuan	1990
3.28	Huangmei	*A Spring Stroll*	Anqing Huangmei Opera Theatre	Zhao Cuihua	Wu Yaling	1993
3.29	Cantonese	*Choosing Qiuxiang*	Hong Kong Yuen Long Cantonese Opera Troupe	Qiuxiang	Chan Sau-hing	1988
3.30	Huangmei	*The Joyous Return*	Anqing Huangmei Opera Theatre	Cui Hua, Cui Xiuying	Huang Zongyi, Li Qiong	1993
3.31	Cantonese	*Hanging a Painting*	Guangdong Cantonese Opera Theatre	Chun Lan, Ye Hanyan	Zhong Yan, Wu Kunru	2006
3.32	Hui	*Crossing Wits*	Anhui Provincial Hui Opera Troupe	White Peony	Li Xiaohong	1991
3.33	Longjiang	*Twice-Locked Mountain*	Heilongjiang Longjiang Opera Experimental Troupe	Maid of Liu Jinding	(unknown)	1991
3.34	Cantonese	*The Fire Phoenix*	Guangdong Cantonese Opera Theatre	White Crane Fairy	Gong Jieying	2006
3.35	Cantonese	*The Fire Phoenix*	Guangdong Cantonese Opera Theatre	White Crane Fairy	Gong Jieying	2006
3.36	Peking	*The Eight Immortals Cross the Sea*	Liaoning Youth Peking Opera Troupe	Goldfish Fairy	Xue Junqiu	1986
3.37	Sichuan	*The Hibiscus Fairy*	Chengdu Hibiscus Sichuan Opera Troupe	Hibiscus Fairy	Yu Haiyan	1988
3.38	Cantonese	*The Red Peony Fairy*	Hong Kong Fook Sing Cantonese Opera Troupe	Red Peony Fairy	Liza Wang	1991
3.39	Peking	*Inn at the Crossroads*	Tianjin Youth Peking Opera Troupe	Liu Lihua, Ren Tanghui	Shi Xiaoliang, Wang Lijun	1990
3.40	Peking	*Inn at the Crossroads*	Tianjin Youth Peking Opera Troupe	Ren Tanghui, Liu Lihua	Wang Lijun, Shi Xiaoliang	1990
3.41	Cantonese	*Hanging a Painting*	Guangdong Cantonese Opera Theatre	Ye Hanyan	Wu Kunru	2006
3.42	Cantonese	*The Haunting of Zhang Sanlang*	Guangdong Cantonese Opera Theatre	Yan Xijiao, Zhang Sanlang	Zeng Xiaomin, Wang Yanfei	2006
3.43	Cantonese	*Blocking the Horse*	Guangdong Cantonese Opera Theatre	Yang Bajie, Jiao Guangpu	Zhu Hongxing, Wu Guowen	2006
3.44	Cantonese	*Blocking the Horse*	Guangdong Cantonese Opera Theatre	Jiao Guangpu, Yang Bajie	Wu Guowen, Zhu Hongxing	2006
3.45	Cantonese	*Lion Tower*	Guangdong Cantonese Opera Theatre	Wu Song	Peng Qinghua	2006
3.46	Peking	*Changban Slope*	Peking Opera Performing Artists Troupe of China	Zhang Fei	Zhang Lianzhang	1985
3.47	Sichuan	*Flooding the Golden Mountain Temple*	Chengdu Hibiscus Sichuan Opera Troupe	White Snake, Green Snake	Ye Changmin, Wang Shibin	1988
3.48	Cantonese	*The Legend of the White Snake*	Hong Kong Elite Cantonese Opera Troupe	White Snake	Chan Wing-yee	1997
3.49	Hui	*Crossing Wits*	Anhui Provincial Hui Opera Troupe	Lü Dongbin	Xu Yousheng	1991
3.50	Peking	*The Eight Immortals Cross the Sea*	Liaoning Youth Peking Opera Troupe	Lü Dongbin	Wu Kun	1986
3.51	Yue	*Finding Mother in a Convent*	Shanghai Yue Opera Theatre	Zhizhen	Jin Caifeng	1991
3.52	Yue	*Finding Mother in a Convent*	Shanghai Yue Opera Theatre	Zhizhen	Jin Caifeng	1991
3.53	Peking	*The Drunken Monk*	Liaoning Youth Peking Opera Troupe	Lu Zhishen	Zhao Hui	1986
3.54	Cantonese	*The Legend of the White Snake*	Hong Kong Elite Cantonese Opera Troupe	Boatman	Yau Sing-po	1997
3.55	Cantonese	*The Dragon Phoenix Battle*	Hong Kong Yin Sang Fai Cantonese Opera Troupe	Qiao Danfeng	Wan Fei-yin	2005
3.56	Cantonese	*The Legend of the White Snake*	Hong Kong Elite Cantonese Opera Troupe	Boatman, Green Snake, White Snake, Xu Xian	Yau Sing-po, Gao Li, Chan Wing-yee, Yuen Siu-fai	1997
3.57	Sichuan	*The Legend of the White Snake*	Chengdu Sichuan Opera Theatre	White Snake, Green Snake	Chen Qiaoru, Zhu Jianguo	1991
3.58	Cantonese	*The Battle of Baqiu*	Guangdong Cantonese Opera Theatre	Zhang Fei	Li Yongbin	2006

English Guide to the Photographs

Photo	Opera Type	Opera/Scene Title	Troupe	Character	Performer	Year
3.59	Kunqu	*Splendour Tower*	Shanghai Kunqu Opera Troupe	Li Cunxiao	Wang Zhiquan	1989
3.60	Peking	*Bringing the Magic Pearl Over the Rainbow Bridge*	Shenyang Peking Opera Theatre	Wave Walker	Li Jingwen	1992
3.61	Cantonese	*Xue Dingshan Thrice Angers Fan Lihua*	Foshan Youth Cantonese Opera Troupe	Soldiers	(unknown)	1997
3.62	Peking	*Tilting the War Carts*	Tianjin Youth Peking Opera Troupe	Gao Chong	Wang Lijun	1987
3.63	Cantonese	*Worshipping the Moon*	Hong Kong Yin Sang Fai Cantonese Opera	Wang Ruilan	Wan Fei-yin	2005
3.64	Peking	*The Cave of Spiders*	Shanghai Peking Opera Theatre	Spider Spirit	Zhou Yang	1992
3.65	Sichuan	*The Legend of the White Snake*	Chengdu Sichuan Opera Theatre	Green Snake	Zhu Jianguo	1991
3.66	Sichuan	*The Legend of the White Snake*	Chengdu Sichuan Opera Theatre	Green Snake, White Snake	Liu Ping, Chen Qiaoru	1991
3.67	Sichuan	*The Legend of the White Snake*	Chengdu Sichuan Opera Theatre	White Snake, Green Snake	Chen Qiaoru, Zhu Jianguo	1991
4.01	Cantonese	*Raid on Hu Village*	Guangdong Cantonese Opera Theatre	Hu Sanniang	Lu Yueling	2006
4.02	Cantonese	*Changban Slope*	Guangdong Cantonese Opera Theatre	Zhao Yun	Wen Ruqing	2006
4.03	Cantonese	*Phoenix Terrace Fortress*	Guangdong Cantonese Opera Theatre	Zhang Xiuying	Zeng Xiaomin	2006
4.04	Sichuan	*The Nine-Tailed Fox Fairy*	Chengdu Sichuan Opera Theatre	Nine-Tailed Fox Fairy	Li Sha	1992
4.05	Peking	*Bringing the Magic Pearl Over the Rainbow Bridge*	Shenyang Peking Opera Theatre	Wave Walker	Li Jingwen	1992
4.06	Peking	*Bringing the Magic Pearl Over the Rainbow Bridge*	Shenyang Peking Opera Theatre	Wave Walker	Li Jingwen	1992
4.07	Cantonese	*The Fire Phoenix*	Guangdong Cantonese Opera Theatre	White Crane Fairy	Gong Jieying	2006
4.08	Cantonese	*The Fire Phoenix*	Guangdong Cantonese Opera Theatre	White Crane Fairy	Gong Jieying	2006
4.09	Peking	*The Eight Immortals Cross the Sea*	Liaoning Youth Peking Opera Troupe	Goldfish Fairy	Xue Junqiu	1986
4.10	Cantonese	*Xue Dingshan Thrice Angers Fan Lihua*	Foshan Youth Cantonese Opera Troupe	Fan Lihua	Li Shuqin	1997
4.11	Cantonese	*Xue Dingshan Thrice Angers Fan Lihua*	Foshan Youth Cantonese Opera Troupe	Xue Dingshan, Fan Lihua	Yuen Siu-fai, Li Shuqin	1997
4.12	Peking	*Wreaking Havoc in Heaven*	Tianjin Youth Peking Opera Troupe	The Giant God	Chen Xiqiang	1990
4.13	Peking	*Wreaking Havoc in Heaven*	Tianjin Youth Peking Opera Troupe	The Giant God, Sun Wukong	Chen Xiqiang, Shi Xiaoliang	1990
4.14	Hebei Clapper	*Lu Wenlong and His Double Spears*	Hebei Clapper Opera Troupe	Lu Wenlong, Yue Yun	Pei Xiaoling, Zhang Kehai	1991
4.15	Hebei Clapper	*The Burning of Pei Yuanqing*	Hebei Clapper Opera Troupe	Pei Yuanqing	Liu Liwei	1991
4.16	Shao	*Monkey Steals the Magic Fan*	Zhejiang Shaoxing Shao Opera Troupe	Sun Wukong	Liu Jianyang	1991
4.17	Peking	*The Cave of Spiders*	Shanghai Peking Opera Theatre	Sun Wukong, Spider Spirit	Zhao Guohua, (unknown)	1992
4.18	Peking	*The Cave of Spiders*	Shanghai Peking Opera Theatre	Sun Wukong, Spider Spirits	Zhao Guohua, (unknown)	1992
4.19	Cantonese	*Shi Xiu Scouts Out Zhu Village*	Guangdong Cantonese Opera Theatre	Shi Xiu, Guard of Zhu Village	Liu Jianke, (unknown)	2006
4.20	Hebei Clapper	*Burning the Camps*	Hebei Clapper Opera Troupe	Huang Zhong	Pei Yanling	1991
4.21	Peking	*Huarong Pass*	Peking Opera Performing Artists Troupe of China	Guan Yu	Li Huiliang	1985
4.22	Longjiang	*Twice-Locked Mountain*	Heilongjiang Longjiang Opera Experimental Troupe	Liu Jinding	Bai Shuxian	1991
4.23	Cantonese	*The Red Peony Fairy*	Hong Kong Fook Sing Cantonese Opera Troupe	Red Peony Fairy	Liza Wang	1991
4.24	Cantonese	*Yuan Chonghuan*	Guangdong Cantonese Opera Theatre	Yuan Chonghuan	Luo Jiabao	1987

Photo	Opera Type	Opera/Scene Title	Troupe	Character	Performer	Year
4.25	Cantonese	*The Legend of the White Snake*	Hong Kong Elite Cantonese Opera Troupe	Crane Spirit, White Snake	Liang Junqiang, Chan Wing-yee	1997
4.26	Peking	*Farewell, My Concubine*	Peking Opera Performing Artists Troupe of China	Xiang Yu, Concubine Yu	Yuan Shihai, Du Jinfang	1985
4.27	Hebei Clapper	*Wu Song's Revenge*	Hebei Clapper Opera Troupe	Wu Song	Pei Yanling	1991
4.28	Peking	*Cleaning Out the Bandit's Lair*	Shanghai Peking Opera Theatre	He Tianbao	Xi Zhonglu	1992
4.29	Peking	*Inn at the Crossroads*	Tianjin Youth Peking Opera Troupe	Ren Tanghui, Liu Lihua	Wang Lijun, Shi Xiaoliang	1990
4.30	Sichuan	*Hua Rong Shoots the Hawk*	Chengdu Hibiscus Sichuan Opera Troupe	Hua Rong	Tang Yong	1988
4.31	Cantonese	*Xue Dingshan Thrice Angers Fan Lihua*	Foshan Youth Cantonese Opera Troupe	Xue Dingshan	Yuen Siu-fai	1997
4.32	Longjiang	*The Romance of the Iron Bow*	Heilongjiang Longjiang Opera Experimental Troupe	Chen Xiuying, Kuang Zhong	Dou Chunfeng, Zhou Jingkui	1991
4.33	Hui	*Drowning the Enemy Troops*	Anhui Provincial Hui Opera Troupe	Guan Yu	Zhang Qixiang	1991
4.34	Cantonese	*The Battle of Baqiu*	Guangdong Cantonese Opera Theatre	Zhang Fei, Zhou Yu	Li Yongbin, Peng Qinghua	2006
4.35	Hebei Clapper	*The Magic Lotus Lantern*	Hebei Clapper Opera Troupe	Chenxiang	Pei Yanling	1990
4.36	Hebei Clapper	*Wreaking Havoc in the Eastern Sea*	Hebei Clapper Opera Troupe	Nezha	Pei Yanling	1991
4.37	Peking	*Tilting the War Carts*	Shenyang Peking Opera Theatre	Gao Chong	Chen Qingguang	1992
4.38	Cantonese	*Women Warriors of the Yang Family*	Hong Kong Tuen Mun Cantonese Opera Experimental Troupe	Yang Qiniang	Poon Wai-ying (Chor Wan-yuk)	1983
4.39	Peking	*Tilting the War Carts*	Tianjin Youth Peking Opera Troupe	Gao Chong	Wang Lijun	1987
4.40	Peking	*Tilting the War Carts*	Tianjin Youth Peking Opera Troupe	Gao Chong	Wang Lijun	1987
4.41	Peking	*Tilting the War Carts*	Shenyang Peking Opera Theatre	Gao Chong	Chen Qingguang	1992
4.42	Peking	*Tilting the War Carts*	Shenyang Peking Opera Theatre	Gao Chong	Chen Qingguang	1992
4.43	Cantonese	*Raid on Hu Village*	Guangdong Cantonese Opera Theatre	Hu Sanniang	Lu Yueling	2006
4.44	Peking	*Raid on Hu Village*	Tianjin Youth Peking Opera Troupe	Hu Sanniang	Li Peihong	1990
4.45	Peking	*Raid on Hu Village*	Tianjin Youth Peking Opera Troupe	Hu Sanniang	Li Peihong	1990
4.46	Cantonese	*Women Warriors of the Yang Family*	Hong Kong Tuen Mun Cantonese Opera Experimental Troupe	Yang Qiniang	Poon Wai-ying (Chor Wan-yuk)	1983
5.01	Peking	*Raid on Hu Village*	Tianjin Youth Peking Opera Troupe	Hu Sanniang	Li Peihong	1990
5.02	Yue	*The Story of the White Rabbit*	Zhejiang Little Flowers Yue Opera Troupe	Liu Chengyou	Xia Saili	1991
5.03	Yue	*The Story of the White Rabbit*	Zhejiang Little Flowers Yue Opera Troupe	Liu Chengyou	Xia Saili	1991
5.04	Sichuan	*Delights of the Mortal World*	Chengdu Hibiscus Sichuan Opera Troupe	White Eel Fairy	Yu Haiyan	1988
5.05	Shao	*Monkey King Battles the White-Boned Demon*	Zhejiang Shaoxing Opera Troupe	Sun Wukong	Liu Jianyang	1991
5.06	Sichuan	*Wresting the Dragon Throne*	Chengdu Sichuan Opera Theatre	Yang Guang	Xiao Ting	1991
5.07	Peking	*Raid on Hu Village*	Tianjin Youth Peking Opera Troupe	Hu Sanniang	Li Peihong	1990
5.08	Hui	*Meeting at the Riverside*	Anhui Provincial Hui Opera Troupe	Zhou Yu	Li Longbin	1991
5.09	Gaojia	*The Trial of Chen San*	Xiamen Jinliansheng Gaojia Opera Troupe	Governor	Zhang Qinghu	1988
5.10	Peking	*The Beheading of a Wicked Husband*	Tianjin Youth Peking Opera Troupe	Bao Zheng	Meng Guanglu	1990
5.11	Yu	*The Story of the Perfumed Sachet*	Henan Provincial Yu Opera Theatre	Zhou Ding	Meng Xiangli	1986
5.12	Yu	*The Story of the Perfumed Sachet*	Henan Provincial Yu Opera Theatre	Zhou Ding	Meng Xiangli	1986

English Guide to the Photographs

Photo	Opera Type	Opera/Scene Title	Troupe	Character	Performer	Year
5.13	Cantonese	*The Merciless Sword*	Hong Kong Chung Sun Sing Cantonese Opera Troupe	Wei Chonghui	Lam Gar-Sing	1993
5.14	Yu	*The Story of the Perfumed Sachet*	Henan Provincial Yu Opera Theatre	Wang Tiancai	Li Bin	1986
5.15	Cantonese	*Accusing the Traitor*	Guangdong Cantonese Opera Theatre	Xia Yuanchun	Xian Jiantang	2006
5.16	Xiang	*Drawing Lots for Life and Death*	Hunan Xiang Opera Theatre	Huang Boxian	Liu Chunquan	1986
5.17	Cantonese	*The Battle of Baqiu*	Guangdong Cantonese Opera Theatre	Zhou Yu	Peng Qinghua	2006
5.18	Gan	*The Grievance of Dou E*	Jiangxi Provincial Gan Opera Troupe	Dou E, Cai Po	Tu Linghui, Hong Liyun	1992
5.19	Chaozhou	*Suing the Husband*	Guangdong Provincial Chaozhou Opera Troupe	Wen Shuzhen	Zheng Jianying	1984
5.20	Gaojia	*The Trial of Chen San*	Xiamen Jinliansheng Gaojia Opera Troupe	Pan Shi	Zhang Lina	1988
5.21	Hebei Clapper	*Shi Xiu Slays an Unfaithful Wife*	Hebei Clapper Opera Troupe	Pan Qiaoyun, Shi Xiu	Xu Heying, Pei Yanling	1992
5.22	Peking	*The Marriage of the Dragon and the Phoenix*	Peking Opera Performing Artists Troupe of China	Sun Quan	Chen Zhenzhi	1985
5.23	Peking	*The Beheading of a Wicked Husband*	Tianjin Youth Peking Opera Troupe	Bao Zheng	Meng Guanglu	1990
5.24	Hui	*Drowning the Enemy Troops*	Anhui Provincial Hui Opera Troupe	Guan Yu, Zhou Cang	Zhang Qixiang, Gu Huamin	1991
5.25	Peking	*Cleaning Out the Bandit's Lair*	Shanghai Peking Opera Theatre	He Tianbao	Xi Zhonglu	1992
5.26	Gan	*Meng Liang Raises Troops*	Jiangxi Provincial Gan Opera Troupe	Meng Liang	Li Weide	1992
5.27	Shao	*The Prime Minister of Wei*	Zhejiang Shaoxing Opera Troupe	Zhai Huang	Zhou Jianying	1991
5.28	Shao	*The Prime Minister of Wei*	Zhejiang Shaoxing Opera Troupe	Zhai Huang	Zhong Guoliang	1991
5.29	Shao	*The Prime Minister of Wei*	Zhejiang Shaoxing Opera Troupe	Zhai Huang	Zhong Guoliang	1991
5.30	Cantonese	*The Haunting of Zhang Sanlang*	Guangdong Cantonese Opera Theatre	Yan Xijiao	Zeng Xiaomin	2006
5.31	Cantonese	*Mourning at the Tomb*	Guangdong Cantonese Opera Theatre	Zhu Yingtai	Liu Li	2006
5.32	Yue	*The Romance of Emperor Han Wu*	Zhejiang Little Flowers Yue Opera Troupe	Wei Zifu	He Saifei	1991
5.33	Cantonese	*The Story of the Purple Hairpin*	Hong Kong Chor Fung Ming Cantonese Opera Troupe	Huo Xiaoyu	Mui Suet-see	1984
5.34	Gan	*The Story of the Wooden Hairpin*	Jiangxi Provincial Gan Opera Troupe	Qian Yulian	Tu Linghui	1992
5.35	Jin	*The Killing of the Imperial Concubine*	Shanxi Provincial Jin Opera Troupe	Liu Guilian, Liu Chengyou, Su Yu'e	Mi Xiaomin, Gao Yalin, Chang Xiangguo	1986
5.36	Cantonese	*At Odds with a God*	Guangdong Cantonese Opera Theatre	Jiao Guiying	Zheng Lipin	2006
5.37	Longjiang	*Twice-Locked Mountain*	Heilongjiang Longjiang Opera Experimental Troupe	Liu Jinding	Bai Shuxian	1991
5.38	Peking	*The Beheading of a Wicked Husband*	Tianjin Youth Peking Opera Troupe	Bao Zheng	Meng Guanglu	1990
5.39	Cantonese	*The Legend of the Red Plum*	Hong Kong Chin Fung Cantonese Opera Troupe	Li Huiniang	Nam Fung	2005
5.40	Peking	*Li Kui Visits His Mother*	Shanghai Peking Opera Theatre	Li Kui	Shang Changrong	1992
5.41	Cantonese	*The Butterfly Lovers*	Hong Kong Chin Fung Cantonese Opera Troupe	Liang Shanbo	Ng Chin-fung	2005
5.42	Peking	*Zhang Fei Honours the Sage Magistrate*	Shanghai Peking Opera Theatre	Zhang Fei	Shang Changrong	1992
5.43	Gan	*Meng Liang Raises Troops*	Jiangxi Provincial Gan Opera Troupe	Meng Liang	Li Weide	1992
5.44	Cantonese	*Escape from the Golden Mountain Temple*	Guangdong Cantonese Opera Theatre	Xu Xian	Li Zhanping (Sima Xiang)	2006
5.45	Chaozhou	*Dr. Happenstance*	Guangdong Cantonese Opera Theatre	Zhang Wuyi	Fang Zhanrong	1991

Photo	Opera Type	Opera/Scene Title	Troupe	Character	Performer	Year
5.46	Hebei Clapper	*Prince Lanling*	Hebei Clapper Opera Troupe	Prince Lanling	Pei Yanling	1992
5.47	Hebei Clapper	*Wu Song's Revenge*	Hebei Clapper Opera Troupe	Wu Song	Pei Yanling	1992
5.48	Cantonese	*Shi Xiu Reconnoiters a Village*	Guangdong Cantonese Opera Theatre	Shi Xiu	Liu Jianke	2006
5.49	Hebei Clapper	*Shi Xiu Slays an Unfaithful Wife*	Hebei Clapper Opera Troupe	Shi Xiu	Pei Yanling	1992
5.50	Hebei Clapper	*Shi Xiu Reconnoiters a Village*	Hebei Clapper Opera Troupe	Shi Xiu	Pei Yanling	1993
6.01	Sichuan		(Face changing performance in a tea-house in Chengdu)	(unknown)	(unknown)	2010
6.02	Sichuan	*Wresting the Dragon Throne*	Chengdu Sichuan Opera Theatre	Yang Guang	Xiao Ting	1991
6.03	Sichuan	*A Palace Interrogation*	Chengdu Sichuan Opera Theatre	Chen Lin	Li Sen	1991
6.04	Sichuan	*The Haunting of Zhang Sanlang*	Chengdu Sichuan Opera Theatre	Yan Xijiao, Zhang Sanlang	Tian Huiwen, Li Zenglin	1991
6.05	Sichuan	*The Legend of the White Snake*	Chengdu Sichuan Opera Theatre	Begging Bowl Spirit	Xiao Ting	1991
6.06	Sichuan	*The Legend of the White Snake*	Chengdu Sichuan Opera Theatre	Begging Bowl Spirit	Xiao Ting	1991
6.07	Sichuan	*The Legend of the White Snake*	Chengdu Sichuan Opera Theatre	Begging Bowl Spirit	Xiao Ting	1991
6.08	Sichuan	*The Legend of the White Snake*	Chengdu Sichuan Opera Theatre	White Snake, Begging Bowl Spirit	Chen Qiaoru, Xiao Ting	1991
6.09	Sichuan	*The Nine-Tailed Fox Fairy*	Chengdu Sichuan Opera Theatre	God of Fire	Zhang Wenming	1992
6.10	Qinqiang	*The Sorrow at West Lake*	Shaanxi Qinqiang Opera Youth Troupe	Li Huiniang	Xiao Ying	1990
6.11	Hebei Clapper	*Zhong Kui Arranges a Marriage*	Hebei Clapper Opera Troupe	Zhong Kui	Pei Yanling	1991
6.12	Sichuan	*The Legend of the White Snake*	Chengdu Sichuan Opera Theatre	God of Fire	Xiao Haiqing	1991
6.13	Sichuan	*The Legend of the White Snake*	Chengdu Sichuan Opera Theatre	White Snake	Chen Qiaoru	1991
6.14	Sichuan	*The Legend of the White Snake*	Chengdu Hibiscus Sichuan Opera Troupe	Weituo	Yu Haiyan	1988
6.15	Sichuan	*The Legend of the White Snake*	Chengdu Hibiscus Sichuan Opera Troupe	Weituo	Yu Haiyan	1988
6.16	Sichuan	*The Legend of the White Snake*	Chengdu Hibiscus Sichuan Opera Troupe	Weituo	Yu Haiyan	1988
6.17	Sichuan	*The Legend of the White Snake*	Chengdu Hibiscus Sichuan Opera Troupe	Weituo	Yu Haiyan	1988
6.18	Sichuan	*Pi Jin Plays the Fool*	Chengdu Hibiscus Sichuan Opera Troupe	Pi Jin	Su Mingde	1988
6.19	Sichuan	*Pi Jin Plays the Fool*	Chengdu Hibiscus Sichuan Opera Troupe	Pi Jin	Su Mingde	1988
6.20	Sichuan	*Pi Jin Plays the Fool*	Chengdu Hibiscus Sichuan Opera Troupe	Du Pishi, Pi Jin	Xiao Daifang, Su Mingde	1988
6.21	Sichuan	*Pi Jin Plays the Fool*	Chengdu Hibiscus Sichuan Opera Troupe	Pi Jin	Su Mingde	1988
6.22	Chaozhou	*A Woodshed Encounter*	Guangdong Provincial Chaozhou Opera Troupe	Li Laosan	Fang Zhanrong	1991
6.23	Chaozhou	*A Woodshed Encounter*	Guangdong Provincial Chaozhou Opera Troupe	Li Laosan	Fang Zhanrong	1991
7.01	Peking	*The Warrior Maiden Mu Guiying*	Liaoning Youth Peking Opera Troupe	Mu Guiying, etc.	Wang Yulan, etc.	1991

Remarks: Performers are identified from left to right.

APPENDIX II

Chinese Guide to the Photographs

Photo	Opera Type	Opera/Scene Title	Troupe	Character	Performer	Year
1.01	京劇	楊門女將	湖北省京劇團	穆桂英、佘太君等	李春芳、甄靜嫻等	1987
2.01	粵劇	花田八喜	香港青年粵劇團	春蘭	鄭詠梅	2008
2.02	梨園戲	董生與李氏	福建省梨園戲實驗劇團	董生、李氏	龔萬里、曾靜萍	2005
2.03	粵劇	拾玉鐲	香港屯門實驗粵劇團	孫玉姣	陳秀卿	1981
2.04	評劇	拾玉鐲	河北省石家莊青年評劇團	孫玉姣	劉鳳芝	1991
2.05	川劇	潘金蓮調叔	成都市川劇院	潘金蓮	陳巧茹	1991
2.06	粵劇	寶蓮燈	香港屯門實驗粵劇團	靈芝	許秋紅	1988
2.07	粵劇	楊門女將	香港東昇粵劇團	楊文廣、穆桂英等	御東昇、御玲瓏等	2012
2.08	粵劇	春草闖堂	香港屯門實驗粵劇團	春草	許秋紅	1985
2.09	河北梆子戲	哪吒鬧海	河北梆子戲劇團	龜丞相	李立水	1991
2.10	河北梆子戲	林沖夜奔	河北梆子戲劇團	林沖	裴艷玲	1992
2.11	京劇	洗浮山	上海京劇院	賀天保	奚中路	1992
2.12	紹劇	相國志	浙江紹興紹劇團	樂燕	孫曉燕	1991
2.13	粵劇	趙子龍百萬軍中藏阿斗	廣東粵劇院	趙雲	盧文斌 (馬亦龍)	2006
2.14	粵劇	逃出金山	廣東粵劇院	許仙	李湛平 (司馬祥)	2006
2.15	粵劇	十八羅漢伏金鵬	湛江粵劇團	金鵬	梁兆明	2005
2.16	粵劇	十八羅漢伏金鵬	湛江粵劇團	金鵬	梁兆明	2005
2.17	粵劇	十八羅漢伏金鵬	湛江粵劇團	金鵬、眾羅漢	梁兆明 (其餘不詳)	2005
2.18	粵劇	鳳台關	廣東粵劇院	張秀英	曾小敏	2006
2.19	粵劇	武松	廣東粵劇院	西門慶、武大郎	文汝清、陳雲聰	2006
2.20	粵劇	活捉張三郎	廣東粵劇院	張三郎、閻惜姣	黃春強、梁曉瑩	2006
2.21	河北梆子戲	火燒連營	河北梆子戲劇團	關興	裴艷玲	1991
2.22	粵劇	楊門女將	香港屯門實驗粵劇團	張彪	陳碧英 (文劍斐)	1983
2.23	京劇	失街亭・空城計・斬馬謖	天津青年京劇團	趙雲	房至剛	1990
2.24	粵劇	戰巴丘	廣東粵劇院	周瑜、張飛	彭慶華、李永彬	2006
2.25	評劇	乾坤帶	河北省石家莊青年評劇團	秦英	趙新城	1991
2.26	龍江	雙鎖山	黑龍江龍江實驗劇團	劉金定	白淑賢	1991
2.27	贛劇	孟良搬兵	江西省贛劇團	楊排風、孟良	涂玲慧、李維德	1992
2.28	徽劇	曹操關羽貂蟬	安徽省徽劇團	關羽	章其祥	1991
2.29	河北梆子戲	雙槍陸文龍	河北梆子戲劇團	陸文龍	裴小玲	1991
2.30	龍江	鐵弓緣	黑龍江龍江實驗劇團	匡忠、陳秀英	周景奎、竇春鳳	1991
2.31	粵劇	廉錦楓	廣東粵劇院	廉錦楓、蚌精	嚴金鳳、陳小嫻	2006
2.32	粵劇	活捉張三郎	廣東粵劇院	張三郎、閻惜姣	黃春強、梁曉瑩	2006
2.33	京劇	挑滑車	瀋陽京劇院	高寵	陳清廣	1987
2.34	贛劇	選馬出征	江西省贛劇團	穆桂英	陳俐	1992
2.35	粵劇	薛丁山三戲樊梨花	佛山青年粵劇團	薛丁山	阮兆輝	1997

Photo	Opera Type	Opera/Scene Title	Troupe	Character	Performer	Year
2.36	粵劇	紅梅記	廣東粵劇院	土地	梁亨賢	2006
2.37	京劇	扈家莊	天津青年京劇團	王英	石曉亮	1990
2.38	粵劇	十八羅漢伏金鵬	湛江粵劇團	金鵬	梁兆明	2005
2.39	粵劇	金蓮搓餅	廣東粵劇院	武大郎、潘金蓮	陳雲聰、岑鳳屏	2006
3.01	贛劇	選馬出征	江西省贛劇團	穆桂英	陳俐	1992
3.02	粵劇	秦瓊觀陣	廣東粵劇院	秦瓊、羅成	嚴雲濤、陳家鼎	2006
3.03	粵劇	秦瓊觀陣	廣東粵劇院	秦瓊	嚴雲濤	2006
3.04	京劇	青石山	瀋陽京劇院	關羽	汪慶元	1992
3.05	粵劇	鳳台關	廣東粵劇院	張秀英	曾小敏	2006
3.06	粵劇	鳳台關	廣東粵劇院	張秀英	曾小敏	2006
3.07	粵劇	攔馬	廣東粵劇院	楊八姐	朱紅星	2006
3.08	粵劇	攔馬	廣東粵劇院	楊八姐	朱紅星	2006
3.09	粵劇	攔馬	廣東粵劇院	楊八姐	朱紅星	2006
3.10	粵劇	攔馬	廣東粵劇院	楊八姐、焦光普	朱紅星、吳國文	2006
3.11	京劇	曹操與楊修	上海京劇院	楊修、曹操	言興朋、尚長榮	1992
3.12	川劇	昭君出塞	成都市川劇院	王昭君	劉萍	1991
3.13	川劇	昭君出塞	成都市川劇院	王昭君	劉萍	1991
3.14	京劇	洗浮山	上海京劇院	賀天保	奚中路	1992
3.15	粵劇	戰巴丘	廣東粵劇院	周瑜	彭慶華	2006
3.16	京劇	鬧天宮	天津青年京劇團	孫悟空	石曉亮	1990
3.17	評劇	花為媒	河北省石家莊青年評劇團	賈俊英、張五可	趙立華、劉秀榮	1991
3.18	黃梅戲	春遊	安慶黃梅戲劇團	趙翠花	吳亞玲	1993
3.19	越劇	回十八	上海越劇院	梁山伯、祝英台	章瑞虹、陳穎	1991
3.20	越劇	回十八	浙江小百花越劇團	梁山伯	方雪雯	1986
3.21	越劇	西廂記	浙江小百花越劇團	崔鶯鶯	陶慧敏	1991
3.22	京劇	貴妃醉酒	遼寧青少年京劇團	楊玉環	劉亞君	1986
3.23	京劇	賣水	遼寧青少年京劇團	梅英	管波	1986
3.24	粵劇	武松打店	香港屯門實驗粵劇團	孫二娘	陸美琴	1981
3.25	京劇	張飛敬賢	上海京劇院	張飛	尚長榮	1992
3.26	呂劇	姊妹易嫁	山東呂劇團	張素梅	高靜	1990
3.27	呂劇	借年	山東呂劇團	愛姐	王媛媛	1990
3.28	黃梅戲	春遊	安慶黃梅戲劇團	趙翠花	吳亞玲	1993
3.29	粵劇	點秋香	香港元朗文協粵劇團	秋香	陳秀卿	1988
3.30	黃梅戲	喜榮歸	安慶黃梅戲劇團	崔華、崔秀英	黃宗毅、李瓊	1993
3.31	粵劇	掛畫	廣東粵劇院	春蘭、葉含嫣	鍾琰、吳琨茹	2006
3.32	徽劇	戲牡丹	安徽省徽劇團	白牡丹	李小紅	1991

Photo	Opera Type	Opera/Scene Title	Troupe	Character	Performer	Year
3.33	龍江劇	雙鎖山	黑龍江龍江實驗劇團	劉金定之女侍	(不詳)	1991
3.34	粵劇	火鳳凰	廣東粵劇院	白鷺仙子	龔潔影	2006
3.35	粵劇	火鳳凰	廣東粵劇院	白鷺仙子	龔潔影	2006
3.36	京劇	八仙過海	遼寧青少年京劇團	金魚仙子	薛俊秋	1986
3.37	川劇	芙蓉花仙	成都市芙蓉花川劇團	芙蓉花仙	喻海燕	1988
3.38	粵劇	楊枝露滴牡丹開	香港福陞粵劇團	紅萼仙子	汪明荃	1991
3.39	京劇	三岔口	天津青年京劇團	劉利華、任堂惠	石曉亮、王立軍	1990
3.40	京劇	三岔口	天津青年京劇團	任堂惠、劉利華	王立軍、石曉亮	1990
3.41	粵劇	掛畫	廣東粵劇院	葉含嫣	吳琨茹	2006
3.42	粵劇	活捉張三郎	廣東粵劇院	閻惜姣、張三郎	曾小敏、王燕飛	2006
3.43	粵劇	攔馬	廣東粵劇院	楊八姐、焦光普	朱紅星、吳國文	2006
3.44	粵劇	攔馬	廣東粵劇院	焦光普、楊八姐	吳國文、朱紅星	2006
3.45	粵劇	武松大鬧獅子樓	廣東粵劇院	武松	彭慶華	2006
3.46	京劇	長坂坡	中國京劇藝術家演出團	張飛	張連長	1985
3.47	川劇	水漫金山	成都芙蓉花川劇團	白蛇、青蛇	葉長敏、王世彬	1988
3.48	粵劇	白蛇傳	香港精英粵劇團	白蛇	陳詠儀	1997
3.49	徽劇	戲牡丹	安徽省徽劇團	呂洞賓	許友升	1991
3.50	京劇	八仙過海	遼寧青少年京劇團	呂洞賓	吳坤	1986
3.51	越劇	遊庵認母	上海越劇院	志貞	金彩風	1991
3.52	越劇	遊庵認母	上海越劇院	志貞	金彩風	1991
3.53	京劇	醉打山門	遼寧青少年京劇團	魯智深	趙輝	1986
3.54	粵劇	白蛇傳	香港精英粵劇團	艄翁	尤聲普	1997
3.55	粵劇	金鳳銀龍迎新歲	香港燕笙輝劇團	喬丹鳳	尹飛燕	2005
3.56	粵劇	白蛇傳	香港精英粵劇團	艄翁、青蛇、白蛇、許仙	尤聲普、高麗、陳詠儀、阮兆輝	1997
3.57	川劇	白蛇傳	成都市川劇院	白蛇、青蛇	陳巧茹、朱建國	1991
3.58	粵劇	戰巴丘	廣東粵劇院	張飛	李永彬	2006
3.59	崑曲	雅觀樓	上海崑劇團	李存孝	王芝泉	1989
3.60	京劇	虹橋贈珠	瀋陽京劇院	凌波仙子	李靜文	1992
3.61	粵劇	薛丁山三戲樊梨花	佛山青年粵劇團	眾兵	(不詳)	1997
3.62	京劇	挑滑車	天津青年京劇團	高寵	王立軍	1987
3.63	粵劇	拜月記	香港燕笙輝劇團	王瑞蘭	尹飛燕	2005
3.64	京劇	盤絲洞	上海京劇院	蜘蛛精	周洋	1992
3.65	川劇	白蛇傳	成都市川劇院	青蛇	朱建國	1991
3.66	川劇	白蛇傳	成都市川劇院	青蛇、白蛇	劉萍、陳巧茹	1991
3.67	川劇	白蛇傳	成都市川劇院	白蛇、青蛇	陳巧茹、朱建國	1991
4.01	粵劇	扈家莊	廣東粵劇院	扈三娘	盧月玲	2006

Chinese Guide to the Photographs

Photo	Opera Type	Opera/Scene Title	Troupe	Character	Performer	Year
4.02	粵劇	長坂坡	廣東粵劇院	趙雲	文汝清	2006
4.03	粵劇	鳳台關	廣東粵劇院	張秀英	曾小敏	2006
4.04	川劇	九尾狐仙	成都市川劇院	九尾狐仙	李莎	1992
4.05	京劇	虹橋贈珠	瀋陽京劇院	凌波仙子	李靜文	1992
4.06	京劇	虹橋贈珠	瀋陽京劇院	凌波仙子	李靜文	1992
4.07	粵劇	火鳳凰	廣東粵劇院	白鷺仙子	龔潔影	2006
4.08	粵劇	火鳳凰	廣東粵劇院	白鷺仙子	龔潔影	2006
4.09	京劇	八仙過海	遼寧青少年京劇團	金魚仙子	薛俊秋	1986
4.10	粵劇	薛丁山三戲樊梨花	佛山青年粵劇團	樊梨花	李淑勤	1997
4.11	粵劇	薛丁山三戲樊梨花	佛山青年粵劇團	薛丁山、樊梨花	阮兆輝、李淑勤	1997
4.12	京劇	鬧天宮	天津青年京劇團	巨靈神	陳璽強	1990
4.13	京劇	鬧天宮	天津青年京劇團	巨靈神、孫悟空	陳璽強、石曉亮	1990
4.14	河北梆子戲	雙槍陸文龍	河北梆子戲劇團	陸文龍、岳雲	裴小玲、張克海	1991
4.15	河北梆子戲	火燒裴元慶	河北梆子戲劇團	裴元慶	劉立偉	1991
4.16	紹劇	三借芭蕉扇	浙江紹興紹劇團	孫悟空	劉建揚	1991
4.17	京劇	盤絲洞	上海京劇院	孫悟空、蜘蛛精	趙國華 (另一演員不詳)	1992
4.18	京劇	盤絲洞	上海京劇院	孫悟空、眾蜘蛛精	趙國華 (其他演員不詳)	1992
4.19	粵劇	石秀探莊	廣東粵劇院	石秀、祝家莊守衛	劉建科 (另一演員不詳)	2006
4.20	河北梆子戲	火燒連營	河北梆子戲劇團	黃忠	裴艷玲	1991
4.21	京劇	華容道	中國京劇藝術家演出團	關羽	厲慧良	1985
4.22	龍江劇	雙鎖山	黑龍江龍江實驗劇團	劉金定	白淑賢	1991
4.23	粵劇	楊枝露滴牡丹開	香港福陞粵劇團	紅萼仙子	汪明荃	1991
4.24	粵劇	袁崇煥	廣東粵劇院	袁崇煥	羅家寶	1987
4.25	粵劇	白蛇傳	香港精英粵劇團	鶴童、白蛇	梁均強、陳詠儀	1997
4.26	京劇	霸王別姬	中國京劇表演家藝術團	項羽、虞姬	袁世海、杜近芳	1985
4.27	河北梆子戲	武松血濺鴛鴦樓	河北梆子戲劇團	武松	裴艷玲	1991
4.28	京劇	洗浮山	上海京劇院	賀天保	奚中路	1992
4.29	京劇	三岔口	天津青年京劇團	任堂惠、劉利華	王立軍、石曉亮	1990
4.30	川劇	花榮射鵰	成都市芙蓉花川劇團	花榮	唐勇	1988
4.31	粵劇	薛丁山三戲樊梨花	佛山青年粵劇團	薛丁山	阮兆輝	1997
4.32	龍江劇	鐵弓緣	黑龍江龍江實驗劇團	陳秀英、匡忠	竇春鳳、周景奎	1991
4.33	徽劇	水淹七軍	安徽省徽劇團	關羽	章其祥	1991
4.34	粵劇	戰巴丘	廣東粵劇院	張飛、周瑜	李永彬、彭慶華	2006
4.35	河北梆子戲	寶蓮燈	河北梆子戲劇團	沉香	裴艷玲	1990
4.36	河北梆子戲	哪吒鬧海	河北梆子戲劇團	哪吒	裴艷玲	1991
4.37	京劇	挑滑車	瀋陽京劇院	高寵	陳清廣	1992

Photo	Opera Type	Opera/Scene Title	Troupe	Character	Performer	Year
4.38	粵劇	楊門女將	香港屯門實驗粵劇團	楊七娘	潘慧瑩 (楚雲玉)	1983
4.39	京劇	挑滑車	天津青年京劇團	高寵	王立軍	1987
4.40	京劇	挑滑車	天津青年京劇團	高寵	王立軍	1987
4.41	京劇	挑滑車	瀋陽京劇院	高寵	陳清廣	1992
4.42	京劇	挑滑車	瀋陽京劇院	高寵	陳清廣	1992
4.43	粵劇	扈家莊	廣東粵劇院	扈三娘	盧月玲	2006
4.44	京劇	扈家莊	天津青年京劇團	扈三娘	李佩紅	1990
4.45	京劇	扈家莊	天津青年京劇團	扈三娘	李佩紅	1990
4.46	粵劇	楊門女將	香港屯門實驗粵劇團	楊七娘	潘慧瑩 (楚雲玉)	1983
5.01	京劇	扈家莊	天津青年京劇團	扈三娘	李佩紅	1990
5.02	越劇	白兔記	浙江小百花越劇團	劉承佑	夏賽麗	1991
5.03	越劇	白兔記	浙江小百花越劇團	劉承佑	夏賽麗	1991
5.04	川劇	人間好	成都市芙蓉花川劇團	白蟮仙姑	喻海燕	1988
5.05	紹劇	孫悟空三打白骨精	浙江紹興紹劇團	孫悟空	劉建揚	1991
5.06	川劇	問病逼宮	成都市川劇院	楊廣	曉艇	1991
5.07	京劇	扈家莊	天津青年京劇團	扈三娘	李佩紅	1990
5.08	徽劇	臨江會	安徽省徽劇團	周瑜	李龍斌	1991
5.09	高甲戲	審陳三	廈門市金蓮陞高甲劇團	知州	張清滬	1988
5.10	京劇	鍘美案	天津青年京劇團	包拯	孟廣祿	1990
5.11	豫劇	香囊記	河南省豫劇院	周定	孟祥禮	1986
5.12	豫劇	香囊記	河南省豫劇院	周定	孟祥禮	1986
5.13	粵劇	無情寶劍有情天	香港頌新聲粵劇團	韋重輝	林家聲	1993
5.14	豫劇	香囊記	河南省豫劇院	王天才	李斌	1986
5.15	粵劇	夏元淳罵奸	廣東粵劇院	夏元淳	冼鑒棠	2006
5.16	湘劇	生死牌	湖南湘劇院	黃伯賢	劉春泉	1986
5.17	粵劇	戰巴丘	廣東粵劇院	周瑜	彭慶華	2006
5.18	贛劇	竇娥冤	江西省贛劇團	竇娥、蔡婆	涂玲慧、熊麗雲	1992
5.19	潮劇	告親夫	廣東潮劇團	文淑貞	鄭健英	1984
5.20	高甲戲	審陳三	廈門市金蓮陞高甲劇團	潘氏	張麗娜	1988
5.21	河北梆子戲	石秀殺嫂	河北梆子戲劇團	潘巧雲、石秀	許荷英、裴艷玲	1992
5.22	京劇	龍鳳呈祥	中國京劇表演家藝術團	孫權	陳真治	1985
5.23	京劇	鍘美案	天津青年京劇團	包拯	孟廣祿	1990
5.24	徽劇	水淹七軍	安徽省徽劇團	關羽、周倉	章其祥、谷化民	1991
5.25	京劇	洗浮山	上海京劇院	賀天保	奚中路	1992
5.26	贛劇	孟良搬兵	江西省贛劇團	孟良	李維德	1992
5.27	紹劇	相國志	浙江紹興紹劇團	翟璜	周劍英	1991

Chinese Guide to the Photographs

Photo	Opera Type	Opera/Scene Title	Troupe	Character	Performer	Year
5.28	紹劇	相國志	浙江紹興紹劇團	翟璜	鍾國良	1991
5.29	紹劇	相國志	浙江紹興紹劇團	翟璜	鍾國良	1991
5.30	粵劇	活捉張三郎	廣東粵劇院	閻惜姣	曾小敏	2006
5.31	粵劇	英台哭墳	廣東粵劇院	祝英台	劉麗	2006
5.32	越劇	漢武之戀	浙江小百花越劇團	衛子夫	何賽飛	1991
5.33	粵劇	紫釵記	香港雛鳳鳴粵劇團	霍小玉	梅雪詩	1984
5.34	贛劇	荊釵記	江西省贛劇團	錢玉蓮	涂玲慧	1992
5.35	晉劇	殺宮	山西省晉劇團	劉桂蓮、劉承祐、蘇玉娥	米曉敏、高亞林、常香果	1986
5.36	粵劇	桂英告廟	廣東粵劇院	焦桂英	鄭麗品	2006
5.37	龍江劇	雙鎖山	黑龍江龍江實驗劇團	劉金定	白淑賢	1991
5.38	京劇	鍘美案	天津青年京劇團	包拯	孟廣祿	1990
5.39	粵劇	再世紅梅記	香港仟鳳粵劇團	李慧娘	南鳳	2005
5.40	京劇	李逵探母	屯門實驗粵劇團	李逵	尚長榮	1992
5.41	粵劇	樓台會	香港仟鳳粵劇團	梁山伯	吳仟峰	2005
5.42	京劇	張飛敬賢	上海京劇院	張飛	尚長榮	1992
5.43	贛劇	孟良搬兵	江西省贛劇團	孟良	李維德	1992
5.44	粵劇	逃出金山	廣東粵劇院	許仙	李湛平 (司馬祥)	2006
5.45	潮劇	無意神醫	廣東潮劇團	張無意	方展榮	1991
5.46	河北梆子戲	蘭陵王	河北梆子戲劇團	蘭陵王	裴艷玲	1992
5.47	河北梆子戲	武松血濺鴛鴦樓	河北梆子戲劇團	武松	裴艷玲	1992
5.48	粵劇	石秀探莊	廣東粵劇院	石秀	劉建科	2006
5.49	河北梆子戲	石秀殺嫂	河北梆子戲劇團	石秀	裴艷玲	1992
5.50	河北梆子戲	石秀探莊	河北梆子戲劇團	石秀	裴艷玲	1993
6.01	川劇		(成都茶樓變臉表演)	(不詳)	(不詳)	2010
6.02	川劇	問病逼宮	成都市川劇院	楊廣	曉艇	1991
6.03	川劇	裝盒盤宮	成都市川劇院	陳琳	李森	1991
6.04	川劇	活捉張三郎	成都市川劇院	閻惜姣、張三郎	田惠文、李增林	1991
6.05	川劇	白蛇傳	成都市川劇院	鐃鉢	曉艇	1991
6.06	川劇	白蛇傳	成都市川劇院	鐃鉢	曉艇	1991
6.07	川劇	白蛇傳	成都市川劇院	鐃鉢	曉艇	1991
6.08	川劇	白蛇傳	成都市川劇院	白蛇、鐃鉢	陳巧茹、曉艇	1991
6.09	川劇	九尾狐仙	成都市川劇院	火神	張文明	1992
6.10	秦腔	西湖遺恨	陝西秦腔青年劇團	李慧娘	蕭英	1990
6.11	河北梆子戲	鍾馗嫁妹	河北梆子戲劇團	鍾馗	裴艷玲	1991
6.12	川劇	白蛇傳	成都市川劇院	火神	蕭海清	1991
6.13	川劇	白蛇傳	成都市川劇院	白蛇	陳巧茹	1991

Photo	Opera Type	Opera/Scene Title	Troupe	Character	Performer	Year
6.14	川劇	白蛇傳	成都市芙蓉花川劇團	韋陀	喻海燕	1988
6.15	川劇	白蛇傳	成都市芙蓉花川劇團	韋陀	喻海燕	1988
6.16	川劇	白蛇傳	成都市芙蓉花川劇團	韋陀	喻海燕	1988
6.17	川劇	白蛇傳	成都市芙蓉花川劇團	韋陀	喻海燕	1988
6.18	川劇	皮金滾燈	成都市芙蓉花川劇團	皮金	蘇明德	1988
6.19	川劇	皮金滾燈	成都市芙蓉花川劇團	皮金	蘇明德	1988
6.20	川劇	皮金滾燈	成都市芙蓉花川劇團	杜皮氏、皮金	蕭代芳、蘇明德	1988
6.21	川劇	皮金滾燈	成都市芙蓉花川劇團	皮金	蘇明德	1988
6.22	潮劇	柴房會	廣東潮劇團	李老三	方展榮	1991
6.23	潮劇	柴房會	廣東潮劇團	李老三	方展榮	1991
7.01	京劇	穆桂英下山破陣	遼寧青少年京劇團	穆桂英等	王玉蘭等	1986

注：演员由左向右排列。

References

Bianji Weiyuanhui, ed. *Zhongguo Dabaike quanshu: Xiqu Quyi*. Beijing: Zhongguo Dabaike quanshu Chubanshe, 1983.

Chen Guofu. *Chuanju Lansheng*. Chengdu: Sichuan Renmin Chubanshe, 1986.

Chen Liming. *Chaoju*. Guangzhou: Guangdong Renmin Chubanshe, 2005.

Chen Youhan. *Xiqu Biaoyan Gailun*. Beijing: Wenhua Yishu Chubanshe, 1996.

Chongqing shi Xiqu Gongzuo Weiyuanhui, ed. *Chuanju Yishu Yanjiu*. Chengdu: Sichuan Renmin Chubanshe, 1981.

Deng Yunjie. *Chuanju Yishu Gailun*. Chengdu: Sichuansheng Shehuikexueyuan Chubanshe, 1988.

Dong Zepu. *Zhongguo Xiqu Biaoyan Yishu Shuyao*. Hong Kong: Man Wah Book Company, 1981.

Fu Weng and others. *Guoju*. Taipei: Hanguang Wenhua Shiye Chubanshe, n.d.

Gao Xin. *Jingju Xinshang*. Shanghai: Shiji Chubanshe, 2006.

Guo Ende and Zhao Huayun, eds. *Shanxi Xiqu Zhezixi Huicui*. Beijing: Zhongguo Xiju Chubanshe, 1989.

Guo Yunlong, ed. *Zhongguo Lidai Xiqu xuan*. Taipei: Hongye Shuju, 1978.

Hu Xuegang. *Wenzhou Nanxi Lungao*. Taipei: Guojia Chubanshe, 2006.

Li Xi, ed. *Zhongguo Xiqu Biaoyan Jishu Shuyao*. Hong Kong: Man Wah Book Company, 1981.

Lin Man-on. *Yueju Mingling Jueji*. Hong Kong: Hong Kong Opera Preview, 2006.

Liu Qi. *Jingju Xingshi Tezheng*. Tianjin: Tianjin Guji Chubanshe, 2003.

Ma Shaobo, Zhang Lihui, Tao Xiong and Hu Sha. *Zhongguo Jingju shi*. Beijing: Zhongguo Xiju Chubanshe, 1990.

Ma Zichen, ed. *Zhongguo Yuju Dacidian*. Zhengzhou: Zhongzhou Guji Chubanshe, 2003.

Mackerras, Colin. *Peking Opera*. New York: Oxford University Press, 1997.

Qi Rushan. *Guoju Tupu*. Taipei: Youshi Wenhua Shiye Chubanshe, 1981.

Shanghai Yishu Yanjiusuo. *Zhongguo Xiqu Quyi Cidian*. Shanghai: Shanghai Cishu Chubanshe, 1981.

Shantou shi Yishu Yanjiushi, ed. *Chaoju Yanjiu*. Shantou: Shantou Daxue Chubanshe, 1995.

Shi Jinan and Zhu Yufen. *Huangmeixi Yishu*. Beijing: Zhongguo Guangbo Dianshi Chubanshe, 1985.

Tu Pei and Su Yi. *Jingju Changshi Shouce*. Beijing: Zhongguo Xiju Chubanshe, 2003.

Wan Fengshu. *Xiqu Shenduan Biaoyan Xunlianfa*. Beijing: Zhongguo Xiju Chubanshe, 1999.

Wang Dingou, Du Jianhua and Liu Changjin. *Chuanju Juehuo*. Chengdu: Sichuan Meishu Chubanshe, 2007.

Wang Shiying. *Xiqu Danhang Shenduangong*. Beijing: Zhongguo Xiju Chubanshe, 2002.

Wu Tongbin. *Jingju Zhishi Shouce*. Tianjin: Tianjin Jiaoyu Chubanshe, 1995.

Xu Huadang, ed. *Zhongguo Xiqu Zhuangshi Yishu*. Beijing: Zhongguo Qinggongye Chubanshe, 1993.

Yan Fuchang, ed. *Chuanju Yishu Yinlun*. Chengdu: Bashu Shushe, 2000.

Yan Ming. *Jingju Yishu Rumen*. Taipei: Yeqiang Chubanshe, 1994.

Yang Youhe. *Chuanju Danjiao Biaoyan Yishu*. Beijing: Zhongguo Xiqu Yanjiusuo, 1959.

Yicai and Qingwang. *Jingju Xinshang Rumen*. Harbin: Harbin Gongcheng Daxue Chubanshe, 1995.

Yu Handong, ed. *Zhongguo Xiqu Biaoyan Yishu Cidian*. Taipei: Guojia Chubanshe, 2001.

Zhang Gansheng. *Zhongguo Xiqu Yishu*. Tianjin: Baihua Wenyi Chubanshe, 1982.

Zhang Geng. *Xiqu Yishulun*. Beijing: Zhongguo Xiju Chubanshe, 1980.

Zhang Yunxi. *Yiyuan Qiushi: Jingju Biaoyan Duozhong Chengshi de Miaoyong*. Beijng: Zhongguo Guangbo Dianshi Chubanshe, 1995.

Zhao Zhishuo, Zhang Yaojia and Yu Yingli. *Zhongguo Chuantong Jingju Fuzhuang Daoju*. Taipei: Shuxin Chubanshe, 1992.

Zhongguo Xiqu Xueyuan. *Xiqu Bazigong*. Beijing: Wenhua Yishu Chubanshe, 1983.

Notes: Page references to photographs are given in bold type, viz. **25***(2.24).*

To assist readers identify characters mentioned in the text, a brief description (in parentheses) has been added after the name of the character, for example, Chen Lin (eunuch), Song Jiang (robber chieftain). Similarly, the terms used to describe different effects, moves, poses and skills are followed by the relevant descriptor, for example, "stiff corpse fall" (move) and "leg twist" (pose).

Accusing the Husband, 145
Accusing the Traitor, **142**(5.15), 143
acrobatics, 16–22, 49, 71
    back flip, 17
    high somersault, 19
actors
    emphasis on, ix, 1, 69
    training, 189
alienation device, 3
All Men Are Brothers, 35
At Odds with a God, **158**(5.36)
audiences, 1, 16, 192
axes, 120

"back crossed double spears" (pose), 28
"back whisk" (move), 78
"backward battering the tiger" (move), 17
"balancing the oil lamp" (skill), 185–7
Bald Eagle Fairy, 67
bandits, 35, 127, 137, 168
Bao, Judge, 140, 149, 159
Battle of Baqiu, The, 24, **25**(2.24), **50**(3.15), **84**(3.58), **119**(4.34), **144**(5.17)
Battle of Red Cliff, 137
battles, 91, 98, 100
    preparation for, 122–9
"beard work" (move), 148, 149, 152
beards, 148–53
    characters without, 144
    designs, 148
Beheading of a Wicked Husband, The, **139**(5.10), **149**(5.23), **160**(5.38)
belts, 167–9
Blocking the Horse, 43, 44–6 (3.07–3.10), **72**(3.43), 73, **73**(3.44)
"board leg pose", 26
"board waist" (pose), 31
boat poles, 81
boats, 34, 80–3
    movement of, 80, 81
Borrowing at New Year, **60**(3.27)
bows and arrows, 115–17
Brecht, Bertolt, 3

Bringing the Magic Pearl Over the Rainbow Bridge, **86**(3.60), **96**(4.05–4.06)
Burning the Camps, **23**(2.21), **108**(4.20)
Burning of Pei Yuanqing, The, **103**(4.15)
Butterfly Lovers, The, 155, 162, **162**(5.41)

Cao Cao (general), 45, 137
Cao Cao and Yang Xiu, 45, **47**(3.11)
Cao Cao, Guan Yu and Diaochan, **29**(2.28)
"carpet work" (skill), 17
carrying chairs, 10
Cave of the Spiders, The, **88**(3.64), **105**(4.17), **106**(4.18)
chairs, 69–74
Changban Slope, 74, **74**(3.46), **94**(4.02)
Chaozhou opera, 165, 188
Chen Lin (eunuch), 172
Chen Shimei (malicious husband), 159
Chen Yong (martial arts master), 117
Chenxiang (son of fairy), 120
Chinese opera
    as cultural achievement, ix
    defined, 2
    development of, 3
    language of, 191–2
    perception of, by Westerners, 16
    styles of, ix, 2
    suggestion as principle of, 3, 15, 37, 91
    women in, 56
Chinese Opera: Images and Stories (by Siu Wang-Ngai with Peter Lovrick), ix, 191
Choosing Qiuxiang, **61**(3.29)
chuanqi (classical drama), 2
"circling the stage" (mime move), 8
Cleaning Out the Bandit's Lair, **14**(2.11), 15, **49**(3.14), **114**(4.28), 150, **151**(5.25)
cloud boards, 89–91
"cloud flip" (move), 18
cloud whisks, 75–80
clouds, *see* cloud boards
clowns, 165, 185–7, 188
Comedy of Eight Errors, A, **4**(2.01)
Cosmic Belt, The, **26**(2.25)

command flags, 84–5
Contemporary Legend Theatre Company (Taiwan), 3
conventions, stage, ix, 1, 192
Cosmic Circlet, 121
costumes (*see also* belts, hats, robes), ix, 140, 159
Crossing Wits, **63**(3.32), **77**(3.49)
Cui Yingying (young maiden), 54

dachushou (fighting style), 94
Delights of the Mortal World, **134**(5.04)
Dong Sheng and Li Shi, 6, **6**(2.02)
Dr. Happenstance, 165, **165**(5.45)
Dragon Phoenix Battle, The, **82**(3.55)
Drawing Lots for Life and Death, 143, **143**(5.16)
Drowning the Enemy Troops, **118**(4.33), 149, **150**(5.24)
Drunken Monk, The, **80**(3.53)
dust whisks, *see* cloud whisks
dwarfs (*see also* "playing the dwarf"), 34–35

Eight Immortals Cross the Sea, The, **66**(3.36), **77**(3.50), 78, 98, **99**(4.09)
Eighteen Crossings, The, **54**(3.19), **55**(3.20)
Eighteen Luohan Pursue the Golden Crane, The, 18, **18–20**(2.15–2.17), 35, **36**(2.38)
"embrace the whisk" (move), 76
emotions, 56, 59
Escape from the Golden Mountain Temple, 17, **17**(2.14), **164**(5.44)
Execution of the Commander, The, **25**(2.23)
"exploring the sea" (special move), 30, 31, 45
eyes, *see* "opening the eye of wisdom"

face changing, **170**(6.01), 171–6
face painting (*see also* face changing), ix, 1, 2
Fahai (Buddhist abbot), 17, 175, 181, 182
Fan Lihua (warrior maiden), 100
fans, 51–8
    magic, 179
Farewell, My Concubine, 112, **112**(4.26)
fighting, 94, 100, 113
Finding Mother in a Convent, **78**(3.51), **79**(3.52)

fire breathing, 177–81
Fire Phoenix, The, **65**(3.34), **66**(3.35), **97**(4.07), **98**(4.08)
flags, 84–8
Flooding the Golden Mountain Temple, **75**(3.47)
Flower Matchmaker, The, 52, **52**(3.17)
fly whisks, *see* cloud whisks
flying tiger flags, 84
Fox Fairy, 94

Gai Liangcai (wicked husband), 145
galloping, horses, 42–3, 45
Gao Chong (general), 31, 85, 88, 121, 123
Gao Junbao (general), 26
gaomao (high somersault), 19
Goddess of Mercy, 68
Golden Crane (bird), 18, 19, 35
golden cymbals, 175
Golden Eagle Prince, 18
Golden Iron Staff, 118
"Golden Melon Warriors", 101
Goldfish Fairy, 78, 98
Green Snake (spirit), 81, 89, 91
Green Stone Mountain, **41**(3.04)
Grievances of Dou E, The, **145**(5.18)
Guan Gong (Guan Yu, deified hero), 118
Guan Sushuang, 100
Guan Yu (general) (*see also* Guan Gong), 28, 42, 108, 120
Guo Yanwei (insurgent leader), 19

Hai Rui (high official), 144
hair (*see also* beards)
    female roles and, 145–7
    loose, 143
    male roles and, 141–4
Han dynasty, 65
handkerchiefs, 59–64
    spinning, 62, 64
Hanging a Painting, **63**(3.31), 71, **71**(3.41)
hats, 138–40
Haunting of Zhang Sanlang, The, 21, **22**(2.20), 31, **32**(2.32), **72**(3.42), **154**(5.30), 172, **174**(6.04)
He Tainbao (warrior), 15, 49, 113, 150
headgear, *see* hats
heavenly beings, *see* supernatural beings
"Hegemon Rises, The" (see also *qiba*), 122
Hibiscus Fairy, 68

Hibiscus Fairy, The, **67**(3.37)
Hong Kong, opera troupes visit, 191
Hong Kong Ballet, The (by Siu Wang-Ngai), ix
"horse ride" (move), 40, 45
horses (*see also* horsewhips), 33, 39, 49
    galloping, 42–3, 45
horsewhips, 39–50, 93
Hu Sanniang (female warrior), 127, 128
Hua Rong Shoots the Hawk, **115**(4.30)
Huang Guiying (mistress), 56
Huarong Pass, **109**(4.21)
hunting, 115
Huo Xiaoyu (young wife), 157

Inn at the Crossroads, **69**(3.39), 70, **70**(3.40), 113, **114**(4.29)
Intoxicated Concubine, The, 54, **56**(3.22)

jade belt, 167
Jia Junying (young man), 52
Jiang Zhong (bully), 165
Jiao Guangpu (exile), 45, 73–4
Journey to the West (by Wu Cheng'en), 88, 105
journeys, 8
    night, 10, 13, 15
Joyous Return, The, **62**(3.30)
juggling, 102

"kicking the spear" (move), 98
Killing of the Imperial Concubine, The, **158**(5.35)
Kneading the Dough, **37**(2.39)
Kuang Zhong (handsome youth), 117
Kunqu opera, 2

ladders, 188–9
language, of the stage, 1, 5, 192
Lanling (prince), 165, **166**(5.46)
"leg twist" (pose), 26
Legend of the Red Plum, The (see also *Story of the Red Plum, The*), 159, **160**(5.39)
Legend of the Water Margin, The, 35, 74, 106, 165
Legend of the White Snake, The, 17, 76, **76**(3.48), 81, **82**(3.56), **83**(3.57), **89**–**91**(3.65–3.67), **111**(4.25), **174**(6.05), 175, **175**–**6**(6.06–6.08), **180**(6.12), 181, **181**(6.13), 182, **182**–**4**(6.14–6.17)
Li Cunxiao (warrior), 84
Li Huiniang (young maiden), 159, 179
Li Kui Visits His Mother, **161**(5.40)

Li Laosan (pedlar), 189
Li Sanniang (mother), 132
Li Yangui (handsome young man), 56
Lian Jinfeng (young maiden), 30, 31, **31**(2.31)
Liang Shanbo (young scholar), 53, 162
Liang Shanbo and Zhu Yingtai, see *Butterfly Lovers*
"lifting the big belt" (move), 167–8
Lin Chong (hero), 13
Lin Chong's Night Flight, 13, **13**(2.10)
Lion Tower, **74**(3.45)
Liu Bei (general), 24, 120, 137
Liu Chengyou (young man), 132
Liu Guilian (warrior maiden), 157
Liu Jinding (warrior maiden), 26, 159
Liu Lihua (innkeeper), 70, 113
love stories, 52–3, 117
Lü Dongbin (immortal being), 64, 76, 78, 98
Lu Wenlong (male warrior), 28, 102
Lu Wenlong and His Double Spear, **29**(2.29), **103**(4.14)
Lu Zhishen (monk and fighter), 79
Luo Cheng (warrior), 42
luohan (ascended beings), 18, 19

mace, 101–2
Magic Fan, Yinyang, 179
Magic Lotus Lantern, 120
Magic Lotus Lantern, The, **10**(2.06), **119**(4.35)
magical beings, *see* supernatural beings
make-up (*see also* face changing), ix, 155
Marriage of the Dragon and the Phoenix, The, **148**(5.22)
masks, 1, 171, 172
Meeting at the Riverside, **137**(5.08)
Mei Lanfang, 3, 54, 112
Mei Ying (maidservant), 56
Meng Liang (military officer), 26, 28, 150, 162, 164
Merciless Sword, The, **141**(5.13)
military, the, 84–5
military opera, 19, 74, 85
mime, 5–15, 40
Ming dynasty, 2
Model Revolutionary Opera, 3
Monkey King (mythical being), 88, 102, 105, 106, 118, 134
Monkey King Battles the White-Boned Demon, **135**(5.05)
Monkey King Steals the Magic Fan, **104**(4.16)

214

moonlight flag, 85
"mountain shoulders" (pose), 24
Mourning at the Tomb, **155**(5.31)
moves and movement (*see also* acrobatics, mime, poses, *qiba*), 35
    special, 30–4
Mu Guiying (female warrior), 10, 33, 108, **190**(7.01)
Murong Yanchao (General), 19

naobo (golden cymbals), 175
naturalist theatre, 1, 5
Nezha (mythical being), 121
Nine-Tailed Fox Fairy, The, 94, **95**(4.04), **177**(6.09)

oil lamp, *see* "balancing the oil lamp"
"opening the eye of wisdom" (effect), 182, 184

paddles, *see* boats
Palace Interrogation, A, **173**(6.03)
Pan Jinlian (ruthless woman), 8, 37, 74
Pan Jinlian Tempts Her Brother-In-Law, **9**(2.05)
Pan Qiaoyun (adultress), 147
Pan Shi (young woman), 147
Pang Tong (magistrate), 58, 162
"pedalling heaven" (pose), 26
Pei Yuanqing (general), 102
Peking opera, 2–3
pheasant tails, 131–7
Phoenix Terrace Fortress, 19, **20**(2.18), **43**(3.06), 94, **95**(4.03)
photographs and photography, ix, 191, 192
Pi Jin Plays the Fool, **185**–6(6.18–6.20), 187, **187**(6.21)
Picking Up the Jade Bracelet, 6, **7**(2.03), **8**(2.04)
"playing the dwarf" (technique), 34, 35, 37
polearm, 107–8, 118
poles, boat, *see* boat poles
poses, 23–8, 31–2
Prime Minister of Wei, The, **15**(2.12), 152, **152**–3(5.27–5.29)
prisoners, 143
props, 5, 39–91

Qian Jin (rich maiden), 143
Qian Yulian (wife), 157
Qianlong emperor, 2
qiba (move), 35
    female, 127–9
    male, 123–6

Qiba ("The Hegemon Rises"), 122
Qin Qiong (general), 42
Qin Qiong Observes the Troops, **40**(3.02), **41**(3.03), 42
Qin Xianglian (young woman), 149
Qin Ying (fighter), 26
Qing dynasty, 2
Qiuxiang (maid), 60
quarterstaff, 105–6
Queen of Spiders, 106

Raid on Hu Village, **36**(2.37), **92**(4.01), **127**(4.43), **128**(4.44–4.45), **130**(5.01), **136**(5.07)
Red Peony Fairy, 68, **68**(3.38), **110**(4.23)
Ren Tanghui (fighter), 70, 113
ribbons, 65–8
robes, outer, 161–7
Romance of Emperor Han Wu, The, **156**(5.32)
Romance of the Iron Bow, The, **30**(2.30), **117**(4.32)
Romance of the Three Kingdoms, The, 58
Romance of the West Chamber, The, 54, **55**(3.21)

sabres, 113–4
Sanbao (handsome man), 52
scripts, 2
Selecting a Horse for War, **33**(2.34), **38**(3.01)
Selling Water, **57**(3.23)
Sharp Fire Spear (weapon), 121
Shi Xiu (fighter), 106, 147, 168
Shi Xiu Reconnoiters a Village, **168**(5.48), **169**(5.50)
Shi Xiu Scouts Out Zhu Village, **107**(4.19)
Shi Xiu Slays an Unfaithful Wife, **147**(5.21), **169**(5.49)
"shooting the wild goose" (special move), 31
"Short-legged Tiger", *see* Wang Ying
Sichuan opera, 171–2, 175, 177, 185
"side step" (move), 10
"side walk" (mime), 13
"singing side walk" (mime), 13
Sisters Switch Marriages, The, **59**(3.26)
Siu Wang-Ngai, ix, 191, 192
sleeves, *see* water sleeves
Snake Spear (weapon), 120
Song Jiang (robber chieftain), 106, 137
Sorrow at West Lake, The, **178**(6.10)
spears, 93–100, 120, 121
    double-headed, 94
spinning, 62, 64
Splendour Tower, 84, **85**(3.59)
Spring Grass (maid), 10

Spring Grass Rushes to Court, **11**(2.08)
Spring Stroll, A, **53**(3.18), **61**(3.28)
stage conventions, *see* conventions
stage technique, 3, 80
"stiff corpse fall" (move), 21
"stormy eyes" (face change), 171
Story of the Perfumed Sachet, The, **139**(5.11), **140**(5.12), **142**(5.14)
Story of the Purple Hairpin, The, **156**(5.33)
Story of the Red Plum, The (see also *Legend of the Red Plum, The*), **35**(2.36)
Story of the White Rabbit, The, **132**(5.02), **133**(5.03)
Story of the Wooden Hairpin, The, **157**(5.34)
Su Yu'e (concubine), 157
Sui dynasty, 134
Suing the Husband, **146**(5.19)
Sun Erniang (female villain), 56, 58
Sun Wukong, *see* Monkey King
Sun Yujiao (country maiden), 6, 8
supernatural beings, 94, 108, 121, 177, 185
    fairies, 67–8, 78, 85, 94, 97
    spirits, 75–6, 78, 89, 182
swords (*see also* sabres), 110–12

tables, 69–70
Tang dynasty, 54, 65
tangma ("horse ride"), 40
tanzigong ("carpet work"), 17
theatre
    Chinese approach to, ix, 1, 3
    Western, 1
"tiger roll" (move), 18
Tilting the War Carts, 31, **32**(2.33), 85, **87**(3.62), 121, **121**(4.37), 123, **123**–6(4.39–4.42)
tresses, *see* hair
Trial of Chen San, The, **138**(5.09), **146**(5.20)
Twice-Locked Mountain, 26, **27**(2.26), 64, **64**(3.33), 108, **109**(4.22), 159, **159**(5.37)

"umbrella whisk" (move), 80

verfremdungseffekt (alienation device), 3

"Waiting for the Command" (move), 123
Wang Boxian (magistrate), 143, 144
Wang Guiying (young woman), 157
Wang Tiancai (poor young scholar), 143
Wang Ying (fighter), 35, 127, 137
Wang Yuhuan (young maiden), 143–4

Wang Zhaojun (princess), 47, 49
Wang Zhaojun Leaves Her Homeland, 48(**3.12**–**3.13**)
Warrior Maiden Mu Guiying, The, **190**(**7.01**)
warriors (*see also* women warriors), 131
water flags, 85
"water hair", 141, 144, 147
water sleeves, 141, 154–60, 161
Wave Walker (fairy), 85, 97
wawa, *see* clowns
weapons, 93–121
Wei Liangfu (musician), 2
Wei Zifu (concubine), 155
Weituo (spirit), 182, 184
Wen Shuzhen (wronged wife), 145
Western drama, 3
    naturalist theatre, 1, 5
Westerners, perception of Chinese opera, 16
White Crane Fairy, 67
White Egret Fairy, 97
White Peony (young maiden), 64
White Snake (spirit), 78, 81
    battles with, 91, 175, 181, 182
    incarnation of, as human, 17, 76, 89, 112
White Tiger (spirit), 115
White-Boned Demon (spirit), 134
women, in Chinese opera, 56
women warriors, 43, 85, 97, 127–9, **190**(**7.01**)
    poses by, 26, 28, 33
    weapons used by, 94, 108, 112
Women Warriors of the Yang Family, **x**(**1.01**), **11**(**2.07**), **24**(**2.22**), **122**(**4.38**), **129**(**4.46**)

Woodshed Encounter, A, **188**(**6.22**), 189, **189**(**6.23**)
Worshipping the Moon, 87(**3.63**), 88
Wreaking Havoc in the Eastern Sea, **12**(**2.09**), 13, **120**(**4.36**)
Wreaking Havoc in Heaven, **51**(**3.16**), **101**(**4.12**), 102, **102**(**4.13**)
Wresting the Dragon Throne, **136**(**5.06**), 137, **170**(**6.02**), 172
Wu Dalang (ugly dwarf), 21, 37
Wu Song (fighter), 8, 37, 74, 165, 167
Wu Song, 21, **21**(**2.19**)
Wu Song's Revenge, **113**(**4.27**), **167**(**5.47**)
Wu Song's Tavern Fight, **57**(**3.24**), 58
wuxi (military opera), 19

Xia Yuanchun (falsely accused prisoner), 143
Xiang Yu (King), 112, 122
Ximen Qing (evil man), 21, 74
Xiuying (young maiden), 117
Xu Xian (young man), 17, 81, 164
Xuanzang (monk), 88, 105, 134
Xue Dingshan (warrior), 34, 100, 115
Xue Dingshan Thrice Angers Fan Lihua, **34**(**2.35**), **86**(**3.61**), **99**(**4.10**), 100, **100**(**4.11**), **116**(**4.31**)

Yan Xijiao (ghost and young maiden), 21, 31, 71, 73, 172
Yang Bajie (female warrior), 43, 45, 73–4
Yang Guang (prince), 134, 137
Yang Paifeng (housemaid and female warrior), 26, 28, 150, 162

Yang Xiong (wronged husband), 168
Ye Hanyan (young maiden), 71
Yinyang Magic Fan, 179
Yu Ji (concubine), 122
Yuan Chonghuan (general), **111**(**4.24**), 112
Yuan dynasty, 2
Yuan opera (*zaju*), 2
Yue opera, 3, 132
Yue Yan (young maiden), 15
Yue Yang (general), 152
Yue Yun (general), 28, 102

zaju (Yuan opera), 2
Zhai Huang (prime minister), 152
Zhang Fei (warrior), 24, 58, 74, 120, 162
Zhang Fei Honours the Sage Magistrate, **58**(**3.25**), **163**(**5.42**)
Zhang Junrui (young scholar), 54
Zhang Sanlang (young man), 21, 31, 71, 73
Zhang Wuke (maiden), 52
Zhang Xiuying (general's wife), 19, 42–3, 94
Zhao Cuihua (maiden), 52, 60
Zhao Yun (general), 24, 93
Zhao Yun Hides the Baby Prince, **16**(**2.13**)
Zhizhen (Buddhist nun), 78–9
Zhong Kui (ghost and official), 179
Zhong Kui Arranges a Marriage, **179**(**6.11**)
Zhou Cang (bodyguard), 149
Zhou Ding (official), 140
Zhou Yu (general), 24, 137, 144
Zhu Yingtai (maiden), 53, 155, 157, 162
Zhuge Liang (master of strategy), 51